Alfarabi, Avicenna, and Averroes, on Intellect

Alfarabi, Avicenna, and Averroes, on Intellect

THEIR COSMOLOGIES, THEORIES OF THE ACTIVE INTELLECT, AND THEORIES OF HUMAN INTELLECT

Herbert A. Davidson

New York *Oxford*
OXFORD UNIVERSITY PRESS
1992

Oxford University Press

Oxford New York Toronto
Delhi Bombay Calcutta Madras Karachi
Kuala Lumpur Singapore Hong Kong Tokyo
Nairobi Dar es Salaam Cape Town
Melbourne Auckland

and associated companies in
Berlin Ibadan

Published by Oxford University Press, Inc.
200 Madison Avenue, New York, NY 10016

Library of Congress Cataloging-in-Publication Data
Davidson, Herbert A. (Herbert Alan), 1932–
Alfarabi, Avicenna, and Averroes on intellect : their cosmologies, theories of the active intellect, and theories of human intellect / Herbert A. Davidson.
p. cm. Includes bibliographical references and index.
ISBN 0-19-507423-8
1. Philosophy, Islamic—Greek influences. 2. Intellect.
3. Fārābī. 4. Avicenna, 980-1037. 5. Averroës, 1126-1198.
6. Philosophy of mind. 7. Cosmology, Islamic. I. Title.
B745.I54D38 1992
153.9—dc20 91-38856

1 3 5 7 9 8 6 4 2

Printed in the United States of America
on acid-free paper

FOR

Mark, Elizabeth, and Abigail

Acknowledgments

Chapters 2, 3, and 4, have grown out of an article published in *Viator* 3 (1972). Chapters 6 and 7 rework articles that appeared in *Viator* 18 (1987) and *Viator* 17 (1986), respectively.

My wife Kinneret read the entire manuscript meticulously and did her best to nudge me in the direction of clarity and logic. My colleagues Hossein Ziai and Michael Fishbein gave me invaluable assistance, the former in the reading of Suhrawardī, and the latter in matters of Arabic. Michael Cohen, formerly of the UCLA Humanities Computing Facility guided me through the hurdles attendant upon the preparation of camera-ready copy. I extend warmest thanks to each of them.

All the translations are my own.

Los Angeles H. A. D.
May 1992

Contents

Alfarabi, Avicenna, and Averroes, on Intellect

1

Introduction

The most intensely studied sentences in the history of philosophy are probably those in Aristotle's *De anima* that undertake to explain how the human intellect passes from its original state, in which it does not think, to a subsequent state, in which it does. Aristotle started from the presupposition that human thoughts reflect the external world without distortion, the antithesis of what would be Immanuel Kant's perspective. Reasoning that the presence of any inborn quality would color thoughts received by the human intellect and hence prevent the intellect from performing its assigned task, he found the human intellect to be a "part of the soul" which has the ability to "become each thing" but in itself originally has "no nature" whatsoever other than the ability to think.[1] Then came the statements that were to echo down through the centuries. Aristotle brought to bear a dichotomy pervading his entire philosophy, positing that the various domains of the physical universe disclose both a "matter" and a "cause" or "agent" (ποιητικόν), which leads the matter from potentiality to actuality; and he inferred that the same distinction must also be "present in the soul." At the side of the intellect that is what it is "by virtue of becoming all things," by virtue of acquiring all thoughts, an intellect must consequently exist that is what it is "by virtue of making all things," by virtue of making all thoughts.[2] The intellect that is what it is "by virtue of becoming all things" came to be known as the *potential* (δυνάμει) or *material* (ὑλικός) *intellect*, and the intellect that is what it is "by virtue of making all things," as the *active intellect* (νοῦς ποιητικός; sometimes also translated as *active mind, active intelligence, active reason, agent intellect, productive intellect*).

Just what Aristotle meant by potential intellect and active intellect—terms not even explicit in the *De anima* and at best implied—and just how he understood the interaction between them remains moot to this day. Students of the history of philosophy continue to debate Aristotle's intent, particularly the question whether he considered the active intellect to be an aspect of the human soul or an entity existing independently of man.[3] W. D. Ross has characterized "the famous

[1]Aristotle, *De anima* 3.4.429a, 10, 21–22; 429b, 6.

[2]Ibid. 3.5.430a, 10–15.

[3]A sample: E. Zeller, *Die Philosophie der Griechen* 2.2, 4th ed. (Leipzig 1921) 573–75 (transcendent); F. Nuyens, *L'évolution de la psychologie d'Aristote* (Louvain 1948) 303–4, 308, 311 (transcendent); W. Ross, *Aristotle*, 5th ed. (London 1949) 153 (transcendent); idem, edition of Aristotle's *De anima* (Oxford 1961) 45–47 (immanent); J. Rist, "Notes on Aristotle *De anima*

doctrine of the active reason" as "perhaps the most obscure and certainly the most discussed of all Aristotle's doctrines."[4] While today the nature of the human potential intellect and active intellect is merely a problem of exegesis, a conundrum exercising historians of philosophy, for two millennia it was a good deal more. Despite, and also undoubtedly because of, the enigmatic quality of his words, the Greek commentators on Aristotle, medieval Islamic, Jewish, and Christian philosophers, and European philosophers as late as the sixteenth century pored over the master's words, seeking in them the key for deciphering man's essence, man's fate, and the structure of the universe.

Alfarabi (d. 950), Avicenna (980–1037), and Averroes (1126–1198) integrate the active intellect and human potential intellect into larger cosmic schemes. In each instance, the physical universe comprises transparent celestial spheres, in which the stars and planets are embedded, and a stationary sublunar world, around which the celestial spheres rotate. A first supreme being consisting in pure thought, and hence an intellect, presides over the entire cosmos; and there follow other beings consisting in pure thought, that is to say, other intellects—or, as they are conventionally termed, *intelligences*—which have the function of maintaining the celestial spheres in motion. The active intellect, the cause of actual human thought, stands at the end of the chain of supernal intelligences. In Alfarabi, Avicenna, and the early Averroes, the intelligences, including the active intellect, are brought into existence through a series of eternal emanations initiated by the First Cause; and Alfarabi and Avicenna understand that the chain of emanations extends to the celestial spheres and brings them into existence as well. All three philosophers locate the human potential intellect immediately after the active intellect in the descending order of existence.

The active intellect plays a towering role in the philosophic systems of Alfarabi, Avicenna, and Averroes. Like the generality of medieval Islamic and Jewish thinkers—and in contradistinction to the majority of Scholastic philosophers—they did not doubt that the active intellect is an incorporeal substance transcending the human soul and occupying a definite spot in the incorporeal hierarchy. Each of them understood that the active intellect leads the human intellect from the state in which it has a potentiality for thinking to a state in which it actually thinks, and each explained the manner by which the active intellect performs that task. Each, in at least some of his writings, also saw in the active intellect the cause of the existence of segments or all of the sublunar world. Each affirmed the possibility of the human intellect's entering a eudaemonic state called *conjunction* with the active intellect, assigned the active intellect a central role in human immortality, and built a rationale for the phenomenon of prophecy around the active intellect. They each thus espoused a cosmic scheme in which a hierarchy of beings consisting in pure

3.5," in *Essays in Ancient Greek Philosophy*, ed. J. Anton (Albany 1972) 506–7 (immanent). See also R. Hicks' edition of Aristotle's *De anima* (Cambridge 1907) lxiv–lxix.

[4]W. D. Ross, edition of Aristotle's *Metaphysics* (Oxford 1924) 1.cxliii. Ross himself changed his mind; see n. 3.

intellect unfolds until the active intellect is reached, in which the active intellect serves as the transcendent cause of a portion or all of the sublunar world, in which the transcendent active intellect leads the human intellect to actuality, and in which the relationship of the active intellect to the human intellect explains phenomena with religious overtones. The active intellect reached its culmination in Avicenna, who saw it as the direct cause of all, or virtually all, existence and all theoretical thought in the sublunar world, as, in effect, the vicar of God on earth.

A direct line of development is easily traced from Alfarabi to Avicenna, and then forward to Averroes, but when one looks back beyond Alfarabi, no immediate predecessor appears. Nevertheless, tendencies that crystallize in Alfarabi and Avicenna, as well as specific propositions advanced by the two, are discernible in the Greek commentators on Aristotle, in Neoplatonic philosophy, and in Arabic writings before Alfarabi. That does not necessarily imply that Alfarabi took material at his disposal and himself molded it into a comprehensive doctrine, which was to be further developed by his successors. The positions Alfarabi put forward may be borrowings from lost philosophic sources and not his own innovations.

The following chapter reviews discussions of intellect in late Greek and early Arabic philosophy not for their own sake but as background for Alfarabi, Avicenna, and Averroes. Chapters 3 and 4 examine the cosmologies, the conceptions of the active intellect, and the theories of human intellect, espoused by Alfarabi and Avicenna, respectively. Chapter 5 studies the reverberations of the theories of Alfarabi and Avicenna, and especially the latter, in subsequent Islamic, Jewish, and Scholastic philosophy. Chapter 6 takes up Averroes' struggles with two issues on which he changed his mind several times: the relation of the First Cause to the rest of the incorporeal hierarchy, and the active intellect's role as a cause of the existence of the sublunar world. Chapter 7 attempts to untangle Averroes' changing stands on another issue. Defining precisely the kind of entity that the human material or potential intellect is had not been a central theme in Alfarabi and Avicenna. Alfarabi barely touched on the question, and Avicenna dealt with it indirectly as part of the more general question of the nature of the human soul. Averroes, by contrast, wrestled with and agonized over the nature of the human potential intellect throughout his career, changing his mind repeatedly. Chapter 7 traces the development of his thought on the issue and then pursues the subject beyond Averroes into subsequent Jewish and Christian thought that fell under his influence. Chapter 8 examines Averroes' treatment of the active intellect's role in leading the human potential intellect to actuality and his treatment of subjects related to the active intellect's leading the human intellect to actuality, namely, conjunction with the active intellect, human immortality, and prophecy.

Problems connected with intellect made up a considerable portion of the overall philosophic enterprise for the three philosophers discussed, and their handling of those problems reveals something of what can be called their philosophic styles. A word about the philosophic style of each may be in place here. Different works of Alfarabi sometimes advance differing positions on a single issue. To account for the discrepancies, scholars have suggested that Alfarabi's writings disclose a development or, alternatively, that some of them express exoteric views, and others, esoteric views. One striking trait exhibited by Alfarabi is that he almost always lays down his positions flatly, without argument. My conjecture is therefore that he may simply have been dependent on whatever sources were available to him when he wrote,[5] and the differing positions he advanced on different occasions may simply reflect the sources from which he was working at any given time. As for Avicenna, he mentions that he had developed an "oriental philosophy" which diverged from the neoplatonized Aristotelianism he usually espoused. Yet nothing of such a distinctively Oriental philosophy has ever come to light. A medieval list of Avicenna's compositions names his *Ishārāt* as the "last" and "best" of them,[6] and the theses espoused in the *Ishārāt*, though formulated in allusive and high-flown language, harmonize completely with what Avicenna's primary philosophic treatises maintain. I accordingly assume that Avicenna was consistent throughout his philosophic career and merely played with alternate formulations.[7] Averroes, like Alfarabi, takes differing stands on certain issues at different times, but in his case the reason is clear. Throughout his lifetime, Averroes labored to attain the truth, which for him was tantamount to recovering Aristotle's intent, and in the course of rethinking issues, he repeatedly changed his mind. Although Averroes' overriding goal was to cut away accretions and return to Aristotle, we shall find that he did not always succeed. On two issues, the relation of the universe to the First Cause and the active intellect's role as a cause of sublunar existence, he gradually does reapproach genuine Aristotelian positions, while on another, the nature of the human potential intellect, he starts with what the consensus of scholars today would deem to be the genuine position of Aristotle and then, in successive works, moves steadily off in the opposite direction, until he arrives at an egregious misreading.

A remark on terminology: Greek and Arabic do not have separate terms for *intellect* and *intelligence*, but a convention originating in the Latin Middle Ages distinguishes the two, applying the term *intelligence* to the incorporeal beings that in the Aristotelian world govern the celestial spheres, and employing the term *intellect* in other contexts. Since the convention has become part of the idiom of the history of philosophy and is useful, I distinguish *intellect* from *intelligence* even though only a single Greek or Arabic word underlies the two terms.

[5]The name of a scholar with whom Alfarabi studied logic has been preserved. See M. Meyerhof, "Von Alexandrien nach Bagdad," *Sitzungsberichte der preussischen Akademie der Wissenschaften, Philosophisch-historische Klasse* 23 (Berlin 1930) 405–8; F. Rosenthal, *The Classical Heritage in Islam* (Berkeley 1975) 50–51.

[6]*The Life of Ibn Sina* (Jūzjānī's biography of Avicenna) ed. and trans. W. Gohlman (Albany 1974) 96–97.

[7]D. Gutas, *Avicenna and the Aristotelian Tradition* (Leiden 1988) 115–130, makes the case against assuming an Oriental philosophy which differed substantially from Avicenna's preserved philosophic system.

2

Greek and Arabic Antecedents

Here I shall examine Greek and early Arabic speculation on the following topics: (1) the stages through which the human intellect can pass; (2) the type of entity the active intellect is; (3) the manner in which the active intellect produces human thought; (4) the active intellect's role in bringing the sublunar world or segments of it into existence; and (5) the rationale that the active intellect furnishes for certain religious phenomena. My object will not be to reproduce the systems of the philosophers discussed but to draw attention to statements and theories that shed light on Alfarabi, Avicenna, and Averroes.

As is hardly surprising, Aristotle constitutes the starting point for understanding Alfarabi, Avicenna, and Averroes; certain post-Aristotelian Greek texts and early Arabic philosophic texts, nevertheless, also contributed to the setting in which they worked. The pertinent post-Aristotelian texts are: Alexander of Aphrodisias' *De anima*[1]; a work entitled *De intellectu*, which is likewise attributed to Alexander,[2] although the attribution has been questioned because of discrepancies between the *De intellectu* and Alexander's *De anima*[3]; Plotinus' *Enneads*[4]; Themistius' Paraphrase of Aristotle's *De anima*;[5] Themistius' Paraphrase of Aristotle's

[1]Alexander, *De anima*, in *Scripta minora* 2.1, ed. I. Bruns (Berlin 1887) 1–100.

[2]Alexander (?), *De intellectu*, in *Scripta minora* 2.1, 106–13. Arabic translation: *Texte arabe du* περι νου *d'Alexandre d'Aphrodise*, ed. J. Finnegan (Beirut 1956), with pagination of the Greek given; and *Commentaires sur Aristote perdus en grec*, ed. A. Badawi (Beirut 1968) 31–42. Neither edition of the Arabic version is wholly adequate. I have translated from my own ad hoc eclectic text, which I base on both editions and their apparatuses, with corrections here and there from the Greek.

[3]P. Moraux, *Alexandre d'Aphrodise* (Paris 1942) 132–42. Moraux later changed his mind and decided that both the *De anima* and *De intellectu* are genuine works of Alexander; see P. Moraux, "Le *De anima* dans la tradition grecque," *Aristotle on Mind and the Senses*, ed. G. Lloyd and G. Owen (Cambridge 1975) 297, 304.

[4]Plotinus, *Enneades*, ed. P. Henry and H.-R. Schwyzer 2 (Paris 1959) contains a useful English translation of the extant Arabic paraphrases of Plotinus, done by G. Lewis.

[5]Themistius, Paraphrase of Aristotle's *De anima*, in *Commentaria in Aristotelem graeca* 5.3, ed. R. Heinze (Berlin 1899). Medieval Arabic translation, with the pagination of the Greek indicated: *An Arabic Translation of Themistius . . . on Aristoteles 'De anima'*, ed. M. Lyons (Columbia, S.C. 1973).

Metaphysics, Book 12[6]; a Greek commentary on Aristotle's *De anima* attributed to John Philoponus[7]; and a different Greek commentary on Book 3 of the *De anima*, also attributed to Philoponus, which is no longer extant in the original but is preserved in a Latin translation.[8] Of these, only the two works carrying Alexander's name—the medieval Arabic philosophers were little inclined to question the names on books and harbored no doubts about Alexander's authorship of either work—and Themistius' paraphrases of Aristotle's *De anima* and of *Metaphysics* 12, are known to have been directly available to the medieval Arabs in Arabic translation. In the case of the *De intellectu* and of Themistius' Paraphrase of Aristotle's *De anima*, the medieval Arabic translations have survived and been published. While no manuscripts of the Arabic translations of Alexander's *De anima* and of Themistius' Paraphrase of *Metaphysics* 12 are known, medieval Hebrew translations from the Arabic have been preserved. Avicenna refers to the views of both Alexander and Themistius on the soul,[9] and Averroes does the same[10]; in addition, Averroes quotes a key passage at length from Themistius' Paraphrase of *Metaphysics* 12.[11] Plotinus and his *Enneads* were not even known by name, but parts of the *Enneads* circulated in Arabic in anonymous and pseudepigraphous paraphrases, the most notable of which is the *Theology of Aristotle*. The *Theology of Aristotle* is cited by Alfarabi as a genuine work of Aristotle's,[12] and Avicenna wrote a commentary on it.[13]

The following Arabic compositions from the period preceding Alfarabi also have some pertinence: a paraphrase of Aristotle's *De anima* attributed to Isḥāq ibn Ḥunain (d. 876); a fragment from a certain Bakr al-Mawṣilī (ca. 900); the writings of Kindi (ninth century); a treatise on the soul, of unknown date, which is attributed

[6]The Greek original and the Arabic translation from the Greek are not extant. Medieval Hebrew translation from the Arabic: *Themistii in Aristotelis Metaphysicorum librum Λ paraphrasis*, ed. S. Landauer, in *Commentaria in Aristotelem graeca* 5.5 (Berlin 1903).

[7]Philoponus, Commentary on *De anima*, in *Commentaria in Aristotelem graeca* 15, ed. M. Hayduck (Berlin 1897).

[8]*Le commentaire de Jean Philopon sur le troisième livre du traité de l'âme d'Aristote*, ed. M. Corte (Liege 1934).

[9]See Avicenna, "Notes" on Aristotle's *De anima*, in *Arisṭū ᶜinda al-ᶜArab*, ed. A. Badawi (Cairo 1947) 98, 101, 114, 116; *Mubāḥathāt*, in *Arisṭū ᶜinda al-ᶜArab*, 120; *Al-Qawl fī Aḥwāl al-Nafs*, in *Majmūᶜ Rasā'il* (Hyderabad 1935) 15.

[10]See below, pp. 268–69, 274–75, 278–80, 282–84, 287, 326.

[11]Averroes, *Tafsīr mā baᶜda al-Ṭabīᶜa* (Long Commentary on *Metaphysics*), ed. M. Bouyges (Beirut 1938–1948) 1492–94.

[12]Alfarabi, *Al -Jamᶜ baina al-Ḥakīmain*, ed. A. Nader (Beirut 1960) 105–6. Also printed in *Alfārābī's philosophische Abhandlungen*, ed. F. Dieterici (Leiden 1890) 28; German translation: *Alfārābī's philosophische Abhandlungen aus dem Arabischen übersetzt*, trans. F. Dieterici (Leiden 1892) 44–45. Although several scholars have tried to interpret away what Alfarabi says, he unambiguously recognizes Aristotle's authorship of the *Theology*.

[13]Avicenna's commentary is printed in *Arisṭū ᶜinda al-ᶜArab* (n. 9 above) 35–74; French translation: "Notes d'Avicenne sur la 'Théologie d'Aristote,'" trans. G. Vajda, in *Revue thomiste* 51 (1951) 346–406.

to Porphyry and extant only in Arabic. Avicenna refers to the Porphyry—or pseudo-Porphyry—treatise, criticizing it harshly.[14]

Of the works that have been mentioned here, the most important for Alfarabi, Avicenna, and Averroes are Alexander's *De anima*, the *De intellectu*, Plotinus' *Enneads*, and Themistius' Paraphrase of Aristotle's *De anima*. As already noted, parts of Plotinus were available to medieval Arabic readers in a paraphrase, and the other three texts were available in translation. Where the Arabic translation or paraphrase of a Greek text diverges from the original, the Arabic version is naturally more germane for our purpose, and I shall usually quote from it.

Stages of Human Intellect

Each natural domain, Aristotle reasoned, discloses a "matter" that is "potentially" everything in the domain, as well as an "agent" that makes everything in the domain; whence he inferred that the soul too must contain an "intellect" that is what it is "by virtue of becoming all things," as well as an intellect that is what it is "by virtue of making all things."[15] Aristotle's wording suggested the qualifications *potential* and *material* for the undeveloped intellectual faculty of the human soul which can become everything, that is, which can think all thoughts, and Alexander of Aphrodisias therefore could, in a single sentence, call the initial state of the human intellect both "potential" and "material" intellect.[16] Commentators and philosophers were to ask what sort of thing the potential or material intellect is. Alexander's reading of Aristotle led him to conclude that it is "only a disposition" in the human organism,[17] whereas Themistius paid heed to statements of Aristotle's pointing in another direction. He learned from Aristotle that the "potential intellect" does "not employ a bodily organ for its activity, is wholly unmixed with the body, impassive, and separate [from matter]."[18] Since anything with those characteristics is perforce an incorporeal substance, Averroes will consistently report that Themistius and others of a similar mind took the human potential intellect to be an incorporeal substance or, in another formulation, a disposition inhering in an incorporeal substance.[19] A modern commentator understands Themistius in the

[14]Avicenna *K. al-Ishārāt wal-Tanbīhāt*, ed. J. Forget, as *Le livre des théorèmes et des avertissements* (Leiden 1892) 180; French translation: *Livre des directives et remarques*, trans. A. Goichon (Beirut 1951), with pages of Forget's edition indicated; Avicenna, *Shifā': De anima*, ed. F. Rahman (London 1959) 240.

[15]*De anima* 3.5.430a, 10–15.

[16]Alexander, *De anima* (n. 1 above) 81.

[17]Ibid. 84.

[18]Themistius, Paraphrase of the *De anima* (n. 5 above) 105.

[19]Cf. below, pp. 269, 279, 287.

same way.[20] The nature of the human potential or material intellect is mentioned only in passing by Alfarabi, it is dealt with indirectly by Avicenna, but it becomes central in Averroes.

Besides noting the existence of human intellect that can become everything, Aristotle remarked on the situation wherein the human intellect has already "become everything"—in other words, already possesses a full repertoire of thoughts—yet is not actually thinking them at the moment. The human intellect in that condition is, Aristotle wrote, "potential in a certain sense," because it is not actually thinking. It is not, however, potential in the same sense as "before learning," because it has undergone a passage to actuality. It is now "able through itself to think," much like the "man of science" who is able to exercise his knowledge at will but does not at the moment happen to be doing so.[21] Alexander's *De anima* and the Arabic Aristotelians who follow Alexander's example applied the term "intellect *in habitu*" (κατὰ ἕξιν, καθῷ ἕξιν, ἐν ἕξει ; *bil-malaka*) to the human intellect when it is in possession of a repertoire of thoughts—though not necessarily a full repertoire—without actually thinking them.[22]

A further distinction, which although not brought out in Aristotle is obvious, was alluded to by Alexander. Alexander commented that intellect *in habitu* stands "between" the pure potentiality of the person who has not begun to acquire intelligible knowledge and the full actuality of the man of knowledge currently engaged in thought.[23] Intellect *in habitu*, the stage in which the human subject has

[20] O. Hamelin, *La théorie de l'intellect d'après Aristote et ses commentateurs* (Paris 1953) 40.

[21] Aristotle, *De anima* 3.4.429b, 5–9. Aristotle also discusses this sense of potentiality in *De anima* 2.5.417a, 22ff.

[22] See Alexander, *De anima* 85–86; *De intellectu* (n. 2 above) 107; *Rasā'il al-Kindī*, ed. M. Abu Rida (Cairo 1950) 1.358 (the notion without the term); Avicenna, below, p. 84. Ghazali, *Maqāṣid al-Falāsifa* (Cairo n.d.) 292; Averroes, Epitome of *De anima*, published as *Talkhīṣ Kitāb al-Nafs*, ed. A. Ahwani (Cairo 1950) 87. Elsewhere, Averroes uses the term intellect *in habitu* in the sense of the human intellect possessed of a repertoire of thoughts, but without the condition that the man is not thinking the thoughts at the moment. See Averroes, *Iggeret Efsharut ha-Debequt* (Arabic original lost), ed. and English trans. K. Bland, as *Epistle on the Possibility of Conjunction* (New York 1982), Hebrew text 12–13 (the English translation, p. 27, incorrectly renders *intellect in habitu* as "acquired intellect"); idem, *Commentarium magnum in Aristotelis de Anima libros*, ed. F. Crawford (Cambridge, Mass. 1953) (henceforth cited as: Long Commentary on the *De anima*) 496–97. Themistius, in his Paraphrase of Aristotle's *De anima* 95, also takes cognizance of the condition in which intellect has undergone a passage to actuality, without its actually thinking at the moment, and he appears to call that state a *habitus*; on 98, however, he appears to use the term intellect *in habitu* in the sense of human intellect when fully actual, rather than when in an intermediate state of potentiality. Alexander and Themistius somehow thought that the term ἕξις, which in the preserved text of Aristotle, *De anima* 3.5.430a, 15, qualifies the active intellect, refers instead to a state or stage of the developing human potential intellect. See G. Rodier's note to the Aristotelian passage in his edition of Aristotle's *De anima* (Paris 1900).

[23] Alexander, *De anima* 85–86.

the power to think at will but is not doing so, may in other words be distinguished from *actual* intellect, the stage in which the human intellect is actually thinking.[24] The stages of human intellect have now increased to three: potential or material human intellect, human intellect *in habitu*, and actual human intellect.

Alfarabi and Avicenna recognized still another stage or state, which they called *acquired intellect*.[25] The term *acquired intellect* reflects nothing in Aristotle. It does appear in the Greek text of Alexander of Aphrodisias' *De anima*, although it is inconspicuous there, serving only as a synonym for intellect *in habitu*, that is to say, human intellect in possession of the ability to think yet not actually thinking.[26] The term becomes significant in the Arabic translations of Alexander's *De anima* and of the *De intellectu* attributed to Alexander.

Both Alexander's *De anima* and the *De intellectu* use a different expression, "intellect from without," a number of times, echoing a perplexing passage in Aristotle's *De generatione animalium*, which refers to intellect that "alone enters [the organism] from without."[27] Both works, as will be seen, deemed it possible for an incorporeal substance, and the active intellect in particular, to enter the human intellect and become the object of human thought; and they called that guise of the incorporeal substance "intellect from without." The sense of the expression is that such an object of thought already was intellect when still outside, and before being thought by, the human intellect, in contrast to intelligible thoughts abstracted from material objects and rendered actually intelligible, and therefore actual intellect, only upon entering the human intellect.

In the Arabic versions of Alexander's *De anima* and the *De intellectu* attributed to Alexander the words *intellect from without* are not translated literally. They are generally rendered as "acquired intellect," and sometimes as "intellect acquired from without."[28] The Arabic versions have an another peculiarity; they substitute the term *acting* (*fāᶜil*) intellect for the more precise term *active* (*faᶜᶜāl*) intellect. Thus, instead of speaking of an *active*, *acquired intellect*, which would show unambiguously that the active intellect is what is qualified as *acquired*, the Arabic translations speak of an "acting, acquired intellect."[29] Although the collocation

[24]Kindi, *Rasā'il* 1.358, draws such a distinction, without the term *in habitu*. The *De intellectu* 107, and Themistius, Paraphrase of the *De anima* 98, do not recognize the distinction between actual intellect and intellect *in habitu*.

[25]On the subject of the *acquired intellect*, see A. Badawi, "New Philosophical Texts Lost in Greek," *Islamic Philosophical Theology*, ed. P. Morewedge (Albany 1979) 4–5; F. Rahman, *Avicenna's Psychology* (Oxford 1952) 90–93; Finnegan (n. 2 above) 172–78; P. Merlan, *Monopsychism Mysticism Metaconsciousness* (Hague 1969) 14–15; and the references they give to earlier literature.

[26]Alexander, *De anima* 82. See E. Zeller, *Die Philosophie der Griechen* 3.1, 5th ed. (Leipzig 1923) 826, n. 2.

[27]*De generatione animalium* 2.3.736b, 28.

[28]Cf. Finnegan (n. 2 above) 172.

[29]Ibid. 186, 187. *De intellectu* 109, describes intellect *in habitu* as "acting."

acting acquired intellect is cloudy, the Arabic translations do say enough to make clear what *acquired intellect* means. According to the Arabic, acquired intellect "exists actually"[30] and is "in itself intellect"[31]; it comes to man "from without"[32]; it "aids the intellect in [man]" and "establishes the *habitus* [for thought] within the material intellect"[33]; it is the factor whereby the potential intellect is "led from potentiality to actuality"[34]; it is "generated in us from without"[35] and "we think it."[36] The descriptions reveal that a transcendent incorporeal entity, and the active intellect in particular, is at issue. The added qualifications "acquired," or "acquired from without," further indicate that the intellect in question somehow belongs to man.

In a word, the Arabic translator of Alexander saw that the expression "intellect from without" denotes the active intellect—or other incorporeal forms—insofar as it somehow enters the human intellect; and for unknown reasons he rendered the expression as *acquired intellect.* The Arabic does not misrepresent the intent of the original, although, by coining the new name, it does draw additional attention to, and permits a misunderstanding of, the aspect of the active intellect—or of another incorporeal form—that enters man.

Plotinus likewise used the term *acquired intellect.* He meant by it intellectual knowledge that is *acquired* by the soul directly from the supernal, cosmic Intellect.[37]

Alfarabi and, in some contexts, Avicenna will employ the term *acquired intellect* to designate not an aspect of the active intellect, or of another incorporeal intelligence, which enters the human intellect, the sense the term has in the Arabic translations of Alexander, but rather an ultimate stage of the human intellect itself, a stage wherein the human intellect enjoys a certain close relationship with the transcendent active intellect. With the addition of the acquired intellect, we have a cadre of four stages: material or potential human intellect, intellect *in habitu*, actual human intellect, and acquired intellect. The cadre does not appear precisely as such in either Alfarabi, Avicenna, or Averroes. Each of them, however, employs a variation of it.

[30]Ibid.

[31]Hebrew translation of the Arabic version of Alexander, *De anima* 90, in Paris, Bibliothèque Nationale, Hebrew MS 894.

[32]Finnegan 191.

[33]Ibid.

[34]Ibid. 191.

[35]Ibid. 186, 194; Hebrew translation of Alexander, *De anima* 91.

[36]Hebrew translation of Alexander, *De anima* 90.

[37]*Al-Shaykh al-Yūnānī*, ed. F. Rosenthal, *Orientalia* 21 (1952) 480–81, paralleling *Enneads* 5.6.4.

The Kind of Entity That the Active Intellect Is

Aristotle's meager remarks on the intellect that is what it is by virtue of "making all things"—subsequently to be known as the active intellect—include both a suggestion that it is, and a suggestion that it is not, a transcendent substance. For he described it as "present in the soul" yet also as "separate [from matter] . . . and, in its essence, actuality."[38] If primary weight be attached to the latter description and the active intellect is understood to exist in an unchanging state of actuality, it would have to be an incorporeal substance independent of the human organism. The statement about its being present *in* the soul would then mean either that an aspect of the essentially transcendent active intellect enters the human soul or else merely that a cause as well as a matter must be assumed *in the case of* soul.[39] Should, by contrast, primary weight be attached to the statement locating the intellect that makes everything "in" the human soul, and should the active intellect exist nowhere but in individual human souls, the description of it as "actuality" in its essence will have to be interpreted away.

Alfarabi, Avicenna, and Averroes, like virtually all Islamic and Jewish philosophers in the Aristotelian tradition, accepted the transcendent interpretation without question. And they did more. They pinpointed the precise place in the incorporeal hierarchy where the active intellect stands—the words *place*, *stands*, and similar terms being used metaphorically here, of course, since incorporeal substances exist outside of space and time. In the medieval Aristotelian universe, a series of incorporeal intelligences parallels the series of celestial spheres, the transparent spherical bodies that carry the planets and stars around the earth. In the version of the Aristotelian scheme of the universe endorsed by Alfarabi, Avicenna, and Averroes, the active intellect, the factor leading the potential human intellect to actuality, is added as a final link to the chain of intelligences. It therein parallels the sublunar world, which stands as the last and least cosmic body, at the end of the series of celestial spheres. The symmetry, as we shall see, can be extended, through the ascription to the active intellect of functions in respect to the sublunar world which are analogous to the functions each intelligence performs in respect to the corresponding celestial sphere.

No known thinker prior to Alfarabi identified the active intellect precisely as the last link in the chain of incorporeal intelligences, but the active intellect was commonly taken to be a transcendent, incorporeal substance. The earliest known philosopher who explicitly[40] construed the active intellect as a transcendent being

[38]Aristotle, *De anima* 3.5.430a, 13, 17–18.

[39]Alexander, *De anima* (n. 1 above) 88, in the course of rewording Aristotle's reason for positing an active intellect, writes that a material factor and an agent must exist "in the case of intellect." Below, p. 20.

[40]Aristotle's *De generatione animalium* 2.3.736b, 28, and the *Eudemian Ethics* 1248a, 25–29, may be read as construing the active intellect as a transcendent being. Theophrastus also

was Alexander. Alexander connected the active intellect implied in Aristotle's *De anima*, Book 3, with the first, incorporeal, ever-thinking cause of the universe established in Aristotle's *Metaphysics*, Book 12. He assumed that the two entities are identical, that the active intellect, the cause of the human intellect's passage from potentiality to actuality, is nothing other than the First Cause of the universe, the deity.[41] Plotinus too, in a sense, construed the active intellect as a transcendent entity. In his cosmology, the First Cause of the universe, called the *One*, eternally radiates, or emanates, from itself a cosmic *Intellect*—which in turn radiates a cosmic *Soul*; and among the functions for which the cosmic Intellect is responsible are those of Aristotle's active intellect.[42] Themistius was a third philosopher who placed a transcendent construction on the active intellect. He rejected the identification of the active intellect as the First Cause of the universe, or, to be more precise, the proposition that the active intellect is the First Cause of the universe and nothing more. His reason was that Aristotle had located the active intellect "in" man's soul.[43] But Themistius also insisted on the transcendent character of the active intellect, or of its primary aspect, because Aristotle had—in an analogy that would be analyzed and reanalyzed through the centuries—compared the active intellect to light.[44] The analogy of light entailed for Themistius that although rays from the active intellect disperse and enter individual men, they have their origin in an external radiating source, in a single transcendent "active intellect" existing outside and above man. In a curious bit of syncretism, Themistius added that the transcendent active intellect, or transcendent aspect of the active intellect, from which rays radiate and enter individual human souls, is the very entity Plato had in mind when he compared the Idea of the Good, the "cause of science and truth,"[45] to the sun, the source of light.[46]

Other instances of the active intellect's being taken as a transcendent substance are recorded in the two commentaries on the *De anima* attributed to John Philoponus. Each of the commentaries lists four theories regarding the active intellect, and one item in each list is of especial interest because it approaches still further what was to be the conception of the Arabic Aristotelians. The Greek

---

seems to have construed the active intellect as a transcendent being; see Themistius, Paraphrase of the *De anima* (n. 5 above) 102.

[41] Alexander, *De anima* 89; cf. the *De intellectu* (n. 2 above) 113.

[42] Cf. A. Armstrong, *The Architecture of the Intelligible Universe in the Philosophy of Plotinus* (Cambridge 1940) 41.

[43] Aristotle, *De anima* 3.5.430a, 13.

[44] Ibid. 15–17.

[45] Plato, *Republic* 6.508.

[46] Themistius, Paraphrase of the *De anima* 102–103. Plotinus, *Enneads* 5.1.8, had identified Plato's idea of the Good with the One, that is to say, with the First Cause, which is beyond Intellect. If Themistius accepts the same equation, his argument that the active intellect cannot be the First Cause of the universe is to be understood as contending only that the active intellect cannot be the First Cause and nothing more, inasmuch as an aspect of it enters the human intellect.

commentary attributed to Philoponus reports that a philosopher named Marinus[47] viewed the active intellect as "something daemonic [δαιμόνιον] or angelic."[48] A parallel statement in the commentary extant in Latin reports that "some" thinkers identify the active intellect not as God but "as a certain other intellect, inferior to Him, positioned close to our [intellect], which radiates upon our souls and perfects them."[49] In both statements, and more explicitly in the second, the active intellect is an incorporeal substance outside man which stands close to man in the hierarchy of existence. Alexander, Plotinus, and Themistius, by contrast, located the active intellect at or near the top of the hierarchy of being.

Little is added by preserved Arabic works prior to Alfarabi.

At least two Arabic works do not recognize the transcendent character of the active intellect. A paraphrase of the *De anima* attributed to Isḥāq ibn Ḥunain speaks of the active intellect as the "actual intellect" and states its functions briefly, without any suggestion that it exists outside the human soul.[50] An obscure contemporary of Alfarabi known as Bakr al-Mawṣilī argues against the proposition that the human intellect obtains knowledge through the action of an incorporeal being outside of man. He contends instead that the "principles" of thought, which are judgments about "the universal things," must be innate to the human intellect. To explain the manner whereby man becomes conscious of the innate principles, Bakr al-Mawṣilī has recourse to a Platonic theory of reminiscence.[51]

Kindi offered two distinct and, very likely, incompatible theories of the cause of actual human thought.

His brief treatise *On Intellect* understands the factor actualizing the human intellect to be a transcendent thinking being, which the treatise calls *first intellect* rather than active intellect and describes as the "cause" of "all intelligible thoughts and secondary intellects."[52] Connections with Alexander have been detected, or are thought to have been detected, in the text,[53] and therefore Kindi might conceivably be reflecting Alexander's position that the active intellect is identical with the First Cause of the universe.

[47]Probably identical with a student of Proclus by that name.

[48]Philoponus (n. 7 above) 535. For the likely context of Marinus' statement, see H. Blumenthal, "Neoplatonic Elements in the *De Anima* Commentaries," *Phronesis* 21 (1976) 81.

[49]*Commentaire* (n. 8 above) 30.

[50]Ahwani (n. 22 above) 168.

[51]S. Pines, "La doctrine de l'intellect selon Bakr al-Mawṣilī," *Studi . . . in onore di . . . Levi della Vida* (Rome 1956) 2.358–361.

[52]*Rasā'il al-Kindī* (n. 22 above) 1.357. Medieval Latin translations of Kindi's *On Intellect*: A. Nagy, *Die philosophischen Abhandlungen des Ja*ᶜ*qub ben Isḥāq al-Kindī* (Münster 1897) 1–11 (significant variants from the preserved Arabic); English translation: R. McCarthy, "Al-Kindī's Treatise on the Intellect," *Islamic Studies* 3 (1964) 125–28; French translation: J. Jolivet, *L'intellect selon Kindī* (Leiden 1971) 1–6.

[53]Cf. E. Gilson, "Les sources gréco-arabes de l'Augustinisme avicennisant," *Archives d'histoire doctrinale et littéraire du moyen âge* 4 (1929) 23–27; Jolivet 31–41.

On a more plausible reading, however, Kindi's *On Intellect* is using the term *first intellect* for the Intellect that is the second hypostasis in the Neoplatonic hierarchy. A number of considerations support that reading: One of the Arabic paraphrases of Plotinus employs the term *first intellect* precisely in the sense of the cosmic Intellect.[54] The Arabic text *On the Soul* attributed to Porphyry employs the term *first intellect* in a Neoplatonic context and presumably again in the sense of the Neoplatonic cosmic Intellect.[55] The Jewish philosopher Isaac Israeli (ca. 850–950) repeats the main points in Kindi's account of intellect[56] but incorporates them into a Neoplatonic hierarchy of Creator-Intellect-Soul-Nature.[57] He apparently, therefore, took Kindi's *first intellect* to be the second of the Neoplatonic hypostases. Ibn Gabirol, a later Jewish Arabic philosopher standing in the Neoplatonic tradition, explicitly applies the term *first intellect* to the hypostasis Intellect, which is subordinate to the First Cause—incidentally adding that philosophers call the same being "active intellect."[58] And popular Neoplatonic literature, in general, uses the terms *first intellect* as well as *active intellect* for the cosmic Intellect of the Neoplatonic hierarchy.[59]

There is finally an unpublished text that, in the judgment of the scholars who called attention to it, is Kindi's work. The text defines "universal intellect" by the same distinctive formula that Kindi's *On Intellect* employed to define "first intellect"; it defines universal intellect, and the treatise *On Intellect* defines first intellect, as "the specificality of things."[60] Assuming that the newly discovered text does belong to Kindi or at least reflects his thought, we have *first intellect* equated with *universal intellect* and presumably equivalent to the Neoplatonic cosmic Intellect.

Such is one way Kindi represents the source of actual human thought. He identifies it as the transcendent first intellect, which appears to be the second hypostasis in the Neoplatonic hierarchy, standing under the First Cause of the universe. In a separate work, entitled *On First Philosophy*, Kindi takes another

[54]See *Theology of Aristotle*, ed. F. Dieterici (Leipzig 1882) 142, paralleling *Enneads* 6.7.2.

[55]W. Kutsch, "Ein arabisches Bruchstück aus Porphyrios (?)," *Mélanges de l'Université St. Joseph* 31 (1954) 268.

[56]A. Altmann and S. Stern, *Isaac Israeli* (Oxford 1958) 35–38.

[57]Ibid. 46–47.

[58]The Arabic original is lost. Medieval Latin translation from the Arabic: S. Ibn Gabirol, *Fons vitae*, ed. C. Baeumker (Münster 1892–1895) 5, §19, p. 294; excerpts from the Arabic in medieval Hebrew translation: *Liqqutim*, ed. S. Munk (Paris 1857) 5, §25.

[59]See Long Version of the Theology of Aristotle, cited by P. Duhem, *Le système du monde* 4 (Paris 1916) 398–401; *Rasā'il Ikhwān al-Ṣafā'* (Beirut 1957) 3.386, chap. 41; Ibn al-Sīd (Baṭlayūsī) *K. al-Ḥadā'iq*, ed. and Spanish trans. M. Asín Palacios, in *Al-Andalus* 5 (1940), Arabic text 77; Spanish translation 118; medieval Hebrew translation: Batlajusi, *ha-ᶜAgullot ha-Raᶜyoniyyot*, ed. D. Kaufmann (Budapest 1880) 27; *K. Maᶜānī al-Nafs*, ed. I. Goldziher (Berlin 1907) 54; F. Rosenthal, "On the Knowledge of Plato's Philosophy," *Islamic Culture* 14 (1940) 399.

[60]Altmann and Stern (n. 56 above) 37–38.

tack. He reasons that since actual human thought comes about when the human intellect unites with the "species and genera of things," that is, with "the universals of things," those universals must be the factor actualizing the human intellect.[61] No indication is given of the ontological status of universals. Kindi's wording does recall Bakr al-Mawṣilī's "universal things" that are innate to the human intellect. But since he speaks of the human intellect's "becoming" actual by uniting with universals, he would seem to exclude its being united with them from the outset. In other words, he seems to exclude universals' being inborn. He might, of course, mean that the universals whereby the human intellect is actualized are embodied in, and supplied by, the transcendent first intellect; for, as was just seen, he describes first intellect as the "specificality of things," which is almost tantamount to saying that first intellect embodies the universals of things. The statement that the "universals of things" actualize the human intellect could, therefore, mean that they do so when communicated by first intellect to the human intellect. The harmonization, like all harmonizations, is tempting, but since the passage describing universals as the cause of actual human thought does not mention a transcendent intellect, we should beware of introducing one. The universals in the passage may simply be concepts abstracted from physical objects; Isaac Israeli, who was dependent on Kindi, outlined a process whereby human concepts are refined from sense perceptions through successive abstractions.[62] Or perhaps the universals Kindi speaks of are abstract concepts subsisting in a Platonic world of ideal Forms. In the passage under consideration, Kindi may, then, very well be dismissing the need for any transcendent agent to lead the potential intellect to actuality. He was fully capable of advocating diverse and inconsistent theories at different times.[63]

Al-Kindi, in sum, offered two theories of the source of actual human thought. According to one, the human intellect is led to actual thought by the transcendent *first intellect*, by which he probably intended the Neoplatonic cosmic Intellect. According to the other, the human intellect is rendered actual by the "universals of things" with no further clarification. In yet another passage that might, at first glance, appear pertinent, Kindi describes the heavenly bodies as the "agent of [human] reason."[64] There, however, he probably meant that the heavens generate the human rational soul with its potentiality for thought,[65] not that the heavens lead the human rational soul to actual thought.

[61]*Rasā'il al-Kindī* (n. 22 above) 1.155. English translation: *Al-Kindi's Metaphysics*, trans. A. Ivry (Albany 1974) 106.

[62]Altmann and Stern 36–37.

[63]Regarding Kindi's eclecticism, see F. Rosenthal, "Al-Kindī and Ptolemy," *Studi ... in onore di ... Levi della Vida* (Rome 1956) 2.438, 446, 454–56.

[64]*Rasā'il al-Kindī* 1.255.

[65]See below, p. 33.

The foregoing survey discloses that post-Aristotelian Greek philosophers who construed the active intellect, the cause of actual human thought, as a transcendent entity identified it with the First Cause of the universe (Alexander); with Plato's Idea of the Good (Themistius); and with the cosmic Intellect that is the second hypostasis in the Neoplatonic hierarchy (Plotinus). Or they took it to be a supernal being located below the deity and close to man in the hierarchy of existence (views recorded in both commentaries on the *De anima* attributed to John Philoponus). Among Arabic philosophic writings prior to Alfarabi, some recognize a transcendent cause of actual human thought, which they call *first intellect* (a work of Kindi's, the text attributed to Porphyry, Isaac Israeli), and others reject or ignore the notion of such a cause (Isḥāq ibn Ḥunain, Bakr al-Mawṣilī). In Kindi alone, one work recognizes a transcendent cause of human thought, while another accounts for the actualization of the human intellect without mention of it. Despite the range of precedents for a transcendent construction of the active intellect or of the cause of actual human thought under another name, no known writer before Alfarabi identifies the active intellect as the last link in the hierarchy of celestial intelligences, which parallels the sublunar world as each incorporeal intelligence parallels its celestial sphere. Alfarabi was the first known philosopher even to assume an entity of the sort, let alone identify it with Aristotle's active intellect.

The Active Intellect as a Cause of Human Thought

The active intellect was originally posited to help explain actual thought in man. Each natural domain, in Aristotle's words, discloses a material factor, and also a "cause" or "agent" that stands to the other as "art" stands to "matter" and "produces everything" in the given domain; and therefore the soul too must contain both an "intellect" that is what it is "by virtue of becoming all things," by virtue of receiving all thoughts, and an intellect that is what it is "by virtue of making all things."[66]

In representing the active intellect as an instance of the cause or agent that produces everything in a given domain, Aristotle's intent would surely appear to be this: In each domain, a cause or agent operates on the material factor and leads it from its state of potentiality to a state of actuality. Similarly, the intellect that is what it is by virtue of making all things is such inasmuch as it performs an operation on the intellect that is potential and resembles matter; and the operation performed by the intellect that makes everything on the potential intellect brings about a new condition in which the latter has become actual and possesses actual thoughts. A fundamental proposition of Peripatetic philosophy would come into play here, namely, as Aristotle explained elsewhere: Whenever "what exists actually is generated from what exists potentially," the transition from potentiality to actuality is effected "by means of what [already] actually is [in possession of the

[66]Aristotle, *De anima* 3.5.430a, 10–15.

characteristic in question]."[67] Obvious as that reading of Aristotle might be, a reading according to which the active intellect performs an action on the potential intellect rendering the latter actual, Alexander of Aphrodisias may not have accepted it, and it has been challenged in modern Aristotelian scholarship.[68] The medieval Arabic Aristotelians, for their part, were certain that when Aristotle compared the active intellect to the cause or agent in any given domain, he meant that the active intellect performs a certain operation on the potential intellect and thereby brings it to actuality.[69]

There remained the task of understanding how the active intellect—which the Arabic Aristotelians took to be a transcendent substance—produces actual thought in the human potential or material intellect.

Aristotle was not of great help. He did offer several observations about actual human thought: The human intellect "thinks the forms in the images [found within the human imaginative faculty]"[70]; "intellect is [related] to what is intelligible as sensation is to what is sense perceptible"[71]; the intellect hence "is receptive of the form" it thinks[72]; "actual knowledge is identical with its object"[73]—in other words, an intellect becomes identical with whatever thought it thinks; although the human intellect receives a form and becomes identical therewith, the intellect is not "affected," or "altered" in the process, and is, moreover, free of affection and alteration to a greater degree than sensation, which likewise, according to Aristotle, is "not affected and altered."[74] The statements tell us that the human intellect takes forms from images in the imaginative faculty, thinks those forms, and becomes identical with them, without being altered in the process.

But as for the role played by the active intellect, Aristotle offered only two undeveloped analogies. First is the analogy already quoted which compares the active intellect to the "art" that acts on matter. Then a few lines later, Aristotle compared the active intellect to "light; for in a certain fashion, light makes potential colors actual. . . ."[75] The analogy with light might well suggest that the active intellect leads the human intellect to actuality by, in some sense, illuminating what is

[67]Aristotle, *Metaphysics* 9.8.1049b, 24–25. Cf. Proclus, *Elements of Theology*, ed. E. Dodds, 2d ed. (Oxford 1963), Proposition 77; that proposition cannot be identified in the material known to have been translated from Proclus' *Elements* into Arabic.

[68]See below, n. 80; W. D. Ross' introduction to his edition of the *De anima* (Oxford 1961) 43, 46–47.

[69]One translation of the *De anima* into Arabic in fact paraphrases Aristotle and has him establish not an intellect that is what it is by virtue of "making all things" but, instead, an intellect "that is an intellect by virtue of making the other [potential or material intellect] think all things"; see Averroes, Long Commentary on the *De anima* (n. 22 above) 437.

[70]Aristotle, *De anima* 3.7.431b, 2; cf. *De memoria* 1, 449b, 31–450a, 1.

[71]Ibid. 3.4.429a, 17–18.

[72]Ibid. 15–16.

[73]Ibid. 3.5.430a, 20.

[74]Ibid. 3.4.429a, 15, 29–31; 3.7.431a, 5.

[75]Ibid. 3.5.430a, 15–17.

intelligible in the world—or, more precisely, what is intelligible in images presented by the imaginative faculty to the human intellect; and the potential intellect becomes actual by, in some sense, viewing the illumined intelligible thoughts. Such a reading of the analogy can find support in Plato's notion, surely known to Aristotle, that man can "look at" the ideal Forms.[76] Aristotle's *De anima* does not, however, trouble to clarify what it has in mind. Having submitted the statements about actual human thought and the bald comparisons to art and light, the *De anima* turns away to other matters and leaves the commentators to their own devices.

Alfarabi, Avicenna, and Averroes have two explanations of the manner by which the active intellect effects actual human thought. In one, the active intellect casts a kind of light on images in the human imaginative faculty and on the potential intellect itself, thereby enabling the intellect to discern what is intelligible in the images. In the other, the active intellect functions as a cosmic transmitter, continually broadcasting all possible intelligible thoughts, and properly attuned human intellects receive intelligible thoughts directly from the active intellect. Antecedents for both explanations can be found in the late Greek and early Arabic sources.

To begin, Alexander of Aphrodisias' *De anima* should be mentioned. Alexander there rewords the Aristotelian grounds for positing an active intellect as follows: "In all things generated . . . by nature[77]. . . there is a matter, . . . which is potentially everything in the given domain," as well as "an agent" (ποιητικόν) that effects "the generation, in the matter, of the things the matter is receptive of." The distinction between matter and agent must also occur "in the case of intellect." Hence, since "a material intellect [ὑλικός τις νοῦς] exists," there "must likewise exist an active intellect [ποιητικὸς νοῦς], which is the cause of the habitus of the material intellect,"[78] that "habitus" being "a form . . . and perfection" of the material intellect.[79] Alexander would seem to be saying that the active intellect acts upon the material intellect and produces a habitus for thought in it. The ensuing account of the active intellect's role in human thought pursues a different line, which is of considerable interest in itself but not pertinent to the Arabic philosophers whom we are studying.[80]

[76]Plato, *Republic* 484C; *Euthryphro* 6E.

[77]More precisely: "In all things generated . . . by nature which do have a matter . . . there is a matter. . . ." Alexander is leaving open the possibility of things that are generated, yet contain no matter.

[78]Alexander, *De anima* (n. 1 above) 88.

[79]Ibid. 85.

[80]Alexander lays down the proposition that whatever has a given characteristic to the "highest degree and preeminently, . . . is the cause of other things' being such." (The converse was affirmed in Aristotle, *Metaphysics* 2.1.993b, 24–26: If something is the cause of other things' having a certain characteristic, it itself possesses the characteristic to a higher degree.) Alexander explains the proposition in a Platonic spirit: When something has a quality "preeminently" and

The *De intellectu*, which was read by the Arabic philosophers as a companion piece to Alexander's *De anima*, makes a number of points about the active intellect's role in producing human thought; and they, although disjointed and probably not even consistent with each other, are highly pertinent.

The first point is put thus in the Arabic translation of the *De intellectu*: What "produces intellectual thinking and leads the material intellect to actuality" is the "active" intellect, a being that is "intellect in actuality" and as a consequence "actually . . . and by its own nature . . . intelligible."[81] The active intellect is, "as Aristotle says, . . . analogous to light,"[82] for "light is the cause making colors that are potentially visible, actually so." If the analogy with light were intended at face value, the active intellect must somehow illumine potential objects of intellect and thereby transform them into actual objects of intellect. But in the present passage, the *De intellectu* ignores the implications of the analogy[83] and draws only the unfocused inference that the active intellect leads the material intellect to actuality: As light makes potential colors visible to the eye, "so too this [active] intellect renders the material intellect, which is in potentiality, an actual intellect." The active intellect renders the material intellect actual "by fixing a habitus for intellecting thought [Greek: the intellecting habitus] in" the material intellect.[84] A similar formulation was just met in Alexander's *De anima*.

In what may or may not be an amplification of the way the active intellect brings the potential intellect to actuality, the *De intellectu* goes on to allude to Aristotle's remark, in *De generatione animalium*, that "intellect alone enters [the organism] from without."[85] The *De intellectu* explains, in the language of the medieval Arabic version: When the active intellect "becomes cause of the material intellect's

---

something else has it "secondarily," "what [has the quality] secondarily receives existence from what [has it] preeminently." He gives two examples: "light," which is "to the highest degree visible" and is the cause of "other things' being visible"; and that which is to "the highest degree and primarily good" and is the cause of "other things'" being good. Applying the rule to intellect, Alexander finds that the transcendent active intellect, which is "preeminently and by its own nature intelligible," can "with reason" be considered the "cause of other things' intelligible thought" (Alexander, *De anima* 88–89). In a word, the active intellect is known to be the cause of human thought not because it is found to do anything, but inasmuch as it is the being with the highest degree of intelligibility.

Alexander adds a further bland consideration: "If" the active intellect is "the first cause" of the universe—as Alexander in fact took it to be—it "would," by virtue of being the cause of the universe, also "be" the ultimate "cause of the existence of all intelligible thoughts." The active intellect may, in other words, be deemed the cause of human thought in the most broad sense of being the cause of everything in the universe (Alexander, *De anima* 89). Neither here nor elsewhere in the treatise does Alexander describe a definite action or operation performed by the active intellect on the human material intellect.

[81]*De intellectu* (n. 2 above) 107–08.

[82]Ibid. 107.

[83]See Moraux, *Alexandre d'Aphrodise* (n. 3 above) 126–27.

[84]*De intellectu* 107.

[85]Aristotle, *De generatione animalium* 2.3.736b, 28.

abstracting, receiving, and conceiving every material form [as an intelligible thought]," it "is called the acting acquired intellect [Greek: the active intellect . . . from without]"; for it is "not any part and power of our soul, but rather appears in us from without."[86] If the statements quoted so far may be correlated, the *De intellectu* maintains that the transcendent active intellect enters man from without, it fixes a habitus for thought in the human intellect, it thereby leads the potential intellect to actuality, and the human intellect begins to think.

Still a further amplification, or perhaps an alternative position, follows. Aristotle had drawn a parallel between intellect and sense perception,[87] and the *De intellectu* plays on the parallel to expound what it calls "Aristotle's"[88] reasons for "introducing an acquired intellect [Greek: the intellect from without]." The exposition begins with the assertion that whenever anything "comes into existence," three factors must be present. These are "something undergoing affection, something active [ποιοῦν, *fā^c^il*], and a third thing, . . . namely, that which is generated . . . from them." In sense perception, the three factors are "the sense faculty, . . . the sense perceptible, and something generated, namely, the perception. . . ." And by analogy, thought too must contain a similar set of three factors. The argument focuses on the second of the factors found in all processes whereby things come into existence, hence in sense perception, and hence in thought as well.

The second factor in all processes is "something active." In sense perception, where the *De intellectu* calls the second factor "the sense perceptible," the text accordingly explains that the factor in question is "something active," an agent enabling the sense faculty to pass to actuality. Since thought requires the same set of factors, it too must have a factor with the character of the second one in sense perception, with the character of the factor rendering the sense faculty actual. And such a factor in thought can be nothing other than "an actual active intellect." Consequently, "just as there exist things that are actually sense perceptible and that render sensation actual, so too there must exist things that, being themselves actually intelligible, render the . . . intellect actual."[89] There must exist "an actual active intellect that renders the hitherto potential intellect capable of thinking," "brings the material, potential intellect to actuality," and renders "all existent things

[86]*De intellectu* 108.

[87]Above, p. 19.

[88]In the sequel, not quoted here, the *De intellectu* ascribes plainly Stoic theories to this "Aristotle"; see below, p. 30. Zeller, followed by Bruns, the editor of the *De intellectu*, therefore ingeniously conjectured that "Aristotle" is a copyist's error for "Aristokles," the name of Alexander's supposed teacher. See Zeller (n. 26 above) 815. P. Moraux, *Der Aristotelismus bei den Griechen* 2 (Berlin 1984) 83 and n. 6, has responded that Alexander had a teacher named Aristotle and that the reference is to him. See also F. Trabucco, "Il problema del de Philosophia di Aristocle di Messene e la sua doctrina," *Acme* 11 (1958) 117, 119.

[89]The Arabic manuscripts are garbled here. My translation is partly conjectural but it is compatible with the Greek original.

intelligible." This factor in thought, which parallels what is actually sense perceptible, and which brings the human intellect to actuality, is an "intellect . . . entering from without," according to the original Greek. It is "acquired from without," according to the medieval Arabic translation.[90]

The *De intellectu* fails to identify what it is that is actually sense perceptible and that makes the sense faculty actual. When Averroes later read the *De intellectu*, he understood that in the case of vision, the actually sense perceptible is light,[91] and the pages in the *De intellectu* coming after the statements just quoted tend to corroborate Averroes' interpretation.

The *De intellectu* now argues the new, unexpected proposition that the human material intellect is not, after all, wholly "passive" but is "active" as well, and further that it develops spontaneously, as the "ambulatory faculty" in man spontaneously passes to actuality with time.[92] To illustrate how the human intellect can be both active and passive, the *De intellectu* expands the repertoire of analogies by comparing the human intellect to an additional phenomenon, fire. Fire has two sides. It has an active side, which "destroys . . . matter," but at the same time it also "feeds on" matter, and "insofar as it feeds on matter, it passively undergoes affection." Similarly, the "acting [*fāᶜil*] intellect in us"—which here means the human material intellect, described in the lines immediately preceding as active—both "separates off" forms through its active side and "takes hold" of them through its passive side. Lest anyone suppose that recognizing an active side of the human intellect leaves the transcendent active intellect otiose, the *De intellectu* insists: Although the human potential intellect develops spontaneously, the active intellect "acquired from without [nonetheless] . . . assists the human intellect." The need for an active intellect is justified through the familiar analogy of light, already mentioned in an earlier passage of the *De intellectu*, and at this point the *De intellectu* extracts a little more from the analogy than it previously did. "Light . . . produces . . . actual sight" and, concomitantly with being "seen itself," renders "color" visible. Human thought similarly requires an active intellect that enters man and becomes "an object of thought" (according to the Greek but blurred in the Arabic translation), thereby "perfecting" the already active material intellect and "fixing the habitus [for thought] in it."[93] In perfecting the human intellect, the active intellect becomes itself an actual object of thought, just as light becomes an actual object of sight in the course of activating the faculty of vision.

In sum, the *De intellectu* first states generally that the active intellect renders the material intellect actual by entering man from without and fixing a habitus for thought in the material intellect; Alexander, or whoever wrote the work, supports

[90] *De intellectu* 110.

[91] Below, p. 325.

[92] Alexander's *De anima* 82, instead contrasts the ambulatory faculty, which becomes actualized naturally, with the intellectual faculty, which does not.

[93] Ibid. 111.

the statement through Aristotle's comparison of the active intellect to light yet ignores the analogy's implications. The *De intellectu* then develops another Aristotelian notion and compares the process of thought to the process of sensation. The parallel with sensation leads to the conclusion that human material intellect is activated by the active intellect in the way that the sense faculty is activated by what is actually sense perceptible. In a final clarification of the nature of actual human thought, the *De intellectu* submits that the material intellect is itself active, like fire, and develops spontaneously, like the ambulatory faculty. But even when recognizing an active side of the human intellect, the *De intellectu* still insists on the need for an external active intellect. The external active intellect enters the material intellect from without and becomes its actual object of thought, as light, besides illumining visible objects, serves as the actual object of vision.

Of interest for us in Plotinus is not his full doctrine of intellect but selected remarks.

Plotinus' cosmic Intellect has a certain resemblance to the Aristotelian active intellect, the cause of actual human thought, and the resemblance increases when the active intellect is taken to be a transcendent substance. It is hardly surprising, therefore, that Plotinus employed what was to become the standard argument for the existence of the active intellect as an argument for the existence of his own cosmic Intellect. In the wording of the Arabic paraphrase of the *Enneads*, an intellect must exist which brings about actual thought in soul, because "potentiality passes to actuality only through a cause that is in actuality similar to [what] the [former is in] potentiality."[94] In the original Greek, the argument is designed to prove that above the hypostasis Soul there stands the hypostasis Intellect. The Arabic paraphrase leaves uncertain, however, whether cosmic Soul or individual human souls are at issue. The anonymous Arabic paraphrase offering the argument might thus be treated as a text belonging to the Peripatetic mainstream, and the argument read as establishing the existence of an already actual intellect that brings the human rational soul to the state of actual thought.

Part or all of human intellectual knowledge is, for Plotinus, communicated to the human rational soul directly by the cosmic Intellect. Plotinus writes that whenever "a soul is able to receive," Intellect "gives" it clear principles, and then "it [the soul] combines" those principles "until it reaches perfect intellect."[95] In other passages the scope of the knowledge communicated by Intellect is broadened beyond "clear principles." In the wording of one of the Arabic paraphrases of Plotinus: "The intellectual sciences, which are the true sciences, come only from Intellect to the rational soul."[96] And the paraphrase known as the *Theology of Aristotle* brings

[94]*Risāla fī al-ᶜIlm al-Ilāhī*, in *Plotinus apud Arabes*, ed. A. Badawi (Cairo 1955) 168, paralleling *Enneads* 5.9.4. For the principle, see above, p. 18, and cf. *Theology of Aristotle* (n. 54 above) 38, paralleling *Enneads* 4.7.8[3].

[95]*Enneads* 1.3.5.

[96]*Risāla fī al-ᶜIlm al-Ilāhī* 169, paralleling *Enneads* 5.9.7.

the matter-form dichotomy to bear, maintaining: Soul has "the status of matter," it "receives the form of" Intellect, and "reason occurs in soul only thanks to Intellect."[97] The original Greek text of the last passage again had cosmic Soul, and not the individual human soul, in view. But Avicenna's comment on the passage as it appears in the *Theology of Aristotle*, shows that he took *soul* in the sense of the human soul, and *intellect* in the sense of the "active intelligences."[98] On such a reading, the human rational soul is a kind of matter that is perfected and receives all its intellectual knowledge through a form coming from an incorporeal intelligence.

Plotinus depicts the situation of the human soul vis à vis the cosmic Intellect through a metaphor that will recur over and over again in Arabic literature. The soul, he writes, contains a sort of mirror wherein images of thought and Intellect are reflected when the soul orients itself properly toward the higher world.[99]

Two more passages deserve to be mentioned. The first, which did not pass into the preserved Arabic paraphrases, says that man has intellectual thoughts (τὰ εἴδη) "in two ways." "In intellect," which seems to mean insofar as the human intellect remains part of the cosmic Intellect, man has intelligible thoughts "all together"; "in soul," that is to say, in his rational soul, which is an offshoot of the cosmic Soul, or perhaps of the cosmic Intellect, he has them "unrolled and discrete, as it were."[100] The second passage says that "the soul contains an acquired intellect [ἐπακτὸς νοῦς; *ᶜaql muktasab*] which illuminates it [that is, which illuminates the soul] . . . and renders it intellectual."[101]

If we do some violence to Plotinus by reading him primarily in the Arabic paraphrase and fitting the scattered quotations together in a synthesis, while ignoring much more that is central to his system, we get the following: A transcendent Intellect has to be assumed in order to account for the passage of the human rational soul from potentiality to actuality. Intellectual knowledge is transmitted directly by the transcendent Intellect to human rational souls that are properly oriented and ready to receive Intellect's bounty. The human intellect is like a mirror in which intelligible thoughts from above are reflected. Thought at a higher level, at the level of Intellect, is all together, which can be taken to mean that it is undifferentiated; at a subsequent level, it is unrolled, which can be taken to mean that thought becomes differentiated as it descends into the human rational soul. The relation of the human rational soul to the intelligible thought it receives is—as Aristotle already suggested and Alexander wrote explicitly—a relation of matter to form; and Plotinus adds that "clear principles" and the "intellectual sciences" constituting the form of the rational soul come directly from the transcendent Intellect. Because thought is acquired by the human intellect from

97 *Theology of Aristotle* 105–6, paralleling *Enneads* 5.1.3.

98 Cf. Avicenna's commentary on the *Theology of Aristotle* (n. 13 above) 72.

99 *Enneads* 1.4.10.

100 *Enneads* 1.1.8. Plotinus held that the human intellect does not descend from the cosmic Intellect into the human body. See Blumenthal (n. 48 above) 73–74.

101 *Al-Shaykh al-Yūnānī* (n. 37 above) 480–81, paralleling *Enneads* 5.6.4.

above, actual human thought is *acquired* intellect. When the foregoing statements, which are made here and there by Plotinus, are thus combined, they prefigure Avicenna's account of the manner whereby the active intellect acts on the human intellect.

Turning to Themistius, we find him laying down the rule that "nothing is perfected by itself" and inferring at once the existence of "an actual, perfect intellect," which leads the human intellect to actuality and perfection. Part of Themistius' justification for assuming a single active intellect for the entire human species is that all men grasp the same "common notions," "first definitions," and "first axioms," without being taught.[102] His intent could be either that the single active intellect communicates the principles of thought directly to the human intellect, or that it enables the human intellect to discern the principles of thought in sense perceptions and extract them from there.

In a possible echo of Plotinus, Themistius describes thoughts as "all together" in the active intellect, while in "the potential intellect they are differentiated." Thoughts that the active intellect "gives undividedly," the human intellect "cannot receive undividedly" but only in a differentiated mode.[103] Nevertheless, despite having described the active intellect as *giving* thoughts undividedly, Themistius does not mean that it conveys thoughts—with the possible exception of the first notions, axioms, and definitions, which were just mentioned—directly to the human mind. So much is plain when he deploys Aristotle's analogy of light in order to explain the interaction of active intellect and potential intellect.

The implication of the analogy receives more attention from Themistius than it did from Alexander. Themistius writes: When "light becomes present in the potential faculty of vision and in potential colors, it turns the former into actual vision and the latter into actual colors." In an analogous manner, the active intellect joins "the potential intellect," acts on it, and acts as well on man's "potential intelligible thoughts"; potential intelligible thoughts, which parallel potential colors, are sense perceptions, mediated by the imaginative faculty and stored in the human memory. The active intellect turns the potential intellect into "actual intellect" and renders potential thoughts "actually intelligible to" the human intellect.[104] In other words, the active intellect, functioning as a sort of light, activates both images in the soul, which are potential thoughts, and the human potential intellect; and it thereby enables the potential intellect to perceive actual thoughts and to become actual itself. Besides exhibiting, after a fashion, how the active intellect renders the human intellect actual, the analogy serves the further purpose of helping Themistius grasp how the active intellect, although a transcendent being, can have been located by

[102]Themistius, Paraphrase of the *De anima* (n. 5 above) 98, 103–4. There is a certain similarity between Themistius' position and the position of the *De intellectu* quoted above, p. 22, since according to both, the active intellect joins the potential human intellect at the beginning of the latter's development.

[103]Themistius, Paraphrase of the *De anima* 100.

[104]Ibid. 98–99.

Aristotle *in* the human soul: The active intellect is in itself one, but it breaks up and enters different human subjects, just as natural light comes from a single source and breaks up in the different subjects receiving it.[105]

Themistius deploys the other Aristotelian analogy too and describes the active intellect as standing to the potential intellect as "art" stands to "matter." He appends a qualification, however: Art and the artisan remain outside the matter they act upon, whereas the active intellect "enters into the potential intellect through and through."[106] Then Themistius pursues the comparison of the human potential intellect with matter along a different line. The several faculties of the soul, he writes, make up a hierarchy in which each level has the status of "matter" in respect to the level above it, while the level above is the lower level's "form." The faculty of "sense perception" serves as matter for the imaginative faculty, the "imagination" as matter for the "potential intellect," and the potential intellect as matter for the "active [intellect]." In the last instance, the active intellect "becomes one with" the potential intellect in the way "matter and form" constitute a single entity. And unlike the intermediate levels of the soul, which are both matter in respect to what comes next and form in respect to what precedes, the active intellect is not the matter of anything else. The active intellect is the soul's form in the "true sense," the "final form," the "form of forms," and in it the process culminates.[107]

The upshot is that the active intellect, or an aspect of the active intellect, enters the potential human intellect, penetrates it through and through, works from within, lights up the potential intellect and also casts a light on images stored in the memory, and becomes the form of the potential intellect. The active intellect is responsible for the first axioms of thought and perhaps conveys them directly to man. After the active intellect has joined the human potential intellect, the compound of the two constructs a corpus of intellectual knowledge. By joining with the potential intellect and "leading it to actuality" the active intellect "effects the intellect *in habitu*, in which universal intelligible thoughts and universal scientific knowledge reside."[108]

In early Arabic philosophy, both Kindi's treatise *On Intellect* and the treatise *On the Soul* attributed to Porphyry maintain that a supernal being communicates actual thought directly to the human intellect. Kindi offers the standard argument for the existence of an agent that produces human thought: Whenever something has a certain characteristic potentially, it can only be actualized by something else already possessing the given characteristic actually; therefore the human soul, which is potentially in possession of intelligible thought, can be rendered actual only "through the first intellect."[109] But Kindi does not merely conclude that actual

[105]Ibid. 103; cf. above, p. 12.

[106]Ibid. 99.

[107]Ibid. 99–100. At several points, the Arabic differs slightly from the Greek, and I have translated the latter.

[108]Ibid. 98.

[109]*Rasā'il al-Kindī* (n. 22 above) 356; cf. ibid. 155.

human thought entails an actual intellect as its cause. Actual thought occurs when the human soul "makes contact [*bāshara*] with intellect, that is, with forms containing neither matter nor imagination"; and first intellect is the intellect with which it makes contact. First intellect "supplies" (*mufīd*) what the human soul "acquires" (*mustafīd*), and the product is "intellect acquired [*mustafād*] by the [human] soul from the first intellect."[110] How the human intellect makes contact with supernal intellect and what role sense perception plays in the process is left unexplained.

The treatise *On the Soul* attributed to Porphyry does not articulate a full theory of intellect but does affirm that thought comes to man directly from a transcendent source. The treatise distinguishes "material intellect," that is, the potential human intellect, from "second, psychic [*nafsānī*] intellect," which is shown by the context to be the human intellect in possession of actual thought[111]; other writers use the term *second intellect* in a similar sense.[112] "Psychic intellect" is "identical with the [transcendent] first intellect when they are in the upper world . . . but is different from it [from the transcendent intellect] when it [the psychic intellect] appears in the body through the medium of the soul."[113] The brief treatise, annoyingly, also uses an alternative terminology and states that human "intellect," with no further qualification, comes "from" the "intelligible world" and serves as "form" of the human soul.[114] Since, however, *intelligible world* is an appellation for the Neoplatonic cosmic Intellect,[115] the statement may be harmonized with the previous quotation as follows: Actual human thought consists in a form that comes to the human soul from the transcendent first intellect, also called *intelligible world*; when the form is still in first intellect, the two are identical; but when manifested in the human soul, the form from above becomes distinct from first intellect and is called *second psychic intellect*. The treatise *On the Soul* further states that the human material intellect can never think without the aid of the "estimative faculty" (*wahm*), a physical faculty of the soul.[116] That statement can be integrated with the others by understanding that when the material intellect contemplates perceptions presented to it by the estimative faculty of the soul, it prepares itself to receive actual intellectual thought from the transcendent Intellect. Avicenna will take a position along those lines.

[110]Ibid. 355–56.

[111]Kutsch (n. 55 above) 268, §§3, 4.

[112]Ibn Gabirol (n. 58 above) 5, §34; Altmann and Stern (n. 56 above) 36. Other senses of *second intellect* appear in the long version of the *Theology of Aristotle*, cited by. S. Stern, "Ibn Ḥasdāy's Neoplatonist," *Oriens* 13 (1961) 88, 91–92; and in Alfarabi, *Risāla fī al-ᶜAql*, ed. M. Bouyges (Beirut 1938) 19. *Rasā'il al-Kindī* 354, also uses the term, but the sense is unclear.

[113]Kutsch 268, §4.

[114]Ibid. §2.

[115]Plotinus, *Enneads* 5.9.9; E. Zeller, *Die Philosophie der Griechen* 3.2, 5th ed. (Leipzig 1923) 584–87.

[116]Kutsch 268, §3.

Here we have seen that a standard argument developed for assuming a cause of the actualization of the human intellect: Whenever something passes from potentiality to actuality, the passage to actuality is effected by an agent that itself already actually possesses the characteristic in question; the passage of the human potential intellect to actuality therefore implies an agent possessing actual thought which brings about the transition (Plotinus, Themistius, Kindi). If the conclusion should be taken to mean that the cause of human thought not only already possesses actual thought but that it consists in such thought, the argument would establish an incorporeal, transcendent cause (Themistius; the argument is not explicit in Plotinus and Kindi, although they do have a transcendent cause of human thought).

One explanation of the way in which the transcendent cause effects actual human thought played on Aristotle's analogy of light. In Themistius' version, which draws the analogy's implications most clearly, the active intellect both casts a light on potential thoughts, which are images in the human soul, and also lights up the potential human intellect; it thereby enables the potential intellect to perceive actual thoughts and to pass to actuality. Another explanation of the way the transcendent cause effects actual human thought represented the transcendent cause as directly furnishing either all human thoughts (probably Plotinus; Kindi; the text attributed to Porphyry) or certain basic thoughts (possibly Themistius). In the spirit of the second explanation, the human soul was described as containing a sort of mirror that reflects the contents of the transcendent intellect (Plotinus), and thought was characterized as *acquired* from the transcendent intellect (Plotinus, Kindi).

Additional motifs encountered here which were to be significant for the Arabic Aristotelians are these: The active intellect is related to the human potential intellect as form to matter (Alexander, Plotinus, Themistius); in bringing the human intellect to actuality, the active intellect enters into man (*De intellectu*, Themistius); thoughts that are all together or undifferentiated in the transcendent intellect are unrolled and become differentiated in the human soul or intellect (Plotinus, Themistius).

The Active Intellect as a Cause of Existence

One work of Alfarabi's, Avicenna generally, and the early works of Averroes not only recognized a transcendent cause that leads human intellects to actuality; they represented the transcendent cause of human thought, the active intellect, as the cause of the existence of part or all of the sublunar world. In Alfarabi and Averroes, the active intellect, besides leading the human intellect to actuality, emanates a range of sublunar natural forms; in Avicenna, the active intellect, which not merely leads the human intellect to actuality but directly emanates all human intelligible thoughts upon properly prepared human intellects, emanates both the matter of the sublunar world and a range of natural forms appearing in sublunar matter. Neither the active intellect of Alfarabi and Averroes, nor that of Avicenna, can be documented prior to their appearance in those philosophers. There were, nevertheless, a number of precedents for tracing both the actualization of the human intellect and the existence of part or all of the physical universe to beings standing above the physical universe on the scale of existence. In at least one of the instances, the two functions, actualization of the human intellect and responsibility for the existence of the physical world, had explicitly been combined in a single transcendent active intellect; the emanation motif was not yet present, however. In another of the instances, the two functions were traced to the supernal region, and the existence of the sublunar world was, moreover, seen as the outcome of an emanative process; but the two functions were not ascribed to the same supernal substance. In this second instance, distinct, though kindred, cosmic entities performed functions very much like those that Avicenna was to combine in a single active intellect.

The work explicitly combining the two functions in a transcendent active intellect is Alexander's *De anima*. As was seen, Alexander there identifies Aristotle's active intellect, the cause of human thought, with the First Cause of the universe.[117] Unlike Aristotle, who had envisaged a First Cause solely of the universe's motion,[118] Alexander characterizes the First Cause as "cause and principle of the existence of all other things,"[119] which must mean that it is responsible for the very existence, and not merely the motion, of the universe. His active intellect is therefore both the cause of actual human thought and the cause, or at least the ultimate cause, of the existence of everything outside itself.

A different combination of the two functions in the active intellect appears at the end of the *De intellectu*, also attributed to Alexander. The section is problematic even in the original Greek and gets further obscured in the Arabic translation. Nevertheless, one can see from the Greek that the *De intellectu* is examining what it knows to be a Stoic theory. The active intellect is described as a divine, but corporeal, substance that permeates the matter of the entire universe without ceasing to perform its own act of thinking. It governs the sublunar world "either by itself" or in cooperation with the "motion . . . of the heavens," by combining and separating the particles of matter from which natural objects are generated. It is thereby also the "cause [of the existence]" (δημιουργός, *khāliq*) of the "potential intellect," a potential human intellect being generated whenever a portion of matter is blended in such a way that the matter can serve as an "instrument" for thought. After bringing the potential human intellect into existence, the active intellect leads it

[117]Above, p. 13.

[118]Cf. E. Zeller, *Die Philosophie der Griechen* 2.2, 4th ed. (Leipzig 1921) 379–81; H. Davidson, *Proofs for Eternity, Creation, and the Existence of God, in Medieval Islamic and Jewish Philosophy* (New York 1987) 281–82.

[119]Alexander, *De anima* (n. 1 above) 89.

to actuality. Actual human thought is, in fact, simply the divine active intellect's thinking through the human intellect.[120]

In the original Greek, the author of the *De intellectu*—or if the work is composite, the author of the pertinent section in the *De intellectu*—proceeds to refute the theory, and in the course of doing so expressly connects it with "the Stoa." The Arabic blurs the refutation beyond recognition, however, and does not translate "Stoa" by the standard Arabic term for that school. In the Arabic, the section might therefore easily be misread as representing the *De intellectu*'s, and hence Alexander's, own view.[121] Even when misread, the theory differs from the position of Alexander's *De anima*. In consonance with its Stoic inspiration, it has the divine active intellect penetrating the material world; Alexander's *De anima*, by contrast, saw the active intellect as transcendent and wholly incorporeal. The theory, moreover, acknowledges only a divine factor working within, and giving form to, the matter of the sublunar world, but not a cause of the existence of all matter, or even sublunar matter; Alexander's *De anima* spoke of a cause of the existence of the entire universe, which presumably means all matter and all form. Still, the theory recorded in the *De intellectu* provided medieval Arabic readers with a further instance of the active intellect's serving as both cause of actual human thought and—by itself or in cooperation with the heavens—the direct cause of all natural objects in the sublunar world, including the potential human intellect.

Plotinus' system traces to the incorporeal realm, although not to a single substance in that realm, both the actualization of the human intellect and the bringing of the physical universe into existence; and several significant threads in Plotinus would be woven together in a new pattern by the Arabic Aristotelians. Intellect, the second hypostasis in Plotinus' cosmic hierarchy, has something of the character of the Aristotelian active intellect and is the source of human intellectual activity.[122] As refracted through the Arabic paraphrases, Plotinus further states that Intellect is "all things, and all things are in it. . . . They are in it as [in] their agent, whereas it is in them as cause."[123] "Intellect is . . . cause of what is beneath it."[124] That is to say, Intellect is the cause of the existence of Soul, the third hypostasis in the cosmic hierarchy; it is the incorporeal model of the physical universe, including the sublunar region[125]; and it is the agent ultimately, although not directly, responsible for the existence of the physical universe. What immediately "engendered matter" is Soul.[126] Inasmuch as matter is "only a recipient," the forms of the four elements—"fire, . . . water, . . . air, . . . earth"—and of physical beings above the level of the elements must, like matter

[120]*De intellectu* (n. 2 above) 112–13.

[121]See further, below, p. 282.

[122]Above, n. 42.

[123]*Risāla fī al-ᶜIlm al-Ilāhī* (n. 94 above) 168 bottom, paralleling *Enneads* 5.9.6.

[124]*Theology of Aristotle* (n. 54 above) 144–45, paralleling *Enneads* 6.7.3.

[125]Cf. Armstrong (n. 42 above) 75.

[126]*Enneads* 1.8.14; 4.3.9. Cf. Zeller (n. 115 above) 603–4.

itself, come "from another." Their immediate source is, again, Soul, which transmits what was given it by Intellect.[127] "Soul emanates [*tufīḍ*] its power over this entire world, . . . and nothing corporeal . . . is free of the power of Soul"; "each body obtains of the power and goodness of Soul in accordance with its ability to receive that power and goodness"; the "goodness" that Soul sends forth is "form," the underlying recipient of the goodness sent forth being "matter."[128] Among the forms bestowed by Soul upon the physical world are human souls, and a human soul makes its appearance whenever a body is properly prepared for receiving one.[129]

Plotinus' Intellect, which was seen to be a direct source of some or all human intellectual thought, is thus also the ultimate cause of the emanation of the entire physical universe. His cosmic Soul is the immediate emanating source of the matter of the universe, including the matter of the sublunar region, and of forms manifested in matter. In the sublunar world, those forms range from the four elements to the human soul. As a team, Intellect and Soul are the source of some or all of human thought, they emanate the matter of the universe, and they emanate natural forms, each portion of matter receiving the natural form for which it is fit.

Themistius was already seen to construe the cause of actual human thought as a transcendent active intellect. His Paraphrase of Aristotle's *De anima*, the work in which he delineates the active intellect's role in human thought, also makes the suggestive remark that "the Soul . . . inserts [ἐντιθέναι, *tarkuz*] [natural] forms in matter."[130] His Paraphrase of Aristotle's *Metaphysics*, Book 12, has more to say. The occasion is a passage in Aristotle's *Metaphysics* which rejects the Platonic doctrine of Forms on the grounds that "man begets a man." Themistius comments: The rule that the progenitor always belongs to the same species as the offspring, that "man is born only from man and the horse from a horse," leaves unexplained the spontaneous generation of a "kind of hornet" from the "bodies of dead horses," of "bees . . . from dead cattle," and similar phenomena. To

[127]*Risāla fī al-ᶜIlm al-Ilāhī* 168, paralleling *Enneads* 5.9.3.

[128]*Theology of Aristotle* 78, paralleling *Enneads* 4.8.6. Cf. Proclus, *Elements of Theology* (n. 67 above) Propositions 122 and 140, and Dodds' note to Proposition 140. *Liber de causis*, which is an Arabic paraphrase of parts of the *Elements of Theology*, states: "The First Cause . . . emanates goodness upon all things in a single emanation [*faiḍ*], but each thing receives of that emanation in accordance with its existence and being. . . . Goodness and virtues differ [in the universe] only by reason of the recipient." See *Liber de causis*, ed. O. Bardenhewer (Freiburg 1882) 95–96, paralleling *Elements of Theology*, Proposition 122.

[129]*Enneads* 4.8.4–6; 4.9.2. The Henry-Schwyzer edition (n. 4 above) has Lewis' English translation of an unpublished Arabic paraphrase of these sections. In Plotinus, individual souls are not completely separated from the Universal Soul; cf. Zeller (n. 115 above) 596–97; E. Brehier, *The Philosophy of Plotinus* (Chicago 1958) 66–68. For some of the problems that arise in Plotinus' philosophy regarding the forms of individual objects, see Zeller 581–82; J. Rist, *Plotinus: The Road to Reality* (Cambridge 1967) 104ff.; A. Armstrong, "Form, Individual and Person in Plotinus," reprinted in his *Plotinian and Christian Studies* (London 1979) chap. 20.

[130]Themistius, Paraphrase of *De anima* (n. 5 above) 115; Arabic translation 211.

explain spontaneous generation, certain "relationships" must be assumed to have "been put in nature" and they are what bring forth not only animals that generate spontaneously but also animals that ostensibly reproduce. Those relationships are "disposed and ready for the generation of any given animal species, whenever they [the relationships] encounter material appropriate for the generation of the given animal." Whence it follows that the formation of the human offspring is the "work" of forces in nature and not of the father; and the forces in nature derive in turn from "the world-Soul, which Plato understands to be generated from the secondary deities and which Aristotle understands to be generated from the sun and the inclined sphere [of the sun's annual motion]."[131]

Thus Themistius too traces both actual human thought and the existence of natural forms, particularly animal souls, to transcendent causes, although not to the same cause, since the world-Soul would rank, for him. below the active intellect in the hierarchy of existence.

In the Arabic world prior to Alfarabi, Kindi discloses musings of the sort that have been cited here from Greek works. In one composition, he was seen to name "first intellect" as the cause of actual human thought. In another, he maintains that the heavens are the cause of generation and corruption in our lower world,[132] the cause of all life in this world,[133] more particularly, the "cause of [man's] being generated," and finally "the agent of [human] reason,"[134] which, the context indicates, means that the heavens bring the potential human intellect into existence. What is significant for us is that the heavens do not—as in Aristotle—produce life and the other phenomena in a merely mechanical fashion.[135] They "grant" (*mufīd*) life, insofar as they themselves possess life, and "make us rational, insofar as they are themselves rational."[136]

Yet another of Kindi's works is concerned with the source solely of the human soul. Instead of tracing the origin of the human soul to the heavens, as in the passage just quoted, it states that the human soul is "of the substance of the creator," and stands in the same relationship to the creator as the "light of the sun to the sun."[137] The creator, in other words, somehow radiates the human soul from

[131]Themistius, Paraphrase of *Metaphysics* 12 (n. 6 above) 7–8. The Arabic translation from the Greek, from which the Hebrew translation was in turn made, has been lost, but the Arabic version of the present passage has been preserved by Averroes, Long Commentary on *Metaphysics* (n. 11 above), 1492–94. Cf. Plato, *Timaeus* 34; Aristotle, *Metaphysics* 12.5 1071a, 15–16, together with Ross' note on the *ecliptic*; *De generatione et corruptione* 2.10.

[132]*Rasā'il al-Kindī* (n. 22 above) 247.

[133]Ibid. 252.

[134]Ibid. 255.

[135]Cf. Aristotle, *De generatione et corruptione* 2.10; Alexander, *De anima* (n. 1 above) 24; Alexander, *Quaestiones*, in *Scripta minora* (n. 1 above), *Quaestio* 2.3; Zeller (n. 26 above) 827–28; Moraux, *Alexandre d'Aphrodise* (n. 3 above) 30–37.

[136]*Rasā'il al-Kindī* 252, 255. The heavens, nevertheless, do not initiate their own actions, the functions they perform being assigned to them by the creator; *Rasā'il al-Kindī* 255.

[137]Ibid. 273.

himself, so that Kindi is here giving a different version of the supernal source of the human soul.

Kindi, then, attributes the processes of generation and corruption in the physical world, life in the physical world, the existence of the human rational soul, and the actualization of the human intellect, to living, rational beings in the higher realms, although not to the same agent within those realms. His works are not even consistent in tracing the same phenomenon to the same cause. For in one text he attributes the actualization of the human intellect to "first intellect," and in another to the "universals of things"[138]; in yet a third text he attributes the generation of the human soul to the rational animate heavens, and in still another to the Creator. The character of his writings should dissuade us from the temptation to harmonize the divergent positions that he embraced on different occasions.

The Arabic Aristotelians, in sum, had precedents for crediting supernal causes with both the actualization of the human intellect and the existence of the entire physical universe (Alexander's *De anima*, Plotinus), or the formal side of the sublunar world (*De intellectu*, Themistius, Kindi). They had a precedent for attributing the two functions specifically to a single transcendent active intellect (Alexander's *De anima*). There were sources for the notion that a material form appears as soon as a portion of matter is properly prepared (*De intellectu*, Plotinus) and for the more specific notion that natural forms are emanated from above upon properly prepared matter (Plotinus). One of Alfarabi's compositions, we shall find, combines in the transcendent active intellect the emanation of a range of natural forms upon properly prepared matter, and the actualization of the human intellect; Avicenna combines in the active intellect the emanation of the matter of the sublunar region, the emanation of natural forms upon properly prepared sublunar matter, and the emanation of all actual human thought; and Averroes' early works take a position close to the position of that one work of Alfarabi's.

Conjunction with the Active Intellect; Immortality

Alfarabi, Avicenna, and Averroes ascribed additional functions to the active intellect, functions with a religious coloring. They explained that human prophecy results from an emanation of the active intellect, they recognized a role for the active intellect in human immortality, and they envisioned a crowning human state wherein the human intellect enters into *conjunction* with the active intellect. I could find no precedent for their explanations of prophetic phenomena. But the role of the active intellect in human immortality and the possibility of the human intellect's entering a state of conjunction with the active intellect again have their antecedents in Greek and earlier Arabic philosophy.

[138]Above, p. 16.

Both those doctrines were already presaged in Aristotle. "Presumably," Aristotle wrote, "it is impossible for the entire [soul] . . . to survive"[139]; "any part" of the soul whose "actuality" (or: entelechy [ἐντελέχεια]) is also the actuality of a part of the body will "plainly . . . be inseparable from the body."[140] "Nothing, however, will prevent" parts of the soul whose "actuality" is not the actuality of the body from surviving the body's demise.[141] Consequently, "nothing will prevent . . . the intellect . . . from surviving"[142]; "intellect . . . apparently does not perish"[143]; "intellect set free" from the body "is alone immortal and eternal," although it does "not remember [anything about this life], since it is impassive, while the passive intellect is destructible."[144] The exact intent of the statements, assuming them to be consistent and to have a single intent, turns on several questions of interpretation, namely, whether "intellect" in each instance means the potential human intellect, the human intellect after it has passed to actuality, or the active intellect; whether or not Aristotle viewed the active intellect as a transcendent being[145]; and whether "passive intellect" in the last quotation is identical with potential intellect. Whatever the correct answers might be, the quotations surely appear to rule out the immortality of nonintellectual parts of the human soul, while strongly suggesting that some aspect of man's intellect can enjoy immortality. If what survives death is the human intellect in a state of actuality, if the active intellect is distinct from the human intellect, and if the active intellect is what renders the human intellect actual, then the active intellect will be the cause leading man to whatever immortality he enjoys.

Aristotle further tantalized his readers with the promise: "Whether or not intellect can, when not itself separate from [spatial] magnitude [that is, when still linked to a human body], think anything that is separate [incorporeal] has to be considered later."[146] The passage seems to pose the possibility of the human intellect's having incorporeal beings as a direct object of thought, that is to say, of the human intellect's not merely thinking propositions about incorporeal beings but taking hold of their very form, as the intellect does when thinking the form of a rock or a tree. An incorporeal being consists in nothing but form; and, in Aristotle's epistemology, intellect is identical with whatever thought it thinks.[147] Therefore, should the human intellect be able to have an incorporeal being, and the active intellect in particular, as the object of its thought, should it be able to take hold of the

[139] Aristotle, *Metaphysics* 12.3.1070a, 26.

[140] Aristotle, *De anima* 2.1.413a, 4–6.

[141] Ibid. 6–7.

[142] Aristotle, *Metaphysics* 12.3.1070a, 24–26.

[143] Aristotle, *De anima* 1.4.408b, 18–19.

[144] Ibid. 3.5.430a, 22–25.

[145] Aristotle's rule that whatever is generated undergoes destruction would appear to limit immortality to an already eternal intellect that enters man from without.

[146] Aristotle, *De anima* 3.7.431b, 17–19.

[147] Above, p. 19.

incorporeal being's form, it would, presumably, be able to become identical with that form—with the active intellect itself. If such is in fact the issue that Aristotle promised to consider "later," nothing in his preserved works ever fulfills the promise.

Alexander's *De anima*, despite its naturalistic treatment of the human material intellect, maintains unequivocally that the human intellect can have incorporeal beings, and the active intellect in particular, as an object of direct thought. And human immortality, for Alexander, is nothing other than the condition in which the active intellect is the object of man's thought.

Alexander's reasoning runs: Things that are compound and consist of matter and form—in other words, physical objects—are potentially intelligible until the intelligible component is separated off from the material substratum and actually thought by an intellect. Only then do the forms of physical objects become actually intelligible. "If," however, things should exist which are forms "without matter or substratum," nothing has to be separated off from a substratum and rendered actually intelligible. Things of the sort would be actually intelligible by their very nature and not made so by any operation performed on them. Now, to be actually intelligible is to be actually thought by a thinking subject. And according to Aristotle, "actual intellect is identical with what is actually thought"; an intellect actually thinking an intelligible thought is identical with whatever thought it thinks. If a form exists independently of matter, is hence actually intelligible by its own nature, and contains nothing apart from what is actually intelligible, the subject thinking it would be wholly identical with it. A pure form would, in other words, be both an actual object of thought and also the subject having it as the object of thought. It would be an incorporeal being having itself as a permanent actual object of thought, an intellect thinking itself.[148]

The proposition that "actual intellect is identical with what is actually thought" has another implication as well. For the rule must also apply to whatever other intellect might have an actually intelligible form, that is, an actual incorporeal intellect, as the object of thought. Hence should a human intellect think an actually intelligible form, it too would become identical with the form. The human intellect would become identical with the incorporeal being that thinks, and is itself identical with, its own form.

The questions remain whether anything exists which is by its very nature actually intelligible and consequently an incorporeal intellect, and whether a being of the sort, something actually intelligible by its own nature, can ever become a direct object of human thought. Alexander's *De anima* answered the first question by establishing the existence of the active intellect, which for Alexander is the First Cause of the universe.[149] His *De anima* does not answer the second, but simply assumes that incorporeal beings and the active intellect in particular can be an object

[148]Cf. *De intellectu* (n. 2 above) 108.
[149]Above, p. 13.

of human thought. A human intellect having the active intellect, the First Cause of the universe, as the object of its thought would undergo something prodigious. It would become identical with the First Cause, which is the object of its thought. It would "in a sense become" the First Cause, in a sense become God.[150]

On becoming identical with the First Cause or another incorporeal being, the human intellect would be rendered as immortal as they are. There is, however, less there than meets the eye.

An incorporeal being "remains indestructible irrespective of being thought [by something other than itself]." Any "intellect," most pertinently a human intellect, having that which is intelligible by its very nature—a form existing independently of matter—as an object of thought becomes identical with, and shares the indestructibility and immortality of, the object of its thought. It becomes equally "indestructible." But here is the rub: The surviving moment in a human intellect having an incorporeal being as the object of its thought cannot be "the underlying and material intellect"; for Alexander understands the material intellect to be a *mere disposition* in the human organism which "perishes together with the soul, whose faculty it is." Nor can "the habitus [for thought] and the power and perfection" of the material intellect survive, even when an incorporeal being is the object of thought.[151] The habitus and perfection of the material intellect perish together with the material intellect, in which they reside.[152] The "intellect" that is indestructible and survives the body is not, for Alexander, the intellectual faculty of the soul at any level or in any guise but the detached human thought of an actual intelligible form—a detached thought identical with its incorporeal object. According to the Greek: "This is the intellect from without which comes to be in us and is indestructible," the intellect "that Aristotle described [in *De generatione animalium* 2.3.736b, 28] as from without."[153]

The Greek text of Alexander's *De anima* thus makes clear that only a detached human thought of an incorporeal being, and no part of the human intellectual

[150]Alexander, *De anima* (n. 1 above) 87–89.

[151]Alexander, *De anima* 90, explains why human intellect with "universals" as the object of its thought cannot survive. He takes for granted, as any good Aristotelian should, that "universals" do not enjoy independent existence. In the external world, they exist solely through the individuals belonging to the class that the universal denotes; in the mental realm, their existence as concepts and universals depends on an intellect's happening to think them; and whenever the intellect or intellects thinking them cease to do so, universals cease to exist as universals. Mathematical concepts, Alexander further explains, are "similar." Their existence also depends on their being thought, and when no intellect thinks them, they cease to exist as actual concepts. (There seems to be a circularity in the argument.)

[152] With this statement, another has to be harmonized. On p. 88, Alexander writes that when the human "intellect *in habitu*" thinks incorporeal "forms, it becomes . . . identical with them."

[153]Ibid. 90–91. The words "that Aristotle described . . . without" are bracketed by the editor of the Greek text, but do appear in the Arabic; see immediately below. For a critique of Alexander's reading of the *De generatione animalium*, see Moraux, *Alexandre d'Aphrodise* (n. 3 above) 105–6.

faculty, attains immortality. Readers of the Arabic translation could, however, have been misled into supposing that Alexander recognized the survival of something more. Intellect *from without*, as we have seen, is an incorporeal form during the time it is an object of human thought. It is so designated because it already was an actual intellect when still outside, and before being thought by, the human intellect; intelligible forms abstracted from material objects are, by contrast, rendered actually intelligible, and become actual intellect, only when in the human intellect. But the Arabic translation of Alexander departs from the original by characterizing the indestructible aspect of man as "the intellect we acquire and which comes to be in us" and, again, as what "Aristotle calls the acquired intellect, which comes to be in us from without."[154] An Arabic reader might therefore have concluded that the immortal moment in man is an advanced stage of intellect which comes to be in man and is called acquired intellect.

A passage in Alexander's *De anima* which may not have appeared in the Arabic translation—the Arabic translation is lost, and the passage is missing in the medieval Hebrew translation from the Arabic—advises "those who are concerned with having something divine in themselves to provide themselves" with the ability to "think what is of that nature."[155] Whether the apotheosis of human thought is a by-product of normal intellectual development or only select intellects achieve it, whether thought with an incorporeal being as object remains with man once he attains it or, on the contrary, it is episodic and each fleeting episode is immortal, whether the event has any cognitive content, mystical[156] or other, whether man is ever conscious of the experience, is all left open.

The *De intellectu*, the other work on the human intellect attributed to Alexander, likewise affirms the possibility of the human intellect's having an incorporeal being as a direct object of thought. The text further takes up an item that Alexander's *De anima* failed to address; it considers the point in human development where thought with the active intellect as object occurs.

One passage says, in the Arabic translation of the *De intellectu*, that "intellect by its own nature [and] acquired from without" (the word *acquired* is added by the Arabic) "enters" into the human intellect, becomes "itself an object of thought," and "helps" render what is potentially intelligible actually so, just as light is itself seen and renders colors visible.[157] Apparently, the active intellect is an object of human thought as soon as the human intellect begins to think. The passage in the *De intellectu* which compared three moments in intellect to three in sensation[158] also implies that the active intellect becomes an object of human thought as a condition of man's beginning to think. There the analogue of the actual object of sensation

[154]Medieval Hebrew translation of medieval Arabic translation (n. 31 above) of Alexander, *De anima* 90.

[155]Ibid. 91.

[156]Moraux *Alexandre d'Aphrodise* 104; Merlan (n. 25 above) 16–20.

[157]*De intellectu* 111.

[158]Above, p. 22.

was the active intellect, which is the actual object of intellectual thought; and since an actual object of sensation, such as light, is present as soon as sensation takes place, the actual object of intellectual thought would by analogy be present as soon as man starts thinking.

Immediately after the comparison of sensation to intellect, the *De intellectu* expresses what appears to be a different view. It states: "The potential intellect, when perfected and grown, has as an object of thought" intellect that is "intelligible by its very nature." "For as the ambulatory faculty, which man possesses from birth, becomes actual with the passage of time, . . . the [human] intellect too, once it is perfected, has things intelligible by their nature as an object of thought."[159] In other words, man's intellect, like his ambulatory faculty, grows spontaneously, and upon reaching maturity it gains a direct concept of incorporeal beings, which are intelligible by their nature. In contrast to the previous passages, where the human intellect has the active intellect as an object of thought at the beginning of the thought process, here the human intellect has unspecified incorporeal beings as an object of thought at some level of perfection. Either the *De intellectu* is simply inconsistent, or it understands the active intellect to be an object of human thought from the beginning of the thought process and other incorporeal beings to be objects of human thought at the end. The *De intellectu* further indicates that the sole immortal aspect in man is the "intellect from without [Arabic: acquired from without]" when it becomes an object of the human intellect.[160]

Alexander's *De anima* recognizes, then, the possibility of the human intellect's having the active intellect as an object of thought and thereby "in a sense" becoming identical with the active intellect. The *De intellectu* implies in certain passages that the active intellect becomes an object of human thought as a condition of human intellectual activity, and states in another passage that the human intellect has "things intelligible by their nature as an object of thought" when the intellect is perfected. The sole immortal aspect in man is, for Alexander's *De anima*, detached human thought having the active intellect as object, and, for the *De intellectu*, the intellect from without, but the Arabic translations of the two works could have misled readers into supposing that Alexander accepted the immortality of something more, of an advanced stage of human intellect called *acquired intellect*.

Themistius, in his Paraphrase of the *De anima*, separates the possibility of the human intellect's conjoining with the active intellect from the question of the active intellect's becoming an object of human thought. On his reading of Aristotle, an

[159]Ibid. 110–11. The reason for the discrepancy may be the composite character of the *De intellectu*.

[160]Cf. *De intellectu* 108, 111. Reference should also be made to a statement in the commentary on Aristotle's *Metaphysics* attributed to Alexander, *Commentaria in Aristotelem graeca* 1, ed. M. Hayduck (Berlin 1891) 714: At moments when "the human intellect" has "knowledge of" and makes "contact" with the "divine intellect," the "divine intellect" is "like a form of the human intellect."

offshoot of the transcendent active intellect joins the potential human intellect—which Themistius construed quite differently from Alexander[161]—at the outset of the intellectual process. The active intellect "enters" the potential intellect, becomes "intertwined with" it[162] and "one with it" in the way "matter and form" combine to become a single entity.[163] The human "I" is a compound of "potential and active [intellect]"—the "essential me" coming from the latter[164]—and only thanks to the emergence of the "compound intellect" does man begin to possess concepts.[165] The active intellect's joining with the human intellect is, therefore, routine and a prerequisite for human thought.

As for the question posed by Aristotle and "left to be considered later," namely, whether "intellect can, when not itself separate from [spatial] magnitude, think anything separate [that is, incorporeal]," Themistius treats it as a topic apart. Inasmuch as Aristotle did not pursue the issue in his *De anima*, Themistius does not pursue it in any detail in his Paraphrase, but he indicates a solution when he reasons as follows: Since the human intellect can "think forms mixed with matter [that is, the forms of physical objects], it plainly is more likely to be such as to think separate [that is, incorporeal] things," which are intelligible by their nature.[166] Themistius says nothing further on the subject.

He does discuss human immortality. Regarding the nonrational parts of the human soul, on the one hand, and the active intellect, on the other, he finds Aristotle to have been unambiguous. The nonrational parts of the soul plainly perish with the body,[167] and the active intellect is an incorporeal, ever-actual being, and hence unquestionably immortal.[168] Human immortality is an issue only as regards the human potential intellect, which lies between the two poles. Aristotle, as Themistius read him, "explicitly" characterized the potential intellect as "unmixed" with the body and "separable" from it.[169] Nevertheless, the immortal element in man is not, Themistius understands, the potential intellect alone but the compound of potential and active intellect. The active intellect is "more separable" from the body "and more unmixed" than the potential intellect, and the potential intellect is its "precursor." When the two intellects join and become one—that is,

[161] See above, p. 9.

[162] Themistius, Paraphrase of the *De anima* (n. 5 above) 98–99. I have translated the Arabic text.

[163] Ibid. 99–100.

[164] Ibid. 100.

[165] Ibid. 99–100, 108.

[166] Ibid. 115 (translating the Arabic text).

[167] Ibid. 105–6. Themistius also quotes Plato to the same effect. Themistius, ibid. 101, 107, distinguished the passive intellect of Aristotle, *De anima* 3.5.430a, 24–25, from potential intellect, explaining that passive intellect is an aspect of the body and mortal, while potential intellect is unmixed with the body and capable of immortality.

[168] Ibid. 99–100.

[169] Themistius read Aristotle, *De anima* 3.4.429a, 24–25, and 429b, 5, as referring to the potential intellect.

when rays proceeding from the transcendent active intellect enter man and join the potential intellect—the potential intellect "shares" the active intellect's immortality.[170] And since the active intellect joins the human potential intellect at least by the time a man grasps the first axioms of thought,[171] the human intellect must already attain immortality at that time. While Themistius, like Alexander, restricts human immortality to the intellectual parts of the soul and makes it contingent on the human intellect's relationship with the active intellect, human immortality has more content for him than for Alexander. The immortal part of man is, for him, not merely a detached thought of an incorporeal being. The immortal part is the individual human potential intellect itself when joined to, and perfected by, the immanent aspect of the active intellect.

The way Plotinus viewed the immortality of the soul is not relevant to the present study but at least one passage in the *Enneads* bears on the conjunction of the human intellect with the transcendent cause that leads the human intellect to actuality. When an individual human soul moves into the realm of Intellect, Plotinus writes, it "becomes one with the object of its thought," which is Intellect, and "enters into unity with Intellect . . . [although] without being destroyed." The given soul and Intellect are then "one," yet they remain "two."[172] The Arabic paraphrase expands somewhat: "When the soul leaves this world and enters the higher world, . . . it unites with" Intellect "without the destruction of its own self. . . . It becomes both intellectual thinker [*ᶜāqil*] and intelligible thought [*maᶜqūl*] . . . because of the intensity of its conjunction [*ittiṣāl*] and union with Intellect." In such a condition, soul and Intellect are "one thing, and two."[173] Although other passages in Plotinus are commonly interpreted as espousing an ecstatic mysticism,[174] there is nothing mystical about the present passage. Nevertheless, the experience spoken of here is not a routine intellectual act. It is a climax, or semiclimax,[175] in the life of the soul, wherein the soul leaves the physical world behind and is absorbed into a higher realm.

Kindi recognizes a similar union of the human soul with the transcendent intellect. As seen earlier, he maintains that contact with first intellect is what renders the human soul "actually intellectual."[176] After making the statement, he continues: "Intellectual form unites with the soul . . . when *it and the intellect* are one."[177] The italicized words are a little ambiguous, but to judge from the context, they mean that in the act of intellectual thought, soul becomes one with first

[170]Themistius, Paraphrase of the *De anima*, 105–6.

[171]Above, p. 26.

[172]*Enneads* 4.4.2.

[173]*Theology of Aristotle* (n. 54 above) 21.

[174]Cf. Zeller (n. 115 above) 666–71; Rist (n. 129 above) 221–27. Merlan (n. 25 above) 79–82 finds an ecstatic element even in union with Universal Intellect.

[175]Union with Plotinus' One would be the climax.

[176]Above, p. 27.

[177]*Rasā'il al-Kindī* (n. 22 above) 356.

intellect. Kindi thereupon adds an opaque qualification: Soul "is both intellectual thinker [*ᶜāqil*; *intelligens*] and intelligible thought [*maᶜqūl*]; consequently, intellect [*ᶜaql*] and intelligible thought are one from the viewpoint of the soul. The intellect that is eternally actual and that leads the soul" from potentiality to actuality "is not, however, one with what thinks it intellectually [*ᶜāqiluhu*]." A marginal gloss or manuscript variant tries to help by explaining: "Thus from the viewpoint of first intellect, the intelligible thought in the soul is not identical with first intellect."[178] Kindi is apparently saying that whenever the human rational soul thinks, and not merely at the culmination of the soul's development, it has "intelligible form" as the object of its thought and the two become one; and since intelligible form is identical with, or part of, first intellect, the human soul can legitimately be described as having become one with first intellect. Yet the union of soul and first intellect obtains only from the viewpoint of the soul, whereas from the viewpoint of first intellect, the soul and first intellect remain distinct. The conception is not an easy one to digest, but it asserts in effect that soul and intellect are one yet remain two. Kindi's position accordingly exhibits a resemblance to the position Plotinus was just seen to express, although Kindi does not limit union with the supernal intellect to the climax of human development as Plotinus did.

A stronger statement on union with the supernal intellect is made by the Arabic treatise *On the Soul* attributed to Porphyry. The treatise posits that the true man is "intellect," and when the human "psychic intellect"[179] exists apart from the body and is present in the "higher world"—that is to say, both before it descends into the material world and after it reascends there—it is completely "one" with first intellect.[180] To bring out the complete unity between the human intellect and first intellect, the text distinguishes such unity from union in a lesser degree. One of the Arabic paraphrases of Plotinus had compared the soul to the air and stated that as air is the place occupied by the radiance of the sun, so the pure soul is a place occupied by the radiance of Intellect.[181] In an apparent reaction to the analogy, the Porphyry text now insists that the human intellect does not "unite with its form" in a manner similar to the "union [*ittiḥād*] of air with radiance." Its union is "purer."[182] The human intellect in the upper world does not, in other words, intermix with first intellect as with something distinct from itself but is wholly identical with first intellect.

To summarize, Aristotle, followed by Alexander and Themistius, restricted human immortality to one or another aspect of the human intellect. In Alexander's *De anima* and the *De intellectu*, the immortal moment in man is a detached human

[178]Ibid. 356–57.
[179]Cf. above, p. 28.
[180]Kutsch (n. 55 above) 268, §4.
[181]*Risāla fī al-ᶜIlm al-Ilāhī* (n. 94 above) 174, paralleling *Enneads* 5.3.9.
[182]Kutsch, §4.

thought with the active intellect or other incorporeal beings as object, at whatever time those beings become an object of human thought. The Arabic translations of Alexander's *De anima* and the *De intellectu* could, however, be read as saying that not merely a detached thought, but a stage of the human intellect called acquired intellect, is immortal. In Themistius, the potential intellect is immortal as soon as the active intellect intertwines with it at the outset of human thought.

The texts cited in this section recognize a conjunction of the human intellect with the active intellect occurring at the beginning of human intellectual development and as a matter of course (*De intellectu*, Themistius), a conjunction with unspecified incorporeal beings upon the perfection of the human intellect (*De intellectu*), or a conjunction with the Neoplatonic cosmic Intellect at the very climax of human intellectual development (Plotinus). The two participants in conjunction can become completely identical with each other (Alexander's *De anima*, the Neoplatonic Arabic text attributed to Porphyry) or remain distinct (Plotinus, Kindi). The Arabic paraphrase of Plotinus explicitly employs the term *conjunction* and brackets *union* with it as a synonym, adding the qualification that neither term means complete identification.

3

ALFARABI ON EMANATION, THE ACTIVE INTELLECT, AND HUMAN INTELLECT

The present chapter deals primarily with four works of Alfarabi which offer a more or less full treatment of the subjects I am considering: *al-Madīna al-Fāḍila* and *al-Siyāsa al-Madaniyya*, which will be treated as representing one position; a work entitled *The Philosophy of Aristotle*, which suggests a second position; and the *Risāla fī al-cAql* (known in Latin as *De intellectu*, *De intellectu et intellecto*, or *De intelligentiis*), which represents yet another. Alfarabi's lost commentary on the *Nicomachean Ethics* will also be touched on briefly. Works attributed to Alfarabi but expressing views very similar to Avicenna's should be omitted from any discussion of Alfarabi, since they are almost certainly not his.[1]

The order in which Alfarabi's works are discussed here is chosen for purposes of exposition. I have no hypothesis about the sequence in which he wrote them.[2]

Al-Madīna al-Fāḍila and *al-Siyāsa al-Madaniyya*

The Emanation of the Universe; The Active Intellect. The universe envisioned by Alfarabi is fashioned of Aristotelian bricks and of mortar borrowed from Neoplatonic philosophy. Aristotle, who of course had no notion of centripetal or centrifugal force, had pictured a universe in which the heavenly bodies are continually borne around a stationary earth by rotating spheres. And he had concluded that the unceasing movements of the celestial spheres must depend on an inexhaustible source of power, and hence upon an incorporeal mover, that in fact each distinct circular movement distinguishable or inferable in the heavens must be due to a distinct sphere with its own incorporeal mover. As Alfarabi and Avicenna were to understand Aristotle, each celestial sphere also has a rational soul, and the continual motion proper to each sphere is an expression of the desire that the

[1]Cf. S. Pines, "Ibn Sina et l'auteur de la Risalat al-Fusus fi'l-Hikma," *Revue des études islamiques* 19 (1951) 121–24; F. Rahman, *Prophecy in Islam* (London 1958) 21. Their remarks apply to other works attributed to Alfarabi which are printed in the Hyderabad editions.

[2]An attempt to trace the chronology of Alfarabi's works is made by T. Druart, "Al-Farabi and Emanationism," *Studies in Medieval Philosophy*, ed. J. Wippel (Washington 1987) 23–43.

sphere's soul has to emulate the perfection of the incorporeal mover. The incorporeal mover was thus deemed the mover of the sphere in the sense that it maintains the sphere in motion as an object of desire. Since the movements of all the heavenly bodies indicated a total of fifty-five primary and subordinate spheres, Aristotle wrote that the total number of incorporeal movers is "in all probability also fifty-five."[3]

The version of the scheme presupposed by Alfarabi gave its attention to the primary celestial spheres and ignored the subordinate spheres—in late Greek and medieval astronomy, although not yet in Aristotle, these were epicyclical or eccentric spheres[4]—that had to be posited in order to explain the full complexity of celestial motion. Alfarabi assumed nine primary spheres and nine incorporeal movers, or intelligences, as they are called in the Middle Ages, which govern them. A slightly different reduction is known from Alexander.[5] The nine main spheres are: an outer, *diurnal* sphere, which rotates around the earth once every twenty-four hours and imparts its daily motion to the spheres nested inside it—an inversion of what modern astronomy sees as the rotation of the earth on its axis; the sphere of the fixed stars, which is carried around the earth once every twenty-four hours by the diurnal sphere and in addition performs its own infinitesimal rotation, a rotation giving rise to the phenomenon that astronomers call the precession of the equinoxes; and the seven spheres carrying the five planets known at the time as well as the sun and the moon. Each of the seven inner spheres participates in the daily motion imparted by the diurnal sphere and in addition performs a rotation peculiar to itself, thereby giving rise to the apparent periodic movements of the sun, moon, and planets around the earth.[6]

Within the translunar region, Aristotle recognized no causal relationship in what we may call the vertical plane; he did not recognize a causality that runs down through the series of incorporeal movers. And in the horizontal plane, that is, from each intelligence to the corresponding sphere, he recognized causality only in respect to motion, not in respect to existence.[7] As the Aristotelian scheme of the universe reappears in Alfarabi, the causal connections not acknowledged by Aristotle are added through a succession of Neoplatonic emanations. An incorporeal First Cause, the deity, stands at the head of the universe and above the movers of the spheres. From the First Cause, a first incorporeal intelligence "emanates"

[3]Aristotle, *Physics* 8.10; *Metaphysics* 12.7–8. For the ingenuity that scholars have expended on Aristotle's statements about the movers of the spheres, see J. Owens, "The Reality of the Aristotelian Separate Movers," *Review of Metaphysics* 3 (1950) 319–22.

[4]J. Dreyer, *A History of Astronomy from Thales to Kepler* (New York 1953) 143.

[5]E. Zeller, *Die Philosophie der Griechen* 3.1, 5th ed. (Leipzig 1923) 827, n. 5.

[6]*Al-Madīna al-Fāḍila*, ed. and English trans. R. Walzer, as *Al-Farabi on the Perfect State* (Oxford 1985) 100–105. The margin of Walzer's text gives the page numbers of the edition published by F. Dieterici (Leiden 1895). German translation: *Der Musterstaat* (Leiden 1900), trans. F. Dieterici, with the pagination of his edition of the Arabic text indicated.

[7]E. Zeller, *Die Philosophie der Griechen* 2.2, 4th ed. (Leipzig 1921) 373–81.

(*yafīḍ*) eternally. The first intelligence has two thoughts, a thought of the First Cause and a thought of its own essence. By virtue of the former thought, the existence of a second intelligence "proceeds necessarily" (*yalzam*), and by virtue of the latter, the existence of the first sphere "proceeds necessarily." The second intelligence similarly has a thought of the First Cause of the universe and of its own essence. It thereby eternally brings forth the existence of the third intelligence and of the second sphere, and the process continues down to the ninth intelligence, from which emanates the ninth sphere, the sphere of the moon.[8] The Neoplatonic inspiration goes beyond causality through emanation. Plotinus' single, grand emanation scheme of (a) the One, (b) Intellect (νοῦς), (c) Soul, (d) material universe is replicated on a smaller scale at every stage of the process. For (a) the deity, called by Alfarabi "the First," eternally emanates (b^1) the first intelligence (*ᶜaql*=νοῦς); and the latter in turn eternally emanates (c^1) what Alfarabi calls both the "soul," and the "intellect," of the first sphere,[9] and also (d^1) the body of the first sphere.[10] The first intelligence initiates a similar subseries by eternally emanating (b^2) the second intelligence, which emanates (c^2) the soul and (d^2) the body of the second sphere. And so forth.

An incorporeal being parallel to the sublunar world was not called for in Aristotle's system, since Aristotle posited his incorporeal causes only to explain the spheres' motions, and in his universe the sublunar world does not move as a whole. In the scheme set forth by Alfarabi, each intelligence is the cause of the existence of a further intelligence like itself, and therefore the ninth intelligence, the mover of the sphere of the moon, might be expected to emanate a tenth with characteristics similar to the intelligences above it. Alfarabi does include the additional emanation. He writes that the ninth intelligence, which governs the sphere of the moon, emanates a tenth intelligence; and the "tenth" is precisely the "active intellect" of Aristotle's *De anima*.[11] The active intellect, the intellect that in Aristotle's words is what it is by virtue of making all things, is thus construed as a transcendent entity with a definite spot in the overall structure of the universe. It is the final link in the chain of celestial intelligences. Alfarabi gives no reason for identifying the last of the emanated incorporeal intelligences as the active intellect. The justification probably was that Aristotle's language[12] and philosophic demonstration[13] show the cause effecting actual thought to itself consist in pure

[8]*Al-Madīna al-Fāḍila* 100–105.

[9]Cf. Alfarabi, *al-Siyāsa al-Madaniyya*, ed. F. Najjar (Beirut 1964) 33–34, 53. Najjar's edition gives the page numbers of the edition published in Hyderabad 1927.

[10]Avicenna will distinguish three separate aspects in the thought of each intelligence, in order to explain the intelligence's emanation of three things—the soul and body of the corresponding sphere and the next intelligence in the series. Alfarabi does not yet have that point.

[11]*Al-Madīna al-Fāḍila* 104–5, 202–3; *Siyāsa* 32.

[12]Aristotle, *De anima* 3.5.430a, 17–18.

[13]The much-repeated argument that whatever produces a characteristic in something else must already actually have the actual characteristic in itself.

actual thought and consequently to be an incorporeal being. Since it is incorporeal, and yet—in contrast to the other incorporeal beings—has its activity directed not toward a celestial sphere but toward man, an inhabitant of the lower world, it can plausibly be identified as the last incorporeal intelligence. None of the preserved Greek commentators had proposed such an identification of the active intellect, although several did offer transcendent interpretations. Nearest to Alfarabi is the anonymous view recorded in the Latin commentary on the *De anima* attributed to Philoponus, according to which the active intellect is an "intellect, inferior to Him [to the Deity], positioned close to our [intellect]."[14]

The following features characterize Alfarabi's translunar universe: The number of primary celestial spheres and of the intelligences governing them is canonized at nine. The first incorporeal cause of the universe does not itself move a celestial sphere but resides beyond the mover of the first sphere. The first cause eternally emanates the first intelligence, and each intelligence eternally brings forth, through a process of emanation, the next intelligence in the series and its own sphere. The series of incorporeal intelligences governing celestial spheres has, as a final link, a tenth intelligence whose activity is not directed to a celestial sphere. And the tenth intelligence is the active intellect posited—or that the commentators found posited—in Book 3 of Aristotle's *De anima* as the cause of the actualization of the human intellect.

Each celestial intelligence, as has been seen, emanates the body and soul of a celestial sphere and the next intelligence in the series. The symmetry leading to the assumption of a tenth intelligence might well suggest that the tenth intelligence has functions analogous to those performed by the intelligences above it. If Alfarabi pursued the suggestion, he would have viewed the tenth intelligence, or active intellect, as the emanating cause of a body, a soul, and a further intelligence, which could appropriately be the body of the sublunar world, the totality of souls existing in the sublunar world, and all intellect within the sublunar world. For reasons about which one can only speculate, Alfarabi's *al-Madīna al-Fāḍila* and *al-Siyāsa al-Madaniyya* assign the active intellect functions related solely to the actualization of the human intellect, whereas his *Risāla fī al-ᶜAql* does add that the active intellect emanates a range of sublunar natural forms, although not the body of the sublunar world. In Avicenna the scheme will blossom into a complete symmetry, in which the active intellect emanates the matter of the sublunar world, natural forms—including nonrational souls and the human soul with its potential intellect—and actual human thought.

Al-Madīna al-Fāḍila and *al-Siyāsa al-Madaniyya* attribute to the heavens, and not to the active intellect, the production of both characteristics of the sublunar world that are invariable and those that vary. Common to the entire sublunar world is an underlying, identical "prime matter." Sublunar matter, according to Alfarabi, is a necessary and eternal product (*yalzam*) of the "power" or "nature"

[14]Above, pp. 14–15.

communicated by the outermost sphere to the spheres beneath it, a power that causes the heavens to perform their common daily motion from east to west. The uniform nature or power communicated by the outer celestial sphere expresses itself—through an unexplained process—at the lowest level of the universe by producing the matter of the sublunar world. Given their common matter, individual physical objects in the sublunar world differ from one another in respect to their substance, and the difference in respect to substance within the sublunar world "proceeds necessarily" from the difference between "substances" within the heavens. Bodies in the sublunar region, moreover, change, and their changes are due to changes in the positions of the heavenly bodies relative to one another, and to changes of their positions relative to the sublunar region. As substances emerge in the sublunar world, they too have powers of their own, and those sublunar powers also interact with one another and with the forces descending from the heavenly region. The heavens are thus the eternal source of the underlying matter of the sublunar world. They eternally produce the four elements. And the interplay of celestial forces and of physical forces within the sublunar world eternally gives rise to further levels of sublunar existence: to "minerals," "plants," "nonrational animals," and "man," the "rational animal."[15]

It is good Aristotelianism to regard the heavens as the cause of generation and corruption in the lower world, and Aristotle even distinguished the effect of the uniform motion of the heavens from the effect of variable celestial motion.[16] Alfarabi's conception also recalls a passage in Kindi.[17] No prior known source, however, represented the heavens as the cause of the very matter of the sublunar world.[18] Alfarabi not only espouses that proposition in *al-Madīna al-Fāḍila* and *al-Siyāsa al-Madaniyya* but in other works assumes it to be the view of Aristotle's *De caelo*[19] and *De generatione et corruptione*.[20]

Human Intellect. Forces descending from the heavens interact with forces arising within the sublunar region to produce beings at each level of sublunar existence, up to and including the human organism, and there stop. They are

[15]*Al-Madīna al-Fāḍila* 132–41; *Siyāsa* 55–56, 62.

[16]Aristotle, *De generatione et corruptione* 2.10.

[17]Above, p. 33.

[18]It is perhaps implied in the material cited by A. Altmann and S. Stern, *Isaac Israeli* (Oxford 1958) 167–69.

[19]Alfarabi, *Philosophy of Aristotle*, ed. M. Mahdi (Beirut 1961) 99; English translation in *Alfarabi's Philosophy of Plato and Aristotle*, trans. Mahdi (New York 1962) 71ff., with pagination of the Arabic text indicated.

[20]*Risāla fī al-ᶜAql*, ed. M. Bouyges (Beirut 1938) 34. Medieval Latin translation, in E. Gilson, "Les sources gréco-arabes de l'augustinisme avicennisant," *Archives d'histoire doctrinale et littéraire du moyen âge* 4.108–126. Partial English translation (paralleling pp. 12–36 of the Arabic text), in *Philosophy in the Middle Ages*, ed. A. Hyman and J. Walsh (New York 1973) 215. Italian translation, with pagination of the Arabic indicated: Farabi, *Epistola sull' intelletto*, trans. F. Lucchetta (Padua 1974).

unable to lead man to his perfection, which is also the highest perfection achievable in the sublunar world. Human perfection consists in the actualization of the human intellect, and to explain the passage of the human intellect from potentiality to actuality, the active intellect must be introduced.[21] In a brief statement of the standard argument for the existence of the active intellect, more fully stated by Alfarabi elsewhere,[22] *al-Madīna al-Fāḍila* contends that the human potentiality for thought cannot "by itself, become actual intellect," it needs "something else to cause it to pass from potentiality to actuality," and what leads it to actuality is perforce "an incorporeal actual intellect."[23] The active intellect "surveys" the handiwork of the heavens, and whenever an object in the sublunar world has "to a certain degree attained freedom and separation from matter, the active intellect tries to purify it from matter . . . so that it arrives at a degree close to the active intellect."[24] Put more straightforwardly, once the forces of nature produce a member of the human species with a potential intellect, the ever-present action of the active intellect automatically begins leading the man's intellect to actuality. In perfecting the human intellect, the active intellect exercises "providence" over man.[25]

Alfarabi recognizes three stages of human intellect. (1) The initial stage is the "natural disposition" for thought, also called "rational faculty," "material intellect," and "passive intellect,"[26] with which all normal men are born. The use of the term *disposition* should be noted, for it suggests adherence to Alexander's conception of the material, or potential, human intellect as a disposition in the human organism and not a substance.[27] (2) When the disposition for thought passes to actuality with the aid of the active intellect, the human intellect becomes "actual intellect," also called "actual passive intellect." (3) At the culmination, the human subject "perfects his passive intellect with all intelligible thoughts" and becomes "acquired intellect."[28] To gain all possible thoughts[29] is no small enterprise for a man of flesh and blood, but the medieval intellectual universe, like the medieval physical universe, was finite, and Alfarabi here assumes that wholly comprehensive knowledge does lie within man's power. As far as I could see, Alfarabi does not use the term intellect *in habitu*.

[21] *Siyāsa* 71.

[22] *Philosophy of Aristotle* 127.

[23] *Al-Madīna al-Fāḍila* 198–201. Cf. above, p. 18.

[24] *Siyāsa* 55.

[25] Ibid. 32.

[26] For the term *passive* intellect as equivalent to *potential* intellect, see Aristotle, *De anima* 3.5.430a, 24–25; Simplicius, Commentary on the *De anima*, in *Commentaria in Aristotelem Graeca* 11, ed. M. Hayduck (Berlin 1882) 219. Themistius, Paraphrase of *De anima*, in *Commentaria in Aristotelem Graeca* 5.3, ed. R. Heinze (Berlin 1899) 101, 107, distinguishes passive from potential intellect.

[27] Above, p. 9.

[28] *Al-Madīna al-Fāḍila* 242–45.

[29] In the *Risāla fī al-ᶜAql*, Alfarabi will make the small qualification that acquired intellect is attained when man masters "all" or "most" intelligible thoughts; below, p. 69.

The term *acquired intellect* in Alfarabi is problematic, because it is not appropriate to the stage of human intellect to which he applies it. As was seen earlier, the term most probably originated in the Arabic translation of Alexander, and there, as well as in Plotinus, who also employed the term, *acquired intellect* designates something coming to man, and hence *acquired*, from above and outside the human realm.[30] The supreme stage of human thought, which Alfarabi calls acquired intellect, is not however acquired from outside. It consists, as will appear, in a body of knowledge constructed by man himself on the foundation furnished by the active intellect.

There happens to be a phase of human intelligible thought which Alfarabi might well have characterized as acquired from without. He draws an analogy between the light of the sun, which renders the faculty of vision actual, and an emission from the active intellect which furnishes the human intellect with the basic principles of thought; and in working out the analogy, he describes the faculty of vision as "acquiring" light from the sun.[31] Inasmuch as the emission from the active intellect which illumines the human material intellect parallels the sun's light, that emission too might aptly be described as *acquired* from the active intellect. But while such a consideration might justify applying the term *acquired intellect* to the initial phase in which the human intellect receives knowledge through the active intellect, it cannot explain Alfarabi's usage, where acquired intellect designates the ultimate stage in which the human intellect possesses a complete body of knowledge; for most human knowledge does not, in Alfarabi's system, come from the active intellect. His choice of the term *acquired intellect* for the highest stage of human intellect therefore remains a puzzle.

As just mentioned, Alfarabi adduces the familiar analogy of light to explain the manner in which the active intellect operates on the human intellect. Although echoes of the *De intellectu* attributed to Alexander and of Themistius are detectable in what he says, he, borrowing perhaps from an unknown predecessor, pursues the implications of the analogy in more detail than we have seen thus far. He does so with the help of Aristotle's theory of vision.

Vision, in Aristotle's optics, requires that light enter the transparent substance of the eye.[32] Alfarabi's version of the light analogy compares the active intellect not to light itself but to its natural source, the sun,[33] and his *al-Madīna al-Fāḍila* accordingly sets the stage for the analogy by noting that "light" (*ḍaw'*) radiated by the sun does four things: It enters the eye, and turns potential vision into actual vision; it comes into contact with potentially visible colors and renders them actually visible; it itself becomes visible to the eye; and it also renders the sun, its source,

[30] Above, pp. 11–12.

[31] *Al-Madīna al-Fāḍila* 200–201; *Siyāsa* 35.

[32] Aristotle, *De sensu* 2, 438b, 7; J. Beare, *Greek Theories of Elementary Cognition* (Oxford 1906) 85–86.

[33] Cf. Plato, *Republic* 508D–E, and Walzer's note in his edition of *al-Madīna al-Fāḍila*, 403.

visible to the eye. The active intellect similarly "is the cause of the imprinting of . . . something" analogous to light "in" the material human intellect. This analogue of light turns the material intellect into actual intellect, transforms potentially intelligible thoughts—"sense perceptions [*maḥsūsāt*] stored in the imaginative faculty"—into actually intelligible thoughts, itself becomes an object of intelligible thought (*ᶜ-q-l*) to the human intellect, and renders the active intellect an object of intelligible thought to the human intellect.[34] Alfarabi's distinction between the active intellect and what it imprints in the material intellect recalls Themistius' distinction between the transcendent side of the active intellect and the side that breaks up and enters individual human intellects.[35] Themistius had, moreover, inferred from the analogy of light that the active intellect leads both the potential human intellect and potentially intelligible thoughts to actuality.[36] Not Themistius, however, but the *De intellectu* attributed to Alexander used the light analogy to make the point that the active intellect itself is an object of human thought.[37]

When the emission from the active intellect which is analogous to light acts upon the human material intellect, or rational faculty, and upon the sense perceptions stored in the imaginative faculty, those sense perceptions undergo a change and become "intelligible thoughts in the rational faculty." The product is "the first intelligible thoughts common to all men, such as [the principles] that the whole is greater than the part, and that magnitudes equal to a single thing are equal to one another."[38] For Themistius too, it will be recalled, the first axioms of thought are the handiwork of the active intellect,[39] and Plotinus stated a similar notion.[40] As *al-Madīna al-Fāḍila* goes on, it places a broad construction on the "common first intelligible thoughts" that the active intellect provides. They comprise "three classes" of propositions: "the principles of scientific geometry"; "the principles whereby one can understand the noble and base in areas where man is to act"; and "the principles used for learning about existent things that do not fall within the domain of human action, their causes, and their degrees—for example, about the heavens, the First Cause, the other primary beings, and what . . . is generated from those primary beings."[41] In other words, the emission from the active intellect transforms perceptions stored in the imaginative faculty into the principles

[34]*Al-Madīna al-Fāḍila* 200–203. Cf. B. Eastwood, "Al-Fārābī on Extramission, Intromission, and the Use of Platonic Visual Theory," *Isis* 70 (1979) 423–25. *Siyāsa* 35–36, has the same analogy, but omits, on the one side, the point that the eye sees the light emitted by the sun as well as the sun, and, on the other, the point that the human intellect has as an object of thought the "thing" emitted by the active intellect as well as the active intellect.

[35]Above, p. 14.

[36]Above, p. 26.

[37]Above, p. 23.

[38]*Al-Madīna al-Fāḍila* 202–3; cf. *Siyāsa* 71–72.

[39]Above, p. 26.

[40]Above, p. 24.

[41]*Al-Madīna al-Fāḍila* 202–5; see apparatus.

of mathematical science, the principles of ethics or practical reason, and the principles of physics and metaphysics. In listing the three classes of first intelligibles, Alfarabi seems to have forgotten the rules of logical reasoning; he must simply have taken them for granted.

Al-Madīna al-Fāḍila draws a division of labor between the active intellect and human initiative. The active intellect provides the "first intelligibles," and man "uses" them to construct a body of knowledge by his own efforts. The division is drawn more fully by the parallel account in *al-Siyāsa al-Madaniyya.*

The *Siyāsa* describes the active intellect as performing its task in a way resembling that in which the heavens perform theirs. The heavens do not perfect all parts of the sublunar world directly and by themselves. Objects within the sublunar world are set in motion by forces descending from above, but they also act on one another; and through the interplay of forces continually descending from the heavens and forces indigenous to the sublunar region—which are themselves ultimately traceable to celestial forces—successively higher levels of existence emerge in the sublunar region.[42] Similarly, the active intellect does not complete the perfection of the human intellect by itself. It rather initiates the development of the human intellect and at subsequent stages contributes further necessary knowledge. It "first gives man a power or principle whereby he strives or can strive, by himself, toward whatever perfections remain for him; this principle consists in the first notions [^{c}*ulūm*; a line later: *ma*^{c}*ārif*] and first intelligible thoughts that arrive in the rational part of the soul." Men differ in their inborn ability "to receive" the common first intelligible thoughts, ranging from those who are unable to receive any to those of sound innate ability who can receive all. Through the common intelligible thoughts that sound men do receive, they "strive toward matters [*umūr*] and acts common to" mankind—presumably toward universal theoretical and ethical, or practical, knowledge. Not only does the active intellect provide the initial "common" intelligible thoughts. It subsequently provides specialized thoughts as well. Certain men have "special" (*khāṣṣ*) innate abilities to receive "special" intelligible thoughts, "whereby they strive" toward one or another "genus" of knowledge, and those special intelligible thoughts, which are the principles of the several sciences, likewise come from the active intellect. Alfarabi elaborates with distinctions regarding the number of thoughts different men are able to receive in each "genus," the differing innate abilities men have for applying the principles of science, variations in the rapidity with which men draw inferences from the principles provided them, and variations in their ability to teach others. It is clear throughout *al-Siyāsa al-Madaniyya* that the active intellect first "gives" man the common principles of thought, subsequently gives certain men the principles of the individual sciences, and in each instance the individual man "by himself" uses the principles he receives from the active intellect in order to

[42]*Siyāsa* 60–62.

"discover whatever can be known by discovery [or perhaps: by deduction, *istinbāṭ*] in a given genus [of science]."[43]

In *al-Madīna al-Fāḍila* and *al-Siyāsa al-Madaniyya*, we find then that an analogue of light emanated by the active intellect enters the human rational faculty or material intellect, turning it into an actual intellect and transforming perceptions stored in the imaginative faculty into actually intelligible thoughts. *Al-Madīna al-Fāḍila* appears to say that all thoughts coming from the active intellect are bestowed at the outset; *al-Siyāsa al-Madaniyya* states that the active intellect provides general principles at the start, and then at subsequent junctures provides the principles of the individual sciences to men capable of receiving them. The discrepancy may however be only in the presentation, with *al-Siyāsa al-Madaniyya* offering the more precise account. At all events, man, through his own effort, constructs a body of science on the foundation furnished by the active intellect. In a different work, Alfarabi depicts Aristotelian physical science as a set of deductions from first principles.[44] If he has the same picture of science in the present works, the active intellect and human intellect divide their tasks inasmuch as the human intellect deduces a corpus of scientific knowledge from the basic propositions of science furnished by the active intellect.

Alfarabi plainly is not maintaining that the active intellect casts a kind of light that enables the human intellect to perceive, as it were, the abstract concept of a dog or a cat, but that the light from the active intellect enables the human intellect to grasp basic scientific propositions. The notion that the active intellect provides man with the principles of thought and science can, perhaps, trace its genealogy to the conclusion of the *Posterior Analytics*, where Aristotle found the source of the "principles" of thought to be "intellect" (νοῦς).[45] For while modern English translations of the *Posterior Analytics* take νοῦς in the passage as "intuition" or "intuitive reason," the tradition that percolated down to Alfarabi when he was writing *al-Madīna al-Fāḍila* and *al-Siyāsa al-Madaniyya* may well have taken νοῦς in the sense of active intellect. Alfarabi's *Risāla fī al-ᶜAql*, as will appear, views the source of the first principles of thought differently, it gives a different account of what the active intellect produces in the human material intellect, and it offers a different interpretation of the end of the *Posterior Analytics* from the one that, I am speculating, may have lain behind *al-Madīna al-Fāḍila* and *al-Siyāsa al-Madaniyya*.

Conjunction with the Active Intellect; Immortality. The three stages of human intellect are, to repeat, material intellect, actual intellect, and acquired intellect. Each stage serves as the "matter and substratum" of the succeeding stage, and when the succeeding stage is reached, the two become "as one thing in the way

[43] Ibid. 71–72, 74–75.
[44] *Philosophy of Aristotle* (n. 19 above) 105.
[45] Aristotle, *Posterior Analytics* 2.19.100b, 12.

that a compound of matter and form is one thing." At the highest stage, when the acquired intellect becomes the form of the actual intellect, acquired intellect in turn serves as "matter for the active intellect," which—apparently immediately—joins the acquired intellect as its form.[46] The characterization of a given level of intellect as the form of a prior level was met in Alexander[47]; and Themistius outlined a full hierarchy in which each successive level of soul is the form of the prior level, with the active intellect supervening as the crowning form.[48] None of those philosophers, however, had the active intellect join the human soul or intellect as its form after the highest stage of human intellect is reached.

Alfarabi employs a variety of formulas to describe the relationship of the active intellect to the acquired intellect. When a man reaches the stage of acquired intellect, and the active intellect joins the acquired intellect as its form, the active intellect "enters into" (*ḥalla fī*) the "man." The active intellect sends forth a new "emanation" on the human subject, rendering him a "philosopher and man of practical wisdom." The human soul becomes "united [*muttaḥid*] as it were" and "conjoined" (*ittaṣala*) with the active intellect, "conjunction with the active intellect" having been "referred to in the *De anima*."[49] In the state of human perfection, man "reaches the degree" of the active intellect, or more precisely arrives "close to the degree of," and at the "closest degree to," the active intellect[50]; the latter phrases are more precise, because even when the human intellect reaches its highest level, "its degree is below that of the active intellect."[51] Nothing Alfarabi says about the union or conjunction of the acquired human intellect with the active intellect contains even a hint of an ecstatic or truly mystical experience.

In spelling out his version of the analogy of light, Alfarabi wrote that the emission from the active intellect renders the active intellect an object of intelligible thought for the human intellect. He submits moreover that not only can corporeal beings like "rocks and plants," which are potentially intelligible, become objects of thought for the human rational faculty; "incorporeal beings," which by their nature are "actual intellects and actually intelligible,"[52] can as well.[53] One might expect Alfarabi's intent to be that the acquired intellect has the active intellect, and perhaps other incorporeal beings, as an object of thought upon conjoining with the active intellect and receiving it as a form. He takes a position along those lines

[46] *Al-Madīna al-Fāḍila* 242–45; *Siyāsa* 79.

[47] Above, p. 20.

[48] Above, p. 27.

[49] *Al-Madīna al-Fāḍila* 244–45; *Siyāsa* 79. My translation of *mutaᶜaqqil* as "man of practical wisdom" is based on Alfarabi, *Risāla fī al-ᶜAql* (n. 20 above) 10, and Alfarabi, *Fuṣūl al-Madanī*, ed. and trans. D. Dunlop (Cambridge 1961) §36. Regarding the man of practical wisdom see Aristotle, *Nicomachean Ethics* 6.5.

[50] *Siyāsa* 32, 35–36, 55.

[51] *Al-Madīna al-Fāḍila* 206–7.

[52] See above, pp. 35–36.

[53] *Al-Madīna al-Fāḍila* 196–99.

elsewhere.[54] But his elaboration of the analogy of light suggests, on the contrary, that the emission from the active intellect renders the active intellect an object of human thought at the outset and not at the end.[55] The *De intellectu* attributed to Alexander had indicated that the active intellect becomes an object of human thought at the beginning of the thought process and had also stated that incorporeal beings—which could still mean the active intellect—become an object of thought of the human intellect at the intellect's maturity.[56] Perhaps Alfarabi understood the active intellect to be an unconscious object of human thought from the start and a conscious object of thought at the stage of acquired intellect. *Al-Madīna al-Fāḍila*, although not *al-Siyāsa al-Madaniyya*, further represents the emission from the active intellect, which illumines the human intellect, as itself an object of human thought. Alfarabi gives no inkling of what that might mean.

The observation that "conjunction with the active intellect . . . was referred to in the *De anima*" is an additional puzzle. Neither Aristotle's *De anima* nor Alexander's work of the same name used the term *conjunction*. The terms *union* and *conjunction*, together with the denial that they involve complete identification with the transcendent Intellect, were met in the Arabic paraphrase of Plotinus known as the *Theology of Aristotle*.[57] But although Alfarabi regarded the *Theology* as a genuine work of Aristotle,[58] he could hardly have mistaken it for Aristotle's *De anima*. Perhaps Alfarabi, or an unknown philosopher upon whom he is dependent, had in mind the passage in Aristotle's *De anima* which promises to consider "later" whether intellect can, when still connected with a human body, have that which is incorporeal as a direct object of thought.[59] Intellect, in Aristotle's epistemology, becomes identical with whatever thought it thinks, and if the tone of Aristotle's promise should be taken to imply an affirmative answer, to imply that the human intellect can indeed have the active intellect as an object of thought, the tone of the promise would presumably imply as well that the human intellect is capable of becoming one with the active intellect. If that promise is the passage in the *De anima* which Alfarabi believes refers to conjunction, he does not accept all the implications; for while he recognizes the possibility of conjunction with the active intellect, he rejects, as we have seen, the possibility of the human intellect's becoming completely one with the active intellect.

[54]Below, p. 69.

[55]Above, p. 50.

[56]Above, pp. 38–39.

[57]Above, p. 41. The denial of an actual identification of the human soul with the transcendent first intellect was also met in Kindi, above, pp. 41–42.

[58]Alfarabi, *al-Jam*[c] *bain al-Ḥakīmain*, ed. A. Nader (Beirut 1960) 105–6; also in *Alfārābī's philosophische Abhandlungen*, ed. F. Dieterici (Leiden 1890) 28; German translation: *Alfārābī's philosophische Abhandlungen aus dem Arabischen übersetzt*, trans. F. Dieterici (Leiden 1892) 44–45.

[59]*De anima* 3.7.431b, 17–19. Above, p. 35.

At the stage of acquired intellect, the "rational part of the soul . . . is very similar to the incorporeal beings," and the "soul" joins the company "of incorporeal beings." For the soul has become "free of matter," can "dispense with matter," and no longer "requires matter for its existence." Since immortality means simply the ability to exist independently of a body, immortality is thus a concomitant of the stage of acquired intellect. The "soul" liberates itself from matter even before the body dies and "remains in that state perpetually," its "eudaemonia [*sacāda*] [being] complete."[60] Whether freedom from matter and human immortality are properties of the stage of acquired intellect as such, or result from the acquired intellect's conjunction with the active intellect, is unclear, and probably insignificant, seeing that conjunction with the active intellect seems to ensue immediately upon man's reaching the stage of acquired intellect.

Human immortality is, then, a product of man's intellectual development and a concomitant of the stage of acquired intellect. Alfarabi accordingly writes that the souls of the ignorant perish.[61] He nevertheless is careful to describe not merely the intellects, but also the souls, of those who have attained intellectual perfection as immortal. Indeed he goes as far as to assert that disembodied souls retain their individuality. Souls remain differentiated from one another inasmuch as the "dispositions" in matter "for [receiving] souls follow the blends [*mizājāt*] of bodies"[62]; and since human bodies are different from one another, the souls following from them are also distinct. As additional souls enter the incorporeal state, "each becomes conjoined with those similar in species, quantity, and quality." As more incorporeal souls join a given class, the pleasure of each soul in the class "increases," for each "has intellectual thought of itself and of the [souls that are] similar to itself, many times over."[63]

Alfarabi also speaks of torments experienced by the disembodied souls of citizens of the "wicked political state." These are souls belonging to men who have fully developed their intellect but are morally vicious.[64] The "vicious characteristics in [their] souls" oppose their intellectual inclinations and tear their souls in two directions, with the result that the "rational part of the soul" is subject to "great pain." As long as men of the sort are alive, their rational faculty is occupied by the flow of messages "that the sense faculties deliver to it," and the pain remains subliminal. Since such men have developed their intellects, and since their intellectual perfection "releases their souls from matter," their souls are immortal. At death, the "rational part" of their souls "separates itself completely from the senses," becomes conscious of its distress, and "remains in great pain for all

[60] *Al-Madīna al-Fāḍila* 204–7 ‚62–63; *Siyāsa* 32, 35, 42.

[61] *Al-Madīna al-Fāḍila* 270–71, 274–75.

[62] Cf. the passage from the *De intellectu* quoted above, p. 30.

[63] *Al-Madīna al-Fāḍila* 262–65; cf. *Siyāsa* 82. The words *these dispositions differ* in the English translation of *al-Madīna al-Fāḍila* are a slip. Alfarabi is saying that *souls* are differentiated.

[64] *Al-Madīna al-Fāḍila* 256–59.

eternity." Further, as additional individuals join the class of suffering souls, they share one another's pain, and the pain of each "increases."[65] We have here an allegorization of hellfire as the torture that human souls suffer in their disembodied state because of residual physical desires, and similar allegorizations are to be found among Arabic writers of a Neoplatonic persuasion.[66]

Although the descriptions of happy and miserable souls in the immortal state appear to be straightforward, Alfarabi is probably dissimulating. In a context not primarily concerned with immortality, he asserts without qualification that upon attaining perfection "the rational part of the soul . . . separates completely from all the other parts of the soul."[67] Seeing that the rational part leaves the other parts behind when it reaches the stage of acquired intellect, immortality must be an affair exclusively of intellect, and the previous physical desires of wicked souls must vanish. Moreover, even in the passage stating that disembodied souls remain differentiated because of their prior attachment to bodies, Alfarabi insists that such souls are free of "accidents affecting bodies insofar as they are bodies." "Anything" by which "body can be described insofar as it is body must be negated of [human] souls that have become incorporeal," and only "terms appropriate to the incorporeal should be predicated of them."[68]

If human souls at the stage of acquired intellect are wholly incorporeal and possess no characteristics of bodies, if, as Alfarabi wrote, the human acquired intellect possesses all intelligible thoughts and hence every acquired intellect has exactly the same thought content, and if an intellect is identical with its thought—then all acquired intellects should be identical. The conclusion should moreover apply to the acquired intellects of wicked as well as of good souls. On the more plausible reading, then, Alfarabi accepted immortality only of the human material intellect or rational faculty after it has become an acquired intellect, with no differentiation between individual immortal acquired intellects. His statements on the immortality of differentiated human souls, whether virtuous or vicious, would on that reading be a stratagem designed to veil his precise views from conservative religious readers.[69]

Aristotle, Alexander, and Themistius restricted human immortality to the intellect, and if my understanding of Alfarabi is correct, he stands in the same tradition. The Arabic translation of Alexander regarded the human acquired intellect

[65]Ibid. 272–75.

[66]*Al-Shaykh al-Yūnānī*, ed. F. Rosenthal, *Orientalia* 24 (1955) 50–51; *Hermetis trismegisti . . . de castigatione animae libellum*, ed. and Latin trans. O. Bardenhewer (Bonn 1873) 110; Kindi, *Rasā'il*, ed. M. Abu Rida (Cairo 1950) 1.278; Isaac Israeli, in Altmann and Stern (n. 18 above) 26–27, 113, 117, 193; Ikhwān al-Ṣafā', *Rasā'il*, pt. 2, §16 (Beirut 1957) vol. 3, p. 79; German translation: F. Dieterici, *Die Anthropologie der Araber* (Leipzig 1871) 155; pseudo-Baḥya, *Kitāb Maᶜānī al-Nafs*, ed. I. Goldziher (Berlin 1907) 65–66.

[67]*Siyāsa* 42.

[68]*Al-Madīna al-Fāḍila* 262–63.

[69]Cf. S. Munk, *Mélanges de philosophie juive et arabe* (Paris 1859) 347.

and nothing else in man as immortal; Alfarabi too ties immortality to the stage of acquired intellect. Alexander and Themistius ascribed a function to the active intellect in human immortality, and Alfarabi does so as well. Yet although the formulas have a similar ring, the conceptions are different. Alexander recognized the immortality only of a detached thought of the active intellect, and Themistius affirmed the immortality of the human potential intellect from the moment the active intellect joins it, that is, from the very beginning of human thought. Alfarabi's position is that immortality accompanies the ultimate stage of human intellect, when man has mastered all science.

Prophecy. Thus far, the active intellect has been seen to operate only on the human intellect. The emanation from the active intellect can, according to *al-Madīna al-Fāḍila*, also pass beyond the intellect to the human imaginative faculty and there produce the natural phenomena that are known in religious nomenclature as prophecy and revelation.

The "imagination" (*mutakhayyila*), Alfarabi explains, is a faculty of the soul located in the heart and standing immediately below, and serving, the rational faculty.[70] It stores "sense perceptions" (*maḥsūsāt*), or the "impressions of sense perceptions," when the objects of perception are no longer present. It manipulates sense perceptions, disassembling them or combining them into configurations that may or may not agree with what exists in the external world. And it can do a "third" thing. It can create "figurative images" (*muḥākāt*), that is to say, images that symbolize, rather than strictly represent, a given object. When the body is asleep and the imaginative faculty is not occupied in receiving perceptions from the senses or supplying images for the use of the intellect, that faculty is especially free to create, and the figurative images it frames are called dreams. The condition of the body at the time may give the imagination direction. If, for example, wetness happens to be preponderant in the body, the imagination may be led to frame a dream concerning water or swimming.[71]

[70]Cf. Aristotle, *De anima* 3.3.428a, 5–12; Zeller (n. 7 above) 545–49. It will appear that Avicenna distinguishes two imaginative faculties, a retentive imagination and a compositive imagination, and the functions that Alfarabi here assigns to the imaginative faculty without further qualification are distributed by Avicenna between the two. See below, p. 89, n. 66. Wolfson, who coined the terms *retentive* and *compositive* imagination, quotes, in addition to a passage in which Alfarabi does not distinguish between the two imaginative faculties, passages from two works attributed to Alfarabi which do have the distinction; see H. Wolfson, "The Internal Senses," reprinted in his *Studies in the History of Philosophy and Religion* (Cambridge, Mass. 1973) 274–76. The second of the two works, *ᶜUyūn al-Masā'il*, is, however, definitely not a genuine composition of Alfarabi's, and the first probably is also not his. It is therefore fairly safe to credit Avicenna with having originated the distinction.

[71]*Al-Madīna al-Fāḍila* 168–69; 210–13. That the human imagination plays a role in dreams was recognized by Aristotle, *De insomniis* 1, but the details stated here by Alfarabi do not appear there.

Alfarabi recognizes two levels of prophetic phenomena, both constituted by an emanation from the active intellect upon the imaginative faculty.[72] The lower of the two levels, labeled specifically as "prophecy" (*nubuwwa*), is enjoyed by men who have not perfected their intellect, whereas the higher, which Alfarabi sometimes specifically names "revelation" (*w-ḥ-y*), comes exclusively to those who stand at the stage of acquired intellect.[73]

He describes prophecy at the lower level as follows: The analogue of "light" which constantly emanates from the active intellect and which every human rational faculty receives, may "emanate from" the rational faculty of the man of imperfect intellect, to the "adjoining" imaginative faculty. Since the rational faculty is twofold, being of "both a theoretical and a practical" character, and since the imaginative faculty adjoins both, knowledge imparted by the active intellect to an inspired imaginative faculty through the rational faculty is twofold as well. It has either practical or theoretical content.

Knowledge of a practical character imparted to the imaginative faculty consists in "sense perceptions" of a certain kind. They are "particulars" that relate to events in the "present" or "future," and that belong to the domain of things which the practical side of the rational faculty "performs by deliberation [*rawiyya*]." In other words, the imagination visualizes present events occurring at a distance and foresees future events; both those sorts of event appear to the imaginative faculty as if they were being perceived by the senses, although in fact they lie beyond the grasp of the sense organs; both sorts are ordinarily accessible to man through deliberation on the part of his practical rational faculty; but in prophecy the imagination also dispenses with the normal processes of deliberation. Under the influence of the active intellect, present and future events sometimes show themselves to the imaginative faculty "as they are"; the imagination perceives an event at a distance or a future event in the exact shape it has or will have when it occurs. Alternatively, events may be recast by the imagination in figurative images.

Knowledge of a theoretical character, the other type of knowledge imparted to the inspired imaginative faculty, consists in "clairvoyance [*kahānāt*] in divine matters." The imaginative faculty gains knowledge of metaphysical truths. Here, when receiving theoretical knowledge, the imaginative faculty must, without exception, recast what it receives in figurative images. For the imagination is a physical faculty, capable of handling only physical impressions, and hence incapable of receiving theoretical truths in their proper, abstract form. The

[72]*Al-Madīna al-Fāḍila* indicates, but does not make wholly explicit, that it envisages two distinct levels of prophecy. The two levels are explicitly distinguished in Alfarabi, *Fuṣūl al-Madanī* (n. 49 above) §89.

[73]In *Siyāsa* 79–80, Alfarabi also uses the term *revelation* for the emanation that the human intellect itself receives from the active intellect when man attains the state of acquired intellect. In *Fuṣūl al-Madanī* §89, the prophecy of the man of imperfect intellect is called *revelation*, and the term *revelation* is applied as well to a kind of knowledge possessed only by the man of perfected intellect, although what that knowledge is, remains unclear.

imaginative faculty "sees, . . . figurative images of incorporeal intelligible [beings] and other supernal beings."[74]

Alfarabi does not explain the process whereby the active intellect furnishes theoretical knowledge or knowledge of distant present events and future events. As regards theoretical knowledge, we may surmise that the active intellect communicates the principles of science to the imaginative faculty, since Alfarabi has already written that it communicates them to the human intellect, whence they might proceed a step further to the imaginative faculty. But he also states that the active intellect "gives" the imaginative faculty, and the imaginative faculty "receives" and "sees," figurative images of the incorporeal intelligible beings and other supernal substances.[75] Perhaps he means that the active intellect imparts theoretical knowledge of the supernal region to the imaginative faculty by conveying the principles of science, including "the principles used for learning about . . . the heavens, the First Cause, [and] the other primary beings"[76]; whereupon the imaginative faculty somehow sees the implications, recast in figurative images, of the scientific principles communicated to it.

As for distant present events and future events, Alfarabi has stated that they belong to the domain where the practical reason exercises "deliberation." Deliberation in Aristotle is a procedure for setting goals and planning the steps to attain them. Since every event is brought about by a concatenation of preceding events, the practical intellect starts with a desired future result, deliberates back from it, discovers the series of causal steps needed to bring it about, and determines the first action to take.[77] In a similar but inverse fashion, Alfarabi intimates, deliberation can proceed forward from immediate circumstances through a series of causal steps to deduce what is occurring at a distance or to predict what will occur in the future. In prophecy, the imagination makes the predictions "without the mediacy of deliberation," that is to say, without laborious step-by-step reasoning. The imagination can dispense with deliberation because of the "action" of the active intellect; the active intellect "gives" knowledge of the events to the imaginative faculty, and the imagination "receives" the knowledge from the active intellect.[78] Alfarabi's intent cannot be that the active intellect itself has direct knowledge of particular objects or events in the physical world, for he accepted the Aristotelian epistemology, which rules out knowledge of the particular by intellect.[79] He presumably understands that the emission from the active intellect conveys the

[74]*Al-Madīna al-Fāḍila* 218–21, 224–25. My translation differs considerably from the English translation at the top of p. 221. Rahman (n. 1 above) 71, quotes from Proclus the theory that the imagination recasts theoretical truths into figurative images.

[75]Ibid. 220–21, 224–25.

[76]Above, p. 51.

[77]Aristotle, *Nicomachean Ethics* 6.5; Alfarabi, *Fuṣūl al-Madanī* (n. 49 above) §§6 (end), 35, 36; Zeller (n. 7 above) 651, n.

[78]*Al-Madīna al-Fāḍila* 220–21.

[79]Zeller (n. 7 above) 210, 568.

principles of practical reason to the imaginative faculty,[80] the imaginative faculty unconsciously applies those principles to circumstances with which it is familiar, and it visualizes the implications.

Practical and theoretical knowledge received by the imaginative faculty occurs either in dreams[81] or, more rarely, in the waking state. When knowledge is produced in the imaginative faculty during the waking state, the imaginative faculty may project images out through the sense faculties into the external world, whereupon the images that the soul itself projected into the world can be perceived by the human subject's sense organ and become "visible" to him. To enjoy both "prophecy" of present and future events and also "prophecy in divine matters," that is to say, a figurative depiction of metaphysical truths, in a waking state, is "the most perfect degree that the imaginative faculty can reach." Lesser degrees are possible and more common.[82]

The characterization of a certain kind of prophecy through the imaginative faculty as that faculty's "most perfect degree" should not be taken to mean that such prophecy has genuine value for man. Alfarabi has already stated that human perfection appertains to the intellect, and he thereby relegates the accomplishments of the nonintellectual faculties of the soul to a lesser status.

The higher of the two levels of prophecy is, according to Alfarabi, incomparably superior to the lower level.[83] In contrast to the lower level, which lies within the power of anyone possessing a receptive imaginative faculty, the higher level is the exclusive province of the fortunate man who has fully developed his intellect and arrived at the stage of acquired intellect. Should a man at the stage of acquired intellect have a receptive imaginative faculty, his imaginative faculty, like the imagination of the prophet at the lower level, is vouchsafed an emanation from the active intellect. Alfarabi adds parenthetically that "since the active intellect itself emanates from the existence of the First Cause, the First Cause" or "God" can be named "as the source of revelation for man, through the active intellect." "The active intellect emanates" its light upon the man's "acquired intellect," whence the emanation descends to the man's "passive [potential] intellect" and from there to his "imaginative faculty." The philosopher with a receptive imaginative faculty gains knowledge of events, becoming a "prophet," a "warner of future events," and one who can "tell what is happening now [at a distance]." Whether he also receives an imaginative depiction of theoretical knowledge is not made clear. Being a

[80]See above, p. 51.

[81]The notion that dreams foretell the future is, of course, an intercultural commonplace. Aristotle discussed the subject in *De divinatione*, which is part of the *Parva naturalia*. A medieval text, entitled *al-Risāla al-Manāmiyya*, "Epistle concerning Dreams," summarized by S. Pines in "The Arabic Recension of *Parva naturalia*," *Israel Oriental Studies* 4 (1974) 120, makes the inaccurate statement that in the "*Parva naturalia* . . . Aristotle called the [divine] force" responsible for true dreams "the active intellect."

[82]*Al-Madīna al-Fāḍila* 222–25.

[83]Alfarabi, *Fuṣūl al-Madanī* (n. 49 above) §89 (end).

philosopher, he must have already mastered science in the proper way, and hence does not need an inspired imaginative faculty to teach him scientific truths in figurative images. Nevertheless, figurative depictions of theoretical truth serve a pedagogical end and might be put to use by the philosopher-prophet. For when the truths of metaphysics are recast figuratively, most notably in the anthropomorphic portrayals of the spiritual realm found in Scripture, they guide members of society who are incapable of abstract philosophical discourse. A philosopher with an inspired imaginative faculty who in addition possesses certain specified gifts of leadership is not only a philosopher-prophet but also a philosopher-king, the only person fully qualified to govern the virtuous state.[84]

Résumé. Alfarabi's *al-Madīna al-Fāḍila* and *al-Siyāsa al-Madaniyya* trace a series of emanations from the First Cause through the incorporeal intelligences and celestial spheres; and they identify the active intellect implied in Aristotle's *De anima* as the last member in the series of ten incorporeal intelligences. The active intellect has responsibilities in regard to the sublunar world, although those responsibilities fall short of the gamut of functions that a fully symmetrical system would dictate; whereas each intelligence emanates the body and soul of its sphere, the active intellect emanates neither the matter nor the formal side of the sublunar world. It is the heavens that produce the matter of the sublunar world and send forth the forces required for the generation of all natural sublunar beings, including man. The active intellect acts only on the human intellect and, when its emanation travels beyond the human intellect, on the imaginative faculty.

The human intellect passes through three stages: material, or passive, intellect, which is characterized as a disposition in man; actual intellect; and acquired intellect. The emanation from the active intellect which is analogous to the light of the sun enables the human material intellect to grasp the first principles of human thought and the principles of the several human sciences. Human effort then has the task of constructing a corpus of intellectual knowledge. In addition to its role of furnishing the first principles of thought and the principles of the sciences, the active intellect plays another role when man reaches the stage of acquired intellect, for at that point the human intellect separates itself from the body and lower parts of the soul, and the active intellect becomes its form. The human acquired intellect enters conjunction with the active intellect, although without becoming completely identical with it, and the human intellect enjoys eudaemonia and immortality.

Finally, the emanation from the active intellect can travel beyond the human intellect, affect the human imaginative faculty, and inspire two levels of prophet. At

[84]*Al-Madīna al-Fāḍila* 244–47, 278–81; cf. *Siyāsa* 79–80, 85. Cf. also *Taḥṣīl al-Sa^c^āda*, ed. J. Al-Yasin (Beirut 1981) 88, 94; earlier edition: *Taḥṣīl al-Sa^c^āda* (Hyderabad 1927) 38, 44. English translation of *Taḥṣīl al-Sa^c^āda*, as *The Attainment of Happiness*, with pagination of the Hyderabad edition indicated, in Mahdi, *Alfarabi's Philosophy of Plato and Aristotle* (n. 19 above).

the lower level, which presupposes no specific level of intellectual attainment, the emanation from the active intellect flows through the man's intellect to his imaginative faculty and gives the imagination knowledge of present and future events and a figurative depiction of theoretical truths. The higher level is reserved for men who have reached the stage of acquired intellect, and whose intellect is in a state of conjunction with the active intellect. If a man at the stage of acquired intellect has a receptive imaginative faculty, the emanation from the active intellect flows again through his intellect, which is now a perfected intellect, to his imaginative faculty, and again produces knowledge of particular future events. When a philosopher-prophet possesses certain gifts of leadership, he becomes a philosopher-king as well.

Nothing said about the active intellect's exercising providence and performing one action or another should be taken to mean that the active intellect chooses when to act and on whom to bestow its bounty. The active intellect radiates its emanation eternally, constantly, and impersonally, just as the intelligences above it eternally, constantly, and impersonally, send forth theirs. The emanation of the active intellect is automatically received by properly prepared intellects and imaginative faculties, and the active intellect automatically conjoins with acquired intellects.

Alfarabi's *Philosophy of Aristotle*

Alfarabi's *Philosophy of Aristotle* is an ostensible sketch of the whole of Aristotle's philosophy with the exception of the *Metaphysics*.[85] When treating the subject of physical causation, the *Philosophy of Aristotle* states that the heavens produce the four elements, and Alfarabi even remarks that such had been proved in Aristotle's *De caelo*[86]; his *al-Madīna al-Fāḍila* and *al-Siyāsa al-Madaniyya* had similarly identified the heavens as the cause of the matter of the sublunar world and of differences in substance within the world, and hence as the cause of the elements. The *Philosophy of Aristotle* further remarks that the souls of individual animals and the forms of individual plants do not come from the translunar realm, but that the former are engendered by parents and the latter by prior individual plants.[87] That statement also is not very far from what the other two works said. They represented living beings as coming into existence not thanks to forms bestowed from above but through the interplay of physical forces operating on the sublunar plane—forces descending from the heavenly bodies and forces indigenous

[85]Alfarabi writes, in *Philosophy of Aristotle* (n. 19 above) 133: "We do not have the science of metaphysics." I take his meaning to be that the corpus of Aristotle's works—or, much more likely, the corpus of summaries of Aristotle's works—from which he was working did not contain the section on metaphysics.

[86]Ibid. 99. Alfarabi does not here mention the existence of prime matter.

[87]Ibid. 129.

to the sublunar world.[88] The actions of parents and seed-bearing plants, which the *Philosophy of Aristotle* gives as the cause of the existence of animal souls and plant forms, are instances of forces indigenous to the sublunar region.

At this point, the *Philosophy of Aristotle* introduces a curious notion, with an unmistakable Platonic flavor. It asserts that whereas the source of individual souls is easily ascertained, "that which in the first instance gave . . . the form of each species," for example "manhood as a whole" or "donkey-hood as a whole," is more difficult. The book suggests four possible alternatives: The source of the species as a whole may be the celestial spheres, the souls of the spheres, the incorporeal movers of the spheres, or the active intellect. Although Alfarabi does not adjudicate among the alternatives, he does state that the solution lies beyond the scope of physical science. Since the celestial spheres are the subject matter of one of the physical sciences, he thereby apparently excludes the possibility of the spheres' being the cause he is seeking.[89] Exactly what Alfarabi means by the source of a species as a whole, and how the souls of the spheres, the incorporeal movers of the spheres, or the active intellect might be the species' source, is uncertain. Yet whatever his meaning might be, the line he takes here in the *Philosophy of Aristotle* differs from that of *al-Madīna al-Fāḍila* and *al-Siyāsa al-Madaniyya*. Those two works drew no distinction between the cause of individual beings and the cause of a species as a whole, recognized no role in the sublunar world for either the incorporeal intelligences or the souls of the spheres, and restricted the function of the active intellect to perfecting the human intellect. The *Philosophy of Aristotle*, by contrast, proposes that each species as a whole has a source beyond the physical realm, whether it be the souls of the spheres, the celestial intelligences, or the active intellect.

When it takes up the active intellect's role in human thought, Alfarabi's *Philosophy of Aristotle* agrees with the position of *al-Madīna al-Fāḍila* and *al-Siyāsa al-Madaniyya*, although it goes into less detail. Alfarabi argues for the existence of an eternal, incorporeal "active intellect" as the being that provides the human intellect with the "first intelligible thoughts," which are again the "principles" of both "theoretical intellect" and "the practical intellectual faculty." The active intellect "engenders the first intelligible thoughts in the potential intellect and gives it a natural disposition for [receiving] the remaining intelligible thoughts."

At the start, then, the active intellect is the "agent" initiating human thought. It is also the "end" toward which men strive, for human perfection is achieved when the human intellect arrives "as close as possible to" the active intellect. Upon a man's reaching perfection, he "becomes substantialized," he "enjoys a certain conjunction [*ittiṣāl*] with the active intellect by having it as an object of thought," and the active intellect becomes his "incorporeal form."[90] The term *acquired intellect*, which in

[88]Abovc, pp. 47-48.
[89]*Philosophy of Aristotle* 129–30.
[90]Ibid. 127–28.

any event was seen to be problematic, is not employed. The *Philosophy of Aristotle* does make a passing allusion to the theory that the active intellect is the cause of dreams foretelling the future.[91]

The *Risāla fī al-ᶜAql*

Alfarabi's *Risāla fī al-ᶜAql*—known in Latin as *De intelligentiis, De intellectu et intellecto*, or *De intellectu*—takes as its formal subject the senses that the term intellect (*ᶜaql*=νοῦς) has among Arabic speakers and in Aristotle's various works. The largest section of the book, and the one of primary interest, begins: The term *intellect* as employed by Aristotle in the *De anima* has four senses: *potential intellect, actual intellect, acquired intellect*, and *active intellect*.[92]

This section of the *Risāla*, which deals with the term *intellect* in Aristotle's *De anima*, includes a brief outline of the emanation of the supernal universe, and the scheme it presents resembles that set forth in *al-Madīna al-Fāḍila* and *al-Siyāsa al-Madaniyya*. The "first principle of all existing things" brings into existence a single incorporeal being, the mover of the outermost sphere. Whereas the First Cause is "unitary in all respects," the incorporeal mover of the outermost sphere contains "two natures," namely its having "itself" as an object of thought and its having the "essence" of its cause as an object of thought. The former nature or thought "gives," and "is the cause of the existence" of, the corresponding celestial sphere, whereas the latter "gives" the next intelligence in the series.[93] We are to understand that each succeeding intelligence similarly has two natures or thoughts, by reason of which it brings forth a sphere and an intelligence. Although the *Risāla* does not, either here or elsewhere, use the technical terminology of emanationism,[94] Alfarabi is plainly describing the emanation by each incorporeal intelligence of its own celestial sphere and of a further intelligence. At the end of the incorporeal hierarchy stands the active intellect of Aristotle's *De anima*.[95] Alfarabi includes an argument showing that the active intellect cannot be the First Cause of the universe, thereby in effect refuting the position of Alexander of Aphrodisias,[96] whom he does not, however, mention by name. The argument is that the active intellect needs the matter of the sublunar world in order to perform its

[91]Ibid. 121.

[92]*Risāla fī al-ᶜAql* (n. 20 above) 12. The *Risāla* also analyzes the sense of the term *intellect* in the following works of Aristotle: The *Posterior Analytics*, which I discuss below; "Book Six of the [*Nicomachean*] *Ethics*," where intellect means *practical* intellect; and "Lambda [Book 12] of the *Metaphysics*," where the First Cause of the universe is called *intellect*. See *Risāla* 8, 9, 36.

[93]*Risāla* 34–35; English translation 221.

[94]Druart (n. 2 above) 25, 34, builds on the absence of emanation terminology in the *Risāla*.

[95]*Risāla* 24; English translation 218.

[96]Above, p. 13.

function and hence is not self-sufficient, whereas the ultimate cause of the universe must perforce be self-sufficient.[97]

The *Risāla* assigns a significantly wider role to the active intellect in natural causation than did the works previously examined. "[Aristotle's] *De generatione et corruptione*," Alfarabi writes, demonstrated that the sublunar world, insofar as it consists of "bodies" and "forces in bodies," is a product of the "heavens."[98] Thus far, we remain within the framework of *al-Madīna al-Fāḍila*, *al-Siyāsa al-Madaniyya*, and the *Philosophy of Aristotle*.[99] But the *Risāla* continues: The "bodies" and "forces" supplied by the heavens serve only as "matters and substrata" upon which the active intellect "acts." Contained within the active intellect are the forms capable of manifesting themselves in the material world below it—as well as the forms of the incorporeal beings above it; and the forms capable of appearing in matter exist in the active intellect in an eternal, incorporeal, and "undifferentiated" mode. To express itself, the active intellect must make those forms manifest, and sublunar matter exists for no other purpose than to permit their manifestation. The active intellect "gives matter the likes of what it contains in its own substance"; that is to say—although technical emanationist terminology is still absent—it emanates natural forms on sublunar matter. Whenever "matter and a substratum" is "ready" for a given natural form, matter receives the form from the active intellect in a "differentiated mode."[100]

Another work of Alfarabi's was seen to credit the "*De anima*" with the un-Aristotelian concept of conjunction with the active intellect,[101] and now the *Risāla* goes on to add the still more surprising observation that the bestowing of natural forms by the active intellect was "something Aristotle proved in his *De anima*."[102] The only passage in Aristotle's *De anima* that might conceivably have suggested an emanation of forms from the active intellect is the sentence characterizing the active intellect as "making all things."[103] But "making everything" there plainly meant making all thoughts. The emanation of forms from the incorporeal realm is much more reminiscent of Plotinus, for whom, however, the cosmic Soul, rather than the active intellect, is the immediate emanating source of natural forms; and the doctrine reappears in the Arabic paraphrases of Plotinus, including the *Theology of*

[97]*Risāla* 33; English translation 220. I take Alfarabi's point to be that the active intellect needs matter to perform its function as a cause of existence, but Alfarabi's argument might also be read as making the point that the active intellect needs matter to perform its function of leading a human intellect to actuality. On the self-sufficiency of the First Cause, see H. Davidson, *Proofs for Eternity, Creation, and the Existence of God, in Medieval Islamic and Jewish Philosophy* (New York 1987) 294–95.

[98]*Risāla* 33–34; English translation 221.

[99]Above, pp. 47–48, 63.

[100]*Risāla* 29–30, 33–34; English translation 219–21.

[101]Above, p. 54.

[102]*Risāla* 30; English translation 219.

[103]Above, p. 9.

Aristotle.[104] The cooperation of the heavens and the active intellect in the production of the sublunar world is reminiscent of another text too, namely, the passage in the spirit of Stoic philosophy at the end of the *De intellectu* attributed to Alexander.[105]

Alfarabi has said that the active intellect instills a form whenever it finds matter and a substratum ready; in other words, the active intellect endues the sublunar world with a range of forms constituting a range of individual natural beings. But what the range is can only be conjectured. As just seen, the heavens are responsible for the emergence in the sublunar world of "bodies" and "forces," which serve as the "matters and substrata" for the operations of the active intellect. In representing the heavens as responsible for the existence of bodies, Alfarabi is saying that the heavens are the cause of something more than the underlying prime matter of the sublunar world; for prime matter is not yet a body, body being a compound of matter and form. He can plausibly be taken as affirming that the heavens are responsible for the existence of the four elements,[106] which are bodies and which serve as the material substratum for everything else generated in the sublunar world. In representing the heavens as responsible as well for the "forces" in bodies, he perhaps means that the heavens in some manner, most likely through their motion, produce the constituent qualities of the four elements. If the role of the heavens in the sublunar world goes no further than producing the four elements and their qualities, Alfarabi's position would be that the active intellect produces all additional natural beings by emanating a full range of natural forms above the level of the elements.

Regarding the active intellect's role as a cause of human thought, the *Risāla* differs again from *al-Madīna al-Fāḍila* and *al-Siyāsa al-Madaniyya*. Like those works, the *Risāla* recognizes three stages of human intellect: an initial stage, now called potential intellect; actual intellect; and acquired intellect. Potential intellect is "a certain soul, or part of a soul, or one of the faculties of the soul, or something whose substance [*dhāt*] is disposed . . . to abstract . . . quiddities . . . and forms."[107] The list of alternatives leaves the correct way of construing the potential intellect undecided, but as the *Risāla* proceeds, it consistently calls the potential intellect a "substance" (*dhāt*). *Al-Madīna al-Fāḍila* and *al-Siyāsa al-Madaniyya* characterized the initial stage of human intellect as a "disposition" and in doing so suggested an endorsement of Alexander's conception, where the initial stage of the human intellect is a disposition in the human organism. The *Risāla* now apparently endorses the contrary construction, which Averroes was to call Themistius'

[104]Above, p. 31. It is noteworthy that two un-Aristotelian conceptions that Alfarabi cites in the name of "the *De anima*," conjunction with the active intellect and the emanation of natural forms from the active intellect, were both most accessible to him in the *Theology of Aristotle*.

[105]Cf. above, p. 30.

[106]Cf. above, pp. 48, 63.

[107]*Risāla* 12; English translation 215.

position, according to which the initial stage of human intellect is indeed a substance.

The "active intellect . . . renders the substance that was a potential intellect an actual intellect, and it renders potential . . . intelligible thoughts actual intelligible thoughts." To explain the active intellect's operation on the human intellect, Alfarabi again adduces the analogy of the sun's light.

The "eye," Alfarabi writes in the *Risāla*, is "potential vision as long as it remains in darkness." When the "light" of the sun, or "actual transparence"—Aristotle having had defined light as the "actuality of . . . the transparent [medium]"[108]—"arrives in [potential] vision and in the air," it makes potential vision, that is, the eye, "actually transparent," and it makes the "air in contact with" the eye "actually transparent" as well. The presence of actual transparence in both the eye and the contiguous medium is a precondition for sight.[109] "Colors," which were "potentially visible," then "become actually visible," and the eye, which was vision in potentiality, becomes "actual vision." Such is the effect of light; and the active intellect acts in a parallel fashion, although Alfarabi does not develop all the implications that the analogy might permit. "The active intellect gives" the "substance that is potential intellect something standing to it [to the potential intellect] as actual translucence [or light] stands to [potential] vision." The "something" given, or emanated, by the active intellect serves as a "principle through which hitherto potentially intelligible thoughts become actually intelligible to" the potential intellect, and the "potential intellect" becomes "actual intellect."[110]

In *al-Madīna al-Fāḍila* and *al-Siyāsa al-Madaniyya*, the analogue of light emanated by the active intellect furnishes the human intellect with certain principles of theoretical reason and with the principles of ethics or practical reason. The *Philosophy of Aristotle* offered an abbreviated version of the same theory, but Alfarabi's *Risāla fī al-ᶜAql* takes a different position.

One of the shorter sections in the book examines the sense that the term *intellect* has in Aristotle's *Posterior Analytics*, and Alfarabi there writes: "In the *Posterior Analytics* . . . Aristotle . . . meant by" intellect "a faculty of the soul through which man obtains certainty in regard to the true, necessary, universal propositions" that are "the principles of the theoretical sciences." Alfarabi, or perhaps a predecessor from whom he is borrowing, has in mind the concluding sentences of the *Posterior Analytics*, where Aristotle determined that the source of the "principles" of science is "intellect" (νοῦς).[111] While Alfarabi's other works seem to have understood the *Posterior Analytics* as saying that the source of human knowledge of scientific principles is the *active* intellect, the *Risāla* here

[108] Aristotle, *De anima* 2.7.418b, 9–10.

[109] See Aristotle, *De anima* 2.7.

[110] *Risāla* 25–27; English translation 218–19. Alfarabi does not explain what in human thought parallels the actually transparent contiguous medium in vision; but Averroes will. See below, p. 318.

[111] Aristotle, *Posterior Analytics* 2.19.100b, 12.

goes on to assert that those principles belong to man "by innate character and nature, or else [appear] at youth, or [appear] in such a way that there is no inkling of whence and how they came."[112] If knowledge of the principles of science is inborn, it does not come from the transcendent active intellect. Nor does the active intellect supply the principles of practical reason. Another of the smaller sections of the *Risāla* treats the term *intellect* in Aristotle's *Nicomachean Ethics*, and there Alfarabi writes that "certainty in regard to . . . the principles" of practical reason derives from "lengthy experience."[113]

The active intellect thus renders potentially intelligible thoughts actually intelligible to the human intellect, but those thoughts are not the first principles of theoretical or practical reason. When discussing the "intelligible thoughts" rendered actual to the human intellect, the *Risāla* calls them "quiddities" and "forms" that the human intellect "abstracts" from matter.[114] Quiddities and forms are concepts. Concepts are therefore what the active intellect enables the human intellect to think. Many of the concepts that the human intellect abstracts out of matter are the same natural forms that the active intellect contains and emanates into matter. The active intellect, in its role as a cause of human thought, hence enables the human intellect to abstract precisely the forms that it emanated into matter in its role as a cause of existence. Whether, and how, the active intellect might enable the human intellect to abstract other, nonnatural and artificial forms, which presumably are not emanated into matter by the active intellect, remains unclear.

In *al-Madīna al-Fāḍila*, Alfarabi wrote that the stage of acquired intellect is reached when man thinks "all" possible thoughts. In the *Risāla* he makes a small qualification and writes that the human intellect reaches the stage of acquired intellect when it possesses "all" or "most" of the intelligible thoughts that can be known through abstraction. The stage of acquired intellect brings with it thought of incorporeal beings, and since such beings are actual objects of thought by their very nature, without the abstraction of any form from a material substratum, the acquired intellect has incorporeal beings as an object of thought simply by "encountering" (*ṣādafa*) them. The *Risāla* does not expressly mention union or conjunction with the active intellect; but it does make the related statement that each stage of human intellect is "like a form" for the previous stage, and incorporeal beings in general, not just the active intellect, are, "as it were, forms" of the stage of acquired intellect.[115] The *Risāla* further agrees with the works examined earlier in describing the stage of acquired intellect as "the closest possible thing to the active intellect,"[116] the implication being that the human intellect falls short of total identity with the active intellect. Thus here too, Alfarabi does not accept the full force of the

[112] *Risāla* 8–9.
[113] Ibid. 9.
[114] Ibid. 12; English translation 215.
[115] Ibid. 20–22; English translation 217.
[116] Ibid. 31; English translation 220.

reasoning that since intellect is identical with whatever thought it thinks, if the human intellect should have the active intellect as the object of its thought, it would become completely identical with the active intellect.

Acquired intellect does not "need the body to serve as its matter in order to exist." Nor does it any longer "have to resort to an act of a faculty of the soul for any of its own actions"; for it contains in itself all—or, at least, most—possible thoughts and can dispense with abstraction. Not being dependent on a body, it attains, even before the body dies, "supreme eudaemonia and the life to come."[117] Immortality is therefore again a concomitant of the stage of acquired intellect and is achieved even before the death of the body. The *Risāla fī al-ᶜAql* does not speak of the immortality of the soul, as distinct from the intellect, and it does not mention prophecy.

Résumé. The *Risāla fī al-ᶜAql* portrays the emanation of the translunar universe as *al-Madīna al-Fāḍila* and *al-Siyāsa al-Madaniyya* did. It differs from those two works in ascribing to the active intellect the emanation of a range of natural forms above the level of the four elements. Alfarabi's *Philosophy of Aristotle*, which maintained that a supernal incorporeal source must be assumed for species as a whole although not for individuals, occupies an intermediate position on the issue, standing between *al-Madīna al-Fāḍila* and *al-Siyāsa al-Madaniyya*, which know nothing about a source of natural forms in the incorporeal realm, and the *Risāla*, which has the active intellect emanate the natural forms of individual sublunar objects.

In the *Risāla*, the active intellect is still the cause of actual human thought. Alfarabi now explains, however, that the analogue of light emitted by the active intellect renders potential concepts actual and hence enables the human intellect to grasp *concepts*. In *al-Madīna al-Fāḍila*, *al-Siyāsa al-Madaniyya*, and the *Philosophy of Aristotle*, the analogue of light emitted by the active intellect enables the human intellect to grasp not concepts but the propositions embodying the first principles of thought and science.

Alfarabi's Commentary on the *Nicomachean Ethics*

Each of Alfarabi's works examined so far understands immortality to be a concomitant of the culminating stage of human intellect. Each also affirms either that the human intellect conjoins with the active intellect at the culminating stage or the related proposition that the active intellect—as well as other incorporeal beings—becomes "as it were," the form of the human intellect at the culminating stage. Alfarabi is reported to have repudiated those propositions in his lost

[117] Ibid.

commentary on Aristotle's *Nicomachean Ethics*. The reports are supplied by Ibn Bājja (Avempace), Ibn Ṭufail, and Averroes.

Ibn Bājja mentions unnamed interpreters who read Alfarabi's Commentary on the *Nicomachean Ethics* as denying an afterlife. For his part, Ibn Bājja rejects the interpretation, although it is uncertain whether he takes issue with the interpretation as such or with the supposition that the Commentary on the *Nicomachean Ethics* represented Alfarabi's final stand on the subject.[118] Ibn Ṭufail makes just a brief remark, which agrees with the interpretation referred to by Ibn Bājja. In Ibn Ṭufail's words: Alfarabi's "Commentary on the Ethics" differed from "*al-Siyāsa al-Madaniyya*"[119] by refusing to admit "human eudaemonia" beyond this world and by branding talk of a hereafter as "raving and old wives' tales."[120] Averroes takes up the matter several times and adds further details.

He writes that even in the Commentary on the *Nicomachean Ethics*, Alfarabi recognized a transcendent active intellect as the factor leading the human intellect to actuality.[121] But then, according to one of Averroes' works, Alfarabi's Commentary on the *Nicomachean Ethics* went on to "assert that man has no perfection other than perfection through the theoretical sciences" and hence "the thesis about man's becoming an incorporeal substance is an old wives' tale."[122] In a second composition Averroes gives the following, slightly different account: What Alfarabi's Commentary on the *Nicomachean Ethics* called "an old wives tale" was "the thesis that we . . . conjoin with the incorporeal intelligence [that is, with the active intellect]."[123] In yet a third composition, Averroes reports:

> In the book on the *Nicomachean* [*Ethics*] Alfarabi appears to have denied that conjunction with the incorporeal intelligences can take place. He stated that such was also the opinion of Alexander. And [he held] that the end for man should not be

[118]Ibn Bājja, *Risāla al-wadā^c*, ed. and Spanish trans. M. Asìn Palacios as "La Carta de Adios," *Al-Andalus* 8 (1943) §2; S. Pines, "The Limitations of Human Knowledge," *Studies in Medieval Jewish History and Literature*, ed. I. Twersky (Cambridge, Mass. 1979) 82, quoting from a text subsequently published by J. Alaoui, in *Rasā'il Falsafiyya li-Abī Bakr ibn Bājja* (Casablanca 1983) 197.

[119]And also from Alfarabi's *al-Milla al-Fāḍila*.

[120]Ibn Ṭufail, *Ḥayy ben Yaqdhān* (*Yaqẓān*), ed. and French trans. L. Gauthier (Beirut 1936), Arabic section 13–14; French translation 12; English translation, with pagination of Gauthier's text indicated: *Hayy Ibn Yaqzān*, trans. L. Goodman (New York 1972) ; Munk (n. 69 above) 348.

[121]Averroes, *Drei Abhandlungen über die Conjunction*, ed. and German trans. J. Hercz (Berlin 1869), Hebrew section 11; German translation 51; Averroes, *Commentarium magnum in Aristotelis De anima libros* (Cambridge 1953] (henceforth cited as: Long Commentary on the *De anima*) 485.

[122]Averroes, *Iggeret Efsharut ha-Debequt* (Arabic original lost), ed. and English trans. K. Bland, as *Epistle on the Possibility of Conjunction* (New York 1982) §14, Hebrew text 108; English translation 85.

[123]*Drei Abhandlungen*, Hebrew section 13; German translation 54. Similarly, ibid., Hebrew section 10; German translation 46.

> regarded as anything other than theoretical perfection. Ibn Bājja, however, explained Alfarabi's statements [in a manner that removes the denial of the possibility of conjunction] and he wrote that Alfarabi's opinion was in fact the same as that of all the Peripatetics. In other words, [on Ibn Bājja's reading, Alfarabi held] that conjunction [with the active intellect] is possible and does constitute the end [for man].[124]

When taken together, the passages quoted thus far from three compositions of Averroes' inform us that the lost Commentary on the *Nicomachean Ethics* agreed with Alfarabi's preserved works in recognizing the transcendent active intellect as the agent leading the human intellect to actuality and in viewing the cultivation of theoretical science as the end of human life. While Ibn Bājja and Ibn Ṭufail report only that Alfarabi rejected—or may have rejected—human immortality, Averroes tells us that Alfarabi rejected both immortality and the possibility of the human intellect's becoming conjoined to the active intellect or other incorporeal beings.

Averroes has additional information, for he records two separate lines of argumentation that supposedly led Alfarabi's Commentary on the *Nicomachean Ethics* to its skeptical conclusions. On three separate occasions, Averroes reports Alfarabi's grounds to have been that "the generated-destructible cannot become eternal."[125] An Aristotelian rule laid down that anything generated must undergo destruction and cannot continue to exist forever,[126] and Alfarabi—as Averroes transmits or reconstructs his reasoning—concluded that inasmuch as the human intellect comes into existence, it inevitably undergoes destruction. On a fourth occasion, Averroes attributes another line of argument to Alfarabi, namely, that a "single disposition cannot . . . receive two different things, nay diametrically opposite things." By its nature, the human intellect receives "intelligible thoughts derived from material objects." Should it also have the "incorporeal intelligences" as an object of thought, it would be a disposition naturally receptive of things diametrically opposite in their character. But no such disposition is conceivable, whence it follows that the human intellect cannot possibly have the active intellect as an object of thought and thereby conjoin with the active intellect. The composition attributing this second line of argumentation to Alfarabi's Commentary on the *Nicomachean Ethics* characterizes the reasoning as "the strongest doubt that can be raised" against the possibility of conjunction with the active intellect.[127]

In sum, Ibn Bājja reports that some scholars had interpreted Alfarabi's Commentary on the *Nicomachean Ethics* as denying an afterlife, but he, Ibn Bājja, questions the interpretation. Ibn Ṭufail repeats the interpretation of the unnamed

[124] Long Commentary on the *De anima* 433.

[125] *Drei Abhandlungen*, Hebrew section 7–8, 13; German translation 27, 36–37, 54; Long Commentary on the *De anima* 481.

[126] Aristotle, *De caelo* 1.12.

[127] *Epistle on the Possibility of Conjunction with the Active Intellect* §14; Hebrew text 108.

commentators referred to by Ibn Bājja. Averroes in different works reports that Alfarabi's Commentary denied human immortality and the possibility of conjunction with incorporeal beings. Since Averroes submits differing versions of Alfarabi's reasoning, and in one spot records, without objection, Ibn Bājja's assessment of the Commentary on the *Nicomachean Ethics*, which would overturn his own, we may suspect that he did not have direct access to the Commentary on the *Nicomachean Ethics* himself. He may have relied instead on bits of secondary information from which he reconstructed Alfarabi's thinking; the sources could have been Ibn Bājja and Ibn Ṭufail, and perhaps someone else who provided the statement about Alfarabi's having cited Alexander to support his position on conjunction. If such is the case, it could be Averroes who inferred Alfarabi's rejection of the possibility of the human intellect's conjoining with the active intellect from Alfarabi's rejection of human immortality.

At all events, the evidence is too thin to make a confident judgment about what Alfarabi in fact said in the Commentary on the *Nicomachean Ethics*. What Averroes believed Alfarabi to have said will play a significant role in his own thought.[128]

Concluding Note

Various texts of Alfarabi, as has been seen, take divergent positions on the functions of the active intellect, the nature of the human intellect, and the ultimate fate of the human intellect. The reasons for the discrepancies can only be conjectured,[129] but the tone of Alfarabi's writings is suggestive. *Al-Madīna al-Fāḍila*, *al-Siyāsa al-Madaniyya*, and the *Philosophy of Aristotle* are not treatises that argue issues through to a conclusion. They read instead like matter-of-fact summaries of familiar positions. The *Risāla fī al-ᶜAql*, although it does argue a number of its positions, has the overall structure of a lexicon. I would accordingly conjecture that Alfarabi worked from different oral or written philosophic sources and summaries at different times, and that the position he took at any one time reflects the texts then before him.

[128]See below, pp. 323, 328–31.

[129]Druart (n. 2 above), who deals with other discrepancies in Alfarabi's writings, suggests that his works form an intentional sequence.

4

Avicenna on Emanation, the Active Intellect, and Human Intellect

In the present chapter I assume that Avicenna's genuine works all reflect a single consistent outlook concerning the issues discussed, although Avicenna sometimes does slip into inconsistency in details.[1]

The Emanation of the Universe; the Active Intellect as a Cause of the Existence of the Sublunar World

Like Alfarabi, Avicenna envisions a translunar region comprising nine primary spheres: an outermost, diurnal sphere, the sphere of the fixed stars, and the seven spheres that contain the planets, the sun, and the moon.[2] Each sphere is again accompanied by an incorporeal intelligence, which is its mover, and Avicenna again knits intelligences and spheres together through a series of emanations. He,

[1]A list of Avicenna's works was compiled by Jūzjānī, a student and long-time companion of Avicenna, and it was subsequently supplemented by longer medieval lists. See *The Life of Ibn Sina* (Jūzjānī's biography of Avicenna), ed. and trans. W. Gohlman (Albany 1974) 13–15, 46–49, 90–113. Still longer lists have been compiled by two modern scholars, Anawati and Mahdavi; and the various lists are discussed by Gohlman 13, and J. Michot, *La destinée de l'homme selon Avicenne* (Louvain 1986) xiii. Almost all of my citations are from works in Jūzjānī's list, which I consider the safest. Avicenna refers at times to an "Oriental," or "Eastern," philosophy developed by him which somehow differed from his standard scheme, but nothing of it has been preserved. Scholars have indulged in wide-ranging speculation, verging on the fantastic, regarding that philosophy. For a sensible discussion of the subject, see D. Gutas, *Avicenna and the Aristotelian Tradition* (Leiden 1988) 115–130.

[2]Avicenna, *Shifā' : Ilāhiyyāt*, ed. G. Anawati et al. (Cairo 1960) 401; French translation, with pagination of the Arabic indicated: *La Métaphysique du Shifā' : livres VI à X*, trans. G. Anawati (Paris 1985); Avicenna, *Najāt* (Cairo 1938) 273. In the present instance, as in most of the citations to be given from the *Najāt*, that work consists of excerpts from the *Shifā'*. Avicenna recognizes secondary spheres and does not reject out of hand the possibility that each secondary sphere has its own intelligence. On such a hypothesis, "the first teacher's [Aristotle's] position" that there are "approximately fifty" intelligences may be correct. But, Avicenna adds, the active intellect will in any event be "the last" in the series.

however, offers his version of the emanation scheme as an explicit solution to a philosophic problem, and his version includes a nuance not found in Alfarabi.

The philosophic problem is encapsulated in the terse formula that "from the one, insofar as it is one, only one can come into existence [*yūjad*]."[3] In Avicenna, the scheme of successive emanations is expressly designed to explain how, given that principle, a plural universe can derive from the wholly unitary First Cause: Plurality enters because the incorporeal beings subsequent to the First Cause have plural thoughts.

Avicenna still locates the ultimate, First Cause of the universe beyond the intelligences that move the celestial spheres. And the First Cause, through its eternal thought of itself, still eternally and continually emanates the first intelligence, which is the mover of the outermost sphere. Alfarabi had differentiated between two aspects in the thought of each incorporeal intelligence, and each intelligence, in his scheme, eternally emanates the next intelligence in the series by virtue of one of the two aspects, while by virtue of the other it emanates a celestial sphere.[4] Avicenna brings to bear a proposition from his metaphysics to the effect that the incorporeal intelligences are possibly existent by reason of themselves, necessarily existent by reason of their cause.[5] The distinction allows him to differentiate between three, and not just two, aspects in the thought of each intelligence; and the addition of the third aspect enables him to account for the presence of both a soul and a body in the celestial sphere emanated by the intelligence.

The first intelligence, in Avicenna's scheme, has the First Cause as the object of its thought, and a second intelligence thereby "necessarily proceeds [*yalzam*] from it." It has itself, insofar as it is a being existing necessarily by reason of the First Cause, as a second object of thought, and it thereby emanates the soul of the outermost sphere. And it has itself insofar as it is possibly existent by reason of itself as a third object of thought, and it thereby emanates the body of the outermost sphere. Or, in a more careful formulation, it has a thought of itself which includes both its being necessarily existent by reason of the First Cause and its being possibly existent by reason of itself, and it thereby emanates the outermost sphere, which is composed of both a soul and a body. The second intelligence similarly

[3] *Shifā' : Ilāhiyyāt* 405. The problem of explaining how a plural universe can derive from a wholly unitary first cause was posed by Plotinus and reappears in one of the Arabic paraphrases of Plotinus. But I have not been able to find the formula that "from one only one proceeds" before Avicenna. See Plotinus, *Enneads* 5.1.6, 5.2.1, 5.3.15, and *Risāla fī al-cIlm al-Ilāhī*, ed. A. Badawi, in *Plotinus apud Arabes* (Cairo 1955) 176–77, which is a paraphrase of *Enneads* 5.3.15. G. Lewis' English translation of the Arabic paraphrases of Plotinus are given in Plotinus, *Enneades*, ed. P. Henry and H.-R. Schwyzer 2 (Paris 1959), facing the Greek original.

[4] Above, p. 46. In *al-Siyāsa al-Madaniyya*, ed. F. Najjar (Beirut 1964) 41, Alfarabi does write that the soul of each of the spheres has three objects of thought: itself, the incorporeal intelligence that is its cause, and the First Cause.

[5] H. Davidson, *Proofs for Eternity, Creation, and the Existence of God, in Medieval Islamic and Jewish Philosophy* (New York 1987) 290–91.

has as objects of its thought: the First Cause, itself as a being necessarily existent by reason of its cause, and itself as a possible being. Through those three thoughts, or aspects of its thought, it emanates the third intelligence, the body of the second sphere, which is the sphere of the fixed stars, and the soul of the second sphere. And so on.[6] The final link in the chain of incorporeal intelligences is the "active intellect governing our souls," that is to say, the active intellect implied in Aristotle's *De anima*.[7]

Avicenna feels called on to explain why the process stops at the active intellect and does "not continue . . . *ad infinitum*." He writes: While it is true that the "necessary proceeding . . . of a multiplicity [of beings] from an [incorporeal] intelligence" implies a multiplicity of aspects in the emanating intelligence, the proposition is "not convertible" and not all intelligences containing the same kind of aspects will bring forth the same kind of effects.[8] What an intelligence emanates depends on its nature and power. As intelligences succeed one another, their power diminishes, and because the active intellect stands low in the hierarchy its power is no longer sufficient to emanate eternal beings like those emanated by the intelligences above it.

Avicenna nevertheless ascribes to the active intellect a set of functions that lend his scheme a symmetry missing in Alfarabi. While the active intellect cannot fully imitate the intelligences above it and eternally emanate the body of a celestial sphere, the soul of a celestial sphere, and an additional incorporeal intelligence, it does emanate lesser analogues. The active intellect is (1) the emanating cause of the matter of the sublunar world, (2) the emanating cause of natural forms appearing in matter, including the souls of plants, animals, and man, and (3) the cause of the actualization of the human intellect. Even these lesser analogues are not the work of the active intellect alone, for in each instance an auxiliary factor participates.

Alfarabi identified the celestial spheres as the cause of the existence of the underlying matter of the sublunar world.[9] Avicenna argues against taking the celestial spheres as the cause, or at least as the sole cause, of sublunar matter; and although he does not mention Alfarabi by name, his argument sounds as if it has

[6] *Shifā': Ilāhiyyāt* 406, 409; *Najāt* 277, 280; *K. al-Ishārāt wal-Tanbīhāt*, ed. J. Forget (Leiden 1892) 174; French translation of *Ishārāt*, with pages of Forget's edition indicated: *Livre des directives et remarques*, trans. A. Goichon (Beirut 1951). The *Isharāt* distinguishes two aspects in the thought of the intelligence, its thought of the First Cause and its thought of itself, and then adds that the second thought is divided in two. Ghazali, *Maqāṣid al-Falāsifa* (Cairo n.d.) 219, distinguishes only two aspects in each intelligence.

[7] *Shifā': Ilāhiyyāt* 407; *Najāt* 278; *Ishārāt* 174; *K. al-Ḥudūd*, ed. and French trans. A. Goichon (Cairo 1963), §26. A. Goichon, *La distinction de l'essence et de l'existence d'après Ibn Sina* (Paris 1937) 237, cites a minor work attributed to Avicenna, which, she reports, identifies the active intellect with the intelligence of the sphere of the moon. If her reading is correct, the discrepancy is sufficient to impugn the attribution to Avicenna. See below, n. 74, for an attempt to read Avicenna as locating the active intellect within the human soul.

[8] *Shifā': Ilāhiyyāt* 407; *Najāt*, 278.

[9] Above, pp. 48, 66.

precisely Alfarabi in mind. He starts with the assumption that a single common material substratum underlies the four elements and every other physical object in the sublunar world.[10] Then he reasons: It may be granted that the characteristic common to all the celestial spheres, that is to say, their circular motion, is an auxiliary factor in producing the single common substratum of the four elements. Nevertheless, the uniform motion of the spheres cannot suffice. For "a multiplicity of things, [even when] agreeing in species and genus, cannot by themselves and without the participation of a unitary . . . factor be the cause of a substance that is the same and unitary in itself." The spheres are individually distinct, and consequently no common characteristic they have can produce the wholly uniform prime matter of the sublunar world. "Hence" another, "unitary" being must participate in the production of prime matter, and such a being can be sought only among "the incorporeal intelligences." The incorporeal intelligences are not the cause collectively, since, as just seen, the cause cannot be a number of individually distinct beings. "Rather, from the last of the intelligences, the one adjacent to us, there emanates [*yafīḍ*], with the participation of the movements of the heavens, something containing the imprint of the forms of the lower world." That is to say, prime matter, with its potentiality for exhibiting the forms of all natural objects in the sublunar world, is eternally emanated by the active intellect with the aid of the movement of the heavens. The factor within the heavens that "aids in the existence of [sublunar] matter" is their common "circular motion"—that is, their common "nature," which expresses itself in circular motion. But how the common circular movement of the heavens contributes is left unclear.[11]

Whatever one makes of Avicenna's reasoning, it certainly reflects a consistency on his part. To the classic Aristotelian proof of the existence of a First Cause from *motion* in the universe, Avicenna added a proof from the *existence* of the universe.[12] To Aristotle's inference of the existence of the celestial intelligences from the *motion* of the celestial spheres, Avicenna added a proof of their existence from the *existence* of the spheres.[13] And now, to the inference—drawn by Aristotle or his commentators—of the existence of the active intellect from the passage, or *movement*, of the human intellect from potentiality to actuality, Avicenna adds an inference of the existence of the active intellect from the *existence* of sublunar matter. Avicenna will also infer the existence of an active intellect from the existence of natural forms in the world and most especially from

[10]Cf. E. Zeller, *Die Philosophie der Griechen* 2.2, 4th ed. (Leipzig 1921) 315ff.; H. Wolfson, *Crescas' Critique of Aristotle* (Cambridge, Mass. 1929) 571–73.

[11]*Shifā': Ilāhiyyāt* 410; *Najāt* 281; *Ishārāt* 175. Ghazali 221, establishes the emanation of prime matter from the active intellect through the principle that one body cannot produce another body; and Goichon's French translation of *Ishārāt* (n. 6 above) 431, n. 5, quotes Ṭūṣī's commentary on that work to the same effect.

[12]Davidson (n. 5 above) 298–304.

[13]*Shifā': Ilāhiyyāt* 407; *Najāt* 278.

the existence of the human soul. He thus consistently supplements Aristotelian proofs from motion with proofs from existence.

All natural forms are contained in the active intellect in a unified, undifferentiated mode,[14] and the active intellect eternally emanates them not through choice but as an eternal, constant, and necessary expression of its being.[15] Avicenna therefore calls the active intellect the "giver of forms."[16] And yet the active intellect is an incorporeal, "unitary" being, and "a unitary [cause] produces only a unitary [effect] in a unitary [subject]." If the active intellect acted upon undifferentiated matter, no differentiation of effect would be possible, and matter would not exhibit a plurality of forms. A "particularizing factor" (*mukhaṣṣiṣ*) must consequently "tip the scales" (*yurajjiḥ*) and "prepare" matter for receiving a given natural form to the exclusion of another. One set of factors "particularizing" matter and preparing it to receive a natural form is the "influences" emitted by the celestial spheres; for although themselves free of qualities, the spheres instill the four basic qualities—ḥeat, cold, dryness, wetness—in matter. Another set is the motions proper to the several spheres, as distinct from the daily motion common to all. The "difference" in the movements of the several spheres "prepares matter for [receiving] divers forms." Still other factors preparing matter for natural forms are forces indigenous to the sublunar world.[17]

At the lowest level, the emanation of the active intellect supplies the forms of the four elements: fire, air, water, and earth. Avicenna explicitly rejects a mechanical hypothesis, espoused by some "who lay claim to this science [of philosophy, or perhaps: of metaphysics]," according to which friction transforms the sublunar matter nearest the celestial spheres into fire, while the forms of the other three elements result directly from their distance from the element fire.[18] The hypothesis would, he submits, entail that each portion of prime matter first exists without the form of any of the four elements and that it then receives a form by virtue of the place it occupies within the sublunar region and the resulting rapidity with which it moves. But, Avicenna contends by way of refutation, matter can never actually exist without the form of an element[19]; further, portions of matter occupy specific spots in the sublunar world and undergo motion only by virtue of possessing their elemental forms, not vice versa. The most plausible theory is therefore that from all eternity, every portion of matter is endued with one or another of the elemental

[14]Below, p. 91. See above, p. 66.

[15]*Shifā': Ilāhiyyāt* 414–15; *Najāt* 284.

[16]*Shifā': Ilāhiyyāt* 413; *Najāt* 283.

[17]*Shifā': Ilāhiyyāt* 410–11, 436; *Najāt* 150, 280–82, 299; *Shifā': Physical Sciences* 2–4, ed. M. Kassem (Cairo 1969) 190–91; *Ishārāt* 175.

[18]An explanation of precisely this sort was suggested by Alfarabi, *Philosophy of Aristotle*, ed. M. Mahdi (Beirut 1961) 104–5; English translation: in *Alfarabi's Philosophy of Plato and Aristotle*, trans. Mahdi (New York 1962) 71ff., with pagination of the original Arabic indicated.

[19]That is to say, prime matter cannot exist solely with "corporeal form." On corporeal form, see Wolfson (n. 10 above) 579–90.

forms thanks to the emanation of the active intellect. A portion of matter with the character predisposing it to receive the form of one of the four elements automatically receives the appropriate form from the ever-present emanation broadcast by the active intellect, and when matter invested with a given form becomes disposed for another form, it receives the new form.

Avicenna offers the following illustration of the transformation of elements into one another: Water, like the other elements, can accommodate a certain latitude of qualities. It can be heated to a certain extent without ceasing to be water. Eventually, though, a point is reached where heat "exceeds the bounds" that water can accommodate. At that point the "relation" of the given portion of matter to the form of fire becomes stronger than its relation to its original form, and the form of water is replaced by the form of fire. The new form comes from without, "emanated" from the active intellect.[20]

Forms above the level of the four elements are similarly emanated by the active intellect and received by properly disposed portions of matter, but Avicenna does not make perfectly clear which forms are, and which are not, emanated. He attributes to the emanation of the "giver of forms and powers," that is, the active intellect, the emergence of all "powers" and "characteristics" that cannot be explained by the constituent elements of a mixture of matter, apparently including even tastes and odors.[21] He further maintains that the forms of plants, animals, and man emanate from the active intellect. When, however, he considers the generation of mist and dry haze, physical compounds ranked immediately above the level of the four elements, he offers a mechanical explanation, with no mention of a role for the active intellect.[22] A most comprehensive statement of the range of forms coming from the active intellect is delineated in Ghazali's summary of Avicenna's philosophy. Ghazali's summary describes the four elements, mist and haze, metals, plants, animals, and man, as all receiving forms emanated by the active intellect.[23]

The form that a given portion of matter does receive depends upon the mixture of the matter; the finer the blend, the more perfect the form. At the lower level of the sublunar hierarchy, the contrariety of qualities in the four elements "prevents them from receiving life." The notion that matter, when not mixed homogeneously, is *prevented* from receiving a higher level of form sounds odd yet is in harmony with Avicenna's viewpoint. Matter, he understands, has the potentiality of receiving all physical forms: It "contains the imprint of the forms of the lower world by way of being acted upon, as the [active] intellect . . . contains the imprint of forms by

[20]*Shifā': Ilāhiyyāt* 413–14; *Najāt* 282–84. One might have expected Avicenna to write that fire first turns water into air.

[21]*Shifā': Physical Sciences* 256–57.

[22]Ibid. 204; *Najāt* 153. *Najāt* 157 mentions the generation of metals, but in too brief a way to infer whether or not Avicenna would assign a role to the active intellect in their generation.

[23]*Maqāṣid* (n. 6 above) 222–24.

way of acting."[24] When a new form is manifested in matter, matter has simply received and exhibited actually what always belonged to it potentially. The physical processes enabling matter to receive progressively higher forms can therefore be regarded not merely as the preparation of matter for those forms but equally as the removal of obstacles that prevented matter from receiving what was rightfully its own.[25] The obstacles are progressively removed, and a given portion of matter is progressively prepared for higher forms, as the movements and influences of the heavens act together with forces within the sublunar world to "destroy" the contrary qualities in a given portion of matter. The constituent elements thereby start to lose their separate identity and to blend into a homogeneous mixture. To the degree that the mixture approaches "the mean that has no contrary," and comes to "resemble the celestial bodies," which contain no contrary qualities, just "to such a degree, does it merit receiving an animating faculty from the incorporeal governing substance." That is to say, successive degrees of homogeneity in a portion of matter dispose the matter to receive successively higher levels of plant or animal form from the emanation of the active intellect.

At the upper limit, the mixture of a portion of matter may go "as far as possible in approaching the mean" and reach the point where "no further destruction of the contrary extremes is possible." It thereupon "receives a substance closely similar, in a certain way, to the incorporeal substance." In other words, when matter is blended to the highest possible degree, it receives a human rational soul, which is an incorporeal substance, in contradistinction to animal and vegetable souls, which consist only in an "animating faculty."[26] The relationship between the body of a celestial sphere, the soul of the sphere, and the corresponding incorporeal intelligence is replicated in man. For the human body stands to the human soul as "the celestial substances" do to the souls that "they receive and are conjoined to," and the human soul stands to the active intellect as the soul of each sphere does to the intelligence that is the cause of the existence of both the sphere's soul and body.[27]

From passages in various works of Avicenna, a set of reasons can be culled showing that the active intellect and no other agent must be the cause of the existence of the human soul. Avicenna contends that the human body cannot, insofar as it is a body, produce its own soul; for a body does not act "insofar as it is a body . . . but only through its powers."[28] Nor can the powers within the

[24]*Shifā': Ilāhiyyāt* 410; *Najāt* 281.

[25]Cf. *Shifā': Physical Sciences* 259–60.

[26]*Shifā': De anima*, ed. F. Rahman as *Avicenna's De Anima* (London, 1959) 261; *Najāt* 191. English translation of *Najāt* 157–93: *Avicenna's Psychology*, trans. F. Rahman (London 1952). The passage cited here appears on p. 67 of the translation.

[27]*Shifā': Ilāhiyyāt* 401; *Najāt* 191, 273.

[28]A contention to the effect that a body, insofar as it is a body, cannot "produce" anything is found in Proclus, Commentary on Plato's *Timaeus*, ed. E. Diehl, 1 (Leipzig 1903) 293; French

human body produce the human soul. They are corporeal, whereas the human soul, as Avicenna will prove,[29] is incorporeal; and the corporeal can never be the cause of the incorporeal,[30] because what stands at a lower level of existence cannot be the cause of what stands at a higher level.[31] In a separate work Avicenna considers and rejects the suggestion that the disembodied souls of past generations produce new human souls. He gives two reasons for rejecting the suggestion—the first of which I could not understand. The second is that disembodied souls as a class cannot produce a human soul, since a class of individuals is divisible, whereas the cause of an indivisible effect cannot be divisible; nor can a single random disembodied soul produce a human soul, since what is random does not act as a cause.[32]

In still another context Avicenna contends that the souls of the celestial spheres cannot be the cause of the existence of other souls, inasmuch as the souls of the spheres operate only through their bodies and a "body cannot serve as an intermediary between one soul and another."[33] And one further passage argues that none of the incorporeal beings above the active intellect can be the cause of the existence of human souls and intellects. The First Cause of the universe cannot be the cause, for it is a simple being and hence produces only a single effect, whereas many human souls and intellects exist. Nor can the incorporeal intelligences associated with the celestial spheres be the cause producing human souls and intellects. For although the intelligences do produce a multiplicity of effects, they do not produce multiplicity within a single species, the nature of the intelligences being to operate on the bodies of the celestial spheres, which are not subject to division. Multiplicity in a single species results, however, only when an agent acts on divisible matter. Of all the incorporeal beings, only the active intellect operates on the divisible matter of the sublunar world, and consequently it alone can produce a multiplicity of things within a single species.[34]

---

translation, with pagination of the original indicated: Proclus, *Commentaire sur le Timée*, trans. A. Festugière, 2 (Paris 1967).

[29]Below, p. 83.

[30]*Shifā': De anima* 228; *Najāt* 185; English translation 59; S. Landauer, "Die Psychologie des Ibn Sīnā," *Zeitschrift der deutschen morgenländischen Gesellschaft* 29 (1876) 335–418, chap. 3. Landauer edits and translates a text that cannot be identified with any item in Jūzjānī's list of Avicenna's works (see above, n. 1), but may be identical with an item in a subsequent medieval list; see Gohlman (n. 1 above) 108–9, item 82. It is equally possible, however, that the text comes from one of Avicenna's followers, and not from Avicenna himself.

[31]*Shifā': Ilāhiyyāt* 409; *Najāt*, 280.

[32]*Mubāḥathāt*, in *Arisṭū ᶜinda al-ᶜArab*, ed. A. Badawi (Cairo 1947) 122, 194.

[33]*Shifā': Ilāhiyyāt* 407–8; *Najāt* 278–79; *Ishārāt* (n. 6 above) 172. The argument, to be precise, is offered as a proof that the soul of one sphere cannot be the cause of the next sphere's soul.

[34]*Shifā': Ilāhiyyāt* 408–9; *Najāt* 279–80.

Résumé. Avicenna's universe has a structure virtually identical with the structure of Alfarabi's. The First Cause of the universe again transcends the intelligences that move the spheres; it emanates the intelligence that moves the outermost sphere; that intelligence emanates the next intelligence in the hierarchy as well as the body and soul of its own sphere; and each succeeding intelligence emanates a similar set of effects. Avicenna, however, offers his version of the scheme specifically in answer to a philosophic problem, the question how multiplicity can have emerged given a single unitary First Cause. By distinguishing three moments in the thought of each intelligence, he is also able to explain a point that was ignored in Alfarabi. He can identify the source of all three of the intelligence's effects—the body and soul of the corresponding sphere as well as the next intelligence. The active intellect is for Avicenna, as it was for Alfarabi, the last in the series of incorporeal intelligences.

As Alfarabi did in *al-Madīna al-Fāḍila* and *al-Siyāsa al-Madaniyya*, Avicenna connects the uniformity and diversity within the lower world to uniformity and diversity within the heavens. But for Avicenna, the heavens are only an auxiliary cause of what exists in the lower world; the active intellect is the primary cause. In an unexplained way the uniformity of celestial motion helps the active intellect to emanate the eternal matter of the sublunar world. Differences in the motions of the spheres and influences emitted by the spheres then prepare sublunar matter for each of the natural forms emanated by the active intellect. While Alfarabi's *Risāla fī al-ᶜAql* had represented the active intellect as the agent that emanates natural forms above the level of the four elements,[35] Avicenna goes beyond the *Risāla* too, for he understands the active intellect to be the cause of the matter as well as the forms of the sublunar world, and to be the cause of the four elements as well as the forms of more complex beings. Avicenna could have arrived at his account of the active intellect's functions by combining in the active intellect functions that Plotinus distributed between the Neoplatonic cosmic Intellect and cosmic Soul.[36] Or he could have started with Alfarabi's *Risāla* and expanded the picture of the active intellect he found there into one in which the functions performed by the active intellect fully parallel those performed by the intelligences above it. As far as I could see, Avicenna never explicitly traces the different products emanated by the active intellect—sublunar matter, sublunar forms, intelligible thought—to different aspects in the active intellect's thought, nor does he indicate whether the active intellect produces what it does through a single emanation or through separate emanations.[37]

[35]Above, p. 66.

[36]Above, pp. 31–32.

[37]Every intelligence above the active intellect has a thought of the First Cause and a twofold thought of itself, hence, three thoughts in all. By virtue of the former thought, it emanates a further intelligence, and by virtue of the other two, it emanates the body and soul of its sphere. The active intellect should, by analogy, also have three thoughts and three emanations.

Avicenna's manner of advancing his positions differs from Alfarabi's, for whereas Alfarabi generally stated positions without justifying them, Avicenna argues his through, with care and at length. Although Avicenna's universe may strike a modern reader as even more bizarre than Aristotle's, it is, like Aristotle's, a carefully argued scientific hypothesis for explaining observed phenomena.

Stages of Human Intellect; the Active Intellect as the Cause of Human Thought

We have seen that as soon as a portion of matter is ready to receive a human soul, it does so from the ever-present emanation of the active intellect. Avicenna advances a set of arguments to establish that the human soul, unlike the other natural forms emanated by the active intellect, is an incorporeal substance, "which does not in any sense exist in a body as a power [or: faculty] or as a form of the body." The burden of the arguments is that intelligible thoughts, by which Avicenna appears here specifically to mean concepts as distinct from propositions, are indivisible and can be present only in an indivisible and hence incorporeal subject. Since the human soul is "the subject" that "receives" intelligible thoughts, the soul must, he concludes, be an incorporeal substance.[38]

At birth, the incorporeal human soul contains no thought whatsoever and has merely an empty potentiality for thinking. As the child grows, the potentiality

---

Suhrawardī, below, pp. 163, 165, does distinguish different thoughts in the active intellect, and assigns an emanation to each thought.

[38]*Shifā': De anima* 209ff.; *Najāt* 174ff.; English translation (n. 26, above) 46–50; *Ishārāt* (n. 6 above) 130; Landauer "Psychologie des Ibn Sīnā" (n. 30 above) chap. 9. On the human soul as the "subject" that "receives" intelligible thoughts, see *Shifā': De anima* 239–40. The proposition that the soul is indivisible since it receives indivisible concepts does not convert, for Avicenna, into the proposition that since the soul is indivisible it can receive *only* indivisible concepts. For as long as the soul operates through the body, it is also conscious of composite propositions and of composite percepts originating in sense perception.

There are problems with a Cartesian flavor in Avicenna's position: If the soul is an indivisible incorporeal substance, how can it receive sense perceptions? If it is an incorporeal substance that does not "in any sense exist in a body," how can it be in a state of potentiality?

The attention of scholars has been attracted to an argument of Avicenna's, which has at least a surface similarity to Descartes' "cogito, ergo sum." Avicenna poses a mental experiment in which a man imagines himself floating in the air under circumstances such that no part of his body touches any other part and he has no sensory experience. The man, Avicenna reasons, will nonetheless be conscious of his existence, whence the conclusion can be drawn that the human soul is the true man and the soul is distinct from the body. See *Shifā': De anima* 16, 255; S. Pines, "La conception de la conscience de soi chez Avicenne et chez Abu'l-Barakat al-Baghdadi," reprinted in his *Studies in Abu'l-Barakāt* (Jerusalem 1979) 185–216; M. Marmura, "Avicenna's 'Flying Man' in Context," *The Monist* 69 (1986) 383–95; T. Druart, "The Soul and Body Problem: Avicenna and Descartes," in *Arabic Philosophy and the West*, ed. T. Druart (Washington 1988) 27–49; and the literature cited by Druart 7–12.

develops. Avicenna distinguishes a series of stages of human intellect, starting from the empty potentiality with which man is born, and he attaches to them names that have been met before. But while the names are familiar, the scheme is peculiar to Avicenna and reflects his understanding of the manner in which human beings think.

Aristotle had called attention to the situation wherein the human intellect has already assembled a repertoire of thoughts yet is not actually thinking them, and Alexander applied the term "intellect *in habitu*" to human intellect in that condition.[39] Avicenna goes further and by the side of the empty potentiality for thought in the newborn distinguishes not one but two stages in which intellect possesses a repertoire of thoughts without actually thinking them. He thus differentiates three stages of human potentiality for thought. To illustrate, he compares the stages of the human potentiality for thought to three senses in which a person may have a potentiality for "writing."

The newborn infant has the potentiality for writing only in the sense that it may eventually learn to write. The infant is accordingly said to have an "unqualified disposition" or "unqualified . . . potentiality" for writing. Later, the "boy matures" and comes to "know the inkwell, the pen, and the letters." Inasmuch as he controls the rudiments and can go on to master the art with "no intermediate" step, he is said to have a "possible potentiality" for writing. At a still higher level stands the "scribe," who is adept with the "[writing] implement," is "accomplished in his art," and can apply the art "at will." When he is not exercising his skill, the scribe has a "perfect" potentiality for writing.

Paralleling the three senses of potentiality in writing are three stages of potential theoretical[40] intellect: (1) "Material" intellect is the wholly "unqualified potentiality" for thought which belongs to "every member of the species." It is a "disposition" (*isti^c dād*) inhering in the incorporeal human soul from birth. (2) "Intellect *in habitu*" (*bil-malaka*) is the "possible potentiality" in which the human subject possesses the "first intelligible thoughts." These are theoretical propositions of the sort man affirms without being able to "suppose that they might ever not be affirmed"; examples are the propositions that "the whole is greater than the part" and "things equal to the same thing are equal to each other." The examples, as will be noted, are the same that Alfarabi's *al-Madīna al-Fāḍila* gave for the principles of thought which the active intellect instills in the human material intellect at the outset.[41] (3) "Actual intellect," despite the name, is a further stage of potentiality—the stage of fully actualized potentiality. It is the "complete [*kamāliyya*] potentiality" that is attained when both "second intelligibles" and "intelligible forms"—that is to say, derivative propositions and concepts—have been added to the "first intelligibles," with the proviso that the human subject is not thinking the

[39]Above, p. 10.
[40]On the practical intellect, see below, p. 88.
[41]Cf. above, p. 51.

propositions and concepts. At the stage of actual intellect, the human subject does not "actually . . . attend to" his knowledge, yet can do so "whenever he wishes." Avicenna has marked off two stages in which the human intellect has acquired intelligible thoughts, but is not attending to them at the moment: the stage of intellectual potentiality paralleling the child who has learned only the letters, and the stage of intellectual potentiality paralleling the accomplished scribe. It would seem that had he chosen to, he could have marked off any number of further gradations.

In addition to the three stages of potentiality for thought, Avicenna distinguishes a level of a different character: (4) "acquired [*mustafād*] intellect," which alone is an "unqualified actuality." At the level of acquired intellect, "intelligible forms" are actually "present" to the man, and he "actually attends" to them. In Alfarabi, the term *acquired intellect* designated the highest stage of human intellectual development, and Alfarabi's choice of the term was problematic, because the highest stage in his scheme of intellect is not in fact acquired from an external source but rather fashioned from below and within, by human effort. Avicenna's acquired intellect is, literally, acquired from the active intellect. The unqualified actuality of thought is "called . . . acquired, because it will be shown . . . that potential intellect passes to actuality" by establishing contact with the active intellect and having "forms acquired from without imprinted" in man's intellect.[42]

The expression "acquired intellect" and even more especially the phrase "acquired from without" recall the Arabic translations of Alexander's *De anima* and of the *De intellectu* attributed to Alexander. Those two works recognized the possibility of the human intellect's having the active intellect or other incorporeal substances as the direct object of its thought, and the Arabic translations of both called detached human thought of an incorporeal substance, and specifically of the active intellect, *acquired intellect* or *intellect acquired from without.*[43] Avicenna rejects the denotation the terms had in the Arabic translations of the two Greek works. He refutes unnamed commentators who "maintained that the . . . active intellect leads our souls from potentiality to actuality . . . by uniting . . . with our souls, becoming their form, and becoming an acquired intellect for us. Then when our bodies pass away, it [the active intellect] remains as it was at the start." The sense the unnamed commentators are here reported to have assigned to the term *acquired intellect* is the one that was assigned by Alexander's *De anima* and the *De intellectu,* in their Arabic versions; and the description of the manner in which the active intellect produces human thought according to the unnamed commentators approximates that of the *De intellectu.*[44] Avicenna adds that for the commentators in question, the factor in man "disposed for receiving the substance [of the active intellect]" is "a corporeal faculty and disposition in the heart or brain"; and some of

[42]*Shifā': De anima* 48–50, 241; *Najāt* 165–66; English translation 33–35; *Ishārāt* 126.
[43]Above, p. 11.
[44]Above, pp. 22–23.

the same commentators had the further "audacity" to identify the active intellect with "the first God." Both those theses were put forward in Alexander's *De anima*.[45]

Avicenna directs two objections against the proposition that the active intellect unites with man and thereby becomes his acquired intellect: If an incorporeal being should unite with man, it would undergo "accidental" motion when the body moved and it would be "circumscribed in the heart or brain." But an incorporeal being cannot undergo motion of any kind, nor can it be physically circumscribed.[46] Further, if the active intellect brought the human soul to actuality by "uniting" with it, the human soul, having become one with the active intellect, would at once know "all intelligible thoughts and be ignorant of nothing." But nothing of the sort happens.[47]

The term *acquired intellect* in Avicenna is most reminiscent of Plotinus, who designated as "acquired intellect" the intellectual knowledge that the soul *acquires* directly from the cosmic Intellect.[48]

While the term *acquired intellect* exactly fits the aspect of human intellect to which Avicenna applies it, an ambiguity does infiltrate his usage. Besides writing that all actual intelligible human thought, no matter how far or how little the human intellect has progressed along the path to perfection, is "acquired" from the active intellect, and that all actual human thought is consequently *acquired* intellect, he also makes the following statements: "At [the level of] acquired intellect, the animal genus and human species are perfected [*tamma*], and the human [intellectual] faculty resembles the first principles of all being [that is, the incorporeal substances]"[49]; the state of acquired intellect is man's "perfection" (*kamāl*)[50]; "acquired intellect, or rather holy intellect, is the head [faculty of the soul], which all the other [faculties] serve, and it is the ultimate end."[51] Phrases of the sort depict acquired intellect as a culmination of human intellectual development, which is what it was in Alfarabi. In a word, Avicenna applies the term *acquired intellect* to two different things, to actual human thought, irrespective of the intellectual progress a man has made, and to actual human thought when human intellectual development is complete.

The cause effecting each of the four degrees of human intellect is the active intellect. To start, the active intellect emanates a human soul endowed with the potentiality for thought upon any receptive portion of sublunar matter. It is thereby the cause of the existence of the human material intellect. Then the active intellect is

[45]Above, pp. 9, 13–14.

[46]The objection would, however, also seem to affect Avicenna's hypothesis that the human soul is an incorporeal substance.

[47]Glosses on *De anima*, in *Arisṭū ᶜinda al-ᶜArab* (n. 32 above) 92–93.

[48]Above, p. 12.

[49]*Shifā' : De anima* 50.

[50]Ibid. 248; *Ishārāt* (n. 6 above) 126.

[51]*Najāt* 168; English translation (n. 26 above) 37.

the factor bringing the material intellect to the stage of intellect *in habitu*,[52] the factor bringing intellect *in habitu* to the stage of actual intellect,[53] and the source of the actual thought constituting acquired intellect, both when acquired intellect means an imperfectly developed intellect's actual thought and when it means actual thought at the completion of human intellectual development.[54] In leading man from one level to the next, the active intellect provides him with the first principles of thought, which are propositions; with abstract human concepts; and with certain other propositions.

We have already seen Avicenna's proof that the active intellect brings the human soul, with its material intellect, into existence. He also proves that the active intellect brings about each of the subsequent levels of human intellect. Both intellect *in habitu* and actual intellect, in Avicenna's sense, are attained when the intellect's previous stage of potentiality thinks new actual thoughts and adds them to its repertoire; and the condition of acquired intellect occurs whenever the human potentiality for thought becomes actual. Each level is therefore the result of a passage from potentiality to actuality. Avicenna postulates, following Aristotle,[55] that "whatever passes from potentiality to actuality" does so "only through a cause that is actually [what the other is potentially]." "There must consequently be a [wholly actual] cause that makes our souls pass from potentiality to actuality in respect to intelligible thoughts,"[56] and the cause is the "active intellect."[57]

The formula just quoted—whatever passes from potentiality to actuality does so only through a cause that is actually what the other is potentially—was already commonplace,[58] but Avicenna draws an inference from it that had not been drawn before. He assumes that one thing renders another actual by "providing the actuality of the second." Inasmuch as the actuality of the human intellect is actual intelligible thought, actual intelligible thoughts must be what the active intellect provides the human intellect. And if the active intellect provides the human intellect with intelligible thoughts, it must consist in them itself.[59] It must "provide and imprint upon the soul the forms of intelligible thought from its own substance."[60] The standard argument for the existence of the active intellect thus establishes not

[52]*Ishārāt* 126–27. Landauer, "Psychologie des Ibn Sīnā" (n. 30 above) 370–71.

[53]*Ishārāt* 126–27.

[54]See below, passim.

[55]Above, p. 18.

[56]*Shifā': De anima* 234. Cf. Avicenna, *Fī Ithbāt al-Nubuwwāt*, ed. M. Marmura (Beirut 1968) 44; English translation: "On the Proof of Prophecies," in *Medieval Political Philosophy*, ed. R. Lerner and M. Mahdi (New York 1963) 114. I am not convinced that the attribution of *Fī Ithbāt al-Nubuwwāt* to Avicenna is correct.

[57]*Najāt* 192–93; English translation 68–69.

[58]Cf. above, pp. 24, 25, 27, 49.

[59]This does not harmonize with Avicenna's statement about the spheres' instilling the qualities of heat, cold, dryness, and wetness, despite being free of those qualities. See above, p.78.

[60]*Najāt* 192, with Rahman's textual correction in the appendix to his English translation (n. 26 above) 125; English translation 68.

merely a cause of human thought. It establishes a cause of human thought that functions as such by communicating thoughts directly from itself to the human intellect. The general thesis—although not either the manner in which Avicenna views the active intellect's operation or his argumentation—could have been known to him most especially from Plotinus but also from Kindi and from the Arabic treatise on the soul attributed to Porphyry.[61]

Everything said so far relates exclusively to theoretical thought. The principles of man's practical intellect do not, according to Avicenna, have their source in the active intellect; they are "commonly accepted views, traditions, opinions, and flimsy experiences."[62] Alfarabi's *Risāla fī al-ᶜAql* had also maintained that the principles of the practical intellect come from experience and not from the active intellect.[63]

The works attributed to Avicenna offer two additional arguments to establish that the active intellect is the direct source of human thought. The first appears in a treatise on the soul, which is believed to be an early work of his. There Avicenna, if he is indeed the author, contends that "experience" cannot be the source of either the first principles of thought—such as the proposition that "the whole is greater than the part," "the impossibility of two contraries' being joined in a single thing," and "the fact that things equal to the same thing are equal to each other"—or the conclusions of logical "demonstration[s]." Propositions of both sorts are universally true, whereas judgments based on experience carry certainty only for the individual instances witnessed or for exactly similar instances.[64] To take an example, although perhaps "all animals we have observed move their lower jaw when chewing," the judgment should not be generalized and applied to species beyond those observed. Here, as it happens, at least one species of animal exists, namely, "the crocodile," which moves not its lower jaw but "its upper jaw when chewing." Since universal judgments carrying the stamp of certainty cannot be grounded in empirical evidence, they must be "acquired" from outside the physical realm, "from a divine emanation that conjoins with the rational soul and with which the rational soul is conjoined." The "[source of the] emanation" must "have in its substance" the "universal intellectual forms" that it "imprints on the rational soul"; and what is of that character is perforce a "self-subsistent, incorporeal, intellectual substance." Universal judgments carrying the stamp of certainty must come to the human intellect directly from an incorporeal being.[65]

The second additional argument showing that the active intellect is the direct source of human thought turns on an analysis of human memory and recollection.

[61]Above, pp. 24–25, 27, 28.

[62]*Shifā': De anima* 207.

[63]See above, p. 69.

[64]For other Arabic thinkers who point out the limitations of empirical knowledge, see Davidson (n. 5 above) 30.

[65]Landauer, "Die Psychologie des Ibn Sinā" (n. 30 above) 370–71; German translation 416–17.

Avicenna's mature philosophic works distinguish five "internal senses" belonging to animal and human souls. All five are physical, operating through different parts of the brain, and two of the five have the function of preserving the perceptions of other senses. The *retentive imagination* (*khayāl; muṣawwira*) preserves sensations processed by the *sensus communis*, which is the internal coordinating faculty for the five external senses; and *memory* (*ḥāfiẓa; dhākira*) preserves the perceptions of the *estimative faculty* (*wahmiyya*), which is the intuitive faculty whereby sheep, for example, recognize the wolf as dangerous and to be avoided.[66]

Now, Avicenna reasons, when a perception is forgotten, it does not disappear from the animal or human organism but remains "stored" in the part of the brain serving either the retentive imagination or the memory. Forgetting is an instance of the soul's ceasing to attend to a percept that is stored in the brain, while recollection is the soul's attending to it once again. But, he continues, whereas the memory and the recollection of sense perceptions are thus amenable to physiological explanation, a different kind of explanation is needed for memory of "intelligible thoughts." Intelligible thoughts—which I understand here to mean concepts—are, as he has proved, indivisible. Being indivisible, they cannot subsist in a divisible substratum and hence cannot be present in a physical organ or known through a physical faculty.[67] They are therefore not stored anywhere in the human organism after they have been learned. Nor can they be "actually present" in the soul when not attended to, since the soul is perforce conscious of whatever thought is actually in it. When not attended to, intelligible forms must exist outside the human soul and outside the physical realm. Avicenna dismisses the Platonic theory of separately existing incorporeal Forms, and having eliminated all the unacceptable alternatives, is left with the conclusion that intelligible thoughts exist in an incorporeal being from which they are "emanated" upon the human soul. Actually to know them is to enter into "conjunction" (*ittiṣāl*) with the incorporeal "principle that gives intellect," in other words, with the "active intellect"; and actual human knowledge of a thought is "acquired intellect." Learning a thought is the process of replacing the soul's original "defective" disposition for the thought with a "perfect [*tāmm*] disposition" that enables the soul to establish conjunction with the active intellect at will. Memory of the thought is the possession of the perfect disposition for it. To recall a thought is to reestablish conjunction with the active intellect vis à vis the given thought.[68]

66*Shifā': De anima* 44–45; *Najāt* 163; English translation 30–31, and endnote; H. Wolfson, "The Internal Senses," reprinted in his *Studies in the History of Philosophy and Religion* (Cambridge, Mass. 1973) 277. The passage cited from the *Shifā'* lists five internal senses: sensus communis; retentive imagination; compositive imagination, the function of which is to work with images in the retentive imagination (see below, p.95); estimative faculty; and memory. The felicitous terms *retentive imagination* and *compositive imagination* were coined by Wolfson.

67*Shifā': De anima* 209ff.; *Najāt* 174–78; English translation 46–50; *Ishārāt* (n. 6 above) 130.

68*Shifā': De anima* 245–48; *Ishārāt* 129; Glosses on *De anima*, in *Arisṭū ᶜinda al-ᶜArab* (n. 32 above) 100–101; *Mubāḥathāt*, in the same volume 230–31; Commentary on the *Theology of*

The foregoing account of intellectual memory and recollection should be combined with Avicenna's earlier statements about stages of potentiality for thinking. Combining them will give the following result: At birth, the human material intellect is an empty disposition for thought. Man progresses to the stage of intellect *in habitu* and then to the stage of actual intellect by entering into conjunction with the active intellect and receiving the active intellect's emanation. Intellect *in habitu* is a perfect disposition for thought vis à vis a minimum corpus of principles of thought, which are propositions; and actual intellect is a perfect disposition vis à vis additional propositions and a full corpus of concepts. The repertoire of thoughts belonging to man at those two stages of potentiality does not exist in either the human organism or the human soul. Thoughts exist in the active intellect. Memory of a thought is the possession of a perfect disposition for thinking a thought, that is to say, the ability, at will, to reestablish conjunction with the active intellect vis à vis the given thought.

Conjunction, Avicenna insists, is not union, and he refutes the thesis that the soul acquires intelligible thought by uniting with the active intellect or with part of it. If the soul became united with the entire active intellect as soon as it knows a single thought, it would—Avicenna has already been seen to argue—immediately contain everything the active intellect contains and know everything the active intellect knows. By virtue of knowing a single thought, it would at once know "all intelligible thoughts and be ignorant of nothing,"[69] and obviously, nothing of the sort happens.[70] Nor can the soul "unite with a part of" the active intellect, since incorporeal beings do not have parts. The soul acquires thought from the active intellect—and this must be the meaning of conjunction with the active intellect and receiving the active intellect's emanation—not through union but by having "an effect [or: impression (*athar*)] of the active intellect displayed in it."[71]

The picture is further fleshed out, and also rendered more complex, by an analysis of a more nuanced phenomenon, the phenomenon of a person's being confident that he can answer a question even before formulating the answer and even if he never answered the question before. The certainty that one can answer a question is not a "potentiality." Inasmuch as the person is certain that he can produce the required answer, he must have some sort of actual knowledge. Nor is the phenomenon a variety of memory, in which the person has a perfect disposition for establishing conjunction with the active intellect, without at the moment being in conjunction with it. For a person may be sure that he can answer a question when he is "near knowing" the answer, although he never gave the answer before.

Aristotle, in the same volume, 73; French translation: "Notes d'Avicenne sur la 'Théologie d'Aristote,'" trans. G. Vajda, in *Revue Thomiste* 51 (1951) 406; Rahman, *Avicenna's Psychology* (n. 26 above) 117–20. A contention curiously similar to Avicenna's is put forward by G. Stout, *God and Nature* (Cambridge 1952) 238–39.

[69]Glosses on *De anima*, in *Arisṭū ᶜinda al-ᶜArab* 92–93; above, p. 86.

[70]*Shifā' : De anima* 241, 247.

[71]Glosses on *De anima*, in *Arisṭū ᶜinda al-ᶜArab* 93.

To account for the situation he has posed, Avicenna draws a distinction similar to one that we met in Plotinus. Plotinus had stated that the man has intellectual thoughts in two ways, at a higher level where thoughts are "all together," and at a lower level where they are "unrolled and discrete, as it were."[72] Avicenna, for his part, explains that the person in the situation of knowing that he can answer a question before articulating the answer already possesses knowledge in "a simple mode" before beginning to make his answer, and as he proceeds to the articulation he recasts his knowledge in "another mode." The simple mode of knowledge belongs to what Avicenna here calls the "absolute intellectual faculty of the soul," or "the simple . . . intellect," or the "faculty of abstract intellect." That faculty "is emanated" from the active intellect when man establishes "conjunction" with the active intellect and is presumably identical with what Avicenna elsewhere calls "the light of the active intellect in us."[73] When man is in the first mode, he is thus in conjunction with the active intellect and receives its emanation. Thoughts within the absolute, or simple, or abstract, intellectual faculty are not differentiated. They are "unitary," with "no sequence of one form after another." Thought in the absolute intellectual faculty hence resembles thought belonging to the "active [celestial] intelligences."[74]

[72]Above, p. 25.

[73]Below, p. 93.

[74]F. Rahman, *Prophecy in Islam* (London 1958) 32–33, quotes Avicenna, *Shifā': De anima* 243, as stating: "This creative knowledge (i.e. the active intellect) belongs to the absolutely noetic *faculty of the soul* resembling the (external) Active Intelligences. . . ." The parentheses and italics are Rahman's. Rahman concludes from his reading of the passage that Avicenna located the active intellect within the human soul and he even submits that Avicenna's theory of "intuitive religious cognition demands that the creative principle of knowledge be in the mind as a part of it." The sentence that Rahman quotes from Avicenna should, however, be translated as follows: Knowledge in the "simple" mode "is knowledge that produces the thing we call cogitative knowledge. . . . It belongs to the absolute intellectual faculty of the soul, [the faculty] resembling the active intelligences." In other words, the absolute intellectual faculty of the human soul, which emanates from the active intellect, brings knowledge in the first or simple mode, that is to say, undifferentiated knowledge; and from undifferentiated knowledge there derives knowledge in the second mode, that is to say, differentiated, or cogitative, knowledge. Although the absolute intellectual faculty that emanates from the active intellect and the undifferentiated knowledge it carries are located by Avicenna within the human soul, Avicenna in no way writes or intimates that the active intellect itself is present in the soul. Nor is there anything in the Arabic text of Avicenna to justify the expression "creative knowledge" in Rahman's translation. Rahman proceeds to quote *Fī Ithbāt al-Nubuwwāt*, a work attributed to Avicenna, which in an old printed edition terms the highest human intellectual "faculty": "active intellect." And Rahman again concludes that Avicenna located the active intellect in the human soul. The editor of the recent critical edition of *Fī Ithbāt al-Nubuwwāt* has, however, chosen a better manuscript reading, according to which Avicenna, or whoever the author was, terms the highest human faculty "acquired intellect" and not "active intellect." See *Fī Ithbāt al-Nubuwwāt*, (n. 56 above) 43; English translation 114. *Fī Ithbāt al-Nubuwwāt* 44, English translation 114, calls the transcendent being that leads the human intellect to actuality "the universal intellect, the universal

The absolute intellectual faculty appears in the soul through an emanation from the active intellect; and a second "emanation" thereupon flows from the absolute faculty, an emanation beginning and terminating within the soul. "Forms" now "emanate" in a "differentiated" mode, and the "sequential arrangement" peculiar to human discourse is born. In acquiring thought, then, man first establishes conjunction with the active intellect, which emanates the absolute faculty; differentiated forms thereupon emanate "upon the soul" from the absolute faculty already in the soul. The person who is confident that he can answer a question before having articulated the answer has entered the first phase. In articulating his answer, he passes to the second.[75]

The innovation that human thought is emanated in two phases is not integrated with what Avicenna writes elsewhere on the subject of human thought. Avicenna does not explain whether at the stage of intellect *in habitu*, which consists in a perfect disposition for thinking the first principles of thought, and at the stage of actual intellect, which consists in a perfect disposition for a full corpus of thoughts, even the first emanation, the one containing undifferentiated thought, disappears from the soul when man is not actually thinking or on the verge of thinking. The more plausible reading of Avicenna would be that both phases disappear from the soul when man is not actually thinking, so that a man must reestablish conjunction with the active intellect and receive the first as well as the second phase of emanation every time he recalls a thought previously learned. Avicenna also does not correlate his theory of the two phases with his conception of acquired intellect; presumably, since acquired intellect is actual thought, it is the end result of both phases. As we shall see presently, the cogitative faculty of the soul plays a central role in human thought, and it will be possible to infer, although Avicenna does not say so explicitly, that the cogitative faculty performs a role in both phases. Avicenna himself recognizes that the notion of two phases in the emanation of thought is problematic. He comments regarding the first phase: "How it is possible for the rational soul to possess a principle that is not the soul and that has knowledge distinct from the soul's knowledge, is a subject for speculation," which everyone "must understand from [his] own soul [or: from (him)self]." Further: "It is a wonder that when someone . . . begins differentiating to another what occurred to him instantaneously, the person, in the very course of instructing [the other], learns the knowledge in the second [differentiated] mode."[76]

To illustrate the way in which the human intellect attains thought, Avicenna deploys several analogies, and the analogy he returns to most frequently is that of light. Like the sun, which is "essentially visible," the active intellect, he writes, is "essentially intelligible." In vision, a ray of light from the sun "conjoins" with

---

soul, and the world-soul." Whether or not one accepts the attribution to Avicenna, the composition has to be read as a watered-down version of Avicenna's philosophic theories.

[75] *Shifā' : De anima* 242–47.

[76] Ibid. 243.

"colors that are potentially visible" and with the human power of sight, which is also potential. The former thereupon "become actually visible," and the latter "actually sees." "Analogously, a power emanates from the active intellect and travels to the potentially intelligible things in the imaginative faculty [*ashyā' mutakhayyala*; properly: in the *compositive* imaginative faculty] in order to render them actually intelligible and to render the potential intellect actual intellect."[77] Abstract concepts result: "When the intellectual faculty gazes on particulars in the imagination [*khayāl*; properly: in the *retentive* imagination] and the light of the active intellect in us shines on them, . . . they become abstracted from matter and its concomitants and are imprinted in the rational soul."[78] The comparison of the active intellect to the sun recalls the formulations of the light analogy in Alfarabi's works; and in the version of Alfarabi's *Risāla fī al-ᶜAql*, concepts are what the lightlike emanation from the active intellect enables the human intellect to abstract from matter.[79]

Avicenna employs the analogy because it had become common, but in his framework, it is no longer apt. His position is not in fact that the emanation from the active intellect enables the human intellect to abstract concepts from images presented by the imaginative faculty, just as the eye sees colors that are illumined by the rays of the sun. Intelligible thoughts, he has maintained, flow directly from the active intellect and are not abstracted at all. He therefore has to qualify the analogy: Images are transformed into universal concepts "not in the sense that they are themselves transported from the imagination [*takhayyul*; properly: the *compositive* imagination] to the human intellect, . . . but in the sense that examining them prepares the soul for the abstract [concept] to emanate upon it from the active intellect." "The light of the active intellect enters into a kind of conjunction with" the rational soul (alternative translation: it enters into a kind of conjunction with forms in the imaginative faculty); and the rational faculty thereby "becomes disposed for abstractions of forms [that are found in the imagination (*khayāliyya*; properly: the *retentive* imagination)] to be generated in it [that is, in the rational faculty] from the light of the active intellect."[80] Activity leading up to the ostensible act of abstraction thus does not come to fruition in a true act of abstraction. It rather prepares the way for the reception of abstract concepts from the emanation of the active intellect.

Avicenna has two additional analogies, and they fit his theory of human thought better. One is a medical variation of the analogy of light and vision, and the other is the analogy of the mirror known from Plotinus.[81] Avicenna compares the preparation of the human intellect for receiving intellectual thought to "treatment" of

[77]*Najāt* 193; English translation 69.

[78]*Shifā': De anima* 235. The discrepancy in assigning the same role to the compositive imagination in one passage and to the retentive imagination in another will be taken up below.

[79]Above, pp. 51, 68, 69.

[80]*Shifā': De anima* 235–36. Cf. *Ishārāt* (n. 6 above) 129; *Mubāḥathāt* (n. 32 above) 239.

[81]Above, p. 25.

the eye. Once treatment has made the eye "healthy," the eye does not of course always see, yet it has the ability to see at will. Similarly, to train the intellect is to bring it to one of the stages of advanced potentiality, in which it can reestablish "conjunction" with the active intellect at will.[82] In the other analogy, the human intellect, once it has the ability to think, is like a mirror. When the intellect faces the active intellect, a thought is reflected in it, while if it turns away to other affairs it loses the reflection.[83]

Résumé. The human soul, Avicenna proves, is an incorporeal substance, received by a properly prepared portion of matter from the ever-present emanation of the active intellect. The active intellect is also the source of abstract concepts, theoretical propositions embodying the first principles of thought, and other propositions that Avicenna does not spell out precisely. Human knowledge pertaining to the practical domain does not come from the active intellect.

At the outset, the soul possesses a blank material intellect, which is an unqualified potentiality and empty disposition for intelligible thought. In order to gain actual intelligible thoughts, man, or the human soul, or the human potential intellect, must conjoin with the active intellect and receive the active intellect's emanation. When a man progresses to the level where he has learned the first principles of thought but is not actually thinking them at the moment, he has attained the stage of intellect *in habitu*. When he goes on to the level where he has a full repertoire of concepts and derivative scientific propositions, again without thinking them at the moment, he has attained actual intellect; actual intellect, despite the name, is an advanced stage of potentiality. Since both intellect *in habitu* and actual intellect result from thinking actual thoughts and placing them in one's repertoire, both result from the active intellect's emanation. All actual intelligible thought, that is, all acquired intellect, is also of course received from the active intellect's emanation. The active intellect is thus the source of the thought constituting all the stages and states of human intellect.

The repertoires of thought at the stages of intellect *in habitu* and actual intellect are not stored in the human soul or anywhere in the human organism. Saying that a man has a repertoire of thoughts consequently does not mean that the thoughts are in any way in him but rather that he can reestablish conjunction with the active intellect vis à vis the given thoughts at will; a perfect disposition for obtaining the thoughts from the active intellect has superseded the empty disposition. Language to the effect that man abstracts thought or that the light of the active intellect transforms potential thoughts into actual thoughts is also not to be taken literally, for the actual thoughts in fact come from the emanation of the active intellect.

[82] *Shifā': De anima* 247.
[83] *Ishārāt* 129.

Imagination, Cogitation, Insight

Aristotle had written that the human intellect "thinks the forms in the images" contained within the human imaginative faculty.[84] His intent, we may assume, was that the imaginative faculty of the soul presents images to the human intellect, and the human intellect takes hold of forms it discovers in those images. By Avicenna's time, the number of internal senses of the human soul had grown, and Avicenna enumerates at least five internal senses, including both a retentive imaginative faculty and a compositive imaginative faculty. The retentive imaginative faculty receives and preserves images from the sensus communis, the faculty coordinating percepts reported by the five external senses. The compositive imaginative faculty "combines images in the retentive imagination with one another and disassembles them, at will."[85]

Avicenna has been seen to state both that man receives intelligible thoughts directly from the active intellect when his intellectual faculty is prepared by the "compositive imaginative faculty" (*ashyā' mutakhayyala*) and that it receives thoughts when it "gazes on particulars in the retentive imagination [*khayāl*]."[86] In the context where the second statement was made, he further writes both that examining images in the "compositive imagination" prepares the intellect to receive thoughts from the active intellect, and again that the rational faculty receives the "abstractions of . . . forms [of images]" that are found in the "retentive imagination."[87] If I have translated the terms correctly, he thus sometimes describes human thought as emanating from the active intellect when the retentive imagination presents images to the human intellect, and at other times, when the compositive imagination does so. Avicenna was, however, frequently inconsistent in handling the internal faculties of the soul.[88] He may, therefore, merely have been careless with terminology, and in the present instance, the terms *retentive imagination* and *compositive imagination* may refer to only a single faculty.[89] As we shall see, the faculty would be the compositive imagination. At all events, Avicenna's position is that the intellect does not extract forms from images, but that the imaginative faculty—or faculties—presents images to the human intellect and thereby "prepares" the human intellect for receiving thoughts from the emanation of the active intellect.[90]

When Avicenna goes more fully into the technicalities of the internal senses' part in human intelligible thought, he employs yet another term and names the

[84]Above, p. 19.

[85]Wolfson (n. 66 above) 274–77; *Shifā' : De anima* 44–45.

[86]Above, p. 93.

[87]*Shifā' : De anima* 235.

[88]Wolfson (n. 66 above) 277–81.

[89]A. Goichon, *Lexique de la langue philosophique d'Ibn Sīnā* (Paris 1938) 118–19, also assumes that Avicenna is not careful in using the terms.

[90]*Mubāḥathāt* (n. 32 above) 232. See above, p. 28.

cogitative faculty (*mufakkira, fikra*) as the internal sense performing the key role. In doing so, he introduces precision, not additional inconsistency. As he explains in his treatment of the internal senses, the same internal sense is "called compositive imaginative faculty [*mutakhayyila*] in reference to the animal soul, and cogitative faculty in reference to the human soul."[91] Cogitative faculty is simply the exact term for the compositive imagination in man. Whether in animal or man, the faculty in question works on images in the retentive imagination, disassembling and combining them to fashion new configurations. It operates through a "ventricle" of the brain[92] and undergoes "movement."[93] It is therefore a physical faculty, not an "intellectual faculty,"[94] and its activity ceases with the death of the body.[95]

The section where Avicenna distinguished two phases of human thought explained that in the first phase, the active intellect emanates an "absolute" or "abstract" intellect, in which thought is not differentiated. Thought becomes differentiated in the second phase, which is an emanation beginning and ending within the soul. Avicenna states clearly that the second phase comes about "through the mediacy of cogitation." From the absolute intellect, which had been emanated in the first phase, the cogitative faculty induces the further emanation of "differentiated forms," it puts those forms into "terms" (*alfāẓ*), and it "arrange[s]" the terms in sequences. Since differentiated knowledge emerges through the mediation of the cogitative faculty, Avicenna terms such knowledge "cogitative," as distinct from the undifferentiated "simple knowledge" of the first of the two phases. Since the soul possesses differentiated knowledge "insofar as it is soul"—whereas it receives the first phase not insofar as it is a soul but by virtue of its intellect—he also calls such knowledge "soul-knowledge" (*nafsānī*).[96]

Avicenna also describes cogitation as "seeking" to establish a "perfect disposition for conjunction with the [active] intellect."[97] The context does not take account of the distinction between two phases of human thought. But if the distinction should nevertheless be applied, the passage would have to be taken as referring to the first phase, since that is where conjunction with the active intellect is established. Avicenna's position would accordingly be that the cogitative faculty plays a role in both phases. In the first phase, it combines and separates images stored within the retentive imagination and presents its handiwork to the human intellect; it thereby

[91]*Shifā': De anima* 45; *Ishārāt* (n. 6 above) 125.

[92]Ibid.

[93]*Ishārāt* 127; *Mubāḥathāt* 239.

[94]*Mubāḥathāt* 232. Avicenna also writes here that when the cogitative faculty serves the intellect, it is related to the "intellect *in habitu*."

[95]*Mubāḥathāt* 231 and passim.

[96]*Shifā': De anima* 241, 243, 247. On p. 241, Avicenna notes that the order in which the terms of a proposition are arranged can be changed without affecting the meaning. "Every man is an animal" seems different to the "retentive imagination" from "*animal* is predicated of every man." Nevertheless, the "pure intelligible thought of both" formulations is "the same."

[97]*Mubāḥathāt* 199; *Shifā': De anima* 247.

prepares the soul for conjoining with the active intellect and receiving the active intellect's emanation. In the second phase, it induces an additional emanation within the soul, an emanation in which thoughts are differentiated, articulated, and arranged sequentially. Avicenna further writes that once the cogitative faculty has enabled the soul to conjoin with the active intellect vis à vis a given thought, the soul can return and "conjoin whenever it wishes."[98] The soul does not have to resort to images and the use of the cogitative faculty in order to reestablish conjunction and rethink the given thought.[99] We can only conjecture whether those statements should apply to both phases of emanation or only the first.

Cogitation helps man progress beyond the stage of material intellect to the subsequent stages. I did not find Avicenna expressly assigning the cogitative faculty a part in forming the stage of potentiality called intellect *in habitu*, but its role is implied, since the cogitative faculty enables man to crystallize thoughts out of the emanation of the active intellect, and intellect *in habitu* is a basic repertoire of human thoughts. The repertoire of thoughts constituting intellect *in habitu* comprises "first intelligibles," that is, propositions embodying the first principles of thought. "Through the cogitative faculty" man thereupon builds on the first intelligibles and "attains the second [intelligibles]," which are derivative scientific propositions; and, we have seen, the cogitative faculty also differentiates concepts out of the emanation of the active intellect. Since the advanced stage of potentiality called "actual intellect" consists in a repertoire of derivative propositions and of concepts, the cogitative faculty hence helps bring man to that stage. When Avicenna wrote that "cogitation seeks" to establish a "perfect disposition for conjunction with the [active] intellect," he could have had in view its role in forming either actual intellect or intellect *in habitu*, each of which is a perfect disposition for a certain corpus of thought. Finally, by helping man receive both propositions and concepts from the active intellect, the cogitative faculty leads man to the condition of "acquired intellect" as well; for acquired intellect consists in the actual thought of propositions and concepts.[100] The cogitative faculty, then, assists man to attain the stage of intellect *in habitu*, the stage of actual intellect, and the condition of acquired intellect.

A composition considered to be an early work of Avicenna's contended that the conclusions of demonstrations are received by the human intellect directly from the active intellect.[101] But Avicenna more frequently credits the cogitative faculty with the formulation of the conclusions of syllogisms, at least in the ordinary course of things. The soul, he writes, arrives at the conclusion of a syllogism when the cogitative faculty differentiates the "middle term" out of the emanation of the active

[98]Ibid.

[99]Answer to a question addressed to Avicenna by Biruni, *Rasā'il Ibn Sīnā* 2, ed. H. Ülken (Istanbul 1953) 3; identical with *Mubāḥathāt* 227–28. Cf. *Shifā': De anima* 223; *Najāt* 183; English translation 56; *Ishārāt* 176.

[100]*Ishārāt* 126–27.

[101]Above, p. 88.

intellect[102] and "combines" the syllogism's components.[103] He apparently means that the human soul starts, for example, with the concepts *man* and *mortal*—or *mortality*; those are concepts that were earlier crystallized out of the emanation of the active intellect through the mediacy of the cogitative faculty. When the soul wants to frame a syllogism, the cogitative faculty presents a new image, thereby preparing the soul to again receive the emanation of the active intellect, although how the cogitative faculty knows which image to present is not clear. The cogitative faculty differentiates the concept *animal*, which can serve as a middle term, out of the active intellect's emanation. And the same faculty formulates the syllogism: all men are animals, and so forth.

Avicenna writes that he was "asked . . . how error can occur" in reasoning if cogitation does nothing more than prepare the soul for conjoining with the active intellect. The foregoing account of the role of the cogitative faculty provides the answer. "Conjunction" with the active intellect is indeed the source of "the terms and concepts," including "the middle [term]." Error therefore does not occur in the concepts. But "combining" the components into a syllogism is the task of the cogitative faculty, which "sometimes does well, sometimes ill."[104] Since the cogitative faculty, a physical faculty of the soul, combines the terms into propositions and the propositions into a syllogism, it and not the active intellect is responsible for the conclusion, and it can make mistakes.[105]

The cogitative faculty, in sum, resides in the brain, and is a physical, not a purely intellectual, faculty. When the soul wants to think a certain thought, the cogitative faculty must present an appropriate image, an image that will prepare the soul for conjunction with the active intellect. The soul is thereby able to receive the active intellect's emanation and think the given thought. Where Avicenna distinguishes two phases of human thought, the cogitative faculty effects the second phase by differentiating concepts out of the first phase and by arranging them in sequences; and his statements about the cogitative faculty's role in establishing conjunction with the active intellect indicate that cogitation is the medium in the first phase too. Among the thoughts the cogitative faculty differentiates out of the active intellect's emanation are the middle terms of syllogisms. After discovering the middle term, the cogitative faculty combines concepts into propositions and propositions into syllogisms. Being a physical faculty, it can err. By assisting man to establish contact with the active intellect, differentiating out concepts, and putting together syllogisms through which further propositions can be inferred, it makes possible the progress from one stage of intellect to the next. But once the human intellect has entered conjunction with the active intellect and learned a thought, the

[102]*Ishārāt* 127; *Mubāḥathāt* 199.

[103]*Mubāḥathāt* 199.

[104]Ibid. The two phases in thought discussed above may be implied here.

[105]Cf. Aristotle, *De anima* 3.6.430b, 26–30.

intellect no longer needs the cogitative faculty to reestablish conjunction with the active intellect in order to rethink the thought.

Notwithstanding its centrality in human thought, cogitation can be partly or wholly dispensed with. The Arabic translation of Aristotle's *Posterior Analytics* 1.34.89b, 10, reads: "Quick-wit [*dhakā'*; ἀγχίνοια] is a certain fineness of insight [*ḥusn ḥads*, εὐστοχία] for seeking out middle [terms] in no time."[106] Avicenna similarly comments that "quick-wit" (*dhakā'*) is "strength of insight [*ḥads*]."[107] Of the two concepts, quick wit and insight, the latter attracted Avicenna's attention, and he depicts it as a natural aptitude which in some men replaces cogitation. Because of Aristotle's definition in the *Posterior Analytics*, Avicenna connects insight particularly with the middle terms of syllogisms, and his statements do not harmonize completely.

Several passages contrast the ability of insight to help man obtain middle terms with the ability of cogitation to do so. The passage making the contrast most fully begins: "Second" intelligible thoughts belonging to the stage of "actual intellect" are inferred from "the first intelligible thoughts" belonging to the stage of "intellect *in habitu*" in one of two ways, either by "cogitation," which is "weaker," or by "insight," which is "stronger." Avicenna elaborates: "Cogitation is a certain movement of the soul among notions [*ma*ᶜ*ānī*]," and especially among those found "within the imaginative faculty [*takhayyul*, which properly means *compositive* imagination]." "It [either the soul or cogitation] seeks" there the "middle term," or "what is analogous to" the middle term. The phrase *what is analogous to* the middle term is surely added by Avicenna because the middle term of a syllogism is, in fact, an abstract concept emanated from the active intellect, rather than an image to be discovered in one of the imaginative faculties. The cogitative faculty therefore does not strictly find the middle term but instead seeks an image that will prepare the soul for the emanation of the middle term from the active intellect. Through the middle term, the passage continues, "knowledge of what is unknown" can be gained. That is to say, once the middle term is differentiated out of the emanation of the active intellect, the soul can frame a syllogism and draw a new scientific conclusion. "Sometimes it"—the soul or cogitation—"succeeds" in its search for the middle term; "sometimes it falls short." "Insight," in contrast to cogitation, is the ability to bring forth both "the middle term" and the conclusion of the syllogism "instantaneously, either through seeking and desire, but without movement," or else "without either desire or movement."[108] The man of insight does not, in other words, need images in order to produce the middle term of a syllogism and the

[106]Medieval Arabic translation of the *Organon*, ed. A. Badawi (Cairo 1948–1952) 2.406. Aristotle's definition is paraphrased in Alfarabi, *Fuṣūl al-Madanī*, ed. D. Dunlop (Cambridge 1961) §46.

[107]*Shifā' : De anima* 249; *Najāt* 167; English translation 36. A similar definition is given in *Najāt* 87.

[108]*Ishārāt* 126–27. A translation of this and other passages on the subject of insight is given by Gutas (n. 1 above) 161–66.

syllogism itself.[109] A person with the highest degree of insight is said to have the "holy faculty [or: holy power]."[110]

In a different work, Avicenna similarly writes that man "learns" "the middle term" of a syllogism in "two ways." One way, that of cogitation, consists in "seeking" and "rummaging" through images; the second, the way of "insight," is "having the middle term occur to mind without seeking" it.[111] Still another passage makes no mention of cogitation, although its role in human thought had been discussed a few pages earlier in the same book. Here Avicenna writes: "The middle term [of a syllogism] arrives in two ways." One way, that of "insight," occurs when the "mind [*dhihn*] extracts the middle term from itself." The second is the conveying of the middle term by a teacher through "instruction." In both instances, Avicenna contends, including the instance where the middle term is transmitted from teacher to student, either the teacher giving instruction or someone standing earlier in the chain of teachers must have discovered the middle term by "insight." Insight is therefore the ultimate source of the middle terms of all syllogisms.[112] In still one more context, where the topic is logical terminology rather than human intellect, Avicenna states: "Insight is a *movement* toward attaining the middle term, when the subject of inquiry has been laid down, or toward attaining the major term [and conclusion of the syllogism], when the middle term has been obtained. In general, it is rapidity in proceeding from something known to something unknown."[113]

In the passages quoted so far, insight enters the scene and makes its contribution after man possesses the first principles of thought constituting intellect *in habitu*: Through insight, man goes beyond the first principles and derives from them a body of syllogistic knowledge. In other passages, Avicenna offers a different characterization of insight, one that recognizes for insight a function in all human intellectual activity, including the soul's initial movement from the stage of material intellect to the stage of intellect *in habitu*.

He portrays insight as an exceptional facility for establishing conjunction with the active intellect and receiving intelligible thought. The human material intellect, as was seen, is an unqualified potentiality and empty disposition for thought, and man progresses beyond the initial empty disposition by establishing conjunction with the active intellect. As man progresses, his ability to reestablish conjunction with the active intellect at will grows, and the subsequent stages of intellect, called

[109]*Rasā'il ibn Sīnā* 2 (n. 99 above) 3.

[110]*Ishārāt* 127.

[111]*Mubāḥathāt* 231.

[112]*Shifā': De anima* 249; *Najāt* 167; English translation 36. In *Najāt* 87, Avicenna defines *dhihn* as "a power [or: faculty] belonging to the soul and disposed for attaining knowledge." See also Goichon (n. 89 above) 132–33. The Arabic translation of *Posterior Analytics* 1.33.89b, 7, uses the term *dhihn* to render διάνοια; see the Arabic translation of the *Organon* (n. 106 above) 2.406.

[113]*Najāt* 87. See also *Mubāḥathāt* 232.

intellect *in habitu* and actual intellect, are therefore "perfect" dispositions for smaller or larger repertoires of thought. Ordinarily, the cogitative faculty must labor to effect the first episode of conjunction vis à vis any given thought, whereupon reestablishing conjunction becomes easy. But insight, Avicenna now writes, is "a powerful disposition" for establishing conjunction with the active intellect without having done so previously. The man of insight, when still at the initial stage of "material intellect," and before ever having established conjunction with the active intellect, already possesses "as it were . . . the second disposition," the perfect disposition or "intellect *in habitu*," which ordinarily only follows conjunction with the active intellect and the creation of a basic repertoire of thought. A high degree of insight is termed "holy intellect."[114] In the same vein, although with less precision, still one more passage describes insight as "a divine emanation and intellectual conjunction," which is reached "without effort [*kasb*]." In this last context Avicenna names a high degree of insight "the power [or: faculty] of [a] holy soul."[115]

If we combine Avicenna's statements on insight—and set aside the passage saying that all middle terms known by man are ultimately traceable to insight as well as the passage that calls insight a "movement"—we find: At the outset, insight permits the soul to establish conjunction with the active intellect without the effort required when conjunction is established through cogitation. Cogitation must labor to effect the first conjunction with the active intellect vis à vis a given thought, and then, after conjunction has been established once, the soul can reestablish conjunction vis à vis the thought without resorting to cogitation again. But the first episode of conjunction with the active intellect, which cogitation has to work for and which gives man the perfect disposition for reestablishing conjunction in the future, is as effortless for the man of insight as reestablishing conjunction is for the man lacking the gift. While still nominally at the stage of material intellect, which is ordinarily an empty potentiality, the man of insight thus already has a perfect disposition for thought equivalent to the standard stage of intellect *in habitu*. Once the man of insight does control the principles of thought belonging to the stage of intellect *in habitu*, his gift enables him to frame syllogisms and infer further propositions without the effort needed when syllogisms are framed through cogitation. The cogitative faculty has to rummage about for an appropriate image, present the image to the intellectual faculty, prepare the soul for conjunction with the active intellect and reception of the active intellect's emanation, and differentiate the middle term of a syllogism out of the emanation. Insight produces the middle terms of syllogisms instantaneously and without recourse to images, probably because of the perfect disposition for conjunction which it brings the soul. Cogitation, moreover, itself draws the conclusion of the syllogism, and being a physical faculty, is subject to error. Insight, by contrast, receives the conclusion

114 *Shifā' : De anima* 248; *Najāt* 166–67; English translation 35–36 (loose).
115 *Mubāḥathāt* 231.

together with the middle term, all—undoubtedly—from the active intellect. Avicenna intimates that insight therefore does not err. Securing not merely the conclusion of a syllogism but the middle term as well is essential, for if insight furnished the conclusion without the rest of the syllogism, it would not provide genuine scientific knowledge.[116] Finally, men vary in their degree of insight, and those who have it to the highest degree are said to possess a "holy faculty" or "holy intellect."

We shall see that insight in the superlative degree is, for Avicenna, the "highest of the powers of prophecy."

Résumé. Cogitation prepares the human intellect for receiving the emanation of the active intellect; it presents an image corresponding to the desired abstract thought, and the human soul or human intellect is thereby readied to conjoin with the active intellect and receive the ever-present emanation. The process parallels the appearance of natural forms in the sublunar world. Just as natural forces prepare a portion of matter to receive a given form from the active intellect, whereupon the form appears automatically, so the cogitative faculty prepares the soul for a given theoretical thought, and the thought is automatically received from the active intellect's emanation.

After man has reached the stage of intellect *in habitu*, the cogitative faculty has the task of preparing the soul for receiving the middle terms of syllogisms from the active intellect's emanation, in order to lead man to the next stage. Avicenna's usual position is that the cogitative faculty itself combines the terms into propositions and the propositions into syllogisms, and it draws the conclusions. That position is at odds with what is assumed to be an early work of Avicenna's, for there the conclusions of all demonstrations are taken to be emanated from the active intellect. Nor does treating certain propositions, including the conclusions of syllogisms, as the handiwork of the cogitative faculty mesh well with Avicenna's insistence that human intelligible thought comes directly from the active intellect. Crediting the cogitative faculty with the conclusions of syllogisms does, however, explain how mistakes can occur. Since the conclusions are formulated by a physical faculty of the soul and do not come from the active intellect, they may go awry.

Cogitation can be replaced by insight, the gift for establishing conjunction with the active intellect effortlessly and instantaneously. When the man of insight is still at the stage of material intellect, he already has "as it were" the intellect *in habitu* of ordinary men. Once insight has supplied the basic principles of thought, it produces both the middle terms of syllogisms and the conclusions, undoubtedly by enabling the soul to conjoin effortlessly with the active intellect. Avicenna intimates that men using insight are exempt from the error affecting cogitative reasoning.

[116]*Shifā': De anima* 250; *Najāt* 167–68; English translation 37.

Conjunction and Immortality

Conjunction. In Alfarabi, acquired intellect was the culminating stage of human intellectual development, and conjunction with the active intellect, the human intellect's crowning condition. In Avicenna, by contrast, conjunction and acquired intellect are quotidian events: The soul is in conjunction with the active intellect and possesses acquired intellect whenever a man thinks an actual thought, regardless of where the man stands on the road to intellectual perfection. The two philosophers differ as well in that, for Alfarabi, the stage of acquired intellect leads to conjunction with the active intellect, whereas Avicenna reverses the sequence. He understands conjunction with the active intellect to be the cause, not the result of attaining acquired intellect: Entering into conjunction with the active intellect and receiving the active intellect's emanation gives man an actual intelligible thought, and actual intelligible thought is acquired intellect. As already seen, Avicenna demonstrates that the quotidian conjunction of the human intellect with the active intellect falls short of true union.[117]

Besides applying the term *acquired intellect* to actual human thought at any level, Avicenna also employs the term in a narrower sense, which approaches Alfarabi's usage. *Actual intellect* was defined by Avicenna as the stage of "complete potentiality" in which the soul has a full repertoire of thoughts, is not actually thinking them, but can do so at will,[118] and acquired intellect, in the narrower acceptation, is actual human thought when man has that complete potentiality. Avicenna undoubtedly had the narrower acceptation in view when he wrote: "At [the level of] acquired intellect, the animal genus and human species are perfected, and the human [intellectual] faculty resembles the first principles of all being [that is, the incorporeal substances]"; acquired intellect is the intellect's "perfection"; "acquired intellect, or rather holy intellect, is the chief [faculty of the soul], which all the other faculties serve, and it is the ultimate end."[119]

In Alfarabi's account, again, the soul at the crowning stage of acquired intellect becomes "free of matter" and can "dispense with matter."[120] Avicenna, as just seen, makes the similar statement that when the soul possesses acquired intellect in the narrower sense, the human intellect resembles the members of the incorporeal realm. In the same vein, he writes that the human soul can and should discard its physical faculties once its intellectual faculty is perfected.

Before attaining control of the entire corpus of possible intelligible thoughts, a man depends on the external and internal senses for refining images and presenting them to his intellect—except of course where a high degree of insight enables him to do without images. Images, presented by the cogitative faculty, prepare the soul

[117]Above, pp. 54, 86.
[118]Above, p. 84.
[119]Above, p. 86.
[120]Above, p. 56.

and the intellectual faculty for conjunction with the active intellect and for receiving the active intellect's emanation. But after a thought has been learned and added to the soul's repertoire, the soul ordinarily requires no additional images to reestablish conjunction with the active intellect and rethink the thought, although Avicenna does append the qualification that a soul sometimes "returns to the imaginative faculties" for help in "strengthening" its hold on a thought. As the human repertoire of thought grows, the soul's dependence on the imaginative faculties, the senses, and the body diminishes. Finally, "when the soul is perfected and powerful, it isolates itself completely in its own activity; and the faculties of sense perception and imagination, as well as the other bodily faculties, [merely] divert it from its [proper] act." The human soul resembles a man of affairs who needs "a mount and gear in order to reach a certain place. Should he be prevented from disposing of them after he arrives, the very means of his arrival will hinder" him from conducting his business. Analogously, once the human soul arrives at its goal and possesses a fully perfected intellect, the physical faculties only distract the soul and intellect from their proper business. They should be discarded.[121]

The human soul possessing acquired intellect in the narrower acceptation thus has established conjunction with the active intellect vis à vis every thought and has no further need of its sense faculties or indeed of the entire human body. Avicenna assumes that the human intellect can ordinarily think no more than one thought at a time.[122] The question arises whether the soul still thinks no more than one thought at a time, when its intellectual development is complete, or whether perhaps it can then receive the entire corpus of possible intelligible thoughts, as a single whole. As far as I could discover, Avicenna does not address the question.

He does speak of a situation in which the human soul "is released from the body," enjoys "permanent conjunction" with the active intellect, becomes "united with" the incorporeal region, "enters into the company" of the incorporeal beings, "becomes of the same substance" as they, and has "the intelligible order of all existence" inscribed in it. The last phrase indicates that the entire corpus of thought available through the active intellect is now present to the soul at once; and the soul, we may suppose, thinks the entire corpus of thought in an undifferentiated mode. This permanent conjunction with the active intellect parallels the conjunction that Alfarabi spoke of. Avicenna clearly understands that permanent conjunction with the active intellect can be achieved after the body dies. He leaves unclear, however, whether permanent conjunction and the ability to think more than a single thought at a time might also be achieved during the life of the body, as Alfarabi held.[123]

[121] *Shifā': De anima* 223; *Najāt* 183 (textually inferior to the *Shifā'*); English translation 56. The image of the rider also appears in *Mubāḥathāt* 232.

[122] *Shifā': De anima* 241, 247.

[123] *Shifā': Ilāhiyyāt* (n. 2 above) 425–26; *Najāt* 293; Landauer, "Die Psychologie des Ibn Sīnā," (n. 30 above) 371; German translation 417.

A further extraordinary intellectual experience awaits the soul. Avicenna writes in one passage that man can have "incorporeal beings" as an object of thought, and in another passage, which may simply be a more precise formulation of the first, that man can have "the active intellect" as an object of thought. In the two instances, if they are two, what enters "in" the human soul is not the incorporeal being or the active intellect itself, that is to say, not the "individual . . . essence [*ḥaqīqa*]" of the active intellect or of another incorporeal being but its "specific . . . essence" and "nature."[124] If the human intellect had the active intellect in its full individuality as an object of thought, the human intellect would become completely identical with the active intellect, intellect being identical with whatever thought it thinks; and that is an outcome unacceptable to Avicenna. What the human intellect has as object of its thought is a simulacrum, the specific essence, of the active intellect. Just how the specific essence of an incorporeal being can be split off from its individual essence is not, however, explained.

Avicenna says nothing to suggest that having the active intellect and other incorporeal beings as a direct object of thought is restricted to the afterlife, yet he also does not explain how the active intellect or other incorporeal beings might become an object of human thought in the present life. They could hardly be accessible to human thought through the process whereby the soul receives the emanation of the active intellect with the assistance of the cogitative faculty. For certainly no sense image presented by the cogitative faculty could prepare the human intellect for differentiating the essence of the active intellect, or the essence of another incorporeal being, out of the active intellect's emanation. We can only conjecture how and when they do become direct objects of human thought, whether perhaps through insight alone and whether only in the afterlife.

In treating quotidian conjunction with the active intellect, permanent conjunction with the active intellect, and thought having the active intellect itself or other incorporeal beings as an object, Avicenna—like Alfarabi in his account of conjunction—envisages no genuinely mystical or ecstatic experience.[125]

[124]*Mubāḥathāt* 134, 135. In an embodied being, the specific essence is the form, and form together with matter constitute the individual. But Avicenna does not explain how the specific essence can differ from the individual essence of an incorporeal being.

[125]*Ishārāt* (n. 6 above) 198–207, is a high-flown description of the man who is an *ᶜārif*. Goichon (n. 6 above) 485–86, translates the term *ᶜārif* as "celui qui connaît l'extase," and on pp. 485 and 497, she translates *ᶜirfān*, an abstract noun from the same root, as "la science secrète" and "la science mystique." L. Gardet, *La pensée religieuse d'Avicenne* (Paris 1951) 147, translates *ᶜārif* as "l'initié ou gnostique." H. Corbin, *Avicenna and the Visionary Recital* (New York 1960) (translation of *Avicenne et le récit visionnaire*) 205, likewise renders the term as *initiate* and *gnostic*. All three discover a full mystical doctrine in the chapter of the *Ishārāt*.

In fact, although the term *ᶜārif* may carry distinctive overtones in Ṣūfī contexts, it simply means *knower*, *man of knowledge*, and the cognate abstract noun simply means *knowledge*. The *Ishārāt* represents the man of knowledge as undergoing a course of "training," as devoting himself completely to "the first truth" and turning away from the "world of falsehood," as having ever more frequent "moments" of "intense experience" in which the "light of the truth" shines on him,

Immortality. As a rule, philosophers in the Aristotelian tradition limited human immortality to one or another aspect of the human intellect. Alfarabi's *al-Madīna al-Fāḍila* did ostensibly affirm the immortality of the entire human soul whose intellect is perfected, but there too the tenor of the reasoning is consistent with the immortality of an aspect of intellect and nothing more. Alfarabi was thus probably dissimulating in *al-Madīna al-Fāḍila* and, in accord with the Aristotelian consensus, recognized the immortality of only an aspect of human intellect, the aspect he called acquired intellect.[126] Avicenna takes another tack. He repeatedly and consistently maintains that the human soul is an incorporeal substance, that the entity receiving thought from the active intellect is the soul as a whole, and that each individual human soul is immortal by its very nature.

Avicenna formulates his arguments for immortality differently in different works. His most comprehensive formulation builds on the proposition that the human soul is an incorporeal substance. With that proposition as the key premise, he undertakes to establish, first, the specific thesis that the destruction of the human body does not entail the destruction of the human soul, and, secondly, the general thesis that the human soul does not contain "the potentiality of being destroyed" and therefore is intrinsically immortal.

Avicenna's proof of the key premise in the argument turned on the prior presupposition that intellectual thoughts, by which he must have meant concepts, are indivisible. His reasoning was that since intellectual thoughts are indivisible, they can be present only in an indivisible, and hence incorporeal, subject; and since intellectual thoughts make themselves present in the human soul, the soul must be an incorporeal substance.[127]

To establish the first thesis of the argument proper, the thesis that the destruction of the body does not entail the destruction of the soul, he distinguishes the three

---

as finally achieving "arrival" (*wuṣūl*, from the same root as *ittiṣāl*, the term for *conjunction*). Other parts of the *Ishārāt*, including the discussion of prophecy, which is offered side by side with the discussion of the *ᶜārif*, restate the positions of Avicenna's technical philosophic works in allusive language, without in any way altering the substance. There is accordingly no reason to read the chapter on the "man of knowledge," despite its high-flown and mystifying diction, as anything other than a description of the philosopher who develops his intellect, dispenses with his sense faculties, and labors toward complete conjunction with the active intellect.

Avicenna may even have been indulging in some playfulness. In *Ishārāt* 199, immediately before the discussion of the man of knowledge, he mentions an allegorical tale "about Salāmān and Absāl"—regarding which, see Corbin, *Avicenna and the Visionary Recital* 204–5—and he remarks that the figure of Salāmān represents "yourself," while the figure of Absāl represents "your degree in knowledge. . . . Then, solve the allegory if you can." Whereupon Avicenna launches into his account of the man of knowledge. He can be read plausibly as inviting perspicacious readers to "solve" not only the allegory of Salāmān and Absāl, but also his own allusive account of the man of knowledge, which follows.

[126]Above, p. 57.

[127]*Shifā': De anima* 209–16.; *Najāt* 174–78; English translation (n. 26 above) 46–50; *Ishārāt* 176ff.; Landauer "Die Psychologie des Ibn Sīnā" (n. 30 above) chap. 9.

conceivable ways in which the relation of the human soul to its body might render the soul dependent on the body in respect to "existence," and he shows that the soul is not related to the body in any of the three ways.

(1) Soul and body are not related in such a manner that the body is the "cause" of the soul's existence. To be more precise, the human body is the cause of the existence of the soul in none of the four Aristotelian senses of cause. The human body is not (1-a) "the efficient cause" bringing the human soul into existence. For a "body effects nothing insofar as it is a body" without qualification but acts solely through "accidents and material forms" inhering in it. Accidents and material forms are, however, incapable of bringing about the existence of a "self-subsistent substance." Inasmuch as the human soul is an incorporeal, and hence self-subsistent, substance, accidents or material forms in a body cannot bring it into existence. The body also is not (1-b) a "receptive," or material, cause of the soul; for, as Avicenna reminds us, he had earlier "demonstrated" that the soul is not "imprinted" in the body.[128] To suppose that something corporeal, the human body, is (1-c) the "formal cause," or (1-d) the "final" cause of the incorporeal soul would be preposterous. The body thus is not the cause of the existence of the soul in any of the four senses of the term. (2) Soul and body are, moreover, not "essentially . . . interdependent for their existence." If they were mutually interdependent, "neither the body nor the soul would [in itself] be a substance." "Yet they are substances." Hence they are not interdependent. (3) Finally, soul and body are not so related that the existence of the soul is logically, as distinct from causally, dependent on the body. The relationship is not, in other words, one in which the soul is the cause of the existence of the body, with the further qualification that whenever the soul exists, the body perforce exists, neither soul nor body existing without the existence of its counterpart. Were soul and body related in that fashion, the existence of the soul would logically—by the rule of *modus tollens*[129]— be dependent on the existence of the body, since whenever the body ceases to exist, the soul would also perforce cease to exist. That body and soul are not related in such a fashion may be seen from the fact that the body deteriorates and dies through a "change" in its own "composition" and not as a result of anything occurring in the soul. The existence of the human soul is, in fine, not (1) causally dependent on the human body, (2) interdependent with the existence of the body, or (3) logically dependent on the existence of the body. Since the soul is in no way "essentially" dependent on the body, it "does not die by [reason of] the death of the body."

The human body does, of course, play a role in the emergence of a human soul, but its role lies in determining the "time" when a soul is crystallized out of the emanation of the active intellect. The "blend" (*mizāj*) of the matter constituting the human body is accordingly an "accidental cause of the soul"; and when an

[128]Cf. above, p. 83.

[129]If A, then B; not B; therefore not A.

accidental cause ceases to exist, what has been produced with its help does not necessarily cease to exist. The circumstance that "one thing has to come into existence together with another thing's coming into existence does not entail that the former cease to exist together with the latter's ceasing to exist."[130]

That is Avicenna's argument for his first thesis, the thesis that the death of the body does not entail the death of the soul. His second and conclusive thesis is "that no other cause whatsoever can bring about the nonexistence of the soul." Stated briefly, Avicenna's contention here is that an object now existent which is subject to destruction in the future, must "contain" two characteristics, the "actuality of continued existence" and "the possibility of being destroyed." The two characteristics are mutually "opposed," and "two distinct factors" in the object must be responsible for them. Objects that exist, and yet are subject to destruction, are therefore composite. Conversely, "simple, incorporeal beings," which are not composite, will be immune to destruction. Since the human soul has been shown to be a simple, incorporeal substance, it is therefore "not subject to destruction."[131]

Avicenna goes on: The Aristotelian "demonstration" of the rule that "whatever is generated will undergo destruction"[132] has no bearing on the conclusion just reached. Aristotle derived the rule from the consideration that generated objects have a "finiteness of potentiality for continued existence." But only objects "generated out of matter and form" have the finite potentiality, and consequently only they are demonstrably subject to destruction. The Aristotelian rule cannot apply to the human soul, since the soul, although generated, is not a compound of matter and form.[133]

Avicenna refuses even to concede that his conclusion runs counter to Aristotle's statements about human immortality in the *De anima.*

In *De anima* 2.1, Aristotle had written that "any part" of the soul whose "actuality" (or: entelechy [ἐντελέχεια])" is also the actuality of a part of the body will "plainly . . . be inseparable from the body"; but "nothing will prevent" a part of the soul whose "actuality" is not the actuality of a part of the body from separating from the body and surviving its death.[134] Although the passage certainly appears to exclude the immortality of the soul taken as a whole, Avicenna reads it as, in fact, endorsing the soul's immortality. He reasons as follows: When Aristotle spoke of a part of the soul that can survive because its actuality is not the actuality of the body, he could not have been referring to the active intellect. The active intellect is an eternal incorporeal being and can hardly be described as "part"

[130]*Shifā' : De anima* 227–31; *Najāt* 185–87; English translation 58–61.

[131]*Shifā' : De anima* 231; *Najāt* 187; English translation 61. Avicenna continues with a very problematic argument, the gist of which is that even if the human soul were assumed to be compound, an underlying substratum of the soul could be isolated which is simple and hence indestructible. See *Shifā' : De anima* 231–32; *Najāt* 187–88; English translation 61–63.

[132]See Aristotle, *De caelo* 1.12.

[133]*Shifā' : De anima* 233; *Najāt* 188–89; English translation 63.

[134]*De anima* 2.1.413a, 4–7. See above, pp. 34–35.

of the soul. Nor could Aristotle have been referring to the human intellectual faculty after it is actualized. For whatever is not "self-subsistent" from the start will never become so by the addition of an attribute; and if the soul and its intellectual faculty were dependent on the body for their existence before they possess actual thought, they would not be "transformed into another substance" and rendered capable of existing independently of the body by virtue of acquiring actual thought. "The man's [Aristotle's] position" must therefore be that the human "soul" itself, the "principle" underlying "all the other faculties of the soul, is what survives and separates [from the body]." The parts of the soul characterized by Aristotle as inseparable from the body would, accordingly, not strictly be parts, Aristotle himself having "viewed the soul as one" and free of parts, but rather faculties that become inoperative when their physical organs disappear.[135]

Human souls are, then, immortal. Avicenna further maintains that souls retain their individuality in the state of immortality, and he refutes the doctrine of transmigration. He contends that souls are differentiated from one another because an individual body must always exist as the occasion for the emanation of a soul from the active intellect; and the original differentiation will carry over into the state of immortality.[136] A similar proposition was put forward in Alfarabi's *al-Madīna al-Fāḍila* but lost its force inasmuch as other theses endorsed in *al-Madīna al-Fāḍila* can accommodate immortality solely of the human intellect, not, however, the immortality of the soul as a whole, let alone the immortality of individual souls.[137] Avicenna disproves transmigration by reasoning: Transmigrating souls would have to attach themselves to bodies disposed to receive them. Yet whenever a portion of matter is capable of receiving a soul, it receives one spontaneously and necessarily from the active intellect's emanation. The doctrine of transmigration thus carries the absurd implication that a single body would have two—or more—souls, the soul emanated by the active intellect and the transmigrating soul or souls.[138]

Whereas Alfarabi saw immortality as a concomitant of the stage of acquired intellect, Avicenna has maintained that the human soul is immortal by its very nature, apart from a man's intellectual development. Nevertheless, although intellectual development does not lead to immortality, it plays a decisive role in immortality for Avicenna as well. It determines which of several grades of immortality each soul attains.

The soul enjoying supreme eudaemonia (*sa^c^āda*) is the one that achieves a perfect disposition for intellectual thought in the present life. A soul of that rank, as

[135]Glosses on Aristotle's *De anima*, in *Arisṭū ^c^inda al-^c^Arab* (n. 32 above) 93–94. See also *Mubāḥathāt* (n. 32 above) 120.

[136]*Shifā': De anima* 225; *Najāt* 184; English translation 58; cf. *Mubāḥathāt* 223.

[137]Cf. above, pp. 56-57.

[138]*Shifā': De anima* 233–34; *Najāt* 189; English translation 64; *Ishārāt* 196–197; *al-Risāla al-Aḍḥawiyya*, ed. and Italian trans. F. Lucchetta as *Epistola sulla vita futura* (Padua 1969) 132–33.

already seen, can dispense with the sense faculties while its body is still alive, and it retains its disposition for intellectual thought when the body dies and the sense faculties cease to operate.[139] "When it [the soul] is released from the body and the body's accidents, it can conjoin with the active intellect in a perfect conjunction. It then experiences intellectual splendor and eternal pleasure."[140] It is "united with" the incorporeal region, "enters into the company" of the incorporeal beings, "becomes of the same substance" as they, and has "the intelligible order of all existence" inscribed in it.[141]

A smaller measure of eudaemonia awaits the soul that attains a degree of intellectual development in the present life but falls short of a perfect disposition for conjunction vis à vis all possible thoughts. Avicenna ventures "merely to state with approximation" what amount of knowledge ensures eudaemonia in the next life; and the amount he proposes turns out to be a considerable segment of physical and metaphysical science. He "thinks" that a "human soul" will enjoy eudaemonia after the death of the body only if it accomplishes the following during its bodily sojourn: It must "have a true conception of the incorporeal principles [of existence]"; be convinced "through demonstration" of the "existence" of the incorporeal beings; know "the final causes of those things [that is, of the celestial spheres] which undergo universal motions"; understand "the makeup of the universe, the relationships of the parts of the universe to one another, and the order that begins with the first principle [of existence and extends] to the last existent being"; comprehend "[natural] providence and the mode" of its operation; be certain of the "existence and unity peculiar to" the First Cause; and grasp the character of the First Cause's "knowledge," which embraces the entire universe without entailing any "plurality and change whatsoever" in the First Cause. That is the minimum. "Then, the more a man grows in perspicacity, the more he will grow in his disposition for eudaemonia."[142]

Souls that remain below the minimum degree of knowledge needed for minimal eudaemonia in the life to come but that have arrived at an appreciation of intellectual activity suffer excruciating "misery" and "pain" after the death of their bodies. These souls have, while associated "with the body," learned through "demonstration" that they are capable of "knowing the essential nature of all [existence]." They have "become aware of the perfection that is the soul's [natural] object of desire" and toward which the soul is "naturally drawn." That is, they are, at a subliminal level, aware of the soul's natural desire for intellectual perfection. As long as they busy themselves with bodily affairs, "their occupation with the body . . . causes them to forget their own essence and their [natural] object of desire." On the death of the body they become conscious of both, and, unhappily,

[139] *Mubāḥathāt* 231.
[140] *Shifā' : De anima* 248.
[141] Above, p. 104.
[142] *Shifā' : Ilāhiyyāt* 429; *Najāt* 296.

the principles of science are now out of reach. The principles of science "are acquired solely by means of the body," that is, with the aid of sense perception and cogitation; and the body "has perished." Souls torn by a desire for intellectual fulfillment which can no longer be realized are racked with pain. Indeed, the "pain" they experience "is as intense as the pleasure" experienced by the fortunate soul that enjoys eternal conjunction with the active intellect.[143] Avicenna does not say whether a soul suffering the pain of frustrated intellectual desire in the next life has its pain tempered by whatever disposition for conjunction with the active intellect it may have equipped itself with in this life.

Finally, there are "simple" souls that have no notion of genuine, intellectual pleasure. On the one hand, they lack the attainments that would permit conjunction with the active intellect in the hereafter and they therefore forfeit intellectual eudaemonia. On the other hand, having no inkling of what intellectual desire is, they are immune to the pain that unfulfilled intellectual desire occasions. Theirs is an afterlife void of both intellectual pleasure and the pain of realizing that intellectual pleasure is beyond them. They resemble a formless "material substratum" and reside in "a kind of peace" for all eternity.[144]

Thus far, we have seen the intellectual factors determining the soul's fate after the death of the body. Avicenna also recognizes ethical factors that bear on the fate of the soul, and in expounding the ethical factors, he offers an allegorization of hellfire not dissimilar to Alfarabi's.[145] He writes: Some souls fail to exercise "sovereignty" over their bodies and instead allow their bodies to rule them—these being precisely the souls that fail to cultivate the intermediate psychological characteristics constituting Aristotelian ethical virtue.[146] When they "separate" from the body at death, such souls are "screened off" by their attraction to the body "from pure conjunction with the locus of eudaemonia," that is, from conjunction with the active intellect. They now become "aware" of "the enormous opposition" between their own "substance," which can only find satisfaction in intellectual activity, and the "bodily characteristic[s]" that they allowed to be ingrained in them and that prevent them from conjoining with the active intellect. The soul's own nature, of which it becomes fully conscious at death, pulls it away from the body, while its immoderate acquired characteristics have enslaved it to the deceased body and the body's concerns. The soul is dragged in two directions and undergoes "confused motions," which "cause it great pain."

Souls of a previously mentioned category, those that recognized the delight of intellectual perfection but had insufficient intellectual accomplishments to satisfy their desire when the body dies, were also found to suffer pain when left without a

[143]*Shifā': Ilāhiyyāt* 427–29; *Najāt* 294–95. Cf. *Ishārāt* 195.

[144]*Shifā': Ilāhiyyāt* 428, 431; *Najāt* 295, 297.

[145]Above, pp. 56–57.

[146]Cf. Aristotle, *Nicomachean Ethics* 2.6; Alfarabi, *Fuṣūl al-Madanī* (n. 106 above) §16. Avicenna is weaving together motifs from both Aristotelian and Neoplatonic ethics.

body. Avicenna assures his readers—and, very likely, himself as well, since he lived a dissolute life and in the end died of dissipation[147]—that the two kinds of pain differ. The pain of unfulfilled intellectual desire endures forever, whereas the pain experienced by a soul subservient to the body and the body's concerns gradually subsides.

He explains: The pain of unfulfilled intellectual desire never ceases, because intellectual desire pertains to the essence of the human rational soul and therefore continues as long as the soul exists. And as long as the desire continues, the pain of being unable to fulfill it also does. By contrast, the pain occasioned by acquired characteristics that enslave a rational soul to its body is due not "to anything necessary, but to something incidental and foreign" to the soul. Psychological characteristics are fixed in the soul by the "repetition" of "physical acts," and acts corresponding to a given psychological characteristic must be repeated constantly if the characteristic is to be preserved. With the death of the body and the "cessation of the [pertinent] acts," the noxious psychological characteristics begin to fade; and the "punishment" consisting in the soul's being drawn to the service of a now deceased body likewise "ceases and fades, little by little." Eventually, "the soul will be cleansed," and it will thereupon gain "the eudaemonia appropriate to it."[148] The last statement, we may understand, means that once a soul is cleansed, it enters upon the fate warranted by its intellectual status. That is to say, souls cleansed of their attraction to the body which possess sufficient intellectual attainments for entering permanent conjunction with the active intellect will thenceforth enjoy eudaemonia. Souls cleansed of their attraction to the body which are conscious of intellectual desire yet are unequipped to satisfy it will, in the afterlife, be liberated from the temporary pain of attraction to their no longer existent body, but they will suffer the unending pain of unfulfilled intellectual desire. Souls cleansed of their attraction to the body which had no inkling of intellectual desire will subsist in an eternal state of rest, void of intellectual content.[149]

Avicenna, finally, records a rationalization of popular religious beliefs regarding the afterlife. He cites the rationalization in the name of "some scholars [*ᶜulamā'*]" and comments that the theory "seems to be . . . true." The theory goes: "Simpleminded souls," as already seen, have no notion of what is "higher." They have no consciousness of the intellectual "perfection" bringing "eudaemonia" to certain men, and hence are immune as well to the frustrated "desire for perfection" bringing "misery" to others. "All their psychological characteristics are directed

[147]Gohlman (n. 1 above) 80–89.

[148]*Shifā' : Ilāhiyyāt* 430–31; *Najāt* 296–97. Cf. *Risāla Aḍhawiyya* (n. 138 above) 208–9.

[149]When describing the pain of sensual simple souls, in *Shifā' : Ilāhiyyāt* 431 and *Najāt* 297, Avicenna does not expressly write that it will come to an end, but that seems to be implied. The pain of a sensual simple soul should also be less than that of a partly enlightened soul. For although the simple sensual soul suffers by reason of the frustration of its physical desires, such a soul, knowing nothing of intellectual desire, will not be dragged in two directions as partly enlightened souls are.

downward and drawn to the body."[150] When simpleminded souls have been indoctrinated in a "belief regarding the hereafter" of the sort "in which the common folk are instructed," they carry the belief with them into the afterlife. There—so the scholars advancing the theory "state"—they experience in their "compositive imaginative" faculty whatever they expect to occur in the life to come. In their disembodied state, "they imagine everything they have come to believe about the conditions in the next world." Although the body has died and the soul's ties to the body have been severed, the soul undergoes experiences through its compositive imaginative faculty which appear exactly like experiences rooted in sense faculties and caused by events in the real world. The circumstance that all is internal to the imaginative faculty and corresponds to nothing in the real world outside does not diminish the effect. Indeed, experiences generated by the imaginative faculty can be "of greater potency and distinctness" than those tied to sense perception, just as "what is dreamed is more vivid . . . than what is sensed."

An obvious objection to the supposition that a disembodied soul undergoes quasi-bodily experiences through its compositive imagination would be that the compositive imagination operates through a physical organ, a ventricle of the brain, and the brain is now dead.[151] But the theory includes an answer to the objection. The disembodied soul is assumed to attach itself to one of the celestial spheres, and "something in the celestial spheres . . . is the organ through which" the soul exercises its compositive imaginative function. A celestial sphere or an aspect of one of the spheres serves as a surrogate brain for the disembodied compositive imagination.[152]

The simpleminded soul experiencing the promises of popular religion through its imaginative faculty will "at the moment of death, experience death." "After death, it imagines itself as the man who just died," as if in a "dream." "It imagines itself buried." It experiences "the resurrection." If it was a "pure," "fortunate" soul, it will experience the "delights of the hereafter," "the garden and the dark-eyed maidens,"[153] and anything else it believes to be its due in the life to come. If it was a "wicked" soul, it will suffer "the punishments" and "pain" that it believes to be its just deserts.[154]

[150]Avicenna presumably understands that although the characteristics of simple souls are directed downward to the body, the pure simple soul, as distinct from the sensual simple soul, does not allow itself to be enslaved by the body.

[151]See above, p. 96.

[152]*Shifā': Ilāhiyyāt* 431–32; *Najāt* 297–98. Cf. *Ishārāt* 196.

[153]See Koran 56:12–22.

[154]*Risāla Aḍḥawiyya* 222–25; *Shifā': Ilāhiyyāt* 431–32; *Najāt* 297–98. *Risāla Aḍḥawiyya* names the faculty through which the soul "imagines" events in the hereafter as "the estimative faculty." Wolfson (n. 66 above) 280, observes that Avicenna's Canon of Medicine treats the compositive imaginative faculty and estimative faculty as one.

The rationalization Avicenna has set forth does not account for the wicked man who has convinced himself that he is good or the righteous man who judges himself to be evil. Would the

Avicenna does not expressly accept or reject the foregoing rationalization of popular religious promises regarding the hereafter. He cites the rationalization once with the remark that he can neither "affirm nor reject" it.[155] Several times he cites it in the name of unnamed "scholars,"[156] and since he deemed himself an independent philosophic authority and did not ordinarily cite in the name of others positions that he espoused himself, his attribution of a theory to others suggests nonacceptance.[157] On the opposite side stands his comment that the rationalization of promises regarding the hereafter "seems to be . . . true," as well as two or three instances where he refers to it without attributing it to anyone else.[158]

The rationalization assumes that after the death of the body, souls can attach themselves to a celestial sphere and employ an aspect of the sphere, never identified more precisely, as a surrogate brain. But when Avicenna refuted the doctrine of transmigration, he contended that a human soul can be linked only to a portion of sublunar matter the composition of which disposes it to receive the given soul; and he further dismissed the possibility of two souls' attaching themselves to a single portion of matter as outlandish.[159] The composition of matter in a celestial sphere plainly is not, in Avicenna's view, such as to dispose the sphere for receiving a human soul, and, moreover, every celestial sphere in his cosmic scheme already has its own soul and would hardly be able to receive additional souls. Since the compositive imaginative faculty could not operate without a brain, and since Avicenna's earlier reasoning would exclude the celestial spheres' serving as a surrogate brain, disembodied human souls should not, in his system, be able to experience the hereafter through their imaginative faculties.[160] Avicenna may have

---

former experience the pleasure that he, in his self-delusion, believed to be his due, and the latter suffer the pain that he, in his humility, believed to be his?

[155]*Mubāḥathāt* 198 (top).

[156]*Shifā': Ilāhiyyāt* 431; *Najāt* 297; *Risāla Aḍḥawiyya* 222–23; an unpublished text translated by J. Michot (n. 1 above) 18, n. 70. Michot's book is an exploration of what he takes to be all the implications of a disembodied soul's having experiences through its imaginative faculty.

[157]Michot 19, n. 70, records two additional instances where Avicenna cites the theories of "scholars" on questions regarding the soul. In both instances, Avicenna plainly does not accept the theories.

[158]Michot 26–27, cites three such instances. In one of the three, *Ishārāt* 196, Avicenna in fact writes only that after death, souls "perhaps" (*la^c^alla*) have the help of a celestial body in imagining the experiences they have been led to expect in the hereafter. Michot, strangely, renders the term meaning "perhaps" as "sans doute." The strongest evidence I found to support a reading of Avicenna as having believed that celestial bodies do serve as surrogate organs for human souls is his Commentary on the *Theology of Aristotle* (n. 68 above) 72; French translation (n. 68 above) 404.

[159]Above, p. 109.

[160]The notion that the soul enjoys physical pleasure in the afterlife through its imagination also conflicts with what Avicenna has said about the pain that results from carrying physical desires into the next world.

recorded the rationalization of promised physical pleasures in the hereafter in order to protect himself against any charge that he was wholly rejecting Islamic accounts of the life to come.

A last remark of Avicenna's deserves attention. At one point, he writes unexpectedly that "a certain sort of ignorance destroys" some souls "forever."[161] He does not explain how the remark might be harmonized with his proofs of the intrinsic immortality of the human soul, nor does he identify the souls subject to destruction. The souls referred to would most plausibly be those lacking all intellectual accomplishments. If they are in fact the souls that perish, then the "kind of peace" enjoyed by simpleminded souls after their bodies die[162] would turn out to be nothing but a euphemism for nonexistence. However it be taken, the statement that ignorance destroys souls runs counter to Avicenna's painstaking philosophic proofs of immortality. If the statement does truly represent his considered position, his position begins to approach Alfarabi's.[163]

Résumé. Conjunction with the active intellect and the resultant state of acquired intellect are integral to all actual human thought. But acquired intellect, besides designating actual human thought at any level of intellectual development, is also the term for human thought at the stage where the soul has a full repertoire of thoughts and can dispense with its body. After the death of the body, a soul possessing acquired intellect in the narrower sense enters permanent conjunction with the active intellect and has "the intelligible order of all existence" inscribed in it, presumably in the undifferentiated mode. Whether the soul with a fully perfected intellect can enter into permanent conjunction with the active intellect during the life of the body or only after the body's demise is not stated by Avicenna.

The immortality of the human soul follows, for Avicenna, from its being an incorporeal substance emanated by the active intellect. Given the intrinsic immortality of the soul, each soul's fate in the world to come is determined by its intellectual attainments in the present life. (1) A soul that in this life gains a perfect disposition for conjunction with the active intellect vis à vis all possible thoughts will enjoy supreme eudaemonia in the next life. (2) A soul that in this life gains a lesser disposition for conjunction yet masters a considerable segment of physical and metaphysical science will also enjoy a degree of eudaemonia. (3) A soul falling below the minimum amount of knowledge needed for conjunction with the active intellect in the next life but aware of the delights of intellectual activity will suffer the eternal pain of unfulfilled intellectual desire. (4) The simpleminded soul, which

---

As will appear presently, Avicenna, in his discussion of prophecy, recognizes the possibility that the souls of the spheres might communicate with the human imaginative faculty, much as the active intellect communicates with the human intellectual faculty. But there he does not contemplate the celestial spheres' serving as surrogate brains.

[161]*Ishārāt* 188.

[162]Above, p. 111.

[163]Above, p. 57.

both lacks intellectual accomplishments and is unaware of the pleasure they bring, will subsist in an eternal state of rest, void of all intellectual content. One comment of Avicenna's suggests that the eternal state of rest, void of intellectual content, may amount to nonexistence.

Souls in each of the categories may, during their stay in the temporal world, have committed the ethical mistake of allowing themselves to become enslaved to the concerns of the body. If they did, they will in the next life suffer the pain of being drawn in one direction by their own nature and in another by the concerns of a body that no longer exists. The pain will pass, however, as the psychological characteristics responsible for the pain gradually fade. Each soul will then enter upon the eternal fate awaiting souls in the category to which its intellectual attainments assign it.

Avicenna further records a rationalization of religious beliefs regarding the hereafter, according to which the postmortal events promised by religion are experienced in the soul's compositive imaginative faculty. I have indicated why he could not, with consistency, have himself accepted that rationalization.

Prophecy

Alfarabi, it will be recalled, found a place for prophetic phenomena in his scheme of intellect: They are the natural effect that the lightlike emanation of the active intellect has on the receptive imaginative faculty of two types of men. In prophecy at the lower level, the active intellect's emanation passes through the rational faculty, and enters the imaginative faculty, of a man who has not fully developed his intellect. It can there produce knowledge of individual events lying beyond the range of the senses, whether present events occurring at a distance or future events, and can also furnish a figurative depiction of theoretical truth. In prophecy at the higher level, which Alfarabi specifically named "revelation," the emanation from the active intellect passes through a human intellect that is fully developed and as a consequence has conjoined with the active intellect. The emanation enters the man's imaginative faculty, and the man again receives knowledge of distant present events or future events; whether he also receives a figurative depiction of theoretical truths is not made clear. Although in both instances, the emanation from the active intellect passes through the intellectual faculty on its way to the imaginative faculty, the human intellect does not at either level participate in the prophetic experience. Prophecy therefore cannot at either level produce genuine theoretical knowledge.[164]

Avicenna likewise recognizes, and attaches the name prophecy to, knowledge that results when the emanation from the active intellect—or another supernal being—acts on the human imaginative faculty. But as an extension of his view that man receives intelligible thought directly from an emanation of the active intellect,

[164] Above, pp. 58–62.

he, unlike Alfarabi, recognizes, and names as prophecy, genuine theoretical knowledge imparted by the active intellect to the human intellect without the human intellect's having to employ standard scientific procedures. That prophets receive theoretical knowledge effortlessly is hardly an original notion[165]; Avicenna's innovation is his explanation of the process. It should go without saying that both intellectual prophecy and imaginative prophecy are, for Avicenna, natural in the sense that any properly prepared human soul attains them.

Intellectual prophecy is due to *insight*. The cogitative faculty, Avicenna wrote, has the function of presenting images to the human intellect and thereby preparing the soul and intellect for conjunction with the active intellect. When conjunction with the active intellect is established, an emanation enters the human intellect, whereupon the cogitative faculty steps in again and differentiates actual intelligible thought out of the emanation. Some men, however, possess *insight*, which is not a faculty of the soul but an aptitude for establishing conjunction with the active intellect and for differentiating out thoughts, effortlessly and without recourse to cogitation.[166] Insight, Avicenna now explains, varies in "quantity," that is to say, in the numbers of "middle terms" of syllogisms which different men of insight can discover without using their cogitative faculty, and in "quality," that is to say, in the "speed" with which different men exercise their gift. From the circumstance that the "variation[s]" are "infinite" and that individuals at the lower "end" of the spectrum "have no insight at all," Avicenna extrapolates and infers that men "must" be found at the upper "end" who possess the gift to a superlative degree, that is, men who "possess insight in regard to all subjects of inquiry, or most," and who can exercise their gift in the "briefest time."

Avicenna further characterizes the man at the top of the spectrum as "burning with insight, that is, with the reception of inspiration from the active intellect." "Forms in the active intellect . . . regarding every subject . . . are imprinted in the man instantaneously or almost so." If the gift of insight furnished the conclusion of a syllogism without the syllogism itself, the recipient would obtain only a "report" of the truth and not "certain, intellectual" knowledge.[167] Avicenna submits that the contrary occurs, that insight enables man to receive, from the active intellect, the "middle terms" and indeed a complete "ordered" syllogism. The man entering conjunction with the active intellect through insight thus gains instantaneous demonstrated scientific knowledge, without having to expend any effort in learning the demonstration. Avicenna was already seen to infuse a religious tone into the discussion by calling insight in a superlative degree: "holy intellect" or "holy power."[168] He further writes that the reception of broad

[165]See Kindi, *Rasā'il al-Kindī*, ed. M. Abu Rida (Cairo 1950) 1. 372–73; trans. R. Walzer in "New Studies on Al-Kindi," reprinted in his *Greek into Arabic* (Oxford 1963) 177–78.

[166]Cf. above, p. 101.

[167]Cf. Zeller (n. 10 above) 232.

[168]Above, pp. 100–102.

instantaneous knowledge from the active intellect through a superlative degree of insight is the "highest of the powers of prophecy," and "the highest level of the human faculties [or: human powers]."[169]

A lesser category of "prophecy" has its focus in the human imagination. The functions of Alfarabi's single imaginative faculty (*mutakhayyila*)[170] were distributed by Avicenna between a retentive imaginative faculty and a compositive imaginative faculty (*mutakhayyila*), the latter of which is, in the case of man, the same as the cogitative faculty. The retentive imagination, in Avicenna's scheme, preserves sense perceptions after they are processed and reported by the sensus communis; and the compositive imagination disassembles and combines images in the retentive imagination to fashion new configurations.[171] The presentation of images by the compositive imagination, or cogitative faculty, plays a clearly delineated role in the overall enterprise of acquiring knowledge, and the compositive imagination is usually kept busy with the tasks assigned it. Under certain circumstances, however, as when the body is asleep, ill, affected by an imbalance of bile, or fearful, the compositive imagination ceases to be occupied in its ordinary tasks. It may also slip free of internal intellectual "discrimination." It then has free rein and can fashion images at random, unchecked. And it can project its images into the retentive imagination and from there into the sensus communis, although I did not find Avicenna explicitly asserting, as Alfarabi did, that images generated within can be projected out through the sense faculties into the air. The soul "hears and sees colors and sounds that have no existence or causes in the external [world]," yet appear as real as the sights and sounds of events actually taking place outside the soul. For whether the soul perceives in the sensus communis an "impression . . . coming from without" or one "coming from within," the percepts are alike. In both instances, the soul perceives an image or "form . . . represented in" the sensus communis.[172]

The images that the compositive imagination fashions when given free rein are usually of no significance. They are induced by the condition of the human body at the time, by earlier concerns of the soul, and even by impressions received from the "celestial bodies." Images of the sort which are induced when the body is asleep are known as "confused dreams."[173]

[169]*Shifā': De anima* 249–250 (see apparatus); *Najāt* 167–68; English translation 36–37; Landauer, "Die Psychologie des Ibn Sīnā" (n. 30 above), chap. 8 (end). Cf. *Ishārāt* 127.

[170]Above, p. 58. Wolfson (n. 66 above) 275–76, and n. 27, quotes, in addition to a passage in which Alfarabi does not distinguish between retentive and compositive imagination, passages from two works attributed to Alfarabi which do draw the distinction. The second of the two works, *ᶜUyūn al-Masā'il*, is, however, clearly not a genuine work of Alfarabi's, and the first is also perhaps not his.

[171]Above, pp. 95–96.

[172]*Shifā': De anima* 170, 172–73; *Ishārāt* 212–14.

[173]*Shifā': De anima* 179–80.

But for fleeting moments in the case of all men and for extended periods in the case of a few, both when the body is asleep and when it is awake, the compositive imaginative faculty enters "conjunction" with the "supernal region" (*malakūt*).[174] The term *supernal region* designates for Avicenna: the souls—not the bodies—of the celestial spheres; the incorporeal intelligences, including, most notably, the active intellect; and perhaps also the First Cause. Just as conjunction of the human intellect with the active intellect results in the soul's receiving an emanation from the active intellect, so the conjunction of the compositive imaginative faculty with the supernal region also brings the soul an "emanation." If the episode is more than momentary, the soul attains a "perception of hidden things, either exactly as they are or recast in figurative images." Those hidden things may be either "intelligible thoughts" or "foreknowledge" of the future.

Avicenna is especially interested in instances of the compositive imagination's entering conjunction with the supernal region during the waking state. Ordinarily, he writes, the compositive imaginative faculty has free rein in the waking state only because a morbid condition—illness, fear, an imbalance of bile—renders the man's "discrimination" inoperative or causes "his soul [to] disregard the [intellect's] discrimination." In some men, however, the "strength of the compositive imaginative faculty and memory" reaches a point where, even though no morbid condition is present, those faculties do not let the "[external] senses" distract them from their "proper activities" of framing new images and preserving a record thereof; a "nobility of soul" in the same men allows the soul to continue "to heed the intellect" as the compositive imagination goes about its business of framing images. The compositive imaginations of these men are highly suited to enter conjunction with the supernal region. When they do, the men are said to enjoy "the prophecy that is peculiar to the compositive imaginative faculty."[175]

Prophecy distinctive to the compositive imagination can accompany the superior category of prophecy, prophecy located in the intellect. If a man blessed with a high degree of insight also possesses a powerful compositive imagination, it is "not farfetched that some of the effects of the holy spirit [that is, conjunction of the human intellect with the active intellect and reception of theoretical knowledge from the active intellect's emanation without recourse to cogitation] should . . . emanate onto the man's compositive imagination." Avicenna has stated that the compositive imagination, upon obtaining information from the supernal region—theoretical truths or knowledge of the future—may see things as they are or recast what is communicated to it in figurative images. When information arriving in the compositive imagination is the handiwork of superior insight and hence of a

[174]*Malakūt* is a Koranic term that was picked up by theological writers. See Koran 6:75; 7:185; 23:88; 36:83; A. Wensinck, "On the Relation between Ghazālī's Cosmology and His Mysticism, *Mededeelingen der Koninklijke Akademie van Wetenschappen* 75.a.6 (1933) 183–84, 191.

[175]Ibid. 173–75, 177; *Ishārāt* 214–15.

theoretical character, it is perforce recast. The passage just quoted continues: When the compositive imagination of the doubly qualified prophet receives the effects of holy spirit, it "depicts them in sense-perceptible and audible images."[176] In other words, the person endowed with both superlative insight and a powerful compositive imaginative faculty fashions, through his compositive imagination, a figurative depiction of the scientific and philosophical truths obtained thanks to insight; the gift of imaginative prophecy recasts in figurative images what the soul learned by the gift of intellectual prophecy. Avicenna undoubtedly has the joining of the two categories of prophecy in mind when he writes elsewhere that the highest class of mankind comprises men whose "soul is perfected as an actual intellect," while the highest subdivision within that highest class comprises those who are "disposed for the level of prophecy" and enjoy "revelation" (*w-ḥ-y*). These men "see" a "form" or "apparition" of "God's angels" and "hear . . . a voice from God and the angels," although no objective sound is present.[177]

A peculiar twist may be noted in the combination of intellectual prophecy with imaginative prophecy. Intellectual prophecy consists in receiving the emanation of the active intellect without recourse to the cogitative faculty, the faculty identical with the compositive imagination, whereas the doubly qualified prophet depicts the fruits of his intellectual prophecy in figurative images precisely because he does receive the emanation of the active intellect through his compositive imagination.[178] At all events, the man endowed with both categories of prophecy utilizes his figurative recasting of theoretical truths to instruct the masses. The majority of mankind is incapable of grasping fundamental metaphysical truths as, for example, the incorporeality of God; and the prophet who accepts political and educational responsibilities teaches his people about God in pictorial images.[179]

Avicenna has offered definitions of intellectual prophecy and imaginative prophecy, and a statement about the figurative depiction of theoretical thoughts

[176] *Shifā' : De anima* 248–49; *Najāt* 167; English translation 36.

[177] *Shifā' : Ilāhiyyāt* (n. 2 above) 435–36; *Najāt* 299.

[178] *Mubāḥathāt* 233, §476, reads: "When we see something in a dream, we first have intelligible thought of it and then have an imaginative perception of it. The reason is that the active intellect emanates the intelligible thought on our intellects, then it [the thought] emanates from it [the human intellect] to our compositive imagination. When, by contrast, we *learn* something, we imagine it first and then think it intelligibly, so that the order is reversed." Avicenna is apparently answering the following question: All human intelligible thought is mediated through the compositive imagination, which is identical with the cogitative faculty. What then is the difference between a theoretical proposition that results when the cogitative faculty crystallizes terms out of the emanation of the active intellect, arranges the terms in propositions, frames a syllogism, and draws a conclusion (see above, pp. 96–98); and an imaginative depiction of a theoretical proposition that results when the emanation of the active intellect passes through the human intellect to the same cogitative faculty, also known as the compositive imagination? The difference, Avicenna is saying, depends on where the process begins and where it ends.

[179] *Shifā' : Ilāhiyyāt* 443. See above, p. 62.

when the two combine. He also seems to recognize the possibility of a depiction of theoretical truths through imaginative prophecy that is independent of intellectual prophecy. In a context where he does not mention the human intellect, he makes the statement, already quoted, that prophecy through the compositive imagination contains intelligible thoughts and foreknowledge of events. In the same section, he further writes that when a man of strong imagination directs his "attention" to "intelligible thoughts, they appear to him."[180] Since the human intellect is not mentioned, Avicenna apparently has in view the reception of intelligible thoughts from a supernal source, without the participation of the human intellect, and the specific source within the supernal region must be the active intellect, seeing that it is what imparts intelligible thought to man. Although he does not express himself very well, Avicenna thus would—like Alfarabi[181]—recognize that the ever-present emanation of the active intellect can communicate theoretical truths to a powerful compositive imagination, irrespective of the human subject's intellectual attainments. Such theoretical thoughts received by the compositive imaginative faculty directly from the active intellect would again invariably be recast in figurative images.

Avicenna goes into somewhat more detail regarding the compositive imagination's knowledge of future events. Events in the sublunar world, including events ostensibly caused by acts of "will," are, in Avicenna's scheme of things, ultimately traceable to the movements of the celestial bodies. Every sublunar event, "whether past, present, or yet to occur," is therefore known in a "universal mode" by "the Creator and the intellectual angels," that is, the incorporeal intelligences, which govern the celestial spheres; and every event is known in a "particular mode" by the "celestial angels," that is, by the "souls" of the spheres. "Human souls" are "more closely related to the angelic substances than they are to their own physical bodies," and they would remain in permanent contact with those substances, were they not dragged down by their bodies. When the body is asleep and the soul is partly released from the bodily activities "dragging it down," it may "behold what is there." The man's compositive imagination can then generate a true dream, which will "most likely" represent future events affecting "the man, his family, his land, and his region." By implication, should a man's compositive imagination be sufficiently strong, it will generate visions representing events of interest to the man, even when the body is awake. Dreams or visions may reveal things either exactly as they are or recast them into images that will have to be "interpreted" and "undergo exegesis" (*ta'awwala*).[182]

The indisputably genuine works of Avicenna do not, so far as I could find, identify the subclass of supernal beings which inspires true dreams of the future. Nevertheless, Avicenna certainly intimates that the souls of the spheres are the

[180]*Shifā' : De anima* 179.
[181]Above, pp. 59–60.
[182]Ibid. 178–80, taken together with *Shifā' : Ilāhiyyāt* 436–37; *Najāt* 299–300.

cause.[183] The souls of the spheres, as was seen, have knowledge of the sublunar world in the "particular mode." They resemble an observer who is "in direct contact" with the object perceived, or "virtually in direct contact," and who "experiences [what he knows] through sense perception."[184] By contrast, the incorporeal movers of the spheres and the active intellect have only a general knowledge of the world. Hence when Avicenna writes that the compositive imagination learns about future events by viewing "what is there," his likely meaning is that the compositive imagination enters into conjunction not with an incorporeal intelligence but with one or another of the souls of the spheres, and that the human compositive imagination thereby receives an emanation from one of the souls of the spheres, and visualize the future. Such an interpretation of Avicenna does raise a problem. In his system, beings consisting in pure intellect produce eternal emanations, and it is therefore consistent for the active intellect to do so as well. His system has not, however, been seen to accommodate an emanation that proceeds from the souls of the spheres. If the interpretation should be correct and Avicenna does take the souls of the spheres as the source of human knowledge of future events, he has sidestepped an anomaly in Alfarabi. Alfarabi stated that the active intellect imparts to the human imagination knowledge of future events and of present events at a distance, but he failed to explain how the active intellect, which has only intellectual, and not particular, knowledge, might communicate what it does not itself know.[185] Identifying the source of the foreknowledge of events as the souls of the spheres, which do have particular knowledge, rather than the active intellect, which does not, would remove the anomaly.

Avicenna recognizes still another category of prophecy, a category that provides him with a rationalization of miracles, while leading him perilously close to the bourne of the occult. The categories of prophecy examined thus far are located in the "perceptive" faculties of the soul. An additional "power" of "prophecy," Avicenna asserts, is located in the soul's "motive . . . faculties." Inasmuch as the human soul is not "imprinted in the matter" of the human body yet is able to "alter [his own] bodily material," it should "not be surprising that a noble, powerful soul" can, by sheer "will," manipulate other bodies. Certain select souls can, as a consequence, "heal the sick and bring illness to the wicked, . . . turn what is not fire into fire and what is not earth into earth," cause "rain" to fall, and the like.

[183]Cf. *Ishārāt* 210–11. Avicenna (?), *Aḥwāl al-Nafs*, ed. A. Ahwani (Cairo 1952) 117, states that the human "practical intellect" employs the "compositive imagination" to "conjoin" with the "supernal soul-substances," that is to say, with the souls of the spheres, and thereby gain knowledge of the future. The book does not, however, appear in the earliest lists of Avicenna's works and is very possibly not genuine, although it is plainly based on Avicenna's thought and writings. A poorer version of the same book, under another title that also does not appear in the early lists, is published in *Rasā'il Ibn Sīnā* 2 (n. 99 above) 109–54.

[184]*Shifā': Ilāhiyyāt* 437. Cf. *Ishārāt* 210–11.

[185]Cf. above, p. 60.

"This is a characteristic linked to the motive faculties . . . of the soul of a prophet who is great in prophecy."[186]

Résumé. Avicenna attaches the name prophecy to a broader range of phenomena than Alfarabi did. He recognizes the possibility of man's attaining instantaneous scientific knowledge without following scientific procedures, something rejected by Alfarabi and to be rejected by Averroes. Through insight, the human soul establishes conjunction with the active intellect effortlessly, and from the active intellect's emanation the soul immediately receives the middle terms of syllogisms, the syllogisms themselves, and their conclusions. The ability to attain broad instantaneous scientific knowledge through insight is the "highest of the powers of prophecy."

In prophecy at a lesser level, a powerful compositive imaginative faculty attains knowledge of "intelligible thoughts" or foreknowledge of the future. When a powerful compositive imaginative faculty is joined to a high degree of insight, that is, when the two kinds of prophecy are combined, the human subject can recast in figurative images the scientific knowledge he learned through intellectual prophecy. The doubly qualified prophet utilizes his figurative depiction of scientific truths to educate the masses, who are incapable of comprehending the truth in a pure form. When a powerful compositive imagination is found in a man of undeveloped intellect, it—apparently—may enter conjunction with the active intellect and receive the emanation of the active intellect directly. It will then receive a figurative depiction of theoretical thoughts that are no longer scientific in character. Finally, the compositive imagination may enter into conjunction with the supernal world, by which Avicenna most likely means the souls of the spheres, and thereby envisage future events of concern for the man either as they are or in a figurative form. All these phenomena make up the "prophecy that is peculiar to the compositive imagination faculty."

In addition to intellectual prophecy and imaginative prophecy, both of which are cognitive phenomena, Avicenna recognizes the possibility of a man's effecting changes in the physical world through an act of sheer will, and he calls that phenomenon prophecy as well.

Details of the several categories and subcategories of prophecy are left vague. Avicenna may simply have been careless, but he also may have deliberately tried to veil his precise intent from casual readers. He may not have wanted them to realize that as he defined each of the categories of prophecy, all intervention by the deity is excluded.

[186]*Shifā' : De anima* 200–201. Cf. *Ishārāt* 219–20.

Summary

In Avicenna's universe is, as in Alfarabi's, existence and thought flow from above to below. The First Cause eternally and unchangingly emanates the incorporeal intelligence that governs the outermost celestial sphere, the incorporeal intelligence governing the outermost sphere emanates another intelligence, and the eternal process continues until the active intellect, the last in the series, is reached. In addition to emanating the next intelligence in the series, each intelligence also emanates the body and soul of the celestial sphere that it governs. The active intellect, although not powerful enough to emanate an unchanging body, a soul to accompany an unchanging body, and a further eternal incorporeal intelligence, does emanate analogues of the three. It emanates the matter of the sublunar world, natural forms in the sublunar world, and human intelligible thought.

The active intellect eternally emanates the underlying matter of the sublunar world with the unexplained participation of the movement of the heavens. Natural sublunar forms subsist in the active intellect in an undifferentiated mode, and whenever influences from the heavens together with forces within the sublunar world blend a portion of matter so as to dispose it for a given natural form, the matter receives the appropriate form from the eternal, ever-present emanation of the active intellect. The active intellect is, as it were, an eternal cosmic transmitter, broadcasting an undifferentiated range of forms, as well as the substratum that can receive them, and properly attuned portions of matter automatically receive the natural forms appropriate to them. The active intellect is accordingly called the "giver of forms." Matter blended to the highest possible degree of homogeneity receives an incorporeal human soul from the active intellect's emanation.

The foregoing is put forward by Avicenna as a demonstrable and demonstrated scientific cosmology.

The human soul, at birth, possesses an empty potentiality for thought, called "material intellect." When a man secures a repertoire of the propositions embodying the first principles of thought but is not thinking them at the moment, he has "intellect *in habitu*." When he secures a full repertoire of abstract concepts and scientific propositions, again without thinking them at the moment, he has "actual intellect." Actual intelligible thought at any level is called "acquired intellect" for the reason that all such thought is acquired from the emanation of the active intellect. The term *acquired intellect* has an additional sense. It designates the "ultimate end" and "perfection" of human intellectual development.

The active intellect is the cause of the existence of the human soul with its material intellect; the passage of the material intellect to the stage of potentiality called intellect *in habitu*; the passage of the intellect to the subsequent stage of potentiality, which is paradoxically called actual intellect; the condition of actual human thought called acquired intellect; and acquired intellect in the special sense of the culmination of human intellectual development.

Actual thought occurs when the human soul enters into "conjunction" with the active intellect, receives the active intellect's emanation, and differentiates a thought out of the emanation. One passage distinguishes two phases in the process: In the first phase, the soul receives the emanation of the active intellect in an undifferentiated mode, and in the second, it induces a further emanation of differentiated thoughts from the undifferentiated emanation already present in the soul. The cognitive operations leading up to the appearance of an intelligible thought serve to prepare the soul and intellect for entering into conjunction with the active intellect, much as the natural processes leading up to the appearance of a form in a portion of matter prepare the matter for receiving the form from the emanation of the same active intellect.

The nonintellectual faculty playing the key role in preparing the soul for conjunction is the *cogitative* faculty, which is the same as the human *compositive imaginative* faculty. The cogitative faculty prepares the soul or intellect for conjunction by presenting images, it then differentiates thoughts out of the emanation of the active intellect, and it arranges thoughts in sequences to frame propositions and syllogisms. Fortunate souls have *insight*, an aptitude that enables them to establish conjunction with the active intellect, crystallize out thoughts, and frame syllogisms, without recourse to cogitation.

When the soul possesses acquired intellect in the narrower acceptation, it has established conjunction with the active intellect vis à vis all scientific thoughts, has no further use for the body or the senses, and should now jettison body and senses. Avicenna speaks of a "permanent conjunction" with the active intellect, a condition wherein the soul not merely thinks all thoughts at will but thinks them all at once. He leaves unclear, however, whether permanent conjunction is reserved for the afterlife or may be enjoyed in the present life as well.

Since the human soul is, for Avicenna, an incorporeal substance, it is immortal by its very nature. Each soul's fate in the world to come is nevertheless determined by its intellectual attainments in the present life. Souls that in this life attain a disposition for conjunction with the active intellect vis à vis all possible thoughts will, in the next life, enjoy a complete permanent conjunction with the active intellect. Those achieving less than a complete disposition for conjunction in this life, yet controlling a considerable segment of physical and metaphysical science, will enjoy a lesser degree of conjunction with the active intellect in the next life. Those falling below the minimum amount of knowledge needed for conjunction with the active intellect in the next life but aware of the delights of intellectual activity suffer the eternal pain of unfulfilled intellectual desire. And simpleminded souls, which both lack intellectual accomplishments and are unaware of the pleasure that intellectual activity brings, reside in an eternal state of rest, void of all intellectual content. A comment made at one point suggests that the eternal state of rest void of intellectual content may in fact amount to nonexistence. If during its sojourn within the temporal world, a soul should have committed the moral fault of enslaving itself to the concerns of the body, it will in the next life suffer the pain of being drawn in one direction by its own nature, and in another by the concerns of its body, which no longer exists. The pain will eventually disappear, however, and each disembodied soul will then enter upon the eternal fate to which its intellectual attainments assign it. Finally, in a rationalization of traditional religious accounts of the hereafter, Avicenna suggests a theory according to which simpleminded souls may in the afterlife experience through their imaginative faculties the physical pleasures and pains promised by popular religion.

Avicenna attaches the name prophecy to three kinds of phenomena. Intellectual prophecy, the "highest of the powers of prophecy," occurs when insight enables a human intellect to establish conjunction with the active intellect effortlessly, vis à vis a wide range of thoughts. The active intellect's emanation immediately imparts to such an intellect the middle terms of syllogisms, the syllogisms themselves, and their conclusions. "Prophecy that is peculiar to the compositive imaginative faculty"—which may or may not be combined with intellectual prophecy—occurs when a supernal emanation gives a powerful compositive imaginative faculty either a figurative version of theoretical knowledge or knowledge of the future, the emanation responsible for the figurative version of theoretical knowledge coming from the active intellect, and that responsible for knowledge of the future, apparently coming from the souls of the spheres. The name prophecy is also attached to a noncognitive phenomenon, to the effecting of changes in the physical world through acts of sheer will.

5

REVERBERATIONS OF THE THEORIES OF ALFARABI AND AVICENNA

Avicenna's Islamic Successors

Avicenna's philosophy was accessible to Moslem readers through the following channels: Avicenna's straightforward philosophic works, notably the *Shifā'* and *Najāt*; his *Ishārāt*, which rephrases his philosophic system in high-flown language; his *Dānesh Nāmah*, a summary of his philosophic system in Persian; allegorical tales he wrote in which human characters and also a bird personify the active intellect and the human intellect or soul[1]; a lengthy restatement of his philosophy by Bahmanyār (d. 1065), one of his students[2]; the better known summary by Ghazali (1058–1111), entitled *Maqāṣid al-Falāsifa*[3]; still another,

[1]H. Corbin, *Avicenna and the Visionary Recital* (New York 1960) (translation of *Avicenne et le récit visionnaire*). Avicenna's allegories, like most specimens of the genre, are flat and uninspired; his own imaginative faculty apparently enjoyed only a minimal measure of emanation from the supernal regions. But *de gustibus non disputandum*, and Corbin 135, may be consulted for a different opinion.

[2]Bahmanyār, *al-Taḥṣīl* (Tehran 1972). See also Behmenjār (Bahmanyār), *R. fī Marātib al-Mawjūdāt*, in *Zwei metaphysische Abhandlungen*, ed. and trans. S. Poper (Leipzig 1851) (arguments for the existence of incorporeal intelligences, souls of the spheres, and the active intellect, and arguments for the incorporeality of the human soul).

[3]Ghazali, *Maqāṣid al-Falāṣifa*, (Cairo n.d.) 218–20 (the emanation scheme as an explanation of a single unitary cause's producing multiple effects, without, however, the nuance of a third aspect in the thought of the intelligences); 221 (emanation of sublunar matter by the active intellect); 222 (preparation of sublunar matter for forms, by the action of the heavens); 222–25 (emanation by the active intellect, the "giver of forms," of forms of elements, mist and haze, minerals, plants, animals, man); 291–92 (the human soul as a "self-subsistent substance," degrees of human intellect, human thought as "acquired" from the active intellect); 299 (intrinsic immortality of the human soul); 302–3 (actualization of the human intellect by the active intellect); 304–5 (true eudaemonia in the afterlife as eternal conjunction of a perfect human intellect with the active intellect); 305 (imagined experience in the afterlife of promises of popular religion, with "some of the celestial bodies" serving as a "substratum for the compositive imagination"); 306–7 (misery in the afterlife as frustrated desire for the pleasures of the body and as the soul's being torn in two directions); 309–12 (true dreams and visions through the compositive imaginative faculty, resulting from conjunction of the human soul with supernal beings); 314, 317–18, 319 (three types of "prophet": men upon whom all "intelligible thoughts" are "emanated"

briefer summary by Shahrastānī (1086–1153)[4]; and the commentary of Ṭūṣī (d. 1274) on the *Ishārāt*.[5]

The picture of the universe that Alfarabi and Avicenna propagated and perhaps created—wherein a distinctive emanation scheme is superimposed on the Aristotelian universe, and wherein the last of the incorporeal intelligences, the transcendent active intellect, performs functions in respect to both the sublunar physical world and the human intellect—is embraced by a fair number of Moslem thinkers. The list of those who assume the picture of the universe common to Alfarabi and Avicenna, or who, more particularly, adopt elements in the scheme peculiar to Avicenna includes: the anonymous authors of a half dozen minor compositions that carry Alfarabi's name yet can be seen by their contents to have been excerpted and paraphrased from Avicenna by persons of modest talents; Ibn Bājja (Avempace) (d. 1138); Ibn Ṭufail (early twelfth century), who, however, overlaid Avicenna's theory of intellect with a patina of mystical knowledge; Averroes, who remained close to Alfarabi and Avicenna in his early works but struggled to break free of them as his thinking matured; and certain works of Suhrawardī. To that list, I shall add Ghazali, a protean figure who is ordinarily regarded as an implacable adversary, rather than an adherent, of Alfarabi and Avicenna. We shall also find that Abū al-Barakāt's philosophic treatise and Suhrawardī's most important work, both of which criticize Avicenna's system sharply, are each in fact a reworking of it.

Of the minor anonymous compositions incorrectly attributed to Alfarabi, the one containing the largest amount of material from Avicenna is a work usually known as *ᶜUyūn al-Masā'il*. It affirms that from the First Cause of the universe, which is wholly unitary, a series of incorporeal intelligences "proceeds" (*ḥ-ṣ-l*). Each intelligence, the composition in question explains, has two aspects—rather than the three distinguished by Avicenna. And in reducing the aspects to two, the composition also conflates two alternative versions of what each of the aspects is: One aspect is the intelligence's "being necessarily existent [by virtue of its cause] and having the First [Cause] as an object of knowledge," and the other is its "being possibly existent [by virtue of itself] and having itself as an object of knowledge."[6]

---

from the "active intellect" rapidly and without a teacher thanks to powerful "insight"; men who are in conjunction with "noble [supernal] substances," and whose compositive imagination thereby becomes able to depict metaphysical truths in figurative images; men who can change nature).

[4]Shahrastānī, *K. al-Milal wal-Niḥal*, ed. W. Cureton (London 1842–1846) 380–84, 417–29; German translation, with the pagination of the Arabic indicated: *Religionspartheien und Philosophenschulen*, trans. T. Haarbrücker (Halle 1850–1851).

[5]Printed in Avicenna, *Ishārāt*, ed. S. Dunya (Cairo 1957).

[6]Alfarabi's two aspects were the intelligence's having the First Cause as an object of thought and its having itself as an object of thought; see above, p. 46. Avicenna's three aspects were: the intelligence's having the First Cause as an object of thought; its having itself, insofar as it is necessarily existent by reason of the First Cause, as an object of thought; and its having itself, insofar as it is possibly existent by reason of itself, as an object of thought. See above, p. 75.

By reason of the former aspect, the next "intelligence" in the series "proceeds," while by reason of the latter aspect there "proceeds" a celestial "sphere," composed of "matter and form."[7] The final link in the chain of intelligences is "the incorporeal active intellect"; it is the cause of the "existence of sublunar souls" and, "through the intermediacy of the [celestial] spheres," of the "four elements."[8] Whenever a "body" is fit for receiving a human soul, "the giver of forms" produces the soul.[9] Since intelligible thoughts cannot be present in a material substratum, the human soul, in which intelligible thoughts are present, must be a "simple incorporeal substance," and, being an incorporeal substance, the soul is capable of "surviving" the "death of the body." The human soul passes from the stage of "material intellect" to that of "intellect *in habitu*," and then to that of "acquired intellect"; and what leads it from "from potentiality to actuality" must be "an incorporeal intellect, namely, the active intellect."[10] "Eudaemonia" and "misery" in the afterlife are "merited," and human souls enjoy the former or suffer the latter through "necessity and justice."[11]

Ghazali is of greater interest. As already mentioned, he wrote a summary of Avicenna's philosophy, and, as will appear, he complemented the summary with a trenchant critique. At another juncture in his life, he composed a comprehensive Kalam work.[12] And his autobiography informs us that his intellectual odyssey

---

Ghazali's summary of Avicenna's philosophy (n. 3 above) 219–20, distinguishes two aspects in each intelligence: its "necessity [that is, its necessary existence] by reason of another" and its "possibility [that is, its possible existence] by reason of itself."

The text we are considering has conflated Alfarabi's two aspects with the two aspects in Ghazali's summary of Avicenna's philosophy. Since *being necessarily existent by virtue of its cause* is not equivalent to *having the First Cause as an object of thought*, and since *being possibly existent by virtue of itself* is equivalent to only part of *having itself as an object of knowledge*—the intelligence, as the text itself recognizes, being both possible and necessary—the two versions of each aspect are not consistent with one another. Below, pp. 150-51, Ghazali's critique of Avicenna's philosophy combines different, but not inconsistent, versions of the aspects in the thought of each intelligence.

[7] *ᶜUyūn al-Masā'il*, in *Alfārābī's philosophische Abhandlungen*, ed. F. Dieterici (Leiden 1890) 56–65, §§7–9; German translation, with same section numbers: *Alfārābī's philosophische Abhandlungen aus dem Arabischen übersetzt*, trans. F. Dieterici (Leiden 1892).

[8] Ibid. §§9, 11.

[9] Ibid. §§21–22.

[10] Ibid. §21. The stages of intellect are a combination of the schemes of Alfarabi and Avicenna. See above, pp. 49, 84–85.

[11] Ibid. §22. Other compositions of a similar character which contain material from Avicenna's theory of intellect are: *Fuṣūṣ al-Ḥikam*, in Dieterici (n. 7 above), 66–83; German translation in Dieterici (n. 7 above), 108–38; and the following, all of which are published in *Rasā'il al-Fārābī* (Hyderabad 1931): *Daᶜāwā al-Qalbiyya* (a different recension of *ᶜUyūn al-Masā'il*); *Fī Ithbāt al-Mufāraqāt*, *R. Zaynūn* ("Zeno's [!] opuscule"), and *Taᶜlīqāt*.

[12] *Al-Iqtiṣād fī al-Iᶜtiqād* (Ankara 1962).

eventually led him into yet one more province, to "Sufism,"[13] a term that may mean either a regimen of God-fearing asceticism or a brand of mystical experience. Averroes belittled Ghazali as one who was "an Asharite with the Asharites, a Sufi with the Sufis, and a philosopher with the philosophers."[14] Unmasking an essential Ghazali ensconced behind the successive guises is not easy.

The work where Ghazali gives the most convincing impression of divulging his final view of things takes its departure from Koran 24:35, a verse playing on the imagery of an oil lamp. Avicenna had interpreted the imagery in the verse as an allegorical representation of the human intellectual process.[15] Ghazali, in the work we are considering, interprets the images in a similar, though not completely identical, manner; but he goes beyond the lamp imagery and the human intellectual process, adducing additional verses, bringing the allegorical procedure to bear on them as well, and weaving an allusive, circuitous account of the structure of the universe. His book is entitled *Mishkāt al-Anwār*, the *Niche of Lights*, a niche in which the oil lamp stands being one of the motifs in the Koranic verse serving as Ghazali's point of departure. The *Mishkāt* employs language from the Sufi mystical vocabulary and ostensibly endorses mystical doctrines. Yet Averroes was to locate the book within the tradition of Islamic Aristotelianism and he berated Ghazali for hypocritically rejecting, or pretending to reject, on certain occasions what the *Mishkāt* and other works of Ghazali espoused.[16] Averroes' reading of the *Mishkāt* has not been taken seriously by recent scholars.[17] It is, nonetheless, correct.

The *Mishkāt* recognizes two classes of men who ascend to the "true heavens" and attain a genuine understanding of God: those who know what they do through means of "scientific knowledge" (*ᶜirfān ᶜilmī*), and those who are in a "state of direct experience" (*ḥāl dhawqī*; *dhawq* literally means "taste").[18] Members of the

[13]*Al-Munqidh min al-Ḍalāl* (Cairo 1962) 172–73; English translation: *The Faith and Practice of al-Ghazali*, trans. W. Watt (London 1953) 54–55.

[14]*Faṣl al-Maqāl*, ed. G. Hourani (Leiden 1959) 28; English translation: *Averroes on the Harmony of Religion and Philosophy*, trans. G. Hourani (London 1961) 61.

[15]Avicenna, *K. al-Ishārāt wal-Tanbīhāt*, ed. J. Forget (Leiden 1892) 126; French translation of *Ishārāt*, with pages of Forget's edition indicated: *Livre des directives et remarques*, trans. A. Goichon (Beirut 1951).

[16]Averroes, *K. al-Kashf*, ed. M. Müller as *Philosophie und Theologie von Averroes* (Munich 1859) 71; German translation, with pagination of the Arabic indicated: *Philosophie und Theologie von Averroes*, trans. M. Müller (Munich 1875); *Tahāfut al-Tahāfut*, ed. M. Bouyges (Beirut 1930) 117; English translation, with pagination of the Arabic indicated: *Averroes' Tahafut al-Tahafut*, trans. S. van den Bergh (London 1954). In *Mīzān al-ᶜAmal*, Ghazali states the rule that a wise man does not disclose his genuine beliefs to anyone except those who are on the same level as he. The Arabic text was not available to me. French translation: *Critère de l'action*, trans. H. Hachem (Paris 1945) 148.

[17]An exception is D. Baneth, "R. Yehuda ha-Levi and Ghazali," (in Hebrew) *Keneset* 7 (1942) 323, n. 6.

[18]Ghazali, *Mishkāt al-Anwār*, ed. A. Afifi (Cairo 1964) 57. English translation (inadequate): *Mishkat al-Anwar (The Niche for Lights)*, trans. W. Gairdner, 2d ed. (Lahore 1952) 106. French

second class, although in danger of falling into the pantheistic error of imagining themselves identical with God, are superior to members of the first class, and Ghazali explicitly encourages readers to "become men of direct experience." Any who cannot are advised to "become men of science."[19] Ghazali, moreover, assures readers that when "intellect is set free of the veil of . . . imagination, it cannot conceivably err; . . . its being set free . . . will be completed after the death [of the body]."[20] He thus ranks the exercise of intellect below direct experience, while at the same time awarding intellect an unambiguous cachet of legitimacy.

The Ḳoranic verse around which Ghazali constructs the *Mishkāt* opens with the words "God is the light of the heavens and the earth," and a little later in the verse, God is called a "light above light." As is hardly surprising, *Mishkāt al-Anwār*, the *Niche of Lights*, makes extensive use of light imagery in representing the nature of the deity and beings subordinate to Him. Employing light imagery for that purpose was hardly original. The Old and New Testaments employ light imagery for describing God,[21] and in philosophy, the application of such imagery to incorporeal beings extends from Plato,[22] through Philo[23] and Plotinus,[24] into the Middle Ages.[25] Especially pertinent here are certain phrases in the Arabic paraphrase of Plotinus known as the *Theology of Aristotle*.

---

translation: *Le tabernacle des lumières*, trans. R. Deladrière (Paris 1981) 53. On the term *dhawq*, which literally means *taste*, see Ibn Ṭufail, *Hayy ben Yaqdhān* (*Yaqẓān*), ed. and French trans. L. Gauthier (Beirut 1936), French section 4, n.1.

[19] Ibid. 78; English translation 148; French translation 78.

[20] Ibid. 47; English translation 90; French translation 44. W. Watt, "The Authenticity of Works Attributed to al-Ghazālī," *Journal of the Royal Asiatic Society* (1952) 38, 44, contends that works betraying "no hint of any contradiction between prophetic knowledge and rational knowledge" cannot belong to the final stage of Ghazali's thought, a stage represented in particular by the *Mishkāt*; for in Ghazali's final stage, direct experience (*dhawq*) is of a wholly different character from reason. What Ghazali says about prophecy in the passages quoted here and below undercuts Watt's contention.

[21] Cf. Psalms 27:1; N.T. 1 John 1:5; 1 James 1:17.

[22] Plato, *Republic* 509.

[23] See F. Klein, *Die Lichtterminologie bei Philon von Alexandrien und in den hermetischen Schriften* (Leiden 1962). (Reference furnished by David Winston.)

[24] Plotinus, *Enneads* 4.3.17; 5.3.12; 5.6.4; 6.8.18; and passim; A. Armstrong, *The Architecture of the Intelligible Universe in the Philosophy of Plotinus* (Cambridge 1940) 54–57. The two passages from *Enneads* 5, appear in the preserved Arabic paraphrases of Plotinus. See *Risāla fī al-ᶜIlm al-Ilāhī*, in *Plotinus apud Arabes*, ed. A. Badawi (Cairo 1955) 175; English translation by G. Lewis, facing the Greek text, in Plotinus, *Enneades*, ed. P. Henry and H.-R. Schwyzer 2 (Paris 1959) 321; *Al-Shaykh al-Yūnānī*, ed. F. Rosenthal, *Orientalia* 21 (1952) 480–81.

[25] C. Baeumker, *Witelo* (Münster 1908) (*Beiträge zur Geschichte der Philosophie des Mittelalters* 3.2) 357–415, 426–34, traces the history of what he calls the metaphysics of light, that is, doctrines in which God is represented as the true, pure light, and hence the source of all other lightlike beings in the universe.

The *Theology of Aristotle* had called the First Cause, or the One: "the first light"[26] and "the light of lights."[27] Taking his cue from the Koranic verse around which he builds the *Mishkāt*, and apparently also from those terms in the *Theology of Aristotle*, Ghazali characterizes God as "the highest, ultimate light," the "true, essential light,"[28] and "the light of lights."[29] In addition, he writes in the *Mishkāt* that the term *light* is a synonym for both "intellect" (*ᶜaql*)[30] and "existence."[31] When he calls God the highest ultimate light and the true essential light, he therefore means either that God is the highest intellect and intellect in the strictest sense, or alternatively that God is the highest existent being and existent in the strictest sense. Ghazali's third phrase, "light of lights," may, in the context of the *Mishkāt*, mean either, again, that God is the highest intellect or highest existent being, or else that God is the source of all other intellects and of all other existent beings. Since God alone is light—that is, existent or intellect—in the most primary sense, to predicate the term *light* of anything else, of beings and intellects standing below the deity as well as of the phenomenon in the physical world commonly called *light*, is, writes Ghazali, to indulge in "pure metaphor."[32] What is metaphorical is not the use of the term *light* to describe God but, paradoxically, the use of the term in the ordinary sense.

In addition to using the terms "first light" and "light of lights," the *Theology of Aristotle* had described the First Cause as "light . . . existing by virtue of itself."[33] When Avicenna's commentary on the *Theology of Aristotle* expounded the passage where the description appears, it spoke of the "necessarily existent [by virtue of itself]," which is "the essence of true light" and which is "light by virtue of itself and light existing by virtue of itself, not by virtue of another."[34] Avicenna saw in the *Theology*'s language an allusion to a proposition lying at the heart of his own philosophy, the proposition that a being must exist which is necessarily existent by virtue of itself and upon which everything existent by virtue of another depends.[35] In the context where Ghazali construes light as a synonym for

[26]*Theology of Aristotle*, ed. F. Dieterici (Leipzig 1882) 51 and 118, paralleling *Enneads* 5.8.3 and 5.8.12. English translation, facing the Greek, in Plotinus, *Enneades* (n. 24 above). The Greek does not, however, have the term *first light*.

[27]*Theology of Aristotle* 44 and 118, paralleling *Enneads* 5.8.1; 5.8.12. The Greek does not have the words *light of lights*. In the Nicene Creed, God is called the "light of light."

[28]*Mishkāt* 41; English translation 79; French translation 37.

[29]Ibid. 60; English translation 111; French translation 56.

[30]Ibid. 43–44; English translation 83; French translation 40.

[31]Ibid. 55; English translation 103; French translation 52.

[32]Ibid. 41, 54; English translation 79, 101; French translation 37, 50.

[33]*Theology of Aristotle* (n. 26 above) 51.

[34]Avicenna, Commentary on the *Theology of Aristotle*, in *Arisṭū ᶜinda al- ᶜArab*, ed. A. Badawi (Cairo 1947) 56–57; French translation: "Les notes d'Avicenne sur la 'Théologie d'Aristote,'" trans. G. Vajda, *Revue thomiste* 51 (1951) 380.

[35]H. Davidson, *Proofs for Eternity, Creation, and the Existence of God, in Medieval Islamic and Jewish Philosophy* (New York 1987) 289–93, 298–304.

existence, he for his part writes that everything existing in the universe exists either "by virtue of itself" or "by virtue of another," that the "first fount" of light is "light by virtue of itself," and that "the true existent being is God, just as the true light is God."[36] Ghazali's wording echoes both the *Theology of Aristotle* and the proposition of Avicenna's philosophy which Avicenna had himself discovered in the *Theology*. In a slightly allusive, but easily decipherable, fashion, Ghazali like Avicenna is saying that whatever exists must be either necessarily existent by virtue of itself or necessarily existent by virtue of another, that something necessarily existent by virtue of itself must exist, and that it is the cause of the existence of everything else in the universe.

In the context where the last passage quoted appears, Ghazali writes as well: A Koranic verse according to which "everything perishes save his [God's] countenance" does not mean that everything "perishes at a particular moment, but rather that it perishes eternally and everlastingly [*azalan, abadan*]."[37] In other words, the world outside God does not actually perish, and in characterizing the world as perishable, Scripture means merely that the world exists eternally by reason of another and not by reason of itself. The statement is astonishing. In his critique of Avicenna's philosophy, Ghazali insists that belief in the past eternity of the world is incompatible with a belief in a First Cause, in the existence of God,[38] and he there brands the belief in "the past eternity [*qidam*] of the world" as heresy.[39] Yet now he says that the world is eternal and everlasting. Perhaps his intent is that the world will exist eternally into the future, not that it has existed from all eternity in the past.[40]

Avicenna had employed the Koranic term *malakūt*, which I translated as *supernal region*, to designate the segment of the universe which includes the souls of the celestial spheres, although not the spheres themselves, the incorporeal intelligences, and perhaps the First Cause.[41] Ghazali's *Mishkāt* asserts that the "world of *malakūt*," also "called the supernal world, the spiritual world, or the light-world," transcends the "heavens."[42] It is the "intellectual [*ᶜaqlī*] . . . world."[43] As for its contents, "the totality of the world of *malakūt*" is "the angels,"[44] "the upper world

[36]*Mishkāt* 54–55; English translation 101–3; French translation 50–52.

[37]Ibid. 55; English translation 104; French translation 52. The verse is Koran 28:88.

[38]Ghazali, *Tahāfut al-Falāsifa*, ed. M. Bouyges (Beirut 1927) 3, §§17, 28; 10, §1. English translation in Van den Bergh (n.16 above) 96, 102, 250. Davidson (n. 35 above) 3–4.

[39]Ghazali, *Tahāfut al-Falāsifa* 376.

[40]A brief work attributed to Ghazali and preserved only in a medieval Hebrew translation offers a standard argument for the past eternity of the world. See Ghazali, *Antworten auf Fragen die an ihn gerichtet wurden*, ed. H. Malter (Berlin 1894) 41–43. That work copies long passages from Ghazali's summary of Avicenna's philosophy and therefore, even if authentic, may be only an exercise and not an expression of Ghazali's personal beliefs.

[41]Above, p. 119.

[42]*Mishkāt* 50; English translation 94–95; French translation 46–47.

[43]Ibid. 65; English translation 122; French translation 64.

[44]Ibid. 50; English translation 95; French translation 47.

is filled with . . . the intellectual, nonphysical [*ma^c^nawiyya*] lights, which are the angelic substances,"[45] the "world of *malakūt* contains lightlike substances . . . known as angels [*yu^c^abbar ^c^anhā bil-malā'ika*]."[46] The "celestial lights" form "a hierarchy," in which the "closest to the primary source most deserves the name 'light' since it is highest in rank."[47]

Two clues slice through the cloud of verbiage. The first is that light is a synonym for intellect. And the second comes when Ghazali discloses the functions performed by the beings making up the supernal world. Each of the "heavens," that is to say, each of the celestial "spheres," is moved by an "angel" that acts "through contact [*mubāshara*]" and by a "divine light" that acts "not by way of contact" but through "command" (*amr*).[48] The supernal intellectual lights, divine lights, angels, and angelic substances, which make up the supernal region, are thus nothing other than the familiar incorporeal intelligences and the rational souls of the spheres, each incorporeal intelligence moving its sphere indirectly—by serving as an object of desire—and each celestial soul moving its sphere directly—through its desire to emulate the perfection of the intelligence.[49] Equating the souls of the spheres and undoubtedly also the incorporeal intelligences with the *angels* of religious nomenclature, as Ghazali does here in the *Mishkāt*, was commonplace. Among others, Avicenna drew the equation,[50] and Ghazali himself remarked in his summary of Avicenna's philosophy that "the souls [of the spheres] and the intelligences . . . are known as celestial spiritual angels [*yu^c^abbar ^c^anhā bil-malā'ika . . .*]."[51] Avicenna, as happens, had also used the term "in contact" (*mubāshar*) to characterize the relation of the souls of the celestial spheres to their respective spheres.[52]

It is, Ghazali stresses, a principle of paramount importance, grasped solely by men of the very highest attainments, that the "outermost celestial body," the "sphere" drawing the other spheres around the earth "once each day," is moved by the command of a being subordinate to the First Cause and not by the First Cause itself.[53] In other words, as Alfarabi and Avicenna had taught, the First Cause of

[45]Ibid. 59; English translation 110; French translation 56.

[46]Ibid. 67; English translation 126; French translation 66.

[47]Ibid. 53; English translation 99; French translation 49.

[48]Ibid. 91; English translation 171–72; French translation 93–94.

[49]Cf. Aristotle, *Metaphysics* 12.7; Avicenna, *Shifā' : Ilāhiyyāt*, ed. G. Anawati et al. (Cairo 1960) 386–87; French translation, with pagination of the Arabic indicated: *La Métaphysique du Shifā' : livres VI à X*, trans. G. Anawati (Paris 1985).

[50]*Shifā' : Ilāhiyyāt* 435.

[51]Ghazali, *Maqāṣid* (n. 3 above) 182. The phraseology is exactly the same as that in the passage quoted in n. 46.

[52]*Shifā' : Ilāhiyyāt* 437.

[53]*Mishkāt* 91; English translation 170–72; French translation 93–94. W. Watt, "A Forgery in al-Ghazālī's *Mishkāt*?" *Journal of the Royal Asiatic Society* (1949) 6–13, 21, questions the authenticity of this section of the *Mishkāt*, because he finds "glaring" differences between it and the earlier sections. I did not see differences in doctrine, and Ibn Ṭufail, Averroes, and Fakhr al-Dīn

the universe is not identical with the incorporeal intelligence that moves the outermost sphere; it transcends the incorporeal movers of the spheres.

The *Mishkāt* does not number the celestial spheres; it merely affirms "a plurality."[54] The "degrees" of supernal "lights," that is to say, the incorporeal intelligences and the souls of the spheres, "resist enumeration" but "do not run to infinity."[55] By that statement, Ghazali may possibly be severing the link between transcendent incorporeal intellects and celestial spheres, and suggesting, as Abū al-Barakāt and Suhrawardī will, that transcendent incorporeal beings exist apart from the incorporeal movers of the spheres and the spheres' souls. He may, however, merely be recognizing, as an early work of Averroes will contend,[56] that incorporeal intelligences and souls should be posited not only for the nine main celestial spheres but for all the spheres, including the secondary, eccentric and epicyclical, spheres; and since the total number of celestial spheres, primary and secondary, had never been ascertained definitively, the total number of intelligences and souls of spheres likewise remains undetermined.

Ghazali, in passages already quoted, called God "the light of lights" and the "first fount" of light. He further calls God the light "illumining everything outside itself," the light from which "all other lights shine in accordance with their [place in the] hierarchy," the "source" from which "light descends to others."[57] The most frequent analogies philosophers employed for illustrating the emanation process were the flowing of water, the radiation of light, and the radiation of heat. By calling God the first *fount* and the *source* from which other lights descend, Ghazali combines two of the three analogies. He nonetheless avoids stating explicitly that God emanated the universe. Instead, using Koranic language, he writes that God "created [*faṭara*] the heavens, the outermost sphere, and [the being] that commands the movement of the sphere."[58] Either Ghazali believed that God brought the world into existence through a process of emanation but hesitated to say so expressly

---

al-Rāzī all refer to the section and treat it as a genuine part of the *Mishkāt*. The pertinent passage in Ibn Ṭufail is *Hayy ben Yaqdhān* (n. 18 above), Arabic section 17; French translation 15; English translation, with pagination of Gauthier's Arabic text indicated: *Hayy Ibn Yaqzān*, trans. L. Goodman (New York 1972). The passage in Averroes is *K. al-Kashf* (n. 16 above) 71. H. Lazarus-Yafeh, *Studies in al-Ghazzali* (Jerusalem 1975) 42, cites the passage in Rāzī.

Ghazali calls the incorporeal mover of the outermost sphere an "obeyed one" (*muṭā*^{c}), and the expression has, strangely, left a line of modern scholars scratching their heads. Ghazali simply means that the soul of the outermost sphere *obeys* the "command" of the first incorporeal intelligence in the sense that it emulates the intelligence and thereby moves the sphere.

[54]*Mishkāt* 91; English translation 170; French translation 93. The English translation sometimes speaks of "seven" spheres, but nothing in the Arabic text justifies the number seven.

[55]Ibid. 53–54; English translation 100–101; French translation 50.

[56]Below, p. 225.

[57]Ibid. 54; English translation 101; French translation 50. See also ibid. 60; English translation 111; French translation 56.

[58]Ibid. 92; the English translation 172, blurs the point; French translation 94. The passage echoes Koran 6:79.

because the notion of divine emanation was suspect in conservative circles; or he did believe that God created the world by fiat; or perhaps he understood that emanation and creation amount to the same thing. The *Mishkāt* betrays no hint of the proposition that from one only one can proceed or of the notion that complexity in the universe derives from the multiple thoughts of the incorporeal intelligences.[59]

The individual lights in the supernal region form a "hierarchy," inasmuch as they are "fueled [*yaqtabis*] from one another." In a different adaptation of the light imagery, Ghazali writes that light in the supernal region is "reflected," as it were, from one surface to another, and thereby successively loses intensity.[60] The angels that move the spheres directly, that is, the souls of the spheres, are related to the "pure divine lights," that is, to the incorporeal intelligences governing them, as "the moon [is related to the sun]" in the physical world.[61] As so often in the *Mishkāt*, the language is elusive. Any doubts about Ghazali's intent are, however, removed by the circumstance that another section of the book uses the term *fueled* as an equivalent of *emanated*.[62] The statement that the supernal lights are fueled from one another accordingly means that the intelligences and souls of the spheres emanate from one another, with an attendant loss of intensity at each successive stage. Similarly, when Ghazali compares the relation of the souls of the spheres to the incorporeal intelligences with the relation of the moon to the sun, he means that just as the moon has no light of its own but reflects the light of the sun, so the souls of the spheres exist solely by virtue of an emanation from the intelligences, again with an attendant loss of intensity.

What we have seen in the preceding paragraphs is that while Ghazali may or may not have understood God to be the emanating cause of what follows Him in existence, he clearly understands the incorporeal intelligences to emanate from one another and the souls of the spheres to emanate from the intelligences.

I could not find the *Mishkāt* addressing the manner in which the physical world receives existence. Ghazali does write that God alone is a being necessarily existent by reason of itself, that God created the spheres and intelligences, that everything outside of God is dependent on Him for its existence. He also writes that the "entire lower world" stands "under the dominion and luminance" of the supernal hierarchy and hence ultimately under the dominion and luminance of God.[63] The physical world thus ultimately depends on God for its existence and is governed, if not brought into existence, through the intermediacy of the intelligences and the souls of the spheres. In an oblique statement, the human "internal" eye, that is, the

[59]Pace Deladrière (n. 18 above) 110–11.

[60]*Mishkāt* 53; English translation 99; French translation 49. On the theme that successive phases of the emanation process are accompanied by a decrease in intensity, see A. Altmann and S. Stern, *Isaac Israeli* (Oxford 1958) 119, 127, 176.

[61]*Mishkāt* 91; English translation 171; French translation 93.

[62]See immediately below.

[63]*Mishkāt* 67; English translation 127; French translation 66.

human "intellect," is described as "from the supernal region"[64] which must mean that it is emanated from one of the higher beings.

"Earthly lights" are "fueled from . . . the celestial lights."[65] "Lights emanate [*tafīḍ*] from" the "lightlike substances . . . known as angels . . . upon human spirits."[66] The source "from which the earthly spirits are fueled" is "the supernal divine spirit," a spirit identical with an "angel" possessing, according to an Islamic tradition, "70,000 faces, each of them with 70,000 tongues."[67] While the first of the three statements may be saying that the human soul is emanated from the celestial region, the second can be seen on its face, and the third is seen from its context, to relate not to the source of the human soul but to the source of its illumination. Elsewhere in the *Mishkāt*, the expression human *spirit* designates the human soul or intellect,[68] or alternatively any of the faculties of the human soul.[69] The statements about human spirits' receiving an emanation from the supernal lights and being fueled by a divine spirit mean, then, that the human soul, or the human intellect, or the human cognitive faculties are illumined by an emanation from the incorporeal realm. More precisely, they are illumined by an emanation from a single "divine spirit" identical with the angel of 70,000 faces. Ibn Ṭufail was to take the angel of 70,000 faces as equivalent to the active intellect, and Ghazali can very plausibly be read in the same way. Even in his critique of Avicenna's philosophy, Ghazali does not reject the existence of the active intellect.[70]

The *Mishkāt* further states: The "word of God," which includes the "Koran" and its "verses," illuminates the human "intellect" and causes it to pass from "potentiality" to "actuality." The "Koran and the books . . . sent down . . . by God," illuminate man's "inner" eye, that is, man's "intellect," and are aptly

[64]Ibid. 49; English translation 93; French translation 46.

[65]Ibid. 53; English translation 99; French translation 49.

[66]Ibid. 67; English translation 126–27; French translation 66. Instances where Ghazali's works speak of God's *emanating* His grace, hence instances where the term *emanation* may have a nontechnical sense, are cited by Lazarus-Yafeh (n. 53 above) 311–12.

[67]Ibid. 52; English translation 98; French translation 49.

[68]Ibid. 43; English translation 83; French translation 40.

[69]Ibid. 76–77; English translation 143–45; French translation 75–76. The passage explains that four of five "degrees of light-like human spirits" are the "sense perceptive spirit," the "imaginative spirit," the "cogitative spirit," and the "intellectual spirit," that is to say, the sense perceptive faculty, imaginative faculty, cogitative faculty, and intellectual faculty. The fifth "spirit" is the "prophetic holy spirit." On p. 46, English translation 87, French translation 42–43, the *Mishkāt* lists five inner senses of the human soul, namely: "retentive imagination, estimation, cogitation, memory [*dhikr*], and conservative memory [*ḥifẓ*]." That list is close to Avicenna's list, but not identical; see above, p. 89, n. 66. It is also similar to, but not identical with, the list of inner senses given in Ghazali's summary of Avicenna's philosophy, the *Maqāṣid*; see *Maqāṣid* (n. 3 above) 284–85, and H. Wolfson, "The Internal Senses," reprinted in Wolfson's *Studies in the History of Philosophy and Religion* 1 (Cambridge, Mass. 1973) 285.

[70]See below, p. 151.

symbolized by the "sun," which enables the external human eye to see.[71] We have not suddenly been transported to the arena of simpleminded scriptualism, for, Ghazali adds, the Koran and other divine books are part of the "supernal world" (*malakūt*).[72] They are "substances" in the supernal "hierarchy."[73] The true divine books are, in other words, not written documents circulating in the physical world but members of the realm of incorporeal intelligences and souls of the spheres. What casts a light on the human potential intellect and leads it to actuality is the supernal being represented by the written Koran, not the document called the Koran. Should, as seems plausible, the Koran represent the active intellect and no other member of the world of incorporeal intellects, Ghazali has repeated the philosophic thesis that the transcendent active intellect sends forth an emanation which acts as light acts upon the eye and which thereby leads the human intellect from potentiality to actuality. Asharite dogmatics held that the Koran, being the word of God, is uncreated.[74] If Ghazali subscribed to the uncreatedness of the Koran when writing the *Mishkāt*, his locating the paradigmatic Koran in the realm of incorporeal intellects would be tantamount to again construing the incorporeal intelligences as coeternal with God.

The "peculiarly human substance" is the human "intellectual spirit," or intellectual faculty. "Through" the intellectual faculty, man obtains "universal, necessary items of knowledge," such as the proposition that "the same thing cannot be both eternal and generated"—in other words, the law of contradiction—and the proposition that what "is affirmed of a thing may be affirmed of its like"—a variation of the principle that things equal to the same thing are equal to each other. Plainly, the intellectual spirit, or faculty, is the human potentiality for thought. The intellectual faculty is followed, in Ghazali's account, by the "cogitative spirit," or faculty, which combines "items of pure intellectual knowledge, . . . draws conclusions from them," combines propositions thus derived, and "acquires a fresh conclusion."[75] That is to say, the cogitative spirit performs functions that Avicenna ascribed to the cogitative faculty of the soul: It takes hold of abstract concepts, employs them to frame syllogisms, deduces conclusions, and then repeats the

[71]*Mishkāt* 49; English translation 92–94; French translation 45–46. Passages in other works of Ghazali which compare the Koran to light or to the sun are recorded by Lazarus-Yafeh (n. 53 above) 291–92. On 293, Lazarus-Yafeh cites a passage where Ghazali compares the Koran to a medication for curing the eye; see above, pp. 93–94, for Avicenna's use of the analogy of an eye medication. On pp. 312–20, Lazarus-Yafeh gives examples of the mirror analogy in Ghazali. That analogy was also met in Avicenna, above, p. 94; but little can be inferred from its reappearance in Ghazali, since it was a commonplace.

[72]*Mishkāt* 49; English translation 94; French translation 46.

[73]Ibid. 70–71; English translation 133–34; French translation 69–70.

[74]H. Wolfson, *The Philosophy of the Kalam* (Cambridge, Mass. 1976) 239, 254, 256, 280–84.

[75]*Mishkāt* 77, taken together with 48; English translation 145–46 taken together with 91–92; French translation 76, taken together with 45.

process.[76] Since Ghazali has been seen to write that the human soul is illuminated by an emanation from the incorporeal region, the cogitative faculty presumably performs its functions thanks to that emanation. Ghazali does not repeat Avicenna's proposition that the soul receives intelligible thoughts directly *from* the emanation illuminating it.

Avicenna had given considerable attention to insight, the aptitude some men have for conjoining with the active intellect effortlessly and without recourse to cogitation, and he had applied to a high degree of insight the terms "holy intellect," "holy faculty [or power]," and "power [or faculty] of [a] holy soul." Should a man "burn" with insight to the extent that he receives broad scientific knowledge from the active intellect effortlessly, the man—Avicenna wrote—enjoys intellectual prophecy, which is the "highest of the powers of prophecy."[77] The Koranic verse using the imagery of a lamp characterized the oil in the lamp "as virtually glowing forth of itself, though no fire touched it." In Avicenna's exegesis of the verse, the oil that glows although virtually untouched by fire symbolizes the "holy faculty" possessed by the man of high "insight."[78] It symbolizes a high degree of the aptitude for effortless conjunction with the active intellect. And a superlative degree of insight constitutes intellectual prophecy.

Ghazali does not explicitly draw Avicenna's distinction between cogitation and insight (*ḥads*) or even use the latter term. He nevertheless makes a similar distinction, writing: The cogitative spirit, or faculty, is of two sorts, that which "requires instruction, prompting, and external aid," and that which is of sufficient "purity" to "prompt itself, as it were, without external aid." When the cogitative faculty reaches "complete purity," man possesses "the holy prophetic spirit attributed to the masters [*walī*]."[79] Another passage puts things a bit differently. It states that the "prophetic holy spirit," the property of "prophets as well as of some masters [*walī*]," operates where "the intellectual and cogitative spirit falls short." The prophetic spirit is "beyond intellect" and "above science."[80]

Thus one passage in the *Mishkāt* identifies the holy prophetic spirit as the pinnacle of a higher sort of cogitative faculty, of the cogitative faculty that can prompt itself without external aid, whereas another passage places the prophetic holy spirit beyond cogitation. What Ghazali mysteriously calls "tablets of the unseen" are "revealed" through the prophetic spirit. Also revealed is knowledge of the type that occupied Alfarabi and Avicenna, namely, the truth about "the next world," and "knowledge of the supernal region [that is, the incorporeal intelligences and the souls of the spheres], the heavens, the earth, and even . . . of the divine

[76]Above, pp. 96–98.

[77]Above, pp. 100–101, 117–18. Avicenna also applied the term *holy intellect* to acquired intellect, in the special sense of the culmination of human intellectual development; above, p. 103.

[78]*Ishārāt* 126. The Koranic verse is 24:35.

[79]*Mishkāt* 81; English translation 153; French translation 81.

[80]Ibid. 77–78; English translation 146–48; French translation 76–78.

nature."[81] Because of the prophetic spirit's ability to go beyond cogitation, or beyond ordinary cogitation, and to prompt itself, Ghazali finds "the prophetic holy spirit" to be symbolized by the oil that, in the Koranic imagery, glows although virtually untouched by fire.[82] Taken together, his statements are suggestive. His prophetic holy spirit, or faculty, goes beyond cogitation, or beyond ordinary cogitation, and prompts itself much as the aptitude of insight does in Avicenna—and in Avicenna a high degree of insight constitutes intellectual prophecy; at least some of the knowledge Avicenna's intellectual prophecy receives from the active intellect is revealed through Ghazali's prophetic spirit; and his prophetic holy spirit or faculty is symbolized by the very Koranic image symbolizing the holy faculty of insight in Avicenna's exegesis. What Ghazali calls holy prophetic spirit sounds suspiciously like a high degree of insight.

Ghazali in addition characterizes prophecy as a "direct experience" (*dhawq*; literally: taste).[83] If he indeed is following Avicenna and recognizes an intellectual prophecy that consists in the exercise of a high degree of insight, he has merely replaced the term *insight* with *prophetic holy spirit* and *direct experience*. Calling insight a direct or immediate experience is by no means inappropriate, for insight is the direct and immediate way of establishing conjunction with the active intellect. Readers of Ghazali who wish to put a more traditional face on the *Mishkāt* will have to interpret the book as intimating that prophecy does not result from a high degree of insight, as Avicenna supposed, but from something different yet strikingly similar, from "direct experience."

Direct experience comes up in another context. Ghazali writes that for certain select men, the "meaning" of the Koranic words "'everything perishes save his [God's] countenance' becomes . . . a direct experience [*dhawq*] and a state." Upon attaining that state, a man's being is overcome by "darkness," is "extinguished," "rendered as naught," and "annihilat[ed]." "All that remains is the One True Being," God.[84] Despite the *mysterium tremendum* with which the passage is freighted, Ghazali stresses that the state and experience he is speaking of do not consist in "becoming one" (*ittiḥād*) with God; rather they consist in "recognizing the unity" (*tawḥīd*) of God.[85] Direct experience is, accordingly, nothing ineffable or ecstatic. It is a heightened human realization that since God alone exists necessarily by virtue of Himself, everything else in the universe, including man, is as naught. If, as I have suggested, the expression *direct experience* is a veiled equivalent of insight, the passages quoted in this paragraph

[81]Ibid. 77; English translation 146; French translation 76.

[82]Ibid. 81; English translation 153; French translation 81.

[83]Ibid. 78; English translation 148; French translation 77–78.

[84]Ibid. 92, English translation 172–73; French translation 94–95. The verse, Koran 28:88, appeared above, p. 133.

[85]Ibid. 92, taken together with 58; English translation 173, taken together with 108 (imprecise); French translation 95, taken together with 55 (likewise not clear).

say that only the person of insight can fully comprehend the unity of God and the nothingness of everything outside of God.

Side by side with intellectual prophecy, Avicenna had recognized a form of prophecy through the human imaginative faculty and had shown how the two forms of prophecy can combine.[86] Ghazali too knows of prophecy through the human imaginative faculty and he likewise shows how it combines with intellectual prophecy. When the body is asleep, he writes, the "domination of the sense faculties" over the "divine inner light," or rational soul, is broken. As a consequence, the senses do not keep the soul "busy," "dragging it to the world of sensation" and "turning its face away from the world of hidden things and the supernal world." "Visions" (*mushāhada*)[87] therefore generally occur—undoubtedly through the imaginative faculty of the soul—when men are asleep. Exceptional souls, those that have become "prophetic lights," can, however, gain control over their sense faculties even in the waking condition, with the result that they are vouchsafed visions from the supernal regions when awake. And should a prophetic soul be "completely perfect, its perception is not limited to the visible form. Its perception goes beyond the visible form to the inner secret."

The vision of the perfect prophetic soul comes about as follows: The "notion" (*ma^cnā*) from the world of hidden things and the supernal world appears first in an "inner vision"; that is to say, the notion from above appears first to the prophet's inner eye, to the intellectual faculty of his soul. The notion may thereupon pass to the "imaginative [*khayālī*] spirit," to the imaginative faculty, where it takes on "a form . . . representing" the notion. In a word, the prophet's intellect receives a *notion*, a theoretical thought, from the supernal region and transmits the thought to the imaginative faculty, which recasts the thought in a figurative image. That is tantamount to Avicenna's thesis that imaginative prophecy frames figurative images of the theoretical truths learned through intellectual prophecy. "This kind of revelation in the waking state requires exegesis [*ta'wīl*], just as [a vision] during sleep requires interpretation [*ta^cbīr*]." [88] To recover the theoretical truths lying beneath the figurative images, one must have recourse to allegorical exegesis.

"The holy prophetic spirit" of the prophets, including Muhammad, initiates a new process of "emanation," a process in which various types of knowledge "emanate upon [other] creatures"[89]; the prophet instructs others. Since Ghazali has affirmed the efficacy of the method pursued by "men of science," and since a figurative depiction of theoretical truths can have no value for those who know the

[86]Above, p. 119.

[87]The term is difficult to pin down. In Ibn Ṭufail, below, p. 147, I translate it as "consciousness," and in Suhrawardī, below, p. 167, I translate it as "direct experience." The context of the present passage shows that Ghazali is speaking of a *vision*.

[88]*Mishkāt* 75–76; English translation 141–43 (imprecise); French translation 74–75. See above, p. 122.

[89]Ibid. 51–52, and cf. 60; English translation 97, and cf. 111; French translation 48, and cf. 56.

truth in the proper way, the purpose of the prophet's figurative depiction must be to aid the unenlightened.

To summarize, when Ghazali's *Mishkāt* is read against the background of Avicenna, an unexpected picture appears, but one that Averroes warned us was there. *Light*, according to Ghazali, is a synonym for both *intellect* and *existence*. God is the highest light, that is to say, the highest intellect and the highest existent being; He is light by reason of itself, that is to say, a being existent by virtue of itself; and He is the first fount or source of light, that is to say, the source of intellect and the source of existence. The supernal region comprises lights, or beings consisting in intellect, also called angels; and they move the celestial spheres either indirectly or directly. In other words, the supernal world comprises the incorporeal intelligences, known as angels in religious parlance, which move the spheres indirectly, and the rational souls of the spheres, likewise known as angels, which move the spheres directly. The mover of the outermost sphere is not God Himself, and comprehending that the First Cause transcends the incorporeal movers of the spheres is of paramount importance. God, in Ghazali's words, "created" the world; nevertheless, when describing the relation of God to the incorporeal intelligences and the souls of the spheres, Ghazali employs analogies from the emanationist repertoire. Two statements in the *Mishkāt* even suggest that the world is eternal.

The *Mishkāt* declares the number of intelligences and souls of the spheres to be unknown, either because Ghazali posits intelligences that are not movers of spheres or because he doubts that the precise number of spheres, primary as well as secondary, can be determined. The intelligences emanate from one another and form a hierarchy, and the souls of the spheres are emanated from the intelligences. Ghazali does not take up the manner in which the physical world comes into existence, except for writing that the human soul is "from" the supernal region. He does treat the manner in which man acquires knowledge. The human intellect is illuminated and brought to actuality by an emanation from the transcendent region and specifically from a single spirit, or angel, or prototypical divine Scripture, these all appearing to be locutions for the active intellect. Superior men possess the prophetic holy spirit, or faculty, which goes beyond cogitation, or beyond ordinary cogitation, and they thereby discover a range of truths of an intellectual character. Ghazali defines the prophetic holy spirit almost exactly as Avicenna defined the holy faculty of insight; and indeed in Avicenna, a high degree of insight brings man intellectual prophecy. Ghazali's prophetic holy spirit and also *direct experience*, an expression he uses to characterize the prophetic holy spirit, are therefore very likely just a high degree of insight. A lesser type of prophecy also is recognized by Ghazali, a type in which the imaginative faculty serves as the medium. Should the man in possession of the holy prophetic spirit be blessed as well with an inspired imaginative faculty, he can recast into figurative images the truths that his intellect receives from the supernal region.

The *Mishkāt*, in fine, incorporates the main lines of Avicenna's system, although on several sensitive particulars Ghazali still cloaks himself so tightly in ambiguity that what he believed can only be conjectured. The attribution of the *Mishkāt* to Ghazali is virtually certain.[90] Another work attributed to him, the authenticity of which is, by contrast, extremely doubtful, paraphrases and even copies verbatim the main points of Avicenna's theory of intellect,[91] without

[90]A doubt has, however, been raised about one section; see above, n. 53.

[91]*Ma*ᶜ*ārij al-Quds* (Cairo 1927): Each level in the hierarchy of existence is "emanated" from the one above it (205). God brought the "intelligence" into existence (203, together with 199). The "souls" that move the "heavens" around the earth stand below the intelligences (151, 199, 202). Arguments drawn from Aristotle and Avicenna for the existence of an incorporeal active intellect responsible for actual human thought (56, 135–36). Arguments drawn from Avicenna for the "substantiality" of the human soul (21–22, 25–32). Arguments drawn from Avicenna to show that the destruction of the human soul is not entailed by the destruction of the body (128–31), and that the human soul is intrinsically indestructible (131–32; cf. above, pp. 106–8). Five internal senses as in Avicenna's *Shifā'* (46–47; cf above, pp. 88–89). The soul can pass through three successive stages of human potentiality for thought, termed material intellect, intellect *in habitu*, and actual intellect; and the three stages parallel three stages in the human potentiality for writing (54–56, copied from Avicenna, *Shifā': De anima*, ed. F. Rahman [London 1959] 48–50; cf. above, p. 84). "Acquired intellect," or "holy intellect," is actual human thought that occurs when the human intellect "conjoins" with an "angel, called an intellect," that is, with the "active intellect," which "emanates intelligible thoughts" upon the human soul (56, 66, 136, largely copied from *Shifā': De anima* 50, 235–36; cf. above, p. 85). "Insight" (*ḥads*) is the aptitude for receiving intelligible thoughts, together "with their demonstrations," without "cogitation" (66); again, insight is the aptitude for receiving the "middle term" of a syllogism, together with the syllogism and its conclusion, "instantaneously or almost instantaneously" (162; cf. above, p. 99). The niche of lights passage (Koran 24:35) is interpreted as Avicenna had interpreted it (58–59; cf. Avicenna, *K. al-Ishārāt wal-Tanbīhāt* [n. 15 above] 126). There are three categories of prophecy: intellectual prophecy, a condition in which a man in possession of "the prophetic holy intellect" (67) "burns with insight regarding every subject, so that the form in the active intellect is imprinted in him instantaneously or almost so" (160–61, copied from *Shifā': De anima* 249; cf. above, p. 117); imaginative prophecy, a condition in which the human practical intellect, aided by the "compositive imagination," conjoins with the souls of the spheres and sees future events prefigured there (153–55; cf. above, pp. 121–22); the ability, possessed by some men, to effect changes in the physical world by the force of their will (164; cf. above, pp. 122–23). A soul that has developed intellectually becomes "united" eternally with the incorporeal region and has "the intelligible order of all existence . . . inscribed in it" (170–71); the soul reaches the threshold for eternal "eudaemonia" only when it controls a considerable body of knowledge (175, copied from Avicenna, *Shifā': Ilāhiyyāt* [n. 49 above] 429); souls that learned to recognize intellectual joy in this life, but failed to attain the minimum level of knowledge, suffer the eternal pain of unfulfilled intellectual desire (172); the "simpleminded" enter into "a kind of peace" in the next world (177, copying *Shifā': Ilāhiyyāt* 431); moral faults cause pain in the next world, but the pain eventually fades away (176–77). (For these last points, see above, pp. 110–12.)

The author or compiler of *Ma*ᶜ*ārij al-Quds* explains that he cites the philosophic, that is, Avicennan, account of the human soul, because "intellect and Scripture" are partners, the former constituting a "foundation," while the latter is a "building" erected on the foundation. Here and

mentioning the source from which it borrows. Additional works attributed to Ghazali, the authenticity of which has been questioned, contain material on the subject of intellect that agrees with what Ghazali writes in the *Mishkāt*.[92]

Turning to Ibn Bājja, we find that his published writings, like the *Mishkāt* and other compositions of Ghazali, do not present their author's positions straightforwardly. The reason, however, is quite different, for unlike Ghazali, Ibn Bājja exhibits no diffidence about disclosing his genuine beliefs. What obscures the positions he attempts to put forward is a barely penetrable literary style, and indeed, with admirable candor, Ibn Bājja himself characterizes one of his works as poorly organized and poorly reasoned.[93] He can nonetheless be descried, through the haze, expounding the nature of the human intellect and related topics as Alfarabi and Avicenna did. On some issues he plainly stands closer to Alfarabi than to Avicenna.

He maintains the following: The celestial spheres are animate rational beings that are governed by incorporeal intelligences[94]; the intelligences are the causes of the spheres' existence[95]; and the "active intellect," the agent effecting actual human

---

there the author does bow deferentially to Scripture or quotes a verse or two from the Koran, but his reasoning is completely philosophic.

D. Baneth (n. 17 above) 317, n. 5, and G. Vajda, "Le ma^c^ārij al-quds," *Israel Oriental Studies* 2 (1972) 470–73, noted the dependence of *Ma^c^ārij al-Quds* on Avicenna.

92*Mīzān al-^c^Amal*, French translation (n. 16 above) lists the inner senses of the soul in the spirit of Avicenna and other works of Ghazali (16–17; see Wolfson [n. 69 above] 284); illustrates the stages of intellect by the stages in a child's learning to write (20; see above, p. 84); defines prophecy as the highest level of human intellectual development, wherein "all essences, or most" are revealed without effort (20; see above, p. 117); affirms the legitimacy of the scientific, i.e., philosophic, method (34–35, 103); calls human intellect the highest of the human faculties and states that it stands to the "first" supernal intellect as light to the sun (97–98), thereby indicating that it is emanated from the first supernal intellect; lays down the rule that a wise man must hide his genuine beliefs (148). *Al-Maḍnūn bihi ^c^alā ghair Ahlihi* contains passages that appear to depend on Avicenna's *al-Risāla al-Aḍḥawiyya*; cf. J. Michot, "Avicenne et le Kitāb al-Madnūn d'Al-Ghazālī," *Bulletin de philosophie médiévale* 18 (1976) 52–55. On the question of the authenticity of the works referred to in this note, see Watt (nn. 20 and 53 above) and Lazarus-Yafeh (n. 53 above). Statements in Ghazali's comprehensive religious work, the *Iḥyā'*, are compatible with what I have pointed out in the *Mishkāt*; see quotations in A. Wensink, *La pensée de Ghazzālī* (Paris 1940) 146–52. But the *Iḥyā'* is intended for a less sophisticated readership and, as far as I could see from a cursory examination, does not have the *Mishkāt*'s theoretical underpinning.

93Ibn Bājja, *Ittiṣāl al-^c^Aql bil-Insān*, ed. and Spanish trans. M. Asín Palacios, as "Tratado de Avempace sobre la unión del intelecto con el hombre," *Al-Andalus* 7 (1942), Arabic section 22; Spanish translation 46–47.

94Ibn Bājja, *Tadbīr al-Mutawaḥḥid*, ed. and Spanish trans. M. Asín Palacios, as *El régimen del solitario* (Madrid 1946), Arabic text 84–85; Spanish translation 123. More explicit in fragments (of questionable genuineness) published by M. Ma^c^ṣūmī as "Ibn Bājjah on the Human Intellect," *Islamic Studies* 4 (1965) 128, 132.

95*Tadbīr al-Mutawaḥḥid*, Arabic text 85; Spanish translation 123.

thought, is an incorporeal being transcending man[96]—although the published texts do not explicitly identify it as the last in the chain of incorporeal intelligences. Besides serving as the agent that effects actual human thought, the active intellect is the cause of the existence of the four sublunar elements[97] and of "souls."[98] The human "potential intellect" or "rational faculty" is a disposition in the human soul[99]—not, as Avicenna held, a substance; actual human thought comes about when the active intellect illuminates images in the human imaginative faculty, which are then perceived by the human intellect[100]—with no mention of an emanation of thoughts directly from the active intellect; human intellectual development culminates in the stage of "acquired intellect,"[101] and acquired intellect is the only immortal aspect of man.[102] At the stage of acquired intellect, the human intellect "conjoins" with the active intellect[103]; in fact all human acquired intellects, for example, those of "Hermes and Aristotle," unite with one another and with the active intellect[104]; and the condition of conjunction and union with the active

[96]*Al-Wuqūf ʿalā al-ʿAql al-Faʿʿāl*, in Ibn Bājja, *Opera metaphysica*, ed. M. Fakhry (Beirut 1968) 107, 109. French translation: T. Druart, "Le traité d'Avempace . . . ," ***Bulletin de philosophie médiévale*** 22 (1980) 75, 77.

[97]Ibid. 107; French translation 75–76.

[98]Ibn Bājja's interpretation of Aristotle, *De generatione animalium* 2.3.736b, 16ff., quoted by Averroes, Commentary on *De animalibus*, Oxford, Bodleian Library, Hebrew MS Opp. 683 (=Neubauer 1370) 155a–b. Averroes quotes Ibn Bājja to the same effect in his Middle Commentary on the *Metaphysics*, Casanatense, Hebrew MS 3083, 109 (108)b. See below, p. 234.

[99]*Ittiṣāl al-ʿAql bil-Insān* (n. 93 above), Arabic text 13; Spanish translation 31; Averroes' report of Ibn Bājja's position on the nature of the material intellect, below, pp. 269, 286.

[100]*Ittiṣāl al-ʿAql bil-Insān*, Arabic text 19; Spanish translation 40. Ibn Bājja, *Risālat al-Wadāʿ*, ed. and Spanish trans. M. Asín Palacios, as "La Carta de Adíos," *Al-Andalus* 8 (1943), Arabic text 35; Spanish translation 79. A. Altmann, "Ibn Bājja on Man's Ultimate Felicity," reprinted in his *Studies in Religious Philosophy and Mysticism* (Ithaca 1969) 85. See above, p. 50.

[101]*Risālat al-Wadāʿ*, Arabic text 38; Spanish translation 84. Maʿṣūmī (n. 94 above) 128, 132. The English translation of Maʿṣūmī 132, lines 29–31, should read: "The superior [sublunar] nature that has a disposition for receiving human perfection has [at the start] a disposition for receiving the human intellect, and then [a disposition] for receiving a divine intellect, that is to say, an intellect acquired from God. . . ." Altmann 93.

[102]Ibn Bājja, *Qawl yatlū Risālat al-Wadāʿ*, in *Opera metaphysica* (n. 96 above) 152. *Ittiṣāl al-ʿAql bil-Insān*, Arabic section 21; Spanish section 45. Altmann 86.

[103]*Ittiṣāl al-ʿAql bil-Insān*, Arabic text 17; Spanish translation 37. *Tadbīr al-Mutawaḥḥid*, Arabic text 61–62; Spanish translation 100–101. Altmann 82–83. On p. 105, Altmann writes that one passage in Ibn Bājja suggests a different view of conjunction, but I have not been able to trace the passage.

[104]*Ittiṣāl al-ʿAql bil-Insān*, Arabic text 15–18, 20–21; Spanish translation 33–38, 43–45. Altmann 77. Ibn Bājja considers the successive levels of intellectual abstraction which can be attained by the human intellect. "The masses" (*al-jumhūr*), he writes, have as an object of their thought "universals" that are closely tied to images in the imaginative faculty. "The student of physical science" performs an additional act of abstraction upon those universals. The student of

intellect constitutes "ultimate human eudaemonia."[105] Man can, with the aid of the active intellect also foresee the future.[106]

Avicenna had, in an experimental mood, garbed segments of his system in brief allegorical tales, and among them is an allegory entitled *Ḥayy ibn Yaqẓān*. *Ḥayy ibn Yaqẓān* means "the Living One, son of the Wakeful One"; the Living One is the active intellect, and it is a son—an emanation—of the ever-wakeful First Cause. In the allegory, the active intellect, personified as an elderly sage, instructs the narrator, who represents the human rational soul, about the nature of the universe.[107] Another, very short piece attributed to Avicenna, the point of which is unclear, is called the *Tale of Salāmān and Absāl*; the title is borrowed from an older story of the same name which apparently came into Arabic from the Greek.[108] Ibn Ṭufail took up Avicenna's allegorical experiment and expanded upon it, composing an extended philosophical novel, which he too entitled *Ḥayy ibn Yaqẓān*. Ḥayy, the hero of Ibn Ṭufail's novel, is no longer an incorporeal intelligence; he is human. The only two other human characters delineated in the novel are named Salāmān and Absāl. Despite the obvious borrowing of the names, the plot of Ibn Ṭufail's novel has nothing in common with Avicenna's tales or with the older *Tale of Salāmān and Absāl.*

Ibn Ṭufail's hero grows from infancy to maturity on a desert island with no human companionship whatsoever. Absāl, the first man he meets, does not arrive on the island until after Ḥayy is fifty years old. Although lacking even a human language in which to formulate his reasoning and express conclusions, the hero is clever enough to discover the existence of the celestial spheres and of a "necessarily

---

metaphysics goes further, performs an act of abstraction upon the concepts proper to physical science, and rises to a level where he thinks thoughts not insofar as they refer to objects in the physical world but—in Ibn Bājja's mystifying words—"insofar as they are themselves existent beings in the universe." And still higher levels of abstraction are possible. If the series of successive abstractions never came to an end, it would run "to infinity—whereas an infinite of such a sort does not exist." The successive abstractions must consequently terminate in "a concept that has no further concept," in a single "first intelligible thought" common to all men. Since all human intellects fortunate enough to reach that level have the same thought, and since intellect is identical with the thought it thinks, all human intellects at the ultimate level become "one in number, with no distinction whatsoever between them." They are, through their thought, "conjoined . . . with the final intelligence [the active intellect]," and the condition thereby gained is "the ultimate eudaemonia." There is an echo here of Plato, *Parmenides* 132A–B. Also see above, p. 56, where Alfarabi writes that all souls in the state of eudaemonia join together.

[105]*Ittiṣāl al-ᶜAql bil-Insān*, Arabic section 17; Spanish section 38.

[106]*Tadbīr al-Mutawaḥḥid*, Arabic section 23–24; Spanish section 54–55. See below, p. 341.

[107]Avicenna, *Traités mystiques*, ed. A. Mehren 1 (Leiden 1889). English translation: Corbin (n. 1 above) 137–50. A detailed exegesis of the composition, with particular attention to the philosophic allusions, is given by A.-M. Goichon, *Le récit de Ḥayy ibn Yaqẓān* (Paris 1959).

[108]Corbin 204, 209–16 (the earlier *Tale*), 224–26 (the *Tale* attributed to Avicenna). A *Tale of Salāmān and Absāl* is also referred to in Avicenna's *Ishārāt*; see above, p. 106, n. 125.

existent" incorporeal cause beyond them, from which everything else "proceeds" (*ṣādir*) and "emanates" (*fā'iḍ*).[109] The hero further infers that each celestial sphere both has a "soul" and is governed by an "incorporeal substance." The incorporeal substance governing the outermost sphere emanates from the First Cause of the universe; the one governing the next sphere emanates from the first emanated incorporeal substance; and the process continues until the "incorporeal substance" governing the sublunar world is reached. This last substance is identical with the being that, according to a tradition also cited in Ghazali's *Mishkāt*,[110] has "70,000 faces, each of them with 70,000 mouths, each of them in turn with 70,000 tongues."[111] Ibn Ṭufail submits that the question whether the universe has existed forever or had a beginning cannot be decided,[112] although in the passage to be quoted immediately below, he allows himself to speak of an "eternal" emanation from God.

Within the sublunar world, he writes, every rank of animated being—"the species of plants, . . . the species of animals, . . . and . . . man"—makes its appearance when a portion of sublunar matter is so blended that it possesses a "disposition" appropriate for the given form or soul, whereupon the "spirit . . . from God," which is an "eternal emanating [source]," supplies the form or soul.[113] A more precise statement locates human souls, and presumably the forms of plants and the souls of animals as well, within the incorporeal substance that governs the sublunar region.[114] Plant forms and animal souls are, in a word, emanated from the active intellect.

The human soul is an "incorporeal . . . substance," not "a power [or: faculty] in a body nor in any sense dependent on bodies." Once it comes into existence, it is therefore immune to destruction.[115] Human souls whose "consciousness" (*mushāhada*)[116] is in "conjunction . . . with the necessarily existent being" will enjoy eternal pleasure after the death of their bodies. Souls that recognized the First Cause and acquired a "desire" for knowledge of the First Cause, but then "turned away," will be torn in two directions after the death of the body and suffer "punishment" and "pain" in the afterlife. If the desire they acquired for knowledge

[109]Ibn Ṭufail, *Ḥayy ben Yaqdhān* (nn. 18 and 53 above), Arabic text 80, 86, 94–95; French translation 60–61, 65, 70–71.

[110]Above, p. 137.

[111]*Ḥayy ben Yaqdhān* 127–29; cf. 99; French translation 92–94; cf. 73. The phrases "la sphère elle-même" and "[la seconde sphère] elle-même" in the French translation, pp. 92–93, should be corrected to "the soul of the sphere" and "the soul of the second sphere." The English translation (n. 53 above) has to be corrected similarly.

[112]Ibid. 81–82; French translation 61–63.

[113]Ibid. 28–29; French translation 25. The passage belongs to the introduction of the book, before Ibn Ṭufail brings his hero on the scene.

[114]Ibid. 130; French translation 94.

[115]Ibid. 92; French translation 69. Cf. Avicenna's wording, above, p. 83.

[116]This is the term that simply means vision in Ghazali's *Mishkāt*, above, p. 141, and that I translate as "direct experience" when it is used by Suhrawardī, below, p. 169.

of the First Cause is strong enough, their pain in the afterlife will eventually fade away and they will gain full consciousness of the object of their desire, while if they are more strongly inclined in the opposite direction, the pain will endure forever. Souls that never "recognized" or "conjoined with . . . the necessarily existent being" will spend an eternal afterlife devoid of both pain and pleasure.[117] "Prophets" recast scientific truths such as the foregoing in "figures," which have the purpose of providing the ordinary run of mankind with "imaginative [versions]" of abstract truth.[118]

What has been quoted thus far is, transparently, another outline of Avicenna's system, with the apparent innovation that the human soul can, and should, conjoin with the First Cause rather than with the active intellect.

Ibn Ṭufail informs us that shortly before writing his philosophic novel, he personally attained a heightened "level" or "state" of understanding and enjoyed "direct experience" (*dhawq*).[119] The heightened state, as he describes it, had affinities both with the experiences of the Sufi mystics and with the "oriental philosophy" that, Avicenna had hinted, supersedes the philosophy of Aristotle.[120] It elevated Ibn Ṭufail above Ibn Bājja's "cogitative investigation" (*baḥth fikrī*) of nature, as well as above the "philosophy" of "Aristotle, . . . Alfarabi, and . . . [Avicenna's] *Shifā'*." "Nothing," nevertheless, "is revealed through it which diverges from what was revealed" by Ibn Bājja's discursive method. Direct experience "differs from the other [discursive method] only in increased clarity."[121]

At an appropriate juncture in the novel, Ibn Ṭufail's hero likewise attains heightened understanding. Through it, he discovers that the incorporeal substances governing the celestial spheres are reflections of the First Cause's existence, analogous to the "form of the sun appearing in a polished mirror." The incorporeal substances are consequently neither "identical" with nor "other" than the First Cause.[122] The hero of the story further sees that the human soul, like the incorporeal intelligences, is neither identical with nor other than God.[123] To characterize something as neither identical with nor other than another thing violates

[117]Ibid. 95–96; French translation 71. Cf. 130–31; French translation 94–95.

[118]Ibid. 136, 146; French translation 100, 108.

[119]Ibid. 4–5, 7; French translation 2–4, 6. The term rendered as "ecstasy" in the English translation simply means "state," as it is rendered in the French translation and in other passages of the English translation.

[120]Ibid. 3–4; French translation 1–2. The French translation, looking ahead to Suhrawardī's "illuminationist philosophy," translates "oriental philosophy" as "philosophie illuminative." Regarding Avicenna's "oriental philosophy," see above, p. 74, n. 1.

[121]Ibid. 5, 11–12; French translation 4, 10. A similar distinction between *investigative science* (*ḥikma baḥthiyya*) and *direct-experience science* (*ḥikma dhawqiyya*) is drawn in a minor work attributed to Avicenna; see D. Gutas, *Avicenna and the Aristotelian Tradition* (Leiden 1988) 77–78. The work in question cannot easily be matched with any of the items in the early lists of Avicenna's writings, and there also are internal reasons for doubting its authenticity.

[122]Ibid. 127; French translation 92.

[123]Ibid. 124; French translation 89.

the law of the excluded middle, the rule that any given thing must be either x or not x, and with palpable satisfaction, Ibn Ṭufail concedes that the revelations of direct experience may prove troublesome to the "bat-minded," who heed only the "rules of intellect."[124]

One additional piece of information about the state of heightened understanding is furnished. That state, Ibn Ṭufail writes, is "unadulterated consciousness [*mushāhada*] and a complete absorption" in God, wherein the "substance" of a man's "soul vanishes, is annihilated, and becomes as naught."[125] The language here is very similar to language used by Ghazali, to whom Ibn Ṭufail moreover acknowledges a debt.[126] I interpreted Ghazali as intimating that the soul's highest experience consists in grasping the nothingness of everything in comparison with the being that is necessarily existent by reason of itself. Ibn Ṭufail is plainly trying to say more, to adumbrate a type of experience further removed from ordinary intellectual knowledge than was direct experience in Ghazali's *Mishkāt*. But like all who try to express the inexpressible, he does not articulate his meaning clearly.

Averroes will be discussed fully in the last three chapters of the present book. His early works will be found to endorse a theory of emanation in the tradition of Alfarabi and Avicenna, and to portray the active intellect's role in the sublunar world much as Alfarabi's *Risāla fī al-ᶜAql* did. Later works of Averroes repudiated his early positions. Throughout his career, he nonetheless explained the manner in which the active intellect leads the human intellect to actuality as Alfarabi had. And throughout his career, he was attracted to subjects connected with the human intellect which were brought to the fore by Alfarabi and Avicenna—the conjunction of the human intellect with the active intellect, immortality of the human intellect, and prophecy through the emanation of the active intellect.

[124]Ibid. 125; French translation 90.

[125]Ibid. 108; French translation 79.

[126]Above, p. 140. In *Ḥayy ben Yaqdhān* 18, French translation 16, Ibn Ṭufail acknowledges his debt to both Avicenna and Ghazali, but adds that books of Ghazali's which "are held back" (*al-maḍnūn bihā*, perhaps an allusion to one of several works with a similar name which are attributed to Ghazali; see above, n. 92), i.e., which are esoteric, had not reached him. He refers to Ghazali's *Mishkāt* in the same context, and although he does not explicitly say that he had read the *Mishkāt*, several passages in *Ḥayy ben Yaqdhān* indicate familiarity with it. Thus, on 4, French translation 2–3, he quotes three Sufi sayings to exemplify the danger of Sufis' being led too far in the direction of pantheism. Exactly the same three sayings were quoted by Ghazali in the *Mishkāt* to exemplify the same danger; see *Mishkāt* (n. 18 above) 57; English translation 106; French translation 54. On 129, French translation 94, Ibn Ṭufail cites the tradition about the angel with 70,000 faces. He understands the angel to be the active intellect, and such apparently had been Ghazali's understanding. And, as we have seen, Ibn Ṭufail, like the *Mishkāt*, further speaks of an "annihilation" of the soul and its becoming "as naught," of a "state [*ḥāl*] of the soul," and of "direct experience" (*dhawq*). But those were common Sufi terms.

The foregoing are thinkers who borrowed from Alfarabi and Avicenna, more especially from the latter. The most penetrating critique of the systems of Alfarabi and Avicenna, again more especially of the latter, was drawn up by Ghazali, the same man who wrote a comprehensive summary of Avicenna's philosophy and whose *Mishkāt al-Anwār* conceals an outline of Avicenna's system. Ghazali entitled his critique *Tahāfut al-Falāsifa* (*Destructio philosophorum*) and published it as a counterpart to his summary, the *Maqāṣid al-Falāsifa*. The critique is concerned primarily with the "metaphysical [*ilāhiyya*] sciences."[127] Consequently, of the positions of Avicenna analyzed in the previous chapter, the one attracting the largest share of Ghazali's attention is the emanation of the universe from the First Cause.

Avicenna's emanation scheme offered itself as a way to harmonize two seemingly incompatible theses, the ultimate dependence of the composite universe on a wholly unitary First Cause, and the principle that, as Ghazali phrases it, "from the one, only one proceeds [*yaṣdur*]."[128] Avicenna accomplished the harmonization by uncovering three distinct aspects in the thought of the incorporeal intelligence emanated by the First Cause and three similar aspects in each successive intelligence. The aspects are the intelligence's thought of the First Cause, its thought of itself as a being necessarily existent by virtue of the First Cause, and its thought of itself as a being possibly existent by virtue of itself; one of the aspects gives rise to the next intelligence in the hierarchy, while the other two give rise to the soul and body of the sphere governed by the intelligence. Ghazali's critique names the aspects, or, to be more precise, misnames them, in a fashion that facilitates refutation.

The refutation goes as follows: (1) If the first emanated intelligence contains distinguishable aspects because its unqualified "existence" is different from its "possible existence," then the First Cause should contain analogous aspects; for its "existence" must be different from its "necessary existence." The First Cause should therefore itself suffice as the immediate source of plurality in the universe. (2) Further, if the "intelligible thought" that the first intelligence has of its cause is different from both its own "existence" and its intelligible thought of itself, with the consequence that the first intelligence contains no less than three aspects, then the intelligible thought that the First Cause has of its effect should also be different from its own existence and from its intelligible thought of itself. The First Cause should accordingly itself contain no less than three aspects and immediately be able to emanate an intelligence, the body of a sphere, and the soul of the sphere. (3) On Avicenna's premises, the first intelligence would in fact have more than the three aspects required to explain the emanation of the next intelligence in the series, of the

[127]Ghazali, *Tahāfut al-Falāsifa* (n. 38 above) 16, §22. English translation in Van den Bergh (n. 16 above) 309.

[128]Ibid. 3, §29; English translation 104. See above, p. 75, for Avicenna's formulation of the principle. As far as I could find, Alfarabi does not employ it.

body of the celestial sphere governed by the first intelligence, and of the soul of the sphere. For the "essence" of the first intelligence, its "intelligible thought of itself," its "intelligible thought of its cause," its being "possibly existent by virtue of itself," and its being "necessarily existent by virtue of another," must, on Avicenna's premises, all be different from one another. The first intelligence should therefore contain not three but five different aspects. (4) The three aspects distinguishable in each intelligence could not—arguing now from the opposite direction—account for everything that is supposed to emanate from the intelligence. The body of the outermost celestial sphere could not be emanated by a single aspect in the first intelligence, since the body of the sphere has several "particular" characteristics, namely: matter; form; a precise size, which, Ghazali's refutation assumes in a Kalam vein, is a distinct characteristic; the differentiation of certain points on the surface as poles, which is still another distinct characteristic. And a single aspect in the second intelligence surely could not emanate the second sphere, the sphere of the fixed stars. For imbedded in the second sphere are "one thousand and twenty odd stars, varying in magnitude, shape, position [on the sphere], color, effects, and unpropitiousness or propitiousness." (5) To say that an intelligence's "being . . . possibly existent" gives rise to the existence of the body of a sphere, its "thought of itself" gives rise to the existence of the soul of the sphere, and its "thought of the First [Cause]" gives rise to the existence of another intelligence, is as ludicrous as saying that a certain "unknown man's . . . being possibly existent" gives rise to the existence of a celestial sphere, and his "having an intelligible thought of himself and of his Maker" gives rise to "two more things." Avicenna's attempt to explain the emanation of the composite universe from a unitary First Cause is, in a word, sheer "nonsense."[129]

Ghazali has no quarrel with the last stage of Avicenna's account of the emanation process, the phase wherein natural forms as well as "accidents and [other] generated things" appearing in the sublunar region are "emanated from the giver of forms, which is an angel, or angels." He merely insists on God's ability to intervene and redirect the customary course of nature.[130] Ghazali does refute the proposition that the souls of the celestial spheres know all particular events before the events occur; and that predictions of the future by prophets in the waking state, as well as by others in true dreams, result from "conjunction" with the souls of the spheres and "viewing" what is foreknown there.[131] Avicenna had stated that events occurring, and to occur, in the sublunar region are known in a "universal mode" by the First Cause and incorporeal intelligences, whereas they are known in a "particular mode" by the souls of the spheres; and he had intimated that the souls

[129]Ibid. 3, §§42, 45, 53, 54–59, 65, 67, 70; English translation 117, 121, 141, 142–44, 149, 150, 152. For the three aspects in the incorporeal intelligence as Avicenna distinguished them, see above, n. 6.

[130]Ibid. 17, §§5, 7, 15–17; English translation 316–17, 326–27.

[131]Ibid. 16, preface and §§6–9; English translation 300, 302–3.

of the spheres are therefore the source of human knowledge of the future. Obviously with Avicenna's words in mind, Ghazali now contends: Each sphere performs a single continuous and unchanging motion, and therefore its soul need not possess particular, as distinct from universal, knowledge of the causes of sublunar events. Still more pertinently, the "created soul" of a sphere could not possibly encompass "infinite particular . . . items of knowledge," since an infinite number cannot be circumscribed. The theory that the human soul learns of future events from the souls of the spheres is, in sum, a "possibility, as long as one does not assume that the items of knowledge [in the celestial souls] are infinite"; but the correctness of the theory remains "unknown" to human reason. Only the adherents of Scripture are free of difficulties, for they have been informed reliably by Scripture that God himself reveals the future to the prophet.[132]

Ghazali also rejects Avicenna's arguments on two other issues.

He refutes the demonstration of the thesis that the human soul is an incorporeal substance, without however objecting to the thesis itself. Avicenna's primary argument had been that intelligible thoughts, being indivisible, can be present only in an indivisible substratum; and since they are present in the human soul, the soul must be an indivisible, and hence incorporeal, substance.[133] Ghazali responds by pointing out that indivisible percepts are present in the estimative faculty of the souls of lower animals. Sheep, for example, perceive the "enmity of the wolf," and the percept *enmity* is indivisible. Yet the sheep's estimative faculty is indisputably a "corporeal faculty." Hence it follows that indivisible percepts can after all be present in a corporeal faculty of the soul.[134]

Ghazali thereupon refutes Avicenna's arguments for the immortality of the human soul. Avicenna's first argument was that since the soul is in no sense dependent on the body, the death of the body does not entail the death of the

[132]Ibid. 16, §§10, 13–15, 17–18; English translation 306–7, 308–9. The translation of §10 is inaccurate. Avicenna's position is discussed above, pp. 121-22.

[133]Above, p. 83. Ghazali, *Tahāfut* 18, §§12–62; English translation 337–55, spins out ten philosophic proofs for the incorporeality of the soul. The first two are versions of what I call the primary proof. Proofs five through eight repeat proofs given by Avicenna for the related proposition that the human rational faculty does not employ a corporeal organ; see *Shifā': De anima* (n. 91 above) 216–19; *Najāt* (Cairo 1938) 178–80; English translation: *Avicenna's Psychology*, trans. F. Rahman (London 1952) 50–53. Proof nine and its source in Avicenna are discussed by M. Marmura in "Ghazali and the Proof for the Immaterial Self," *A Straight Path* (Hyman Festschrift) (Washington 1988) 195–205. Ghazali's *Maqāṣid* (n. 3 above) 292–97, has ten arguments—three of which he calls "apodictic demonstrations, while the remaining seven are "convincing . . . indications"—that the soul does not employ a corporeal organ, and the ten are similar to, but not identical with, the ten arguments for the incorporeality of the soul listed in the *Tahāfut*.

[134]*Tahāfut* 18, §15; English translation 337–38 (inaccurate). This is the "second stage" of Ghazali's refutation. The "first stage" is the objection that the human soul might be an atom, and hence both indivisible and corporeal—an objection that Ghazali acknowledges will not carry weight for philosophers; see ibid. §§13, 26–27; English translation 337, 342.

soul.[135] Ghazali responds that since each soul is attached to a particular body, some factor plainly "particularizes out" a given soul for the body; "it is not farfetched" that the factor—whatever the factor should be—"is a condition for the continued existence" of the soul; therefore, when the nexus between body and soul is severed and the factor attaching the soul to the body is removed, the soul might very possibly perish. Moreover, even if the existence of human souls is not dependent on the existence of bodies, God or some other cause may be able to destroy human souls.[136] Avicenna's second and more general argument for immortality reasoned that objects actually existing yet subject to destruction contain two distinct characteristics, the actuality of continued existence and the possibility of being destroyed; two distinct factors in the object must be responsible for the two characteristics; but the soul, a noncomposite substance, cannot contain distinct factors, and consequently cannot have the possibility of being destroyed.[137] To that argument, Ghazali replies that the "possibility" of existing or of being destroyed is merely a "judgment of the intellect" and not something subsisting in the object. Noncomposite, incorporeal objects therefore might very well contain the possibility of being destroyed and might be subject to destruction.[138]

Ghazali, in short, refutes Avicenna's explanation of the manner in which the incorporeal realm emanates from the First Cause, his explanation of the manner in which prophets foresee the future, his proof of the incorporeality of the human soul, and his proof of immortality. Nevertheless, nothing said here contradicts what we found in *Mishkāt al-Anwār*, where Ghazali accepted virtually all of Avicenna's picture of the universe; for Ghazali is not rejecting the structure of the universe depicted by Avicenna or even the possibility that God produces everything outside himself through a series of emanations. He is merely rejecting Avicenna's explanation of the process. He certainly is not excluding the incorporeality and immortality of the human soul but only Avicenna's proofs.

We have examined Islamic philosophers following in the wake of Alfarabi and Avicenna as well as the most comprehensive refutation of Avicenna. Scraps from Avicenna are also found here and there in other Islamic writers,[139] and criticisms,

[135]Above, pp. 106–7. *Tahāfut* 19, §1; English translation (Averroes' paraphrase of Ghazali's discussion) 356–57.

[136]*Tahāfut* 19, §§8, 11–13.

[137]Above, p. 108.

[138]*Tahāfut* 19, §§19–20, taken together with *Tahāfut* 1, §87; English translation 60.

[139]A few examples, without pretense of exhaustiveness: *Ma^cārij al-Quds*, a text attributed to Ghazali; see above, n. 91. Ibn Sab^cīn, summarized by A. Mehren, "Correspondance du philosophe soufi Ibn Sab'in avec l'empereur Frédéric II," *Journal asiatique* 14 (1879) 359 (in Mehren's paraphrase: the active intellect, which "presides over the movement of the moon," emanates the "several species of intelligence"); 381–82 (an outline of the levels of human intellect which is a hybrid of the schemes of Alfarabi and Avicenna). Āmidī, *Ghāyat al-Marām* (Cairo 1971) 20 (reference to the "philosopher's position" that the "active intellect, which exists together with the

often in the tone of Ghazali's critique, are likewise to be found.[140] Much more noteworthy, however, is a line of thinkers which branches off from the line of Avicenna's adherents and which continues within Persian Islam up to the present century.

The branching off took place through Abū al-Barakāt (d. ca. 1160)—who may be classified loosely as an Islamic philosopher since he converted to Islam from Judaism late in life, apparently after writing his magnum opus—and through Suhrawardī (1155–1191). Abū al-Barakāt saw himself as an independent thinker who burst the bonds of those whom he calls "Aristotle" and the Aristotelian "school," although the doctrines that in fact concern him are all distinctive to Avicenna. With a touch of peevishness, Abū al-Barakāt complains of his adversaries that they "make statements as if [what they relate were] revealed truth, which cannot be challenged. . . . If only they would say: 'Matters may be thus or otherwise.' . . . Should their opinions come from a revelation, they ought to mention the fact."[141]

---

body of the sphere of the moon," brings "substantial forms and human souls" into existence when portions of sublunar matter are ready to receive them); 285–86 (the philosophers', that is, Avicenna's, proof of the immortality of the human soul); 288, 290–91 (the philosophers' theory of the afterlife, including the experiencing of the promises of religion through the imaginative faculty); 297 (the philosophers'—again Avicenna's—refutation of the transmigration of the soul, with Āmidī's response). Ījī, *Mawāqif* (Cairo 1907) 1.246; German translation and discussion: J. van Ess, *Die Erkenntnislehre des ᶜAḍuḍaddīn al-Īcī* (Wiesbaden 1966) 295 (the philosophers' theory that the transcendent being responsible for "generated things in our world" also "emanates" human intelligible thoughts).

Writers adopting a Neoplatonic cosmic scheme sometimes apply the term *active intellect* to the cosmic Intellect, which is emanated directly by the One. Examples: the redaction of the *Theology of Aristotle* known as the "Long Version," cited by P. Duhem, *Le système du monde* 4 (Paris 1916) 398; Ibn al-Sīd (Baṭlayūsī) *K. al-Ḥadā'iq*, ed. and Spanish trans. M. Asín Palacios, in *Al-Andalus* 5 (1940), Arabic text 77; Spanish translation 118; medieval Hebrew translation: Batlayusi, *ha-ᶜAgullot ha-Raᶜyoniyyot*, ed. D. Kaufmann (Budapest 1880) 27; Miskawayh, *Le petit livre du salut*, ed. S. Asima and trans. R. Arnaldez (n.p. 1987), Arabic text 82, 101; French translation 47, 61.

140Shahrastanī, summarized by W. Madelung, "Aspects of Ismāᶜīlī Theology," reprinted in Madelung, *Religious Schools and Sects in Medieval Islam* (London 1985) 61 (criticism of Avicenna's emanation theory). Fakhr al-Dīn al-Rāzī, *Muḥaṣṣal* (Cairo 1978) 201 (refutation of Avicenna's emanation theory, mainly in a Kalam spirit, but including an argument in the spirit of Ghazali's critique); 227–28 (refutation of Avicenna's arguments against the transmigration of the soul); 228–29 (refutation of Avicenna's proof of the immortality of the soul, with echoes of Ghazali's critique). Fakhr al-Dīn al-Rāzī, *K. al-Arbaᶜīn* (Hyderabad 1934) 267–70 (a recasting of Avicenna's argument showing the human soul to be an incorporeal substance, followed by a refutation of the argument). Āmidī, *Ghāyat al-Marām* (Cairo 1971) 42–43 (refutation, in the spirit of one of Ghazali's criticisms, of Avicenna's explanation of the emergence of plurality out of a wholly unitary First Cause); 294–96 (refutation, following Ghazali, of the philosophers', that is, Avicenna's, arguments for immortality). Ījī, *Mawāqif* 7.256–257 (critique of Avicenna's emanation theory in the spirit of Ghazali's critique).

141Abū al-Barakāt, *K. al-Muᶜtabar* (Hyderabad 1939) 3.158.

As often happens, the man is less independent than he would have us believe. Abū al-Barakāt lays out his main philosophic treatise on the model of Avicenna's treatises, and the structure of his universe likewise plainly derives from Avicenna. In effect, he accepts Avicenna's framework, then picks holes in it and proposes alternative possibilities. His argumentation also is obviously dependent on Avicenna's but is less rigorous, and one can hardly believe that philosophic considerations alone led him to the new alternatives. His rationale appears rather to have been that Avicenna had hypothesized the existence of various unobserved beings in the universe, and other, more numerous unobserved beings might be hypothesized instead. He is saying, as it were, to Avicenna: "There are more things in heaven . . . than are dreamt of in your philosophy." Considering that Avicenna's system was highly speculative, undermining it through speculative alternatives was fine poetic justice. Yet Avicenna's system, with all its exotic appurtenances, was designed as a rational explanation of natural phenomena, such as the movements of the heavenly bodies, the emergence of new objects in the physical world, and the development of individual human intelligence. A healthier move forward, from a scientific standpoint, would have been a more economical explanation of the same phenomena, an explanation reducing, rather than expanding, the number of speculative, unobservable entities.

Be that as it may, Abū al-Barakāt's universe consists of concentric spheres rotating around a stationary sublunar region. Incorporeal beings move the spheres; the First Cause transcends the movers of the spheres; and the universe is eternal.[142] The principle that "from one, insofar as it is one, only one can proceed [*yaṣdur*]" is accepted by Abū al-Barakāt as "true."[143] Once the principle is given, he faces the question how plurality in the universe might develop out of a wholly unitary First Cause. He records the theory according to which an incorporeal intelligence "proceeds" from the First Cause by virtue of the First Cause's having itself as an object of thought; the first intelligence's thought contains three aspects, its thought of its cause, its thought of itself as possibly existent by reason of itself, and its thought of itself as necessarily existent by reason of cause; from the three aspects there "proceed" a second "intelligence," the "body of the first sphere," and the "soul of the first sphere"; the process continues "until the last sphere, the sphere of the moon, is reached"; and the last in the series of incorporeal intelligences is the "active intellect," the "effect" of the "intelligence" governing the sphere of the moon.[144] But Abū al-Barakāt dismisses the theory.

He contends, in a possible echo of one of Ghazali's objections to Avicenna,[145] that the unitary First Cause itself could have brought forth the universe through a

[142]Ibid. 162, 167. P. 162, lines 17–18, states explicitly that beings emanating directly from God are eternal.

[143]Ibid. 156.

[144]Ibid. 151.

[145]Above, p. 150.

plurality of aspects in its own thought. The process may, Abū al-Barakāt proposes, have gone instead as follows: The First Cause brings "a first intelligence" into existence. By virtue of having the first intelligence as the object of its thought, a new aspect enters the First Cause's thought, all in an eternal mode, and from the new aspect "another being proceeds." The First Cause thereupon, and still in an eternal mode, has that second being as an object of its thought and, by virtue of the additional aspect of its thought, brings forth yet another being. And the reciprocal process continues until the ranks of existent beings are filled.[146]

In Avicenna, each celestial sphere has a soul, but Abū al-Barakāt protests that his adversaries have, "without grounds, neglected all the stars, [ascribing to them] neither intelligences nor souls." The stars embedded in the celestial spheres are, he contends, alive and radiate light. They therefore deserve having souls attributed to them no less than do the spheres themselves.[147]

Abū al-Barakāt further refuses to recognize a single active intellect as the cause of the existence of all souls in the sublunar world. He contends first that a single cause would not suffice even for the existence of human souls, not to speak of the souls of other creatures, and secondly that the causes of the existence of human souls must be sought not among the incorporeal intelligences but in another echelon of the hierarchy of existence.

From the differing "conditions and actions" observable in divers human souls, he infers that human souls differ from one another in their "substances" and "quiddities." The differences in the substances and quiddities of souls then show him that either "every human soul has its individual [supernal] cause" or, as is "more likely," each "class" of human souls has "a single cause from which they [the members of the class] proceed."[148] Human souls thus receive their existence from a plurality of causes.

As to what the multiple causes are, Abū al-Barakāt contends that "bodies" could not produce the different classes of human soul, since bodies "insofar as they are bodies" are not "the efficient causes of anything." The causes cannot be "accidents," which exist through bodies; "for a cause must be of a more perfect existence than its effect," and hence anything "having its existence through a body . . . cannot be the cause producing an incorporeal substance." Avicenna too had ruled out the possibility of human souls' having bodies or accidents in bodies as the cause of their existence, but he had gone on to contend that the souls of the spheres as well cannot be the cause of the existence of the human soul and that only an incorporeal intelligence, and specifically the active intellect, can be the cause.[149] Abū al-Barakāt's radical and original departure consists in reversing the weight Avicenna placed on arguments that rule out the souls of the spheres, and that

[146]*K. al-Mu^c^tabar* 3.156, 159.
[147]Ibid. 157, 167.
[148]Ibid. 152–53.
[149]Above, pp. 80–81.

establish an incorporeal intelligence, as the cause of the existence of human souls. The immediate cause of the existence of human souls cannot, in Abū al-Barakāt's judgment, be "the holy substances that have no link with bodies," in other words, the incorporeal intelligences, including the substance "called the active intellect." For in every instance, "an effect is similar to its cause, and everything belonging essentially to the effect comes from the cause." Incorporeal intelligences, which do not operate through bodies, are too dissimilar from human souls, which do operate through bodies, for the intelligences to be taken as the immediate cause of the existence of human souls. The cause of each class of human soul must accordingly be one of the "celestial souls," that is, a soul of a celestial sphere or the soul of a star imbedded in one of the spheres.[150] A considerable number of celestial souls is involved, one "superior" to and "more noble" than another, and each responsible for the existence of a corresponding class of souls in the human hierarchy.[151]

The number of "spiritual angels" has now grown well beyond the figure that Avicenna contemplated. The roster includes: the incorporeal intelligences, whose precise contribution to the movement of the celestial spheres is left unexplained; the souls of the "spheres we know and those we do not know"; and the souls of the "visible and nonvisible stars." As just seen, the causes of human souls are found among the souls of the spheres and the souls of the stars. Abū al-Barakāt remarks that the "angel[s]" serving as "cause" and "preserver" of the "other animal souls, the plant souls, and the mineral powers," are "probably" distinct from the celestial souls taken into consideration thus far and therefore they too have to be added to the roster of translunar spiritual beings.[152]

Abū al-Barakāt has been seen to employ the proposition that the human soul is an incorporeal substance. In Avicenna, the proposition rested on the consideration that indivisible incorporeal thoughts are present in the human soul and anything in which something indivisible is present is equally indivisible.[153] Abū al-Barakāt likewise points to a kind of knowledge that cannot be present in a body yet is in the human soul. But as another expression of his independence and originality, he seeks out a different kind of knowledge that, while incapable of being present in the body, is present in man's soul; and he hits upon knowledge of a wholly unexpected sort. He reasons: If a certain thing is present in another and the second in a third, then the first is also present in the third. Hence, if the human soul resided in the body, anything in the soul would likewise be "in" the body; any percept in the human soul would be present in the body as well. Now, a large physical object cannot be contained within a smaller physical object, and by the same token the percept of a large physical object cannot be contained within a smaller physical object. The human soul does, however, receive percepts of enormous objects,

[150]*K. al-Mu^c tabar* 2.388–391.
[151]Ibid. 3.213.
[152]Ibid. 167, 216.
[153]Above, p. 83.

such as "the heavens." Since those percepts cannot be present in a man's body, man's soul too does not exist in the body. Abū al-Barakāt goes on to argue that the human soul does not exist within a spirit that envelops the human body. He concludes, as Avicenna did, that the human soul is "an incorporeal substance," with the healthy proviso that the soul does "act through the body."[154]

The dominant philosophic school, Abū al-Barakāt reports, construed the transcendent active intellect as the "teacher of mankind," that is, as the cause of actual human intelligible thought. Just as the "light of the sun renders potentially visible things actually visible" and makes "the potential [faculty of] vision actually see," so too—in his account of the dominant theory—"a power emanates from the active intellect on images [present within the soul] which are potentially intelligible, rendering them actually intelligible" and the same power thereby "renders the potential intellect an actual intellect." Abū al-Barakāt's report adds a hint of Avicenna's thesis that intelligible thoughts themselves come from the active intellect, rather than being abstracted from images: The philosophers, he writes, compared the active intellect not merely to the sun and a "lamp" but also to a "mirror" in which things "can be seen."[155] The suggestion is that, for the philosophers, the human soul in some sense sees intelligible thoughts in the active intellect.

In Abū al-Barakāt's judgment, the active intellect's role as a cause of actual human thought is only a "supposition and intuition [*ḥads*]." It rests on an often cited Aristotelian principle,[156] which, in our author's formulation, affirms: When "actuality" follows "upon potentiality," the new actuality must come from an agent that already is an "actuality" free "of potentiality." Abū al-Barakāt casts doubt on the principle by adducing an instance where it does not—or apparently does not—apply: A seed "becomes an actual tree by itself" and without the participation of "another [actual] tree." "By the same token the soul may perhaps pass to its perfection by itself, without there being . . . anything with the actual characteristic in question, which leads it to actuality." After the dialectical dust settles, Abū al-Barakāt reveals, however, that he holds fast to a principle very similar to Aristotle's. His version states that whatever is found in an effect must exist in "the first cause [of the effect], actually and eternally."[157] And despite

[154] *K. al-Mu*^{c}*tabar* 2.364–366. *K. al-Mu*^{c}*tabar* 2.403, 407, 411, and passim, does away with the faculties of the soul and contends that a "single" human soul, which is the "essence of man," is the percipient subject in the case both of sense perceptions and intelligible thoughts, both of which Abū al-Barakāt calls "mental forms." Pines suggests that Abū al-Barakāt was led to his conception of the human soul by Avicenna's "floating man" argument. See above, p. 83, n. 38; S. Pines, "La conception de la conscience de soi chez Avicenne et chez Abu'l-Barakāt al-Baghdādī," reprinted in his *Studies in Abu'l-Barakāt* (Jerusalem 1979) 221–30.

[155] Ibid. 2.408.

[156] Above, p. 18.

[157] The only difference I see between Abū al-Barakāt's principle and his formulation of Aristotle's principle is that his principle looks to the ultimate cause, rather than the immediate cause, of the actualization of the effect.

having written a few lines earlier that the human soul may perhaps pass to actuality through its own power, he does not in the end exempt actual human thought from his version of the principle. His concluding position is that the appearance of intelligible thought in the human soul always requires an external cause, and although in some cases the immediate external cause is a human teacher, all human intelligible thought ultimately goes back to an agent eternally endowed with actual thought. With some hesitation, Abū al-Barakāt identifies the beings that "bring about the existence of" the various classes of human soul as the ultimate causes of the thought of their respective classes.[158] He does not say whether he understands intelligible thoughts to emanate directly from the supernal causes or whether those causes emit a kind of light that illuminates images in the human soul and enables the soul to abstract intelligible thoughts from the images.

From the proposition that the human soul is an incorporeal substance, not dependent on a body for its existence, Abū al-Barakāt, like Avicenna, infers its intrinsic immortality.[159] Different classes of souls have different supernal causes for their existence in Abū al-Barakāt's scheme, and after the death of the body, each soul, whether good or bad, returns to its source and "conjoins" with the cause of its existence. A soul's fate in the afterlife thus depends in the first instance on its own innate character: Its innate character determines the rung on the supernal hierarchy, the "home" and "company," the "given spot and specific level," to which it returns. But the quality of the existence awaiting the soul upon its return is determined by its "scientific and ethical" attainments during its earthly sojourn. A soul that has grown "close" to its cause—although never "equal with it," since that is impossible—by acquiring knowledge and purifying itself from "bestiality" and "corporeality," will enjoy "eudaemonia." A soul that, by contrast, is "wretched in its filth . . . and defective because of its ignorance" will, upon returning to its source, find itself in a "neighborhood" where it is "hated," "despised," and "shunned." It will be like a "stranger" who happened upon a "land, the language of whose people he does not understand," and the "customs and religion of which" he does not comprehend. The stranger who is wholly "alienated" from those around him suffers pain; the soul that returns to its supernal source with characteristics completely unlike those of the celestial being with whom it must henceforth eternally associate suffers far greater pain, for its pain is endless and more intense.[160]

It is, writes Abū al-Barakāt, a "property" of the human soul to "behold what is hidden," that is, to foresee the future. Avicenna had indicated that the source of

[158]*K. al-Mu*[c]*tabar* 2.411–412. Abū al-Barakāt's nuanced position is that some human souls are led to actuality by human instructors, some by human instructors as well as by transcendent causes, and some fortunate souls exclusively by the transcendent causes. In all cases, however, the ultimate causes of human thought are the transcendent causes of the existence of the human souls. A crucial line on 412 appears to be corrupt.

[159]Ibid. 440.

[160]Ibid. 3.213–214, 216.

human knowledge of the future is the souls of the spheres,[161] and Abū al-Barakāt makes a very similar discovery. He reasons that the source of human foreknowledge must, on the one hand, be "incorporeal substances," which have "intelligible" thought; only beings possessed of intelligible thought can comprehend events that have not yet come to pass. On the other hand, the source must also be "sense perceptive," since what has no familiarity with the world of sensation can have and convey no information about physical events in their particularity. The source of human knowledge of the future—and, Abū al-Barakāt appears to say, revealed knowledge of theoretical truths as well—is hence "most likely" identical with "the causes [of the existence] of [human] souls." In other words, souls of the celestial spheres and of the stars imbedded in spheres, which Abū al-Barakāt has taken to be the causes of the existence of human souls and the probable ultimate cause of human intelligible thought, are also the most likely source of human knowledge of the future. Knowledge of the future comes to man when the human soul and the supernal source communicate with each other as "one soul to another," and the human soul "beholds what is present in the [supernal] soul." Since when man is awake, his senses distract his soul and prevent it from focusing its attention to the supernal source, communication of knowledge of the future usually occurs in sleep and through dreams. Occasionally, however, men receive knowledge of the future when awake, "by way of inspiration [*ilhām*]."[162]

To summarize: Avicenna's mark on Abū al-Barakāt is unmistakable. Abū al-Barakāt pictures a physical universe consisting of celestial spheres and a sublunar region as Avicenna and Alfarabi did, and like them, he takes the universe to be eternal. Following Avicenna, he recognizes the need to harmonize the principle that from one only one proceeds with the unitary nature of the First Cause. He locates the cause of the existence of human souls, as well as of the forms of other animate and inanimate sublunar beings, in the supernal realm. After some dialectical give-and-take, he establishes an ultimate supernal cause of each human soul's intelligible thought and suggests strongly that the supernal cause of human thought is identical with the supernal cause of the soul's existence. He deploys a peculiar adaptation, or perhaps perversion, of Avicenna's reasoning to prove that the human soul is an incorporeal substance. Like Avicenna, he deduces the intrinsic immortality of the human soul from the proposition that the soul is an incorporeal substance. Again like Avicenna, he has the impersonal workings of the laws of nature consign morally and intellectually perfected souls to a eudaemonic eternity in the company of the cause of their existence, and souls that fail to develop intellectually or are morally defective, to posthumous suffering. His explanation of human foreknowledge through true dreams, and occasionally even in the waking state, reflects Avicenna's explanation of the same phenomena.

[161] Above, p. 122.

[162] *K. al-Mu^c^tabar* 2.419–422.

But Abū al-Barakāt remodels the structure he has borrowed. To solve the problem of plurality in the universe, he proposes that the First Cause itself might have multiple thoughts and thereby produce multiple effects. He peoples the incorporeal domain with many more incorporeal beings than Alfarabi or Avicenna had dreamt of. He splits up the functions of the active intellect among an indeterminate number of supernal beings, by distributing the responsibility for producing different classes of human souls among the souls of the spheres or souls of the stars, and by recognizing still other unspecified supernal beings as the causes of the existence of minerals, plants, and animals. His system, in a word, is a looser version of Avicenna's system, with a host of new nonphysical entities squeezed in.

Suhrawardī has left a number of works, but here I shall deal with three: *Āvāz-i Par-i Jibra'īl*, an allegorical tale in Persian, which has been translated into English under the title *The Sound of Gabriel's Wing*; *Kitāb al-Talwīḥāt*, which means "Elucidations"; and *Ḥikmat al-Ishrāq*, which means "The Science [or: Philosophy] of Illumination."

The Sound of Gabriel's Wing is a sketch of Avicenna's philosophy, garbed in a transparent allegory. The *Talwīḥāt* praises Avicenna as "the finest of the later [philosophers]"[163] and, like *The Sound of Gabriel's Wing*, follows him closely. *Ḥikmat al-Ishrāq*, by contrast, rejects Avicenna's picture of the universe in favor of an alternative picture. In *Ḥikmat al-Ishrāq*, Suhrawardī moreover reports that although he had once been an adherent of the "Peripatetic" school, that is to say, of Avicenna's version of Aristotelian philosophy, he had subsequently seen the light.[164] It would therefore seem natural to take the allegorical tale and the *Talwīḥāt* as earlier works, and *Ḥikmat al-Ishrāq* as later. But the hypothesis cannot stand without qualification, for the *Talwīḥāt* refers to the discussion of a certain topic "in *Ḥikmat al-Ishrāq*"[165] and also refers to an additional work of Suhrawardī's, which both criticizes Avicenna and explicitly calls attention to the corrections of Avicenna's philosophy that are made in *Ḥikmat al-Ishrāq*.[166]

[163] Suhrawardī, *K. al-Talwīḥāt: Metaphysics*, in *Opera metaphysica et mystica*, ed. H. Corbin (Istanbul 1945) 69. On 74, Suhrawardī narrates a dream in which Aristotle appeared to him, and in answer to a question stated that none of the "philosophers of Islam" reached even "one thousandth part" of Plato's "level." See Corbin's introduction, viii–ix.

[164] Suhrawardī, *Ḥikmat al-Ishrāq*, in *Oeuvres philosophiques et mystiques*, ed. H. Corbin (Teheran 1952) 10, 156, translated by Corbin in Suhrawardī, *Opera* x–xi.

[165] Suhrawardī, *K. al-Talwīḥāt: Physics*, Los Angeles, UCLA Library, Minasian Collection, Arabic MS 845, 158. My colleague Hossein Ziai helped me read the manuscript and all in all was generous with his knowledge of Suhrawardī.

[166] Suhrawardī, *K. al-Talwīḥāt: Metaphysics* 59, refers to *Kitāb al-Mashāri*^{c} *wal-Muṭāraḥāt*, and the latter (in *Opera*, n. 163 above) 361 and 453, refers, in turn, to criticisms of Avicenna in *Ḥikmat al-Ishrāq*. *K. al-Mashāri*^{c} *wal-Muṭāraḥāt* 401 and 505, also mention Suhrawardī's "book" entitled "*Ḥikmat al-Ishrāq*."

Suhrawardī's *Ḥikmat al-Ishrāq*, for its part, remarks that a mastery of the "method of the Peripatetics" is a precondition for the new way.[167] The suggestion has accordingly been made that Suhrawardī designed a single course of study in which the presentation of Avicenna's theories serves as a propaedeutic for the supposedly more profound "Science of Illumination."[168] An equally plausible explanation may, however, be that the allegorical tale as well the *Talwīḥāt* are indeed earlier works but that after rethinking matters, Suhrawardī returned to the *Talwīḥāt* and added a few cross-references.

In *The Sound of Gabriel's Wing*, a young man, who obviously represents the human soul, leaves the women's quarters of his house; the women's quarters represent the domain of sense perception. On his way to the men's quarters, to the domain of intellect, the young man meets an elderly sage,[169] who is clearly the active intellect, the cause of human intellectual development. An allegorical tale of Avicenna's entitled *Ḥayy ibn Yaqẓān*, which was referred to earlier, also represented the human soul by a young man in search of instruction, and the active intellect by an elderly sage who instructs the youth.[170] In Suhrawardī's tale, the sage is described as the last in a line of ten handsome old men, who are "incorporeal" beings that come from "nowhereland"[171]; he is, in other words, the last of ten incorporeal intelligences, which derive from a Being that exists outside of time and space. Each of the other old men is the teacher of the next in line and is responsible for the next one's "investiture"[172]; in other words, each emanates the intellectual substance of the one following it. Each old man moreover possesses a millstone, and all except the tenth has a single child who administers the millstone[173]; that is to say, each of the first nine intelligences possesses a celestial sphere and engenders a soul that governs the sphere. The child keeps one eye on its millstone and the other on its father[174]; the soul of each celestial sphere moves its sphere out of its desire to imitate the corresponding incorporeal intelligence.

The millstone belonging to the tenth elder, the elderly sage who instructs the youth, has four layers—the natural places of the sublunar elements. And this elder sends not one but numerous children to his millstone—the active intellect emanates the rational souls of the sublunar world. When those children complete their term in the lower world, they rejoin the source of their existence, never to return again.

[167]*Ḥikmat al-Ishrāq* (n. 164 above) 258.

[168]Corbin, in Suhrawardī, *Opera* ix, xv.

[169]Persian text: *Āvāz-i Par-i Jibra'īl*, in Suhrawardī, *Oeuvres philosophiques et mystiques* 2, ed. S. Nasr and H. Corbin (Tehran 1970) 207–23. English translation: *The Mystical and Visionary Treatises of Suhrawardi*, trans. W. Thackston (London 1982) 27. I have relied on Thackston's translation and on help that Hossein Ziai gave me with the Persian text.

[170]Above, p. 146.

[171]Thackston 27.

[172]Ibid. 28.

[173]Ibid. 28–29.

[174]Ibid. 29.

Although the tenth elder is never changing, he has an Abyssinian slave girl—the matter of the sublunar world—who, when receptive, conceives his offspring.[175] In other words, souls and natural forms are crystallized out of the never-changing emanation of the active intellect when matter is properly disposed to receive them.

In a digression, the young man representing the human soul notices a bowl with eleven layers, at the bottom of which there lie some water and sand. The first of the eleven layers has no "luminous node"; it obviously symbolizes the outermost, diurnal sphere, in which no star is imbedded. The second layer has many such nodes; it symbolizes the second celestial sphere, which contains the fixed stars. The next seven layers have one node each and symbolize the spheres of the seven planets. The final two layers, which represent the sublunar elements of fire and air, are the handiwork of the tenth old man himself, as are the water and sand at the bottom of the basin, which represent the elements water and earth.[176] In other words, as Avicenna held, the forms of the four elements are emanated by the active intellect.

As for the Gabriel of the tale's title, he is another symbol for the active intellect.[177] Suhrawardī's *Talwīḥāt*, as will appear, distinguishes three aspects in the active intellect's thought, but here Suhrawardī simplifies and writes that Gabriel has two wings, or aspects. Gabriel's left wing contains some darkness, because it embodies "nonexistence" and "possible existence." The left wing, or aspect, is, in other words, the thought that the active intellect has of itself as a possibly existent being. That aspect casts a "shadow"; it brings forth the matter of the sublunar world. The right wing embodies Gabriel's relation to God and is pure light; it is the active intellect's thought of the necessity of its existence by reason of the First Cause. Through it, Gabriel, or the active intellect, brings forth "luminous souls" in the lower world and also transmits "essences" (*ḥaqā'iq*) to the human mind[178]; the active intellect emanates human souls and concepts constituting human intellectual thought. According to still another statement in the allegory, not merely souls but everything that comes to be in the lower world has its source in Gabriel's wings.[179]

The allegory thus follows Avicenna as well as Alfarabi in recognizing nine incorporeal intelligences, which emanate one from the another. The intelligences are the emanating source of the souls of the spheres and, although Suhrawardī does not explicitly say that they emanate their "millstones," presumably of the spheres as well. From the ninth intelligence, the active intellect emanates. The active intellect is presumably the emanating cause of the matter of the sublunar world, it emanates all natural forms appearing in sublunar matter, from the forms of the four elements to human souls, and it emanates human intelligible thoughts. That conception of the active intellect is distinctive to Avicenna.

[175]Ibid.
[176]Ibid. 28.
[177]See below, p. 174.
[178]Thackston 32–33.
[179]Ibid. 30.

Suhrawardī's *Talwīḥāt* speaks a more conventional philosophic language and puts more flesh on the skeleton. Suhrawardī writes there: The observed movements of the heavens are to be explained by celestial "spheres." Each sphere is moved jointly by a "soul," which produces movement through its "desire" to "imitate" a corresponding intelligence, and by the "intelligence" that is "the object of [the soul's] desire." The incorporeal "intelligence" has the same "relation" to the "soul of [its] sphere" that "the active intellect" has "to our [human] souls." "The later philosophers," that is to say, Alfarabi and Avicenna, set the number of intelligences as equal to the "number of the general spheres"; they fixed the number at nine, there being nine main spheres. Aristotle, by contrast, had espoused the "superior" position that the number of intelligences is equal to "the movements of all the spheres, both general and particular"; in other words, he assumed intelligences not only for the main spheres but also for each of the subordinate spheres—eccentric or epicyclical—needed to account for the full complexity of celestial motion. He therefore recognized "more than fifty intelligences."[180] The information that Aristotle recognized "approximately fifty" intelligences could have been found by Suhrawardī in Avicenna.[181]

The *Talwīḥāt* calls the First Cause: "light" and "light of all light,"[182] terms that recall expressions in the *Theology of Aristotle* and Ghazali[183]; and also "the pure good" (*al-khair al-maḥḍ*),[184] a term echoing the title of the Arabic version of the *Liber de causis* (*K. al-Īḍāḥ li-Aristūṭālīs fī al-Khair al-Maḥḍ*, that is, *Aristotle's Exposition regarding the Pure Good*). The *Liber de causis* is a paraphrase of Neoplatonic theorems drawn from Proclus' *Elements of Theology*.[185] "From the First True [Being], only one can proceed [*yaṣdur*]," and "they," that is, the later philosophers, accounted for plurality and corporeality in the universe as follows: "Through the intelligible thought" that the "first effect" has of "the necessity of its existence"—through its thought of itself as a being necessarily existent by reason of the First Cause—"another intelligence . . . is produced." "Through its intelligible thought of the possibility [of its existence] in respect to itself," the intelligence brings "the body of the outermost celestial sphere" into existence. And through its "intelligible thought of its own quiddity," it brings "the soul of the [outermost] sphere" into existence. The process replicates itself. From the "second" intelligence there emanate a further "intelligence, the sphere of the fixed stars, and the soul" of that sphere, "and so on, until the nine spheres are complete."[186] The three

[180]*K. al-Talwīḥāt: Metaphysics* (n. 163 above) 57–59.

[181]Above, p. 74, n. 2.

[182]*K. al-Talwīḥāt: Metaphysics* 91, 93.

[183]Above, p. 132.

[184]*K. al-Talwīḥāt: Metaphysics* 91.

[185]*Liber de causis*, ed. and trans. O. Bardenhewer, as *Ueber das reine Gute* (Freiburg 1882) 11–12.

[186]Suhrawardī, *K. al-Talwīḥāt: Metaphysics* 63–64. For the aspects in the thought of each intelligence according to Avicenna and others, see above, p. 128, n. 6.

aspects in the thought of each intelligence are, as will be noted, delineated somewhat differently here from the way Avicenna delineated them.

There is a "tenth intelligence." "Through its intelligible thought of the possibility [of its existence]," the tenth intelligence—the active intellect—brings forth "the common matter" underlying the four sublunar "elements"; through its "intelligible thought of its quiddity," it brings forth "the forms" in sublunar matter, including "plant" and "animal" souls; and through its thought of "the necessity" of its existence by reason of the "[First] Cause," it brings forth "our rational souls." Avicenna had written that the general circularity of motion which is shared by all the spheres "aids" the active intellect in the emanation of the underlying matter of the sublunar world, while the differences between the several circular motions performed by the individual spheres prepare sublunar matter for the emanation of the full range of natural forms from the active intellect.[187] Suhrawardī uses almost the same words, writing: The "circular motion . . . common" to the heavens is an "aid" in bringing forth the "single matter" common to the four sublunar elements, while the "diversity in the [spheres'] motions" prepares sublunar matter for receiving a "diversity of kinds of forms" from the active intellect's "emanation."[188]

The emanation flowing from the "giver [of forms]," that is, the active intellect, remains unchanging through "eternity" and expresses itself "in accordance with the disposition" of the "recipient." Hence, the natural form that in every instance crystallizes out of the emanation of the active intellect is determined by the blend of the portion of sublunar matter receiving the form. When a portion of sublunar matter is blended to the highest degree of homogeneity, it receives a human soul.[189]

[187]Above, p. 77, Avicenna did not expressly distinguish three aspects in the thought of the active intellect.

[188]Suhrawardī, *K. al-Talwīḥāt: Metaphysics* 64; *K. al-Talwīḥāt: Physics* (n. 165 above) 163. Suhrawardī's *K. al-Mashāri^c wal-Muṭāraḥāt* (in *Opera*, n. 163 above) 449–52, also poses the problem of corporeality and plurality in the universe. There too Suhrawardī assumes that the First Cause contains no plurality in itself and that "what is one in all respects cannot be the cause of plurality . . . or of a body, since bodies . . . are [composed of two factors, namely] matter and form." As to how plurality and corporeality do emerge, *K. al-Mashāri^c* gives an abbreviated statement of the "Peripatetics[']," that is, Avicenna's, solution, which is close to the version of the emanation theory just quoted from the *Talwīḥāt*. In *K. al-Mashāri^c*, however, Suhrawardī raises one of the objections advanced in Ghazali's refutation of Avicenna. (See above, p. 151.) He contends that "the sphere of fixed stars contains thousands of stars. . . . There must, consequently, be a plurality in the causes of those stars, and the three aspects in the second effect [in the second emanated intelligence, which governs the sphere of the fixed stars] will not do." Furthermore, each of the other celestial spheres also contains more multiplicity than can be accounted for by three aspects in the intelligence assumed to govern it. These and other difficulties in Avicenna's emanation theory can, according to *K. al-Mashāri^c*, "only be solved through the procedure of the Science of Illumination [*Ḥikmat al-Ishrāq*]." Suhrawardī then concludes the discussion with a brief sketch of the solution that his *Ḥikmat al-Ishrāq* will offer.

[189]*K. al-Talwīḥāt: Metaphysics* 76.

The human rational soul can have a "potentiality" for thought at "three levels," and they are exactly the three stages of potentiality for thought that Avicenna delineated[190]: The infant is born with a "first disposition" for thought, called "material intellect." When the human soul develops and controls the "first intelligible thoughts," thereby readying itself for learning the "second [intelligible thoughts] through cogitation or insight," it attains "intellect *in habitu*." And the final level of potentiality, called "actual intellect," is the "advanced disposition," in which intelligible thoughts are not present to the soul, but the soul can make a full range of thoughts "present whenever it wishes, . . . without searching." When "intelligible thoughts" are "present in actuality" and not merely potentially, man possesses the "perfection" called "acquired intellect."[191]

"The soul does not lead itself from potentiality to actuality." To demonstrate that the factor "perfecting" our soul and "bringing it to actuality" is an "intellectual substance" called the "active intellect" with which "we conjoin," Suhrawardī adduces Avicenna's argument from the phenomenon of intellectual memory. And repeating an analogy of Avicenna's, he writes that "our souls are like a mirror"; when a human soul faces in the correct direction, it reflects what is in the active intellect, but it loses the reflection when it turns away.[192]

The *Talwīḥāt* establishes the incorporeality of the human soul through the same arguments that Avicenna deployed for the purpose.[193] Suhrawardī also offers an "argument for the impossibility of the transmigration [of the soul]" which is a condensation of Avicenna's argument against transmigration. His version goes: "When the body has a blend [of matter] which is such that it [the body] merits a soul from the giver [of forms]," it receives the soul; were a "transmigrating soul [also] to join the body, a single animal would have two souls"; since such a situation is obviously preposterous, the transmigration of souls is impossible.[194]

After the death of the body, the souls of "men of science who have attained superior [ethical] qualities" enter a state of "conjunction and unity . . . with the active intellect" and with souls similar to themselves. They thereby enjoy the highest degree of "eudaemonia."[195] The *Talwīḥāt* does not spell out all the possible fates in the afterlife which Avicenna had distinguished, but it is intrigued by the rationalization that, Avicenna had reported, "some scholars" (*ᶜulamā'*) gave of traditional accounts of the hereafter and that, he had commented, "seems to be . . . true."[196] Suhrawardī records the same rationalization, again in the name

[190]Above, p. 84.

[191]*K. al-Talwīḥāt: Physics* 153.

[192]*K. al-Talwīḥāt: Physics* 136–37. (The leaf is misbound, and should follow p. 154.) For Avicenna's argument from the phenomenon of intellectual memory, see above, p. 89. For the mirror analogy in Avicenna, see above, p. 94.

[193]*K. al-Talwīḥāt: Physics* 159–62; see above, p. 83.

[194]*K. al-Talwīḥāt: Metaphysics* (n. 163 above) 81; see above, p. 109.

[195]*K. al-Talwīḥāt: Metaphysics* 73, 94.

[196]Above, pp. 112–14.

of "some scholars," and he calls it "a fine statement." In Suhrawardī's formulation, "the body of the heavens serves as a substratum for the compositive imaginations of different classes of happy and miserable" souls in the hereafter, these being souls that, in the present life, acquired no "conception of the intellectual world" and whose "link to bodies was never severed." Should the souls in question be "simpleminded, good, and chaste," their imagination enables them to experience "marvelous, handsome pictures and forms,"[197] such as "a garden constructed of" precious stones, "dark-eyed maidens," and "the like."[198] Nonvirtuous simpleminded souls have experiences in the afterlife which accord with their deserts.[199]

Finally, the *Talwīḥāt* recognizes the three kinds of phenomena to which Avicenna attached the name prophecy.

"Insight" (*ḥads*), in Suhrawardī's definition, is the aptitude for discovering the "middle terms" of syllogisms with little effort. Men vary in the aptitude, and some "exceed others in the quantity and quality [of their insight]," with the result that they enjoy an "intensity of conjunction with the active intellect."[200] Since there is "no limit" to the amount of insight that a man might possess, a man "may come into existence who, through his insight, comprehends the larger part of [the corpus of] intelligible thoughts, without a teacher and in a brief time." At the top of the spectrum stands the "holy . . . soul, powerful [in its insight], such as [belongs] to the prophets."[201] Here we have intellectual prophecy, replete with phrases borrowed from Avicenna.[202]

The *Talwīḥāt* further recognizes the type of prophecy that is centered in the compositive imaginative faculty, although I did not find Suhrawardī using the name *prophecy* in connection with it. The "compositive imaginative faculty," he writes, is charged with "framing figurative images." Usually, the raw material for such images is furnished by sense perceptions, which make their way from the external sense organs, through the several internal senses, to the compositive imagination. But when bodily "concerns" fall away, the soul may turn in the "direction of holiness," whereupon something "hidden" from the incorporeal region may be "engraved" upon the compositive imagination. The route traveled by an impression engraved upon the compositive imagination from above is the reverse of that traveled by sense perceptions. The impression coming from above is transmitted by the compositive imagination to the "memory,"[203] and from the memory it "passes to the retentive imagination." The retentive imagination "exercises control

[197]*K. al-Talwīḥāt: Metaphysics* 89–90.

[198]Ibid. 92, 95.

[199]Ibid. 89.

[200]*K. al-Talwīḥāt: Physics* 165; *K. al-Talwīḥāt: Metaphysics* 95.

[201]*K. al-Talwīḥāt: Physics* 165.

[202]See above, pp. 117–18.

[203]The introduction of "memory" at this point does not accord with Avicenna's scheme of internal senses; see above, p. 89, n. 66.

over the . . . sensus communis, so that a form . . . is inscribed there." What finally takes shape in the sensus communis may be "a form of utmost beauty" which "whispers" secrets to the soul—an unmistakable allusion to the Moslem prophet's vision of the angel Gabriel.[204] Alternatively, what appears may be a loud call or written message. Or it may be an exact pictorial representation of the "thing that is hidden." Or, again, the hidden things revealed to the soul may be recast in "figurative images." When the soul retains an impression exactly as it received from above, it has a "true dream" or a "straightforward revelation [*waḥy*]." When, by contrast, the soul recasts what it received into figurative images, it has "a revelation requiring exegesis [*ta'wīl*] or a dream requiring interpretation [*ta^c^bīr*]."[205]

As for the content of the hidden things communicated to the soul from above, the single example Suhrawardī gives is "predictions" of the future. Avicenna had suggested that the specific supernal source of predictions of the future are the souls of the celestial spheres, and Suhrawardī—like Abū al-Barakāt—explicitly reasons that the souls of the spheres are indeed the source. The souls of the spheres, he explains, are the only supernal beings with sufficiently detailed knowledge of the laws governing physical events to be able to foresee, and to convey predictions of, particular future events. They therefore must be the source of the imaginative faculty's knowledge of those events.[206]

The third phenomenon classified by Avicenna as a kind of *prophecy* was the effecting of changes in the physical world by an act of sheer will. The *Talwīḥāt* recognizes that noncognitive phenomenon too, although I again did not find Suhrawardī calling it prophecy. "Some souls," he writes, possess a "divine power" of such strength that "matter obeys them as their own bodies do." Such souls can therefore "act on the blend and [the four basic] qualities [of matter, that is, heat, cold, dryness, and dampness]." Since a physical object's "character" is determined by the underlying qualities and blend of matter of which the object is made, those powerful souls can, by changing the qualities and blend, bring about a transformation of physical objects and "effect . . . marvels."[207]

In sum, the *Talwīḥāt*, like the allegorical tale of Suhrawardī's examined previously, portrays a universe whose structure is identical with that of the universe portrayed by Avicenna and Alfarabi. The *Talwīḥāt* further follows Avicenna closely in explaining the emergence of the complex universe from a wholly unitary First Cause, the active intellect's role as cause of the matter and forms of the sublunar world, the stages of human intellectual development, the role of the active intellect in producing actual human thought, the fate of souls after the death of their

[204] Koran 2:97.
[205] *K. al-Talwīḥāt: Metaphysics* 103–4.
[206] Ibid. 99.
[207] Ibid. 97.

bodies, and the nature as well as the types of prophecy. Other, briefer works of Suhrawardī also do nothing but summarize Avicenna's system.[208]

Suhrawardī's *Ḥikmat al-Ishrāq* announces a new departure. *Ḥikmat al-Ishrāq* means "Science of Illumination," and in the pages to follow, I shall use the Arabic term to designate the book, and the English expression "science of illumination" to designate the doctrine that Suhrawardī expounds there.

Ḥikmat al-Ishrāq grounds itself in the notion, which was encountered earlier in Ghazali and Ibn Ṭufail and which was a Sufi commonplace, that "direct experience" (*mushāhada*) rather than discursive thinking constitutes the high road to metaphysical truth. Suhrawardī tells us that he was himself vouchsafed direct experience of the divine "light" subsequent to his "Peripatetic" period. His *Ḥikmat al-Ishrāq* is designed exclusively for those on whom the "divine flash has appeared and for whom the appearance [of the divine light] has become habitual"; uninitiated readers will consequently "draw no benefit whatsoever" from the book. Any who "desire only a [discursive] investigation" (*baḥth*) should go to the "Peripatetics," that is, to Avicenna and his adherents, for there they will find the "finest" and "most solid" version of discursive philosophy.[209]

Yet it is not the entire science of illumination that direct experience reveals but only the basic premises. Once they are given, the "illuminationist" thinker must "build" his system on them.[210] The science of illumination thus is a *science* in the technical sense that it is a body of knowledge erected by human reasoning upon a set of presuppositions—presuppositions discovered through direct experience.[211] Nor does Suhrawardī regard himself as the first to have beheld the divine "lights." He lists a number of eminent predecessors, and they are a bizarre crew. "Hermes [Trismegistos],"[212] "Plato," "Zarathustra," the mythical "faithful, blessed king Kay

[208]Suhrawardī's *K. al-Lamaḥāt*, ed. E. Maalouf (Beirut 1969), and *Fī Iᶜtiqād al-Ḥukamā'* [*On the Philosophers' Creed*], in *Oeuvres* (n. 164 above), are brief summaries of Avicenna's philosophy. Pp. 119–21, 141–43, 147, in the former work, and pp. 267–71, in the latter work, cover the points presented here. In addition to *The Sound of Gabriel's Wing* other allegorical tales translated by Thackston (n. 169 above) incorporate motifs from Avicenna.

[209]*Ḥikmat al-Ishrāq* (n. 164 above) 12–13, 156; translated in Corbin's introduction 29–30, 33–34. Pp. 258–59, translated in Corbin's introduction 58, outline a regimen for experiencing the revelatory light. Corbin, *Avicenna and the Visionary Recital* (n. 1 above) 42, quotes a remark that another of Suhrawardī's allegories makes about Avicenna's limitations. See also above, p. 131, where Ghazali encouraged readers to "become men of direct experience [*dhawq*]," while advising those who are incapable of direct experience to "become men of science"; and above, p. 148, where Ibn Ṭufail contrasted his own direct experience with Ibn Bājja's "cogitative investigation" (*baḥth fikrī*) of nature.

[210]*Ḥikmat al-Ishrāq* 13.

[211]See Alfarabi's notion of science, above, p. 53.

[212]For Arabic texts carrying Hermes' name as their author, see A. Festugière, *Révélation d'Hermès Trismégiste* 1 (Paris 1950) appendix 3 (by L. Massignon). The most substantial Arabic philosophic text with Hermes' name is known as *Hermetis trismegisti . . . de castigatione animae libellum*, ed. and Latin trans. O. Bardenhewer (Bonn 1873). (It has nothing

Khosrow,"[213] and "Empedocles,"[214] to whom several minor Neoplatonic texts were attributed, are all credited with having viewed the divine lights before Suhrawardī.[215]

Although Suhrawardī does not list Avicenna among those who had experienced the divine light, he acknowledges that a mastery of the "method of the Peripatetics" is a precondition of the illuminationist experience;[216] and echoes from Avicenna reverberate through his *Ḥikmat al-Ishrāq*. Had Suhrawardī been frank in listing the thinkers who in truth inspired his new scheme, he would also have included at least two more names, those of Ghazali and Abū al-Barakāt. Arguments from Ghazali's critique of Avicenna, as set forth in *Tahāfut al-Falāsifa*, prepare the ground for the central doctrine of *Ḥikmāt al-Ishrāq*; the spirit of Ghazali's *Mishkāt al-Anwār* will be apparent in the application of light terminology to the incorporeal beings, and in the name *light of lights* which Suhrawardī chooses for the First Cause; and the spirit of Abū al-Barakāt will be apparent in the proliferation of supernal entities which constitutes the book's central doctrine. Occasional, albeit critical, references to Abū al-Barakāt disclose that Suhrawardī knew his work.[217] Anyone with Suhrawardī's education can be presumed to have been familiar with the writings of Ghazali.

Suhrawardī's *Ḥikmat al-Ishrāq* establishes the existence of a "light of lights" (*nūr al-anwār*), that is to say, a first, self-subsistent, being, through one of the standard proofs of the existence of a First Cause, the proof from the impossibility that causes—or, in the parlance of the book, "lights"—should "regress . . . to infinity."[218] The book goes on to borrow Avicenna's proof for the unity and noncomposite character of the First Cause in order to establish that the "light of

---

in common with the Greek Hermetic corpus.) Apart from a few instances of light imagery, nothing in it could have led Suhrawardī to name Hermes as one of his predecessors.

[213]H. Corbin, *En islam iranien* 2 (Paris 1971) 160–81, tries to explain the relevance of Kay Khosrow, but not all readers will find his explanation plausible.

[214]The largest collection of medieval fragments carrying Empedocles' name is preserved in a Hebrew translation from the Arabic, published by D. Kaufmann, *Studien über Salomon ibn Gabirol* (Budapest 1899) 1–51. The fragments include the following statements that Suhrawardī might have found harmonious with his *Ḥikmat al-Ishrāq*: The deity is "the first pure true light" (31); the higher world is "a light-like world, full of light" (29); "the soul is light-like, and its world is pure light" (ibid.). Information regarding pseudo-Empedocles is given in *Encyclopaedia of Islam*, new ed., s.v. Anbaduḳlīs.

[215]*Ḥikmat al-Ishrāq* 157–58; partly translated in Corbin's introduction 34–35.

[216]Ibid. 258.

[217]*K. al-Mashāri*^{c} *wal-Muṭāraḥāt* (in *Opera*, n. 163 above) 436, 468, 471. The second and third passages do not explicitly name Abū al-Barakāt. All three are critical of Abū al-Barakāt and appear to have in view his explanation of the emanation of a plural universe from a unitary First Cause; see above, p. 156. They were called to my attention by H. Ziai. *K. al-Talwīḥāt: Physics* (n. 165 above) 137, makes an oblique reference to Abū al-Barakāt and his theory of human perception.

[218]*Ḥikmat al-Ishrāq* (n. 164 above) 121: "Subsistent lights, arranged in an ordered chain, cannot regress to infinity." See Davidson (n. 35 above) 336–43.

lights is one, contains no condition within its substance, . . . and is affected by no characteristic."[219] The "light of lights" is superlatively "beneficent" inasmuch as it is an "emanating [cause] by virtue of its essence" and not for any other reason.[220] Since the "light of lights" is free of composition, "multiplicity" cannot "proceed" from it. "The first thing to proceed from it is a single incorporeal light"—a first incorporeal intelligence—which "also . . . does not contain . . . plural aspects."[221] The perennial question hence rears its head: How do plurality and also corporeality emerge in the universe, given a unitary and incorporeal First Cause that emanates only a unitary and incorporeal first effect?[222]

The *Ḥikmat al-Ishrāq* begins its solution of the problem of plurality in the universe as Avicenna had done and as Suhrawardī had himself done in the *Talwīḥāt*, but with the difference that Suhrawardī here distinguishes only two aspects in the thought of the first intelligence and dresses up what he says in the peculiar language of the book. The first emanated light—in other words, the first emanated intelligence—has an intelligible thought of "its wealth and its necessity [of existence] through the light of lights." From that thought "there proceeds [*yaḥṣul*] another incorporeal light," or incorporeal intelligence. In addition, the first emanated light, or intelligence, has "an intelligible thought of its poverty [that is, its dependence and possible existence], which is a dark characteristic in it." "By the darkness" of the first intelligence, Suhrawardī adds, he does not "in the present instance . . . mean" genuine darkness; he means the intelligence's being a "light not through itself" but solely by virtue of its cause. From this second thought of the first intelligence, "there proceeds a shadow, that is to say, the outermost celestial sphere [*barzakh*]."[223] Earlier we saw Gabriel's left wing, the aspect of the active intellect embodying its possible existence by reason of itself, similarly described as containing darkness and as casting a shadow, the shadow being the matter of the sublunar world.[224] To translate what Suhrawardī has said back into the language of Avicenna's philosophy, the two aspects in the first emanated light, or first intelligence, are its thought of itself as necessarily existent by virtue of its cause and its thought of itself as possibly existent by virtue of itself; and those two thoughts give rise to a second emanated light, or intelligence, and the body of the outermost sphere. Suhrawardī, as will presently be seen, explains the origin of the sphere's soul in an original manner.

[219]Ibid. 122–23. See Davidson (n. 35 above) 296–97, for Avicenna's proof of the unity and noncomposite nature of the being that is "necessarily existent by reason of itself," which is Avicenna's term for the First Cause.

[220]*Ḥikmat al-Ishrāq* 134.

[221]Ibid. 126, 132.

[222]Ibid. 133–34.

[223]Ibid. "Wealth" and "poverty" are defined on 107, and *barzakh* is defined on the same page as "body." Suhrawardī's definition of wealth comes from Avicenna, *Ishārāt* (n. 15 above) 158.

[224]Above, p. 163.

Ghazali had, in his critique of Avicenna, argued that a single aspect in the second incorporeal intelligence could not emanate the second of the celestial spheres, the sphere of the fixed stars. For besides its own body, the sphere of the fixed stars contains "one thousand and twenty odd stars, varying in magnitude, shape, position [on the sphere], color, effects, and unpropitiousness [*nuḥūs*] or propitiousness [*su*c*ūd*]."[225] Suhrawardī's *Ḥikmat al-Ishrāq* now contends in the same vein: The stars in "the sphere of the fixed stars" are so numerous that man cannot "delimit" them, and they must therefore have as their causes "numbers of aspects which cannot be delimited by us." But no single "one of the higher" lights has anything remotely approaching the requisite "plural aspects." The explanation of the "Peripatetics," that is, of Avicenna, according to which a single aspect in an incorporeal intelligence brings the sphere of the fixed stars into existence, consequently collapses.[226]

In another of his criticisms, Ghazali had argued that on a consistent application of Avicenna's assumptions, the incorporeal intelligences would have to have more than the three aspects of thought which Avicenna distinguished.[227] Suhrawardī's *Ḥikmat al-Ishrāq* makes a similar point, and his purpose, unlike Ghazali's, is constructive.

Suhrawardī submits that the number of "lights"—incorporeal intelligences—emanating from one another far exceeds the nine recognized by Alfarabi and Avicenna. There are "more than ten, twenty, one hundred, [even] two hundred [incorporeal lights, or intelligences]." And that is not all. The thought of each successive light in the hierarchy has more aspects than the thought of the one preceding it. The second emanated light, or intelligence, "will receive the light descending from the light of lights twice, once directly from it [that is, from the light of lights], and another time by virtue of the first [emanated] light." The third in the series has a fourfold refraction of light, for it receives the light shining from the light of lights, a reflection from the first emanated light, and the duplex reflection from the second emanated light. And as the series continues, the aspects of light continually "redouble."[228] Furthermore, each reflection of light in each intelligence redivides, thanks to the aspects in the intelligence which were already distinguished—the intelligence's "wealth," or necessary existence, and its "poverty," or possible existence—as well as through, new, additional aspects that Suhrawardī now introduces.[229] The total number of aspects in the totality of intelligences is thus enormous.

The systems of Alfarabi and Avicenna—and a possible interpretation of Aristotle's system—placed two classes of entity between the First Cause and the

[225] Above, p. 151.
[226] *Ḥikmat al-Ishrāq* 139. For a similar argument in *K. al-Mashāri*c, see above, n. 188.
[227] Above, pp. 150–51.
[228] *Ḥikmat al-Ishrāq* 140.
[229] Ibid. 142.

celestial spheres: incorporeal intelligences and souls of the spheres. Suhrawardī's science of illumination posits three, not two, tiers of supernal lights. The first tier, the one described in the previous paragraph, is "vertical"; that is to say, its members emanate one from another seriatim, exactly like the incorporeal intelligences in Alfarabi and Avicenna, although with the difference that, as just seen, they are far more numerous and contain many more aspects.[230] From some aspects in the members of the first tier, there "proceed the fixed stars, the sphere [of the fixed stars],"[231] and other unknown "wonders" in and above the sphere of the fixed stars.[232] From other aspects in members of the first tier, there emanates a second tier of "lights." Lights in the second tier, deriving as they do from the first tier and not from one another, no longer form a vertical series but rather "stand all on the same level." They are called, most mysteriously, "the masters of icons of species and of spheres, [masters] of the talismans of simple [elements] and what is compounded out of the elements, and [in general, masters] of whatever exists below the sphere of the fixed stars."[233] Suhrawardī seems to mean that some members of the second tier are responsible for the existence of the celestial spheres standing below the sphere of the fixed stars as well as the stars borne by those spheres. And, he notes, whether a star has "propitiousness" (*sa^c^diyya*) or "unpropitiousness" (*naḥsiyya*) depends on the character of the aspect in the first tier which gives rise to the member of the second tier which in turn brings the given star into existence.[234] Other members of the second tier share among themselves the functions of Avicenna's active intellect. They contain the forms—the "icons" and "talismans"—of the four sublunar elements, of inanimate compounds from the four elements, and of the various plant and animal species, and they emanate those forms onto the matter of the sublunar world.

From still other aspects of members of the second tier of lights, a third tier "proceeds." These are the "incorporeal lights" that "govern the spheres [*barāzikh*], without existing in them," and that cause the spheres' "motions."[235] They are simply the souls of the spheres under a new name. The "light of lights" and all members of the three tiers have existed from eternity[236]; they are "unchanging"[237]; and the mode of action of each of the higher lights consists in eternally "emanating [*fayyāḍ*] through its essence."[238] Hence they are as impersonal as the First Cause,

[230]Ibid. 144.

[231]Ibid. 143.

[232]Ibid. 149.

[233]Ibid. 143–44, 179. The first and second tiers are both "dominant" (*qāhir*) lights, in contrast to the third tier, which are the "governing" (*mudabbir*) lights, that is, lights governing the celestial bodies.

[234]Ibid. 143.

[235]Ibid. 145–46, 183.

[236]Ibid. 172–74, 178, 181.

[237]Ibid. 200.

[238]Ibid. 117.

the intelligences, and the souls of the spheres, in the systems of Alfarabi and Avicenna.[239]

Suhrawardī has followed the lead of Abū al-Barakāt on two scores, in exploding the frame of Avicenna's cosmology and letting the inhabitants of the incorporeal region reproduce luxuriantly, and also in distributing the emanation of natural sublunar forms among a number of transcendent entities. He differs sharply from Abū al-Barakāt, however, regarding the manner in which plurality and corporeality emerge in the universe. Abū al-Barakāt had proposed that when the unitary First Cause has the first being it eternally brings into existence as an object of thought, it can, by virtue of that thought, eternally bring another being into existence; it can then have the new being as an object of thought and thereby eternally bring a further being into existence; and so forth. One of Suhrawardī's works that makes reference to the Science of Illumination cites Abū al-Barakāt's explanation of plurality and corporeality within the universe, in Abū al-Barakāt's name. Suhrawardī there rejects the explanation disdainfully on the grounds that the wholly unitary and unchanging First Cause can be directly responsible for nothing more than a single emanated intelligence.[240] In the same vein, Suhrawardī's *Ḥikmat al-Ishrāq* insists—as Avicenna had done—that plurality, composition, and corporeality emerge only through "intermediaries."[241]

From the human soul's consciousness of itself, *Ḥikmat al-Ishrāq* concludes that the soul is an incorporeal substance,[242] and in harmony with the terminology of the book, Suhrawardī calls the human soul an "incorporeal light governing in man."[243] As in Avicenna and in Suhrawardī's *Talwīḥāt*, a human soul appears when a portion of sublunar matter is tempered to the degree that it has "the most perfect blend" (*mizāj*) and complete "balance" of qualities; as soon as a portion of matter is prepared for receiving a human soul, it immediately receives one from a being called the "giver."[244] The being that *gives* human souls is one of the second tier of supernal "lights," a light with a number of titles, namely: "Gabriel," the "spirit of holiness," "the giver of knowledge [or: science (*ᶜilm*)] and succor," and "the bestower of life and virtue."[245] The term "giver" echoes "giver of forms," Avicenna's sobriquet for the active intellect when considered as the emanating source of sublunar forms; the term "Gabriel" was the name assigned the active intellect in Suhrawardī's allegory, entitled *The Sound of Gabriel's Wing*; and producing human souls and imparting knowledge to them are familiar functions of the active intellect. What we have here, then, is plainly a version of the active

[239]Pace Corbin (n. 164 above) 44, and elsewhere.

[240]*K. al-Mashāriᶜ wal-Muṭāraḥāt* (in *Opera*, n. 163 above) 436, 468, 471.

[241]*Ḥikmat al-Ishrāq* 144.

[242]Ibid. 112, 114.

[243]Ibid. 154. Similarly on 201.

[244]Ibid. 200–201.

[245]Ibid. 160, 200–201, taken together with 143.

intellect. By calling his version the *giver* of knowledge, Suhrawardī suggests that it is the direct source of human thought, but he does not pursue the subject.

Since the human soul is an incorporeal substance, it is immortal by its very nature and is unaffected by the death of the body.[246] Suhrawardī reports Avicenna's refutation of the doctrine of transmigration[247]; yet although he employed the refutation in his own *Talwīḥāt*, in the present work he notes possible rebuttals.[248] In the end Suhrawardī's *Ḥikmat al-Ishrāq* takes no definitive stand on the issue, giving as its reason that the "arguments" on both sides are "weak."[249]

When delineating the fates of human souls in the afterlife, *Ḥikmat al-Ishrāq* betrays dependence on Avicenna once again, although it—like the *Talwīḥāt*—does not spell out the posthumous fates of all the categories of souls distinguished by Avicenna. Suhrawardī writes: To the extent that a soul "increases in light," that is, in intellectual perfection, it throws off its ties to its body, grows in desire for the higher realms, and acquires "a habitus for conjunction with the world of pure light."[250] Upon leaving its deceased body, a soul with a habitus for conjunction becomes an "adjunct of the [supernal] lights." Avicenna had described the eudaemonia enjoyed by the perfect rational soul in similar language, although without the imagery of light.[251] Suhrawardī adds that "infinite illuminations," from the "light of lights" and the other supernal lights, "reflect" upon the fortunate soul that conjoins with them,[252] and such a soul may "suppose" that it has become "identical" with those lights, although in fact it retains its individuality.[253] The fate of souls whose intellect is well developed but which are morally deficient is not explored.

Avicenna had recorded, and Suhrawardī's *Talwīḥāt* endorsed, the theory that after the death of the body the imaginative faculty of a simpleminded soul allows it to undergo what was promised by popular religion. The human imaginative faculty needs a physical organ in order to function, and, the theory went, the celestial spheres serve as the imaginative faculty's posthumous organ.[254] Suhrawardī's *Ḥikmat al-Ishrāq* goes a step further. It envisions an entire, objectively existing "other world," a world of "images" (*muthul*) and "disembodied specters" (*ashbāḥ mujarrada*), where certain souls receive their "imagined eudaemonia" in the hereafter.[255] The images contained in the world of images are "not Plato's Forms."

[246]Ibid. 222–23.

[247]Ibid. 218.

[248]Ibid. 218–21.

[249]Ibid. 222, 230.

[250]Ibid. 223–24.

[251]Above, p. 110.

[252]*Ḥikmat al-Ishrāq* 226, 255.

[253]Ibid. 228.

[254]Above, p. 167.

[255]*Ḥikmat al-Ishrāq* 232, 234, 243. F. Rahman calls attention to statements in Ibn al-ᶜArabī and Ghazali which may have contributed to Suhrawardī's conception. See Rahman, "Dream, Imagination, and ᶜĀlam al-Mithāl," *Islamic Studies* 3 (1964) 171–72.

For unlike Platonic Forms they are "dependent" and not "steadfast," which seems to mean that they have no permanence but continually come into existence and pass out of existence.[256] In order to become "manifest," they moreover need "the higher [celestial] bodies."[257] How the images are brought into existence to serve individual souls, how the celestial spheres enable the images to manifest themselves, and how images adapt themselves to the tastes of the souls spending an eternal afterlife in their presence, are not, as far as I could see, explained. Perhaps the celestial bodies still serve as the imaginative faculty's posthumous organ.

Human souls whose intellect is undeveloped, or insufficiently developed, go "to the world of images" when they are "released" from their bodies, and there "the resurrection of the dead . . . and all the promises of the prophets are fulfilled."[258] "Happy [*su^cadā'*] average" souls—which probably means souls whose intellectual development is insufficient to merit an afterlife in the world of lights—and "chaste" souls—which probably means good souls whose intellect is completely undeveloped—delight in whatever "fine food, shapes, and sounds" please them. Souls destined to "misery," endure "shadows . . . in proportion to their ethical qualities." These conditions "continue forever," for the world of images and the celestial bodies serving as the images' medium are immune from destruction.[259]

Suhrawardī congratulated himself on his personal direct experience of the supernal lights, and he encourages others to tread the same path.[260] In addition, *Ḥikmat al-Ishrāq* mentions two other types of supersensory perception achievable during the life of the body, each of which has a realm inferior to the supernal lights as its object. Since these two other types relate to lesser realms, they are, by implication, inferior to the direct experience of the supernal lights with which, Suhrawardī would have us believe, he had been graced.

One of the two lesser types of supersensory perception is the portion of "prophets and masters," who perceive "hidden things" of an extraordinary visual, audible, and even olfactory character. Such experiences are not objective in the sense that they are accessible to the external sense organs, but they are objective in that the things experienced subsist in the "world of images."[261] The organ through

[256]Ibid. 230–32.

[257]Ibid. 230.

[258]Ibid. 229–30, 234.

[259]Ibid. 229–30.

[260]Ibid. 252–53.

[261]Ibid. 240–41. *K. al-Mashāri^c wal-Muṭāraḥāt* (in *Opera*, n. 163 above) 494–96 (called to my attention by H. Ziai) speaks of the visions that the "virtuous" have through the "world of Heraqlia." The description clearly echoes Avicenna's account of visions of the supernal world which are mediated through the imaginative faculty; see above, pp. 119–20. Suhrawardī insists, however, that the visions he is referring to go far beyond what the "Peripatetics," that is, Avicenna, had in mind. "Heraqlia" reappears in *Ḥikmat al-Ishrāq* 254, and the commentators quoted in the notes on that passage take it to be part of the world of images. But as far as I could see, the description of Heraqlia does not, in either passage, match the description of the world of images.

which the prophet and holy man perceive the contents of the world of images and the import of what they perceive are among the many items that Suhrawardī leaves unexplained. The other lesser type of supersensory perception recognized by *Ḥikmat al-Ishrāq* is knowledge of the future. Avicenna had intimated that since the souls of the spheres are the only supernal beings in possession of particular knowledge, they must be the source of human knowledge of future events, and Suhrawardī's *Talwīḥāt* explicitly espoused that position. The *Ḥikmat al-Ishrāq* now explains in a similar vein that since all events in the sublunar world are traceable to the movements of the heavens, the "celestial bodies"—as distinct from their souls—contain "impressions of . . . events" to take place on earth. A human soul that frees itself from the distractions of its "external and internal senses" including the "compositive imaginative faculty [*takhayyul*]" joins the company of the "lights"—members of the third tier of supernal lights—that govern the celestial spheres. Such a soul joins the company of the souls of the spheres and there it "beholds the impressions of events in the celestial bodies." Whether the view of what is imprinted in the spheres occurs in a "true dream"—as is common—or in a wakeful vision, the human "memory" may retain what it sees and thereby obtain a picture of the future "which does not need exegesis [*ta'wīl*] and interpretation [*ta^c^bīr*]." Alternatively, the "compositive imaginative faculty" may recast what the soul beheld into another, figurative shape. In the latter instance, "exegesis" (*tafsīr*) and "inference" must be called upon to recover precisely what the soul saw.[262]

The different forms of supersensory perception that Suhrawardī recognizes in *Ḥikmat al-Ishrāq* —direct experience of the world of lights and the two forms of lesser supersensory perception—can be read as a revision of Avicenna's scheme of prophecy. He has replaced Avicenna's highest form of prophecy, intellectual prophecy, with direct experience of the world of lights; the substitution was suggested by Ghazali and Ibn Ṭufail.[263] And he has recognized prophecy through the imaginative faculty in two guises: first as "prophecy" through contact with the world of images; secondly as the soul's perceiving the future events inscribed in the celestial spheres and in some instances recasting what it sees through its compositive imaginative faculty. When treating the imaginative prophecy that discloses future events, Suhrawardī speaks of the soul's "behold[ing]" what is in the spheres, and of the need to apply "exegesis" and "interpretation" in instances where the imaginative faculty has reshaped what was seen. Those terms come from Avicenna.[264]

Avicenna had given credence to a noncognitive preternatural phenomenon that he classified as an additional kind of prophecy, namely, the possibility of a human soul's effecting changes in the physical world by the sheer power of will. *Ḥikmat al-Ishrāq* also refers to that phenomenon. In one of many obscure passages in the

[262]*Ḥikmat al-Ishrāq* 236–37.
[263]Above, pp. 140, 148.
[264]Above, p. 121.

book, Suhrawardī writes that certain men "are able to bring stable images into existence," and those images take "whatever form they [the men] wish." In some fashion the apparitions created by men are related to the higher "world" of "images."[265] Suhrawardī does not, however, explain what the relation is or how the apparitions are created.

To summarize, Suhrawardī's *Ḥikmat al-Ishrāq* bases the existence of an incorporeal First Cause not on direct experience but on a standard proof of the existence of God, the argument from the impossibility of an infinite regress of causes. The book repeats the proposition that the First Cause of the universe, being wholly unitary and noncomposite, can produce only one effect. Like Alfarabi and Avicenna, it explains that plurality, composition, and corporeality, in the universe emerge through the intermediacy of incorporeal beings subsequent to the First Cause. The First Cause emanates a single incorporeal being, and the first emanated incorporeal being produces plural effects by reason of plural aspects in its thought.

Once he reaches that point, Suhrawardī begins to plot a different course. He repeats Ghazali's criticism that a single aspect, or even two or three, in an incorporeal intelligence would not suffice as the cause of the sphere of the fixed stars. And he explains the full complexity of the universe by positing that the incorporeal world comprises many more incorporeal beings, and the incorporeal beings subsequent to the first emanated intelligence contain many more aspects, than Avicenna contemplated. The added intelligences and added aspects in them are the source of the enormous multiplicity in the universe. In another departure from Avicenna, Suhrawardī distributes the functions of Avicenna's active intellect among a number of incorporeal beings belonging to a second tier of lights, one member of the second tier emanating human souls while others emanate the various natural forms. Still other members of the second tier emanate all except the outermost sphere, the stars embedded in the spheres, and the souls of the spheres, these last constituting a third tier of lights.

Again in harmony with Avicenna, Suhrawardī's *Ḥikmat al-Ishrāq* construes the human soul as an incorporeal substance—basing the incorporeality of the human soul on a philosophic demonstration that is, however, different from Avicenna's demonstration. It refuses to credit Avicenna's refutation of the transmigration of the soul, yet it does not endorse transmigration either. It consigns human souls that have acquired a "habitus for conjunction" with the incorporeal world to the everlasting world of lights. Simple souls experience the promises of popular religion after the death of their bodies but not merely through their imaginative faculty. The souls in question go to their reward in an actually existent world of images—although with the celestial spheres still serving as the medium whereby the images manifest themselves. *Hikmat al-Ishrāq* replaces Avicenna's intellectual prophecy with direct experience, and it recognizes lesser forms of supersensory perception that parallel Avicenna's imaginative prophecy.

[265]*Ḥikmat al-Ishrāq* 242–43.

The Science of Illumination rests, by Suhrawardī's pronouncement, upon a direct experience of the transcendent lights. But the felicitousness of light imagery for describing supernal beings had been known from time immemorial. Ghazali in particular had made extensive use of light imagery when describing the incorporeal domain in his *Mishkāt*, and the appellation "light of lights" for the First Cause could have been learned by Suhrawardī from the *Mishkāt*. The formulation of the critical flaw in Avicenna's explanation of complexity in the universe also comes from Ghazali, and not from any direct experience that Suhrawardī might have had of the transcendent lights. *Hikmat al-Ishrāq*'s tactic for circumventing the flaw in Avicenna's explanation, by allowing supernal beings and their aspects to proliferate, was suggested by another of Ghazali's criticisms of Avicenna and was a central motif in Abū al-Barakāt. Abū al-Barakāt further showed how the functions of Avicenna's active intellect might be distributed among a number of transcendent beings.

Perhaps direct experience revealed to Suhrawardī that the supernal lights are divided in three, rather than two tiers, and that the total number of lights runs into the hundreds.

After Suhrawardī, a line of Iranian thinkers, inspired by him and by Avicenna, extends up to the twentieth century.[266] The best known is the seventeenth-century thinker Mullā Ṣadrā, who, in his treatment of the issues relating to intellect, quarries materials from Avicenna, from Suhrawardī's science of illumination, and from Sufi and Shiite thought, then cements them together with original ideas of his own.[267] Some of the other Iranian thinkers whose work is accessible show a similar eclecticism, tempered by a smaller measure of originality.[268] The literature is very difficult to evaluate, however. It lies encased in weighty Arabic and Persian tomes, much of which is unpublished; and assessment is made harder by the proclivity of modern scholars who study the literature to lose their scholarly objectivity and convince themselves that they have happened on the wisdom of the ages.[269]

[266]Corbin (n. 163 above) xlvii–xlix, lix; T. Izutsu, *The Concept and Reality of Existence* (Tokyo 1971) 57, 64–65; J. Morris, *The Wisdom of the Throne* (Princeton 1981) (an introduction to, and translation of a work of Mullā Ṣadrā) 46–49.

[267]See F. Rahman, *The Philosophy of Mullā Ṣadrā* (Albany 1975) 10–13, 85–87 (a peculiar emanation theory); 198–99 (a peculiar theory of the relation of souls to bodies); 234–35 (Avicenna's notion that emanation of knowledge from the active intellect has two phases; cf. above, pp. 91–92); 240–41 (the active intellect as cause of sublunar existence, and intellectual knowledge through union with the active intellect); 248 (afterlife of undeveloped souls and evil souls in the world of images); 254 (a peculiar version of the afterlife of developed souls in the realm of the intelligences). See also Mullā Ṣadrā, *Le livre des pénétrations métaphysiques*, ed. and French trans. H. Corbin (Tehran 1964); Morris (n. 266 above).

[268]See H. Corbin, *La philosophie iranienne islamique aux xvii*^e^ *et xviii*^e^ *siècles* (Paris 1981).

[269]See Corbin (n. 163 above) xliii, Corbin (n. 164 above) 58, and Corbin (n. 213 above) 35–39, all on Suhrawardī; Izutsu (n. 266 above) 61, on Suhrawardī and his followers; 68–69 and 149,

Résumé. Avicenna's thinking on the problems relating to intellect was available to readers of Arabic and Persian in a number of versions and summaries. Of writers who followed Avicenna in their own philosophies, the most unexpected is Ghazali. Ghazali is commonly regarded as an implacable foe of Avicenna, yet his *Mishkāt al-Anwār* reproduces much of Avicenna's system, partially disguised in allusive language. Another work that follows Avicenna while clothing its thinking in unconventional language is Ibn Ṭufail's philosophic novel; but Ibn Ṭufail, in contrast to Ghazali, apparently does attempt to go beyond Avicenna in ranking direct experience above discursive thought as the preferable road to human understanding. Ibn Bājja stands in the tradition of Avicenna and Alfarabi and borrows from both. As will be seen in the next chapter, Averroes' early works endorse a theory of emanation and a conception of the active intellect which are related to the positions of Alfarabi and Avicenna, while his later works strain to break free of the influence of those positions. The final chapter of the present book will find Averroes explaining the active intellect's effect on the human intellect in a manner similar to Alfarabi.

The most thoroughgoing refutation of Avicenna was drawn up by Ghazali, who thus dances around Avicenna in three capacities, as a summarizer, a critic, and a covert adherent.

Abū al-Barakāt fashions a partly new system by starting with Avicenna's framework, then stretching it to the bursting point. From the outlook of the present study, his most significant innovations are his allowing the population of the supernal region to proliferate and his distributing of the active intellect's functions among a number of supernal beings. Some of Suhrawardī's works carefully reproduce Avicenna's system. But Suhrawardī's Science of Illumination is another attempt to burst the framework of Avicenna's philosophy by adding a host of new incorporeal entities, by distributing the functions of the active intellect among a number of supernal beings, and by elevating direct experience of the incorporeal realm to the apex of human cognitive activity. In the centuries after Suhrawardī, a long line of Iranian thinkers construct their systems out of materials borrowed from him and from Avicenna.

Reverberations in Medieval Jewish Philosophy

Alfarabi's thought on the issues with which we are concerned entered the medieval Jewish world through translations of his works into Hebrew[270] as well as

---

on Sabzawārī; quotations from two modern Persian writers on the greatness of Mullā Ṣadra and the superiority of Persian philosophy in general, in Rahman (n. 267 above) 22; S. Nasr, *Ṣadr al-Dīn Shīrāzī and His Transcendent Theosophy* (Tehran 1978) 93–94, on Mullā Ṣadrā; Morris (n. 266 above) 27–31, on Ibn ^{c}Arabī and Mullā Ṣadrā.

[270] M. Steinschneider, *Die hebräischen Uebersetzungen des Mittelalters und die Juden als Dolmetscher* (Berlin 1893) 290 (*al-Siyāsa al-Madaniyya*) and 294 (*Risāla fī al-^{c}Aql*).

indirectly through the writings of Jewish philosophers who read Arabic and borrowed from him. In the case of Avicenna, the translation of his own works was not a major route of entry. Only one of his comprehensive philosophic works was translated into Hebrew in the Middle Ages, the translation was not done until the middle of the fourteenth century, and it apparently attracted little attention.[271] His thought became known to the medieval Jewish world through the writings of Jewish philosophers who read him in the original, through the Arabic text and Hebrew translation of Ghazali's summary,[272] and through the Hebrew translations of Averroes' early commentaries, which espoused a cosmology similar to Avicenna's.[273]

Although Alfarabi's works were more easily available to the medieval Jewish thinkers, Avicenna left the stronger mark both on genuine philosophers and on those who merely dabbled in philosophy. For a number of reasons—because the earliest Jewish writers who adopted or referred to positions deriving from Avicenna did not mention him by name, because his thought was largely mediated through others, because his positions often intertwine with Alfarabi's—Jewish thinkers following in his path do not generally realize that they are doing so. It may be mentioned here that an even stronger mark on medieval Jewish philosophy would subsequently be made by Averroes.

The Jewish philosophers who did most to introduce Avicenna's thought into the Jewish milieu were Judah Hallevi (ca. 1085–ca. 1140), Abraham Ibn Daud (ca. 1110–ca. 1180), and Maimonides (1135–1204), all of whom read Arabic and wrote their philosophic works in that language. The works of Hallevi and Maimonides were quickly translated into Hebrew. Ibn Daud was translated toward the end of the fourteenth century.

Hallevi's religious opus takes the form of a dialogue in which a "philosopher," a Moslem, a Christian, and a Jew set forth their several creeds before the king of the Turkish Chazar (in Hebrew: Cuzar) nation. The Jewish participant, who serves as Hallevi's spokesman, refutes the philosopher's creed in the course of presenting his own worldview, and the dialogue concludes with the king's conversion to the Jewish faith. The speech placed in the mouth of the "philosopher" together with supplementary information about the tenets of "philosophy" furnished by the Jewish interlocutor outline a cosmology and a theory of human intellect.

Hallevi tells us that the "philosophers" counted "more than forty" motions in the network of celestial "spheres." "Speculation" led the philosophers to affirm that celestial motion, being circular, must be "voluntary"; that each spherical motion therefore derives "from a soul"; that "each soul has an intelligence," or "incorporeal

[271] The work was the *Najāt*, the shorter version of his entire philosophy. See Steinschneider 285.

[272] Ibid. 299.

[273] Ibid. 144 (Commentary on *De generatione animalium*); 154 (Epitome of the *Parva naturalia*); 159 (Epitome of the *Metaphysics*).

angel" to direct it; and that "the last stage [in the chain of intelligences] . . . is the active intellect," which "governs this lower world."[274] "All" derives from the "First Cause, not through the pursuit of any goal on its [the First Cause's] part, but as an emanation, wherein a second cause [the first intelligence] emanates from it [that is, from the First Cause], followed by a third echelon of beings [the sphere and intelligence emanated by the second cause] and then a fourth. Causes and effects are interlinked, they succeed one another in a chain, . . . and the interlinking is eternal."[275]

Because the philosophers accepted the rule that "from the one only one can proceed [*yaṣdur*]," they had to explain how a multifaceted universe can emerge from a wholly unitary First Cause. They "assumed an . . . angel that emanates from the First [Cause]. Then they stated that the angel has two attributes, one of which is its knowledge of its own existence, . . . while the other is its knowledge that it has a cause. [By virtue of the two attributes,] two things necessarily come from the angel, namely, an[other] angel and the sphere of the fixed stars. From this [second angel's] having an intelligible thought of the First [Cause], there necessarily comes another angel, while from its having an intelligible thought of itself, there necessarily comes the sphere of Saturn. And so on, until the moon and, following it, the active intellect." "People" suppose that the foregoing is "demonstrat[ed]," because it carries the prestige of "the philosophers of Greece."[276]

Unlike the other incorporeal intelligences, the active intellect—continuing Hallevi's account of the philosophers' creed—produces "neither an angel nor a sphere."[277] Hallevi records no opinion regarding the origin of sublunar matter. The give-and-take in the dialogue does bring forward the hypothesis—which had been advanced by Alfarabi and refuted by Avicenna[278]—that a portion of sublunar matter becomes one or another of the four natural elements simply by virtue of its closeness to, or distance from, the innermost celestial sphere.[279] "Necessity," Hallevi writes, led the philosophers to reject the hypothesis. They realized that since the four elements differ from each other in "form," and not merely in accidental qualities, the cause of the elements' existence must be of a nature capable of instilling substantial forms. They accordingly concluded that the "active intellect . . . gives . . . the forms" of the four elements, "just as it gives the forms

[274]Hallevi, *K. al-Radd wal-Dalīl fī al-Dīn al-Dhalīl* (henceforth cited as *Cuzari*) ed. D. Baneth (Jerusalem 1977) 5, §21. Medieval Hebrew translation: *Sefer ha-Cuzari*, ed. A. Ṣifroni (Tel Aviv 1964 [?]); German translation: *Das Buch Kusari*, trans. D. Cassel (Leipzig 1869); English translation: *Book of Kuzari*, trans. H. Hirshfeld (London 1905) (inadequate). The discussion of Hallevi offered here is partly based on my article "The Active Intellect in the *Cuzari* and Hallevi's Theory of Causality," *Revue des études juives* 131 (1972) 351–96.

[275]*Cuzari* 1, §1.

[276]Ibid. 4, §25.

[277]Ibid. 5, §14.

[278]Above, p. 78.

[279]*Cuzari* 5, §3.

of plants and animals"; and the philosophers therefore "call" the active intellect "the giver of forms."[280] Regarding "minerals," Hallevi records a difference of opinion. The generality of philosophers understood that when the elements are "mixed" by physical forces into "divers blends, . . . the elements merit divers [mineral] forms from the giver of forms." "Some," however, held the contrary opinion that the characteristics of minerals do not come from a transcendent cause and emerge "solely from the blend." All concurred that as the blends of sublunar matter become "finer" and "still . . . finer," matter receives the forms of "plants" and "animals." When the qualities in a portion of matter reach full "equilibrium," the "form . . . called the passive, material intellect" is "emanated,"[281] and a member of the human species comes into existence.

Such is Hallevi's account of the philosophers' cosmology. Most of what he reports is common to Alfarabi, particularly as Alfarabi set forth his thinking in the *Risāla fī al-cAql*,[282] and to Avicenna. But certain features are distinctive to Avicenna, namely: the principle that from the one only one can proceed; the rejection of the hypothesis that distance from the innermost celestial sphere is the sole factor engendering the forms of the four elements; the tracing even of the forms of the four elements to the active intellect; the term *giver of forms*. The philosophers' cosmology, as Hallevi reports it, is nonetheless not identical with Avicenna's cosmology. Hallevi's philosopher distinguishes only two aspects in the thought of each intelligence, which was Alfarabi's position, rather than three, which was the position of Avicenna.[283] When describing the emanation of the translunar realm, the philosopher omits the outermost starless, diurnal sphere and accompanying intelligence which were recognized by both Alfarabi and Avicenna—although Hallevi does appear to recognize a starless diurnal sphere and its intelligence elsewhere in the dialogue.[284] And Hallevi's account of the views of the philosophers fails to recognize, or forgets to mention, a role for the active intellect as the cause of the existence of sublunar matter.

The philosopher in Hallevi's dialogue complements his cosmology with a theory of human intellect. A "passive" or "passive material intellect,"[285] also called

280Ibid. 5, §4.

281Ibid. 5, §10.

282Above, pp. 65–67.

283Ghazali's summary of Avicenna's philosophy also recognizes only two aspects in each intelligence, but they are different from the aspects that Hallevi's philosopher distinguishes; see above, n. 6.

284*Cuzari* 5, §2, where Hallevi speaks in his own name, refers to the "outermost sphere, which rotates once every twenty four hours and makes the other spheres rotate with it"; he seems to be distinguishing the diurnal sphere from the sphere of the fixed stars. According to *Cuzari* 5, §14, the philosophers believed that there are "eleven levels" of incorporeal existence, and the "emanation stops at the active intellect." The eleven levels must be the First Cause, the intelligence of the diurnal sphere, the intelligence of the fixed stars, the intelligences of the seven planetary spheres (including the sun and moon), and the active intellect.

285*Cuzari* 1, §1.

"potential" intellect,[286] is, according to the philosopher, emanated from the active intellect upon any portion of sublunar matter that is disposed to receive such an intellect; *passive intellect* was a term used by Alfarabi,[287] but not Avicenna, for the human potential or material intellect. The philosophers construe the "[human] soul" as "an intellectual substance, which does not occupy space and is not subject to generation and destruction."[288] If no weight is placed on the term *generation*, Hallevi here closely reflects Avicenna's thinking. Avicenna took the human soul to be an incorporeal substance that comes into existence together with the human body and therefore is in a sense generated; but he held that once the human soul exists, it is exempt from the laws of generation and destruction.[289] A long chapter in the dialogue consists of excerpts from a medieval Arabic psychological work that scholars take to be an early composition of Avicenna's. There Hallevi copies from his source a "philosophic" proof of the proposition that the human soul is a "self-subsistent [incorporeal] substance." The proof, which is the same as that advanced by Avicenna in his unquestionably genuine works, runs as follows in Hallevi's version: "Intelligible thought[s]" become present in the human soul; intelligible thoughts are indivisible; anything in which something indivisible makes itself present must be equally indivisible; therefore the human soul is an indivisible substance possessing "the attributes of the divine substances."[290]

Elsewhere Hallevi represents the philosophers as maintaining that when "existent beings" become "intelligible in the potential intellect," the potential intellect is transformed into "actual intellect, and then acquired intellect."[291] Those are the stages of human intellect as Alfarabi distinguished them.[292] "The ultimate eudaemonia for man" is attained when the human intellect reaches its highest stage of development[293]; that is a sentiment shared by Alfarabi, Avicenna, Ibn Bājja, and others of an Aristotelian persuasion.

The chapter of the dialogue consisting of excerpts from the psychological work attributed to Avicenna copies from its Arabic source an argument showing that universal judgments cannot be validated by human "experience." The reasoning, as Hallevi restates it, is that empirical experience can never be exhaustive and hence can never encompass all the instances covered by a universal judgment. Since experience cannot encompass all the instances covered, it cannot be what validates

[286]Ibid. 4, §19.

[287]Above, p. 49.

[288]*Cuzari* 5, §14.

[289]Above, pp. 106–8. Alfarabi's *Risāla fī al-ᶜAql* also termed the human intellect a substance, but not an incorporeal substance; above, p. 67.

[290]*Cuzari* 5, §12. Cf. S. Landauer, "Die Psychologie des Ibn Sīnā," *Zeitschrift der deutschen morgenländischen Gesellschaft* 29 (1876) 335–418, chap. 9. Landauer identified the text as the source of *Cuzari* 5, §12. For the argument in Avicenna, see above, p. 83.

[291]Ibid. 4, §19.

[292]Above, p. 49.

[293]*Cuzari* 4, §19.

the judgment. But if universal judgments are not validated by experience, they must come "from a divine emanation that conjoins with the rational soul." The "[source of the] emanation" must itself contain "the universal intellectual form" that it "imprints on the rational soul." And "what contains an intellectual form . . . is an incorporeal, intellectual substance."[294] The source of human universal judgments is consequently an incorporeal substance—the active intellect. Hallevi does not describe the way in which the philosophers understood the active intellect to produce intelligible thought in the human intellect.

When the philosopher makes the initial formal presentation of his views, he does state that the intellect of the "perfect" man enters into a "conjunction-union" with the active intellect, whereupon "the man appears to be the active intellect, with no distinction between them." The "soul of the perfect man becomes one with the [active] intellect" and the man joins the "company of Hermes, Asclepius, Socrates, Plato, Aristotle," and other luminaries, who also have become "one with the active intellect."[295] At a later point in the dialogue, when again recording the views of the philosophers, Hallevi puts things differently. He has the philosophers maintain that human intellect at its culmination becomes merely "close to the active intellect."[296] The statement to the effect that the human intellect at its crowning stage becomes identical with the active intellect harmonizes with Ibn Bājja's position.[297] The other statement, to the effect that the human intellect at its crowning stage becomes close to the active intellect but not identical, reflects the position of Alfarabi and Avicenna.[298] Hallevi also ascribes inconsistent positions on human immortality to the philosophers. One passage has the philosophers maintain that the human soul is immortal by its nature,[299] while other passages report the philosophic view to be that human immortality is contingent on a person's attaining the stage of acquired intellect.[300] The former is Avicenna's position,[301] and the latter, the position of Alfarabi as well as Ibn Bājja.[302]

Finally, Hallevi's account of the views of the philosophers takes notice of intellectual prophecy and prophecy through the imaginative faculty, both of which it represents as natural phenomena resulting from conjunction with the active intellect.

The section of the book excerpted from the psychological work attributed to Avicenna reports that the philosophers believe: "In some men . . . conjunction"

[294]Ibid. 5, §12, based on the text published by Landauer (n. 290 above) chap. 10. The argument in Landauer's text is quoted above, p. 88.

[295]Ibid. 1, §1; 4, §10 (end). Cf, above, pp. 56, 145.

[296]Ibid. 4, §19.

[297]Above, p. 145.

[298]Above, pp. 54, 109.

[299]*Cuzari* 5, §12, the chapter consisting in excerpts from the work attributed to Avicenna, which is published by Landauer (n. 290 above).

[300]Ibid. 4, §19. Similar sentiments are expressed in 5, §14, and 1, §1.

[301]Above, pp. 106–8.

[302]Above, pp. 56, 145.

with the active intellect frees "the rational faculty" from reliance on "syllogistic and discursive reasoning" and permits the rational faculty to acquire knowledge through "inspiration [*ilhām*] and revelation [*waḥy*]." "That property . . . is called holiness, . . . and such [a rational faculty] is called the holy spirit."[303] The passage plainly has in view the prophecy that, according to Avicenna's unquestionably genuine works, consists in a man's dispensing with the services of his cogitative faculty and acquiring theoretical knowledge through insight; those works of Avicenna, moreover, called the exercise of a high degree of insight in prophecy: *holy spirit*.[304] When Hallevi's philosopher makes his own formal presentation, he informs the Chazar king that upon the latter's entering into "conjunction . . . with the active intellect," the active intellect "may reveal to you . . . hidden knowledge, through true dreams and accurate imaginative [visions]."[305] Here the reference is to prophecy through the imaginative faculty, it being the faculty that frames dreams and imaginative visions. The content of the dreams and visions is not stated. A third passage reports: "The philosophers maintain" that "prophecy" occurs when a man's "thoughts [*afkār*] are purified" and his soul "conjoins with the active intellect—also called the holy spirit or Gabriel—whereupon the soul is inspired [*yulham*]." "Either in sleep, or between sleep and wakefulness," the prophet then "may imagine . . . that someone speaks to him. The prophet hears the speaker's words in an imaginative mode within his soul, rather than with his ears; he sees the speaker in the inner faculty of his soul [*wahm*], rather than with his eye"; and people "say that God spoke to him."[306] The reference is obviously again to prophecy through the imaginative faculty, but as in the previous instance, specific content is absent.

Hallevi's philosopher thus recognizes both intellectual and imaginative prophecy through the active intellect, without, however, saying enough about imaginative prophecy to allow us to determine whether he recognized both the form that supplies knowledge of the future and the form that recasts theoretical truths into figurative images. Intellectual prophecy was Avicenna's doctrine. Both Alfarabi and Avicenna described an imaginative prophecy that results from conjunction with the active intellect and that depicts theoretical truths figuratively.[307] Alfarabi, Avicenna, and Ibn Bājja all recognized an imaginative prophecy that furnishes predictions of the future, although only Alfarabi and Ibn Bājja, and not Avicenna, traced those predictions to an emanation coming from the active intellect.[308]

Hallevi's account of the philosophers' cosmology, as we saw previously, combined features common to Alfarabi and Avicenna with a number of features

[303] *Cuzari* 5, §12, based on the text published by Landauer (n. 290 above), chap. 8 (end).

[304] Above, p. 119.

[305] *Cuzari* 1, §1.

[306] Ibid. 1, §87.

[307] Above, pp. 119–20.

[308] Above, pp. 59, 122, and below, p. 341. In Avicenna, the emanation furnishing predictions of the future apparently comes from the souls of the spheres.

distinctive to Avicenna and at least one feature distinctive to Alfarabi. His account of the philosophers' theory of human intellect, which has just been examined, also contains a number of theses peculiar to Avicenna, but almost all of them are excerpted from a single Arabic work written by Avicenna or a member of his school. Aside from the excerpts, the only item distinctive to Avicenna in the philosopher's theory of intellect is the construction of the human soul as an incorporeal substance. Other theses concerning intellect derive from Alfarabi, and one or two, perhaps, from Ibn Bājja. On a pair of issues, immortality and the possibility of the human intellect's becoming wholly identical with the active intellect, Hallevi carelessly credits the philosophers with contradictory positions.

Inasmuch as Hallevi lists various historical and legendary Greek philosophers, most frequently Aristotle,[309] but mentions the name of no Arabic philosopher, he must have believed that the cosmology and theory of intellect which have been outlined reflect either the general worldview of Greek philosophy or, specifically, Aristotle's system. What he has in fact presented is an eclectic set of doctrines drawn from the Arabic Aristotelians. Since he was a physician, he should have at one time read some philosophy, philosophy being a component of the medical curriculum. Yet with the exception of the psychological work attributed to Avicenna which he excerpted, he could hardly have had a serious philosophic treatise before him when he wrote his dialogue. He must have relied on notes, or on his recollection of earlier reading, lectures, and conversations.

Having recorded the philosophers' creed, Hallevi, through his spokesman in the dialogue, refutes it and expounds his own position.

He criticizes the philosophers' theory of successive emanations on three scores, two of which go back to Ghazali's critique of Avicenna's version of the theory. Ghazali had, in one of his objections, contended that, on Avicenna's premises, no less than five different aspects might be distinguished within the first intelligence, rather than the three aspects through which Avicenna had explained the emanation of the next intelligence in the incorporeal hierarchy, the emanation of the body of the celestial sphere governed by the first intelligence, and the emanation of the soul of the sphere. In another of his objections, Ghazali had scoffed that ascribing the existence of the body of a sphere, the existence of the soul of the sphere, and the existence of an additional intelligence, to three aspects of an intelligence's thought is as preposterous as saying that a certain "unknown man's . . . being possibly existent" gives rise to the existence of a celestial sphere, and that the man's "having an intelligible thought of himself and of his Maker" gives rise to "two more things."[310]

Hallevi, for his part, submits that the emanation theory he recorded in the name of the philosophers "can be objected to, on several grounds." One objection is that "it may be said: Why does not something necessarily come from Saturn's

[309] *Cuzari*, 4, §25 (end); 5, §14 (end).
[310] Above, p. 151.

[intelligence's] having what is above it as an object of thought, and something else from its having the first angel as an object of thought? The emanations of Saturn's [intelligence] will then add up to four." In other words, the intelligence of the sphere of Saturn should have not only the First Cause and itself as objects of thought but also "what is above it"—a vague phrase that perhaps refers to the sphere of the fixed stars—as well as the first intelligence, which, in Hallevi's account of the philosophers' cosmology, is the intelligence governing the sphere of the fixed stars. The intelligence of Saturn should thus have four objects of thought and as a consequence emanate four distinct beings, which is more than the number of beings it emanates according to the philosophers.[311] In a second objection Hallevi asks: "How can we suppose that when something has an intelligible thought of itself, a sphere necessarily comes forth from it, and when something has an intelligible thought of the First [Cause], an angel necessarily comes forth? Were it so, when Aristotle asserts that he has himself as an object of thought, we should demand that a sphere emanate from him, and if he asserts that he has the First [Cause] as an object of thought, we should demand that an angel emanate from him!"[312] Hallevi's third objection addresses an issue that Avicenna had raised and was satisfied he solved, namely, the need to explain why the process ceases at the active intellect.[313] Hallevi wonders: "Why does the emanation cease? Is it because of inadequacy in the First [Cause]?"[314]

Hallevi proceeds to question the very existence of intelligences and souls of spheres. In one of the sections of the dialogue which state his own beliefs, he does grudgingly refrain from rejecting the common equation of "the eternal angels" of religious tradition with the "beings whose existence the philosophers recognize." "We have," he writes, "no reason for either rejecting or accepting" the philosophers' intelligences.[315] His final summation of his own beliefs does not, however, leave the matter in doubt. There he asserts: The "philosophers . . . divide the divine world into degrees" and thereby "multiply deities," but "let us not give heed" to such scandalous notions. Anyone "deceived by" the philosophers into accepting the existence of intelligences and the souls of the spheres is a "heretic," since he encroaches upon the unity of God. "For us, everything" beyond the corporeal

[311]The present passage does not mention a diurnal sphere and corresponding intelligence above the sphere of the fixed stars and its intelligence. See above, pp. 182–83. Conceivably, however, a reference to the diurnal sphere has fallen out of our text or perhaps Hallevi copied his refutation of the philosophers' theory of emanation from notes that did take the diurnal sphere and its intelligence into consideration. Then his objection to the theory would be: The intelligence of the sphere of Saturn should have four objects of thought: itself; the intelligence "above it," that is, the intelligence of the sphere of the fixed stars; the first angel, that is, the intelligence of the diurnal sphere; and the First Cause.

[312]*Cuzari* 4, §25.

[313]See above, p. 76.

[314]*Cuzari* 4, §25.

[315]Ibid. 4, §3.

realm "is a [single] divine degree; there is only a [single] deity, who governs the corporeal [world]."[316]

Hallevi further rejects the philosophic proposition that the human soul is "an intellectual substance, which does not occupy space and is not subject to generation and destruction." He presupposes that if human souls were intellectual substances, as his adversaries conceive of such substances, souls would all be exactly of the same character and could not be individuated; and he reads out the absurdities that ensue: "How [on the philosophers' assumption] might my soul be distinguished from your soul, or from the active intellect, the [incorporeal] causes, and the First Cause?"[317] If souls were not individuated, "one [man] would know the other, his belief, his innermost thoughts." And each man would possess all possible "intelligible thoughts at once, as God and the active intellect do." There are anomalies of another sort as well: If the human soul were an intellectual substance, it could not forget. Men would not lose consciousness when they fall asleep, become intoxicated, have brain fever, suffer brain concussions, grow old and feeble. And so on.[318]

Finally, Hallevi lays bare distasteful consequences of the supposition that human immortality depends on intellectual perfection: If "the human soul becomes separate from the body and indestructible" only through "a total knowledge of existent beings," no one qualifies, for there is "much that . . . the philosopher [himself] does not know of what is in the heavens, the earth, and the sea." If, by contrast, "a little knowledge suffices, then every rational soul is separate [from the body and immortal]; for the first principles of thought are innate to the soul," and therefore every rational soul has some intellectual knowledge. And "if," testing one more hypothesis, "the soul separates itself [and gains immortality] by grasping the ten [Aristotelian] categories together with whatever principles of thought are more comprehensive than they, the rationale being that all existent beings" are in a general sense "subsum[ed]" under the ten categories and the more comprehensive

316 Ibid. 5, §21.

317 S. Pines, "Shīᶜite Terms and Conceptions in Judah Halevi's *Kuzari*," *Jerusalem Studies in Arabic and Islam* 2 (1980) 216–17, understands this argument to imply that human souls are not, in the view of the philosophers, identical with one another; and he sees a discrepancy between that implication of the argument and the statement of the philosopher, quoted above, p. 185, to the effect that the souls of perfect men do become identical with one another. Even granting the implication, it is hard to see a discrepancy. The argument here is that if human souls were incorporeal substances, they would be identical with one another from the outset, which is preposterous; the statement of the philosopher there is that human intellects become identical with one another at the climax of their development. As pointed out above, p. 185, discrepancies are discoverable in Hallevi's presentation of the views of the philosophers. The discrepancies do not, however, support Pines' suggestion that Parts 1 and 5 of the *Cuzari* reflect different philosophic systems.

318 *Cuzari* 5, §14. The question how men can have private thoughts if all souls are one goes back to Plotinus, *Enneads* 4.9.1. English translation of the Arabic paraphrase of the passage, in the Henry-Schwyzer edition of Plotinus (n. 24 above) ad locum.

principles, "then that is an easy kind of knowledge, to be acquired in a day." But "it is farfetched that man should be transformed into an angel in a single day."[319]

Such are Hallevi's objections to the philosophers' cosmology and theory of intellect. When Hallevi sets forth his own beliefs, he shows himself to be yet another thinker who remained under the spell of Arabic Aristotelianism to a greater extent than he imagined or acknowledged.

He borrows the terminology of his opponents and states that "the First Cause . . . is in its essence intellect [or: intellect by reason of itself]."[320] Although he hesitates, as we have seen, to identify the angels of religious tradition with the philosophers' incorporeal intelligences, he allows himself language appropriate to the intelligences when describing the "angels" of tradition: They are "actual intellect"[321] and make up the "world of intellect."[322] Hallevi does depart from Alfarabi and Avicenna on other issues concerning the supernal region. In place of successive necessary emanations, which he refuted, he submits that God, through an act of "will, . . . instantaneously created the numerous things [constituting the universe]"[323]; "the universe . . . came into existence by God's will, when He wished and as He wished"[324]; the "spiritual angels are created" specifically from something that Hallevi calls "the spirit of God" or the "holy spirit."[325] Instead of the incorporeal intelligences' moving the celestial spheres, Hallevi understands that the "First Cause," without intermediaries, produces the "order and arrangement seen in . . . the heavens"[326]; "the heavens perform [their functions] solely through God's will, with no . . . intermediate . . . causes between" them and God[327]; the "divine thing [*amr ilāhī*]. . . governs the spheres."[328] By *divine thing*, Hallevi means a projection of God into the universe, and he seems to conceive of the *divine thing* specifically as a divine emanation—an emanation that for him, of course, neither is necessary and eternal nor has the status of a distinct substance.[329] He is saying that God, or a projection

319Ibid.

320Ibid. 5, §20 (4). Similarly in 2, §2 (end).

321Ibid. 4, §3.

322Ibid. 4, §25.

323Ibid. 4, §26.

324Ibid. 5, §14.

325Ibid. 4, §25.

326Ibid. 5, §20.

327Ibid. 4, §3.

328Ibid. 4, §25.

329Ibid. 4, §25. The term *amr* of God goes back to Koran 7:54, 17:85, where it means God's "command," and the term plays a role in various strands of Islamic theology. For the divine *amr* in Hallevi, see I. Goldziher, "Le amr ilāhī chez Juda Halévi," *Revue des études juives* 50 (1905) 32–41; Davidson (n. 274 above) 381–95; Pines (n. 317 above) 172–80.

My article contends from internal evidence that the basic sense of the divine *amr* in Hallevi is an emanation from God. Other Arabic texts use the term *amr* in that sense. Ibn Ṭufail (nn. 18, 53 above) Arabic section 28; French translation 25, speaks of "the spirit from the *amr* of God"

of God, or an emanation sent forth through an act of God's will, causes the heavens to rotate.

The infiltration of Arabic Aristotelianism, and particularly of Avicenna, into Hallevi's thought becomes broad and unmistakable when Hallevi turns to the generation of natural objects in the sublunar world. He too is convinced that "the elements, the moon, the sun, and the stars" exercise an "effect" on the matter of the sublunar region "by way of heating, cooling, moistening, and drying" matter.[330] "Mixture[s]" (*mizāj, imtizāj*; Hebrew: *mezeg*, *himmazeg*) of matter thereby become "balanced" to varying degrees, portions of matter become "prepared" for new forms, and each portion of matter receives the "form of [whatever] animal or plant it deserves."[331] But natural forces, although they prepare matter for a given form, are not capable of "efficient" causation."[332] "The instilling of form as well as the evaluation [of the correct form for each portion of matter], the bringing forth [of a new object], and everything involving wisdom [directed] toward a goal," can proceed only from a "wise and powerful" agent.[333] Hallevi thus arrives at the proposition that sublunar forms come from an agent transcending the forces of nature.

The wise and powerful agent that instills forms in matter can, however, no longer be the active intellect, for in doing away with the incorporeal intelligences, Hallevi did away with the active intellect as well. "God" is the agent who "gives everything [the form] that it deserves."[334] The "wisdom" and "providence" of "[God] the giver of forms" is, he posits, "one and . . . the same" at all levels of the universe. A "unitary" divine "wisdom" and "divine thing" (*amr ilāhī*) manifest themselves—or, manifests itself—differently at each level of the universe; and the differing manifestations of the unitary divine wisdom and divine *thing* are determined by the "difference [in the receptivity] of matter." "The differences between things" are due to "differences in their matter."[335] Hallevi does not usually employ the language of *emanation* in contexts where he sets forth his own understanding of the emergence of natural forms, but in some instances he does.[336] Since he also stresses that "God gives every [portion of] matter the best form it can receive," that God "is beneficent and does not withhold . . . His governance"

---

which "eternally emanates on all existent beings" and which expresses itself differently, depending on the preparation of matter for receiving it. Pines 177, calls attention to a Shiite text where the term *amr* has the sense of a divine emanation.

[330]Ibid. 1, §77. Both celestial forces and forces indigenous to the sublunar world are "intermediate causes," that is, causes acting semi-independently but ultimately dependent upon God, and always subject to divine intervention. See ibid. 5, §20.

[331]Ibid. 3, §§23, 53.

[332]Ibid. 5, §20 (2)

[333]Ibid. 1, §77.

[334]Ibid. 5, §10 (end).

[335]Ibid. 4, §25; 5, §20 (3). Cf. above, pp. 30–31, 79–80.

[336]Ibid. 2, §26; 4, §§3, 25.

from anything capable of receiving it,[337] Hallevi must mean that whenever matter is prepared to receive a form, the form is unfailingly crystallized out of the *divine thing*, the undifferentiated projection of God into the universe, or divine emanation. The statement that the "instilling of form as well as the evaluation" of the form suitable for a given portion of matter proceed from a "wise and powerful" agent cannot, therefore, envisage an individual evaluation of each portion of matter and an individual decision as to what form the matter deserves. Rather—such must be Hallevi's intent—God devised the universe in such a way that each portion of matter automatically receives whatever form is appropriate to it.

In his account of the views of the philosophers, Hallevi reported that they trace even the forms of the four elements to a supernal giver of forms, and he concurred although, we have now seen, he differs as to who the giver of forms is. Avicenna was the philosopher who traced even the forms of the four elements to a transcendent cause. Unprepossessed readers will have to conclude that Hallevi has adopted Avicenna's position on the appearance of sublunar forms and has merely added the proviso that they come from God and not the active intellect. Hallevi saw his relationship to his philosophic adversaries differently. He saw his opponents making a significant concession to revealed religion: "The philosophers were forced to affirm that the *divine thing* gives these [sublunar] forms," but they mistakenly "call" the *divine thing* "the intellect that is the giver of forms."[338]

Hallevi has, then, accepted the proposition that each portion of sublunar matter receives, from a transcendent source, the form for which it is prepared. When the qualities of a portion of matter are fully "balanced," the matter is "prepared" for a "rational soul," and a rational soul is unfailingly furnished by an "emanation" (*ifāḍa*; Hebrew: *a-ṣ-l*) coming from the "beneficent . . . divine thing [*amr ilāhī*]." Hallevi describes the human rational soul as an "incorporeal substance" (*jawhar mufāraq*), which does not occupy "place" and which resembles the "substance of the angels."[339] We have already seen that the angels are pure intellect. He does not explain how his conception of the human soul differs from the philosophers'—that is, Avicenna's—construction of the human soul as an incorporeal substance, nor how the objections he raised against Avicenna's position may be deflected from his own.

Employing concepts that plainly go back to Alfarabi and Avicenna, Hallevi further speaks of the "conjoining" of "spiritual [human] souls" with "God," with the "spirit of God," with the "divine light," with the "divine thing," or with "spiritual [beings]"[340]; of souls' "knowing truths without instruction and, indeed,

[337]Ibid. 5, §20 (3).

[338]Ibid. 5, §4.

[339]Ibid. 2, §26.

[340]Ibid. 1, §95; 2, §14; 3, §20; 4, §25. The notion of *conjunction* with God or with a member of the incorporeal hierarchy was already entrenched in Jewish philosophic and theological literature by Hallevi's time. A tenth-century Judeo-Arabic text states that the soul of Moses "united with the world of the Rational Soul before it separated from its body," and that, in general,

through minimal cogitative thought [*fikra*]," thanks to their conjunction with God[341]; of a "eudaemonia" (*sa^c^āda*) of the human soul "in the next world"[342]; of souls' prophesying as a result of conjunction[343]; of prophecy through "an inner eye, . . . which may be identical with the imaginative faculty [*mutakhayyila*] when it is under the control of the intellectual faculty."[344] Hallevi says little about these phenomena, beyond insisting that they are the fruit not of human intellectual development but of the performance of ritual acts,[345] and that they are closed to most human souls. Conjunction, eudaemonia, and prophecy are reserved for a narrow human elite. They lie solely within the grasp of men upon whom the divine thing governing the universe has emanated a nature higher than mere human intellect, of men who therefore constitute "virtually a different species."[346] When a

---

"the separation" of souls from bodies, "when the latter are still alive, . . . is a conjunction [*ittiṣāl, dibbuq*] and union with the supernal worlds" and with "the divine light." Arabic text: G. Vajda, "Nouveaux fragments arabes du commentaire de Dunash b. Tamim," *Revue des études juives* 113 (1954) 41; medieval Hebrew translation and French translation: G. Vajda, "Le commentaire kairouanais sur le 'Livre de la Creation,'" *Revue des études juives* 107 (1946–1947) 150, 155–56. Solomon Ibn Gabirol (eleventh century), who espoused a Neoplatonic philosophic system, described the human soul's "eudaemonia" (Hebrew: *haṣlaḥa*) as consisting in the human "substance's uniting" with the "spiritual" or "intelligible substances," and the human "form's conjoining [*debequt*; *adiunctio*] with their forms." The Arabic original is lost. Medieval Latin translation from the Arabic: Ibn Gabirol, *Fons vitae*, ed. C. Baeumker (Münster 1892-1895) 3, §56, pp. 204–5; excerpts from the Arabic in medieval Hebrew translation: *Liqqutim*, ed. S. Munk (Paris 1857) 3, §§37–38. Slightly later, Baḥya Ibn Paquda, *al-Hidāja* (*al-Hidāya*) (*Ḥobot ha-Lebabot*) ed. A. Yahuda (Leiden 1912) 10.1, speaks of the superior soul's desire to "conjoin with" (*tattaṣil*; *tiddabeq*) God's "light." Abraham Ibn Ezra, a contemporary of Hallevi, refers to a conjunction of a superior human soul both with God and with the "supernal soul, which is the soul of the heavens"; and he writes that conjunction can take place either upon the death of the body or before, and that in the latter instance prophecy can result. A. Ibn Ezra, Bible Commentary, Exodus 6:3; Deuteronomy 11:22; Psalms 1:3; 16:8; 49:16; 139:18.

To render the Arabic root underlying the cluster of words meaning *conjoin*, *conjunction*, and the like, the medieval translators of philosophic works from Arabic into Hebrew chose the Hebrew root *d-b-q*, which a number of Biblical verses, such as Deuteronomy 4:4, 11:22, 30:20, use for the notion of man's—as distinct from the human soul's—*cleaving* to God. As a consequence, *conjunction* acquired a scriptural resonance in Hebrew which it has retained ever since From the Middle Ages on, every Hebrew writer who speaks of the soul's *conjoining* with the active intellect or God is at the same time incidentally offering an interpretation of the biblical *cleaving* to God.

[341]Ibid. 1, §95.

[342]Ibid. 2, §14.

[343]Ibid. 1, §109; cf. 4, §15.

[344]Ibid. 4, §3.

[345]Ibid. 3, §53.

[346]Ibid. 1, §§39–42, 103; 4, §3. The plant realm is characterized by the "natural thing," the animal realm by the "soul-thing," and the ordinary run of mankind by the "intellectual thing," that is, by the possession of the intellectual faculty; ibid. §§31–35. The elite segment has, in addition to the "intellectual thing," a higher principle called the "divine thing" (*amr ilāhī*); and *divine thing* in the other sense, in the sense of the projection, or emanation, from God which governs the universe, emanates (*yufiḍ*) the human *divine thing* upon properly prepared matter in the mother's

member of the elite—which is coterminous with the Israelite nation[347]—actualizes his nature by fulfilling religious precepts, he achieves conjunction and the related phenomena.

To summarize: Hallevi attributes to the "philosophers" an eclectic cosmology and theory of intellect, fashioned out of theses drawn from Alfarabi and Avicenna. He was not oppressed by a compulsion for consistency, and he allows his account of the philosophers' theory of intellect to contradict itself on at least two significant points. After setting forth the philosophers' creed, Hallevi refutes its key constituents, namely: the theory of successive emanations; the very existence of incorporeal intelligences that move celestial spheres; the proposition—which we know to be specifically Avicenna's—that the human soul is an incorporeal substance; and the proposition, not wholly compatible with the construction of the human intellect as an incorporeal substance, that immortality is contingent upon intellectual attainments.

Despite the harsh tone in which he criticizes his philosophic adversaries, Hallevi incorporates much of their picture of the universe into his own. In agreement with his adversaries, he represents the deity and the angels of religious tradition as consisting in pure intellect. In opposition, he asserts that God created the universe outside Himself without the aid of intermediaries, and that God Himself, or the *divine thing*, which is a projection from God and not a distinct substance, governs the celestial spheres. Again in agreement with his adversaries, he explains that sublunar natural objects come into existence when the interaction of celestial forces and forces indigenous to the sublunar region blend matter and prepare it for a given form, whereupon the appropriate form is unfailingly provided by a transcendent source. But then, again correcting his adversaries, he maintains that sublunar forms are furnished by the unitary, undifferentiated *divine thing*, which is a projection or emanation from God, and that God is therefore the giver of forms. No independent substance called the active intellect participates, and indeed no such substance exists. Whenever the blend of a portion of matter is sufficiently balanced to receive a human soul, one is emanated, and the human soul is, as in Avicenna, an incorporeal substance. Following Alfarabi and Avicenna, Hallevi recognizes a supreme state of conjunction, which, however, is conjunction with God and the *divine thing*, rather than with the active intellect; prophetic knowledge through conjunction; and eudaemonia in the next life. Hallevi reserves those phenomena for a narrow segment of mankind, for men whose constitution enables them to receive an emanated nature superior to mere human intellect. And he maintains that

---

womb. See my article on Hallevi (n. 274 above) 382–85. I suggest there, 393–95, a reason why the term *divine thing* is used by Hallevi to characterize the human elite: The human elite are those in whom the "divine thing" in the sense of the unitary emanation proceeding from God and governing the universe has its purest manifestation.

For the notion of a divine degree of mankind, in a variety of contexts, see the references in the same article, 383, n. 1, and Pines (n. 317 above) 181–84 and passim.

[347]Ibid. 2, §14.

conjunction, eudaemonia, and prophecy are enjoyed only by those who bring their superior nature to actuality through ritual, rather than intellectual, activity.

Abraham ibn Daud, who lived and wrote a generation after Hallevi, is not of interest because of any profundity or originality in his thought. But he is the earliest Jewish philosopher known to have consciously borrowed from the Arabic Aristotelians. He portrays a familiar universe, with the deity producing, through a chain of causation, the incorporeal "intelligence[s] or angel[s]," the "souls" of the celestial spheres, and the "spheres." The last of the intelligences is the "active intellect," the existence of which can be inferred from the transition of the "human soul from . . . potential intellect to . . . actual intellect."[348] Scripture, as read by Ibn Daud, confirms the picture of the universe outlined thus far.[349]

The philosophers, he continues, were hard put to harmonize the unitary character of the First Cause with their rule that "for plurality to proceed from the one in a primary fashion [that is, directly] is [judged] impossible by the intellect." They solved their dilemma by assuming that while the First Cause emanates only "a single thing, called an *intelligence* in their terminology and an *angel* in the language of the Law," the thought of the intelligence contains three aspects. Those three aspects in the intelligence's thought give rise to three effects, to the "body of the [outermost] sphere," the "soul of the [outermost] sphere," and an additional incorporeal "unmoved mover"; and the process continues until the incorporeal "mover . . . of the sphere of the moon" produces the "active intellect."[350] Ibn Daud is "skeptical" about the foregoing explanation of plurality in the universe, dismissing it as mere "assertions, the proofs of which we do not find demonstrable." In his judgment, the manner whereby God brought forth a plural universe lies beyond human comprehension.[351]

Like Alfarabi, he writes that the "existence" of the underlying "common matter" of the sublunar region comes "from the outermost sphere."[352] He leaves unclear whether the forms of the four elements and of inanimate natural objects emerge out

[348]The original Arabic text is lost. Medieval Hebrew translation: *Emunah Ramah*, ed. and German trans. S. Weil (Frankfurt 1852), Hebrew text 58, 62, 64; German translation 73, 78, 81. There is also an English translation: Ibn Daud, *The Exalted Faith*, trans. N. Samuelson (Rutherford, N.J. 1986). Mantua, Biblioteca della comunità israelitica, Hebrew MS 81, contains what is often described as another translation of the book, but what is in fact only a different recension of the same translation. The Mantua manuscript's version is poorer than that of the printed edition, but here and there helps to correct the latter. I have not seen T. Fontaine, *In Defense of Judaism, Abraham Ibn Daud* (Assen 1990).

[349]Ibid., Hebrew text 67–68; German translation 84–85.

[350]Ibid. 63–64, 67; German translation 79–80, 84 The distinction of three aspects is peculiar to Avicenna, but Ibn Daud does not describe the aspects exactly as Avicenna did.

[351]Ibid. 67; German translation 84.

[352]Ibid. 64; German translation 80. Ibid. 10, German translation 14, describes God as having created matter as well as the elemental forms. There is, however, no contradiction if we understand that God performed His act of creation through the intermediacy of the sphere and active intellect.

of the mixture, or are emanated from above.[353] But regarding the forms of plants, animals, and man, he allows no ambiguity: The forms of animate beings come from without.[354] "God has emanated the giving of forms to an intellectual substance," to the "active intellect," which serves as "the giver of forms," and the active intellect "emanates" whatever form of a living being each "blend" of matter is "prepared" to receive. The active intellect's function as the source of sublunar form is, in Ibn Daud's view, another philosophic proposition confirmed by Scripture.[355]

He proves, as Avicenna did, that the human soul is an incorporeal substance,[356] that the human soul must be immortal because it is in no sense dependent on the body,[357] and that transmigration is impossible because it would entail two souls in a single body, namely, the soul required by the "blend" of matter and the transmigrating soul.[358]

At birth, he writes, man possesses "potential intellect." Upon learning the "first principles of thought through divine inspiration, such as the proposition that two things equal to the same thing are equal to each other, and the impossibility of two contraries' being combined in the same respect in the same subject," the human faculty for thought becomes "actual intellect." When it draws the inferences that can be made from the first principles of thought and masters the "sciences," it becomes "acquired intellect."[359] So far, the scheme and the terminology are Alfarabi's.[360] Ibn Daud goes on: Since the cause leading the human intellect from potentiality to actuality must itself contain "in actuality" the concepts it brings forth, "the active intellect," the factor leading the human intellect to actuality, must be an incorporeal, "simple substance." Here again, "Scripture and philosophy concur."[361] The active intellect stands "to human souls as light stands to [the faculty of] vision." Just as light activates the faculty of vision, the active intellect

[353]The printed edition 10, German translation 14, speaks of the *emanation* of the elements, but the term *emanation* is missing in the version of the Mantua ms.

[354]Ibn Daud's reason is that if forms arose solely from the mixture of qualities in matter, natural objects would be infinite in their variety and would not lend themselves to a taxonomy of species and genera.

[355]*Emunah Ramah*, Hebrew text 32, 36–37, 44, 64–67, with help of the Mantua ms.; German translation 41, 46–47, 57, 80–84.

[356]Ibid. 34, 37, 58, with corrections from the Mantua ms.; German translation 44, 47, 73. Ibn Daud reasons, as Avicenna did, that indivisible concepts make themselves present in the human soul; that indivisible concepts can be present only in an indivisible, and hence noncorporeal, subject; and that "the human soul, which does contain intellectual thought," is therefore not "a body," a "power in a body," or a "corporeal form." He also repeats Avicenna's arguments showing that the human intellect does not employ a physical organ.

[357]Ibid. 37–38; German translation 48. See above, p. 107. Ibn Daud's formulation loses some of the cogency of Avicenna's reasoning.

[358]Ibid. 39; German translation 49. See above, p. 109.

[359]Ibid. 37; German translation 47.

[360]See above, pp. 49, 67.

[361]*Emunah Ramah*, Hebrew text 58; German translation 73.

activates the intellect by, for example, "awakening [or: inspiring]" the soul "to the first principles of thought, such as the proposition that two things equal to the same thing are equal to each other."[362] Apart from the possible suggestion here that the first principles of thought come directly from the active intellect, I did not see Ibn Daud stating that thoughts emanate directly from the active intellect upon the human intellect.

He knows of a type of prophecy in which the "[compositive] imaginative [faculty]"[363] enables the human "rational soul to receive from the supernal substances what is hidden" and thereby foresee the "future,"[364] and another type in which the incorporeal intelligences "appear . . . in corporeal forms" to souls that have "arrived at complete perfection."[365] The first type, prophetic predictions of the future through the imaginative faculty, recalls what we found in Alfarabi and Avicenna; but Ibn Daud describes the second type in too oblique a fashion to connect it with anything specific in either of those philosophers. He recognizes, as well, the extraordinary noncognitive ability classified by Avicenna as another form of prophecy, namely, as he puts it, the ability of "souls of highest virtue" to "change existent beings" in the physical world.[366]

All in all, the general lines of Ibn Daud's scheme of the universe and theory of intellect are common to Alfarabi and Avicenna. Two details, the celestial origin of sublunar matter and the terminology for the stages of human intellect, come from Alfarabi. Many of the other details, including much of the argumentation, come from Avicenna.

In Moses Maimonides, we encounter, one more time, a translunar universe consisting of celestial spheres, the souls that move them, and the incorporeal intelligences—or "angels," in religious parlance[367]—that inspire the souls to do so.

[362]Ibid. 60; German translation 75–76. See above, pp. 51 (Alfarabi) and 92–93 (Avicenna). The doctoral dissertation of Amira Eran makes a convincing case for taking *ilhām* to have been the Arabic term standing behind the Hebrew term that I translate as: "awakening [or: inspiring]." The Hebrew is *zarez* and elsewhere the term *he*^c^*ara* is used as its equivalent.

[363]Ibid. 70; German translation 88. Both redactions of the Hebrew translation use the term *meṣayyer* (=Arabic: *muṣawwira*; see above, p. 89), which earlier in the Hebrew text 29, German translation 37, had designated the *retentive imagination*. But the functions ascribed here to the faculty operative in prophecy show that Ibn Daud, like Avicenna, has the *compositive imagination* in mind.

[364]Ibid. 70–71, translated with the help of the Mantua ms.; German translation 88–89.

[365]Ibid. 85; German translation 107.

[366]Ibid. 93; German translation 118. See above, p. 122.

[367]Maimonides, *Dalālat al-Ḥā'irīn* (henceforth cited as *Guide*) 2.6. Edition and French translation: *Le guide des égarés*, ed. and trans. S. Munk (Paris 1856–1866); a corrected edition of the Arabic text: I. Joel (Jerusalem 1930); medieval Hebrew translation: *Moreh Nebukim*, trans. Samuel ibn Tibbon, ed. Y. Ibn Shmuel (Jersualem 1981); yet another edition of the Arabic text, with modern Hebrew translation: *Moreh Nebukim*, ed. and trans. J. Kafah (Jerusalem 1972); English translation: *The Guide of the Perplexed*, trans. S. Pines (Chicago 1963). Munk's

Beyond the incorporeal intelligences that move the spheres resides a transcendent First Cause,[368] and it brings the first intelligence into existence through an "emanation" (*faiḍ*; Hebrew: *shefa*ᶜ), *emanation* being the term for all action performed by an incorporeal being.[369] The first intelligence "emanates" the next intelligence in the series, its own celestial sphere, and the soul of its sphere. And each succeeding intelligence does the same, until the intelligence of the moon emanates the "tenth" intelligence, called the "active intellect." That an active intellect exists may be inferred from the "passage of our intellect from potentiality to actuality" as well as from the "appearance of the forms of generated-destructible beings."[370]

In one of its capacities, the active intellect emanates the matter of the sublunar world.[371] Influences descending from the spheres as well as forces within the sublunar world then act upon sublunar matter and "prepare" it for a form[372]; and whenever matter has the "blend" (*mizāj*, *imtizāj*; Hebrew: *mezeg*, *himmazegut*) appropriate to a given natural form, the form appears. No sublunar form can, however, emerge from below, out of the blend of matter, for "what produces a form must itself be an incorporeal form." "All" sublunar forms—which has to mean forms down to the level of the four elements—consequently have an incorporeal source, outside the physical world. Like the matter of the sublunar world, forms come from the ever-present and never-changing emanation of the active intellect, and the active intellect is accordingly termed the "giver [*mu*ᶜ*ṭī*] of forms."[373]

---

translation is one of the two or three best modern translations ever made of a medieval Arabic or Hebrew philosophic text.

368Ibid. 2.4. Maimonides proves the point by showing that the movers of the spheres have a composite essence, whereas the First Cause must be wholly free of composition.

369Ibid. 2.12.

370Ibid. 2.4. When speaking in his own name, Maimonides does not explicitly say that each intelligence emanates the soul, as well as the body, of its sphere, but that is certainly implied.

371Ibid. 2.4 and 11.

372Ibid. 1.72; 2.10 and 12.

373Ibid. 2.12; 18 (1). *Mishneh Torah: Yesode ha-Torah* 4.6; English translation: *Mishneh Torah* 1, ed. and trans. M. Hyamson (New York 1937). Maimonides' reasoning is that changes in the blend of a portion of matter, which are due to physical causes, are gradual and continuous, whereas the change from one natural form to another is instantaneous and sudden; the cause producing natural forms must therefore be of a kind completely different from physical causes. Since the argument applies to all natural forms, including those of the four elements, and since Maimonides expressly writes that "all" forms emanate from the active intellect, he must be saying that even the forms of the four elements come from the active intellect. H. Wolfson, "Hallevi and Maimonides on Design, Chance, and Necessity," reprinted in his *Studies in the History of Philosophy and Religion* 2 (Cambridge, Mass. 1977) 34, quotes a passage in *Guide* 2.19 as evidence for Maimonides' having recognized the movements of the heavens as the cause of the forms of the four elements. Because of the evidence cited here to the contrary, the passage in the *Guide* should be read as saying merely that celestial motion prepares sublunar matter for receiving the forms of the four elements, whereas the active intellect is the agent producing the forms.

Much of the picture sketched thus far is unknown prior to the Arabic Aristotelians, and in crediting the active intellect with the emanation of sublunar matter and "all" sublunar forms, Maimonides has endorsed theses peculiar to Avicenna.[374] Nevertheless, he names "Aristotle" as the author of the scheme,[375] and he further maintains that the scheme is—with a qualification—shared by Scripture.[376]

"Aristotle and all those who philosophized" further subscribed, in Maimonides' words, to the "proposition . . . that from what is simple, only one simple thing can proceed necessarily [*yalzam*]." Burdened with that proposition, "Aristotle" did his best to explain how a multifaceted universe can have emanated from a wholly noncomposite First Cause. The explanation Maimonides attributes to Aristotle turns out to be the emanation theory that we know from Alfarabi and Avicenna, and Maimonides finds the explanation wanting.

In his critique of the emanation theory of Alfarabi and Avicenna, Maimonides reasons, firstly, that since anything proceeding necessarily from what is noncomposite must be equally noncomposite, nothing complex could ever emerge in the manner supposed. If the series of emanated beings flowing by necessity out of the noncomposite First Cause were to descend "through thousands of stages," no stage would contain a greater degree of composition than the preceding one, and the "last" emanated being would be as "simple" as the first. Secondly, even granting the distinction of "two" aspects—as Maimonides reports the theory—in the thought of each emanated intelligence, the two aspects would not suffice. As will be recalled, Ghazali's critique of Avicenna included the contention that a single one of the "three" aspects in the first intelligence could not account for the body of the first sphere, because the first sphere is not uniform but consists of matter, form, and other characteristics; and a single aspect in the second intelligence certainly could not account for the full complexity of the second celestial sphere, since the second sphere contains a "thousand and twenty odd stars."[377] Maimonides argues in the same vein: (1) In necessary emanation, "a correspondence always obtains between cause and effect," so that "a form cannot proceed necessarily from matter, nor matter from form." Consequently, even granting the distinction of aspects in the incorporeal intelligences, the intelligences could, in the manner that the theory supposes, produce only what is incorporeal like themselves, and the corporeality of the spheres and of the sublunar world remains unaccounted for. (2) If an additional concession be made and it is granted that an aspect of an incorporeal intelligence can produce something corporeal, the theory could still not explain the existence of the

[374]In *Guide* 2.18 (1), Maimonides cites Alfarabi's *Risāla fi al-ᶜAql* regarding the active intellect's role in producing natural forms; but the range of forms that he ascribes to the active intellect clearly reflects Avicenna's position.

[375]Ibid. 2.4 (end); 6 (end); 22. Maimonides does recognize that setting the number of spheres, or main spheres, at nine is post-Aristotelian; see 2.4 and 9.

[376]Ibid. 2.5 and 6.

[377]Above, p. 151.

spheres. Most of the spheres consist of at least four factors, the matter and form of the body of the sphere, as well as the matter and form of the star embedded in the sphere; and a single aspect could not give rise to a fourfold product. And (3) the complexity of the sphere of fixed stars would remain completely unexplained, since that sphere contains stars of various types, each of them composed of matter and form.[378]

Maimonides was careful to formulate the rule motivating the theory of successive emanations as the impossibility of more than one effect's *proceeding necessarily* from a noncomposite cause. Both Alfarabi and Avicenna did in fact use the term "proceed necessarily" (*yalzam*) in expounding the emanation of intelligences and spheres.[379] The upshot of Maimonides' critique is, accordingly, that the corporeal and complex universe cannot have emanated "necessarily" from the unitary First Cause. He does not dispute that the First Cause, or God, brings the first intelligence into existence through an act of emanation, that the first intelligence brings its sphere and the next intelligence into existence through a further act of emanation, and so on through the series. His conclusion is only that emanation takes place not through eternal necessity but through a noneternal act of will.[380]

A human soul, like every other natural sublunar form, is crystallized out of the emanation of the active intellect whenever sublunar matter is ready to receive one. Maimonides characterizes the "human rational faculty" as "a power in a body," as a "disposition" in the human organism, and as "inseparable from" its body,[381] although not inseparable in the sense of being distributed through the human body.[382] He thereby parts ways with Avicenna, who had argued that the human soul is an incorporeal substance. Perhaps he is consciously following Ibn Bājja. Ibn Bājja had construed the human intellect as a disposition in the human organism,[383] and Maimonides explicitly cites him in connection with another detail related to the human intellect.[384]

Maimonides does not formally list the stages through which the human intellect progresses, but he does distinguish between "potential" or "material intellect,"

[378] *Guide* 2.22.

[379] Above, pp. 46, 75.

[380] Maimonides' finding that God initiated the emanation of the universe through an act of will serves as the nerve of a carefully wrought "argument" for the creation of the world. After establishing that the universe must have been emanated through an act of will, he adds the further premise that necessity entails eternity, whereas will entails an agent's acting after not having acted. Maimonides concludes that the universe outside of God, being the result of an act of will, cannot be eternal, but must have been created. See *Guide* 2.21 and 22; H. Davidson, "Maimonides' Secret Position on Creation," in *Studies in Medieval Jewish History and Literature*, ed. I. Twersky (Cambridge, Mass. 1979) 34.

[381] *Guide* 1.70 and 72.

[382] Ibid. 2, introduction (11). See A. Altmann, *Von der mittelalterlichen zur modernen Aufklärung* (Tübingen 1987) 67.

[383] Above, p. 145.

[384] *Guide* 1.74 (7).

which is the human rational faculty before it begins to think, "actual intellect," which is human intellect when thinking any intelligible thought,[385] and acquired intellect. Actual human intelligible thought comes, as in Avicenna, "from the emanation of the active intellect."[386] Avicenna had explained the process whereby a man acquires actual intelligible thought as the man's entering into "conjunction" (*ittiṣāl*) with the active intellect and receiving the active intellect's emanation.[387] Maimonides similarly writes that man obtains intelligible thought through "conjunction [*ittiṣāl*; Hebrew: *hiddabeq*] with the divine [active] intellect, which emanates upon him and from which the form [the intelligible thought] comes into existence."[388] He does not, however, employ another formula of Avicenna's, the characterization of all actual human thought as *acquired* intellect. A human intellect that has already passed to actuality, yet is not at the moment actually thinking, is described by Maimonides as neither "actual intellect," on the one hand, nor an unqualified potentiality, on the other. It is in a state of potentiality "close" to actuality and resembles the "skilled scribe when he is not writing."[389] Avicenna had used the analogy of the skilled scribe to make the same point.[390]

The human "acquired intellect," in contrast to the human potential intellect, is "not a power in a body" but rather is "completely separate from the body, and emanates upon it." It is related to the individual "man" as "God is [related] to the world"[391]; it thus apparently is something substantial. The only other passage in Maimonides which employs the term classifies acquired intellect as an "intellectual virtue" and contrasts it with human intellect when man possesses no more than the "first principles" of thought.[392] The statements, when taken together, though not

[385]Ibid. 1.68.

[386]Ibid. 2.4 and 37; 3.8.

[387]Above, p. 89.

[388]*Guide* 3.8. Altmann (n. 382 above) 80–81, 83, takes note of Maimonides' statements, but does not accept what they expressly say, in order to avoid reading Maimonides as tracing all actual human thought to an emanation from the active intellect. B. Kogan, "What Can We Know. . . . Maimonides on the Active Intelligence and Human Cognition," in *Moses Maimonides and His Time*, ed. E. Ormsby (Washington 1989) 127, interprets Maimonides in what I consider to be the correct way, although without quoting the passages in Maimonides which I find to be distinctive of Avicenna's conception.

[389]Ibid. 3.51.

[390]Avicenna distinguished three stages of human potentiality for thought and illustrated them by three senses in which a man may have a potentiality for writing. The third stage of potentiality for thought parallels the "scribe" who is "accomplished in his art" and who can apply the art of writing "at will," but is not at the moment exercising his skill; see above, p. 84. Maimonides, *Millot ha-Higgayon*, Hebrew and Arabic texts, ed. and trans. I. Efros as *Maimonides' Treatise on Logic* (New York 1938), chap. 11, illustrates three senses of *potentiality* in general by the three senses in which, according to Avicenna, a man may have the potentiality for writing; but Maimonides makes no reference there to human intellect.

[391]Ibid. 1.72.

[392]Maimonides, *Thamāniya Fuṣūl* (*Shemonah Peraqim*), ed. and German trans. M. Wolff, as *Acht Capitel* (Leiden 1903) chap. 2. Medieval Hebrew translation: *The Eight Chapters of*

very informative, do tell us that acquired intellect is an advanced stage or state of human intellect, that it is something incorporeal, and that it exists independently of the human body. Maimonides further writes that man's "final perfection" consists in attaining "actual intellect" and he adds that such a condition comes about when one "knows everything a man can know about all existent things."[393] Actual intellect in this sense, as man's final perfection, is different from actual intellect in the sense previously employed by Maimonides, in the sense of a human intellect actually thinking any thought whatsoever,[394] and very plausibly is equivalent, in Maimonides' terminology, to *acquired* intellect. The term *acquired intellect* would, then, denote for Maimonides—as it did for Alfarabi and as one acceptation of acquired intellect did for Avicenna—human intellect at the culmination of its development.

Maimonides does not mention the proposition that when human intellectual development is complete, man enters into permanent *conjunction* with the active intellect.[395] But he does know of a closely related state, the human intellect's having incorporeal beings[396] and the active intellect in particular as a direct object of thought. He writes: The "intellect" belonging to the rational soul of a celestial sphere—which is an intellect brought into existence by "the emanation" of the incorporeal intelligence accompanying the sphere—enables the sphere to "know [*yudrik*] the incorporeal [intelligence] and have it as an object of conceptual thought [*yataṣawwaruhu*]." In a parallel fashion, the human "actual intellect," which comes "from the emanation of the active intellect," enables man to "know the active intellect."[397] If we can assume that *actual* intellect in the present passage is again the human intellect at the culmination of its development, Maimonides is saying that just as the rational soul of a celestial sphere has a direct concept of its incorporeal intelligence, so too a perfect human intellect has a direct concept of the active intellect.

Possessing actual intellect at the level of "final perfection" is, for Maimonides, the "sole . . . cause" of human immortality.[398] That statement meshes with

---

Maimonides, ed. and trans. J. Gorfinkle (New York 1912). Maimonides' statement is based on Alfarabi, *Fuṣūl al-Madanī*, ed. and trans. D. Dunlop (Cambridge 1961) §7. See Altmann (n. 382 above) 80.

[393] Ibid. 3.27.

[394] The two senses of actual intellect in Maimonides seem to correspond to the two senses of acquired intellect in Avicenna.

[395] The closest I found was a statement to the effect that the patriarchs enjoyed a "union [*ittiḥād*] of their intellects with knowledge [*idrāk*] of" God. *Guide* 3.51.

[396] Maimonides, Commentary on Mishnah, *Abot* 3.17 (20), cited by Altmann (n. 382 above) 77; and perhaps *Mishneh Torah*: *Yesode ha-Torah* 4.8. Altmann 84, again does not take the statements at face value.

[397] *Guide* 2.4. See also 1.62, where Maimonides writes that "knowledge" (*idrāk*) of the active intellect cannot be forgotten. He is there echoing Ibn Bājja, *Risālat al-Wadā*ᶜ (n. 100, above) §15.

[398] Ibid. 3.27. Similarly in 2.27.

statements already quoted, to the effect that the human potential intellect is a "power" in the body whereas acquired intellect is "completely separate from the body." Maimonides nonetheless recognizes at least some gradation in the intellectual attainments qualifying man for immortality. In one passage he writes that although "prophets and virtuous men fall short of" the biblical Moses in intellectual perfection, they too gain intellectual immortality and the "enormous pleasure" attendant thereon,[399] and in another he notes that the prophets themselves differed considerably in their intellectual attainments.[400] How far one may fall below absolute human intellectual perfection without losing immortality is left unclear. Despite his insistence on the enormous pleasure awaiting the human intellect in its afterlife,[401] Maimonides cites without demurral the opinion of Ibn Bājja that individuality and all distinction between human intellects is inconceivable after the body's demise.[402]

The statements about human intellect discussed until this point are occasional remarks that have to be pieced together in order to give us anything even approximating a theory. The only topic relating to the human intellect which Maimonides addresses in a systematic fashion is prophecy. His procedure there is to set forth what he calls the "philosophers' view" and then to add the theological provisos that, in his opinion, render it acceptable.

He writes that should a man develop his intellect, but lack a sufficiently strong and healthy "imaginative faculty" (*mutakhayyila*), the rational faculty alone receives the emanation of the active intellect—an emanation whose ultimate source is "God"—and the outcome is a "man of science." Should, on the contrary, a man possess the requisite imaginative faculty and not develop his intellect, the emanation from the active intellect will pass through the rational faculty and act solely on the imagination. The outcome now is a "statesman," a "lawgiver," a "clairvoyant" (*kāhin*; Hebrew: *qosem*), an "augur," or a "man of true dreams." The inclusion of true dreams in the effect of the active intellect's emanation upon the imaginative faculty recalls the descriptions of imaginative prophecy that were met in Alfarabi and Avicenna,[403] but Maimonides refuses to dignify a phenomenon restricted to the imaginative faculty with the name of *prophecy*.[404] True prophecy, in his account, takes place only when the rational and imaginative faculties together enjoy the

[399]Ibid. 3.51 (end).

[400]Ibid. 2.36.

[401]See Commentary on Mishnah, *Sanhedrin* 10.1; *Mishneh Torah: Hilkot Teshubah* 8.6–7. See above, p. 109–10.

[402]*Guide* 1.74 (7), taken together with 2, introduction, proposition 16; 1.70. Ibn Bājja's position, is discussed above, p. 145. On the subject of immortality in Maimonides, see Altmann 85–91.

[403]Above, pp. 61, 119.

[404]The point is made very sharply by Maimonides in *Sefer ha-Miṣwot*, negative commandments §31; English translation: *The Commandments: Sefer ha-Mitzvoth of Maimonides*, trans. C. Chavel (London 1967).

emanation of the active intellect.[405] The emanation from the active intellect must come "first to the rational faculty and then emanate upon the imaginative faculty."[406]

For a man to qualify for true prophecy, "the substance of his brain" must be, "from birth, in a state of complete balance, by reason of the purity of its matter and its blend." The man's imaginative faculty, which is a function of a part of the brain, will as a result be superlatively strong and healthy. The man must "study, . . . pass from potentiality to actuality, and procure a human intellect in a perfect state." He must in addition possess ethical virtue, so that he can withstand the blandishments of corporeal pleasures. And he must direct all his attention to "knowledge of the secrets of the universe, . . . knowledge of the universe's causes, . . . and . . . knowledge of God." If such a man's "imaginative faculty becomes active, and there reaches it an emanation from the [active] intellect commensurate with the man's" intellectual attainments, he "will see God and His angels" and learn "true opinions and general modes of government [*tadbīr*; *hanhaga*] for the welfare of mankind." The prophetic experience may occur in a "dream" or in a "vision"; when it occurs in a vision, the imaginative faculty "sees the thing as if outside [the soul]," and the image "originating in it [that is, in the imaginative faculty] seems to arrive through external perception." The person vouchsafed the experience stands at the "highest human level and the ultimate perfection possible for his species."[407]

What Maimonides has described as "true prophecy" is imaginative prophecy in the case where the active intellect's emanation affects the imaginative faculty of a man of perfect intellect. Under the influence of the active intellect, the prophet's imaginative faculty "sees," as it were, God and the incorporeal intelligences; that is to say, his imaginative faculty depicts theoretical truths figuratively. And Maimonides emphasizes, undoubtedly because of the legal bias of the Jewish religion, that codes of law are also revealed to the prophet.[408] He has not yet mentioned predictions of the future through true prophecy but does so in a nearby passage.

Besides the primary qualifications for prophecy, there are, he writes, secondary qualifications, and one of them is the aptitude of "intuition" (*shuᶜūr*) or "insight" (*ḥads*). Intuition, or insight, enables certain men to draw rapid inferences from known events and predict the future, and when the men are prophets, intuition, or insight, enables them to "foretell future events in the shortest time." What is more

[405]*Guide* 2.37. For God as the ultimate source of the emanation, see above, p. 61. Maimonides, like Alfarabi, does not distinguish between a retentive and a compositive imagination.

[406]Ibid. 2.36.

[407]Ibid.; Commentary on Mishnah, *Sanhedrin* 10.1; *Mishneh Torah: Yesode ha-Torah* 7.1 (where the participation of the imaginative faculty is not stated explicitly but only implied). On seeing God's angels, see above, p. 120.

[408]*Guide* 2.36.

important, it also "undoubtedly" enables "true prophets" to attain "theoretical knowledge" in instances where "a man could not by mere speculation learn the causes [that is, the premises] from which the proposition follows."[409] Prophecy, in other words, produces genuine theoretical knowledge, as distinct from the mere figurative depiction of theoretical truths. Genuine theoretical knowledge through prophecy recalls Avicenna's intellectual prophecy, but Maimonides' version has peculiarities of its own. Avicenna's intellectual prophecy consisted in the intellectual faculty's receiving the emanation of the active intellect effortlessly, thanks to insight, and the result was scientific propositions. In Maimonides' version, both the human intellect and imaginative faculty must participate in receiving the active intellect's emanation, with the aid of insight; and the result is theoretical knowledge lying beyond ordinary human science, beyond the furthest limit to which the human intellect can reach by itself. Maimonides does not state whether insight brings the prophet effortless knowledge of ordinary scientific truths as well. Since he has said that a man must already master all science before receiving prophecy, he would perhaps reject prophetic knowledge of ordinary scientific truths.[410]

The foregoing is Maimonides' account of the philosophers' position on prophecy, and it becomes the core of his own position. The emanation from the active intellect which ultimately derives from God, the participation of the imaginative faculty, true dreams regarding the future and a figurative depiction of theoretical truth as the contents of imaginative prophecy—those elements come from Alfarabi and Avicenna. Peculiar to Avicenna is the contribution of the aptitude of insight, which enables the prophet to receive the emanation of the active intellect effortlessly and thereby acquire genuine theoretical truths. Two significant elements in Maimonides' account of the philosophers' position on prophecy do not, however, come from Alfarabi, Avicenna, or any other known philosopher, and probably are original with him. They are the refusal to dignify the effect of the active intellect on the imaginative faculty alone with the name of prophecy, and the assertion that through insight, the prophet can attain theoretical knowledge beyond the realm of ordinary science. Maimonides' personal position on prophecy is completed when he adds his two theological provisos to the philosophic position. The provisos are (1) that prophecy is not a completely automatic and natural phenomenon, for God can, if He so wishes, stay the effect of the active intellect's emanation on the rational and imaginative faculties, and thereby prevent those who are qualified for prophecy from receiving it; and (2) that the philosophic theory of prophecy in no way covers the prophecy of Moses.[411]

[409] Ibid. 2.38. The other secondary qualification is bravery. In 2.16 (end), Maimonides' example of theoretical knowledge through prophecy is prophetic knowledge of the creation of the world.

[410] *Guide* 2.38 (end). Above, p. 203, Maimonides did recognize degrees in the prophets' intellectual attainments.

[411] Ibid. 2.32; 35.

To summarize, the structure of the universe and emanation of the universe from the First Cause, which Maimonides attributes to Aristotle and says is shared by Scripture, the range of the active intellect's functions, which he likewise attributes to Aristotle and discovers in Scripture, his statements about human intellect, which he implies are drawn from Aristotle or from the "philosophers" generally, and the theory of prophecy which he explicitly attributes to the philosophers and around which he builds his own position on prophecy, these all derive from the Arabic Aristotelians, rather than from Aristotle himself. Maimonides' main philosophic work, the *Guide for the Perplexed*, refers to Alfarabi and Ibn Bājja several times by name,[412] while never mentioning Avicenna. Yet of the Arabic Aristotelians, Avicenna is the one from whom Maimonides borrows most, both in recording the views of the philosophers and in delineating his own positions.

Theses and details in Maimonides for which Avicenna is the source include the explicit formulation of the principle that from the one only one can necessarily proceed, the emanation of the matter of the sublunar region from the active intellect, the emanation of all sublunar forms from the active intellect, and the designation of the active intellect as the *giver of forms*. In construing the human rational faculty as a power or disposition in the human organism, Maimonides does not follow Avicenna and may be consciously borrowing from Ibn Bājja. His terms for the stages of human intellect—potential or material intellect, actual intellect, acquired intellect—are not defined very precisely, but his use of the terms reflects Alfarabi's usage more than Avicenna's. The thesis that man obtains actual intellectual thought by entering into conjunction with the active intellect and receiving the active intellect's emanation brings us back again to Avicenna. The possibility of the human intellect's having the active intellect as a direct object of thought is common to Alfarabi, Avicenna, and Ibn Bājja, as is Maimonides' account of the centrality of the imagination in prophecy. The part played by insight in securing theoretical knowledge for the prophet effortlessly is, however, one more point borrowed from Avicenna, although Maimonides works out the notion of prophetic theoretical knowledge in his own way.

Through a few carefully placed corrections, Maimonides transforms the deism of the Arabic Aristotelians into a rationalistic theism: With the help of arguments drawn from Ghazali's critique of Avicenna, he refutes the emanation scheme of Alfarabi and Avicenna, insofar as the scheme assumes emanation to occur necessarily. He can then conclude that the emanation of the universe from the First Cause takes place not by necessity but through an act of will, and is hence noneternal. Having established that the deity possesses will, he can also reserve for the deity the possibility of intervening in the prophetic process and staying the effect

[412]See Pines' introduction to his translation of the *Guide* (n. 367 above) lxxix, civ, cvii. In a letter to Judah Ibn Tibbon, Maimonides ranks Avicenna below Alfarabi as a philosopher. See Steinschneider (n. 270 above) 42; A. Marx, "Texts by and about Maimonides," *Jewish Quarterly Review* 25 (1935) 380.

of the active intellect's emanation. And he exempts the prophecy of the biblical Moses from the philosophic definition of prophecy on no other grounds than the text of Scripture. Regarding human immortality, an issue with obvious ramifications for religion, Maimonides' rationalism outweighed any religious scruples. He writes that human immortality is the exclusive outcome of man's intellectual development and he refrains from defending the individual immortality of the human soul or intellect.

Résumé. Hallevi outlines a picture of the universe and a theory of human intellect, both of which he attributes to unnamed philosophers. He criticizes those philosophers harshly but thereupon turns around and incorporates much of their thinking into his own view of things. Ibn Daud and Maimonides also present accounts of the structure of the universe and the nature of the human intellect in the name of Aristotle or unnamed philosophers. Unlike Hallevi, they openly accept the schemes they set forth, although with significant reservations. What is common to the three men is revealing. Each knew Arabic and could have read Avicenna if texts were available. Each submits his account of the views of the philosophers as if it were the system of Aristotle or, in some sense, an official philosophic system. Each account is in fact an eclectic combination of doctrines from the Arabic Aristotelians. Avicenna is not mentioned by Hallevi, by Ibn Daud, or by Maimonides in his main philosophic work. Yet in each of the eclectic accounts, Avicenna's positions predominate.

From the thirteenth century onward, Jewish philosophy was conducted almost exclusively in Hebrew, and Jewish thinkers learned their philosophy primarily from Hebrew translations of Maimonides and Averroes. Key works of Alfarabi continued to circulate in Hebrew translation. There was, by contrast, virtually no direct acquaintance with Avicenna, at least as regards the subjects we are studying.[413] Nevertheless, through the medium of Hallevi, Ibn Daud, Maimonides, and one or two others who read Avicenna in Arabic, that philosopher left a solid mark on subsequent Jewish philosophy. The following theses deriving from Alfarabi and more especially from Avicenna appear among Jewish philosophic writers from the thirteenth to the sixteenth centuries: the theory of successive emanations, which is often cited for the purpose of refuting it[414]; the identification of the active intellect

[413]On the translations into Hebrew of the works of Alfarabi and Avicenna, see above, nn. 270, 271.

[414]Gersonides, *Milḥamot ha-Shem* (*Die Kämpfe Gottes*) (Leipzig 1866) 5.3.8; English translation of *Milḥamot* 1–4: Levi ben Gershom, *The Wars of the Lord*, trans. S. Feldman (Philadelphia 1984–1987); Abraham Shalom, *Neweh Shalom* (Venice 1575) 1.14, 21b; see H. Davidson, *The Philosophy of Abraham Shalom* (Berkeley 1964) 47–48; Leone Ebreo, *Dialoghi d'Amore*, ed. S. Caramella (Bari 1929) 281–84 (noncommittal); discussed by H. Davidson, "Medieval Jewish Philosophy in the Sixteenth Century," in *Jewish Thought in the Sixteenth Century*, ed. B. Cooperman (Cambridge, Mass. 1983) 127–28.

as the last of the incorporeal intelligences[415]; emanation of the matter of the sublunar world from the active intellect[416]; emanation of sublunar forms from the active intellect upon properly blended matter[417]; the appellation "giver of forms" for the active intellect[418]; the human soul as an incorporeal substance[419]; the emanation of human intelligible thought from the active intellect[420]; prophecy through an emanation of the active intellect arriving in the human intellect and giving rise to instantaneous theoretical knowledge[421]; foreknowledge of the future through prophecy, or merely true dreams, through an emanation upon the human imaginative faculty from either the active intellect,[422] or the souls of the celestial spheres[423]; and human eudaemonia as conjunction with the active intellect or with God.[424]

[415]*Ruaḥ Ḥen* (Berlin 1930) 3, p. 9; Shem Ṭob Falaquera, *Moreh ha-Moreh* (Pressburg 1837) 141; Mūsā al-Lāwī, untitled treatise, trans. G. Vajda, "Un champion de l'avicennisme," *Revue thomiste* 48 (1948) 507; Gersonides, *Milḥamot* 1.6, 45; 5.3.13 (the strange thesis that the active intellect comes into existence through a collective emanation of all the intelligences).

Medieval Jewish philosophers who accept a Neoplatonic picture of the universe sometimes attach the name *active intellect* to the Neoplatonic cosmic intellect. Examples: S. Ibn Gabirol, *Fons vitae* (n. 340 above) 5, §19, p. 294; *Liqqutim* (n. 340 above) 5, §25; pseudo-Baḥya, *K. Maᶜānī al-Nafs*, ed. I. Goldziher (Berlin 1907) 54; proto-Cabalistic texts cited by A. Farber, "On the Sources of Moses de Leon's Early Kabbalistic System," in *Studies in Jewish Mysticism, Philosophy, and Ethical Literature* (Tishby Festschrift) (Jerusalem 1986) 77–78, 82 (in Hebrew).

[416]Mūsā al-Lāwī 507.

[417]*Ruaḥ Ḥen* 10, p. 39; Moses ben Naḥman, Commentary on the Pentateuch, Leviticus 17:11; English translation: *Commentary on the Torah*, trans. C. Chavel (New York 1971–1976); Mūsā al-Lāwī 507; Gersonides, *Milḥamot* 1.6, 41; 1.8, 50; 5.3.13, 289; A. Shalom, *Neweh Shalom* 7.2.4, 112a; 7.2.6, 115b; Davidson, *Philosophy of Abraham Shalom* 51–52.

[418]*Ruaḥ Ḥen* 10, p. 39; Gersonides, *Milḥamot* 1.6, 43; M. Isserles (a sixteenth-century rabbinic scholar), *Torat ha-ᶜOla* (Lemberg 1858) 1.6b.

[419]In the eleventh century, Baḥya Ibn Paquda (n. 340 above) 2.5; 10.1, construed the human soul as a "simple" or "light-like spiritual substance." Above, p. 192, Hallevi was seen to construe the human soul as an incorporeal substance. After Maimonides, similar constructions of the human soul are found in: Ḥasdai Crescas, *Or Ha-Shem* (Vienna 1859) 2.6.1, 53b–54a; Joseph Albo, *Sefer ha-ᶜIkkarim* (*ha-ᶜIqqarim*), ed. and trans. I. Husik (Philadelphia 1946) 4.29, pp. 283–85; A. Shalom, *Neweh Shalom* (n. 414 above) 8.9, 144a; 11.8, 198b; Davidson, *Philosophy of Abraham Shalom* (n. 414 above) 82–83.

[420]Shem Ṭob Falaquera, *Sefer ha-Nefesh*, ed. and trans. in R. Jospe, *Torah and Sophia* (Cincinnati 1988), chap. 18, pp. 313 (Hebrew text), 346 (English translation).

[421]*Ruaḥ Ḥen* 4, p. 13. Gersonides, *Milḥamot* 2.4. A. Shalom, *Neweh Shalom* 6.1, 88b–89a; 6.5, 93b; but see 6.2, 89b; Davidson, *Philosophy of Abraham Shalom* 95–99.

[422]*Ruaḥ Ḥen* 4, p. 13.

[423]Gersonides, *Milḥamot* 2.6, 114. Gersonides, ibid. 2.2–3, explains that prophetic foreknowledge results from an emanation of the active intellect on the human intellect. In 2.6, he maintains that nonprophetic foreknowledge through dreams must result from an emanation of the souls of the spheres upon the human imaginative faculty. Although Gersonides had no direct acquaintance with Avicenna, this latter thesis recalls Avicenna's position.

[424]*Ruaḥ Ḥen* 3, pp. 10–11; Shem Ṭob Falaquera, *Moreh ha-Moreh* (n. 415 above) 141–42; Gersonides, *Milḥamot* 4.4, 165 (conjunction only in a loose sense; see ibid. 1.12).

Alfarabi and Avicenna seem even to have infiltrated the theosophical doctrine known as the Cabala. The distinctive doctrine of the medieval Cabala is an emanation process taking place within God Himself. Through the internal emanation, ten divine aspects emerge. The tenth and last of the aspects serves as the channel through which existence, human souls, and the holy Law are emanated into the realm outside of God;[425] and human eudaemonia consists in reascending to a state of conjunction with one or another of the divine aspects.[426] Those plainly are not the philosophic doctrines we have been examining, but the similarities can hardly be fortuitous.

Reverberations in Scholastic Philosophy

In the twelfth century, the Latin world received a cornucopia of translations of Greek and Arabic philosophic works. Among them were Alfarabi's *Risāla fī al-ᶜAql*, known variously as *De intellectu*, *De intellectu et intellecto*, and *De intelligentiis*[427]; the parts of Avicenna's most comprehensive work which bear most directly on our subject, namely, the *De anima* and *Metaphysics* of the *Shifā'*[428]; and Ghazali's summary of Avicenna's philosophy. The pertinent parts

[425]Moses ben Naḥman, Commentary on the Pentateuch, Genesis 1:11, 26; 2:7 (in his commentary on Leviticus 17:11, Moses ben Naḥman mentions the philosophers' theory that the active intellect emanates animal souls); Jacob ben Sheshet, cited by G. Vajda, *Juda ben Nissim ibn Malka* (Paris 1954) 77 (what the philosophers supposed to be an active intellect located at the end of the hierarchy of intelligences is "according to us" a part of the godhead); M. Recanati, Commentary on the Pentateuch, Genesis 1:26; 11:4; Exodus 3:13. On medieval attempts to coordinate the cabalistic aspects of God with the philosophic incorporeal intelligences, see A. Altmann, "Moses Narboni's 'Epistle on Shiᶜur Qomā,'" in Altmann (n. 382 above) 146–47.

[426]Moses ben Naḥman, Commentary on the Pentateuch, Deuteronomy 11:22; I. Tishby, *Mishnat ha-Zohar* 2 (Jerusalem 1961) 292–93, 302–5; G. Scholem, "Devekuth or Communion with God," *Review of Religion* 14 (1949–1950) 115–17, 120–22, and 129–30 (where Scholem is surprised that although eighteenth- and nineteenth-century Polish Hasidism deemphasized intellectual values, many in the movement describe *conjunction* [*debekut*] as "reached by a fixation of one's" thought [*maḥshavah*] or intellect [*sekel*] on God); G. Scholem *Kabbalah* (New York 1974) 174–76.

A. Abulafia, who is commonly (and perhaps incorrectly) classified as a Cabalist, speaks repeatedly of the conjunction of the human intellect with the active intellect, although what the active intellect means from him is not clear to me; see passages quoted by M. Idel, *The Mystical Experience in Abraham Abulafia* (Albany 1988) 128–33.

[427]The Latin text is edited by E. Gilson, in "Les sources gréco-arabes de l'augustinisme avicennissant," *Archives d'histoire doctrinale et littéraire du moyen âge* 4 (1930) 108–26.

[428]The Latin translation of *Shifā': De anima* (n. 91 above) has been preserved in no less than fifty manuscripts, found in the libraries of ten European countries. The text was edited by S. van Riet, as *Liber de anima seu sextus de naturalibus*, 2 vols. (Louvain 1968–1972); the manuscripts are described in vol. 1, 105*–112*. *Shifā': Ilāhiyyāt* (n. 49 above) was translated into Latin as *Liber de philosophia prima sive scientia divina*; it was edited by S. van Riet, 2

of the *Shifā'* as well as Ghazali's summary were translated in the middle of the century, and Alfarabi's *Risāla* was probably translated at about the same time.

The translations of Avicenna have been preserved in an impressive number of manuscripts, the manuscripts are spread throughout the libraries of Europe, and citations of Avicenna by scholastic philosophers also abound. There are thus good grounds for supposing that, whether in their own right or as an interpretation of Aristotle, his writings aroused considerable interest. Nevertheless, Avicenna's impact was not large in the areas that concern us, and Alfarabi's impact was still smaller.

Two minor Latin texts do follow Avicenna on certain pivotal points. The first of the two is a small composition dating from the late twelfth or early thirteenth century, which is entitled *De causis primis et secundis et de fluxu qui consequitur eas* or, in other manuscripts, *De primis et secundis substantiis et de fluxu earum.* The author is unknown; one of the three manuscripts names no author, while the others credit Avicenna himself with the authorship.[429] When treating the derivation of the universe from the First Cause, the composition states that the first caused intelligence contains two aspects, its being "possible in itself" and its having "an intellectual nature in itself." From the two aspects there flow—if I understood correctly—"the corporeality . . . of the outermost heaven" and the "outermost heaven's form," or "soul."[430] The terminology and the distinction between the cause of the sphere's body and the cause of its soul plainly come from Avicenna, yet Avicenna's position is not represented at all precisely. The text does not, for instance, mention the first intelligence's thought of its cause, the first intelligence's thought of itself as a necessarily existent being, or the emanation of the next intelligence in the hierarchy.[431] A later passage reproduces a different thesis of Avicenna's more faithfully. Human thought, the anonymous author here tells us, takes place when "the active intellect," which embodies "the multitude of forms, . . . conjoins" with the "potential intellect" in a certain mode "of conjunction." (Alternative, possible translation, which will reflect Avicenna even more closely: when "the potential intellect . . . conjoins" with "the active intellect. . . .") Through conjunction with the active intellect, the potential intellect is

---

vols. (Louvain 1977–1980). Twenty-five manuscripts containing the entire text, and distributed through the libraries of Europe, have been preserved, and other manuscripts have fragments; see van Riet, vol. 1, 124*–125*, 128*–129*.

429R. de Vaux, *Notes et textes sur l'Avicennisme Latin* (Paris 1934) 63–64, 68–69. The text was printed together with Latin versions of several works of Avicenna—including the *De anima* and *Metaphysics* of the *Shifā'*—and Alfarabi's *De intellectu* (called *De intelligentiis*) in a volume published in Venice, 1508. De Vaux 63–140, provides a critical, annotated edition of the text.

430De Vaux 74, 101.

431Avicenna, *Shifā': Ilāhiyyāt* (n. 49 above) 405; Latin: *Liber de philosophia prima* (n. 428 above) 2.481. Cf. above, n. 6.

"illuminated, . . . receives a form from the active intellect," and becomes "actual."[432]

Both the passage regarding the emanation of the outermost sphere and the passage regarding the emanation of human thought repeat theses lying at the heart of Avicenna's philosophy. They are woven together with less distinctive theses of Avicenna but also with paraphrases or quotations from other sources—from the *Liber de causis*, from Augustine, from John Scotus Erigena, and, through Erigena, from Gregory of Nyssa and pseudo-Dionysius the Areopagite.[433] The *Liber de causis* is a paraphrase of sections of one of Proclus' works, and Erigena as well as pseudo-Dionysius betray Neoplatonic inspiration. To some extent, they therefore share a common background with Avicenna. The anonymous author of our work does not, however, integrate Avicenna's positions with what he takes from his other sources and merely concocts an emanationist pot pourri.

The second minor text that follows Avicenna carries the stereotyped title *De anima*. Some, although not all, of the manuscripts name Dominic Gundissalinus, a man who participated in the translation of Avicenna into Latin, as the author,[434] but a study of the contents has unearthed elements that do not sit well with the attribution to Gundissalinus.[435] This second composition borrows much more from Avicenna than the previous one. Once again, though, Avicenna's views are tempered with material of a different provenance and different character.

Without ever mentioning Avicenna by name, the Latin *De anima* repeats his argument from the premise that the soul serves as the substratum for indivisible thoughts to the conclusion that the soul is an indivisible, and hence incorporeal, substance[436] and also his arguments for the immortality of the human soul.[437] The treatise refers to the "philosophers[']" proof that human "souls . . . are created by the angels," although with the stipulation that God, acting through the instrumentality of the angels, has ultimate responsibility for creating souls.[438] It copies, virtually verbatim, Avicenna's three stages of human potentiality for thought, these being the "material intellect," "intellect *in habitu*," and "actual intellect." Like Avicenna, it illustrates the three stages by three levels in the human potentiality for writing. It quotes Avicenna's thesis that when the human potential intellect

432De Vaux 78, 130. See Avicenna, *Shifā': De anima* (n. 91 above) 235–36; Latin translation (n. 428 above) 2.128; above, p. 93.

433De Vaux 65–66, 72–80.

434J. Muckle, "The Treatise De Anima of Dominicus Gundissalinus" (annotated edition of the text), (henceforth cited as: Gundissalinus [?], *De anima*) *Mediaeval Studies* 2 (1940) 28–29.

435De Vaux 144–45.

436Gundissalinus (?), *De anima* 37–39, paralleling *Shifā': De anima* 209–19; Latin translation of *Shifā'* 2.81–98. See above, p. 83. On p. 37, the Gundissalinus text repeats Avicenna's floating man argument; see above, p. 83, n. 38.

437Gundissalinus (?), *De anima* 61–63, paralleling *Shifā': De anima* 227–33; Latin translation of *Shifā'* 2.113–124. See above, pp. 107–8.

438Gundissalinus (?), *De anima* 51.

"conjoins with" the active intellect in "a certain mode of conjunction, . . . a *species* [that is, a conceptual copy] of [intelligible] forms, which is acquired from without, is imprinted in" the human intellect. And it accordingly calls actual human thought "intellect acquired [*adeptus*] from without."[439] As it proceeds, the treatise reproduces Avicenna's analysis of the situation in which a person is confident that he can answer a theoretical question even before formulating the answer, and Avicenna's argument from the phenomenon of intellectual memory; and it finds, as Avicenna did, that to learn a thought is to "acquire a perfect disposition for conjoining [at will] with the active intellect" vis à vis the given thought.[440] Finally, it explains that "insight" (*subtilitas, ingenium*) is an inborn aptitude for "conjoining with the [active] intellect" effortlessly. A man who "burns with insight" receives "from the active intellect [the answers to] all questions, imprinted firmly [in himself], instantaneously or almost so," and in receiving knowledge, the man of insight is vouchsafed "the middle terms" as well as the conclusions of syllogisms. Theoretical knowledge through superlative insight is a "mode of prophecy, . . . higher than all the powers of prophecy; . . . [it is] appropriately called holy intellect, . . . [and] is a higher level" than any other human "power [or: faculty]."[441]

The passages that have been quoted cover all the significant aspects of Avicenna's theory of intellect. The final chapter in the treatise then suddenly veers off on another tack. Borrowing a distinction from Boethius, the author differentiates between human "science," which falls within the scope of man's "intellect," and human "wisdom," which is a brand of knowledge attainable only through a different human faculty called "intelligence." Earlier, the treatise had affirmed that since a high degree of insight enables the human intellect to conjoin effortlessly with the active intellect and receive immediate theoretical knowledge, insight constitutes the highest human power. It now, by contrast, submits that the soul's true goal is not "science" at all but "wisdom," and the soul reaches that goal when the "eye of the soul, which is intelligence," contemplates "the creator" thanks to a light radiated by God himself—"wherefore the prophet says: 'O Lord, in your light we shall see light.'"[442]

439Ibid. 87–88, paralleling *Shifā': De anima* 48–50; Latin translation of *Shifā'* 1.95–99. The Latin translation exists in two slightly different versions (van Riet, *Liber de anima*, n. 428 above, 1.109*), and in one version—probably the original—acquired intellect is termed *intellectus accommodatus* rather than *intellectus adeptus*.

440Gundissalinus (?), *De anima* 91–94, paralleling *Shifā': De anima* 241–47; Latin translation of *Shifā'* 2.138–149. See above, p. 89.

441Gundissalinus (?), *De anima* 95–96, paralleling *Shifā': De anima* 249–50; Latin translation of *Shifā'* 2.151–153. See above, pp. 117–18. The Latin translation of the *Shifā'* falls into some confusion in its handling of the term *insight*.

442Gundissalinus (?) *De anima* 98–99; cf. Gilson (n. 427 above) 85–92. The verse is Psalms 36:10.

The *De anima* attributed to Gundissalinus thus reproduces and apparently subscribes to Avicenna's theory of intellect, yet the author or, conceivably, a correcting hand felt that Avicenna could not be allowed to stand by himself. Earlier we saw Islamic writers of a mystical bent overlaying Avicenna's theory of intellect with the doctrine of a *direct experience* that surpasses intellectual thought. In a similar fashion, the present text overlays Avicenna's theory with the doctrine, inspired by an older Christian theology, of an intellectual activity surpassing ordinary ratiocination.

When we turn to other Scholastic philosophers, we find that neither the structure of the translunar world envisioned by the Arabic Aristotelians, nor the emanation scheme of Alfarabi and Avicenna, won a sympathetic reception.[443] The emanation of natural forms in general from the active intellect and the emanation of human souls in particular, theses that could have been learned from either Alfarabi's *Risāla fī al-ᶜAql* (*De intellectu*) or Avicenna, did gain a very limited following. John Blund (d. 1248) distinguishes the "first giver of forms" from the "intelligence" that, according to "a number of writers," serves as the intermediary of the first giver of forms.[444] By *first giver of forms*, Blund plainly means the First Cause. He then writes that when matter is properly prepared to receive a human soul, a soul is "emanated from the first giver of forms." His position is, in a word, that human souls are indeed emanated from without upon properly prepared matter but that the source is God Himself.[445] Albert the Great (1206–1280) has left an enormous corpus of writings, encompassing borrowings that are not always fully assimilated and, as a result, not always consistent. He repeatedly lays down the principle that

[443]Examples: William of Auvergne dismisses, on both religious and philosophic grounds, the explanation of celestial motion through a desire that souls of the spheres have to imitate incorporeal intelligences. He contends that the supposition of intelligences and souls of spheres arrogates to them functions properly belonging to the deity; and the supposition that desire to emulate an intelligence might induce a celestial soul to make its sphere rotate continually is, from a logical standpoint, "ridiculous" and "impossible." The reasoning is curiously similar in spirit to that of Judah Hallevi. William also rejects the emanation of human souls from the active intellect. See E. Gilson, "Pourquoi Saint Thomas a critiqué Saint Augustin," *Archives d'histoire doctrinale et littéraire* 1.49–51; De Vaux (n. 429 above) 26, n. 1; 31–32. John Blund, who on other issues betrays the influence of both Aristotle and Avicenna, rejects the existence of celestial souls and explains the motion of the spheres by their "nature." See John Blund, *Tractatus de anima*, ed. D. Callus and R. Hunt (London 1970) §10. Albert the Great, whose vast corpus is not always consistent, sometimes argues against the construction of the active intellect as the tenth and last of the incorporeal intelligences, but in one work does recognize celestial intelligences and an intellect "universally active in the lower world." See Albertus Magnus, *De intellectu* 2.9, in *Opera omnia*, ed. A. Borgnet 9 (Paris 1890) 516; A. Schneider, *Die Psychologie Alberts des Grossen* (Muenster 1903–1906) (*Beiträge zur Geschichte der Philosophie des Mittelalters* 4.5–6) 72–73, 189, 360. Aquinas refutes the emanation scheme of "Avicenna," the conception of the active intellect as a transcendent being, and "Avicenna['s]" argument from intellectual memory. See *Summa contra gentiles* 2.42, 74, 76; *Summa theologiae* 1.47.1; 1.79.3, 4, 6.

[444]John Blund, *Tractatus de anima*, §344.

[445]Ibid. §361.

from one only one can proceed but probably never had the intention of accepting its applicability to the deity.[446] Sometimes he rejects the emanation of natural forms from the active intellect, while elsewhere, on the contrary, he accepts the emanation of natural forms from the "intelligence," or from the "active intellect." Here, he is simply inconsistent.[447] Regarding the human soul in particular, he in one work refutes the notion that the last of the intelligences is the source of the human rational soul and instead identifies God as the source.[448] In other works, he apparently conflates the active intellect of the Arabic Aristotelians, the cosmic Intellect of Neoplatonic philosophy, and the deity; and he calls God "the giver of forms."[449] Whatever Albert in fact believed, of interest for us are the threads drawn from Avicenna which he intertwines with other notions.[450]

Alfarabi and Avicenna probably made their strongest mark upon the Latin world by helping convince a fair number of thirteenth-century Scholastics that the active intellect, in the original sense of the agent leading the human potential intellect to actuality, is an incorporeal being transcending the human soul. Credit for teaching the transcendent construction of the active intellect to the Latin world has to be shared, however, for that construction could also have discovered in the *De intellectu* attributed to Alexander of Aphrodisias, which circulated in Latin by the end of the twelfth century[451]; the *Fons vitae* of Solomon Ibn Gabirol (Avicebron), which was translated by the same circle that rendered Avicenna's writings in Latin and which evoked considerable interest; and Averroes' Long Commentary on the *De anima*, which was translated about 1230 and which also was widely read. Ibn Gabirol espoused a Neoplatonic scheme of First Essence/Intellect/Soul/Nature, rather than the emanation scheme of Alfarabi and Avicenna; but he attached the name "active intellect" to the cosmic Intellect, the second hypostasis in his Neoplatonic hierarchy, and thus joined the company of those endorsing a transcendent active intellect.[452] In 1267, when the transcendent construction already had a certain following, one more work, Themistius' Paraphrase of the *De*

[446]M. Grabmann, *Mittelalterliches Geistesleben* 2 (Munich 1936) 288–89, 292–93, 301–9.

[447]Schneider 340–41. Sometimes Albertus makes clear that he was recording philosophic doctrines without intending to affix his own endorsement; see Grabmann 294–97. L. Kennedy, "St. Albert the Great's Doctrine of Divine Illumination," *The Modern Schoolman* 40 (1962) 35–37, proposes a development in Albert's positions regarding the manner in which man acquires knowledge.

[448]Albertus, *De intellectu et intelligibili* 1.1.4, in *Opera omnia* 9.481–483. English translation: *Selections from Medieval Philosophers* 1, ed. and trans. R. McKeon (New York 1929) 334–38.

[449]Schneider 73–78.

[450]The statements quoted in the previous two notes can be harmonized by understanding that the deity, also known as the active intellect, the cosmic Intellect, and the giver of forms, is the agent who creates human souls. See Schneider 78–80.

[451]G. Théry, *Autour du décret de 1210: 1—Alexandre* (Le Saulchoir 1926) 82–83.

[452]S. Ibn Gabirol, *Fons vitae* (n. 415 above) 5, §19, p. 294; excerpts in medieval Hebrew translation: *Liqqutim* (n. 415 above) 5, §25.

anima, was translated into Latin and added its support. Themistius envisaged a single transcendent active intellect from which rays proceed and enter the souls of individual men.[453]

Among the Scholastics who were exposed to the Latin translations of Alfarabi, Avicenna, and the others, William of Auvergne (d. 1249) rejected the existence of an active intellect "that generates human souls," as well as the existence of an active intellect, whether located inside or outside the human soul, that leads the human faculty for thought from potentiality to actuality. He however did, following the lead of Augustine, recognize a "light . . . from above," that is to say, a light from God, which illuminates the human intellect.[454] A report transmitted by Roger Bacon suggests that, with the notion of God's being the illuminator of the human soul as a fulcrum, William was maneuvered, in public disputations, into accepting the appellation *active intellect* for God.[455] Bacon further reports that in the course of a disputation, Adam of Marsh (d. between 1259 and 1269), whose writings have not been preserved, explicitly equated the active intellect with God, and that Robert Grossteste (1175–1253) was a third thinker who acquiesced in the equation.[456] Alexander of Hales (d. 1245) accommodates an active intellect located in the human soul with a divine illumination from without. He accounts for ordinary human intelligible thought through the internal active intellect; and he holds that man needs the illumination from God for supernatural, as distinct from natural, knowledge. He moreover concedes indirectly that since God is the source of the supernatural illumination, God may be called the "active intellect."[457]

Albert the Great's writings contain both passages insisting that the active intellect exists within the human soul and other passages recognizing a transcendent active intellect. Since Albert further explains that the internal active intellect requires the aid of a divine illumination in order to perform its function of producing intelligible thoughts, his differing statements on the location of the active intellect have been harmonized as meaning that the external active intellect, presumably the deity himself, enables the internal active intellect to do its work.[458] Some statements of Albert's regarding the active intellect nevertheless resist harmonization. In one spot, he carefully refutes Avicenna's argument from intellectual memory, together

[453]Themistius, *Commentaire sur le Traité de l'âme d'Aristote, traduction de Guillaume de Moerbeke*, ed. G. Verbeke (Leiden 1973) vii. Regarding Themistius' position, see above, p. 14.

[454]Gilson (n. 443 above) 58–59, 71, 79; De Vaux (n. 429 above) 26, n. 1.

[455]Gilson (n. 443 above) 71, 76–77, 81–83.

[456]Ibid. 81, n. 1. Gilson 91, finds that Grossteste's writings recognize Augustine's doctrine of divine illumination, but do not explicitly identify God as the active intellect.

[457]Ibid. 86, n. 2. Alexander takes up a possible argument in favor of an incorporeal active intellect, and he responds that the argument shows only that man needs an illumination from God for supernatural knowledge. He neither rejects nor expressly accepts the implication that God may therefore be called the external active intellect.

[458]Schneider (n. 443 above) 343–48.

with the argument's conclusion that the human intellect receives intelligible thoughts directly from the active intellect, and that "to learn" a thought is "to acquire a perfect aptitude for conjoining with the active intellect."[459] Elsewhere, by contrast, he argues wholly in the spirit of Avicenna not only that actual human thought depends on an incorporeal agent but that intelligible forms emanate directly from the incorporeal agent upon the human soul.[460] And in still other statements, he echoes Alfarabi more than Avicenna—although he chooses to cite Averroes, rather than either Alfarabi or Avicenna, as his authority.[461] He affirms that upon the human intellect's attaining perfection, the "incorporeal . . . active intellect" "conjoins with the [human] possible intellect as its form"; "this compound" of the two intellects "is called divine, acquired [*adeptus*] intellect by the Peripatetics"; and the human intellect can then have "incorporeal" substances as the object of its thought.[462]

John Peckham (d. 1292) is an additional philosopher recognizing both an immanent and a supernal active intellect. For he locates a "created active intellect" in the human soul; and he also maintains that the human intellect cannot pass to actuality in respect to any intelligible thought without the aid of an external "light," that the "light" or "sun" illuminating the human intellect is "God," and that therefore "God" is the "active intellect of which the Philosopher [Aristotle] spoke."[463] Various works of Roger Bacon (d. after 1292) likewise affirm an immanent active intellect, a supernal, incorporeal active intellect, and the identification of the supernal active intellect with God. Since, however, the disparate statements appear in different works of Bacon and are not coordinated by him, scholars have differed as to how he should be read. He has, on the one hand, been understood as affirming an immanent active intellect side by side with an external active intellect, and identifying the latter as God[464]; on the other hand, his differing statements on the active intellect have been taken as reflecting different, successive phases in his thought."[465]

To cite the example of one more Scholastic writer, Roger Marston (end of the thirteenth century) submits that the position "of the philosopher [Aristotle]

[459]Ibid. 209–11.

[460]Ibid. 341–42. L. Kennedy (n. 447 above) 29, n. 40.

[461]L. Kennedy, "The Nature of the Human Intellect according to St. Albert," *The Modern Schoolman* 37 (1960) 130–31, nn. 57, 60, 61. Regarding the manner in which man obtains intelligible thought, Albertus writes: ". . . conveniemus in toto cum Averroe."

[462]Ibid. 130–33.

[463]Gilson (n. 443 above) 99–104. Peckham expresses approval of "Avicenna['s]" construction of the active intellect as an "incorporeal intelligence," adding his own qualification that the active intellect is God; but at least in the citations provided by the secondary literature, he does not repeat what is distinctive in Avicenna, namely, that thoughts emanate directly from the active intellect, which he identifies with God, on to the human soul.

[464]E. Gilson, *History of Christian Philosophy in the Middle Ages* (New York 1955) 304. T. Crowley, "Roger Bacon and Avicenna," *Philosophical Studies* (Dublin).

[465]D. Salman, "Note sur la première influence d'Averroès," *Revue néoscolastique de philosophie* 40 (1937) 205–8; T. Crowley, *Roger Bacon* (Louvain 1950) 165–66.

regarding the active intellect" is in "harmony" with "the position of Saint Augustine regarding the light" from above which illumines all human souls. The human intellect, in other words, requires a light from God to perform its activity, as Augustine taught; and God is, by virtue of furnishing the light, none other than the transcendent active intellect of the Aristotelians.[466]

In sum, several thirteenth-century Scholastics posit two distinct active intellects, one internal and the other external (Alexander of Hales, Albert the Great, John Peckham, Roger Bacon). A line of Scholastics identify the active intellect with God, usually alluding at the same time to the old Augustinian notion that God is a light, or provides a light, illuminating the human soul (William of Auvergne, Adam of Marsh, and Robert Grossteste, all on the report of Roger Bacon; Alexander of Hales, by implication; Albert the Great; John Peckham; Roger Bacon; Roger Marston). While the works of Alfarabi and Avicenna can be credited with a role in transmitting a transcendent construction of the active intellect to Scholastic philosophy, other philosophic works translated into Latin from Greek or Arabic also helped propagate that construction.

Thomas Aquinas (1225–1274) accepted the argument for the existence of an active intellect that leads the potential intellect to actuality, but he rejected the transcendent construction of the active intellect and located the active intellect exclusively within the human soul.[467] After the thirteenth century, the theory of an incorporeal active intellect transcending the human soul was kept alive only among the adherents of Averroes.[468]

[466]E. Gilson, "Roger Marston: un cas d'augustinisme avicennisant," *Archives d'histoire doctrinale et littéraire* 8 (1933) 38–41. On 41, Gilson quotes a passage where Marston accepts "Augustine's doctrine" that "all things are thought in an eternal light" as well as Aristotle's position that intelligible thoughts ("species") are abstracted from images in the imaginative faculty of the soul; and Marston adds that "Avicenna's" position, according to which "intelligible forms are emanated upon our intellect by way of being imprinted," may also "be true." Gilson calls the yoking of Augustine's theory of divine illumination with the identification of God as the active intellect: "augustinisme avicennisant." A true *augustinisme avicennisant* would, however, have God, the active intellect, emanating thoughts directly on the human intellect, and virtually none of the Scholastics whom Gilson cites as examples of the phenomenon espouse the direct emanation of thoughts. His term *augustinisme avicennisant* has been criticized; see F. van Steenberghen, *La philosophie au XIIIe siècle* (Louvain 1966) 17–18.

[467]Aquinas, *Summa contra gentiles* 2.76–78; *Summa theologiae* 1.79.3–7.

[468]Bits and pieces of Avicenna's theory of intellect survive in fifteenth- and sixteenth-century Latin writers. Examples in: S. Swiezawski, "Notes sur l'influence d'Avicenne sur la pensée philosophique latine du XVe siècle," in *Recherches d'Islamologie* (Anawati-Gardet Festschrift) (Louvain 1977) 299–30; F. Lucchetta, "Recenti studi sull'Averroismo padovano," *L'Averroismo in Italia*" (Rome 1979) 114.

Summary

A number of Islamic thinkers either summarized Avicenna's emanation scheme and theory of intellect for the use of Arabic readers, incorporated Avicenna's theses into their own writings, or garbed Avicenna's system in unconventional attire. The last group is the most interesting, and its most unexpected representative is Ghazali. Although Ghazali had, at one stage, drawn up a thoroughgoing critique of Avicenna's philosophy, his *Mishkāt al-Anwār* reproduces much of Avicenna's system, disguised in allusive language. Ibn Ṭufail's philosophic novel likewise presents a good part of Avicenna's system in an unconventional mode. As for other avowed Islamic Aristotelians, Ibn Bājja borrows from both Alfarabi and Avicenna, and on several critical issues takes a stand closer to the former. Averroes' early works, as will be seen in the next chapter, endorse an emanation scheme and a conception of the active intellect which come from Alfarabi and Avicenna; and, as will appear in the final chapter of the book, Averroes, throughout his career, explained the active intellect's effect on the human intellect in a manner similar to Alfarabi.

Abū al-Barakāt took his departure from Avicenna but stretched Avicenna's framework to the bursting point. From the outlook of the present study, his most significant innovations are his allowing the population of the supernal region to proliferate and his distributing of the active intellect's functions among a number of supernal beings. One of Suhrawardī's works faithfully reproduces Avicenna's system, and another decks Avicenna's system out in allegorical attire. But Suhrawardī's Science of Illumination is a fresh attempt to burst Avicenna's framework. Suhrawardī there adds a host of new incorporeal entities to Avicenna's intelligences and souls of the spheres, he distributes the functions of the active intellect among the newly minted supernal beings, and he elevates direct experience of the incorporeal realm to the apex of human cognitive activity. In the centuries that follow, a line of Iranian thinkers fashion their systems out of materials quarried from Suhrawardī and Avicenna.

Judah Hallevi, Abraham Ibn Daud, and Moses Maimonides were the first Jewish philosophers to adopt theories of Alfarabi and Avicenna. Hallevi outlines a picture of the universe and a theory of human intellect which he ascribes to unnamed philosophers, he criticizes the unnamed philosophers harshly, and he then turns around and constructs his own worldview out of conceptions borrowed from them. The thesis that most caught Hallevi's fancy was the emanation of natural forms upon properly prepared sublunar matter. Natural forms, Hallevi agrees, are indeed emanated from without, but God and not the active intellect is the giver of forms. Ibn Daud and Maimonides endorse, with certain reservations, the picture of the universe and theory of intellect that they set forth in the name of Aristotle and unspecified "philosophers." Maimonides, for instance, accepts: the scheme of successive emanations espoused by Alfarabi and Avicenna, with the proviso that a genuine act of will by the deity initiates the process; the emanation of all natural forms including the human soul from the active intellect; the emanation of all human intelligible thoughts from the active intellect; and an adaptation of Avicenna's theory of prophecy. Although neither Hallevi, Ibn Daud, nor Maimonides lets slip that Avicenna is his primary source, Avicenna dominates in each instance. From the thirteenth to the sixteenth centuries, various combinations of theses deriving from Alfarabi and more especially from Avicenna appear in Jewish philosophic writers; and Alfarabi and Avicenna seem even to have infiltrated the theosophical doctrine known as the Cabala.

In Scholastic philosophy, the impact of Avicenna was modest and that of Alfarabi even smaller. An anonymous text entitled *De primis et secundis substantiis* repeats two significant items from Avicenna: a fragment of his emanation scheme and the central thesis of his theory of human intelligible thought. A second text, entitled *De anima* and perhaps written by Dominic Gundissalinus, copies copiously from Avicenna's theory of human intelligible thought. Both texts, however, overlay Avicenna with doctrines of a more traditional Christian character. The emanation from above of natural forms and of the human soul in particular, which could have been learned from either Alfarabi's *Risāla fī al-ᶜAql* or from Avicenna, reappear in John Blund and Albert the Great. Both Blund and Albert noticed what Judah Hallevi had seen, that philosophy could be relegated to its proper station as the handmaiden of religion, if God himself is identified as the giver of forms. Persuaded in part by Alfarabi and Avicenna, a number of Scholastics recognize an incorporeal active intellect transcending the human soul which leads the human intellect to actuality—either side by the side with an additional active intellect that exists within the soul, or to the exclusion of an internal active intellect. Those accepting a transcendent active intellect which leads the human intellect to actuality generally identify it too with God.

6

Averroes on Emanation and on the Active Intellect as a Cause of Existence

General Considerations

The present chapter will examine Averroes' attempts to determine, first, the causal connections obtaining within the realm of incorporeal intelligences, and, secondly, the active intellect's role as a cause of existence in the sublunar realm. Averroes treats those two related subjects a number of times in his commentaries on Aristotle and in other compositions. As he returns to the two subjects on successive occasions, he endeavors to pare away post-Aristotelian accretions that, he had become convinced, colored his previous efforts, and to recover the genuine Aristotelian doctrine embodying—so he assumes—philosophic truth. We shall find that the enterprise of recovering the genuine Aristotle leads him to revise and re-revise his thinking.

Something has to be said about his commentaries on Aristotle. That Averroes wrote commentaries on Aristotle in three distinguishable modes is well known. In general—although there are variations—the so-called Epitome or Compendium reorganizes the material of a given Aristotelian work and recasts it in Averroes' own words; the Middle Commentary paraphrases an Aristotelian text almost sentence by sentence; and the Long Commentary, a genre Averroes employed for only a few important Aristotelian works,[1] quotes each passage of the Aristotelian text in extenso and proceeds to expound it at considerable length. Where the commentaries can be dated, the Epitomes are found to belong to his early, and the Long Commentaries to his later, career.[2] Sometimes, after having completed his Epitome of a given Aristotelian work, Averroes changed his mind on an issue and expounded his revised position in the Long Commentary or Middle Commentary on the same work. On occasion, he then went back to the Epitome and added annotations that reflect his rethinking of the issue. Averroes' Epitome of the *De anima* will be seen in the next chapter to be one such instance. His Epitome of the

[1]E. Renan, *Averroès et l'Averroisme* (Paris 1866) 62.
[2]Ibid. 60–61.

Physics is another.[3] In both cases, certain passages can be surmised to be later annotations incorporated into the original text, since manuscripts containing the passages exist side by side with manuscripts from which they are missing. One of the annotations incorporated into the Epitome of the *De anima* carries us beyond surmise, however, for it explicitly directs readers to Averroes' Long Commentary on the *De anima*, where, Averroes writes, readers can find his revised position on the subject.[4]

Averroes' Epitome of the *Metaphysics*, which plays a central role in the present chapter, is a third instance. Several Arabic manuscripts of the Epitome of the *Metaphysics* contain interpolations correcting positions advanced in the original version. In one such passage, which appears in some but not all of the Arabic manuscripts, Averroes expressly disavows the arguments "I [originally] gave," and manuscripts of the medieval Hebrew translation of the Epitome mark the passage as a "gloss."[5] In a second passage, which happens to have been incorporated into all

[3]H. Davidson, "Averroes on the Active Intellect as a Cause of Existence," *Viator* 18 (1987) 193. Averroes, *Epitome de Fisica*, trans. J. Puig (Madrid 1987), which according to a reviewer discusses the issue, is not available to me.

[4]See below, p. 270.

[5]I did not examine the Arabic manuscripts of the Epitome but did use four printed editions, each of which follows a different manuscript tradition. One manuscript, found in Madrid, contains the passage I refer to here, without the designation "gloss"; see Averroes, *Compendio de Metafisica*, ed. with Spanish trans. C. Quirós Rodríguez (Madrid 1919) 4, §60. A text published by M. Qabani (Cairo ca. 1903) and based on a single Cairo manuscript does not have the passage. The two German translations—*Die Metaphysik des Averroes*, trans. M. Horten (Halle 1912), and *Die Epitome der Metaphysik des Averroes*, trans. S. Van den Bergh (Leiden 1924)—do not translate the passage; see Horten 192 and Van den Bergh 135. Horten had only the edition of Cairo 1903). Van den Bergh had both that Cairo text and the Quirós text, but supposed the passage in question to be "ein späterer Zusatz"; see his appendix, 317–18. It is indeed a later addition but one written by Averroes himself.

A third Arabic text, which has the present passage and other additions to the original Epitome but is not identical with the Madrid manuscript, was published in *Rasā'il Ibn Rushd* (Hyderabad 1947). A fourth text was published by U. Amin as *Talkhīṣ mā ba^{c}da al-Ṭabī^{c}a* (Cairo 1958). (The term *talkhīṣ* is misleading, because it properly designates a Middle Commentary, rather than an Epitome.) Amin consulted the Madrid and Hyderabad editions, which have Averroes' later corrections, and the Cairo manuscript underlying the Qabani text, which does not; but in the main he follows a second Cairo manuscript, which also lacks the added corrections. (Yet a third Cairo manuscript exists; see Amin's introduction, 1–2.)

Some eight or nine manuscripts of the Hebrew translation are extant, of which I was able to examine three. Madrid, Escorial Hebrew MS G1-14, 103b–104a, and Munich, Staatsbibliothek, Hebrew MS 108, 113b–114a, contain the present passage and both have, within their texts, the notation "gloss" near the beginning of the passage and the notation "end of gloss" (*^{c}ad kan ha-haggaha*) near the end. In both, the former notation appears a few lines too early and the latter a few words too late. The manuscripts must consequently stem from an earlier manuscript in which the passage was already incorporated into the text, while the notations still remained in the margin. The third Hebrew manuscript that I examined contains the passage without the notations; see below, n. 32.

known manuscripts of the Epitome—those that do, as well as those that do not, incorporate the other corrections—Averroes comments that he "had clarified" the topic at hand in his "Commentary" (*sharḥ*), that is to say, his Long Commentary, on the *Metaphysics*.[6] The corrections do in fact reflect positions espoused in the Long Commentary. They are thus undoubtedly notes written by Averroes after the completion of the original Epitome and incorporated into the text by him or by scribes.

The two subjects to be discussed in this chapter—the causal relations obtaining within the supernal hierarchy, and the active intellect's role as a cause of existence in the sublunar realm—were integral to the systems of Alfarabi and Avicenna. Averroes was acquainted with Alfarabi's writings and refers by name to the *Risāla fī al-ᶜAql*,[7] the work of Alfarabi's which is most pertinent here. He seems to have had only limited direct knowledge of Avicenna's writings,[8] but he nonetheless possessed a fair understanding of Avicenna's system, largely through Ghazali's restatement of it. He also knew the works of Ibn Bājja (Avempace), a philosopher nearer to his time, who stood in the tradition of Alfarabi and Avicenna.[9] In both issues to be discussed, Averroes originally took positions close to Alfarabi and Avicenna and subsequently, after rethinking matters, rejected those positions.

The Qabani and Amin texts and the German translations more or less represent the original Epitome. The Quirós and Hyderabad editions, the third Cairo manuscript consulted by Amin, and the medieval Hebrew translation incorporate Averroes' later corrections. I was not able to use the text of the Epitome of the *Metaphysics* in the Chester Beatty collection, MS 4523.

In the following notes, references to the Epitome of the *Metaphysics* with no further qualification are to the Quirós text, and references to the German translation are to Van den Bergh. An appendix in Quirós' edition lists the differences between his text and the earlier Qabani edition.

B. Nardi, who read the Epitome in a Latin translation from the Hebrew, saw that the Epitome—that is, the sections representing the original text—state different positions from Averroes' later writings. He mistakenly inferred therefrom that the Epitome is not a genuine work of Averroes. See B. Nardi, "Sigieri di Brabante nella Divina Comedia," *Rivista di filosofia neo-scolastica* 3 (1911) 532, n. 2; reprinted as *Sigieri di Brabante nella Divina Comedia* (Spiante 1912) 17, n. 2.

6 See below, p. 241.

7 Averroes, *Drei Abhandlungen über die Conjunction*, ed. and German trans. J. Hercz (Berlin 1869), Hebrew text 7, German translation 27. Averroes refers to Alfarabi's *Philosophies of Plato and Aristotle* (see above, pp. 63–64; the *Philosophy of Plato* is a companion of the *Philosophy of Aristotle*) in the Long Commentary on the *Metaphysics* 7, comm. 31, and 12, comm. 18; Arabic text: *Tafsīr mā baᶜda al-Ṭabīᶜa*, ed. M. Bouyges (Beirut 1938–1948) 886, 1499. English translation of Long Commentary on *Metaphysics* Book 12, with pagination of Arabic indicated: C. Genequand, *Ibn Rushd's Metaphysics* (Leiden 1984). French translation of same, with pagination of the Arabic indicated: A. Martin, *Averroès, Grand commentaire de la Métaphysique d'Aristote* (Paris 1984).

8 See H. Davidson, *Proofs for Creation, Eternity, and the Existence of God, in Medieval Islamic and Jewish Philosophy* (New York 1987) 319, 334.

9 See above, p. 141.

The Emanation of the Universe

Averroes' original Epitome of the *Metaphysics* advocates an emanation scheme that diverges only in particulars from the schemes of Alfarabi and Avicenna. Averroes takes for granted that stars and planets do not travel through space freely but are imbedded in rotating celestial spheres.[10] In one departure from Alfarabi and Avicenna, which is of secondary importance for our purpose, he rejects the existence of a diurnal sphere beyond the sphere of the fixed stars, that is to say, a sphere without stars of its own which draws the entire celestial region around the stationary earth once every twenty-four hours. He judges such a sphere, empty of all stars, to be "improbable" or "rather impossible," inasmuch as "spheres exist only for the sake of stars," and inasmuch as the daily rotation of the heavens can be accounted for satisfactorily through a rotation of the sphere of the fixed stars itself, with no additional sphere beyond it.[11]

Having made the reservation about the existence of a diurnal sphere lying beyond the sphere of the fixed stars, Averroes reasons as follows: The continuous rotation of the celestial spheres resembles neither the motion of the physical elements, which move to their natural place, nor animal motion, which is induced by "sensation" and "imagination"; for both those sorts of motion attain a goal and cease.[12] Seeing that the spheres do not move as the physical elements or animals do, their continuous and unending motion must, for lack of any other explanation, be effected by a rational soul. Spherical motion must result from a "desire" accompanying an "intellectual conception" in a rational soul belonging to the sphere. Further, since the object of desire of a rational soul is perforce at a higher level of perfection than the soul harboring the desire, the object that the rational soul of the sphere conceives, and whose concept induces desire, must be an incorporeal being.[13] The existence of the souls of the spheres and of the incorporeal intelligences is hereby established, the soul acting as the direct, and the intelligence as the indirect, mover of the sphere. In the very act of conceiving the perfection of the incorporeal intelligence, the soul of a celestial sphere desires, for itself and its sphere, a state of perfection which is as close to the perfection of the incorporeal intelligence as possible. And because motion is a more perfect state for a body than rest, motion being a manifestation of life, the desire to emulate the intelligence expresses itself in constant circular motion.[14] Each sphere must have its own incorporeal intelligence, which serves as its "own object of desire," since each performs its own unique motion.[15]

[10]Epitome of the *Metaphysics* (n. 5 above) 4, §6; German translation 108.

[11]Ibid. §§15–16; German translation 113.

[12]Ibid. §§7–8; German translation 108–9.

[13]Ibid. §§8–9; German translation 109–10.

[14]Ibid. §27; German translation 118 (inexact).

[15]Ibid. §17; German translation 113.

In a second departure from Alfarabi and Avicenna, the Epitome of the *Metaphysics* does not mention, and plainly rejects, a cause of the existence of the bodies[16] of the spheres. As for the forms or souls of the spheres, Averroes writes that each intelligence "gives the sphere its form,"[17] and that the form, or soul, of the sphere "proceeds" (*ṣadara*) from the corresponding intelligence.[18] He also writes, in a somewhat different conception, that the form, or soul, of each sphere consists in nothing other than the "intelligible thought" the sphere has of its intelligence,[19] and the sphere—which must mean the soul of the sphere—thereby receives its "form" and "essence." By virtue of furnishing the form, or soul, and essence of its sphere—although not the sphere's body—the intelligence may be deemed the sphere's "efficient [cause]" (*fāᶜil*).[20]

Averroes advances arguments to establish that the intelligences constitute a causal hierarchy in which every link is responsible for the existence of the next.[21] Then he goes on: "More than one" effect "proceeds" (*ṣadara, lazima*) from each celestial intelligence, since the intelligence "provides [both] the form" of its own sphere and the "existence of the [incorporeal] mover of the next sphere."[22] That is, the intelligence emanates both the soul of the sphere with which it is associated and the next intelligence in the series. Yet an old, familiar rule affirms that "from the one . . . only one can proceed [*ṣadara*]."[23] It follows that the intelligences associated with celestial spheres, having multiple effects, are not wholly one but contain "parts."[24] The ultimate source of the unity that knits the universe together must, however, be unqualifiedly unitary, and, because of the rule that only one thing proceeds from what is unitary, the ultimate source of unity in the universe can have a single effect and nothing more.[25] As a consequence, the First Cause of the universe cannot be any of the intelligences coordinated with celestial spheres. The

[16]Averroes, *De substantia orbis*, ed. and trans. A. Hyman (Cambridge, Mass. 1986), Hebrew text 26, English translation 79, states that the "sphere is a simple body, not composed of form and matter." Ibid., Hebrew text 27, English translation 82, states that the "celestial body" serves as "matter," or more correctly "subject," for its "incorporeal form." *De substantia orbis* is a collection of Averroes' essays on the nature of the heavens, which are not known to be extant in the Arabic, and which have been preserved in a medieval Hebrew translation. The essays are not wholly consistent, and very likely stem from different periods in Averroes' career.

[17]Epitome of the *Metaphysics* 4, §29; German translation 119. Averroes uses the phrases "form" of the sphere and "soul" of the sphere interchangeably. Cf. ibid. §§54, 57; German translation 131, 133.

[18]Ibid. §54; German translation 131.

[19]Ibid. §29; German translation 119.

[20]Ibid.

[21]Ibid. §§32; 36; German translation 120–22.

[22]Ibid. §54; German translation 131.

[23]Ibid. §59; German translation 135. Cf above, pp. 75, 150.

[24]Ibid.

[25]Ibid. 4, §§38, 53; German translation 123, 130. Cf. Aristotle, *Metaphysics* 12.10.1075a, 11–25; Plotinus, *Enneads* 6.5.1; 6.9.1; 6.9.3.

First Cause, or "God," must—as Alfarabi and Avicenna held—be a substance unassociated with any sphere and transcending all the intelligences that move spheres.[26]

Averroes' original Epitome of the *Metaphysics* thus agrees with Alfarabi and Avicenna in setting a First Cause beyond the intelligences that move the spheres. The wholly unitary First Cause once again eternally emanates a single incorporeal being. Although the first emanated intelligence consists, like its cause, in pure thought, its thought is multifaceted. From the first intelligence there eternally emanate a second intelligence as well as the form or soul, but not the body, of the outermost sphere.[27] And the process replicates itself through the series of intelligences and spheres.[28]

In one further qualification of the scheme common to Alfarabi and Avicenna, Averroes adds that where the complex motion of any of the planets points to a subsystem of secondary spheres interacting with each other and with the main planetary sphere, the intelligence coordinated with the main sphere must eternally bring forth not only the next main intelligence and the form of its own sphere but the first of the secondary intelligences in the subsystem as well. That secondary intelligence then brings forth the form or soul of its secondary sphere and a further secondary intelligence; and so on, until the full complement of secondary intelligences and souls of the secondary spheres is filled.[29] Finally, from the intelligence of the lunar sphere, the last of the primary intelligences eternally "proceeds" (*ṣādir*). It is the "active intellect," the cause of actual human thought, whose existence Aristotle posited in the *De anima*.[30]

Such is the cosmology that Averroes endorses in the original text of his Epitome of the *Metaphysics*. It breathes the same spirit as the comologies of Alfarabi and Avicenna.

A passage already referred to, which is found in some although not all of the available Arabic manuscripts of the Epitome of the *Metaphysics*,[31] which is found as well in the medieval Hebrew translation, and which is labeled by some Hebrew

[26]Epitome of the *Metaphysics* 4, §54; German translation 131–32.

[27]Ibid. §54; German translation 131–32.

[28]Ibid. §61; German translation 135–36.

[29]Ibid. §§22, 35, 57; German translation 116, 121 ("Prinzip," six lines up, is a typographical error for "Beweger"), 133–34. Averroes recognized eccentric spheres in the Epitome of the *Metaphysics*, but expressed doubts about both eccentric and epicyclical spheres in the Long Commentary on the *Metaphysics*; see A. Sabra, "The Andalusian Revolt against Ptolemaic Astronomy," in *Transformation and Tradition in the Sciences* (I. B. Cohen Festschrift), ed. E. Mendelsohn (Cambridge 1984) 139–42.

[30]Ibid. §62; German translation 136.

[31]The passage appears in the Madrid manuscript underlying Quirós' text, in the Hyderabad printed text, and in the third Cairo manuscript, as recorded in Amin's apparatus, 153. See above, n. 5.

manuscripts as a gloss,[32] repudiates much of what has been said. Averroes there calls the "method" he expounded in the original Epitome a theory of "recent philosophers of Islam such as Alfarabi," and possibly also of "Themistius . . . and Plato." He characterizes the lengthy arguments "I gave" in the original text not as his own but as "the most solid" that those philosophers had "adduced." And he brands the method of the aforementioned philosophers as "defective." Averroes' reversal does not concern the structure of the heavens, or the existence of intelligences and souls of spheres.[33] What he revises is the relation of the intelligences to one another, their relation to the First Cause, and the First Cause's place within the hierarchy.

[32]Madrid, Escorial Hebrew MS G1-14, 103b; Munich, Staatsbibliothek, Hebrew MS 108, 113b–114a; see above, n. 5. Paris, Bibliothèque Nationale, Hebrew MS 918, 145a, has the passage but without the notation "gloss."

[33]At least one of the essays in Averroes' *De substantia orbis* states that the spheres have only a single percipient substance associated with them; that is to say, they do not have both a soul of their own and an intelligence coordinated with them. See *De substantia orbis* (n. 16 above), Hebrew text 23, English translation 70. But another of the essays, ibid., Hebrew text 48, English translation 113–15, appears, on the contrary, to assign a soul and incorporeal intelligence to each sphere. Here I am relying on a passage in Averroes' *Tahāfut al-Tahāfut*, where he advocates the theory adumbrated in the later annotations to the Epitome of the *Metaphysics* which I am discussing. The passage in question ascribes a *conception* to each of the spheres and distinguishes the sphere's conception from the *mover* of the sphere; and, what is especially to the point, it expressly ascribes to the outermost sphere a conception of its mover. The implication is that the spheres have souls doing the conceiving which are distinct from the intelligences moving the spheres; and that the outermost sphere, in particular, has a soul which is distinct from its mover. The passage reads: "We find that all the celestial spheres, in their [common] diurnal movement, and the sphere of the fixed stars as well, have the same concept [that is, a concept of the mover of the sphere of fixed stars, which in Averroes' later thought is identical with the First Cause]. For they all undergo that [common diurnal] motion by reason of a single mover, the mover of the sphere of fixed stars. We further find that the spheres have divers movements peculiar to each, whence it follows that their movements are due to movers divers in one respect, and united in another. They [the movers] are united insofar as their movements [*their* may refer either to the incorporeal movers or to the spheres; see Bouyges' apparatus] are linked to the movement of the first sphere." See Averroes, *Tahāfut al-Tahāfut*, ed. M. Bouyges (Beirut 1930) 231; English translation with pages of the original Arabic indicated: *Averroes' Tahafut al-Tahafut*, trans. S. Van den Bergh (London 1954). I think Averroes is assuming that each celestial soul, with the exception of the soul of the outermost sphere, has two objects of desire. One of the two objects of desire, the intelligence moving the outermost sphere, that is, the intelligence that is identical with the First Cause of the universe, induces the soul of the sphere to move its sphere around the earth once every twenty-four hours, while the other object of desire, the intelligence paralleling the sphere, induces the soul of the sphere to produce the sphere's own peculiar motion. The incorporeal movers of the spheres are "united" in the sense that they all contribute to a single interlocking system, as explained in Aristotle, *Metaphysics* 12.10; *Metaphysics* 12.10, is clearly alluded to in the continuation of the passage just quoted from the *Tahāfut al-Tahāfut*. Averroes, Long Commentary on the *Metaphysics* 12, comm. 44; Arabic text 1649, also appears to recognize souls of the spheres, but that passage is even more difficult than the passage quoted here from the *Tahāfut al-Tahāfut*.

He makes the following statements: Alfarabi and the others did not realize that the rule affirming "from one only one can proceed [*ṣadara*]" is "valid" exclusively for the "efficient [cause]" in the strict sense of the term; it is not valid for the "formal cause" or "final cause," even when they may be regarded, in an extended and analogical sense, as an "efficient cause."[34] The "problem at hand" may be put as the question "whether more than one concept . . . can be framed" of the being that is "one and simple," and hence "whether more than one thing can receive its perfection" from a simple, absolutely unitary being. The answer to those questions must be negative to render the theory of Alfarabi and the others "true." Should the answer be affirmative, as Averroes intimates it is, their theory will be "false." "We have," the annotation closes, "discussed the subject elsewhere."[35]

Averroes' remarks are not so intimidatingly enigmatic as they may at first appear. He is saying: To demonstrate their picture of the universe, Alfarabi and philosophers taking the same line would have to establish that an absolutely unitary being can exercise causality in just a single fashion, solely as an efficient cause in the strict sense—in other words, by engendering its effect by direct action. If such were the case, the rule that from one only one can proceed would apply to the First Cause, the First Cause could have only one effect, and multiplicity in the universe would have to enter at a subsequent stage. In fact, however, an absolutely unitary being may, and does, serve as the immediate cause of multiple effects not by directly engendering them but in another manner—very much as the intelligences were described, in Averroes' early view, as furnishing the celestial souls' essence by offering themselves as an object of thought.[36] The first unitary being can act on the incorporeal intelligences as a formal cause, providing them with form insofar as each intelligence enjoys a conception of the first being proportionate to the intelligence's level of existence.

Averroes is suggesting that each intelligence has some stratum of existence in its own right, a stratum that one of his later works does expressly recognize as a quasi-material aspect of the incorporeal intelligence.[37] The inchoate aspect of the intelligence eternally turns its intellectual gaze,[38] as it were, upon the First Cause. The conception it thereby gains becomes its eternal form, the form through which it

[34]See Aristotle, *Physics* 2.3.

[35]Epitome of the *Metaphysics* 4, §60; German translation, appendix, 317–18. Themistius took a position on the generation of sublunar forms which is pertinent to the active intellect's role as a cause of sublunar forms; see above, p. 32, and below, p. 251. But I do not know why Averroes mentions him in the present connection.

[36]Cf. above, p. 224.

[37]Averroes, *Commentarium magnum in Aristotelis de Anima libros*, ed. F. Crawford (Cambridge, Mass. 1953) (henceforth cited as: Long Commentary on the *De anima*) 409–10; cf. H. Wolfson, "Averroes' Lost Treatise on the Prime Mover," reprinted in his *Studies in the History of Philosophy and Religion* 1, ed. I. Twersky and G. Williams (Cambridge, Mass. 1973) 426, n. 60; below, p. 291.

[38]Cf. Plotinus, *Enneads* 1.7.1; 1.8.2.

receives perfection in proportion to its rank in the hierarchy of existence. We may conjecture that, in Averroes' mature view, the soul of each celestial sphere receives its full measure of existence through its conception of the corresponding intelligence.

The rule that from one only one proceeds thus need not—and, Averroes intimates, does not—apply to the First Cause of the universe, nor need the First Cause initiate a process of emanation. Each incorporeal intelligence may receive its form and be perfected at its own level through its unique conception of the First Cause; and the latter may endow all rungs of the incorporeal hierarchy, and not just the first intelligence, with form and thereby also with a full measure of existence.

The emanation scheme espoused by Averroes' original Epitome entailed as a corollary that the First Cause of the universe transcends the incorporeal movers of the spheres. Seeing that all the intelligences, including the intelligence moving the outermost celestial sphere, have multiple effects, none of them, the original Epitome contended, can be the ultimate cause of the universe; for the ultimate cause is absolutely unitary and, producing its effect by a process of emanation, can have only one effect. If, however, the First Cause is now no longer construed as an emanating cause, and if it does after all have multiple effects in the way Averroes has described, the corollary vanishes. The mover of the outermost sphere, which Averroes has been seen to identify as the sphere of the fixed stars,[39] might indeed be the wholly unitary First Cause of the universe; and nothing will have to transcend the incorporeal movers of celestial spheres. The First Cause would move the sphere of the fixed stars by presenting itself to the rational soul of the sphere as an object of desire,[40] much as it imparts perfection to the intelligences—as well as to the soul of the sphere of fixed stars—by presenting itself as an object of thought.

What Averroes adumbrates in the annotation to the Epitome of Aristotle's *Metaphysics*, he affirms outright in the Middle and Long Commentaries on the *Metaphysics*, as well as in his *Tahāfut al-Tahāfut* (*Destructio destructionum*). The Long Commentary on the *Metaphysics*, which he tells us he wrote in his "old age,"[41] makes the point most fully and most sharply.

Averroes contends there that emanation is not a true category of efficient causation and, moreover, that efficient causation is wholly foreign to the incorporeal domain. "Men of our time," he writes, "are accustomed to assert that from such and such an [incorporeal] mover, another [incorporeal] mover proceeds or emanates or necessarily comes forth [*ṣadara, fāḍa, lazima*]," or else they say the same using "similar expressions." Language of the sort is not, however,

[39]That in his later thought Averroes still rejected a diurnal sphere beyond the sphere of fixed stars is clear from *Metaphysics* 12, comm. 44; Arabic text (n. 7 above) 1649; and from the passage in *Tahāfut al-Tahāfut* quoted above in n. 33.

[40]See above, n. 33.

[41]Long Commentary on the *Metaphysics* 12, comm. 45; Arabic text 1664.

applicable to incorporeal entities. In the first place, *procession*, *emanation*, and the like are "ostensibly attributes of efficient causes [*fā^cil*], but they are not so in reality"; for "nothing proceeds from" an efficient cause, and efficient causation consists merely in "leading what is potential to actuality." Seeing that emanation is not in fact a kind of efficient causation, and hence no kind of causation whatsoever, emanation should not be sought at any level of the universe. In the second place, since the incorporeal realm "contains no potentiality," no "efficient cause" at all can operate there. The whole notion of emanation is, then, to be dismissed as illegitimate, and quite apart from that, the category of efficient causation cannot be used to explain the existence of the incorporeal realm.[42]

As a consequence, the unitary First Cause must operate on the world of intelligible beings not as an efficient cause but in a different manner, in the way that the "object of intelligible thought is the cause of the subject thinking intelligible thoughts," in other words, in the way that the object of thought furnishes the thought content of the subject thinking it. The ultimate cause of the universe acts as a cause in the sense that the "intelligences" have "an intelligible thought" and "concept" of it and thereby receive their "perfection." Since "divers beings" receive their thought and concept of the first being in "divers" and "differing" degrees, depending on their rank in the hierarchy of existence, the ultimate, absolutely simple cause can, and does, have multiple effects.[43]

As for the argument whereby "later" philosophers inferred the existence of a being transcending the movers of the spheres, its "invalidity" should now be apparent to "anyone with the slightest training in the science [of metaphysics]."[44] The argument had been that "from the mover of the first heaven, there proceed the soul of the first heaven and the [incorporeal] mover of the next sphere"; but "from what is one and absolutely simple, only one can emanate or proceed"; the incorporeal mover of the first, outermost sphere, from which more than one thing does emanate, is therefore "necessarily not simple"; the "first substance," which is the ultimate cause of the universe, must, however, "be absolutely one and simple";

[42]Ibid. comm. 44; Arabic text 1652.

[43]Ibid.; Arabic text 1648–49, 1652; *Tahāfut al-Tahāfut* 231; Middle Commentary on the *Metaphysics*, Casanatense Hebrew MS 3083, 115 (114) a–b; appendix to Averroes' *Iggeret Efsharut ha-Debequt* (Arabic original lost), ed. and trans. K. Bland, as *Epistle on the Possibility of Conjunction* (New York 1982), Hebrew text 151; English translation 111 (the printed text is defective, and I used Paris, Bibliothèque Nationale, Hebrew MS 947, the readings of which are recorded in Bland's apparatus); Wolfson (n. 37 above) 421–22. The translation of the passage in the *Tahāfut al-Tahāfut* should be corrected to read: ". . . and it is not impossible that it [the First Cause] should be something unitary, of which a plurality of things have differing conceptions, just as [conversely] it is not impossible that a plurality should be grasped in a single conception."

That in the present stage of his thought Averroes still viewed the intelligences as forming a hierarchy is clear from Long Commentary on the *Metaphysics* 12, comm. 44; Arabic text 1649; *Tahāfut al-Tahāfut* 232; and *Epistle on the Possibility of Conjunction* 151.

[44]Long Commentary on the *Metaphysics*, 12, comm. 44; Arabic text 1648.

hence the mover of the first sphere, which is not absolutely unitary, must "have a cause prior to it" and is not the First Cause; and the First Cause, which transcends even the mover of the outermost sphere, engenders it alone through an eternal process of emanation.[45] Such is the argument that Averroes' Long Commentary on the *Metaphysics* attributes to the "later" philosophers; and it is the argument that his original Epitome had advanced in its own name but that the annotation interpolated into the Epitome had attributed to Alfarabi, to other Islamic philosophers, and tentatively to Themistius and Plato.[46] In the Long Commentary, Averroes dismisses the argument as invalid and "delusory" for the reason the Long Commentary has already given, namely, that "neither procession [*ṣudūr*, *luzūm*] nor efficient causation occurs [in the intelligible world]."[47]

The argument supposedly showing that the mover of the outermost sphere cannot be the First Cause of the universe is thus baseless. Moreover, Averroes adds, an incorporeal substance that does not move a sphere is intrinsically implausible, for, "as Aristotle wrote, if [incorporeal] substances existed which did not move [spheres], their actuality [*fiᶜl*] would be in vain"[48]; the First Cause would exist in vain, if it did not move a sphere. Averroes' Long Commentary on the *Metaphysics* accordingly concludes that the supposition of a "first substance" transcending "the mover" of the outermost sphere, the sphere of the fixed stars, is "false." The intelligence moving the outermost sphere is the First Cause.[49] As for the active intellect, although it is no longer the product of a process of emanation, it still stands at the end of the hierarchy of incorporeal beings.[50]

Résumé. Averroes' original Epitome of the *Metaphysics* sets forth an emanation scheme similar to that of Alfarabi and Avicenna. The First Cause transcends the incorporeal intelligences that move the celestial spheres; an intelligence eternally

[45]Ibid.; Arabic text 1648–49.

[46]See above, p. 226.

[47]Long Commentary on the *Metaphysics* 12, comm. 44; Arabic text 1649. Cf. Middle Commentary on the *Metaphysics* (n. 43 above) 115 (114) a–b; *Tahāfut al-Tahāfut* 179–80; Wolfson (n. 37 above) 422.

[48]Perhaps a reference to Aristotle, *Metaphysics* 12.8, 1074a, 22–23. In Aristotle, where the intelligences are not causes of existence, it is understandable why they would exist in vain if they had no spheres to move. But since Averroes, even in his mature thinking, continues to misread Aristotle, by still agreeing with his Islamic predecessors that the First Cause is the cause of the existence of all subsequent intelligences, it is hard to see why the First Cause would exist in vain if it had no sphere to move.

[49]Long Commentary on the *Metaphysics* 12, comm. 44; Arabic text 1648. Cf. Wolfson 425.

[50]Long Commentary on the *Metaphysics* 12, comm. 38; Arabic text 1612–13; Long Commentary on the *De anima* (n. 37 above) 442. The Long Commentary on the *De anima* does not, to be precise, place the active intellect at the very end of the incorporeal hierarchy; for it locates the material human intellect—which Averroes there construes as a single eternal substance shared by all men—directly after the active intellect in the incorporeal hierarchy.

emanates from the First Cause; the first intelligence and those subsequent to it contain multiple aspects, which enable each of them to produce multiple effects, specifically, the soul of the corresponding celestial sphere and the next intelligence in the series; the active intellect, the final rung in the incorporeal hierarchy, emanates eternally from the intelligence associated with the lunar sphere. Averroes does diverge from his predecessors on particulars. He dismisses the notion of a diurnal sphere beyond the sphere of the fixed stars, and he does not construe the intelligences as the emanating cause of the bodies of the spheres. He also supplements the scheme by extending the emanation thesis to the subsystems of spheres which astronomers assumed in order to explain the full complexity of celestial motion.

Averroes' more considered position is adumbrated in an interpolation in the Epitome of the *Metaphysics* and is articulated in the Long Commentary—as well as being affirmed in the Middle Commentary on the Metaphysics and in the *Tahāfut al-Tahāfut*. Averroes now does away with the emanation of incorporeal beings. He explains that the First Cause serves as the cause of all the incorporeal intelligences, inasmuch as each of them has a thought of the First Cause and thereby receives its form. And having liberated himself from the emanation thesis, he also does away with the hypothesis of a being beyond the movers of the spheres. Since a wholly unitary being may after all have multiple effects, there is no reason why the intelligence associated with the outermost sphere may not be the wholly unitary First Cause of the universe.

Averroes seems to envision a hierarchy of eternal and independently existing, quasi-material strata for the intelligences, quasi matters that involve no potentiality. Each stratum has a unique eternal conception of the First Cause, which is different from the conceptions constituting the essences of the other intelligences, and each thereby gains for its intelligence the eternal perfection proportionate to the intelligence's rank within the incorporeal hierarchy. We have here a strange collection of entities that are free of potentiality yet need to be perfected, that do not emanate from one another yet arrange themselves in a hierarchy. Averroes has been led to posit them, because he has, on the one hand, rejected the emanationism of his Islamic predecessors, while, on the other, continued to interpret Aristotle's First Cause as the cause of the very existence, and not merely the motion, of the universe.

At all events, the active intellect still stands at the end of the incorporeal hierarchy. Like the other incorporeal beings in the hierarchy, it possesses some sort of existence in its own right and eternally receives its proper degree of perfection through the intelligible thought that it has of the First Cause.

The Active Intellect as a Cause of Existence: Epitomes of the *Parva naturalia* and the *Metaphysics*

Averroes also rethought the range of functions performed by the active intellect.[51]

As was seen in an earlier chapter, certain of Alfarabi's works recognized no role for the active intellect in bringing forth sublunar beings, but Alfarabi's *Risāla fī al-ᶜAql* described the active intellect as emanating a range of natural forms above the level of the four elements—the human form, animal forms, plant forms, and probably certain inanimate forms. Avicenna went further and represented the active intellect as giving forth from itself, through a process of emanation, the material substratum of the entire sublunar world and all, or virtually all, natural forms in the sublunar world. Averroes' early position on the functions of the active intellect is close to that of Alfarabi's *Risāla fī al-ᶜAql*.

Averroes states his original position unambiguously in the Epitome of the *Parva naturalia*. The context where the subject comes up does not require him to deal with the source of sublunar matter, but he cites two works of Aristotle, the *De generatione et corruptione* and the *De generatione animalium*, in order to determine the source of the various classes of sublunar forms.

The pertinent chapter of Aristotle's *De generatione et corruptione* had traced the processes of "generation" and "destruction" within the sublunar region to two movements of the heavens around the earth: the daily movement of the entire celestial system, on the one hand, and the periodic movement of the sun, on the other. The former, being uniform, causes—according to Aristotle—the uniformity in natural sublunar processes; the latter, which at one season of the year brings the sun nearer to the earth and at another season carries it away, causes the diversity.[52] With that chapter in mind, Averroes writes in his Epitome of the *Parva naturalia*: "It is proved [*tabayyana*]" in Aristotle's *De generatione et corruptione* that individual portions of matter receive the forms of one or another of the four elements "thanks to the movements of the celestial bodies," and that "homoeomeric bodies"—basic natural compounds in which the elements are blended and their qualities tempered[53]—are brought into existence when the movements of the heavens work together with the natural movements of the elements themselves to

[51]Gersonides, *Milḥamot ha-Shem* (*Die Kämpfe Gottes*) (Leipzig 1866) 5.3.1, observes that Averroes' works express three different views on the active intellect's role in the generation of sublunar objects.

[52]Aristotle, *De generatione et corruptione* 2.10; H. Joachim's notes on the chapter, in his edition (Oxford 1922). Averroes' Epitome of the *De generatione et corruptione* explicitly brings the planets into the process; see Middle Commentary and Epitome of the *De generatione et corruptione*; medieval Hebrew translation from the Arabic, ed. S. Kurland (Cambridge, Mass. 1958) 121–22; English translation, trans. S. Kurland (Cambridge Mass. 1958) 133.

[53]Organic material—plant and animal cells of various sorts—is included in the class of homoeomeric bodies. See H. Bonitz, *Index Aristotelicus* (Berlin 1870) 510b, lines 35–42; A. Peck's edition and translation of *De generatione animalium* (Cambridge, Mass. 1942) xlviii–xlix.

mix the elements into homogeneous blends.[54] As soon as matter is mixed in the requisite way, the form of an element or of a homoeomeric body is, ipso facto, present.

The pertinent passage in Aristotle's *De generatione animalium* was murky, and Averroes read it with the help of Ibn Bājja's interpretation.

The *De generatione animalium* stated that a physiological factor called soul-heat—characteristic of animals but also appearing in inanimate nature—is sufficient to explain both sexual reproduction and spontaneous generation. Soul-heat, which is related to the heat of the sun, engenders plants and animals and also the nonintellectual side of human life. "Intellect alone"—and Aristotle did not indicate whether he meant the human potentiality for thought or actual intelligible thought—must, since it is not a bodily function, be something "divine" entering "from without."[55]

Those statements would seem to express a straightforward, naturalistic view of the origin of life below the level of human intellect and rule out any transcendent source of plant and animal forms. A few lines later, however, Aristotle went on to speak of a "soul-like principle" (φυσικὴ ἀρχή), which accompanies the male semen, and added that the soul-like principle is sometimes "separable" from "body," sometimes "inseparable." It is separable in the case of animals having "something divine. And what is called *intellect* is of such a sort."[56] The Greek text is obscure, to say the least,[57] and the only known medieval Arabic translation, which may or may not be the one that Averroes and Ibn Bājja used,[58] makes things worse. Instead of a "soul-like principle" in semen, the Arabic speaks of "a power of the origin [*ibtidā'*] of soul" which is carried by the "seed" of the "body of the male semen." "It"—gender and context make "origin" the probable antecedent—is "separate from the body [of the semen] . . . and is something divine"; and "what is of this character is called intellect."[59] While the Greek said that the soul-like principle is sometimes separable from matter—and just what that means is debatable—the Arabic drops the qualification *sometimes* and says that the "origin

[54]Averroes, Epitome of the *Parva naturalia*, Arabic text, ed. H. Blumberg (Cambridge, Mass. 1972) 76; medieval Hebrew translation, ed. H. Blumberg (Cambridge, Mass. 1954) 49–50; English translation, trans. H. Blumberg (Cambridge, Mass. 1961) 44–45.

[55]*De generatione animalium* 2.3.736b, 21–737a, 5; Peck 586–89.

[56]Ibid. 737a, 7–11.

[57]F. Nuyens, *L'évolution de la psychologie d'Aristote* (Louvain 1948) 38–39, gives a plausible interpretation. He punctuates and reads the text in such a way that only the inseparable, and not the separable, soul-principle is described as carried by the semen.

[58]Averroes complained about the poor quality of the translation of the *De partibus animalium* and *De generatione animalium* which he used; see M. Steinschneider, *Die hebräischen Uebersetzungen des Mittelalters und die Juden als Dolmetscher* (Berlin 1893) 144.

[59]Aristotle, *The Generation of Animals: The Arabic Translation*, ed. J. Brugman and H. Lulofs (Leiden 1971) 64.

of soul" which is carried by the seed of the semen is separate from matter and hence divine.[60]

The way Ibn Bājja and others understood the Arabic text is reported in Averroes' Commentary on the *De generatione animalium*, a work not known to exist in the original Arabic but preserved in a medieval Hebrew translation. "They supposed" Aristotle's meaning to be that "the principle [Hebrew: *hatḥala*=Arabic: *mabdā'*] of the power in the substance of the seed [or: semen] which [and again the antecedent is unclear] bestows the soul and brings it into existence" is a "separate [incorporeal; *nibdal*=*mufāraq*] power." Although the language is cumbersome, the intent is clear. On Ibn Bājja's reading of Aristotle, souls in the sublunar world come from an incorporeal substance. To justify his interpretation, Ibn Bājja and the others cited—according to Averroes' report—the Aristotelian rule[61] that the agent bringing something into existence must already actually itself have the characteristic it brings into existence. "What produces heat" is, for example, "heat"; what "produces soul" must consequently be a "soul." Since male semen plainly "does not contain actual soul," the Aristotelian rule would imply that the agent producing actual soul is distinct from, and transcends, the semen. On Ibn Bājja's reading, then, when Aristotle spoke of something separate from the body of the male semen and divine, which is the origin of soul, he meant an incorporeal agent that contains in itself the souls of all living beings and imparts them to sublunar matter.[62]

Returning now to Averroes' Epitome of the *Parva naturalia*, we find that Averroes there follows the interpretation of Aristotle which he reported in the name of Ibn Bājja. The Epitome of the *Parva naturalia* states: "It is . . . proved in the *De animalibus*"—*De animalibus* being the name for Aristotle's three zoological works taken as a unit—that in instances where "individual plants and animals . . . reproduce," their "causes" are the "seed and the active intellect"; and in instances where plants and animals do not reproduce but are generated spontaneously, their causes are the "elements, the celestial bodies, and the active intellect."[63] That is to say, plant and animal seed, in the one instance, and the effect of celestial motions upon the elements, in the other, render a portion of matter

[60]As the Arabic translation renders the text, the attribute *separable* qualifies "soul-like principle" and the attribute *inseparable* qualifies "seed." The thing that is "inseparable" from body is therefore not "the origin of soul" but the "seed" in the male semen.

[61]*De generatione animalium* 2.1.734b, 21–22. Above, p. 18.

[62]Averroes, Commentary on *De animalibus*, Oxford, Bodleian Library, Hebrew MS Opp. 683 (=Neubauer 1370) 155a–b. The work of Ibn Bājja's in which Averroes finds the interpretation is that philosopher's *De anima*. Averroes may, as he often does, be giving what he understands to be the implications of Ibn Bājja's statements, rather than what Ibn Bājja expressly said. The Commentary on the *De animalibus* looks like a Middle Commentary, but M. Steinschneider (n. 58 above) 144, n. 258, cites some evidence for classifying it as an Epitome. Averroes' Middle Commentary on the *Metaphysics* (n. 43 above) 109 (108)b, also refers to Ibn Bājja's interpretation of the *De generatione animalibus* .

[63]Averroes, Epitome of the *Parva naturalia* (n. 54 above), Arabic text 76–77; Hebrew translation 50; English translation 45.

receptive of a particular organic form, and when a portion of matter is thus prepared, it receives the appropriate form from the emanation of the incorporeal active intellect.[64]

Averroes' Epitome of the *Parva naturalia*, in short, relates two Aristotelian passages, one in *De generatione et corruptione* and one in *De generatione animalium*, to distinct classes of sublunar existence. On Averroes' reading, the passage in *De generatione et corruptione* which traces the processes of generation and destruction to the movements of the heavens has in view forms below the level of living plants and animals. The passage in the *De generatione animalium*, which Averroes understands to affirm an incorporeal source of plant and animal forms, has only the forms of animate beings in view, and it traces them, in instances of both sexual reproduction and spontaneous generation, to the active intellect. The position Averroes here takes on the functions of the active intellect agrees, more or less, with the line adopted by Alfarabi's *Risāla fī al-ᶜAql*,[65] but his reference to the *De generatione animalium* indicates that he was relying on Ibn Bājja's interpretation of that work of Aristotle's.

Averroes also treats the active intellect's role in the sublunar world in his Epitome of the *Metaphysics*, and there the situation is more complex. The original version of the Epitome of the *Metaphysics* sees the active intellect as the cause of certain sublunar natural forms, with an unexpected nuance. Then annotations added in some manuscripts repudiate Averroes' early position, just as annotations in the same manuscripts repudiated Averroes' early endorsement of the theory of successive incorporeal emanations.

As already seen, the original Epitome of the *Metaphysics* outlines a process of emanation wherein each incorporeal intelligence brings forth the next intelligence in the incorporeal hierarchy as well as the form or soul of its own celestial sphere.[66] The process, the Epitome goes on, extends into the sublunar world. Averroes excludes an emanation of the underlying matter of the sublunar world. When he had outlined the translunar emanation process, he did not recognize a cause of the existence of the bodies of the spheres,[67] and in the same vein, he contends that an "efficient cause" (*fāᶜil*) of the underlying matter of the sublunar world is inconceivable. An efficient cause, the original Epitome reasons, "produces a thing by providing it with the substance through which it is what it is—in other words, by providing it with form. In itself, however, the prime matter [of the sublunar world] has no form, thanks to which it might have an efficient cause. Furthermore, prime matter cannot conceivably have another matter [from which it is fashioned],

[64]Averroes, Epitome of the *De anima*, ed. A. Ahwani as *Talkhīṣ Kitāb al-Nafs* (Cairo 1950) 88, similarly assumes that the active intellect is the cause of the "existence" of the material human intellect.

[65]Above, pp. 66–67.

[66]Above, pp. 224–225.

[67]Above, p. 224.

because it is itself the first matter." That is to say, anything material not made from a prior matter is not made at all, prime matter is not made from a prior matter, hence prime matter can have no efficient cause.[68] The underlying matter of the sublunar world is, therefore, the product of neither the active intellect nor any other agent.

Matter does, in a sense, have a formal and final cause. In the first place, since the forms of the four elements invest indeterminate matter with a determinate character, and since matter exists for the purpose of allowing the elements to emerge, the forms of the elements are the "immediate . . . formal and final . . . cause of the existence of prime matter." In the second place, since the "celestial bodies" bring forth the elemental forms in prime matter, the celestial bodies can be taken as the ultimate formal and final cause of the existence of prime matter.[69] And the matter of the lower world has a cause "in another respect" as well. For the term *matter* is predicated of translunar and sublunar matter in one of the several modes of "priority and posteriority"[70]; the "prior" in any class can be deemed the "cause of the existence of the posterior"; and "therefore the matter of the celestial bodies is in this sense too the cause of the existence of sublunar matter."[71]

Thus the underlying matter of the sublunar world has no true efficient cause, although it can be described as having a cause in various loose senses. When the Epitome of the *Metaphysics* turns to the cause of the forms of the four elements, it endorses a naturalistic theory that Alfarabi had espoused and Avicenna had rejected.[72] Averroes explains that, as "proved in [Aristotle's] *De caelo*,"[73] the rapid movement of the celestial spheres heats the matter furthest from the center of the sublunar world and closest to the innermost sphere; "heat entails lightness"; and lightness constitutes "the form of fire." The outermost sublunar matter, which is moved most rapidly, therefore becomes fire. The innermost matter, the matter farthest from the celestial spheres, is not moved or heated, remains heavy, and, heaviness being the form of earth, becomes earth. Intermediate matter assumes the form of air or water, depending on its relative lightness or heaviness.[74] The appearance of "homoeomeric" bodies, blended compounds constituting levels of existence immediately above the four elements, is likewise amenable to a naturalistic explanation. Homoeomeric bodies "have been shown" in Aristotle's "physical science" to "require" nothing for their existence beyond the effect that celestial movement exercises on the four elements.[75]

[68]Epitome of the *Metaphysics* (n. 5 above) 4, §68; German translation 139.

[69]Ibid.

[70]Regarding priority and posteriority, see Aristotle, *Metaphysics* 5.11.

[71]Epitome of the *Metaphysics* 4, §69; German translation 139. See the passage quoted from Alexander, above, p. 20, n. 80.

[72]Above, p. 78.

[73]Perhaps a reference to *De caelo* 4.4.

[74]Epitome of the *Metaphysics* 4, §63; German translation 136–37.

[75]Ibid. §65; German translation 137.

Since the existence of the four elements and of homogeneous blends of the elements can be accounted for through the interaction of physical forces, the "aforementioned science"—physics—requires us "to introduce a principle from without" only for "the existence of plants and animals." Plants and animals exhibit "faculties," such as the "nutritive soul," which perform "determinate acts working toward a given end." The emergence of those faculties "can be attributed neither to the elements," which possess only primitive physical qualities, nor to the organism's "individual progenitor; for the progenitor furnishes merely . . . the receptive matter or the instrument," as for example, "semen [which is an instrument], and menstrual blood [which is the receptive matter]." If organic forms do not emerge from within, they must enter from without, supplied by an external "principle."[76]

Averroes' Epitome of the *Metaphysics* has so far limned somewhat more circumstantially the position that his Epitome of the *Parva naturalia* sketched. The underlying matter of the sublunar world, Averroes has again explained, cannot conceivably have an efficient cause of its existence. The forms of the four elements are brought into existence by the motion of the celestial region, and natural homoeomeric compounds come into existence when the elements are, in turn, mixed by celestial motion. But the forms or souls of living beings are crystallized out of the emanation of the active intellect when a given portion of matter becomes disposed to receive a given form, as when female menstrual blood is fertilized by male semen.

Whereupon Averroes adds an unexpected scholium. The foregoing, he writes, "has been proved in physical science," while from the standpoint of metaphysics, the active intellect must be credited with a wider role. For "material forms" can instill in matter only equally "material" forms, not "forms separate [from matter]," and a "particular material object can produce only a particular thing like itself." The "factor" (or: notion; *maᶜnā*) in a sublunar physical object rendering it "intelligible"—that is, the form of the physical object, which can be abstracted from the object and grasped by the mind as an intelligible thought—is, however, neither material nor particular. The celestial bodies, themselves material objects possessing material forms, consequently cannot instill in matter the form that the human intellect abstracts and comprehends as an intelligible thought. From what Averroes calls the metaphysical, and what we might prefer to call the epistemological, perspective, the "active intellect" must therefore be assumed to "give" not just the

[76]Ibid. §66; German translation 137–38. Cf. Aristotle, *De generatione animalium* 1.20.729a, 9–11; 28–33. In *Metaphysics* 9.7.1049a, 2, and elsewhere, Aristotle seems to regard semen as the material from which the animal is generated, Ross' commentary *ad locum* explains that Aristotle is just speaking imprecisely and according to popular notions. D. Balme, "Development of Biology in Aristotle and Theophrastus: Theory of Spontaneous Generation," *Phronesis* 7 (1962) 95–96, takes the passages as evidence that the *Metaphysics* represents a stage in Aristotle before he developed his biological thinking.

forms of plants and animals but all other forms capable of becoming objects of thought, including the forms of "the simple bodies," or elements.[77]

Averroes has propounded the unusual thesis that as long as a philosopher works in physical science, he can account for the existence of the four elements and of inanimate compounds through physical factors and he has to attribute only the existence of plants and animals to the active intellect. When the philosopher shifts to the science of metaphysics, which inquires into physical objects' intelligibility,[78] he finds, on the contrary, that he must construe the active intellect as the source of all forms, down to the level of the elements.

Thus far, the position taken by the Epitome of the *Metaphysics* in its original version.

At several junctures, the manuscripts of the Epitome which contain the annotation repudiating Averroes' original position on the emanation of the incorporeal realm also have annotations repudiating his original position on the active intellect's role in producing sublunar forms. The manuscripts are especially revealing in one spot where Averroes defends the Aristotelian proposition that the agent engendering an individual animal always belongs to the "same species" as the offspring it engenders[79] or is at least "similar and analogous" to its offspring. The "semen . . . moving the menstrual blood so that it becomes" a living animal might, Averroes observes, appear to constitute a counterexample, since semen obviously is not an animal belonging to the same species as the animal born of the fertilized female. But in fact, he writes, the agent standing behind the semen does conform to the rule. The reasoning whereby Averroes makes the point is put differently in the different manuscripts.

[77]Ibid. §67; German translation 138; cf. ibid. 2, §§36–37 (a line has dropped out of the text in §37); German translation 44–45. Averroes goes on to insist that he has neither backslid into Platonism nor forgotten the Aristotelian dictum that each "man is generated by a man and the sun" (cf. Aristotle, *Physics* 2.2.194b, 13; *Metaphysics* 7.9.1034a, 21–25). "What is generated essentially," he explains, "is the individual," and its generating cause is another individual, "whereas the form is generated" not essentially but "accidentally" (cf. Aristotle, *Metaphysics* 7.8.1033b, 5–8; 15.1039b, 20–26). Thus "an individual man," the thing generated essentially, is brought into existence by "the individual sun and an individual man." The man's form, his "humanity," is "generated in him accidentally"; it is brought into existence by "humanity abstracted from matter [and inhering in the active intellect]." The difference between the systems of Plato and Aristotle, as Averroes views them at the present stage of his thinking, is accordingly as follows: On the Platonic position, the incorporeal Form produces the individual *essentially*, that is to say, it is the "immediate" cause, whereas on the Aristotelian position, one individual produces another individual essentially, and the new individual's form supervenes in an *accidental* generation.

[78]Aristotle, *Metaphysics* 4.3; Wolfson, "The Classification of Sciences in Medieval Jewish Philosophy," reprinted in his *Studies* (n. 37 above) 518.

[79]See Aristotle, *Physics* 2.2.194b, 13.

The Arabic manuscripts preserving the reasoning in its original form—they are the same manuscripts that remain faithful to Averroes' early position on translunar emanation[80]—read:

> The mover that necessarily has to be of the same quiddity as what is moved [that is, as the offspring] or analogous and similar thereto is the ultimate mover. For the ultimate mover is what gives the immediate mover the power whereby it moves [and engenders the offspring]. In the case of semen, the ultimate mover is the father,[81] and in the case of [fertilized] eggs the ultimate mover is the [male] bird—with, however, the proviso that these factors have been proved to be insufficient without a principle from without, as proved in physical science.
>
> As for animals and plants that are generated spontaneously, their generation results from the heat of the stars, yet that heat is not the ultimate cause of their coming into existence. Here too, it has been proved, a mover analogous [to the organism being generated] exists which gives the organism its substantial form. The reason why the ultimate mover is not, in this instance, of the same quiddity as what is moved [and engendered, but only analogous and similar thereto], is that the mover is, as has been proved, incorporeal.[82]

The Arabic manuscripts incorporating the corrections read:

> The mover that necessarily has to be of the same quiddity as what is moved [that is, as the offspring] or analogous and similar thereto is the ultimate mover. For the ultimate mover is what gives the immediate mover the power whereby it moves [and engenders the offspring]. In the case of semen, the ultimate mover is the father, and in the case of [fertilized] eggs the ultimate mover is the [male] bird—with, however, the proviso that these factors have been proved to be insufficient without a principle from without. *The latter is the celestial bodies in Aristotle's view, which is the correct one, or the active intellect in the view of many of the later philosophers.*[83]
>
> As for animals and plants that are generated spontaneously, *the ultimate mover is, in Aristotle's system, the celestial bodies through the mediacy of soul-powers emanating from them, or else the active intellect as the later philosophers interpret him* [*Aristotle*]. . . .[84]

[80]See above, n. 5.

[81]Cf. Aristotle, *De generatione animalium* 1.22.

[82]Quirós Rodríguez edition (n. 5 above) 2, §§27–28, and apparatus; Amin edition (n. 5 above) 46–47.

[83]Quirós Rodríguez's edition implies that the Madrid manuscript continues with the words: "as proved in physical science." If the edition can be relied on, the scribe who interpolated the gloss in the Madrid manuscript must have worked mechanically and did not realize that the gloss superseded the reference to physical science.

[84]Quirós Rodríguez edition 2, §§27–28, and apparatus; Amin edition 47, apparatus; Hyderabad edition (n. 5 above) 50.

Of the Hebrew manuscripts that I examined, two have the emended version of the text,[85] and one conflates the emended version with the original text.[86]

What has happened is plain enough. In the original version of the text, the first of the two paragraphs explained that in sexual reproduction, the ultimate agent belonging to the same species as the offspring is not the semen but the father; and it added that physical science—Aristotle's *De generatione animalium* as interpreted by Ibn Bājja—shows the true ultimate agent to be a substance outside the sublunar world, that is, the active intellect, from which plant and animal forms emanate. A subsequent annotation stated that in the correct, Aristotelian view, the ultimate mover is the celestial bodies, although many later philosophers did identify the ultimate mover as the active intellect. The second paragraph originally explained that in spontaneous generation, where there is no father and hence no agent belonging to the same species as the offspring, the ultimate mover analogous to the offspring is an incorporeal being—the active intellect. Averroes later added an annotation, which again stated that the ultimate mover analogous to the offspring is, in the correct, Aristotelian view, the celestial bodies, which emanate physical soul-powers, although later philosophers did interpret Aristotle as affirming that the active intellect is the ultimate mover. The annotations emending Averroes' original position must have been penned into the margins of one or more manuscripts of the Epitome. In the case of the first paragraph, one or more scribes, but not all, incorporated the annotation into the text—while dropping the phrase "as proved in physical science." In the case of the second paragraph, the scribes substituted the annotation for the words it supersedes. Since the Hebrew manuscripts vary in their handling of the annotations, the Hebrew translator must have had a manuscript in which the annotations were still appended to the text and not yet incorporated. He left them as marginal notes. One Hebrew scribe substituted the annotation to the second of the two paragraphs for the passage meant to be superseded, while another conflated the emendation with the original version.

At further junctures, manuscripts of the Epitome of the *Metaphysics* incorporate additional glosses repudiating Averroes' original position on the active intellect. The first of the additional glosses is a minor parenthetic sentence.[87] A second appears after a passage discussed earlier which accounts for the forms of homoeomeric bodies without assuming an external incorporeal source.[88] The original version there continues with a paragraph stating that an incorporeal source must be assumed for the forms of plants and animals; and then the next paragraph makes the statement that from the metaphysical viewpoint, an external source must be assumed not only for organic but for all natural forms, including the forms of the

[85]Munich, Staatsbibliothek, Hebrew MS 108, 98a–b; Madrid, Escorial, Hebrew MS G1-14, 80b.

[86]Paris, Bibliothèque Nationale, Hebrew MS 918, 126b.

[87]Epitome of the *Metaphysics* (n. 5 above) 2, §36.

[88]Above, p. 236.

four elements, since otherwise their intelligibility could not be accounted for.[89] In two Arabic manuscripts[90] as well as in the medieval Hebrew translation, an annotation correcting Averroes' original position has been inserted just before those two paragraphs. The annotation ends with the same transitional clause as the second of the two paragraphs,[91] which indicates that it was meant to replace them. In a third Arabic text the annotation does replace the two paragraphs.[92] Other manuscripts, those reflecting the original Epitome, lack the annotation altogether.[93] What the annotation says is that animate beings, no less than homoeomeric bodies, receive their forms from the "celestial bodies." The celestial bodies "give life" to the world, and they alone can do so, for "one thing gives another only what it contains in its own substance," and therefore only a "body by its own nature animate" can "move matter to an animate perfection." Aristotle accordingly "introduced . . . an incorporeal principle" into his picture of the sublunar world "solely [to account] for the human intellect."[94]

A final passage in the Epitome, one found in all the preserved manuscripts, reiterates that "there is no need . . . to introduce incorporeal forms in connection with anything generated [naturally] . . . except for the human intellect." The passage concludes by directing readers to Averroes' "[Long] Commentary" (*sharḥ*) on the *Metaphysics*, where he treated the subject more fully.[95] We undoubtedly here have a gloss that happened to be incorporated into all the known manuscripts, including the manuscripts that generally reflect the original text of the Epitome.

Résumé. Averroes' Epitome of the *Parva naturalia* takes the forms of the elements and of homoeomeric bodies to be the product of celestial motion. The movements of the heavens heat sublunar matter to various degrees and thereby turn it into the four elements, and they mix the elements into a variety of configurations, the forms of homoeomeric bodies being nothing other than those configurations. The same Epitome traces all plant and animal forms to the active intellect. The Epitome of the *Metaphysics* has preserved at least two positions. Its earlier position was that from the standpoint of physical science, a philosopher must "introduce" the active intellect to account for plant and animal forms, while other, inanimate forms are explicable by the movements of the heavenly bodies. But from a metaphysical, or epistemological, standpoint the appearance of all natural sublunar forms, animate as well as inanimate, must be ascribed to the active intellect, because only forms deriving from a source consisting in pure thought can themselves become objects of intellectual thought. Annotations incorporated into the Epitome

[89] See above, p. 237.
[90] The Madrid and third Cairo manuscript (n. 5 above).
[91] The clause is: "Since matters are as we laid down. . . ."
[92] The Hyderabad edition (n. 5 above).
[93] The manuscripts on which the two published Cairo texts are based (n. 5 above).
[94] Epitome of the *Metaphysics* 4, §65.
[95] Ibid. 2, §39.

of the *Metaphysics* repudiate the earlier position. The celestial bodies now are not merely the cause of inanimate natural forms. They are, through physical soul-powers that they emanate, the ultimate cause of animate forms, in instances of both sexual reproduction and spontaneous generation. According to the annotations, an incorporeal cause has to be "introduced" only to account for human intellect. That statement might on its face mean either that an incorporeal cause must be posited to explain the appearance of the human potential intellect, or to explain the passage of the human intellect from a state of potentiality to actuality.

The Active Intellect as a Cause of Existence: The Commentary on *De generatione animalium*

Averroes, as was seen, records Ibn Bājja's interpretation of the passage in the *De generatione animalium*, where Aristotle spoke of a "soul-like principle" accompanying the male semen which is sometimes "separable" from "body," and sometimes "inseparable." The soul-like principle is separable, Aristotle wrote, in the case of animals having "something divine; and what is called *intellect* is of such a sort."[96] On Ibn Bājja's reading, the passage in Aristotle recognizes an incorporeal source of plant and animal forms. The composition where Averroes reports Ibn Bājja's interpretation is his own Commentary on the *De generatione animalium*. In contrast to the Epitome of the *Parva naturalia* and original Epitome of the *Metaphysics*, which follow Ibn Bājja, when the Commentary on the *De generatione animalium* discusses the pertinent passage in Aristotle, it refutes Ibn Bājja's interpretation.

Averroes contends: To suppose that "an incorporeal form" imparts plant and animal forms from without and "creates form[s] in matter" would be to backslide into the Platonic "doctrine of Forms,"[97] with the attendant absurdity that "something would come out of nothing." To support his contention, Averroes cites "Aristotle in Book 7 of the *Metaphysics*." He apparently means, as Aristotle argued in *Metaphysics* 7,[98] that Platonic ideal Forms, which do not exist on the physical plane, can in no way help explain the appearance of new forms in matter, since the appearance of new forms occurs completely within the physical plane. An explanation of the appearance of physical forms solely through Platonic Forms would accordingly be no explanation at all and would be tantamount to having forms come into existence without a cause.

There remains the more nuanced theory that celestial movements and other natural forces act upon matter until it possesses a "blend-form" (Hebrew: *ṣura*

[96]Aristotle, *De generatione animalium* 737a, 7–11. Above, p. 233.

[97]Cf. above, n. 77.

[98]See Aristotle, *Metaphysics* 7.8; also Aristotle, *Metaphysics* 13.5, 1080a, 3–4: "Even if there are Forms, nothing can come into existence unless there is something to originate motion."

mizgit=Arabic: *ṣūra mizājiyya* or *ṣūra imtizājiyya*), that is to say, a certain blend of the four elements, whereupon the "active intellect" automatically "gives" the appropriate "soul-form." Averroes, as we saw, embraced a theory of the sort in early works. His Commentary on *De generatione animalium* now refutes it. The theory would hold water, he reasons, only if the same "term" could be "predicated . . . univocally" of the blend-form after it receives a soul from the active intellect and of the blend-form before the soul was present—only if, to invent an example of our own, a fertilized human ovum could be called an ovum after receiving a human soul in the same sense as before. In fact, however, terms are perforce predicated equivocally in the two instances, just as the "term *flesh*" is predicated "equivocally" of the flesh of a living being and of the flesh of the dead.[99] Averroes leaves his reasoning truncated, but since, as will appear presently, he develops it fully elsewhere,[100] we can complete it for him. His point, put briefly, is this: If we look only at the physical substratum receiving a soul, we find the substratum itself undergoing a critical change at the moment of receiving the soul, so great a change that to describe the substratum by the same term after as well as before the change would be to use the term equivocally. Inasmuch as the change in the substratum undoubtedly takes place on the physical plane, it must be explained by a physical factor. The form appearing in the substratum must be due to the same physical factor, and not to the action of an incorporeal being, which functions on a wholly different plane.

The upshot of Averroes' rereading of Aristotle's *De generatione animalium* is, accordingly, that the soul of an organism emerges through a process within the physical world, a process in which the "engendering agent . . . alters matter potentially containing the form until it produces the form in matter actually." To identify just what the engendering agent is, Averroes adduces the Aristotelian concept of *soul-heat*,[101] a concept that he neglected in his early treatment of the appearance of organic forms, perhaps because he was not yet familiar with *De generatione animalium*.[102] Souls, he writes, are brought forth by a "soul-heat" or "soul-power" in matter. Paraphrasing the text of Aristotle's which he is expounding, he adds that soul-heat is unrelated to the heat of the element fire and belongs instead to "the genus of the celestial nature."[103] It is produced by a causal process going back to the "sun and the celestial spheres," and is identical with the physiological factor that "Galen" called the "formative [power]."[104] In cases of

[99] Averroes, Commentary on the *De animalibus* (n. 62 above) 155b. For the equivocation in predicating the term *eye* of the organ of a living being and that of a dead being, see Aristotle, *De generatione animalium* 2.1.735a, 8.

[100] Below, pp. 247-48.

[101] See above, p. 233; Peck (n. 53 above) 580–84.

[102] Averroes' Epitome of the *De anima* (n. 64 above) 7, seems to refer to soul-heat, but I find the meaning of the passage unclear.

[103] Cf. Aristotle, *De generatione animalium* 2.3.736b, 35–737a, 1.

[104] Cf. Galen, *De naturalibus facultatibus* 1.6.15.

organic reproduction, it is present in the seed of a plant or in the male semen, both of which are generated from a "residue" of the body's "nourishment,"[105] while in spontaneous generation, where seed and semen play no role, it is present in a "natural residue," that is to say, in decaying material.[106] It operates on an appropriate portion of matter to bring into actuality the soul that is already latent and potential there.[107]

The proposition that "soul-heat in seed . . . produces a soul" may seem, on the surface, to contradict the Aristotelian principle that "the agent . . . must agree in name and definition with its effect,"[108] which is a version of the broader principle that only what is itself of a certain character in actuality can produce something having the same character. Averroes resolves the apparent contradiction by explaining that although the agent producing a given actual form must indeed be the same in form as its product, it "need not exist in the same sort of matter as the matter in which it produces the [new actual] form." For example, the agent that produces an actual form of a bed in wood is the actual form of *bed* residing not in another piece of wood but in the "soul of the craftsman." The macrocosmic analogue of the form in the craftsman's soul, the analogue of the agent that truly produces the bed, is plainly different from soul-heat; soul-heat, which operates on the physical plane, parallels instead the "craft" by which the craftsman fashions the bed.[109] Averroes does not explicitly say what he understands the analogue of the actual form in the soul of the craftsman to be. He does write, however, that the cause "engendering" soul-heat "is perforce an incorporeal power," an "intellect . . . distinct from" and standing below the First Cause of the universe[110]; the language unmistakably echoes Aristotle's reference to a soul-like principle accompanying semen which is "separate," "something divine," and of the nature of "intellect."[111] I take Averroes' meaning to be that the analogue of the form in the mind of the craftsman, and hence the true agent producing a natural object, is a form contained in the incorporeal agent which is the ultimate cause of soul-heat. Since the incorporeal agent is subordinate to the First Cause, it would have to be either the active intellect or one of the incorporeal intelligences—and much more likely the former. If I have understood Averroes correctly, his present account therefore traces the source of soul-heat back beyond the sun and the celestial spheres to either the active intellect or, possibly, the movers of the spheres. The active intellect or the movers of the spheres employ soul-heat in a manner analogous to that in which the craftsman employs his craft.

[105]Cf. Aristotle, *De generatione animalium* 1.18.725a, 3.

[106]Ibid. 3.11.762a, 13–15.

[107]Averroes, Commentary on the *De animalibus* 154b–155b.

[108]Cf. Aristotle, *Metaphysics* 7.9.1034a, 22; 12.3.1070a, 4–5.

[109]The craftsman analogy is from Aristotle, *De generatione animalium* 1.22.730b, 14; 3.11.762a, 17.

[110]Averroes, Commentary on the *De animalibus* 155b–156a.

[111]Above, p. 233.

The Commentary on the *De generatione animalium*, in sum, argues strenuously that what endows plants and animals with their souls is not an emanation from the active intellect or any other incorporeal being but a physical factor, called soul-power or soul-heat, operating within matter. Yet notwithstanding its insistence upon a physical factor as the immediate cause of the forms of living beings, the present work still cannot do without an incorporeal agent. Either the active intellect or the incorporeal movers of the celestial spheres engender soul-heat and employ it to impart form, as the actual form of a bed in the mind of the craftsman employs the craftsman's craft to fashion a bed. Averroes' Middle Commentary on the *Metaphysics*, which was completed five years after the Commentary on the *De generatione animalium* and which refers to it by name, suggests a similar position.[112]

The Active Intellect as a Cause of Existence: The Long Commentary on the *Metaphysics* and *Tahāfut al-Tahāfut* (*Destructio Destructionum*)

Averroes treats the provenance of natural forms most fully and systematically in his Long Commentary on the *Metaphysics*. The position he takes there agrees with the annotations to the Epitome on the *Metaphysics* and goes a step beyond the Commentary on *De generatione animalium.*

For the first time Averroes has something specific to say about Avicenna. "Avicenna" and others, he reports, maintained that "a wholly nonmaterial . . . agent," namely, the "active intellect," also called the "giver of forms," "creates the form" of every natural object and "fixes the form in matter."[113] A minor argument supporting an incorporeal source of natural forms would be that when fire ensues upon rapid motion, "we cannot say we see motion engendering the substantial form of fire; consequently, the form of fire . . . must come into existence thanks to the [incorporeal] giver of forms."[114] That argument is simplistic, but Averroes also formulates a more sophisticated argument with which his opponents might buttress their position.

It rests on the Aristotelian principle that has governed every stage of the discussion, the principle that the "potential becomes actual only through something already actual in the same genus or species." The argument is especially plausible in cases of spontaneous generation, where "animals . . . and plants" are found to "pass from potentiality to actuality" in the absence of any "seed" born of a

[112]Middle Commentary on the *Metaphysics* (n. 43 above) 109 (108)b. For the dates of composition of these works, see Renan (n. 1 above) 61.

[113]Long Commentary on the *Metaphysics* 7, comm. 31; 12, comm. 18; Arabic text (n. 7 above), 882, 1496, 1498.

[114]Long Commentary on the *Metaphysics* 7, comm. 31; Arabic text 883.

progenitor "similar . . . in form" to the new organism. Since no agent already actually endowed with the requisite form can be discovered within the physical setting, "it would seem that [incorporeal] substances and forms must exist, which give forms to the [spontaneously] generated animals and plants."[115]

The argument can, Averroes continues, be extended to plants and animals capable of reproducing and even to inanimate substances, down to the level of the four elements. The reasoning would be that "the substantial forms in each and every object are something added to the blend-forms [*ṣuwar mizājiyya*]," the forms on the physical level which represent nothing more than a mixture of material components. Something must bring those substantial forms into existence. In the generation of plants, however, the "seed does not contain a soul actually, but only potentially, and whatever is potential requires something actual [to lead it to actuality]." Nothing actually possessing the form—or "soul"—of the new plant and able to produce the same kind of form in the plant is present within the physical setting.[116] Similarly—to add an example that Averroes was seen to offer elsewhere,[117] although he does not use it here—when male semen fertilizes female menstrual blood, the semen does not contain an actual soul which then produces another actual soul within the blood.

Carrying the argument down to the lowest rung of the incorporeal realm, the proponents of an incorporeal giver of forms may contend that even in the generation of the four elements, no physical substance endowed with the element's form acts directly on the substance possessing the form potentially. When actual fire, for example, ostensibly ignites another substance and produces fire in it, the "active" factor in the first substance, in the actual fire, is the "quality" of "heat," and heat alone is communicated to the second substance. Yet the "substantial form" of fire is "lightness,"[118] not heat, and the lightness of the first substance is never brought to bear on the second. The form of the one substance thus does not operate on the other substance, nor is the form of the second generated by contact with the form of the first. To suppose that the "generation of the form of fire" is not effected by a substantial form but is "attendant upon the generation of the fiery heat, as accidents are attendant upon the generation of a form" would be a "reprehensible" (*shaniᶜ*) thesis. The only remaining thesis, so the argument concludes, is that the form of the newly generated fire, as well as of a newly generated plant or animal, comes from the "incorporeal" realm.[119]

The foregoing considerations, writes Averroes, may even be thought to support the Platonic theory of Forms. And they are the foundation underlying Avicenna's theory that all natural forms—the "soul-forms" of plants and animals, whether they

[115]Ibid.; Arabic text 881.

[116]Ibid.; Arabic text 881–82.

[117]Above, p. 237.

[118]See above, p. 236.

[119]Long Commentary on the *Metaphysics* 7, comm. 31; 12, comm. 18; Arabic text 882, 1496. Similarly, *Tahāfut al-Tahāfut* (n. 33 above) 407.

reproduce sexually or are engendered spontaneously, the "substantial forms of homoeomeric" compounds, and the "substantial forms of the elements"—come "from the active intellect, which Avicenna calls the giver of forms."[120]

Averroes' Long Commentary on the *Metaphysics* undertakes to settle the issue by proceeding solely in accordance with the "propositions and principles" of Aristotle's philosophy; for Aristotle's system is the one "that involves fewest doubts, that most firmly reflects reality, . . . and that stands at the furthest remove from contradiction."[121] Aristotelian propositions and principles lead Averroes to reject an incorporeal source of any sublunar natural form.

The train of reasoning through which Averroes brings the issue to its final denouement is somewhat abstruse. He reasons as follows: When an object comes into existence, to regard its "form" and "substratum" as "two actually" distinct entities would be "absurd"; if the form were completely distinct from the substratum, form and substratum would constitute not a single object but two. That means that when a portion of matter possessing a physical *blend-form* receives a new, substantial form, whether the form of an inanimate object, a plant, or an animal, the portion of matter becomes something completely different from what it was before the new form appeared. As put by Averroes, to call matter that possesses a blend-form the *substratum* of the supervening substantial form before as well as after it receives the substantial form would be to employ the term *substratum* "equivocally." Two inferences can be drawn: The substratum of a substantial form exists as the substratum, in the strict sense, only from the moment when it receives the form; and the agent bringing an object into existence produces neither "form by itself nor the substratum without the form," but rather brings "both into existence together" and as a single object.

Consequently, there can be no more than one agent. For "if the substratum of the form [in the sense just defined] came into existence through an agent and the form through another, a single product would, insofar as it is a unity, come into existence through two agents, which is absurd." Any object coming into existence must therefore have a single agent, which simultaneously both brings the substratum into existence—by rendering a portion of matter the substratum of a given form—and also produces the new form in the substratum. Inasmuch as the agent bringing the material substratum into existence does its work on the physical plane, it must be physical. It must be either "a body possessing an active quality, or a power . . . operating through a body possessing an active quality." And the same agent, acting on the physical plane, is what brings forth the form in the substratum. The agent bringing forth any natural form is consequently physical.[122]

[120]Long Commentary on the *Metaphysics* 7, comm. 31; Arabic text 882. Averroes' language does not mean that plants and animals lack "substantial" forms, but rather that their "soul-forms" are a specific kind of substantial form.

[121]Long Commentary on the *Metaphysics* 12, comm. 18; Arabic text 1497.

[122]Ibid. 7, comm. 31; Arabic text 884–85.

The conclusion Averroes' Long Commentary on the *Metaphysics* draws and, inevitably, discovers in Aristotle is then that new natural forms are brought into existence by physical agents, that "material forms generate material forms."[123] The form of any emerging natural object was already present within the portion of matter that is going to turn into the object; in fact, "all . . . forms are potentially present in prime matter"; and the "agent," which is physical, "produces the compound of matter and form . . . by moving matter . . . until what is potentially form therein passes to actuality." The agent accordingly does not "introduce anything from without into the matter." For example, a portion of matter to be ignited already contains fire in potentiality, and "fire comes into existence" because either "motion" or other actual "fire" brings the potential fire within the matter to actuality. Similarly, an animate being comes into existence because "forms existing in the agent that generates the animal . . . bring . . . the forms in matter [that is, in the mother's menstrual blood and, ultimately, in prime matter itself] from potentiality to actuality."[124]

The generation of living beings does differ from the generation of inanimate objects in one respect, inasmuch as *soul-heat* or an equivalent also plays a role there. When plants and animals reproduce, the agent leading the potentiality to actuality is a "soul-heat" inhering in the seed or semen. Soul-heat is "generated" in the seed by the mature parent plant and in the semen by the male parent, acting, in each instance, together with the heat of the "sun" or, to be more precise, with the heat of the sun "blended" with the heat of the other stars—whence Aristotle's dictum "that man is generated by a man and the sun." Where plants and animals do not reproduce but are generated spontaneously "from decayed material" (*ᶜufūna*), the "decayed material serves in place of the seed," and the surrogate of soul-heat is a heat "generated" by the "heat of the sun blended with the heat of the other stars."[125] Soul-heat or its surrogate suffices to bring living beings into existence.

Averroes does not forget that Aristotle's *De generatione animalium* spoke of a "power of the origin of the soul," which power or origin is "something divine" and "called intellect."[126] Ibn Bājja had read the words as referring to an incorporeal *giver of forms*. The original version of Averroes' Epitome of the *Metaphysics* as well as his Epitome of the *Parva naturalia* had agreed and identified the active intellect as the agent producing the souls of animate beings.[127] Averroes' Commentary on the *De generatione animalium* dismissed the notion of an incorporeal giver of forms but still understood the passage in Aristotle to refer to an

[123]Ibid.; Arabic text 883. Averroes' proof text in Aristotle is *Metaphysics* 7.9, 1034b, 10, according to which: Our "reasoning shows that form is not generated," and what comes into existence is not the form itself, but the substance consisting of form and matter; see Averroes, ibid. 884.

[124]Ibid. 12, comm. 18; Arabic text 1499–1500, 1505.

[125]Ibid. 12, comms. 13 and 18; Arabic text 1464, 1501–2.

[126]Above, p. 233.

[127]Above, pp. 234–35.

"incorporeal power" that "engenders" soul-heat, soul-heat being the proximate cause bringing plant and animal forms into existence.[128] The Long Commentary on the *Metaphysics* now recognizes no incorporeal power that engenders soul-heat, although it does remark blandly that just as all natural forms exist potentially within matter, so too "in a sense, they exist actually in the prime mover."[129] From the standpoint of the Long Commentary on the *Metaphysics*, the expression "divine" power "called intellect" celebrates the wondrous physical powers within soul-heat. The powers in soul-heat are not, of course, "separate [from matter, that is, incorporeal]" nor do they "have themselves as objects of intellectual thought." Being corporeal, they have no consciousness at all. Nevertheless, they are appropriately described as "divine," "intellect," and "inspired" because they "drive toward an end" and "generate" organisms in an "intelligent manner."[130]

Such is Averroes' explanation of the provenance of natural forms in his Long Commentary on the *Metaphysics*. Despite the care with which the Long *Metaphysics* explores the subject, Averroes leaves the mechanics of plant and animal generation obscure at several points. He speaks of "forms" inhering in seed which impart the "forms of things generated from seed,"[131] of soul-heat's being "possessed of form," and of "powers in seed" or, more precisely, powers associated with the "heat of the seed," which "produce living beings."[132] No clarification is forthcoming as to whether the forms in seed or in the soul-heat contained in seed are the same as the powers, as they presumably are,[133] or whether the forms and powers are perhaps related to each other in a different fashion. Again, Averroes—reflecting similar statements in Aristotle[134]—stresses concerning both the aforementioned forms and the aforementioned powers that they are not "soul" and "ensouled in actuality," but are so only "in potentiality." Consequently, the Aristotelian rule that the potential becomes actual only through something actual in the same genus or species is not to be taken *au pied de la lettre* and "in every respect."[135] Averroes knows that factors in a state of potentiality do not initiate action within an Aristotelian universe,[136] yet he fails to identify any factor already in a state of actuality and carried by seed or semen which brings forth actual plant and animal souls.[137] He is vague on another item as well, never

[128]Above, p. 244.

[129]Long Commentary on the *Metaphysics* 12, comm. 18; Arabic text 1505.

[130]Ibid. 7, comm. 31, and 12, comm. 18; Arabic text 884, 1500–1501.

[131]Ibid. 7, comm. 31; Arabic text 883.

[132]Ibid. 7, comm. 31, and 12, comm. 18; Arabic text 884, 1500–1501. Cf. Aristotle, *De generatione animalium* 1.21.729b, 4–9.

[133]Cf. below, p. 252.

[134]Cf. Aristotle, *De generatione animalium* 2.1.735a, 8–9.

[135]Long Commentary on the *Metaphysics* 12, comm. 18; Arabic original 1500–1501.

[136]Cf. above, p. 245.

[137]Aristotle, *De generatione animalium* 2.2.734b, 20–735a, 4, explains that the male parent is the factor, already an animal in actuality, which sets the semen in motion, whereupon the

indicating exactly what soul-heat operates on in the various categories of generation. In animal reproduction, Averroes had remarked in an earlier work, male semen acts on female menstrual blood[138]; translated into the present scheme, that would mean that the power or form in the soul-heat of the male semen brings a potential animal form in the female menstrual blood to the state of actuality. What soul-heat acts on when seeds germinate, or when a surrogate of soul-heat is engendered within decayed material, remains unclear.

At all events, Averroes' Long Commentary on the *Metaphysics* unambiguously excludes the active intellect or any other incorporeal agent from the process whereby natural forms emerge; no incorporeal being serves as either the emanating source of animate forms, which was the position of Averroes' early works, or as the source of soul-heat, which was the position of his Commentary on *De generatione animalium.* In inanimate nature—according to Averroes' final view of things—mechanical physical forces bring forms already existing potentially in matter to a state of actuality. In the sector of animate nature where plants and animals reproduce, the physical agent is soul-heat, which is generated in seed and semen by the parent plant or animal in conjunction with the sun and stars. And in the sector of animate nature where generation occurs spontaneously, the physical agent is a surrogate of soul-heat, instilled in decayed material exclusively by the heavenly bodies. Soul-heat and its surrogate carry an unconscious, physical form or power, which somehow leads the forms of plants and animals potentially in matter to a state of actuality.

The origin of natural forms is discussed by Averroes in other works as well. His Long Commentary on the *Physics* touches on the subject in passing and seems to reflect the same position as the Long Commentary on the *Metaphysics*. Averroes there mentions "the formative powers that Aristotle called soul-powers in *De animalibus* [in other words, in *De generatione animalium*]" and that "are brought into existence . . . by the heavenly bodies."[139] Averroes' *Tahāfut al-Tahāfut* (*Destructio destructionum*) has more to say.

The *Tahāfut al-Tahāfut* is Averroes' answer to Ghazali's *Tahāfut al-Falāsifa* (*Destructio philosophorum*). Ghazali's object had been to refute the central theses of Avicenna's philosophic system, which he regarded as the most authoritative

---

motion in the semen actualizes the female menstrual blood. See Peck (n. 53 above) 583. In plants, Aristotle explains that the male and female factors are combined in the seed; *De generatione animalium* 1.23.731a, 1–14. But it is unclear what active agency initiates development in a dormant seed. It is still more unclear what Aristotle might have seen as the factor, already having the form of an actual animal or plant, which produces a new animal in instances of spontaneous generation; see Peck 584–85, and Balme (n. 76 above) 101–2. Balme senses a drift toward materialism in Aristotle's treatment of spontaneous generation in *De generatione animalium.*

[138] Above, p. 237.

[139] Averroes, Long Commentary on the *Physics* 8, comm. 47.

version of Aristotelian philosophy. In response, the *Tahāfut al-Tahāfut* dismisses some of Ghazali's arguments as sophistical; rejects others as cogent only in reference to an Avicennan but not a genuine—that is to say Aristotelian—philosophic system; defends the Aristotelian system as the most accurate description of the universe; and insists on the harmony, indeed identity, of Aristotle's philosophy with an enlightened reading of Scripture. Since the *Tahāfut al-Tahāfut* envisages a broader, and hence less scientific as well as more conservative, readership than Averroes' commentaries on Aristotle, the book sometimes expresses itself nontechnically and circumspectly.

At several junctures where the issue of sublunar forms arises, the *Tahāfut al-Tahāfut* lists possible theories. In one passage, Averroes remarks that some philosophers "construed" the source of natural forms as "an intellect"; "some, . . . as a soul"; "some, . . . as the body of the heavens"; and "some, . . . as the First [Cause]."[140] In another passage, he contrasts just two positions.

Certain philosophers, he writes, were "of the opinion that the giver of the forms of inanimate bodies and the giver of souls is an incorporeal substance, [that is,] either an intelligence or an incorporeal soul." By *intelligence*, Averroes is alluding to Avicenna's active intellect, and by *incorporeal soul*, to Themistius' world soul.[141] Other philosophers, he goes on, were "of the contrary opinion and maintained that forms are produced in bodies by bodies possessing similar forms." "Avicenna and additional Islamic philosophers"—but "none of the early philosophers"[142]—held the former position, "and their argument was that a body can produce in a body only heat or cold, wetness or dryness." Although Averroes does not spell out the argument, his Long Commentary on the *Metaphysics* has told us how it should go: If bodies can produce only qualities, if fire for instance can produce only heat, whereas lightness and not heat is the form of fire, then one portion of matter cannot be what produces the form of fire in a second portion of matter.[143] Avicenna and those of a similar mind accordingly concluded that "an incorporeal being . . . produces substantial forms [that is, the forms of nonanimate natural substances] and, a fortiori, animate forms."[144]

Philosophers taking the contrary line maintained that "living bodies produce living bodies" and "one animal . . . gives birth to another," as "sense perception [in fact] testifies." Where spontaneous generation occurs, "the celestial bodies are, in their opinion, what give life" to plants and animals. The philosophers in question "have arguments going beyond sense perception" to support their position, but the arguments "are not appropriate for the present context."[145] The reference to

[140]*Tahāfut al-Tahāfut* (n. 33 above) 212. By the philosopher who construed the source of natural forms as a soul, Averroes presumably means Themistius; see immediately below.

[141]See above, p. 32.

[142]*Tahāfut al-Tahāfut* 579.

[143]Above, p. 246.

[144]*Tahāfut al-Tahāfut* 407–8.

[145]Ibid. 408.

the celestial bodies' giving life to plants and animals that are generated spontaneously recalls the proposition, in the Long Commentary on the *Metaphysics*, that the celestial bodies produce the surrogate of soul-heat which, in turn, engenders spontaneously generated organisms. Averroes does not expressly adjudicate between the positions of Avicenna and the earlier philosophers, because "this is not the proper place to investigate" the issue, and anyone who does desire to know the truth should "approach the topic through its [proper] gate,"[146] in other words, through a systematic study of metaphysics. Nevertheless, if sense perception testifies that one animal gives birth to another, as Averroes was just seen to write, it is fairly clear that an incorporeal giver of forms is not what brings animals into existence[147]; and Averroes has intimated that soul-heat generated by the parent in seed is what does.

On a superficial reading, one section in the *Tahāfut al-Tahāfut* might seem to reveal Averroes espousing a totally different line and even indulging in occultism. He seems to envisage myriads of disembodied souls floating about in the world and interacting with bodies.[148]

The section at issue takes up Ghazali's contention that the "philosophers" cannot demonstrate the immortality of the soul. In the course of his rebuttal, Averroes writes: No genuine philosopher "disputes" the existence, within the sublunar world, of "souls that create every species . . . of animal, plant, and mineral." Again: "No philosopher disputes" the existence within the lower world of a "celestial heat bearing powers that generate animals and plants." The "souls" of the first sentence must be identical with the "powers" borne by celestial heat of the second sentence, because, Averroes also writes, the "heat" emanated by the heavens contains "souls that create both sublunar bodies and the souls inhering in those bodies."

Averroes goes on: The existence of "this . . . creative . . . soul" or power is "most apparent . . . in animals that do not reproduce," although it can be inferred as well for "animals that do reproduce." The creative souls or powers borne by celestial heat may be conceived in two possible ways. They might be thought of "as themselves becoming joined to the bodies they generate," in other words, as working within matter to transform it into animate bodies. On such a construction, when "bodies [of organisms] are destroyed" the souls or powers

146Ibid. 524.

147Averroes shows his respect for sense perception, ibid. 211, where he contrasts the "philosophers" with those who put forward their views "without demonstration and indeed often even contradict things perceived by the senses." (Van den Bergh's translation is misleading.)

148Scholars who have had difficulty with the section in question are: Van den Bergh (n. 33 above) 2.202–203; R. Arnaldez, "La pensée religieuse d'Averroès: III," *Studia islamica* 10 (1959) 37–38; A. Tallon, "Personal Immortality in Averroes' Tahafut al-Tahafut," *New Scholasticism* 38 (1964) 355–56; G. Hourani, "Averroès Musulman," in *Multiple Averroès*, ed. J. Jolivet (Paris 1978) 29–30; C. Touati, "Les problèmes de la génération et le rôle de l'intellect agent chez Averroès," in *Multiple Averroès* 163–64.

associated with them would "return to their spiritual matters and to their subtle unperceivable bodies." Alternatively, creative souls might be thought of as not themselves joining bodies in the sublunar world. They would then "occupy an intermediate rank between the souls of the celestial bodies and the sublunar souls in physical bodies," and they would act on bodies from without. Since they would on that conception "hold . . . sway [*taslīṭ*] over sublunar souls and bodies," there "arose the belief in spirits [*jinn*]." Either of the two conceptions will permit a belief in disembodied souls. Therefore anyone "who maintains the survival of the soul . . . should locate it in a subtle [*laṭīfa*] matter, in the soul-heat emanating from the celestial bodies."[149]

The references to celestial heat, creative souls or powers borne by celestial heat, spiritual matter, subtle nonperceivable bodies, and subtle matter are certainly bewildering, and undoubtedly deliberately so, considering that another section of the book dismisses individual human immortality as completely impossible.[150] Averroes' intent can hardly be misread, however, once he equates the subtle, unperceivable matter with the soul-heat emanating from the celestial bodies. In an allusive fashion, he is saying again, as he did straightforwardly in the Long Commentary on the *Metaphysics*, that a physical factor called soul-heat brings forth organisms, whether they reproduce or are generated spontaneously. Where organisms reproduce, the sun and stars share the bringing forth of soul-heat with the male parent or parent plant; where they are generated spontaneously, a surrogate of soul-heat is produced exclusively by the sun and stars. Soul-heat carries within itself powers that can, if one likes, be called *souls*,[151] but anyone with a

[149]*Tahāfut al-Tahāfut* 577–79. Thābiṭ ibn Qurra reportedly held that at death, a human soul attaches itself to a "subtle body"; see Avicenna, *al-Risāla al-Aḍḥawiyya*, ed. and trans. F. Lucchetta, as *Epistola sulla vita futura* (Padua 1969), 114–15, 224–25.

To a certain extent, Averroes may have chosen language echoing the Neoplatonic notion—which he would not have dreamt of accepting literally—of a "vehicle" (ὄχημα) or "body" acquired by the soul as it descends from its supernal home to earthly exile. See Plato, *Timaeus* 41E, 69C (which Neoplatonic interpretation distorted); Plotinus, *Enneads* 4.3.15; Proclus, *Elements of Theology*, ed. E. Dodds (Oxford 1963) §209; Dodds' excursus, ibid. 315–21; H. Lewy, *Chaldean Oracles and Theurgy* (Cairo 1956) 183–85; H. Blumenthal, "Neoplatonic Elements in the De Anima Commentaries," *Phronesis* 21 (1976) 70–71. J. Bidez, *Vie de Porphyre* (Leipzig 1913) 89–90, finds in Porphyry the additional notion that demons subsist in a vehicle similar to that carrying the human soul.

[150]*Tahāfut al-Tahāfut* 27–29.

[151]Curiously, Averroes did have a precedent, although he most likely did not realize it. In *De generatione animalium* 3.11.762a, 21–22, Aristotle wrote that since "soul-heat" pervades water and earth, "all things are in a way full of soul"; the passage echoes Thales, who, as Aristotle reports, "thought that all things are full of gods" (Aristotle, *De anima* 1.5.411a, 7–8). Aristotle's intent was that spontaneous generation can occur because *pneuma* is present in water, which in turn is present in the earth; and soul-heat pervades pneuma. The preserved Arabic translation of the *De generatione animalium* does not however keep the phrase "full of soul," stating instead that everything is "full of soul power." See Aristotle, *The Generation of Animals; The Arabic Translation* (n. 59 above) 129. Averroes' paraphrase of the passage in his Commentary on *De*

philosophic training will immediately realize that those so-called souls are physical and unconscious powers.[152]

Of the two hypotheses for construing the souls or powers in soul-heat—according to one of which, the souls or powers themselves enter bodies, while according to the other, souls or powers in soul-heat occupy an intermediate rank between celestial souls and the souls of plants and animals—the former hypothesis would seem to be supported by Averroes' Long Commentary on the *Metaphysics*.[153] The *Tahāfut al-Tahāfut*, with all its mystifying language, has simply reaffirmed the theory of soul-heat, which bears powers or, if one should prefer, souls, and which works within matter. The powers, or souls, lead potential forms of plants and animals to a state of actuality. When a plant or animal dies some of its soul-heat, carrying the aforementioned powers or souls, survives—undoubtedly for no more than a limited time, seeing that it is an object composed of matter and form and all such objects decay. Anyone who so wishes may comfort himself in the thought that the subtle unperceivable substance called soul-heat, together with the unconscious powers in soul-heat which brought forth his human form, will outlive his body. Scientists and philosophers will, however, seek their assurance of immortality elsewhere. The *Tahāfut al-Tahāfut* closes its discussion of human immortality with the comment that "among the strongest" grounds for the belief is the ability of the "material [human] intellect" to make a "universal judgment." A "substance of that description," a substance capable of making universal judgments, is "completely nonmaterial" and consequently indestructible. Philosophers and scientists will, in other words, take no comfort in the survival of soul-heat. They understand that the only genuine survivor of the body is the human material intellect—which despite its name is, according to the last stage of Averroes' philosophy, a nonmaterial substance existing independently of the soul.[154]

Summary

The original version of Averroes' Epitome of the *Metaphysics* outlines a cosmic system similar to the systems of Alfarabi and Avicenna. Averroes does depart from Alfarabi and Avicenna in rejecting an outermost diurnal sphere empty of all stars, and in rejecting the emanation of the bodies of the celestial spheres. Nevertheless, the core of the emanation theory that went back at least to Alfarabi remains. Averroes still understands that the First Cause of the universe eternally emanates from itself an incorporeal being consisting in pure thought; the emanated being, the

---

generatione animalium (n. 62 above) 174a, renders the passage as follows: Since earth and water are permeated with "soul-heat," they are "full of generating soul power."

[152]See above, p. 249.

[153]See above, p. 248–49.

[154]*Tahāfut al-Tahāfut* 579. See below, p. 289.

first intelligence, contains multiple aspects and through them eternally emanates two things, the form, or soul, of the first sphere and a further incorporeal being consisting in pure thought; the second incorporeal intelligence emanates two similar effects; and so on. As for the place of the First Cause of the universe within the scheme, Averroes agrees with his predecessors that the First Cause must transcend the incorporeal intelligences associated with celestial spheres. Because of the rule that "from one only one can proceed," the wholly unitary being at the head of the causal chain can have no more than a single effect. Since each of the intelligences governing celestial spheres has at least two effects, and hence is not wholly unitary, the ultimate cause of the universe, which must be wholly unitary, resides beyond the movers of the spheres.

The process of emanation unfolds eternally step-by-step through the series of celestial intelligences. The intelligence governing the sphere of the moon eternally brings forth the form or soul of its sphere and the final intelligence in the incorporeal hierarchy. That final intelligence is, once again, the *active intellect*, the entity Aristotle posited on the grounds that an intellect must exist which is what it is "by virtue of making all things"—by virtue of making all thoughts.

Averroes' Epitome of the *Parva naturalia* and the original version of his Epitome of the *Metaphysics* view the active intellect as the cause of a considerable segment of sublunar existence. Averroes does not go as far as Avicenna had gone. Just as he recognized no cause of the existence of the bodies of the celestial region, so too he maintains, and undertakes to prove, that sublunar matter can have no cause of its existence. He moreover states that from the perspective of physical science, the forms of the four elements and the forms of blends of the four elements—homoeomeric compounds—can be accounted for by natural forces. But the forms of animals and plants, those capable of reproducing as well as those generated spontaneously, cannot, according to his early works, arise from the interplay of natural forces. They must be produced by an agent existing outside the physical realm. Averroes' original position thus is that in sexual reproduction, plant seed or male sperm prepares a portion of matter for a plant or animal form; in spontaneous generation, the action of the heavenly bodies prepares matter for a form; and in each instance, the portion of matter so disposed automatically selects the appropriate form out of the ever-present emanation of the active intellect. Having delineated the role of the active intellect from the standpoint of physical science, Averroes adds in the early version of his Epitome of the *Metaphysics* that from the metaphysical—or epistemological—perspective, physical forces cannot, after all, account even for the forms of the four elements or the forms of natural compounds. Since the human mind extracts intelligible forms from natural substances below the animal and plant level, those forms too must, from the metaphysical perspective, be ascribed to a source consisting in intelligible thought. In other words, the forms of all natural substances must be attributed to the active intellect.

Such was Averroes' early position on the emanation of intelligences and celestial souls, and on the functions of the active intellect in the sublunar world.

His later position on the emanation of intelligences and spheres is set forth in annotations incorporated into his Epitome of the *Metaphysics* and in the Long Commentary on the *Metaphysics*, as well as being mentioned in the Middle Commentary on the same book and alluded to in the *Tahāfut al-Tahāfut*. Averroes now abandons the emanation thesis. He contends that, in general, beings do not proceed or emanate from one another. And even if emanation were a genuine subcategory of efficient causation, the incorporeal realm could not be emanated, because efficient causation is foreign to incorporeal beings.[155] Since the rule that from one only one proceeds applies solely to efficient causes, and the First Cause is not an efficient cause, the rule does not apply to it. In Averroes' final picture of the universe, each intelligence possesses a stratum of existence in its own right, the underlying stratum eternally turns its mental gaze upon the unitary First Cause, and the conception of the First Cause which each thereby receives endows it with the measure of perfection befitting its rank in the cosmic hierarchy. Inasmuch as a unitary cause can have more than one effect in the fashion Averroes has described, the objection to taking the intelligence governing the outermost sphere as the First Cause of the universe vanishes. Averroes therefore concludes that the First Cause is identical with the intelligence moving the outermost sphere. He still identifies the active intellect as the last in the series of incorporeal intelligences, although the active intellect is no longer the outgrowth of a process of emanation.

Averroes also retreats from his original position on the active intellect's role as a cause of sublunar natural forms. He does so in a number of works, notably in annotations to the Epitome of the *Metaphysics*, in the Commentary on *De generatione animalium*, in the Long Commentary on the *Metaphysics*, and in *Tahāfut al-Tahāfut*. An intermediate and a final position can be discerned.

His most carefully thought-out argument against taking the active intellect as the source of sublunar forms, an argument given in two works, reasons that the substratum of a new substance exists as such only from the moment when it receives its new form. Because the substratum, in that sense, and the form constitute a single object, a single agent must bring the substratum and form into existence together and through a single act. The substratum of any given sublunar form is brought into existence—that is to say, is rendered a substratum—by an agent that operates on the physical plane and is hence physical. Since the natural form, whether of an inanimate object, a plant, or an animal, is brought into existence by the same agent that brings the substratum into existence, it too is brought into existence by a physical agent.

155John of Jandun and Alexander Achillini followed Averroes in excluding efficient causation from the incorporeal realm. By contrast, Marcantonio Zimara, who had Averroes' Epitome of the *Metaphysics* in a sixteenth-century translation from the Hebrew, interpreted Averroes as having traced the existence of the translunar region to an efficient causation initiated by God. See A. Maurer, "John of Jandun and the Divine Causality," *Mediaeval Studies* 17 (1955) 189, 195–96.

Averroes concludes that all natural forms exist potentially in prime matter. Forms of the four elements and forms of homoeomeric compounds are elicited from matter by physical forces. Forms of plants and animals are brought to actuality by soul-heat or a surrogate of soul-heat, which in instances of organic reproduction is borne by plant seed or male semen, and in instances of spontaneous generation appears in decaying material. Averroes' intermediate and final positions regarding the appearance of sublunar forms relate to soul-heat. His intermediate position, advanced in the Commentary on *De generatione animalium*, is that soul-heat is engendered in seed or semen and decaying material by an incorporeal substance subordinate to the First Cause—presumably, the active intellect. His final position is that where organisms reproduce, soul-heat is engendered in seed or semen by the parent in conjunction with the heat of the sun, blended with the heat of the other stars; and where they do not reproduce, a surrogate of soul-heat is instilled in decaying material exclusively by the sun and the stars. The active intellect plays no role, and its function accordingly shrinks back to what Aristotle established in the *De anima*, to the actualization of the potential human intellect.

On the subjects discussed in the present chapter, as elsewhere, Averroes strove to liberate himself from mistaken interpretations of Aristotle and mistaken philosophic theories, especially those propounded by his Islamic predecessors. In banishing emanation and efficient causation from the incorporeal realm and in denying that the natural forms of the sublunar world emanate from the active intellect, Averroes' later works undoubtedly do capture Aristotle's intent better than the earlier works. Whether Averroes should also have revised his understanding of the type of entity the active intellect is, whether he should, in other words, have read Aristotle as recognizing no active intellect outside the individual human person, is one of a class of questions that scholars will debate into the indefinite future.

Although paring away accretions and recovering the genuine Aristotle was the leitmotif in all of Averroes' later philosophic activity, and although he succeeded to a considerable degree in the subjects considered here, one should not generalize and suppose that his maturer works consistently attain a more accurate understanding of Aristotle. On the issue of the potential, or material, human intellect, which is the subject of the next chapter, Averroes' efforts led him not toward a more accurate interpretation of Aristotle, but in what the consensus of modern scholars would consider to be the very opposite direction.

7

Averroes on the Material Intellect

Introduction

Aristotle, as we have seen, posited an intellect in man which is "potential"[1]; which "is what it is by virtue of becoming all things,"[2] that is, by virtue of learning all thoughts; and which is a kind of "matter."[3] But nothing Aristotle said about what came to be known as the potential or material intellect reveals the kind of entity he supposed it to be, and one can only guess whether the question concerned him at all. The question of the nature of the potential human intellect did capture the attention of Alexander of Aphrodisias and Themistius, and they reached opposite conclusions. Alexander construed the human potential or material intellect as a mere *disposition* in the human organism, and Themistius construed it as a *substance*. The issue did not, however, carry any special import for Averroes' Arabic predecessors. Alfarabi described the potential intellect as both a "disposition" and a "substance,"[4] and justified neither description. Avicenna took up the nature of the human material intellect only indirectly, in the course of treating a different issue that preempted the question of the material intellect's nature. He maintained that the human soul, and not merely the intellect, is "an incorporeal substance," which is brought into existence together with the generation of each human body.[5] The published works of Ibn Bājja (Avempace) also evince little interest in the nature of the potential intellect, although he plays a significant role in Averroes' treatment of the subject. A comment in one of Ibn Bājja's works, which is corroborated by Averroes' report of Ibn Bājja's position, places him close to Alexander.

In contrast to his Islamic predecessors, Averroes was haunted by the issue, and successive works find him struggling with it and moving restlessly from one position to another. The differing positions regarding the potential human intellect which Averroes espoused at different times not only disclose a good deal about his own philosophic development and style; they were of great consequence for the

[1] Aristotle, *De anima* 3.4.429a, 16.
[2] Ibid. 5.430a, 14–15.
[3] Ibid., 10–11.
[4] Above, pp. 49, 67.
[5] Above, pp. 83, 107.

history of philosophy. Averroes' writings launched two movements reaching into the fifteenth and sixteenth centuries, not in the Islamic world, where he was ignored, but in the Jewish and Christian philosophic communities. The nature of the human intellect was a prime concern of both movements, and quirks of history delivered different compositions, representing different stages of his thought, to the Hebrew and Latin readers. Two Averroistic traditions resulted, each growing up around a partial reading of Averroes and his position on the human potential or material intellect.

Averroes invariably poses the question of the potential human intellect against the background of Aristotle, Alexander of Aphrodisias, Themistius, and Ibn Bājja.

Aristotle and the others, and indeed all writers in the Aristotelian tradition, worked from the unquestioned presupposition that the human intellect reflects objective reality with no distortion. Aristotle reasoned that should the intellect man is born with have "some quality" before it begins to think, the quality already present there would "prevent and block" the intellect's operation; the ingrained coloring would prevent the intellect from exactly mirroring reality. Since, as he presupposed, the human intellect does mirror reality exactly and hence can have no quality at the outset, he concluded that the part "of the soul called intellect . . . is no existent thing before it thinks" and again that, being free of qualities, it is "not mixed . . . with the body" but is "separate" therefrom.[6] The phrase "separate" from the body or from matter is an Aristotelian way of saying "incorporeal." A reader who fixes on the characterization of the human potential intellect as not mixed with the body and as separate, or incorporeal, will obtain a very different notion of it from one who fixes on the characterization of the potential intellect as "no existent thing."

To help explain how the human intellect is at the outset "potentially [everything] thinkable but actually nothing at all," Aristotle compared it to a "tablet," which is receptive of writing and "on which nothing is so far actually written."[7] The intellect, like the writing tablet, is receptive of thought yet at the beginning of its career has no intellectual thought inscribed upon it. In one further statement, which was to be quoted and requoted through the centuries, Aristotle posited that the human intellect is "impassible," that it does not suffer "affection" or alteration as it performs its function. Even nonintellectual levels of human perception, Aristotle had determined, perform their tasks without undergoing affection and alteration. Seeing that the lower faculties of the soul do not suffer affection, the intellect, which is "unmixed" with the body, certainly cannot.[8]

Alexander of Aphrodisias gave heed to Aristotle's description of the initial stage of human intellect as being no existent thing before it thinks. He reasoned as follows: "Whatever is receptive of forms of a certain sort cannot have any of them

[6]Aristotle, *De anima* 3.4.429a, 18–429b, 5.

[7]Ibid. 429b, 30–430a, 2.

[8]Ibid. 429a, 15, 29–30. See G. Rodier's commentary on 429a, 15, in his edition (Paris 1900).

in its own nature; for the copresence of its own form would prevent its receiving the other form. . . . Now, all things are known by the intellect. . . . Therefore, the material intellect" can originally contain no form in itself and "must be no thing actually, but everything potentially." Being nothing in actuality, nothing substantial or even real, the material intellect can be "only a disposition . . . for receiving [intelligible] forms."

Having come this far, Alexander saw that Aristotle's analogy of the writing tablet needed emendation. Aristotle had compared the material intellect to a tablet; yet a tablet is "already an existent being" before it is written on, whereas the material intellect, as just seen, is not describable as actually existent before it begins to think. To rescue the analogy, Alexander added a distinction between the "unwritten tablet itself" and "the unwritten character of the tablet." The true analogue of the tablet itself, he submitted, is the "soul" or, if one prefers, the entire human "subject." The "material intellect" corresponds not to the tablet but "rather to the unwritten aspect of the tablet," that is, to the "disposition for being written on." "When written upon, . . . the writing tablet" does "undergo affection." The "disposition" that the tablet has for receiving writing, by contrast, "undergoes no affection when it is brought to actuality; for it is not some [actual] subject [or substratum]," and only something actual, only a subject or substratum, can be described as being *affected.* "By the same token the [material] intellect," which parallels the disposition the tablet has for receiving writing, "undergoes no affection [when it thinks], inasmuch as it does not belong to the class of actual beings."[9]

Alexander, then, understood the material intellect to be merely a disposition in the human soul, and nothing whatsoever actual in itself; for just that reason, it undergoes no affection. Since the material intellect is a "power" in the soul, it is, in Alexander's view, "destroyed together with the soul [when the soul is destroyed]." As was seen in an earlier chapter, Alexander did accommodate a certain attenuated type of human intellectual immortality. He could, however, attribute no survival to the potentiality for thought with which man is born.[10]

Themistius likewise rehearsed Aristotle's phrases, but instead of fixing on the characterization of the intellect as "no existent thing," he paid heed to the characterization of it as "not mixed" with the body and "separate." The "potential intellect," Themistius understood, does "not employ a bodily organ for its activity"; it is "wholly unmixed with the body, impassive, and separate [from matter]." From the potential intellect's being unmixed with the body and separate from matter, he inferred that it is not "destructible."[11] And he drew support for his interpretation from Theophrastus. As reported by Themistius, Theophrastus had also repeated

[9]Alexander, *De anima*, in *Scripta minora* 2.1, ed. I. Bruns (Berlin 1887) 84–85.

[10]Ibid. 90; above, p. 37.

[11]Themistius, Paraphrase of Aristotle's *De anima*, in *Commentaria in Aristotelem Graeca* 5.3, ed. R. Heinze (Berlin 1899) 105. Medieval Arabic translation, with the pagination of the Greek indicated: *An Arabic Translation of Themistius . . . on Aristoteles 'De anima'*, ed. M. Lyons (Columbia, S.C. 1973).

the Aristotelian description of the potential intellect as "separate" from matter.[12] He had, moreover, tried to explain how the potential intellect might "come from without and be superadded, as it were, and nonetheless be naturally linked" to man. His proposal was that the intellect does not in fact come "from without . . . by way of being superadded, but rather by way of being included together with the original generation" of a man.[13] In other words, for Theophrastus as reported by Themistius, something from without joins man at birth and constitutes the human intellect. Since an indestructible entity separate from matter could be nothing other than an incorporeal substance, Averroes consistently writes that Themistius and those of a similar mind construed the potential intellect as an incorporeal substance or, alternatively, as a disposition inhering in such a substance.[14]

Finally, there was Ibn Bājja. Aristotle had established a connection between the human soul's intellectual faculty and imaginative faculty, on the grounds that the human intellect can operate only if the imaginative faculty of the soul presents it with images.[15] Ibn Bājja—in the only pertinent statement that I was able to find in his published writings—accordingly stated that the term "rational faculty" denotes "in the first instance, spiritual forms insofar as they are able to receive intellect."[16] By "spiritual forms," Ibn Bājja meant forms, or images, in the imaginative faculty of the soul.[17] Either by reading out the implications of that statement and similar statements in Ibn Bājja or by drawing on sources no longer extant or still undiscovered—as, for example, Ibn Bājja's *De anima*, the published text of which breaks off tantalizingly in the middle of the discussion of intellect[18]—Averroes reports that Ibn Bājja construed the material intellect as a disposition located in the imaginative faculty of the soul.

Averroes thus found himself before two poles, both of which are grounded in Aristotle. At the one extreme stood Alexander and Ibn Bājja, who construed the potential human intellect as a mere disposition either in the human subject, in the human soul, or specifically in the imaginative faculty of the soul. At the other extreme stood Themistius, who construed the potential intellect as a nonmaterial substance, which exists independently of the physical man and joins him at birth.

[12]Ibid. 108.

[13]Ibid. 107; French translation in E. Barbotin, *La théorie aristotélicienne de l'intellect d'après Théophraste* (Louvain 1954) 249. Cf. E. Zeller, *Die Philosophie der Griechen* 2.2, 4th ed. (Leipzig 1921) 848–50; Barbotin 187–90. The word *linked* is from the Arabic translation.

[14]A similar interpretation of Themistius is offered by O. Hamelin, *La théorie de l'intellect d'après Aristote et ses commentateurs* (Paris 1953) 40.

[15]Aristotle, *De anima* 3.3.427b, 16; 8.432a, 8–9; *De memoria* 1.449b, 31.

[16]Ibn Bājja, *Fī Ittiṣāl al-ᶜAql bi'l-Insān*, ed. and Spanish trans. M. Asín Palacios, *Al-Andalus* 7 (1942), Arabic text 13–14; Spanish translation 31.

[17]Ibn Bājja, *Tadbīr al-Mutawaḥḥid*, ed. and Span. trans. M. Asín Palacios, as *El régimen del solitario* (Madrid 1946), Arabic text 19–21; Spanish translation 50–52.

[18]Cf. A. Altmann, "Ibn Bājja on Man's Ultimate Felicity," reprinted in his *Studies in Religious Philosophy and Mysticism* (Ithaca 1969) 76, n. 7.

Averroes' repeated attempts to resolve the exegetic and philosophic issues—to determine Aristotle's intent and to satisfy himself on the true nature of the material intellect—led him from the first of the two poles to an intermediate position and then to the other pole.

No less than seven of Averroes' compositions treat the subject of human intellect formally—while others do so incidentally—and the nature of the material intellect comes up in all seven.

Three of the seven are commentaries on Aristotle's *De anima*. Averroes, as is well known, wrote commentaries on Aristotle's works in three modes, in what are called Epitomes, Middle Commentaries, and Long Commentaries. The *De anima* was one of the handful of Aristotelian works significant enough to elicit all three, and they had their several fates.

(1) The Epitome of the *De anima* is preserved in the Arabic original and in a medieval Hebrew translation. Two editions of the Arabic text were at my disposal, one of which has an apparatus recording the variant readings of two Arabic manuscripts.[19] The Hebrew is still unpublished.[20] There are seven passages, ranging in length from a few lines to a paragraph, that appear in some of the Arabic manuscripts and the unpublished Hebrew translation but not in other manuscripts; and manuscripts that agree regarding a given passage do not necessarily do so regarding the remaining. In all, a total of four configurations or versions of the Epitome can be distinguished.

(2) The Middle Commentary on the *De anima* exists only in manuscript. The Arabic original has survived in two manuscripts written in Hebrew characters,[21] and two separate medieval Hebrew translations have been preserved in a number of

[19]The edition containing the apparatus was published as *Talkhīṣ Kitāb al-Nafs*, ed. A. Al-Ahwani (Cairo 1950). The other edition that I used is printed in the collection called *Rasā'il Ibn Rushd* (Hyderabad 1947). Bibliographies list a further edition by N. Morata (Madrid 1934), but I could find no trace of its actually having been published. The edition of S. Gomez Nogales (Madrid 1985) was not available to me, but J. Alaoui, *Al-Matn al-Rushdī* (Casablanca 1986) 53, n. 8, describes it as inadequate. Spanish translation: *La psicologia de Averroes*, trans. S. Gomez Nogales (Madrid 1987). The term *talkhīṣ* properly designates the Middle Commentary and is therefore not the correct term for the present item; and Alaoui contends that the work is not strictly an epitome either. Ahwani's version is based on manuscripts found in Cairo and Madrid, and I relied on his apparatus to recreate the character of the two manuscripts. The Hyderabad edition does not have a scientific apparatus, but the notes indicate that it too is based on two manuscripts. Chester Beatty collection, Arabic MS 4523, fol. 111b ff., has the same readings as the Hyderabad text.

[20]For the manuscripts, see M. Steinschneider, *Die hebräischen Uebersetzungen des Mittelalters und die Juden als Dolmetscher* (Berlin 1893) 147. I examined three manuscripts in microfilm and found that they all have the same text.

[21]Paris, Bibliothèque nationale, Hebrew MS 1009; Modena, Hebrew MS 41. Regarding the latter, see C. Bernheimer, *Catalogo dei manoscritti orientali della Biblioteca Estense* (Rome 1960) 55. I shall cite the Arabic text from the Paris manuscript, and the Hebrew text from Paris, Bibliothèque nationale, Hebrew MS 947.

exemplars.[22] In addition, a Latin manuscript has been identified which contains a late translation into that language, made from the Hebrew and not from the Arabic.[23] I consulted both manuscripts of the Arabic original, as well as manuscripts of both Hebrew translations but did not use the derivative Latin translation.

(3) The Long Commentary on the *De anima* is not known to have survived in the original Arabic, although excerpts have been discovered. It was translated into Latin in the Middle Ages, and an admirable edition of the Latin translation has been published.[24] A Hebrew translation of the Long Commentary circulated at the end of the fifteenth century, and a single manuscript of a Hebrew translation has been preserved which, scholars have shown, is derivative, made not directly from the Arabic, but from the Latin.[25] Whether the Hebrew translation circulating in the fifteenth century was identical with the presumably late translation from the Latin which has been preserved is a matter of conjecture. It is clear, however, that Jewish philosophers prior to the fifteenth century who were restricted to Hebrew texts knew nothing of a Long Commentary.[26] They relied for their understanding of Averroes' theory of intellect on the Epitome, the Middle Commentary, and the compositions that remain to be described.

Averroes' commentaries on Aristotle's *De anima* naturally encompass the entire Aristotelian work and deal with intellect only when they reach the point where Aristotle does so, in *De anima* 3.4 and 3.5. Besides his commentaries on the *De anima*, Averroes composed briefer pieces that do not treat the subject of the soul in general but are devoted exclusively to specific problems regarding intellect. While none of the briefer compositions have been preserved in Arabic, they all can be

[22]Steinschneider 148–49.

[23]See J. Vennebusch, "Zur Bibliographie des psychologischen Schrifttums des Averroes," *Bulletin de philosophie médiévale* 6 (1964) 94.

[24]Averroes, *Commentarium magnum in Aristotelis de Anima libros*, ed. F. Crawford (Cambridge, Mass. 1953) (henceforth cited as: Long Commentary on the *De anima*). The translation probably was done by Michael Scot. Sixteenth-century editions of Averroes add an alternate and clearer rendering of two critical sections—Book 3, comms. 5 and 36—by Jacob Mantino. Mantino's translations into Latin were generally done from the Hebrew, but the source from which he translated these two sections into Latin is puzzling. The suggestion has been made that a medieval Hebrew translation of just the two sections may have existed; see H. Wolfson, "Plan for the Publication of a *Corpus commentariorum Averrois in Aristotelem*," reprinted in his *Studies in the History of Philosophy and Religion* 1 (Cambridge, Mass. 1973) 446. Another possibility is that a Hebrew translation from the Arabic of *De anima*, Book 3, did exist in the fifteenth century; see Wolfson 447. A third possibility is that Mantino was retranslating into Latin from the late Hebrew translation, which had itself been made, shortly before, from the Latin version; Wolfson contests that possibility. Still another possibility is that Mantino simply rephrased and fleshed out the two critical sections in Michael Scot's translation in order to render them more readable.

[25]Wolfson 448–49; Crawford xi–xii.

[26]Shem Ṭob Falaquera, who knew Arabic well, translates a passage from the Arabic text. See Falaquera, *Moreh ha-Moreh* (Pressburg 1837) 145.

matched with items in the lists of Averroes' works drawn up by medieval Arabic bibliographers.[27] These compositions are:

(4) A piece entitled *Epistle on the Possibility of Conjunction* (Hebrew: *Iggeret Efsharut ha-Debequt*) that is to say, on the possibility of the human intellect's conjoining with the active intellect. The *Epistle* has survived only in a medieval Hebrew translation, which has been published.[28]

(5) and (6) Two other short pieces, again on the theme of conjunction with the active intellect. Like the previous item, they are not known to exist in the original Arabic and have been preserved thanks to a medieval Hebrew translation, which has been published.[29] The first of the two was translated from the medieval Hebrew version into Latin in the sixteenth century.[30] And there also exists a curious composition in Latin, known as *Averrois Tractatus de animae beatitudine* (*Averroes' Treatise on the Well-being of the Soul*), which reworks the two pieces into a single treatise and attempts to palm the product off as a genuine work of Averroes.[31]

(7) A commentary on sections of Alexander's *De intellectu*, which once again is known only in Hebrew translation. It too has been published.[32]

[27]Regarding items 4, 5, and 6, see S. Munk, *Mélanges de philosophie juive et arabe* (Paris 1859) 435, 437; E. Renan, *Averroès et l'Averroïsme* (Paris 1866) 66–67. Regarding item 7, see Renan 70, 462–63.

[28]See Steinschneider (n. 20 above) 191–97. None of the manuscripts has the composition by itself; two medieval Jewish philosophers, Moses Narboni and Joseph Ibn Shem Ṭob, wrote commentaries on it, and the manuscripts interweave the text of Averroes with either one or the other commentary. Ibn Shem Ṭob undoubtedly took his text from Narboni. Half of the text was published in the last century as: Averroes, *Ueber die Möglichkeit der Conjunktion*, ed. L. Hannes (Halle 1892). The entire text was published recently as: *The Epistle on the Possibility of Conjunction*, ed. and trans. K. Bland (New York 1982). To correct the editions, which are poor, I have used Paris, Bibliothèque Nationale, Hebrew MS 947, the readings of which are recorded in Bland's apparatus.

[29]Published as the first and second items in Averroes, *Drei Abhandlungen über die Conjunction*, ed. and German trans. J. Hercz (Berlin 1869). The author of the third of the items in Hercz was not Averroes, but his son, and of the three, the third, which is the least original of the compositions, is alone known to exist in the original Arabic; it is published in Ahwani (n. 19 above) 119–24. The three compositions were translated into Hebrew by Samuel Ibn Tibbon as part of his still unpublished commentary on the Book of Ecclesiastes.

[30]Steinschneider (n. 20 above) 200. The most convenient edition is found in vol. 9 of *Aristotelis opera cum Averrois commentariis* (Venice 1562–1574), reprinted in Frankfurt 1962.

[31]See H. Davidson, "*Averrois Tractatus de Animae Beatitudine*," in *A Straight Path* (Hyman Festschrift), ed. R. Link-Salinger (Washington 1988) 57–73.

[32]"Averroes' Commentary on the *De intellectu* attributed to Alexander," ed. H. Davidson, *Shlomo Pines Jubilee Volume* 1 (Jerusalem 1988) 205–17. Like the *Epistle on the Possibility of Conjunction* (item 4), the commentary on the *De intellectu* never appears by itself in the manuscripts. It always is interwoven with one of two medieval Hebrew commentaries, composed by the same two thinkers who wrote the two commentaries on the *Epistle*.

The three commentaries on the *De anima* are typically Averroistic in tone and style, and their genuineness can hardly be doubted. The genuineness of the other compositions is corroborated, as already mentioned, by lists of Averroes' works in the medieval Arabic bibliographers. I take all seven compositions, with the possible exception of the *Epistle on the Possibility of Conjunction*, to be genuine.[33] The conclusions to be drawn here will not, however, be affected substantially if the genuineness of any of the compositions, apart from the three commentaries on the *De anima*, should be challenged.

The Epitome of the *De anima* and the *Epistle on the Possibility of Conjunction*

The textual situation of the Epitome of the *De anima* is complex. In seven places within the section on intellect, certain manuscripts have passages that are absent in other manuscripts, and some of the passages are plainly comments written at a later date and incorporated into the original text. One Arabic manuscript, now in Madrid, has all the passages that can be considered additions.[34] The medieval Hebrew translation agrees with the Madrid manuscript, except that it lacks a single passage found there; the passage in question is, however, not strictly an interpolation within the section on intellect but an appendix. An Arabic version of the Epitome, which was printed in Hyderabad and is based, it seems, on two manuscripts, lacks two of the added passages found in the Madrid manuscript and in the Hebrew, and also lacks the appendix. Finally, a further Arabic manuscript, now in Cairo, lacks all but one of the additions in the Madrid manuscript and in the Hebrew, has a passage of its own which is missing in all the other versions, and—if the apparatus of the printed edition is correct[35]—does have the aforementioned appendix.

Despite the complexity, the underlying situation is clear. The text without the additions—or at least without the significant ones—and including the passage preserved only in the Cairo manuscript, represents the Epitome as Averroes originally wrote it; and at least some[36] of the additions found in the Madrid manuscript of the Arabic text and in the Hebrew translation are corrections that Averroes made subsequently, after having rethought the subject. Whether the

[33]Doubts may be raised about the *Epistle*, because it defines its problem very differently from the way other works of Averroes define the same problem, and because it deploys a highly dialectical argumentation, which is untypical of Averroes. See below, p. 324, n. 38, and p. 328, n. 49.

[34]The same manuscript also contains the version of Averroes' Epitome of the *Metaphysics* which has the latter additions; see above, p. 221.

[35]See Ahwani (n. 19 above).

[36]Ahwani 82–83, seems to be a mere variant and not a later addition. An appendix to the Epitome of the *De anima*, ibid. 90–95, does not appear in all versions, but also does not seem to be a later correction.

appendix is also a later addition or belongs to the original Epitome is of no consequence for us. In a word, the Cairo manuscript more or less represents the original Epitome, whereas the Madrid manuscript and the Hebrew translation incorporate Averroes' later corrections. The judgment that Averroes underwent a change of heart is not conjectural, for one of the added passages explicitly states that he completely revised his position sometime after having written the Epitome. With the explicit statement as a guide, the character of the other additions cannot be missed.

The Epitome as originally written puts forward an argument in several steps, leading to the conclusion that the material human intellect is a disposition residing in the human organism. The argument begins by examining the characteristics of "theoretical intelligible thoughts," a term covering, for Averroes, both *concepts* (*taṣawwur*) and *propositions* (*taṣdīq*). Averroes takes as granted that an intelligible thought has the ontological status of neither a physical object nor an accident, in the Aristotelian sense. Once those alternatives are put aside, the only remaining possibility is that an intelligible thought is a "form." Averroes proceeds: Intelligible thoughts are undeniably different from two other kinds of form, forms of physical objects and "soul-forms" (*ṣuwar nafsāniyya*), the latter being the forms constituting the nonintellectual levels of perception in the soul.[37] Nevertheless, unless one were to accept the Platonic theory of ideal Forms, a theory whose "absurdities . . . Aristotle set forth in the Metaphysics,"[38] intelligible thoughts must be acknowledged to share two crucial traits with forms of physical objects and forms in the soul at subintellectual levels of perception, both of which Averroes terms "material" forms.

First, like material forms, intelligible thoughts "follow upon change." They are the outgrowth of a series of processes, namely, "sensation," the refining of sense perceptions in the "imaginative faculty," and the "repeated" reporting of percepts to the "memorative faculty." The dependence of intelligible thoughts on process and change is unmistakable in the case of concepts openly tied to experience. We acquire a "universal," such as the concept *color* or the concept of a given animal species, only after perceiving appropriate individual objects with our external senses and refining the perceptions within the soul. That is the reason why the "blind man" never acquires the concept "color" and inhabitants of the northern

[37]Averroes lists the following differences, ibid. 75–78; Spanish translation 198–201: (a) Intelligible thoughts seem to enjoy no existence apart from their intelligible existence; that is to say, they do not exist as objects in the external world. (b) An intelligible thought has an infinite denotation. (c) In the act of intelligible thought, the perceiving subject is identical with the perceived object. (d) No *affection* occurs in intelligible thought (see, however, above, p. 259). (e) The perceiving subject, the intellect, becomes stronger with age. Averroes' expression *soul-forms* probably derives from the term *spiritual forms*, which Ibn Bājja uses for all levels of abstraction within the soul below the level of intellect. See the reference to Ibn Bājja, above, n. 17.

[38]Ahwani 81; Spanish translation 204. Cf. Aristotle, *Metaphysics* 1.9; 7.8; 13.4–5.

regions never acquire the concept "elephant"; they lack the perceptions with which to start. But even the first principles of thought, the primary propositions "whereof we have no inkling when and how they arrive"—such as the proposition that a whole is greater than any of its parts—originate in the same way. Although an adult no longer, perhaps, recalls the "individual" events from which he derived the first principles of thought, those principles belong to the same "genus" as the other "intelligible thoughts" and therefore must likewise have their origin in sense perception. They too, must—as Aristotle, whom Averroes does not mention, had argued[39]—grow out of the processes of sensation, imagination, and memory, and they too are consequently dependent on change.[40]

The second trait intelligible thoughts share with material forms is that the concepts possessed by different men are "rendered plural by the plurality of their substrata" and are accordingly subject to "enumeration." The substrata to which they are "essentially" linked are the imaginative faculties of individual human souls, as evidenced by the circumstance that when someone's "imaginative faculty is destroyed" his "comprehension is defective," and again that the "loss of imaginative forms" entails the "forgetting" of intelligible thoughts.[41] Inasmuch as the concept of a given species possessed by one man is "linked to images of individuals distinct from the [images of] individuals" to which the thought of the same species is linked in another—inasmuch as it is linked to images in the imaginative faculty of a different soul—the intelligible thoughts possessed by the one man are plainly not identical with those of the other.[42]

Since intelligible thoughts are contingent upon change and are linked to individual human subjects, they are, after all, in a sense "necessarily possessed of matter." They consequently "come into existence and are destroyed."[43] But when something comes into existence, a "disposition" for its existence precedes its actual existence. A disposition for thought must accordingly exist in man prior to actual human thought. Dispositions do not exist in a "disembodied" state, and the human disposition for thought must therefore be present in a "subject." "That subject cannot be a body," because intellectual thoughts were seen "not to be material" in the full sense, "in the respect wherein corporeal forms are material." Nor can the subject be "an intellect." An intellect consists in actual thought, whereas the human disposition for thinking is intelligible thought only potentially; and "whatever is some thing potentially cannot contain any of the same thing actually." Being neither a body nor an intellect, the subject of the human disposition for thought must be the

[39]Aristotle, *Posterior Analytics* 2.19.

[40]Ahwani 79; Spanish translation 202.

[41]Ibid. 80–81; Spanish translation 203–4.

[42]Ibid. 81; Spanish translation 204. The argument derives from Ibn Bājja, *Fī Ittiṣāl al-ᶜAql bi'l-Insān* (n. 16 above), Arabic text 15, 17; Spanish translation 33, 37. To take an example, the concept *elephant* in one man is linked to images distinct from the images to which the concept *elephant* is linked in another man.

[43]Ibid. 80, 82; Spanish translation 203, 205.

only entity remaining, namely, "a soul." "None of the faculties of the soul can more plausibly be taken as the subject of intelligible thought than forms [images] in the imaginative faculty; for intelligible thoughts have just been shown to be linked to those forms, to exist when they are present, and not to exist when they are absent." The analysis of human thought, pursued, Averroes is confident, without prepossession, thus reveals the precise nature of the human material intellect. The "human material intellect" is "the disposition within imaginative forms for receiving intellectual thoughts."[44] The disposition for thought does differ from other dispositions in the soul in one important respect: It is not "mixed with the imaginative forms" serving as its substratum.[45]

As a concluding note, preserved only in the manuscript that on the whole gives the original text of the Epitome without the interpolations, Averroes cites Aristotle's analogy of the writing tablet, and since he is construing the material intellect as a disposition, not a substance, he formulates the analogy with Alexander's emendation.[46] He does not state that Aristotle had compared the human potentiality for thought to a writing tablet, as Aristotle had in truth done, but rather that "Aristotle compared the disposition in the imaginative faculty for receiving intelligible thoughts to the *disposition* in the writing tablet. The soul, which serves as the substratum of the disposition [for thought, is what] parallels the tablet." As for Aristotle's statement that the potential intellect is impassive and does not undergo affection, Averroes, again like Alexander, takes the impassivity and freedom from affection to be due simply to the potential intellect's being a mere disposition: "Inasmuch as the disposition [for thought] is nothing in actuality and does not exist *in* a body, it undergoes no affection [or alteration] whatsoever when [intelligible] forms are generated in it."[47]

The original text of the Epitome identifies the theory that the human intellect is not a substance but a disposition as "Alexander's . . . view,"[48] and Alexander is the source of Averroes' version of the writing tablet analogy as well as of his explanation of the sense in which the potential human intellect is impassive. Ibn Bājja, however, was the philosopher who located the human disposition for thought specifically in the imaginative faculty, and, as will appear presently, one of the annotations incorporated into the Epitome does name Ibn Bājja as the inspiration of the position taken in the original Epitome. A different work of Averroes' also reports that Ibn Bājja was the philosopher who construed the material intellect as a disposition specifically in the imaginative faculty of the soul, in contrast to Alexander, who construed the material intellect, more generally, as a disposition in

[44]Ibid. 86; Spanish translation 209.
[45]Ibid. 87; Spanish translation 210.
[46]See above, p. 260.
[47]Ahwani 88; Spanish translation 211.
[48]Ibid. 86; Spanish translation 209.

the human soul or in man.[49] Strands of argumentation in the Epitome can, moreover, be traced to Ibn Bājja.[50]

As for "Themistius and other earlier commentators"—presumably, Theophrastus—as well as "Avicenna and others" who maintained that the material intellect is "eternal,"[51] the original Epitome expressly rejects their conception. On their approach, the subject in which the human disposition for thought resides could be neither a "body" nor a "soul," because both bodies and souls are generated-destructible and not eternal.[52] The subject would have to be an "intellect." But if the subject in which the disposition for thought resides were an intellect from the outset, the subject would already "have in actuality the character it [in fact] has potentially; and that is impossible, since potentiality and actuality are contraries."[53]

In brief, the Epitome establishes through an analysis of human thought that the potential or material human intellect can be nothing other than a generated-destructible disposition residing in the imaginative faculty of the soul, or, as Averroes puts it, in the forms, or images, making up the contents of the imaginative faculty. To take the potential human intellect as an eternal substance would entail the absurdity of a thing's being potential and actual at the same time.

After the Epitome examines additional topics relating to human intellect, Averroes closes the discussion with the words: "The discourse on the rational faculty is here complete."[54] But the versions of the Epitome most consistently incorporating Averroes' later corrections thereupon add a paragraph in which Averroes confesses: "What I have written about the material intellect," construing it as a disposition in the imaginative faculty of the soul, "is what previously appeared to me correct." That was the position "Ibn Bājja was first to advocate," and Ibn Bājja "misled me." When I subsequently "pressed my investigation of Aristotle's words, I realized that the material intellect cannot be the substance containing the faculty [for thought] in *which* anything actual whatsoever, that is, any form whatsoever, is present." The antecedent of the pronoun *which* in the last sentence is unclear, and the sentence is awkward. But Averroes is plainly saying that the human disposition for thought cannot after all reside within something such as the human soul, or the imaginative faculty of the soul, which has its own actual form. The reason is Aristotle's old argument: "If such were the case," if the disposition for thought resided in a substratum that has its own form, the actual form present there would interfere with the intellect's operation, and the intellect "would not be able to receive all forms"

49Alexander, *De anima* (n. 9 above) 83, does state that intellect uses images presented to it by the imaginative faculty, but he does not expressly locate the intellect *in* the imaginative faculty.

50Ahwani (n. 19 above) 81, 83. See n. 42 above.

51Ahwani 83–84; Spanish translation 206–7. In fact, Avicenna maintained that the human soul with its material intellect is generated; above, p. 107.

52There is an exception, since the celestial sphere is an eternal body.

53Ibid. 85; similarly on 86. Spanish translation 208–9.

54Ibid. 90; Spanish translation 213.

without distortion. Contrary to what "we stated earlier in the book, . . . percepts [or: notions (*ma^cānī*)] in the imaginative faculty" are not therefore "the subject [of the human disposition for thought]." The imaginative faculty's role in thought is merely that of a repository from which images are drawn for presentation to a material intellect existing independently of it; the imaginative faculty is not analogous to an "eye" that sees—to a percipient subject—but to the "visible" object presented to the eye. Aristotle, it now turns out, not only had no thought of construing the material intellect as a disposition residing in a part of the soul but "explicitly affirmed that the material intellect is eternal."[55] The purported explicit statement is undoubtedly Aristotle's characterization of the intellect that man is born with as not "mixed" with matter and "separate."[56] Averroes here reads Aristotle's word's as affirming that the material intellect is a separate, that is, incorporeal, and hence eternal, substance.

Averroes, then, repudiates his original position because of the old Aristotelian consideration that the human intellect cannot at the outset contain any actual quality or any form of its own and also because of Aristotle's purportedly explicit characterization of the material intellect as eternal. Although Averroes no longer accepts the position originally stated in the Epitome, he explains that he refrained from rewriting the book for two reasons: "One is that scholars have already made copies of it; the second is that the Epitome [as originally written] is a good account of doubts that can be directed against Aristotle's treatment" of the material intellect and therefore retains heuristic value. "Anyone wishing to ascertain" Averroes' "true opinion on the question" is invited to consult his "[Long] Commentary [*sharḥ*] on Aristotle's *De anima*," where he "expounds [the subject] in full."[57]

Whereas the original Epitome determined that the material intellect cannot possibly be an eternal substance and must be a disposition in the imaginative faculty of the soul, the interpolated note at the conclusion of the discussion of intellect thus repudiates Averroes' original position on both scores. Of the other interpolations in the Epitome, two in particular expand on Averroes' change of heart.

The first of the two is incorporated into the text immediately after the original version of the Epitome decides that the material intellect can be nothing other than a disposition residing in the imaginative faculty of the soul.[58] Averroes reverses himself there, as he does in the passage just examined, but on somewhat different grounds. He reasons that in thought, "the notion perceived by the imaginative faculty [*al-ma^cnā al-mutakhayyal*] is identical with the notion intellected [*al-ma^cnā al-ma^cqūl*]." He means that what is digested at each level in the process of abstraction is presented to the subsequent level for further refinement; hence

[55]Ibid.

[56]Above, p. 259.

[57]Ahwani 90; Spanish translation 214.

[58]The passage is missing in the Hyderabad edition and in the Chester Beatty manuscript. If Ahwani's apparatus is accurate, this is the only one of the later corrections appearing in the Cairo manuscript.

percepts refined by the imaginative faculty are what it in turn presents before the intellectual faculty to be turned into an object of thought. If the intellectual faculty were a disposition within the imaginative faculty, whenever the imaginative faculty places an image before the intellect, it would be presenting part of itself to be refined and digested by a faculty that inheres in itself. "Something would be receiving itself," which is impossible.

"Perhaps," the passage continues, the material intellect is "as Aristotle states, a substance that is all intelligible thoughts in potentiality" but nothing in actuality. "Intelligible thoughts" would accordingly "be linked to two subjects." One of the two, the subject in the strict sense, is "eternal and bears the same relation to intelligible thoughts that prime matter bears to physical forms"; it is an eternal substance, wholly potential at the start, and receptive of new thoughts much as prime matter is receptive of forms. The "second" subject is something "generated-destructible, to wit, the imaginative forms. For in a certain sense they are a subject [of human intelligible thoughts, intelligible thoughts being linked to the soul through them], although in another sense they are a mover" setting the human thought process in motion.[59] The material intellect, Averroes is suggesting, may well be an entity of a sort that the original text of the Epitome, directly prior to the interpolation, refused to contemplate, namely, an eternal substance which is nonetheless not an actual intellect. That will be the position of Averroes' Long Commentary on the *De anima*. The Long Commentary will also develop the notion that human intelligible thought has two subjects.

A few lines later, the manuscripts preserving Averroes' corrections have the second of the more significant interpolations into the body of the Epitome. "Indeed," the interpolated passage states, "it would be better" to regard "images [in the imaginative faculty] as motive, rather than as receptive." It would, in other words, be better to regard them as the factor moving the intellect to think rather than as the recipient of intelligible thought or as the substratum of the human disposition for thought. Because the "commentators" judged the construction of the material intellect as a disposition residing in the soul or in the imaginative faculty to be "problematic, . . . they construed the material intellect as an eternal substance of an intellectual nature . . . whose existence . . . is potential, . . . [and] whose relation to intelligible thoughts is like that of physical matter to forms." Their solution, however, is also problematic—although not for the reason the Epitome originally gave, not because the material intellect is pure potentiality, whereas an eternal substance would perforce be an actual intellect, and therefore an eternal material intellect is a self-contradictory notion. The commentators' position that the human material intellect is an eternal substance is problematic because it would have man, a destructible being, "perfected" through the presence in him of an eternal substance, an entity completely different from himself. The issues, Averroes goes on, are so subtle that "adjudication between the two positions demands a broader

[59] Ahwani 86–87; Spanish translation 209–10.

discussion than . . . the present epitome will allow. Let us return to the place where we were."[60]

In sum, when composing the Epitome of the *De anima*, Averroes analyzed human intelligible thoughts, found them to be generated-destructible, inferred that they must come into existence in a *disposition*, and identified the subject in which the disposition resides as the imaginative faculty of the soul. Symptomatic of the line he took is the way in which he put the analogy of the writing tablet. He formulated the analogy with Alexander's emendation, explaining that Aristotle had not compared the human material intellect to the writing tablet itself, the human intellect not being a substance, but rather to the tablet's disposition for receiving writing. The Epitome as originally written flatly excluded the possibility of the material intellect's being an eternal substance; if it were an eternal substance, it would, in the view of the original Epitome, perforce be an actual intellect, consisting in actual thought, whereas the human material or potential intellect is a potentiality for thought, not actual thought.

That was what the Epitome of the *De anima* originally said. At one or more[61] subsequent dates, Averroes returned to the Epitome. In a note attached to the end of the discussion of intellect, he blamed Ibn Bājja for having misled him. There and in notes attached to the body of the text, he offered two grounds for not construing the material intellect as a disposition in the imaginative faculty: Forms already present in the imaginative faculty would prevent the material intellect from thinking intelligible thoughts without distortion. And were it true that the imaginative faculty presents images to an intellectual faculty inhering in itself, something would "receive" itself, which is impossible. Averroes now construed the material intellect—and understood Aristotle to have done the same—as an unusual sort of eternal substance, a substance of a sort that the original Epitome dismissed out of hand. He construed it as an incorporeal substance in a state of total potentiality, independent of the human organism, and receptive of intelligible thoughts in the manner that prime matter is receptive of physical forms. The notes that Averroes attached to the original text of the Epitome or wrote in the margins of his copy were incorporated by scribes into some manuscripts of the Epitome but not into others.

Averroes' *Epistle on the Possibility of Conjunction* with the active intellect takes the same line as the original Epitome of the *De anima*. Averroes asserts there that the "material intellect has been proved in [Aristotle's] *De anima* . . . to be a mere disposition, not perfected by any form whatsoever," rather than a substance. The supposed proof rests on the Aristotelian consideration that the prior presence of a form would prevent the material intellect from performing its function of mirroring

[60]Ibid. 87; Spanish translation 210–11.

[61]The passage just cited in n. 60 is more cautious than both the Long Commentary and the interpolation at the end of the Epitome, and it might conceivably represent a tentative stage.

the external world without distortion—the very consideration adduced by one of the additions to the Epitome for the purpose of proving the contrary thesis that the material intellect is an eternal substance in a state of pure potentiality.[62] What Aristotle had contended was simply that the material intellect can contain no form. His contention might help to define the material intellect as a mere disposition only with the added premise that intellectual substances in a state of pure formless potentiality do not exist; the *Epistle on the Possibility of Conjunction* must therefore be presupposing the added premise. At all events, Aristotle's supposed proof, as reported by the *Epistle*, runs: If the material intellect already had a form of its own, the presence of the "form would either prevent the material intellect from receiving the forms of [all] objects or else would alter [and distort] the forms" of objects which the intellect "receives."[63] Since the material intellect cannot have a form of its own, it must be a blank disposition.

The *Epistle on the Possibility of Conjunction* goes on to ascertain the location of the material intellect within man from the circumstance that "intellect *in habitu*," the level at which man can think at will, is "perfected through imaginative notions [*ᶜinyanim medummim=maᶜānī mutakhayyala*]." That is to say, the human intellect acquires its store of intelligible thoughts through contemplating images presented by the imaginative faculty. Inasmuch as "imaginative forms [images] are the substratum of intelligible thoughts, the potentiality for receiving intelligible thoughts or so-called material intellect must be connected" with those forms, or images.[64] The material intellect must be a disposition "connected . . . to the imaginative soul."[65] Such being the nature of the material intellect, Averroes cites the analogy of the writing tablet with Alexander's emendation. The human disposition for thought, he writes, is "joined to imaginative forms as the disposition in the writing tablet is connected with the tablet."[66]

Writers in the Aristotelian tradition knew that the human intellect cannot be "mixed" with the human organism, for the oft-repeated reason that were it mixed, the mixture would prevent it from perceiving intelligible thoughts without distortion.[67] Averroes' *Epistle on the Possibility of Conjunction* coins a pair of terms to express the relationship precisely. The *Epistle* styles the link between the intellectual faculty and the imaginative faculty a "connection of existence" (*heqsher meṣi'ut*), as distinct from a "connection of admixture" (*heqsher ᶜerub*).[68] Although "joined" to the imaginative faculty solely in a "connection of existence" and

[62]Above, pp. 269–70.

[63]*Epistle on the Possibility of Conjunction* (n. 28 above), Hebrew text 4; English translation 23.

[64]Ibid., Hebrew text 12–13. The English translation incorrectly renders *intellect in habitu* as "acquired intellect."

[65]Ibid., Hebrew text 102.

[66]Ibid., Hebrew text 108.

[67]Above, p. 259.

[68]*Epistle on the Possibility of Conjunction*, Hebrew text 13; English translation. 28.

not "of admixture," the human potentiality for thought remains dependent on the imaginative faculty of the soul not just in one but in "two" respects: Imaginative forms "are as it were the substratum" of the faculty of thought, because the material intellect is present in man through them. They are, moreover, the motive factor setting the thought process in motion; for the faculty of thought must, in order to perform its operation, "contemplate" and "look at" images presented by the imagination, the intellect being activated by images in the imaginative faculty "as sensation" is activated by "sensata." Averroes concludes that since "speculative intelligible thoughts"—actual human intelligible thoughts—are dependent upon imaginative forms, and the latter are "generated-destructible, speculative intelligible thoughts are likewise generated-destructible." He doubtless means as well that the disposition for thought, or material intellect, which is equally dependent on the imaginative faculty, is also generated-destructible.[69]

The *Epistle on the Possibility of Conjunction*, in fine, construes the material intellect as a generated-destructible, blank disposition linked to the imaginative faculty of the human soul. The *Epistle* accordingly belongs to the same stage of Averroes' thought as the original Epitome of the *De anima.*

A Minor Composition on Conjunction and the Middle Commentary on the *De anima*

Neither the Epitome of the *De anima* in its original form nor the *Epistle on the Possibility of Conjunction* identifies Ibn Bājja as the proponent of the position it endorses. As already seen, an annotation added to the Epitome does name Ibn Bājja as the philosopher who inspired Averroes when he originally wrote that work, and elsewhere Averroes names Ibn Bājja as the philosopher who construed the material intellect as a disposition located specifically in the imaginative faculty, in contradistinction to Alexander, who construed it, more generally, as a disposition residing in the human subject or the human soul. One of the minor treatises of Averroes' which discusses the subject of conjunction with the active intellect—a treatise that became part of the Latin composition known as *Tractatus de animae beatitudine*—construes the material intellect as a disposition in the human soul without specifying that the disposition is located in the imaginative faculty. And there Averroes names Alexander as the philosopher whom he is following.

The treatise in question sets forth the constructions placed by Themistius and Alexander on the material intellect and sums up Alexander's view with the sentence: "The nature of this part of the soul is nothing but the disposition [for thought] present in the soul."[70] Alexander arrived at his conception because Aristotle had "compared" the material intellect "to the disposition in a writing tablet, which is

[69]Ibid.

[70]*Drei Abhandlungen* (n. 29 above), Hebrew text 5; German translation 17–18.

receptive of writing" (the antecedent of the pronoun *which* is unclear).[71] Taking the human soul to be the analogue of the writing tablet, Alexander naturally enough construed the faculty of thought as a disposition in the soul. Once he did so, he further "determined . . . that this human disposition is, like other dispositions, generated together with the generation of the soul"[72] and hence mortal, undergoing destruction when the soul does.

Such, according to the treatise we are considering, was Alexander's reading of Aristotle. Aristotle himself, Averroes here observes, "made no explicit statement" on the issue. The observation is accurate, although it conflicts with Averroes' own report, in one place, that Aristotle had proved the material intellect to be a mere disposition,[73] and his contrary report, in another place, that Aristotle had "explicitly" characterized it as an eternal substance.[74] Aristotle, the present treatise acknowledges, did describe the material intellect as "separate [from the body]," and the description could be taken to mean that the material intellect "is absolutely separate [from matter]," or incorporeal. But the description of the material intellect as separate can also easily be harmonized with Alexander's position, since Aristotle may merely have meant that the material intellect is "not a power existing within [and distributed through] the body and [thereby] divisible by virtue of the body's being divided."[75]

Nothing explicit, then, is forthcoming from Aristotle. Yet "it does appear from Aristotle's principles," Averroes here writes, that Alexander's position is correct and "the material intellect is a mere disposition." For if the material intellect were a "substance receptive of the forms of existent objects, intelligible thoughts would"—and the reasoning is unclear[76]—turn out to be "self-subsistent existent beings," whereupon all the objections Aristotle drew up against Plato's theory of self-subsistent intelligible Forms would ensue.[77]

Whereas the original Epitome of the *De anima* and the *Epistle on the Possibility of Conjunction* took the material intellect to be a disposition located in the imaginative faculty, the present treatise on conjunction joins Alexander in defining it as a disposition in the human soul, without specifying the imaginative faculty as the disposition's locus.

[71]For the writing tablet analogy, see above, pp. 260, 268.

[72]*Drei Abhandlungen*, Hebrew text 5; German translation 18–19.

[73]Above, p. 273.

[74]Above, p. 270.

[75]*Drei Abhandlungen*, Hebrew text 6, following the reading of ms. A; German translation 24–25.

[76]Possibly, the unstated argument is the same as that given in the Long Commentary, below, p. 287.

[77]*Drei Abhandlungen*, Hebrew text 5–6; German translation 20–21. Averroes' second minor treatise on conjunction—the second of the three *Abhandlungen*—takes no clear stand on the material intellect.

Averroes' Middle Commentary on the *De anima* is another problematic text. Averroes there discusses the human intellect at length, and in the center of the discussion stand two pages that carefully analyze the positions of Alexander and Themistius and reach an unusual conclusion. The two-page section decides that the material intellect is a hybrid entity, a mere disposition within the human organism in one respect, yet an eternal substance in another. We can visualize Averroes throwing up his hands in frustration and, unable to withstand the arguments on either side, accepting both as at least partly right. Medieval Jewish philosophers generally saw nothing in the Middle Commentary on the *De anima* beyond the hybrid or, as one of them puts it, "intermediate"[78] position, and they took the hybrid position to represent Averroes' considered opinion on the material intellect.

Unlike the Epitome on the *De anima*, the Middle Commentary has not, as far as I could discover, been preserved in variant versions that might reveal evidence of interpolation. Nor do the manuscripts contain an admission, like that in some manuscripts of the Epitome, of a change of heart by Averroes. Nevertheless, when the Middle Commentary is read without the two-page excursus, it assumes a very different visage. The disparity between the text when read without the excursus and the conception that the excursus articulates testifies, I believe, to interpolation here as well.

When we consider the text without the excursus, we find Averroes putting forward the standard argument for the material intellect's being "completely unmixed with any material form," that is, "unmixed with the subject in which it exists": If the material intellect "were mixed with any form, . . . the form of the subject with which it is mixed would either block the forms that the faculty receives, or else . . . would alter the forms being received; and in that case the forms of things would not be present in the intellect accurately. Seeing that intellect by its nature receives the forms of things without distortion, it must itself be a faculty unmixed with any form whatsoever."[79] Averroes hereupon draws the inference that we have seen him draw from the same argument in another work.[80] "Such being the character of the intellect under consideration, it has no nature other than that of a mere disposition [*isti*ᶜ*dād faqaṭ*]." The human disposition for thought resides, of course, within the human organism or human soul and hence is "in a subject." Still, "since the disposition for thought is not mixed with" the subject to which it is linked, "that subject is not potential intellect." Material or potential intellect is not "some thing in which the disposition [for thought] inheres," not a subject or substratum bearing the disposition but solely the disposition unmixed with anything else.[81]

[78]Levi Gersonides, Commentary on Averroes' Epitome of the *De anima*, Oxford, Bodleian Library, Hebrew MS Opp. add. 4° 38, 245b.

[79]Averroes, Middle Commentary on the *De anima* (n. 21 above), Arabic text, 143b–144a; Hebrew translation, 218b–219a.

[80]Above, p. 273.

[81]Middle Commentary on the *De anima*, Arabic text 144a; Hebrew translation 219a.

Having concluded that the material intellect is a mere disposition, the manuscripts of the Middle Commentary which I examined contain the aforementioned excursus, which determines that the material intellect is a hybrid entity and not a mere disposition after all. Then the manuscripts return to Averroes' line-by-line paraphrase of Aristotle's *De anima*, with the words: "Inasmuch as its nature is what has been stated, namely . . . a mere disposition. . . ."[82] The text following the excursus thus betrays no knowledge of the unusual conclusion that immediately precedes in the manuscripts. A later passage in the Middle Commentary also knows nothing of the excursus. As Averroes' paraphrase proceeds, it arrives at the point where Aristotle posed and solved a certain difficulty. The difficulty, in Averroes' restatement, is that human thought will apparently be impossible should two propositions maintained by Aristotle be accepted. Aristotle had, on the one hand, affirmed that receiving new thoughts is a kind of "affection,"[83] and—as Averroes explicates Aristotle's intent—everything experiencing affection exists within, and is part of, a material substratum. Yet Aristotle had, on the other hand, determined that the material intellect is "simple," or incorporeal, and "not subject to affection."[84] How might a human intellectual faculty that is incorporeal and immune from affection think, if thought is a kind of affection, and every affection occurs within a material substratum? Aristotle's own solution to the apparent contradiction is opaque,[85] and Averroes reformulates it.

He explains: When intellectual thought is described as a kind of affection, the term "affection" is not used in a strict sense but in the "broader sense" of "reception."[86] The description simply means that the intellectual process consists in the "reception" of intelligible thoughts. Since the human disposition for thought is not mixed with a material substratum, since the recipient of intelligible thought is a "mere disposition" and not any underlying "thing whatsoever" besides the disposition, no material substratum is, in truth, involved in thought, and no "alteration at all" occurs. The human disposition for thought "is, as Aristotle said, analogous to the *disposition* in the writing tablet for receiving writing." Even there, no alteration of the disposition takes place. And "just as the disposition in the surface of the tablet is not mixed with the tablet," and the "tablet's receiving writing" hence involves no "affection" in the disposition, so too the human

[82]Ibid., Arabic text 145a; Hebrew translation 220a. I have given the reading of the Hebrew translation. The Arabic manuscript I used has: "Inasmuch as the nature of the intellect is what has been stated, namely . . . a mere disposition." The pronoun "its" in the Hebrew is a *lectio difficilior* since there is no antecedent in the immediately preceding excursus. There is, however, an antecedent in the immediately preceding text when the excursus is ignored. I conjecture that some time after the excursus was added to the text, an Arabic scribe changed "its nature" to "the nature of the intellect" in order to remove the awkwardness.

[83]Aristotle, *De anima* 3.4.429b, 25.

[84]Ibid. 22.

[85]See, e.g., Rodier's commentary.

[86]Aristotle, *De anima* 2.5.417b, 2–16, does in fact distinguish two senses of *affection*.

disposition for thought is unmixed with the human organism and undergoes no affection or alteration in the process of thought.[87]

All the passages quoted thus far from the Middle *De anima* unqualifiedly construe the human material intellect as a mere disposition residing in the human organism or human soul. Averroes has again given the metaphor of the writing tablet with Alexander's emendation, comparing the material intellect to the disposition in the tablet for receiving writing rather than to the tablet itself. And he has employed the analogy of the disposition in the writing tablet to explain why the material intellect does not undergo affection, maintaining—strangely perhaps, but exactly as Alexander had done and as he too had done in another work—that the disposition in the writing tablet is unmixed with the tablet and consequently also does not suffer affection.

When the excursus in the center of the discussion of intellect is ignored, Averroes' Middle Commentary on the *De anima* thus consistently construes the material intellect as a "mere disposition" in man.[88] The Middle Commentary does recognize that the human intellect operates on forms presented by the imagination[89]; it does not, however, connect the disposition for thought specifically to the imaginative faculty. The Middle Commentary on the *De anima* thereby aligns itself, in the passages quoted so far, with the minor treatise on the subject of conjunction discussed just previously and not quite with Averroes' Epitome in its original form and his *Epistle on the Possibility of Conjunction*. Although those two compositions construed the material intellect as a disposition, they located the disposition, with Ibn Bājja, specifically in the imaginative faculty of the soul.

As for the excursus, it appears immediately after the Middle Commentary on the *De anima* first concludes that the material intellect is a mere disposition. The excursus reads: "Such is Aristotle's conception of the passive intellect[90] on Alexander's exegesis. The remaining commentators, by contrast [that is, Themistius and his party], understood Aristotle's statement to the effect that the material intellect must

87 Middle Commentary on the *De anima* (n. 21 above), Arabic text 145b–146a; Hebrew translation 220b–221a.

88 Ibid., Arabic text 148a; Hebrew translation 222b, which appears after the excursus, may however be a reference to the hybrid position.

89 Ibid., Arabic text 146b; Hebrew translation 221b.

90 The term *passive intellect* comes from Aristotle, *De anima* 3.5.430a, 24–25. See Alfarabi, above, pp. 49, 61. Below, p. 294, Averroes again uses the term *passive intellect* as equivalent to *potential intellect*. But his Long Commentary on the *De anima*, which advocates a different conception of the potential intellect from that given here, distinguishes potential intellect from passive intellect. By passive intellect, Averroes writes there, Aristotle meant "imaginative forms insofar as the cogitative faculty operates on them." See Long Commentary (n. 24 above) 449; and cf. ibid. 89, and n. 140 below. A similar construction of the term *passive intellect*, as distinct from *potential intellect*, is found in Themistius, with whom Averroes more or less aligns himself in the Long Commentary. See Themistius, Paraphrase of *De anima* (n. 11 above) 101, 105, 107; Arabic translation 183, 191, 195; and Averroes, Long Commentary on the *De anima* 446.

be unmixed [with matter]" differently. On their reading, the statement, far from indicating that the material intellect is a mere disposition, excludes its being so. A disposition has to exist somewhere and Alexander's mere disposition in the soul could—since the soul is, in its turn, the form of the body—be nothing other than "an attendant characteristic [*lāḥiq*] of matter" and hence "part of a material object." If Aristotle established that the material intellect is not—despite its being called *material*—mixed with matter, whereas Alexander's mere disposition could inhere in nothing other than matter, the material intellect cannot be a mere disposition. "And in general, . . . what is disposed to receive an intelligible thought must be intellect" and belong to the incorporeal and not the physical domain. The commentators who rejected Alexander's position accordingly took the material human intellect to be a "disposition existing within an incorporeal substance" distinct from man, rather than a disposition residing in the human organism.[91]

Their view, however, "also has odious" implications, implications in the spirit of objections Averroes has been seen to raise elsewhere against Themistius. First, construing the material intellect as a disposition within an incorporeal substance supposes "an incorporeal substance" existing not in a state of pure actuality but "in [a state of] disposition and potentiality"; yet every student of Aristotle's philosophy knows that "potentiality is a property [*lāzim*] of material objects," and incorporeal substances in a state of potentiality do not exist.[92] Secondly, to construe the potential intellect as Alexander's opponents do entails an anomaly. For if the material intellect is, or inheres in, an incorporeal and hence eternal substance, "the first entelechy of the intellect," the undeveloped intellect with which man is born, would be "eternal." The "final" entelechy, the realization of the first entelechy, would be "generated-destructible," since the intelligible thoughts man acquires as he perfects his intellect come into existence and later disappear at death. An eternal being would attain its realization as something destructible, and that is an anomalous, if not self-contradictory, proposition.[93]

"After assigning the due share of doubts to each position," Averroes arrives at a "combination" (Arabic: *jam*ᶜ; Hebrew: *qibbuṣ*). His solution he proposes recalls Theophrastus' remarks on the material intellect, as reported by Themistius.[94] Even more distinctly, it echoes a section in Alexander's *De intellectu*, where a theory is recorded in the name of "Aristotle" and is also attributed to "the men of the Stoa"[95]; the Arabic translation of the *De intellectu* renders the latter phrase enigmatically

[91]Middle Commentary on the *De anima*, Arabic text 144a; Hebrew translation 219a.

[92]Cf. above, p. 269.

[93]Middle Commentary on the *De anima*, Arabic text 144a–b; Hebrew translation 219a.

[94]Above, p. 261.

[95]Alexander (?), *De intellectu*, in *Scripta minora* 2.1, 110. Arabic translation: *Texte arabe du* περι νου *d'Alexandre d'Aphrodise*, ed. J. Finnegan (Beirut 1956), with pagination of the Greek given; and *Commentaires sur Aristote perdus en grec*, ed. A. Badawi (Beirut 1968) 36 (for an adequate text, both editions have to be used). Regarding the name of Aristotle, see below, n. 105.

and calls the theory in question the view "of some members of the shaded area [*al-miẓalla*]," ***shaded area*** not being the standard Arabic term for the *Stoa*. The theory recorded there took the human intellect to be "compounded" of two parts: first, a "potentiality," which grows out of the "mixture" of elements constituting a human organism and which serves as an "instrument" for the "divine intellect"; and secondly, the ubiquitous divine intellect, which is "present in all bodies" and employs any properly blended portion of matter as its instrument.[96] Despite the precedents, which Averroes must have known, the excursus in his Middle Commentary on the *De anima* mentions neither Theophrastus nor the *De intellectu*.

"The [material] intellect," according to the excursus, "is in one respect a disposition [within man, which is] free of all material forms . . . and in another respect an incorporeal substance clad in the disposition." As Averroes expands upon the initial statement, which is hardly crystal clear, he employs two slightly different formulations. One formulation refers to no disposition already existent in the human recipient and states that the "human disposition [for thought]" is engendered "in the incorporeal intellect by virtue of its conjoining with man." The alternative, and undoubtedly more precise, formulation does speak of a disposition for thought already present within the human soul which awaits the entrance of the incorporeal intellect from without: "The material intellect is something compounded of the disposition found in man, and an [incorporeal] intellect conjoined with the disposition."[97]

Averroes has no difficulty identifying the incorporeal intellect that joins man and brings him the faculty for thought. It is the being immediately above man in the hierarchy of existence, the very entity that also brings about the actualization of the human intellect, in other words, the "active intellect." That is to say, the active intellect has a transcendent and an immanent guise, the latter being the active intellect when joined to a disposition for thought rooted in the newly born human soul. Insofar as the active intellect "is conjoined" with the innate human "disposition, it perforce becomes potential intellect, which cannot have itself as a direct object of thought, but can think what is other than itself, namely, material objects. Insofar as it is not conjoined with the human disposition, it perforce remains actual intellect, having itself, and nothing in the physical world, as an object of thought." Intellectual development takes place as the active intellect in its transcendent guise brings a given human potentiality for thought, which is the same active intellect in its immanent guise, to actuality.[98]

The new conception, which combines the positions of Themistius and Alexander, recommends itself to Averroes because it sidesteps the difficulties that each of those positions involved when standing by itself. "We escape [Themistius'

[96]*De intellectu* 112; Arabic translation: Finnegan 195, Badawi 40.

[97]Middle Commentary on the *De anima*, Arabic text 144b; Hebrew translation 219b.

[98]Ibid.

error of] positing an incorporeal being that contains a disposition in its substance" and hence does not exist in a state of pure actuality. For the human capacity for thought, as now conceived, inheres in the incorporeal substance not by virtue of the latter's "nature" but by virtue of the incorporeal substance's "conjoining with a[nother] substance that does contain the disposition essentially, namely, man." "We also escape [the error of] the potential intellect's being a mere disposition," with the attendant inevitability of locating the human intellect in a physical substratum; for we "assume . . . an [incorporeal] being in which the disposition is, in an accidental fashion, engendered."[99] The untoward implications of locating the human disposition for thought in an incorporeal being are thus removed by locating the disposition, *essentially*, within the human organism, and the untoward implications of locating the human disposition for thought in the human organism are removed by locating the disposition for thought, in an *accidental* fashion, in the incorporeal active intellect. As will appear in the next section, Averroes' Long Commentary on the *De anima* solves the problems surrounding the material intellect in a different but analogous fashion. The Long Commentary recognizes two *subjects* of human thoughts, one incorporeal and one located within the human organism, and it distributes incompatible characteristics of the human material intellect between the two subjects.

One more position on the material intellect has here been added to the spectrum of positions espoused by Averroes at different times. The original text of Averroes' Epitome of the *De anima* and his *Epistle on the Possibility of Conjunction* subscribed to Alexander's theory with Ibn Bājja's nuance. They construed the human material intellect as the disposition for thought inhering in the human imaginative faculty; and Themistius' theory that the human disposition for thought is an eternal incorporeal substance, or that it exists within an eternal substance, was ruled out, on the grounds that such a substance would already be actual intellect and could not possibly possess a potentiality for thought. A brief tract of Averroes' on the subject of conjunction with the active intellect subscribed to Alexander's theory without Ibn Bājja's nuance; it construed the material intellect as a "mere disposition" attached to the human soul without linking it specifically to the imaginative faculty. The original text of Averroes' Middle Commentary on the *De anima*, if I have read it correctly, took the same stand. Now the excursus in the center of the Middle Commentary's discussion of intellect contends that the material intellect cannot, after all, be a mere disposition, since a mere disposition could be nothing other than an attribute of matter. Nor can the human disposition for thought inhere in an incorporeal substance. For incorporeal substances do not exist in a state of disposition and potentiality, and locating the human disposition for thought in an incorporeal substance would, moreover, involve the anomaly of an eternal "first entelechy" that is crowned by a generated-destructible "final" entelechy. The excursus concludes that each person's material intellect is in some accidental

[99]Ibid., Arabic text 144b–145a; Hebrew translation 219b–220a.

fashion engendered in the incorporeal active intellect when the active intellect joins a disposition already present in the human subject.

Besides these three positions, the interpolations in the text of Averroes' Epitome of the *De anima* were seen to recommend a fourth. They construed the material intellect as an incorporeal substance, without any qualification.

Averroes' Long Commentary on the *De anima* and His Commentary on Alexander's *De intellectu*

Averroes' Long Commentary on the *De anima* refutes the positions of Alexander and Ibn Bājja, does not mention the compromise position of the Middle Commentary, and arrives at what is in effect Themistius' position.

In the contexts where Averroes embraced Alexander's view, he reported that Alexander construed the material intellect as a mere disposition existing in, yet unmixed with, the human organism, and he emphasized that construing the material intellect as a disposition in man does not conflict with Aristotle's characterization of the human intellect as "separate" from matter.[100] The excursus in Averroes' Middle Commentary on the *De anima*, which departed from Alexander's view without rejecting it completely, shifted somewhat in evaluating Alexander; for the excursus contended that the mere disposition Alexander spoke of would perforce inhere in a material substratum as an "attendant characteristic" and hence be "part of a material object." Averroes' Long Commentary on the *De anima* not only contends that Alexander's mere disposition cannot be conceived in any other fashion than as inhering in a material substratum. It goes a step further and prepares the ground for its refutation of Alexander by reporting that Alexander himself expressly construed the material intellect as a "generated faculty," which "like other faculties of the soul" is produced "*in* the body . . . by the mixture [of the body's components]."[101]

The Long Commentary on the *De anima* discovers a naturalistic and materialist conception of the material intellect in two works of Alexander. It discovers such a conception at the "beginning of [Alexander's] *De anima*,"[102] where Alexander applied the Aristotelian definition of soul as "the first entelechy of a natural body furnished with organs" to soul in general, including soul endowed with the "reasoning" faculty; Alexander concluded that soul in general is "inseparable from body."[103] And the Long Commentary discovers the same conception of the material intellect in a passage of Alexander's *De intellectu* referred to a little earlier,

100See above, pp. 273, 275.

101Long Commentary on the *De anima* (n. 24 above) 394. Differing interpretations of Alexander's theory of intellect extend into modern scholarship; see P. Thillet, "Matérialisme et théorie de l'âme et de l'intellect chez Alexandre d'Aphrodise," *Revue philosophique de la France et de l'étranger* 171 (1981) 13–14.

102Long Commentary on the *De anima* 394.

103Ibid. 396–97; Alexander, *De anima* (n. 9 above) 16–17. Cf. Aristotle, *De anima* 2.1.

the passage recording a theory in the name of both "Aristotle" and, according to the Greek, the "men of the Stoa." As Averroes here reports, the *De intellectu* affirmed: "When . . . body is mixed in a certain fashion, something . . . disposed to serve as the instrument of the intellect that permeates the mixture . . . [and that indeed permeates] all body is generated. . . . The instrument [that is generated] . . . is called potential intellect."[104] The Greek text of the *De intellectu* makes clear that the author of the work does not accept the theory, but Averroes, with only an inadequate Arabic translation at his disposal, can hardly be blamed for taking the theory to be one that Alexander ascribed to Aristotle and himself endorsed.[105] Averroes' Long Commentary on the *De anima* cites the passage to clinch its materialist and naturalistic reading of Alexander, a reading in which Alexander took the material intellect to be an epiphenomenon of the physical human organism.[106]

Averroes supposes that Alexander was led to his conception of the material intellect because he took note of Aristotle's definition of soul as the "first entelechy of a natural body furnished with organs," and assumed that the definition covers the rational soul, and also because he saw certain "problems" in construing the human intellect as an incorporeal substance.[107] On earlier occasions, the difficulties in construing the human intellect as an incorporeal substance had convinced Averroes too that the human intellect must in fact be of a different nature. The Long Commentary on the *De anima* will, however, undertake to solve the difficulties. As for the Aristotelian definition of soul, it should not, Averroes writes, prejudge the issue, since Aristotle had added the qualification that the definition does not apply to all faculties of the soul.[108] The considerations that led Alexander to view the material intellect as a generated faculty in the body are therefore, Averroes now believes, surmountable.

Other considerations, primarily of an Aristotelian character, refute Alexander. "O Alexander," Averroes apostrophizes, how could you have imagined that

[104]Cf. *De intellectu* (n. 95 above) 112; Arabic translation: Finnegan 195, Badawi 40.

[105]The preserved Greek text of the *De intellectu* is itself problematic, for it has "Aristotle" agreeing with the "men of the Stoa" on the completely un-Aristotelian thesis that a divine intellect permeates all matter. To remove the incongruity, Zeller proposed the ingenious correction to "Aristokles," which was the name of Alexander's teacher. P. Moraux disputed the correction and suggested instead that the reference is to a teacher of Alexander's who was named Aristotle. See above, p, 22, n. 88. Readers of the medieval Arabic translation had, of course, neither the information nor temperament to make either conjecture. The Arabic translation, moreover, blurs the reference to the Stoa. And to make matters worse, the Arabic garbles a sentence in which the author of the *De intellectu*, be it Alexander or someone else, asserted that basic philosophic considerations "seem to me to clash" with the theory; see *De intellectu* 113; Arabic translation: Finnegan 198, Badawi 41.

[106]Long Commentary on the *De anima* 394.

[107]Ibid. 396–97.

[108]Ibid. 397. Cf. Aristotle, *De anima* 2.1.413a, 3–7.

Aristotle took the material intellect to be "a mere disposition"?[109] By maintaining that man's "discriminating, perceptive faculty," his intellect, can arise spontaneously out of the "substance of the elements" and "without an external mover" to bring it forth, Alexander approached the ranks of the un-Aristotelian and unenlightened "who deny [the operation of] efficient causes" and explain events in the physical universe solely through "material causes."[110] His conception, moreover, runs counter to "Aristotle's words." For Aristotle characterized the material intellect as "separate [from matter], . . . not subject to affection, . . . and not mixed with the body,"[111] whereas the material intellect, as Alexander conceives it, grows out of the material side of man and would necessarily be subject to affection like other modifications of matter. Most decisively, Alexander's position is precluded by Aristotle's "demonstration" of the nature of the material intellect.[112] The demonstration Averroes has in mind is the protean argument that begins by showing the material intellect to be free of any form of its own. In one of Averroes' earlier works, the argument concluded by finding the material intellect to be a disposition and nothing else,[113] but an interpolation into the Epitome of the *De anima* carried the argument to the opposite conclusion.[114] In the Long Commentary, the argument now reaches the conclusion at which it arrived in the interpolation in the Epitome. Averroes reasons: Since the material intellect is "receptive" of "all material forms," it cannot contain "the nature of those material forms in itself." Consequently, it cannot be a "body," a "form in a body," or "at all mixed with matter."[115]

Averroes continues: Alexander attempted to harmonize his view of the material intellect with Aristotle's determination that the material intellect is "neither subject to affection, nor an individual object, nor a body or faculty in a body." He did so by drawing a distinction between the "disposition" for thought and the "substratum of the disposition."[116] Whereas the substratum, the human organism, is indeed corporeal and subject to affection, Alexander—and Averroes as well in earlier works, although he is silent here about that chapter of his philosophic development—explained that the disposition for thought, taken by itself and distinct from the substratum, is neither of those things. To reinforce the distinction between the human disposition for thought and its substratum, Alexander—and Averroes in his early works as well[117]—emended Aristotle's analogy of the writing tablet. The human "material intellect," with Alexander's emendation, "resembles

[109]Long Commentary on the *De anima* 443.
[110]Ibid. 398.
[111]Ibid. 395. Cf. Aristotle, *De anima* 3.4.429a, 15–25, and above, p. 259.
[112]Ibid.
[113]Above, p. 273.
[114]Above, pp. 269–70.
[115]Long Commentary on the *De anima* 385–86, 396.
[116]Ibid. 395.
[117]Above, pp. 268, 273, 274–75, 277.

the disposition in a tablet not yet written upon, rather than the tablet disposed [for writing]."[118] Alexander contended that only the tablet, as distinct from the disposition for receiving writing, is subject to affection; similarly, the substratum underlying the disposition for thought is subject to affection, but the disposition itself is not.

Averroes' Long Commentary on the *De anima* dismisses the distinction between disposition and substratum, and the emendation of the writing tablet analogy, as quibbles: "What Alexander says is nothing."[119] If Aristotle had meant that the disposition for thought is not material and not subject to affection merely inasmuch as dispositions in material substrata are not strictly material, then he could have made the same point about "any disposition whatsoever." Any disposition in the physical world and any disposition in the soul might be described "as neither a body, nor an individual form existing in a body," on the grounds that, strictly speaking, only its substratum and not it, in itself, is corporeal. Since Aristotle made his point exclusively in regard to the disposition for thought, he surely had something more significant in mind. He was surely speaking about "the subject of the disposition," and not the "disposition itself" taken in isolation. He meant that the subject, the substance containing the disposition for thought, is neither a body nor mixed with matter. And indeed, the demonstration whereby Aristotle showed the disposition for thought to be unmixed with matter reveals as much. Aristotle reasoned that "whatever receives something cannot actually contain anything of the nature of the thing received," and that "proposition . . . manifestly" has in view the substratum itself, not the disposition inhering in it. If the recipient of thought must be free of material forms, it is the substratum of the faculty for thought, not the disposition inhering in the substratum, which must be free of forms and unmixed with matter. Alexander's version of the writing tablet analogy is therefore equally "false." Aristotle's intent was to compare the material intellect to a "tablet insofar as it is disposed" for receiving writing, not to the "disposition in the tablet."[120]

In brief, Alexander, according to Averroes' Long Commentary on the *De anima*, construed the material intellect as an epiphenomenon of the human body. Averroes had once accepted a construction of that kind, although with the materialism softened. The Long Commentary rejects the construction of the material intellect as a disposition in the human organism because, Averroes finds, it clashes both with Aristotle's statements concerning the material intellect and Aristotle's demonstration of the material intellect's unmixed character. As a corollary of his refutation of Alexander's position on the material intellect, Averroes in the Long Commentary also rejects Alexander's distinction between the disposition for thought and the subject of the disposition for thought, and Alexander's emendation of the writing tablet analogy.

[118]Long Commentary on the *De anima* 395.

[119]Ibid.

[120]Long Commentary on the *De anima* 430–31.

Regarding Ibn Bājja, the Long Commentary on the *De anima* reports: "He seems, from the plain sense of his words, to believe that the material intellect is [nothing other than] the imaginative faculty insofar as it is disposed" for the "notions it contains to become actual intelligible thoughts; . . . no other faculty . . . is the substratum of intellectual thoughts" in man.[121] By locating the disposition for thought in a faculty of the soul, Averroes understands, Ibn Bājja wished to "escape the absurdities attaching themselves to Alexander." Alexander, in the words of the present passage of the Long Commentary, construed the "substratum receiving intelligible forms" as either a "body fashioned from the elements or a faculty in the body"[122]; that is to say, he construed the material intellect as a part of the human body or as a faculty inhering in it. And Averroes conjectures that in locating the material intellect in a faculty of the soul rather than in the body, Ibn Bājja was consciously fleeing Alexander's extreme materialism. Despite the small improvement, Ibn Bājja fares no better at the hands of the Long Commentary than Alexander did. His position is dismissed as "plainly absurd," for three reasons.

It is ruled out by the double-edged argument that Averroes deployed, at different times, on both sides of the question, and that the Long Commentary has been seen to adduce against Alexander. As the Long Commentary puts the argument one more time, "the material intellect cannot have any actual form, because its . . . nature is to receive [all] forms." Since the imaginative faculty is a form in the soul, if the material intellect existed in, or was identical with, the imaginative faculty, the material intellect would possess a material form before it began to think and it could not perform its function without distortion. A second reason given by the Long Commentary for rejecting Ibn Bājja's position was met in one of the interpolations in Averroes' Epitome of the *De anima*. The Long Commentary contends, as the interpolation in the Epitome did, that inasmuch as the intellectual faculty operates on images presented by the imaginative faculty, if the intellectual faculty were nothing other than a guise of the imaginative faculty, a faculty would be operating on images presented to it by itself. "A thing would receive itself and the mover would be the same as what is moved," which is impossible.[123] The third reason for rejecting Ibn Bājja's position is that images presented by the imaginative faculty were shown by Aristotle to stand to the rational faculty as "an object of sensation [stands] to the subject of sensation."[124] On Ibn Bājja's construction, the imaginative faculty and the images it contains would correspond not to the object but to the subject of sensation. Ibn Bājja's identification of the material intellect with the imaginative faculty is consequently untenable.[125]

[121] Cf. above, p. 261.
[122] Long Commentary on the *De anima* 397.
[123] Cf. above, pp. 270–71.
[124] Cf. Aristotle, *De anima* 3.7.431a, 14–15.
[125] Long Commentary on the *De anima* 398.

Seeing that the positions of Alexander and Ibn Bājja entail such absurdities, how could Averroes have subscribed to them in earlier works? He confesses that he was "for a long time" misled, and that Ibn Bājja had likewise been misled, by the manner in which philosophy was pursued in their time. "Modern" philosophers "disregard Aristotle's works . . . and especially [his book] on the soul, believing the book to be unintelligible," and they "study the works of the commentators" instead.[126] Because he had at first imitated the philosophers of his day, abandoning the fount of science and studying not Aristotle's *De anima* but secondhand works on the human soul and intellect, Averroes had been seduced into accepting either Alexander's construction of the material intellect as a mere disposition in man or Ibn Bājja's construction of it as a disposition specifically in the human imaginative faculty. Only after decades of reflection did Averroes realize the untenability of both positions.

Themistius is left. "Theophrastus, Themistius, and many commentators," Averroes writes, accepted at face value Aristotle's argument showing the material intellect to be separate from matter and unmixed with the body. They construed the material intellect as a "substance" that is "neither generated nor destructible," in other words, as an eternal, incorporeal substance. Yet their position also occasions "no few questions."[127]

There is, to begin, the following objection: The factor leading the human intellect from potentiality to actuality, namely, the active intellect, is an eternal being. If the material intellect too is eternal, the product of the active intellect's operation on the material intellect must likewise be so. "For when the agent is eternal, and what is acted on is eternal, the product must be eternal." Now the material intellect—as revealed by philosophic analysis and established by Aristotle—contemplates images that the imaginative faculty presents, and through the action of the active intellect it raises them to the level of intelligible thoughts. Those images, for their part, are previously generated in the imaginative faculty through a process of abstraction starting with sense perception. Should the eternal active intellect act upon the eternal material intellect through all eternity, the material intellect must transform the images it contemplates into intelligible thoughts timelessly. The images presented by the imaginative faculty and contemplated by the material intellect would, therefore, from time immemorial have been transformed into thoughts. The sense perceptions in which the images are grounded would also have to be eternal. And the physical objects in the external world which the sense perceptions mirror would have to be so as well. Themistius' position would have the wholly paradoxical upshot that the physical objects underlying sense perception are not generated-destructible, as they are seen to be, but eternal.[128]

[126]Ibid. 470.

[127]Ibid. 389, 391.

[128]Ibid. 391–92. The difficulty is raised again on p. 399, as a possible objection to what Averroes there finds to be Aristotle's position.

A further objection to Themistius—which was already met in Averroes' Middle Commentary on the *De anima* and which is not completely consistent with the foregoing—is "very difficult" to answer. If the material intellect is an incorporeal being and does not exist in matter, and if matter is the principle whereby things of the same character are distinguished from each other, there can be only one material intellect for the entire human species. The material intellect is, by definition, the "first perfection [or: entelechy] of man," and the "theoretical intellect," the human intellect after it has acquired a complement of intelligible thoughts, "is the final perfection." Each man plainly has his own personal theoretical intellect, and his theoretical intellect comes into existence and is destroyed. In "his final perfection," each man is therefore "an individual" and "generated-destructible." If man's final perfection is individual and generated-destructible, his first perfection must presumably be the same. Hence "it would seem" that man's first perfection, the material human intellect, cannot be a single, eternal incorporeal substance.[129]

Averroes poses yet another objection: If the material intellect is incorporeal, there can, as just seen, be only one for the entire human species. But human intellects must be individual, for otherwise whatever intelligible thought any given person thinks, all mankind would think, and whatever thought one person forgets, all mankind would forget; and such obviously is not the case. Since each man has his own individual intellect, the material intellect cannot, it would seem, be a single incorporeal substance.[130]

The positions of Alexander and Ibn Bājja being completely unacceptable and the position of Themistius and his party having such unhappy implications, where does the truth lie? Although Averroes had wrestled with the issue throughout his philosophic career, his Long Commentary still submits its conclusions tentatively and apologetically: "If my thesis is not the complete [truth], it will be a beginning. Therefore I bid colleagues who see what is written here to set down their doubts."[131]

Averroes takes Aristotle as his lodestar, "since everything that can be said about the nature of the material intellect appears absurd except what Aristotle said—and even what he said raises . . . questions!"[132] Returning to Aristotle, Averroes credits the argument that since the human potentiality for thought "receives all material forms," and "every recipient . . . must be free of the nature of what it receives," the substratum receiving material forms in the guise of intelligible thoughts cannot "have any material form in its own nature." From the standpoint of

[129]Ibid. 392–93. Cf. above, p. 279. This difficulty too is raised again on p. 399, as a possible objection to what Averroes finds to be Aristotle's position. Mantino's translation (n. 24 above) has *primus actus* and *ultimus actus* instead of the *prima perfectio* and *postrema perfectio* of the Scot translation.

[130]Long Commentary on the *De anima* 393. The argument derives from Ibn Bājja, *Fī Ittiṣāl al-ᶜAql bi'l-Insān* (n. 16 above), Arabic text 15; Spanish translation 33.

[131]Long Commentary on the *De anima* 399.

[132]Ibid.

the Long Commentary the argument leads to the conclusion that the aspect of man receiving intelligible thoughts can be "neither a body nor a form in a body" nor "in any respect mixed with matter."[133] Inasmuch as it is not a body, it is ungenerated and indestructible, that is to say, eternal.[134] Inasmuch as it is not mixed with matter, the principle whereby objects of the same character are individuated and subject to enumeration, the material intellect cannot—contrary to what Averroes' original Epitome of the *De anima* expressly affirmed[135]—be "enumerated through the enumeration of individual men."[136] Individual men do not, in other words, possess individual material intellects. Rather, "one" material intellect is somehow shared by all mankind.[137]

The interpretation of Aristotle accepted here by Averroes is—except for a subsidiary issue to be taken up presently—identical with Themistius' position on the nature of the human material intellect, as Averroes read Themistius. The difficulties that Averroes noted in Themistius' position therefore also affect Aristotle's position as Averroes now interprets it,[138] and they demand a solution. Averroes' solution turns on the distinction between two "subjects" of human thought.

He explains that images in the imaginative faculty constitute one subject; they are the "mover"[139] in the thought process and also the referent for intelligible thoughts, intelligible thoughts being "true," by virtue of corresponding to images in the imaginative faculty.[140] The eternal material intellect is the other subject. It is the "recipient" in the thought process, the factor permitting intelligible thoughts to enter the realm of real existence and become "existent things."[141] The second of these factors, Averroes asserts—in stark contradiction to a point he made in the original Epitome of the *De anima*[142]—never attaches itself to man "essentially and primarily, but joins" him only through its partner, "only by . . . joining with

[133]Ibid. 385–86.

[134]Ibid. 389, 406; cf. 87.

[135]Above, p. 267.

[136]Long Commentary on the *De anima* 402.

[137]Ibid. 399.

[138]Averroes, ibid., repeats the first two of the possible objections to Themistius' position as problems also affecting Aristotle's position.

[139]But they are not to be confused with the *active intellect*, which also moves the human intellect. An image acts as a mover as color does in the visual process, whereas the active intellect does so as light does in the visual process. Cf. Aristotle, *De anima* 3.5.430a, 16–17, and below, p. 316.

[140]Long Commentary on the *De anima* 400, 406. On 449, Averroes states that the function is performed not just by one, but by three faculties, namely, "ymaginativa et cogitativa et rememorativa," and he connects the term *passive intellect* with those faculties; cf. above, pp. 95–96. In Avicenna, the cogitative faculty was central to the thought process; see above, p. 98.

[141]Long Commentary on the *De anima* 400.

[142]Above, p. 267.

forms in the imaginative faculty."[143] To solve the difficulties he posed, Averroes distributes ostensibly incompatible characteristics of the human potentiality for thought between the eternal material intellect and the noneternal human imaginative faculty.

The question how a temporal process of abstraction can take place, seeing that the transcendent cause effecting thought and the material intellect receiving it are eternal, is answered as follows: Human thought is indeed eternal in a certain respect, but it is generated-destructible in another. It is eternal "in respect to . . . the material intellect," since material intellect always possesses actual human thought. It is nonetheless generated-destructible "in respect to the subject by virtue of which" it is "true," that is, in respect to images in the imaginative faculty, as seen from the fact that whenever a man and his imaginative faculty perish, the man's consciousness of intellectual thoughts ceases.[144] The eternal active intellect's operation on the eternal material intellect therefore does in a sense give rise to an eternal product, while a genuine, noneternal process of abstraction takes place as well.

The question how a single eternal material intellect can serve the entire species, while each man's final perfection, his theoretical intellect, is individual and generated-destructible, and the further question how a single material intellect can be posited for all mankind without entailing all mankind's possessing identical thoughts, are handled in a similar fashion. In answer to the latter question, Averroes writes that what links actual thought to individual men and renders it amenable to enumeration is plainly not "the part playing the role of matter, as it were [in the thought process], that is to say, the material intellect"; the common material intellect serving the entire human species is not what makes possible the private thoughts of individual men. Actual thought does, however, link itself to individual men and become subject to enumeration through "the part . . . playing, in some fashion, the role of—as it were—form," that is to say, by virtue of "images" in the imaginative faculty.[145] Through images in the imaginative faculty, the soul becomes conscious of intelligible thoughts. Consequently, although men share a common material intellect, each still owns his personal, individual actual thoughts, and thoughts are not shared.

As for the question how man's final perfection can be individual and destructible, if man's first perfection is common to the entire human species and eternal, Averroes explains that the "generation and destruction" of human thoughts[146] occurs "in respect to the plurality affecting them"—insofar as each set of thoughts belongs to a human "individual" possessing an individual imaginative faculty.

[143]Long Commentary on the *De anima* 486.

[144]Ibid. 401. On p. 477, Averroes also explains, with an allusion to Aristotle, *De anima* 3.5.430a, 23–25, why human memory ceases at death.

[145]Ibid. 404–05.

[146]Here Averroes speaks specifically of the first propositions of thought, but on p. 408, he extends the proposition to all scientific-philosophic knowledge.

Human thoughts are nonetheless not "unqualifiedly" generated-destructible, because they are exempt from generation and destruction "from the side of their being unified"; they are exempt from generation and destruction insofar as they are present to the material intellect. Each individual man's final perfection, his theoretical intellect, is consequently individual and does perish in one sense, while in another sense, in the sense that a material intellect common to all mankind receives the totality of human thought, "we can say that the theoretical intellect is common to all [*unus in omnibus*]" and "eternal."[147]

Averroes has not yet told us what sort of entity the human material intellect is. He does so when addressing still another philosophic problem attendant upon his present interpretation of Aristotle.

The problem is a version of an objection that his earlier works raised against Themistius' construction of the human material intellect as an incorporeal substance. The human material intellect is distinguished in having, or being, a *potentiality* for thought, and Averroes' early works had asked how it can be conceivable, as Themistius would have us believe, that an incorporeal substance exists in a state of potentiality. What is at heart virtually the same question is put by the Long Commentary on the *De anima* thus: The material intellect "must be assumed to be some thing" in possession of the capacity for thought. It does not itself contain a form, for if it did, the form would interfere with, or distort, its receiving new forms, that is, new thoughts. Now, anything that is an existent being without possessing a form has "the nature of prime matter." Yet, for the material intellect to have the nature of prime matter is "unimaginable," since prime matter plainly does not have the power to think. "How, moreover, can anything of such a character be described as incorporeal [*abstractum*]?"[148]

Averroes solves this last problem by uncovering a class of existence which he had overlooked in his earlier works. Philosophers, he writes, generally recognize three classes of existence: the matter of physical objects, the form of physical objects, and incorporeal substance. But a "fourth genus" of existence "escaped many modern" philosophers, for "just as sensible existence is divided into form and matter, so too must intelligible [incorporeal] existence be divided into analogues" of form and matter. The existence of a quasi matter in the nonmaterial realm can be learned from the "incorporeal forms," or intelligences, that "move the celestial bodies." Aristotle's book on "First Philosophy," his *Metaphysics*, established that the incorporeal movers of the spheres must be "of the same number" as the spheres;[149] and a plurality of incorporeal intelligences is, Averroes reasons, tenable only if they are individuated and subject to enumeration thanks to the presence in them—or, to be precise, in all but the mover of the first, outermost sphere—of a quasi-material constituent. Whereas the celestial intelligences are compounds of

147Long Commentary on the *De anima* 407.

148Ibid. 399.

149Cf. Aristotle, *Metaphysics* 12.8.

intelligible form and this quasi matter, the eternal human material intellect consists solely in the same quasi matter.[150] Within the hierarchy of incorporeal existence, which is crowned by the First Cause and descends rung by rung through the incorporeal movers of the spheres to the entity known as the *active intellect*, the material intellect is the very lowest rung, less "noble" than, and located immediately below "the active intellect." The "material intellect . . . is the last of the incorporeal intelligences."[151]

The human material intellect is, then, an eternal substance, the lowest rung in the incorporeal hierarchy. It attaches itself to the human organism in a nonessential fashion by joining with the human imaginative faculty, and it plays the role of recipient in the intellectual process; the manner in which it functions as recipient will be examined in the following chapter.[152] Images in the imaginative faculty have, by contrast, the role of mover in the process—much as colors are the mover in the visual process.[153] And those images are what intellectual thoughts refer to, an intellectual thought being deemed "true" because it is abstracted from, and corresponds to, them. Arguments showing human thought to be eternal have in view human thought belonging to the material intellect, whereas arguments showing it to be generated-destructible and individual have in view human thought insofar as it belongs to the imaginative faculty of an individual man.

When Averroes states that the actual thoughts men think temporally are present to the material intellect eternally, he does not mean that the material intellect possesses human thoughts through itself. Thoughts pertaining to the physical realm—as distinct from thought of incorporeal entities[154]—reach the material intellect only with the help of the imaginative faculties of individual men. The eternity of thought of the material intellect signifies that since the human species is eternal, since at every moment individual men exist who possess the basic propositions of human thought, and since moreover men presumably also always exist who think philosophic thoughts, the material intellect at every moment contains a full range of actual human thoughts. The eternity of the material intellect's thought of the physical world is, accordingly, not a single continuous fiber, nor does it spring from the material intellect. It is wholly dependent on the ratiocination and consciousness of individual men, the complete body of possible thoughts of the physical world being supplied at any given moment by individuals living at that moment, and the continuity of the material intellect's thought through infinite time

[150]Long Commentary on the *De anima* 409–10. The notion of a quasi matter in the intelligences recalls the cosmology of Ibn Gabirol (Avicebron).

[151]Long Commentary on the *De anima* 442; see textual apparatus there.

[152]Below, p. 318.

[153]Cf. Aristotle, *De anima* 3.5.430a 16–17.

[154]Long Commentary on the *De anima* 486 appears to say that the material intellect, in its own right ("in natura istius intellectus materialis"), always possesses thought of the incorporeal beings. I do not see how that proposition can be harmonized with Averroes' insistence, above, p. 288, that the incorporeal material intellect can have no form of its own.

being spun from the thoughts of individuals alive at various moments.[155] Averroes never explains when and how the material intellect becomes associated with the individual human organism; how human effort can move the material intellect to do its bidding, seeing that the material intellect is an eternal substance only tenuously associated with man; nor how the material intellect, the recipient of actual human thoughts, reciprocates and endows individual man with an intellectual consciousness.[156]

The position on the material intellect which Averroes adopts in the Long Commentary on the *De anima* is Themistius' position, as Averroes understands it, with a correction and an addition. Themistius, Averroes writes in the Long Commentary, construed the material intellect rightly but missed a critical detail; he did not realize that actual human thought, or human "theoretical intellect," although in one respect eternal, is in another respect generated-destructible.[157] Averroes also does something that Themistius did not do, in construing the material intellect as a quasi-material incorporeal substance and assigning it a precise place in the incorporeal hierarchy. He identifies it as the last of the incorporeal intelligences, standing directly below the active intellect in the hierarchy of existence.

The position Averroes arrives at in the Long Commentary on the *De anima* is precisely the position he sketched in passages interpolated into the Epitome. There too he construed the material intellect as an eternal substance in a state of potentiality; he described it as one of two subjects in the thought process, playing the role of recipient, whereas images in the imaginative faculty perform the role of mover; and he referred readers to the Long Commentary for a fuller exposition.[158]

Averroes also recommends what seems to be the same theory in his Commentary on Alexander's *De intellectu*. After "long study and rigorous application," he writes there, he arrived at a conception of the material intellect which he had never "seen . . . in anyone else." In the new conception, the material intellect is a "single power common to [all] individual . . . human . . . souls." In an attempt to clarify his meaning, Averroes compares and contrasts *material intellect* to

[155] Ibid. 407–8, 448. For a somewhat similar notion, see John Philoponus, *Commentaire sur le De anima d'Aristote*, ed. G. Verbeke (Louvain 1966) 52.

[156] The last point is pressed by Thomas Aquinas, *Summa contra gentiles* 2.59. It seems to be recognized by Averroes himself in Ahwani (n. 19 above) 87 (bottom); Spanish translation 211. The translator's note records several manuscript readings, the second of which supports my suggestion. I find the interpretation offered by the translator in the note and in his introduction to be farfetched.

[157] Long Commentary on the *De anima* 406. In the Arabic text of his Long Commentary on the *Metaphysics*, Averroes writes that he "proved . . . in the *De anima* . . . that the material intellect is generated-destructible." If the reading is correct, Averroes cannot be referring to the Long Commentary on the *De anima*. Very possibly, however, the word *not* has dropped out. The printed medieval Latin text has: "non est generabilis et corruptibilis"; and the word *not* has plainly dropped out a few lines later (line 11) in the Arabic. See *Tafsīr mā ba^cda al-Tabī^ca* (Long Commentary on the *Metaphysics*), ed. M. Bouyges (Beirut 1938–1948) 1489 and apparatus.

[158] Above, pp. 269–71.

natural species. A natural species, he writes, comprises "individuals [existing] in actuality" but does not, in the Aristotelian scheme of things, have independent existence. Since it exists solely through the individuals, the natural species in itself exists only "potentially." The reverse, Averroes submits, is true of material intellect, for the material intellect "is species in actuality and individual [only] potentially." This two-part notion by which Averroes characterizes material intellect—species in actuality, and individual potentially—is strange. Averroes explains the first half as meaning that a "single," common material intellect serves all mankind, and in attaching itself to "individual men" does not become individualized; it remains what it was before, namely, "species in actuality." The second half is perhaps equivalent to saying, as Averroes did in the Long Commentary on the *De anima*, that the material intellect does not join man in an essential and primary sense.[159]

When a man is born, the Commentary on the *De intellectu* goes on, the material intellect is "generated in respect to him, without being generated in itself," and when a man dies, the material intellect "is destroyed in respect to him but not in itself." The material intellect is thus something—not called *substance* in the present text—"common" to all mankind, "unmixed with the body, . . . separate therefrom [that is, incorporeal]," not "subject to enumeration," and "in itself not generated and destructible."[160] Averroes' Commentary on the *De intellectu* has little more to say on the subject, apart from a few sentences that might have been helpful were they not patently corrupt.[161]

A position along the same lines is intimated as well in Averroes' *Tahāfut al-Tahāfut* (*Destructio destructionum*). The *Tahāfut al-Tahāfut* states that "according to most" philosophers, the human "potential intellect . . . is eternal." Again: Aristotle, reasoning from the potential intellect's "having everything as an object of thought," proved that the "passive"[162] or potential intellect is "ungenerated and indestructible."[163] The Aristotelian proof alluded to is undoubtedly the familiar argument that since the potential intellect can think the form of every object in the physical world, it contains no material form in itself; containing no such form in itself, it is separate from matter, or incorporeal, and hence immune to generation and destruction. Another possibly pertinent passage in the *Tahāfut al-Tahāfut* affirms that the "proof" for the unity of all human intellect is "strong."[164] From the

[159]Above, p. 289.

[160]Commentary on *De intellectu* (n. 32 above) 211–12.

[161]On 212, Averroes could be saying that the material intellect exists only as long as human individuals exist. If such is the meaning, the text takes a different position from the Long Commentary on the *De anima*, but the passage is undoubtedly corrupt.

[162]See above, n. 90.

[163]Averroes, *Tahāfut al-Tahāfut*, ed. M. Bouyges (Beirut 1930) 6, 180; English translation, with pagination of the original Arabic indicated: *Averroes' Tahafut al-Tahafut*, trans. S. Van den Bergh (London 1954).

[164]Ibid. 574.

context, Averroes could be saying that a single identical *active* intellect serves all mankind.[165] If, however, he is speaking of a single potential or material intellect serving mankind, he has in the *Tahāfut al-Tahāfut* alluded to the main points he laid down in his Long Commentary on the *De anima.* He has indicated that the material or potential intellect is a single, incorporeal, eternal substance shared by the entire human species.

Summary

At various times, Averroes embraced at least four positions on the human material intellect. His Epitome of the *De anima* and his *Epistle on the Possibility of Conjunction* endorse what Averroes knew as Ibn Bājja's position, the theory that the material intellect is a disposition for thought joined to, but not mixed with, the imaginative faculty of the human soul. A brief piece on the possibility of conjunction with the active intellect and—if my reading of the text is correct—the original version of the Middle Commentary on the *De anima* endorse Alexander's conception of the human intellect as a mere disposition for thought not mixed with the human body or linked to any specific part of the body or soul. An excursus in the Middle Commentary states that "after assigning the due share of doubts" to the positions of Alexander and Themistius, Averroes settled on a "combination" of the two. He decided that a material intellect is engendered for each individual man when the transcendent active intellect joins an inborn human disposition for thought; the ability to think human thoughts is thereby, in some accidental fashion, generated in the active intellect.

In the Long Commentary on the *De anima,* Averroes confesses that when he was younger he had been misled by relying inordinately on Aristotelian commentators instead of Aristotle himself. The Long Commentary refutes both Alexander, who is now painted in more materialist hues than previously, and Ibn Bājja. It does not mention the compromise position of the Middle Commentary, although the distinction between the two subjects of human thought in the Long Commentary does have a certain resemblance to the compromise position advanced there. In effect, the Long Commentary endorses Themistius' position, as Averroes understands it, construing the human material intellect as a single incorporeal, eternal substance that becomes attached to the imaginative faculties of individual men in some nonessential fashion. Averroes adds that the material intellect stands directly below the active intellect in the hierarchy of existence, as the last of the incorporeal intelligences. The position of the Long Commentary reappears in glosses incorporated into Averroes' Epitome of the *De anima* and is alluded to in his *Tahāfut al-Tahāfut.* His Commentary on the *De Intellectu* propounds the same conception or a related one.

[165] Ibid. 27–29, lends itself to that interpretation.

Arguments that a given work adduces to establish its conception of the material intellect are sometimes employed to the same end in other works[166]; sometimes, the same argument is employed to contrary ends[167]; and sometimes an identical conception will rest on different arguments in different works.[168] Three strands of argumentation in particular merit attention because of their persistence. (1) Aristotle had reasoned that any prior coloring in the potential human intellect would prevent it from thinking all thoughts without distortion. In Averroes' early discussions of the nature of the material intellect, Aristotle's reasoning helps prove that the material intellect can be nothing other than a mere disposition[169]; in later stages the same reasoning leads to the contrary conclusion that the material intellect cannot possibly be a mere disposition and must be nothing other than an incorporeal substance.[170] (2) In early works, the contention that a wholly intellectual substance cannot exist in a state of potentiality supports the construction of the material intellect as a mere disposition, and the contention is cited as well to support the intermediate position of the Middle Commentary.[171] Averroes does not forget the contention when concluding in the Long Commentary that the material intellect is an eternal intellectual substance. There, however, he counters it by uncovering a hitherto overlooked class of existence. He finds that the incorporeal realm contains a quasi matter, so that an incorporeal substance, and the material intellect in particular, can after all exist in a state of potentiality.[172] (3) When construing the material intellect as a disposition, Averroes invariably adduces Aristotle's analogy of the writing tablet with Alexander's emendation; he compares the material intellect not to a writing tablet but to the disposition that the tablet has for writing.[173] When in the Long Commentary he finally decides that the material intellect is an eternal substance rather than a disposition, he reconsiders the analogy. He insists now that Aristotle compared the material intellect to the substance of the writing tablet and not to the disposition in the tablet. Since it is the substance receiving human thoughts—the analogue of the tablet itself—which must be unmixed with matter, the material intellect must be an incorporeal substance.[174]

Where exact dates can be assigned to Averroes' commentaries, his Epitomes have been found to be early and his Long Commentaries late.[175] In the case of the commentaries on Aristotle's *De anima*, an annotation incorporated into the Epitome

[166]See above, pp. 269, 286.

[167]See immediately below.

[168]See arguments taking the material intellect to be a mere disposition, above, pp. 267, 273.

[169]See above, pp. 273 and 276.

[170]See above, pp. 269, 286.

[171]See above, pp. 269, 279.

[172]Above, p. 291.

[173]See above, pp. 268, 273, 274–75, 277.

[174]Above, p. 285.

[175]See Munk (n. 27 above) 431–32; Renan (n. 27 above) 60–61; Alaoui, *Al-Matn al-Rushdī* (n. 19 above) 49–58.

expressly states that Averroes rethought the subject of the material intellect after writing the Epitome, and that the Long Commentary offers his revised position.[176] The Long Commentary for its part—and also the Commentary on Alexander's *De intellectu*, which is related to the Long Commentary—informs us that it is the fruit of lengthy study.[177] The Epitome of the *De anima* is thus plainly earlier than the Long Commentary. The relative date of the excursus in the Middle Commentary vis-à-vis the Long Commentary can only be conjectured. It is highly tempting to suppose that Averroes started at one extreme, progressed to the intermediate, compromise position of the Middle Commentary, and subsequently went on to the other extreme; in presenting Averroes' theories, I have observed that sequence. Several considerations suggest that here temptation is safely succumbed to. Whereas the body of the Middle Commentary subscribes to Alexander's position, the excursus criticizes Alexander and by implication Ibn Bājja as well. The excursus is therefore presumably later than all the works in which Averroes follows Alexander or Ibn Bājja. The excursus knows nothing, however, of a fourth class of existence, eternal intellectual substance in a state of potentiality, which Averroes uncovered in the Long Commentary and which enabled him to construe the material, or potential, intellect as an incorporeal substance. Moreover, it offers a much scantier treatment of the human intellect than the Long Commentary, which embodies Averroes' most exhaustive and carefully reasoned treatment.

At an early state of his thought, we can conclude with a fair degree of confidence, Averroes followed Ibn Bājja and construed the material intellect as a disposition in the imaginative faculty of the soul. Somewhat later—if we rely on the general assumption that he wrote the Middle Commentaries after the Epitomes—he construed the material intellect, with Alexander, as a disposition in the soul without specifically locating it in the imaginative faculty.[178] Still later, he arrived at the intermediate theory that an individual material intellect is engendered whenever the active intellect joins the inborn disposition awaiting it in an individual human soul. At what we can presume was the crowning stage of his thought, he construed the human material intellect as a single eternal substance shared by all men, consisting in the quasi matter that analysis can discover in other incorporeal beings and standing immediately below the active intellect in the hierarchy of existence.

A curious twist may be noted. Averroes struggled throughout his career to recapture Aristotle's intent, and the previous chapter saw him succeeding. After repeatedly wrestling with the pertinent issues, he finally did away with the emanation of incorporeal beings from one another, the existence of a First Cause beyond the incorporeal movers of the spheres, and the emanation of sublunar

[176]Above, p. 270.

[177]Above, pp. 287, 294.

[178]Averroes accepted Alexander's position in the original version of the Middle Commentary on the *De anima*, if my analysis was correct, and he is generally thought to have written his Middle Commentaries after the Epitomes.

natural forms from the active intellect. Those are plainly non-Aristotelian conceptions, and by eliminating them Averroes liberated himself from a number of misreadings of Aristotle. The present chapter has shown that in seeking to recapture Aristotle's intent concerning the potential, or material, human intellect, and in heeding, as he writes, the words of Aristotle himself rather than the commentators, Averroes moved not toward what the consensus of modern scholarship would take to be the historically correct interpretation of Aristotle but in the opposite direction. He started with a material intellect that is a faculty of the soul and concluded with something foreign to Aristotle, a single eternal, incorporeal material intellect that joins each man from without.

As a consequence, Averroes' final picture of the sublunar world, while more naturalistic than his early picture in one respect, is less so in another. In his early career, Averroes understood that sublunar forms, including the human soul, emanate from the transcendent active intellect, but he gave a naturalistic explanation of human material intellect. In his final view of things, he eliminates the emanation of sublunar forms, maintaining that the forms of inanimate and animate beings are drawn out of sublunar matter by the action of natural forces. The material intellect, which he before explained naturalistically, has now, however, turned into a single incorporeal being that continually irrupts into the physical world to serve individual men.

The next chapter will show that at all stages of his career, Averroes credited the transcendent active intellect with the actualization of the human intellect, and that almost all his works recognize the possibility of some kind of conjunction of the human intellect with the active intellect.

Averroes' Theories of Material Intellect as Reflected in Subsequent Jewish and Christian Thought

As far as is known, Averroes' Long Commentary on the *De anima* was not available in Hebrew before the fifteenth century, and the Hebrew translation was even then not widely disseminated. Scholastic philosophy, by contrast, had no work of Averroes' on intellect except for the Long Commentary.[179] Jewish philosophers who could not read the Long Commentary in the original Arabic or in the Latin translation—and it was they who constituted the mainstream of medieval Jewish philosophy—consequently received a picture of Averroes wholly at variance with the picture prevalent in Scholastic circles and accessible to the few Jewish

[179]The Middle Commentary on the *De anima* was translated from Hebrew into Latin, but only at a late period; see n. 23 above. Two small compositions on the theme of conjunction with the active intellect were translated into Latin, probably from the Hebrew; see Davidson, *Averrois Tractatus de Animae Beatitudine* (n. 31 above). No evidence has been discovered of Scholastic writers' using them, however, and I assume that they were not translated before the fifteenth century.

philosophers who could read the Arabic or Latin versions. Thus Moses Narboni (fourteenth century), Levi Gersonides (1288–1344), and Shem Ṭob Ibn Shem Ṭob (late fifteenth century), all careful students of Averroes, assume that the compromise theory set forth in the Middle Commentary is Averroes' considered position on the material intellect.[180] Averroes, each of them reports, understood that a material intellect is engendered when the transcendent active intellect attaches itself to the inborn disposition of an individual man. Narboni accepts Averroes' position as he records it.[181] Gersonides rejects it and instead endorses what he calls Alexander's position,[182] although as he pursues the subject, his conception turns out not to be precisely Alexander's position either but the position Averroes attributed to Ibn Bājja: Gersonides determines that the human disposition for thought is linked specifically to the imaginative faculty of the soul.[183] Shem Ṭob Ibn Shem Ṭob likewise endorses Alexander's position.[184] He, however, interprets Alexander and Averroes' Middle Commentary in a fashion that blurs the difference between them.[185]

Of the Jewish philosophers who used Latin texts, Hillel b. Samuel of Verona (ca. 1220–1295) did not go directly to Averroes' Long Commentary on the *De anima*. He relied instead on a more readable, secondary account, Thomas Aquinas' *De unitate intellectus contra Averroistas*. Besides Aquinas, Hillel also employed the Hebrew version of Averroes' two small compositions on the conjunction of the human intellect with the active intellect.[186] But although one of the two compositions describes the material intellect in a wholly different way from Aquinas' account of Averroes, which is based on the Long Commentary, Hillel ignored the disparity and read the conception recorded by Aquinas into the Hebrew pieces. He accordingly reports without qualification that Averroes construed the material intellect—or as he also puts it, the human soul[187]—as a single incorporeal

[180]These writers understand the reference to Averroes' "Commentary" in one of the interpolations to Averroes' Epitome (above, p. 270) as a reference to his *Middle* Commentary on the *De anima*, rather than to his *Long* Commentary, which was not known in Hebrew.

[181]Moses Narboni, *Ma'amar be-Shelemut ha-Nefesh*, ed. A. Ivry (Jerusalem 1977) 123–25. See H. Davidson, "Averroes and Narboni on the Material Intellect," *AJS Review*, 9 (1984) 182–84.

[182]Levi Gersonides, Commentary on Averroes' Epitome of the *De anima* (n. 78 above) 247b; *Milḥamot ha-Shem* (*Die Kämpfe Gottes*) (Leipzig 1866) 1.3, p. 20. English translation of *Milḥamot* 1–4: Levi ben Gershom, *The Wars of the Lord*, trans. S. Feldman (Philadelphia 1984–1987).

[183]*Milḥamot ha-Shem* 1.5.

[184]Shem Ṭob Ibn Shem Ṭob, Commentary on Maimonides' *Guide* (Warsaw 1930) 1.68, 100a; *Be'ur ha-Koaḥ ha-Dibberi*, Paris, Bibliothèque nationale, Hebrew MS 898, 144a.

[185]Shem Ṭob Ibn Shem Ṭob, *Be'ur ha-Koaḥ ha-Dibberi* 144a, 146b.

[186]See above, p. 264, nos. 5 and 6; Hillel b. Samuel, *Sefer Tagmule ha-Nefesh*, ed. J. Sermoneta (Jerusalem 1981) 1.6, notes; Davidson, *Averrois Tractatus de Animae Beatitudine* (n. 31 above) 68–70.

[187]Hillel b. Samuel 1.5, p. 60.

substance common to all mankind.[188] Borrowing arguments from Aquinas, Hillel refutes the doctrine of the unity of the human intellect or human soul.

The fifteenth century, at last, saw a Jewish philosopher, Elijah Delmedigo, who could navigate through the Latin version of Averroes' Long Commentary on the *De anima*. Delmedigo bases his discussion of intellect almost exclusively on the Long Commentary.[189] He records Averroes' construction of the human material intellect as a single eternal substance common to all mankind, and with arguments drawn from the Long Commentary, he defends Averroes in detail.[190]

The Long Commentary on the *De anima* was translated into Latin around 1230, and in the second half of the century, the theory of material intellect propounded in the Long Commentary achieved notoriety. Albert the Great read the Commentary but for some reason did not at first realize that Averroes was positing a single potential, or material, intellect for all mankind.[191] Others did understand fully. Aquinas discussed Averroes' theory in several works, and his *Summa contra gentiles*, doing something that not all the other works do, names Averroes as the protagonist. "Averroes," the *Summa contra gentiles* states, took the "possible intellect by which the soul thinks" to be a "separate [incorporeal]" substance, a substance not joined to the human body as its "form."[192] The first part of the report is, except for the change of terminology to *possible* intellect, precisely what we encountered in the Long Commentary, and the second part is probably implied there, since it is hard to see how a single material intellect serving all mankind might be the form of each individual man. Nevertheless, Averroes did not explicitly say that the material intellect is not man's form. He did write that the material intellect is not "a body" or a "form in a body,"[193] but those expressions do not necessarily exclude the material intellect's being the human form, the organizing principle constituting man's essence and making him what he is.[194] Aquinas, after all,

[188]Ibid. 1.7, p. 101.

[189]He also cites John of Jandun.

[190]Elijah Delmedigo, Paris, Bibliothèque nationale, Hebrew MS 968, 120a, 135b.

[191]Albertus Magnus, *De anima*, 3.11, in *Opera omnia* 5, ed. A. Borgnet (Paris 1890) 386a. R. Miller, "An Aspect of Averroes' Influence on Albertus Magnus," *Mediaeval Studies* 16 (1954) 60–61 (Miller 65, does not formulate Averroes' position correctly); D. Salman, "Note sur la première influence d'Averroès," *Revue néoscolastique de philosophie* 40 (1937) 208. Salman 205–8, 209–11, infers from the writings of Roger Bacon and Adam of Buckfield that they too read Averroes without realizing that he envisaged a single material intellect for the entire human species.

[192]Thomas Aquinas, *Summa contra gentiles* 2.59; cf. *Summa theologiae* 1.76, art. 1.

[193]See above, p. 284.

[194]Other pertinent passages are: Long Commentary on the *De anima* 160, where, commenting on Aristotle's statement, *De anima* 2.2.413b, 26, that the intellect is "another genus of soul," Averroes writes that the intellect is "another genus of soul, and if called soul, it will be by equivocation"; and the passages quoted above, p. 283, at note 108, and p. 290, at n. 143.

likewise insisted that the human intellect is not a "material form."[195] In any event, the proposition that the material, or potential, intellect is not the true form of man, and is at most man's form in some loose, extended sense, came to be one of the touchstones of Latin Averroism.

Playing devil's advocate, the *Summa contra gentiles* lists five considerations that Averroes and philosophers of the same mind might adduce to support their position; and the list includes arguments that Averroes in fact put forward, alongside others that he did not. The first of the five considerations is "Aristotle's words" to the effect that intellect is "separate, unmixed with the body, simple, and not subject to affection." Such descriptions might seem to imply that the possible or potential human intellect is not the "body's form." The second is that if "possible intellect had any form or nature of sensible things in itself," it would be prevented from thinking all thoughts without distortion; whence it might seem to follow that possible intellect cannot "be mixed with the body or be the actuality or form of any body."[196] Both considerations were advanced by Averroes to establish that the potential intellect is an incorporeal substance,[197] although not to prove that the material intellect cannot be the human *form*. The remaining three considerations listed by Aquinas are not from Averroes and must be either arguments current in Latin circles or arguments that Aquinas himself framed as hypothetical support for his adversaries. Aquinas dismisses the arguments and judges the Averroist position to be "foolish and impossible," because—put briefly—what experiences human intellectual thought would, on Averroes' conception, be an entity distinct from man and not the human subject; and because, somewhat similarly, intelligible thought is the distinctively essential moment in man, the moment making him what he is, and consequently the possible or potential intellect, which enables man to achieve intelligible thought, must be man's *form*.[198]

Averroes, Aquinas further reports, identified the link between man and the potential intellect existing apart from him as the "image" (*phantasma*) in the imaginative faculty; he characterized images in the imaginative faculty as a "kind of subject" of human thought[199]; the "cogitative faculty," which operates in concert with the "imaginative faculty" and "memory," was dubbed by him the human "passive intellect"; and he identified passive intellect as the part of man endowing the child with its "human species."[200] All but the last of the statements reflect views expressed by Averroes in the Long Commentary on the *De anima*. All are duly refuted by Aquinas.

[195]Thomas Aquinas, *Summa contra gentiles* 2.69; *Tractatus de unitate intellectus contra Averroistas*, ed. L. Keeler (Rome 1936) §83; English translation, with the same section divisions: *On the Unity of the Intellect against the Averroists*, trans. B. Zedler (Milwaukee 1968).

[196]Aquinas, *Summa contra gentiles* 2.59.

[197]Above, pp. 284, 288.

[198]Aquinas, *Summa contra gentiles* 2.59; *Summa theologiae* 1.76.1, resp.

[199]Ibid. See above, pp. 289–90.

[200]Aquinas, *Summa contra gentiles* 2.60. See above, nn. 90 and 140.

The Averroes that Aquinas' *Summa contra gentiles* depicts is, unmistakably, closely akin to the genuine Averroes of the Long Commentary on the *De anima*. But Averroes' visage has been altered, most notably in being burdened with the proposition that the potential intellect does not constitute man's form, a proposition perhaps implied, yet never expressed, in the Long Commentary.

A certain William of Baglione, writing in Paris about the same time as Aquinas, devoted a *quaestio* to the proposition that "intellect is one in number for all men" as the "Commentator [Averroes] laid down." William too draws up a list of possible arguments that might support the proposition; they are borrowed from thinkers as strangely diverse as Aristotle, Augustine, and Anselm, but include as well a rewording of considerations taken from Averroes himself. William rejects Averroes' position both on theoretical grounds and because of its "perniciousness" for religion.[201]

Although the renowned Dominican, Thomas Aquinas, and the obscure Franciscan, William of Baglione, gave short shrift to Averroes' theories, Averroes won adherents in Paris. Ecclesiastical authorities were not in the least pleased, because of the ramifications that his theories had for individual immortality and for the summoning of individual human souls to the last assize. In 1267 and 1268, Bonaventure remonstrated against errors growing out of an improper use of philosophy, and among them was the proposition that "one intellect" serves "all [men]." Bonaventure's tone suggests that he was attacking doctrines actually espoused by Christian thinkers.[202] In 1270, Stephen Tempier, bishop of Paris, formally "condemned and banned" thirteen errors "together with all who might teach . . . or maintain them." The first of the errors was that "the intellect of all men is one and numerically identical."[203] At approximately the same time, a member of the Dominican order sent Albert the Great, who was then residing in Germany, a list of fifteen theses, already "opposed in many assemblies," and he asked for Albert's comments. The first of the fifteen was once again the proposition "that the intellect of all men is one and identical in number"; and Albert's response shows that he now understood the unity of the human potential intellect to be at issue.[204]

The year 1270 also saw the publication of Aquinas' monograph, *De unitate intellectus contra Averroistas*. There Aquinas speaks of an "error" recently embraced by "many" and "taking its source in the words of Averroes," to wit, the proposition that "the intellect that Aristotle called *possible*," but that Averroes "called by the inappropriate name *material*," is a "substance . . . separate from

[201]I. Brady, "Background to the Condemnation of 1270: Master William of Baglione," *Franciscan Studies* 30 (1970) 35–45.

[202]F. Van Steenberghen, *Maître Siger de Brabant* (Louvain 1977) 36, 42–43.

[203]P. Mandonnet, *Siger de Brabant et l'Averroïsme Latin* 1 (Louvain 1911) 111; H. Denifle and A. Chatelain, *Chartularium universitatis Parisiensis* 1 (Paris 1899) 486–87.

[204]Mandonnet 1.105; 2 (Louvain 1908) 29ff. Mandonnet 1.106, dates the list of theses sent to Albertus in 1270, but others date it a few years later; see Van Steenberghen 122–24.

the body," "one for all men," and not "joined to the body as its form."[205] In 1277, Bishop Tempier, apparently acting at the pope's behest, formally condemned a much longer list of theses than the list of 1270.[206] The theses now at issue were, in the language of the condemnation, "manifest and execrable errors." They were taught by scholars "in the [Faculty of] Arts at Paris who overstep the borders of their Faculty," by dealing with subjects belonging to theology, and who dare, moreover, to maintain that things can be "true according to philosophy but not so according to the Catholic faith—as if there were two contrary truths!" Included among the theses condemned was the proposition that the "substance of the soul" as well as the "active and possible intellects are eternal" (no. 109), and the further proposition that "the intellect is numerically one for all men" (no. 32).[207]

Solid information is available about only a single figure who was a member of the Faculty of Arts and whose teachings resemble the execrable errors censured by Tempier and refuted by Aquinas. He is Siger of Brabant. A manuscript listing the theses condemned in 1277 bears the heading "Against the heretics Siger and Boetius [of Dacia]."[208] An early manuscript of Aquinas' *De unitate intellectus contra Averroistas* names Siger as Aquinas' antagonist. And another manuscript of the *De unitate* contains the remark that Aquinas wrote the treatise "in 1270, against Siger of Brabant and . . . others."[209]

Two compositions dealing specifically with the human intellect carry Siger's name, and excerpts from a third composition of his which deals with the human intellect are provided by a later author. A fourth composition of Siger's, although not taking the human intellect as its primary subject, also treats the human intellect at some length. A considerable scholarly literature has developed around Siger, offering divergent judgments on the dates of his writings, their relation to Aquinas' *De unitate intellectus contra Averroistas*, and their Averroistic character. Whatever one makes of the man, he clearly followed Averroes at certain stages of his career, although never blindly.

A work of his entitled *Quaestiones in tertium de Anima*, perhaps the protocol of a course of lectures, treats questions regarding the human intellect in a typically Scholastic format.[210] Siger sets down arguments for and against given theses, states his own stand, draws distinctions, and rebuts the considerations seemingly in

[205]Thomas Aquinas, *De unitate intellectus* (n. 195 above) §1. Themistius, whom Averroes had cited to support his position, is cited by Aquinas in §§51–53, in support of his own position that the potential intellect "is part of the human soul."

[206]Mandonnet 1.212–213; Van Steenberghen 146, 148–49.

[207]Mandonnet 2.175, 184–85 (nos. 117, 129); Denifle and Chatelain 543, 545, 549. English translation: *Medieval Political Philosophy*, ed. R. Lerner and M. Mahdi (New York 1963) 337–54.

[208]Mandonnet 1.220. See Van Steenberghen 155, for other manuscripts mentioning Siger and Boetius.

[209]Zedler (n. 195 above) 6.

[210]Van Steenberghen 339–47.

opposition. On the nature of the human "intellect"—glossed more precisely as the "potentiality" for thought[211] and qualified as "possible"[212]—the *Quaestiones* repeats the materialist and naturalistic account of Alexander which Averroes' Long Commentary gave. Alexander, Siger writes, construed the human intellect as "the highest material form," a form that emerges spontaneously from the "finest degree of mixture [of the physical elements]." He "alone . . . among all the commentators on Aristotle . . . took the [potential] intellect to be generated."[213] Aristotle and Averroes, by contrast, determined that "one" potential human intellect, not subject to enumeration, serves all mankind.[214] It joins individual men through the human imaginative faculty, without entering into the human organism and employing a human organ.[215] What has been said thus far comes directly from Averroes.

The human "intellect," Siger further contends without reference to Averroes, can contain no matter, for unlike material objects, which are "potentially intelligible," the human intellect is "in itself actually intelligible and, moreover, capable of having itself as an actual object of thought [*se ipsum actu intelligens*]."[216] The conclusion that the potential human intellect is free of matter is wholly in the spirit of Averroes' Long Commentary on the *De anima*, but the argument from the "actually intelligible" character of the potential intellect which leads to the conclusion is not. Ostensibly quoting Averroes, Siger goes on to draw a distinction that also would have struck Averroes as strange. Siger submits that "intellect perfects the body . . . through its [the intellect's] power" and not "through its [the intellect's] substance," the reason being that the human intellect does not come into contact with, and "use," the body.[217]

Averroes had, with little ado, inferred the eternal existence of the potential human intellect from its incorporeality.[218] Siger divides the issue of the intellect's eternal existence into two formal questions, the question whether the human intellect was

[211]Siger de Brabant, *Quaestiones in tertium de anima; De anima intellectiva; De aeternitate mundi*, ed. B. Bazán (Louvain 1972) 5.

[212]Ibid. 30.

[213]Ibid. 11–12.

[214]Ibid. 2, 26–27.

[215]Ibid. 23, 25, 56. Intellect joins man through the circumstance "quod intelligit ex intentionibus imaginatis."

[216]Ibid. 20.

[217]Ibid. 23–24. The editor refers to Averroes, Long Commentary on the *De anima* 160, where, however, Averroes by no means says all that Siger represents him as saying. Both the argument that the "rational soul" must be incorporeal since "it knows itself" and the notion that the "rational soul perfects the [human] animal not through substance but through act [ἐνεργείᾳ]," are to be found in John Philoponus, Commentary on the *De anima*, ed. M. Hayduck, *Commentaria in Aristotelem Graeca* 15 (Berlin 1897) 14, 206. Parts of Philoponus' Commentary were translated into Latin in the thirteenth century, but these sections are not known to have been translated.

[218]Above, p. 289.

"made" from all eternity or "at a certain moment" (*novum, de novo*) in the past, and the additional question whether the human intellect is "destructible" in the future. In answer to the first question, he represents Aristotle as having maintained that the human potential intellect is, like the world, an "immediate product" of "the First Cause"; that every immediate product of the eternal unchangeable First Cause is an "eternal product"; and that, consequently, "the human intellect is, like the world, an eternal product" of the First Cause.[219] Augustine's position, by contrast, was that the entire human soul, including the intellect, was "created at a certain moment" and is "not eternal." After some scholastic give-and-take, Siger concludes a bit gingerly that "Aristotle's position is more probable than Augustine's."[220] In answer to the other question, Siger determines that the human intellect receives future eternal existence and gains immortality "solely from the First Cause."[221] As for the human "speculative intellect," or theoretical intellect, that is to say, actual thoughts acquired by the potential intellect, it, "as Averroes states, is destructible in respect to a given man, and yet eternal in respect to itself and in an unqualified sense."[222]

In exploring one more issue, Siger dismisses the notion that beings consisting in intellect contain a material side. Among his reasons is the consideration that if intellect contained "matter it would not be actually intelligible, but only potentially so." Siger probably has in view Scholastic thinkers who distinguished a form and matter within the human rational soul.[223] He could conceivably, though, also be distancing himself from Averroes, who had maintained in the Long Commentary on the *De anima* that all incorporeal beings except the First Cause contain a quasi-material side, and the human material intellect consists in that quasi matter.[224]

In short, Siger reports that Averroes recognized a single incorporeal potential intellect for all mankind, that the potential intellect joins men through images in their imaginative faculty, that the human speculative, or theoretical, intellect is destructible insofar as it is connected with individual men but otherwise eternal. Those positions come from Averroes' Long Commentary on the *De anima*. Siger's reasoning in support of the past and future eternity of the human potential intellect does not, by contrast, derive from Averroes, nor does his affirmation of the "actually intelligible" character of the potential human intellect.

Siger's *Quaestiones in tertium de Anima,* the text we have been examining, is dated by scholars before 1270, the year in which Aquinas wrote his *De unitate intellectus contra Averroistas*. As already mentioned, Aquinas' *De unitate intellectus* undertakes to answer Averroes and certain Latin "Averroists" who

[219]Siger, *Quaestiones in tertium de Anima* (n. 211 above) 5–6. Perhaps Siger was taking a work such as the *Theology of Aristotle* as a genuine Aristotelian work.

[220]Ibid. 5, 8.

[221]Ibid. 17.

[222]Ibid. 29. Cf. above, p. 290.

[223]E.g., Roger Bacon. See E. Gilson, *History of Christian Philosophy in the Middle Ages* (New York 1955) 302.

[224]Ibid. 20. See above, p. 291.

affirmed that the "possible" or "material" intellect is a "substance . . . separate from the body," "one in all men," and not "joined to the body as its form." The thesis that the potential intellect is not joined to the body as its form, which is nowhere articulated in Averroes' Long Commentary on the *De anima*, is not stated in so many words by Siger in the work just examined either, although Siger probably implies the thesis when he writes that the human intellect does not "perfect" man "through its [the intellect's] substance."[225] On the issue of the potential intellect as the human form, Aquinas' *De unitate intellectus* therefore at most addresses the implications of Averroes' Long Commentary and Siger's *Quaestiones in tertium de Anima*. Even apart from the issue of the potential intellect as the human form, the *De unitate intellectus* does not stand as a direct critique of the positions taken by Siger in the *Quaestiones* or, for that matter, in any of Siger's known works. Conceivably, Aquinas was refuting a lost work of Siger's such as one that an early fourteenth-century writer, John Baconthorpe, refers to.[226] Alternatively—the suggestion has been made[227]—Aquinas may have had in view listeners' accounts of lectures conducted by Siger or other adherents of Averroes.

Whoever Aquinas' Parisian adversary was in the *De unitate intellectus*, Siger reportedly composed a surrejoinder. Agostino Nifo, writing in 1492, quotes from a work entitled *De intellectu*, which, he says, Siger sent to Aquinas in "response" to the latter's *De unitate intellectus*.[228] Siger in the *De intellectu*, as well as other philosophers—so Nifo informs us—took, "as it were, . . . an intermediate stance [*mediare*] between the Latins [Scholastics] and the Averroists." The term *Averroists*, the context shows, designates those who, like Aquinas' Averroists, maintained both that a single potential intellect serves all men, and that the potential intellect is not the human form. In Nifo's account, Siger's *De intellectu* accepted the "indivisibility, immateriality, and unity of the intellect" from the Averroists. From the Latin scholastics, Siger accepted the proposition that the material intellect is "the form furnishing existence [*constituens*] to man [in general] and also to this [particular] man . . . thus giving existence [*dare esse*] to [both] individual and species."[229] Whereupon Nifo undermines his analysis with a qualification. Siger, he writes, did not suppose that the potential intellect by itself furnishes existence to an individual man; the potential intellect does so only in concert with man's "cogitative" faculty, "only by joining with images in the imaginative faculty." The human potential intellect is, hence, "primarily and essentially" the "first perfection of man [in general]." Merely "accidentally, and in respect to their final perfection,

[225]See above, p. 304.

[226]M. Chossat, "St. Thomas d'Aquin et Siger de Brabant," *Revue de philosophie* 24 (1914) 556–58; J. Etzwiler, "Baconthorpe and Latin Averroism," *Carmelus* 18 (1971) 241–44.

[227]Van Steenberghen (n. 202 above) 59.

[228]The text is quoted in B. Nardi, *Sigieri di Brabante nel pensiero del Rinascimento italiano* (Rome 1945) 18.

[229]Ibid. 18–19.

is it the actuality and perfection of Socrates, Plato, and other [individuals]."[230] Nifo is trying to sweeten the proposition that the eternal potential intellect is not man's form, while in effect acknowledging that for Siger, the potential intellect is in the strict sense the form solely of the species as a whole. Only in cooperation with the imaginative faculty and in an accidental sense is the potential intellect also the form of the individual.

Still a third text of Siger's, entitled *De anima intellectiva*, deals with the nature of the material intellect, and this text has been preserved.[231] Scholarly consensus dates it after both the *Quaestiones in tertium de Anima* and the *De intellectu*,[232] and Siger may well have been under attack at the time, since he expresses himself with extreme circumspection and barely mentions Averroes. The *De anima intellectiva* speaks of "intellective soul," the "intellective" part of the soul, and "intellect," apparently using the terms interchangeably. Siger establishes that the intellective soul is "not composed of matter and form, is not a material form, but is free of matter, and," although it has a cause of its existence, "subsists through itself" (*per se subsistens*).[233] It is consequently eternal.[234] Concerning the critical question whether the "intellective soul is the perfection [or: entelechy] and form of the [human] body," Siger offers another of his distinctions. He represents Aristotle as having maintained that the "act of intelligible thought," and hence "the intellective soul, is in one respect united to the body and in another respect separate therefrom."[235] In the strict sense, the human intellective soul, being incorporeal and having no "corporeal organ," is plainly not something "united to the body as a form, giving existence [*dans esse*] to the body" and actually present therein "like shape in wax."[236] And yet, although "the intellective soul is, in its being, separate from the body, . . . in its operation [*in operando*] . . . it is united [with the body], because it thinks nothing without a body and without an image [in the imaginative faculty]."[237] In the sense, then, that it *operates* through the body, but in that restricted sense alone, the intellective soul may—according to Siger's account of the view of Aristotle—be "called" the body's "form" or "entelechy."[238]

230Ibid. 20. *Final perfection* apparently means perfection accruing to an individual, thanks to its belonging to a class. Above, pp. 279, 288, Averroes uses the terms *final perfection* and *final entelechy* in the more normal sense of the realization of the potentiality represented by the *first* perfection or entelechy.

231Van Steenberghen 364–74.

232Van Steenberghen 99; Nardi, *Sigieri di Brabante nel pensiero del Rinascimento italiano* 33. Mandonnet 1 (n. 203 above) 175, on the contrary, takes it to be the target of Aquinas' *De unitate intellectus* and hence prior to 1270.

233Siger, *De anima intellectiva* (n. 211 above) 89–90. See ibid. 93: "Nothing prevents what is necessary and eternal from having a cause of its necessity and eternity."

234Ibid. 89–95.

235Ibid. 80.

236Ibid. 78.

237Ibid. 84.

238Ibid. 87.

Concerning a second critical question, "whether the intellective soul is rendered multiple by virtue of the multiplicity of human bodies" or whether a single such soul serves all mankind, Siger's *De anima intellectiva* professes uncertainty. Siger is uncertain what the "Philosopher [Aristotle] thought"; and he is equally uncertain in which direction "natural reason" points, since arguments can be mustered on each side. On one side stands the convincing argument that nothing whose nature is "separate from matter" and "existent through itself" can be enumerated, whence it would follow that the "intellective soul" is not subject to enumeration. Yet countervailing arguments can also be adduced—for example, the argument that if all men had the same intellect they would have identical knowledge.[239]

Siger's *De anima intellectiva* thus treats both questions, the question of the intellective soul as the body's form and the question of the unity of all such souls, cautiously; he states only Aristotle's position, and not his own, on the first and does not even venture to decide what Aristotle's position was on the second. He, moreover, offers his obeisance to the Church on both. If the "position of the holy Catholic faith" opposes the "position of the Philosopher" on the issue of the intellective soul as the human form, he "willingly" bows to faith.[240] And he similarly defers to the Church on the unity of the human intellective soul. His philosophic treatment of this question is prefaced with the words: "According to the [Catholic] truth, which cannot be false, intellective souls are undoubtedly rendered multiple through the multiplicity of human bodies."[241] The discussion ends with the milder declaration that since rational arguments can be adduced on both sides of the issue and since Aristotle's view is unclear, "adherence ought to be given to faith, which surpasses all human reason."[242] Modern scholars have differed, and will surely continue to differ, in assessing the sincerity or disingenuousness of Siger's submission to orthodox belief.[243]

One further work carrying Siger's name, the *Quaestiones super librum de Causis*, is not primarily concerned with the human intellect but does devote a section to it.[244] Siger there finds that the "intellective soul" is the "perfection [or: entelechy] and form of the body," without any reservation to the effect that the intellect is the human form solely in some loose sense.[245] More startling, the present text sets forth arguments in favor of, and opposed to, the thesis that there "is one intellect" for "all men"; observes that the "Commentator [Averroes] . . . took intellect to be one in number" for "all men"; professes uncertainty as to Aristotle's view; observes that in any event, "whatever he

[239]Ibid. 101–2, 107–8.
[240]Ibid. 88.
[241]Ibid. 101.
[242]Ibid. 108.
[243]See Van Steenberghen (n. 202 above) 243–52.
[244]Ibid. 377–83.
[245]Siger, *Quaestiones super librum de causis*, ed. A. Marlasca (Louvain 1972) 106.

[Aristotle] thought, he was a man and could err"; and then concludes flatly that the unity of the human intellect is "heretical in our faith and irrational" to boot. All Catholic Christians therefore "should steadfastly believe that it [the potential human intellect] is rendered multiple through the multiplicity of men."[246]

To recapitulate: Critiques and condemnations disclose the presence in thirteenth-century Paris of philosophers who followed Averroes' Long Commentary on the *De anima* and construed the human material, or potential, intellect as a separate—that is to say, incorporeal—substance common to all mankind. The philosophic and ecclesiastical critiques reveal that Averroes' Latin adherents went beyond the express words of the Long Commentary. Most notably, the thesis that the potential intellect is not properly the human *form*, at best an implication to be drawn from Averroes, was prominent from the start. Siger of Brabant, the only certifiable target of the anti-Averroistic fulminations, propounded the theory of a single, common incorporeal material intellect in two works; in a third work, he attributed the theory to Aristotle, while deferring, for his own part, to the Catholic faith; and finally in a fourth work, he recanted completely, pronouncing the unity of the human potential intellect to be unacceptable on rational and theological grounds. As for the issue of man's proper form, each of Siger's four works handles it differently. The first of the four affirms that the potential intellect "perfects the body" through the intellect's "power" but not through its "substance," thereby implying that the potential human intellect is not truly man's form. The second, which is lost, reportedly maintained that potential intellect is "primarily and essentially" the form of the human *species* inasmuch as it furnishes existence to mankind as a whole; nevertheless, inasmuch as the potential intellect furnishes existence to *individuals* in cooperation with the human cogitative faculty, it is "accidentally" the actuality, perfection, and form, of individual men. The third work attributes to Aristotle, without itself endorsing, the proposition that the potential intellect can be called the human form in the attenuated sense of *operating* through the body, although it is not truly the body's form. The fourth work, in which Siger recants his Averroism, declares the potential intellect to be man's form, without reservation.

Between 1281 and 1284, Siger was assassinated in Italy by a "somewhat demented" companion.[247] Despite his apparent recantation and violent death, the doctrines of Averroes' Long Commentary on the *De anima* were borne on high by a line of Christian thinkers extending into the sixteenth century. The tradition survived so long and so stubbornly in the face of repeated attempts to suppress it that its perdurability is no less a sociological than a philosophic phenomenon. Writers belonging to the tradition reason that the possible or potential intellect—or intellective part of the soul, or intellective soul—is separate from matter, that is to say, incorporeal, and eternal; that one potential intellect serves all mankind; that the

[246]Ibid. 108–15.

[247]Mandonnet 1.280–286; Van Steenberghen 159.

potential intellect joins an individual man through his cogitative faculty and through images in his imaginative faculty; and that, as an incorporeal entity serving all mankind, it is the form of an individual man solely in some attenuated sense. Building on those premises, Averroes' adherents wrestle with a private cycle of questions, such as the precise sense in which the potential intellect can be taken as the form of an individual man, the question whether the potential intellect alone constitutes human intellect or whether it does so in partnership with the active intellect, and the question whether the potential intellect is identical with, or related to, a quasi-material moment in the celestial intelligences. Meticulous philosophic investigations are often punctuated with cheerful submission to the Catholic faith. The philosophers involved, so their common protestation goes, have drawn their conclusions as a mere academic exercise and without endorsing them. The construction of the material intellect as a single incorporeal being shared by all mankind, together with the notion of two possibly incompatible truths, one philosophic and the other religious, are the most distinctive doctrines, indeed the defining doctrines, of the movement commonly called Latin Averroism.

The end of the thirteenth century and first quarter of the fourteenth century found the Averroist theory of intellect espoused by the following philosophers, all of whom are known to have been, or can be presumed to have been, active in Paris: the authors of anonymous commentaries on the *De anima*,[248] Giles of Orleans,[249] John of Goettingen,[250] Anthony of Parma,[251] Thomas Wilton,[252] Marsilius of Padua (in very general terms),[253] John of Jandun,[254] and, in some contexts, Walter Burley.[255] During the years 1320–1350, the tradition was transplanted to Bologna, where it found a new, congenial home. The central Averroist positions were repeated, and the cycle of issues was debated, by Angelo of Arezzo,[256]

[248]*Trois commentaires anonymes sur le Traité de l'âme d'Aristote*, ed. M. Giele et al. (Louvain 1971) 75, 513–14 (the preceding section in the latter composition argues the opposite, anti-Averroist position); Z. Kuksewicz, *De Siger de Brabant à Jacques de Plaisance* (Wroclaw 1968) 102–4. Kuksewicz provides extensive and highly valuable extracts from the original texts.

[249]Kuksewicz 100–101.

[250]Ibid. 121–24, 129–30, 138, 140.

[251]Ibid. 149–55, 162, 167, 170.

[252]Ibid. 182, 186.

[253]Ibid. 201.

[254]See immediately below.

[255]A. Maier, *Ausgehendes Mittelalter* 1 (Rome 1964) 107–20; Kuksewicz 245–47. A. Uña Juárez, "Aristotles y Averroes en el siglo xiv," *Antonianum* 52 (1977) 689–94, cites passages where Burley apparently rejects Averroes' theory of intellect. Z. Kuksewicz, "The Problem of Walter Burley's Averroism," *Studi sul xiv secolo in memoria di Anneliese Maier* (Rome 1981) 341–377, cites passages to show that Burley took different stances on the human material intellect in different contexts, and one stance was unambiguously Averroistic. Burley was reportedly in Bologna in 1341; see Maier 120.

[256]M. Grabmann, *Mittelalterliches Geistesleben* 2 (Munich 1936) 267; Kuksewicz (n. 248 above) 318.

Thaddeus of Parma,[257] and Jacob of Placentia.[258] As already seen, the Averroist theory of intellect elicited opposition almost from its first appearance in a Latin setting. Apart from Bonaventure, Aquinas, and William of Baglione, the thirteenth- and fourteenth-century critics included Albert,[259] Giles of Rome,[260] William of la Mare,[261] John Peckham,[262] Peter of Trabes,[263] Raymond Lull,[264] Duns Scotus,[265] Simon of Faversham (early fourteenth-century Oxford),[266] and William of Alnwick (early fourteenth-century Bologna).[267] The church added its formal condemnation at the Council of Vienne in 1311.

The most influential and best known of the thirteenth- and fourteenth-century Averroists was John of Jandun. He was the primary link in the transmission of Averroist thought from Paris to the Bolognese and subsequent schools,[268] and centuries later was still studied, his commentary on Aristotle's *De anima* being published several times in the sixteenth century. And he was the quintessential Latin Averroist. He explores the characteristic issues, adopts the characteristic attitudes, and defends the characteristic positions, often echoing the language of Siger's Averroist phase and, on one of the central questions,[269] explicitly naming Siger as an authority.

Jandun knows Alexander of Aphrodisias through the "Commentator Averroes" and, following Averroes' Long Commentary on the *De anima* as well as Siger, he puts an extreme materialist interpretation on that ancient philosopher. Alexander, he reports, held that the finely modulated "composition and mixture of [physical]

[257]Thaddeus, *Quaestiones de anima*, ed. S. Vanni Rovighi (Milan 1951) q. 4, 29; q. 5, 53–63; Kuksewicz (n. 248 above) 319–21, 338.

[258]Kuksewicz (n. 248 above) 353–56, 358, 360, 362–63, 370, 393–94.

[259]Mandonnet 2 (n. 204 above) 30–35.

[260]Giles of Rome, *Errores philosophorum*, ed. J. Koch and trans. J. Riedl (Milwaukee 1944) 22–23; *De plurificatione intellectus possibilis* (not available to me).

[261]C. Krzanic, "Grandi lottatori contro l'Averroismo," *Rivista di filosofia neo-scolastica* 22 (1930) 172–73.

[262]John Peckham, *Quaestiones tractantes de anima*, in *Beiträge zur Geschichte der Philosophie des Mittelalters* 19.5–6, ed. H. Spettmann (Münster 1918) 38–40, 49; Krzanic 179–80.

[263]Krzanic 203–5.

[264]O. Keicher, "Raymundus Lullus und seine Stellung zur arabischen Philosophie," in *Beiträge zur Geschichte der Philosophie des Mittelalters* 7.4–5 (Münster 1909) 53, 130, 133–35.

[265]Duns Scotus, *Opus oxoniense* 4.43.2; in Duns Scotus, *Philosophical Writings*, ed. A. Wolter (Edinburgh 1962) 137–38.

[266]D. Sharp, "Simonis de Faversham: *Quaestiones super tertium de anima*," *Archives d'histoire doctrinale et littéraire* 9 (1934) 321–22, 327–29.

[267]Maier (n. 255) 1–22.

[268]Vanni Rovighi (n. 257 above) xiii; S. MacClintock, *Perversity and Error* (Bloomington 1956) 8–9.

[269]John of Jandun, *Super libros Aristotelis de anima* (Venice 1587) 3, q. 5, col. 245. John quotes from the *De anima intellectiva*, but calls it *De intellectu*.

elements in the human body" brings forth from itself "this marvelous and noble [material] form, namely, the intellect." Hand in hand therewith goes the proposition that the human intellect is man's *substantial* form: "Alexander's opinion" was that "the intellective soul is the substantial form giving existence . . . to the human body, and it is joined to the body in respect to existence, like the shape in wax."[270] "Aristotle and the Commentator [Averroes]," by contrast, concluded that since the human intellective soul is "separate" from the body, it is not the factor "giving specific substantial existence [*esse*]" to man and hence not the "substantial form of the human body." From the philosophically correct standpoint, the potential human intellect can accordingly be termed human *form* only in a loose sense, insofar as the potential intellect is a factor "operating within" man through "images" in the "imaginative" or "cogitative" faculty of the soul.[271]

Such, according to John of Jandun, were the conclusions of Aristotle and Averroes on the question of the potential intellect as human form. On the other perennial question, the unity of the human potential intellect, those two preeminent philosophers—John reports—established that "one intellect" serves all men, that it is "not rendered multiple or numerable through the multiplicity of bodies," and that "all men think through" the same, single potential intellect.[272] Opponents had of course argued the contrary thesis, but after examining the counterarguments meticulously, Jandun determines that the Averroist position "cannot be shaken by demonstrative reasoning."[273] Whereupon, having made an uncompromising case for both the unity of the human intellect and its not being the human form, Jandun pays conventional obeisance to the "Catholic position." On the grounds of "mere faith," he declares that the human intellect is not after all "one in number for the whole of mankind," that it is after all "enumerated . . . by virtue of human bodies' being enumerated," that it is "the perfection [and form] giving existence" to the human body. Whatever one may think about other Averroists' sincerity, John of Jandun's tongue is set unmistakably in cheek. Nothing could be more bitingly sarcastic than his remark: "I cannot prove" the Catholic belief "through any demonstrative argument, because I do not know that such is possible. Should anyone know that proving it is possible, let him rejoice!"[274]

The Bolognese tradition was by no means the swan song of Averroes' theory of human intellect in the Latin world. At Erfurt in the fourteenth century, two philosophers are known to have upheld the Long Commentary's theory of human intellect—a single incorporeal potential intellect serving all mankind; and in the subsequent century, a professor at the University of Kraków added his

[270] Ibid. cols. 234–35; MacClintock 56–58; above, p. 307.

[271] John of Jandun cols. 239–41; above, p. 307.

[272] Ibid. q. 7, col. 258.

[273] Ibid. col. 269.

[274] Ibid. cols. 269–70; cf. q. 5, col. 246.

endorsement.[275] But in the fifteenth and sixteenth centuries, the hotbed of Latin Averroism was northern Italy and especially Padua. Fresh humanist zephyrs were supposed to be blowing away the medieval cobwebs, yet an impressive series of fifteenth- and sixteenth-century Italian philosophers continued to analyze and defend an Averroist theory of intellect. They include Paul of Venice,[276] Nicoletto Vernias (at least in his early career),[277] Alexander Achillini,[278] Tiberio Bacielieri,[279] Agostino Nifo (in his early career),[280] Geronimo Taiapietra,[281] Marcantonio Zimara,[282] Marcantonio Genua,[283] and Antonio Bernardi della Mirandola.[284] Philosophic and ecclesiastical opposition naturally enough also continued.[285] And at the turn of the sixteenth century, Pietro Pomponazzi struck out upon a new tack; he rejected Averroes' position and argued for a materialist conception of the human intellect in the spirit of Alexander of Aphrodisias.[286] He and his followers were, appropriately, styled Alexandrians.[287]

[275]Z. Kuksewicz, "Commentarium super Libros *De anima* by an Anonymous Averroist," *Studia mediewistyczne* 17 (1977) 69–70; Kuksewicz, "L'influence d'Averroès sur les universités en Europe centrale," in *Multiple Averroès*, ed. J. Jolivet (Paris 1978) 276–77, 279–80; Kuksewicz (n. 248 above) 466–67.

[276]Nardi, *Sigieri di Brabante nel pensiero del Rinascimento italiano* (n. 228 above) 125–27; repr. in Nardi, *Saggi sull' Aristotelismo Padovano* (Florence 1958) 86–88.

[277]Nardi, *Saggi* 99, 108–9; E. Mahoney, "Nicoletto Vernia on the Soul and Immortality," in *Philosophy and Humanism* (Kristeller Festschrift), ed. E. Mahoney (Leiden 1976) 145–49.

[278]Nardi, *Sigieri di Brabante nel pensiero del Rinascimento italiano* 71–76; repr. in *Saggi* 205–10; also *Saggi* 230.

[279]Nardi, *Sigieri di Brabante nel pensiero del Rinascimento italiano* 141–44.

[280]Ibid. 21. E. Mahoney, "Agostino Nifo's Early Views on Immortality," *Journal of the History of Philosophy* 8 (1970) 453–55, understands that Nifo merely credited Averroes' interpretation of Aristotle as an accurate interpretation, without committing himself to it as a correct account of the human intellect.

[281]Nardi, *Saggi* 302–5; F. Lucchetta, "Recenti studi sull' Averroismo padovano," in *L'Averroismo in Italia* (Rome 1979) 116.

[282]Nardi, *Saggi* 349–52.

[283]Ibid. 452.

[284]Nardi, *Sigieri di Brabante nel pensiero del Rinascimento italiano* 157–58.

[285]Renan (n. 27 above) 364–66, 390–91, 430–31; Nardi, *Sigieri di Brabante nel pensiero del Rinascimento italiano* 45, and *Saggi* 98, 101, 109, 357; Lucchetta 113, 119.

[286]P. Pomponazzi, *De immortalitate animae*, ed. G. Morra (Bologna 1954) 48–69, 144–45; English translation in E. Cassirer, P. Kristeller, and J. Randall, *Renaissance Philosophy of Man* (Chicago 1948) 286–97, 334. Pomponazzi dealt with the question of the nature of the human intellect in several works, written over a number of years. On one reading, he took ever more materialist views of the human intellect; see Randall 276; B. Nardi, *Studi su Pietro Pomponazzi* (Florence 1965) 21–23, 149–70, 182–99. But a more recent study of his thought finds that he was a follower of Alexander at an early date; see A. Poppi, *Saggi sul pensiero di Pietro Pomponazzi* (Padua 1970) 45–46, 90–91. Poppi 50, quotes from a contemporary of Pomponazzi who had sentiments similar to his regarding Alexander.

[287]For the term *Alexandrians*, see Renan (n. 27 above) 402–3, and Randall, *Renaissance Philosophy of Man* 266.

The positions at which Averroes arrived in the last stage of his thought and which he put forward tentatively and hesitatingly in his Long Commentary on the *De anima*, positions completely ignored in the Arabic world and virtually unknown in Jewish circles, thus helped mold European philosophy for an astonishing stretch of three centuries.

8

Averroes on the Active Intellect as the Cause of Human Thought

The Passage of the Human Intellect to Actuality

Although he repeatedly revised his position on the active intellect's role as a cause of sublunar existence,[1] Averroes remained firm throughout his career regarding the active intellect's nature. Like his predecessors among the Arabic Aristotelians, he consistently construed it as an incorporeal substance transcending the human soul; and he took for granted that it is the last link—or, in his Long Commentary on the *De anima*, which raises the material intellect to the status of the last of the eternal incorporeal substances, the penultimate link—in the hierarchy of incorporeal intelligences.

To establish the transcendent character of the active intellect, Averroes' various works adduce what was already a commonplace argument. As Averroes puts the reasoning in one passage, anything passing to a state of actuality cannot do so "by itself" and therefore needs an agent or "mover that will lead it from potentiality to actuality." Since the human material intellect does become actual, the material intellect needs such an agent. Since, moreover, any agent, or "mover, gives to that which is moved only the likes of what it has in its own substance," the agent leading the human potentiality for thought to actuality must have actual intelligible thought in its substance. It must be "an [actual] intellect."[2] The context of this

[1] Above, chap. 6.

[2] Averroes, Epitome of the *De anima*, published as *Talkhīṣ Kitāb al-Nafs*, ed. A. Ahwani (Cairo 1950) 88; Spanish translation: *La psicologia de Averroes*, trans. S. Gomez Nogales (Madrid 1987) 212. (I have simplified the reasoning for the incorporeal character of the active intellect.) Similarly in: Averroes, *Drei Abhandlungen über die Conjunction*, ed. and German trans. J. Hercz (Berlin 1869), Hebrew text 3, 11; German translation 3, 51. Latin reworking of the same text (see above, p. 264): *Averrois Tractatus de animae beatitudine*, printed in vol. 9 of *Aristotelis opera cum Averrois commentariis* (Venice 1562–1574, reprinted in Frankfurt 1962). Averroes, Middle Commentary on the *De anima*, Arabic text in Hebrew characters, Paris, Bibliothèque Nationale, Hebrew MS 1009, 146b; medieval Hebrew translation: Paris, Bibliothèque Nationale MS 947, 221b. Averroes, Commentary on Alexander's *De intellectu* (medieval Hebrew translation from the Arabic, which is lost), ed. H. Davidson, *Shlomo Pines Jubilee Volume* 1 (Jerusalem 1988) 214 (the argument is put in Alexander's mouth).

particular passage does not require Averroes to identify the active intellect's place within the incorporeal hierarchy, but he does so elsewhere.[3]

As for the manner in which the active intellect leads the human material intellect to actuality, two models were available from which Averroes could choose. Alfarabi, deploying an analogy that had been suggested by Aristotle and developed by his followers, portrayed the active intellect as emitting a kind of light, which affects both images in the imaginative faculty and the human material intellect itself. When the analogue of light illumines the potentially intelligible images as well as the potentially thinking material intellect, it renders them actual; the intellect discerns intelligible thoughts—basic principles of thought according to some of Alfarabi's writings, and concepts according to his *Risāla fī al-ᶜAql*—which are latent in the images.[4] Avicenna found, by contrast, that images in the imaginative faculty merely prepare the human intellect for receiving intelligible thoughts, whereas the thoughts themselves—which include abstract concepts of all natural objects and at least some propositions—are emanated directly by the active intellect upon properly disposed human intellects.[5]

Averroes, in all stages of his career, follows the lines of Alfarabi's explanation, although without troubling himself with the distinction between the source of light and light emitted by the source. He writes, for example: "The active intellect" functions, "in a certain sense," as "light" does. Natural light "transforms [potential] colors [in the surface of a physical object] into actual colors" and also "imparts to the pupil of the eye" the quality of "transparency" (*ishfāf*),[6] which allows it to see them. "Similarly," the active intellect renders "individual impressions in the imaginative faculty . . . actually intelligible" and also "imparts to the material intellect something analogous to transparency," which enables the material intellect to "receive intelligible thoughts."[7] By illuminating both the material intellect and the intelligible thoughts latent in images, the active intellect enables the material intellect to behold the intelligible thoughts and think them. The intelligible thoughts spoken of here are presumably concepts, rather than propositions, since they are compared to colors and not to judgments about colors. Other compositions of Averroes represent the active intellect either as a light that illuminates images in the imaginative faculty,[8] or as a light that illuminates the human intellect itself.[9]

[3]*Compendio de Metafisica*, ed. and Spanish trans. C. Quirós Rodríguez (Madrid 1919) (henceforth cited as: Epitome of the *Metaphysics*) 4, §62; German translation: *Die Epitome der Metaphysik des Averroes*, trans. S. van den Bergh (Leiden 1924) 136.

[4]Above, pp. 51, 69.

[5]Above, pp. 88, 90, 93.

[6]Regarding transparency in the eye as a condition for vision, see Aristotle, *De sensu* 2; J. Beare, *Greek Theories of Elementary Cognition* (Oxford 1906) 85–86; above, p. 68.

[7]Middle Commentary on the *De anima*, Arabic text 146b; Hebrew translation 221a–b.

[8]*Drei Abhandlungen* (n. 2 above), Hebrew text 11–12; German translation 51–52.

[9]Ibid., Hebrew text 3; German translation 3; Averroes, Commentary on *De intellectu* (n. 2 above) 213, 214.

Averroes' fullest account of the active intellect's effect on the material intellect is naturally enough found in the work containing his fullest overall treatment of soul and intellect—the Long Commentary on the *De anima*. As was seen in the previous chapter, the Long Commentary is the composition that construes the material intellect as a single incorporeal substance serving all mankind.

From the circumstance that man passes from the potentiality for thinking intelligible thoughts to actually thinking them, the Long Commentary draws the familiar inference and deduces the existence of an "active intellect," which "makes what is potentially intelligible, actually intelligible."[10] Since every agent producing something has in itself the actual character it produces, since the active intellect "produces all intelligible forms [intelligible thoughts]," and since intelligible thoughts are free of matter, the active intellect must likewise be "separate" from matter, that is to say, incorporeal.[11] The manner whereby the active intellect enables the human intellect to think intelligible thoughts resembles the process whereby light renders colors visible. "Just as vision is not moved by colors until they have become actual, a situation occurring only when light is present, light being that which leads colors from potentiality to actuality, so too notions [*intentiones=ma^{c}ānī*] in the imaginative faculty do not move the material intellect until they have become actually intelligible." Images in the imaginative faculty are rendered actually intelligible through the presence of something "that is actual intellect," in other words, through an active intellect that illuminates the images.[12]

What the Long Commentary on the *De anima* has said so far is routine. When that work expands on the analogy of light, it introduces a new twist.

"The active intellect," Averroes writes, stands to the potential, or material, intellect as "light to the transparent [*diaffonum*]"; and "material forms [in the imaginative faculty]" stand to the material intellect

> as color to the transparent. For just as light is the entelechy [*perfectio*] of the transparent, so the active intellect is the entelechy of the material [intellect]. Just as the transparent is not moved by color nor receives it unless illuminated, so the material intellect does not receive intelligible thoughts of objects in the physical world except when it [the material intellect] is perfected and illuminated by the active intellect. And just as light renders potential color actual and capable of moving the transparent, so the active intellect renders notions [in the imaginative faculty] which

[10]Averroes, *Commentarium magnum in Aristotelis de Anima libros*, ed. F. Crawford (Cambridge, Mass. 1953) (henceforth cited as: Long Commentary on the *De anima*) 438. The Arabic translation of Aristotle's *De anima* 3.5.430a, 10–15, on which Averroes is commenting here, gives a double translation of the words: "[an intellect] by virtue of making all things, a sort of habitus, like light." Averroes accordingly reads the passage in Aristotle as referring to three, and not two, aspects of intellect, namely, material intellect, intellect *in habitu*, and active intellect.

[11]Long Commentary on the *De anima* 441.

[12]Ibid. 439.

are potentially intelligible, actual and capable of being received by the material intellect.[13]

Light, Averroes is stating, prepares the ground for vision by doing two things. It illuminates potential colors, thereby transforming them into actual colors and making them actually visible; and it attaches itself to, and illuminates the "transparent," thereby permitting the *transparent* to receive actually visible colors. The active intellect exercises an analogous effect on images in the imaginative faculty of the soul and on the material intellect.

At first reading, one might suppose that Averroes is again comparing the material intellect to the eye and saying that the active intellect illuminates the material intellect in the way light illuminates the eye, renders it transparent, and enables it to see. The passage does not, however, mention the eye, and, as far as I could discover, no comparison of the material intellect to an eye is drawn in the Long Commentary on the *De anima*. The key to the passage lies in the clause: "light is the entelechy of the transparent." In analyzing the phenomenon of vision, Aristotle's *De anima* determined that both the eye itself and the medium extending from the eye to the object seen must be illuminated; and he explained that when the medium is illuminated it becomes "receptive of color." Those observations helped him formulate a definition of light. "Light," on the definition, is the "actuality of . . . the transparent [medium] insofar as [it is a] transparent [medium]"[14] For example, if air is the medium, light is the entelechy of the air insofar as it is a transparent medium, although not insofar as it is air. When Averroes' Long Commentary comes upon the definition of light in the course of interpreting Aristotle's *De anima*, Averroes rephrases it slightly, writing: "The essence of light is the entelechy [*perfectio*] of the transparent [medium], insofar as [it is a] transparent [medium]."[15]

The Long Commentary's statement that "just as light is the entelechy of the transparent, so the active intellect is the entelechy of the material [intellect]" accordingly affirms that the active intellect stands to the material intellect as light stands to the medium, not as light stands to the eye. After he construed the material intellect as an incorporeal substance that does not attach itself to man "essentially and primarily,"[16] Averroes apparently could no longer accept the comparison of the material intellect to an animal organ. He therefore compares the material intellect not to the eye, but instead to the medium, which is distinct from the seeing subject. The Long Commentary on the *De anima* was, in the previous chapter, seen to describe the material intellect as the "recipient in the thought process."[17] Averroes

[13]Ibid. 410–11; cf. also 499.

[14]Aristotle, *De anima* 2.7.418b, 9–10, 26–27. Alfarabi mentioned the transparent visual medium in one of his analogies between a source of light and the active intellect; see above, p. 68.

[15]Long Commentary on the *De anima* 236.

[16]Above, p. 289.

[17]Above, p. 292.

is now telling us that the material intellect is the recipient in the way the medium in the visual process receives color.

The material intellect thus receives intelligible thoughts as the transparent visual medium receives colors, and the material intellect enables the individual human soul to become conscious of intelligible thoughts as the transparent visual medium presents colors to the eye and enables the eye to see them. Comparing the material intellect to the visual medium, rather than to the eye, does not, as will appear, exclude the material intellect's having its own thoughts of the physical world.[18]

Aristotle had located both aspects of intellect, the potential and the active, "in" the soul,[19] while Averroes' Long Commentary on the *De anima* construes both the active and material, or potential, intellects as eternal substances existing independently of human souls. To resolve the apparent discrepancy between its position and Aristotle's, the Long Commentary locates the functions performed with the aid of the two intellects, and not the two intellects themselves, in the human soul. Actual thought, Averroes writes, comes about thanks to an act of abstraction performed through the active intellect, and an act of reception performed through the material intellect. Both the "operations, . . . [of] abstracting intelligible thoughts and [of receiving and] thinking them," are "subject to our will."[20] Falling as they do under the control of the human will, both operations therefore occur "within us, . . . even though the agent and recipient are eternal substances."[21] The question that cries out for an answer, namely, how a transient human soul can induce the eternal active intellect and eternal material intellect to do its bidding, is never addressed.

The Long Commentary on the *De anima* maintains, then, much as other works of Averroes did, that the active intellect illuminates both the material intellect and images in the imaginative faculty of the soul; and the result is actual human abstract thoughts, that is, concepts. The material intellect is now compared, however, to the

[18]Below, p. 333. Also above, p. 292.

[19]Aristotle, *De anima* 3.5.430a, 13. Above, p. 12.

[20]Cf. Aristotle, *De anima* 2.5.417b, 23–24.

[21]Long Commentary on the *De anima* (n. 10 above) 439 and also 406. In *Iggeret Efsharut ha-Debequt* (Arabic original lost), ed. and trans. K. Bland (New York 1982) as *Epistle on the Possibility of Conjunction with the Active Intellect*, §6, Averroes states that the active intellect penetrates the material intellect and works from within, its "status over against the material intellect" resembling that of a "potter . . . penetrating into clay, as Themistius wrote" or that of "the form of fire in the burning object, as Alexander drew the analogy." For Themistius, see above, p. 27. The reference to Alexander may be an interpretation of the passage quoted above, p. 23. Averroes, Long Commentary on the *Metaphysics* 12, comm. 17; Arabic text: *Tafsīr mā ba*c*da al-Ṭabī*c*a*, ed. M. Bouyges (Beirut 1938–1948) 1489–90, describes the interaction of the active intellect and material intellect, but both the text and description are problematic. English translation of Long Commentary on *Metaphysics* Book 12, with pagination of Arabic indicated: C. Genequand, *Ibn Rushd's Metaphysics* (Leiden 1984). French translation of same, with pagination of the Arabic indicated: A. Martin, *Averroès, Grand commentaire de la Métaphysique d'Aristote* (Paris 1984).

medium in vision rather than to the sense organ; it is through the medium of the material intellect that the human soul gains intelligible thoughts of objects in the physical world. Although the active intellect and the material intellect are, in the constructions placed on them by the Long Commentary, eternal substances existing independently of the human soul, the processes of abstracting, receiving, and thinking human thoughts are initiated by the human will and can therefore be described as taking place within the soul.

A final passage deserving attention adds a few more brush strokes to the picture. The passage states that "intelligible thoughts come about in man in two ways." One of the two ways gives rise to the "first principles of thought, of which we know neither when, whence, nor how they come about."[22] The other gives rise to the "intelligible thoughts" that are derived "from already known principles [of thought]." Averroes expressly calls thoughts of the former sort "propositions" (*propositiones*); and thoughts of the latter sort, being derived from the first principles, are undoubtedly propositions as well. He therefore appears to be supplementing his previous account of the origin of abstract concepts with an account of the origin of propositions.[23] The first principles of thought, he goes on, come about "naturally," that is, with no exercise of will, and they are given "by . . . an incorporeal intelligence, the active intellect." Intelligible thoughts belonging to the other class come about by "an exercise of will," and are "produced from already known principles [of thought] and the active intellect."[24] Averroes further notes, as he had when treating abstract concepts, that these "theoretical thoughts"—the two sorts of proposition—"are joined to us through forms in the imaginative faculty."[25]

The overall picture painted by the Long Commentary is, in sum, that the active intellect bestows the first principles of thought upon man without any human effort or exercise of will. Through an exercise of will, the human soul can induce the eternal transcendent active intellect to illuminate both images in the imaginative faculty and also the eternal material intellect, which is joined to man in a nonessential fashion. The material intellect thereby receives actual concepts, in the way that the medium in the visual process receives actual colors, and concepts are made available for the soul to contemplate. The human soul can in addition exercise its will and induce the active intellect to help it derive secondary propositions from the first principles. Both concepts and propositions are linked to the soul through images in the imaginative faculty, and it is through those images that the soul becomes conscious of both concepts and propositions.

None of what the Long Commentary on the *De anima* has said about the active intellect's role in human thought is especially original. The Long Commentary has

[22]See above, pp. 51, 84, 267.

[23]Long Commentary on the *De anima* 455, commenting on Aristotle, *De anima* 3.6.430a, 26, refers to the "well-known" dichotomy of *concept* and *proposition*.

[24]Ibid. 496. On 496–497, Averroes calls the first principles of thought "intellect *in habitu*."

[25]Ibid. 500.

taken commonplaces about the active intellect, which Averroes' earlier works also adduced, elaborated them a bit, and adapted them to accommodate an eternal material intellect.

The Possibility of Conjunction with the Active Intellect; Immortality

Conjunction. Earlier chapters uncovered several issues that dogged Averroes throughout his philosophic career. One further issue with which he struggled continually was the possibility of the human intellect's having the active intellect as a direct object of thought and thereby entering into *conjunction* (*ittiṣāl*) with the active intellect. Besides taking the issue up in his commentaries on Aristotle and his commentary on Alexander's *De intellectu*, Averroes devoted three opuscules—assuming him to be, in fact, the author of all three—specifically to conjunction.[26]

The only peg in Aristotle to which the twin phenomena—the human intellect's having the active intellect as an object of thought, and its conjoining with the active intellect—could attach themselves was hardly sturdy. Aristotle's *De anima* made the promise: "Whether or not . . . intellect . . . can, when not itself separate from [spatial] magnitude [that is, when linked to a human body], think anything separate [that is, incorporeal] has to be considered later."[27] None of Aristotle's preserved works consider the matter again.[28] To extract from Aristotle's words the doctrines we are concerned with here, one must assume that the implied answer to the question he posed is affirmative, that the human intellect can accordingly have an incorporeal intellect, and the active intellect in particular, as a direct object of thought, and that the human intellect can, by virtue of being identical with whatever it thinks, become identical with, or perhaps to some lesser degree conjoin with, the active intellect. Averroes, for his part, was not always sure what Aristotle's promise even meant,[29] and he learned about the subject not from Aristotle but from Aristotle's successors.

A number of post-Aristotelian voices affirmed the possibility of the human intellect's having the active intellect as an object of thought and the possibility of its conjoining with the active intellect. Alexander's *De anima* taught that the human

[26]For the bibliographical information, see above, p. 264.

[27]Aristotle, *De anima* 3.7. 431b, 17–19.

[28]Aristotle, *De memoria* 450a, 7–9, however, implies a negative answer to the question posed in *De anima* 3.7.

[29]Long Commentary on the *De anima* 480–81. When composing the Long Commentary, Averroes used two translations of Aristotle's *De anima*, which did not agree on the passage in question. In *Drei Abhandlungen* (n. 2 above), Hebrew text 7; German translation 30, Averroes alludes to the passage in Aristotle, with the statement: "In the *De anima*," Aristotle "promised to investigate the question [of conjunction], . . . but his discussion has not been preserved." *Epistle on the Possibility of Conjunction* (n. 21 above) §13, 101–2, also takes the Aristotelian passage to be a promise of a later discussion of conjunction.

intellect may have the active intellect as a direct object of thought at some point in its development and "in a sense" thereby become identical with the active intellect.[30] The *De intellectu* attributed to Alexander indicated in certain passages that the active intellect becomes an object of human thought as a condition of human intellectual activity, and in one passage maintained that the human intellect has "things intelligible by their nature as an object of thought" at the culmination of its development.[31] Themistius posited an intertwining of the active intellect with the human material intellect as a prerequisite of all human thought; and when discussing the possibility of man's having incorporeal substances as an object of thought, he put forward the following a fortiori argument: Since the human intellect "can think forms mixed with matter [that is, forms of physical objects, which have to be abstracted from their material substrata], it plainly is more likely to be such as to think incorporeal things," which are intelligible by their nature and are ready to be thought without having to be abstracted.[32] Alfarabi and Ibn Bājja held that at the culmination of its development, the human intellect has the active intellect as an object of thought and conjoins with the active intellect.[33] Avicenna understood conjunction with the active intellect to be a prerequisite for all human thought, but in addition he too recognized a culminating state in which the human intellect enters into a "perfect" and "permanent conjunction" with the active intellect. And he also recognized the possibility of the human intellect's having the active intellect as an object of thought.[34] The positions taken by these philosophers were not in complete harmony. Alfarabi and Avicenna, for example, did not view conjunction as a consequence of having the active intellect as an object of thought, and they stressed that human intellects in conjunction with the active intellect remain distinct from it. Ibn Bājja did take conjunction to be a consequence of having the active intellect as an object of thought. And he held fast to the rule that intellect is identical with whatever thought it thinks, and therefore concluded that a human intellect having the active intellect as an object of thought and hence conjoined with the active intellect is rendered identical with the active intellect. Notwithstanding the differences, Averroes heard a choir of support for the possibility of both of the phenomena we are considering.

Alfarabi's Commentary on the *Nicomachean Ethics* was the only dissenting philosophic voice known to Averroes. Ibn Bājja reported that certain scholars had read Alfarabi's Commentary on the *Nicomachean Ethics* as rejecting the immortality of the human soul[35]; Ibn Ṭufail expressly stated that the Commentary on the *Nicomachean Ethics* dismissed immortality as an old wives' tale[36]; and Averroes

[30]Above, pp. 36–37.
[31]Above, pp. 38–39.
[32]See above, pp. 39–40.
[33]Above, pp. 54, 69, 145.
[34]Above, pp. 103–5.
[35]Above, p. 71.
[36]Above, p. 71.

reports that the Commentary on the *Nicomachean Ethics* rejected not just immortality but also the phenomenon that, he understood, brings it about—the conjunction of the human intellect with the active intellect.

Averroes may at first have been unsure about the possibility of the human intellect's having the active intellect as an object of thought and conjoining with it. His Epitome of Aristotle's *Metaphysics* exhibits skepticism about the possibility, and the body of his Epitome of Aristotle's *De anima* broaches the subject without committing itself to one side or the other. By contrast, an appendix to the Epitome of the *De anima*, Averroes' Long Commentary on the *De anima*, his Long Commentary on the *Metaphysics*, and his three opuscules on conjunction all affirm the possibility of the twin phenomena. His Commentary on the *De intellectu* presents the case in favor of the possibility, and tacitly concurs. In each instance, having the active intellect as an object of thought is the means to conjunction, and conjunction is, as in Ibn Bājja, the goal. The meaning Averroes attaches to conjunction varies; and the Long Commentary on the *De anima* in particular, since it construes the human material intellect not as an aspect of the human organism but as a single eternal substance serving all mankind, has to rethink the whole subject. The arguments Averroes advances also vary from work to work, and the ways in which he handles the challenge of Alfarabi's Commentary on the *Nicomachean Ethics* do so as well. Yet once his initial hesitation passes, he tenaciously upholds the possibility of conjunction in some form or other. If it were legitimate to speak of dogmas in Averroes, the possibility of conjunction with the active intellect would rank high on the list.

To define the issue, Averroes adduces the Aristotelian distinction between different senses of *cause*. Three of the four Aristotelian causes[37] come into play. The issue of "conjunction," Averroes writes, comes down to the question whether the active intellect is the cause of the human "material intellect's becoming an actual intellect . . . merely as an *efficient* [cause] and mover, . . . like the light of the sun, which . . . leads [the potential power of vision] to actuality. . . . Or whether perhaps it [also] is a cause as form and end [that is, as a *formal* and *final* cause of the human material intellect], in the way that the incorporeal intelligences stand to the souls of the celestial spheres." The intelligences are the formal causes of the souls of the spheres "inasmuch as . . . the concept [of the intelligence possessed by the soul of each sphere] . . . perfects" the sphere's soul; and they are the final causes of the souls of the spheres inasmuch as the "desire" that the soul of each sphere has "to imitate" the accompanying intelligence motivates the sphere's soul to perform its proper act.[38] The issue of conjunction thus reduces itself to the

[37] Aristotle, *Physics* 2.3.

[38] *Drei Abhandlungen* (n. 2 above), Hebrew text 3–4; German translation 3–5. I have corrected the Hebrew text with the aid of the version in Ibn Tibbon's Commentary on Ecclesiastes, Parma, Hebrew MS 272 (2182). The second of the three *Abhandlungen* defines the issue in similar terms; see *Drei Abhandlungen*, Hebrew text 11; German translation 51. Averroes' Long Commentary on the *De anima* (n. 10 above) 502, does so as well. And the same way of putting the issue is

question whether the human material intellect can ever enter into a relationship with the active intellect wherein the latter becomes the material intellect's formal cause, by virtue of the material intellect's acquiring a concept of the active intellect which becomes its ultimate form, and whether the two can enter into a relationship wherein the active intellect serves as the material intellect's final cause, by inspiring in the material intellect a desire to resemble the active intellect.[39] What is pivotal for Averroes is the first half of the question—whether the active intellect can become the material intellect's formal cause by virtue of the material intellect's acquiring a concept of it. If such should occur, the material intellect would be conjoined with the active intellect.

As already mentioned, Averroes evinces hesitation in his Epitome of the *Metaphysics*. That was a work containing Averroes' early acceptance of the emanation of the incorporeal intelligences from one another and the emanation of a range of sublunar forms from the active intellect.

In the Epitome of the *Metaphysics*, Averroes writes that human concepts have "material things . . . as [their] underlying substratum"; in other words, human concepts are rooted in perceptions of objects belonging to the material realm.[40] Even the "intelligible thought that man has of the principles [that is, of incorporeal substances], he has with reference" to things in the material world; human intelligible thoughts regarding the incorporeal substances grow out of concepts that are rooted in sense perceptions and therefore they too are ultimately rooted in sense perceptions. "Some philosophers [*qawm*] did believe that man's intellect can have a conception of the essence of the active intellect as it truly is, with the result that we would become identical with the active intellect." Should that occur, however, "the effect would become identical with the cause." Averroes is implying the following reasoning: Since intellect is identical with whatever thought it thinks, the human

---

alluded to in Averroes' Long Commentary on the *Metaphysics* 12, comm. 38; Arabic text (n. 21 above) 1612.

[39]The *Epistle on the Possibility of Conjunction* (n. 21 above), which breathes a different spirit from Averroes' other works, also plays on the notion that the active intellect can serve as the human intellect's *final cause*; see ibid. §14, pp. 110–11. *Epistle* §4, and §5, pp. 35–36, defines the issue with the aid of a distinction between *perfection of existence* or *conjunction of existence*, on the one hand, and *perfection of cognition* or *conjunction of cognition* (*hassaga=idrāk*), on the other. Averroes—if we accept the *Epistle* as a genuine work of his—reasons that when one considers any two successive levels in the soul, such as the faculty of sensation and the imaginative faculty, one finds that the lower is perfected by the higher and conjoins with it in respect to *existence*, inasmuch as the lower serves as matter for the higher, which is its form. And the higher is perfected by the lower and conjoins with it in respect to *cognition*, inasmuch as the higher has the lower as an object of perception; the imaginative faculty, for example, has sense perceptions as the object of its perception. The issue of conjunction with the active intellect is reduced to the question whether the human intellect can enjoy conjunction with the active intellect not only in respect to existence but also, despite standing at a level below the active intellect, by having cognition of it.

[40]Cf. above, pp. 266–67.

intellect would, if it had the active intellect as the object of its thought, become identical with the active intellect—and such in fact was Ibn Bājja's stance; but the active intellect is the human intellect's cause, both inasmuch as it emanates human souls endowed with human intellects and as it leads human intellects to actuality; if the human intellect had the active intellect as an object of thought it would consequently become identical with its cause. A few lines later, Averroes treats the possibility of an effect's becoming identical with its cause as absurd.[41] The present composition thus appears to reject the possibility of the human intellect's having the active intellect as an object of thought and thereby conjoining with the active intellect—at least in the sense of becoming identical with the active intellect, which is the only sense Averroes here takes notice of. I did not see why Averroes failed to contemplate the possibility of the human intellect's gaining a concept of the active intellect in the way that the soul of each celestial sphere gains a concept of the corresponding intelligence, while remaining distinct from the intelligence.

In the series of works where Averroes upholds the other side of the issue and does affirm the possibility of conjunction with the active intellect, he borrows arguments from Alexander's *De intellectu*, from Themistius, and from Ibn Bājja.

Averroes' version of the *De intellectu*'s argument[42] begins by assuming three moments in sense perception: "a recipient, that is, the sense faculty; what is received, that is, the perception; and a mover, that is, the actual object of sensation [existing] outside the soul." In the most pertinent instance, vision, the mover and actual object of sensation is light. "There must," by analogy, "be three [moments] of the same sort in intellect: a receptive intellect, . . . that is, the material [human intellect]; an intelligible thought, that is, the theoretical [intellect, to wit, the actual thought present in the human intellect]; and an agent, that is, the incorporeal intellect." The argument, as Averroes fleshes it out, needs two further premises. A premise "entailed by" the analogy between intellect and sense perception "must be added, . . . namely, that since the sense faculty can receive the actual object of sensation [as when the sense of vision perceives light], the potential intellect should be able to receive the actual intellect, that is, the incorporeal [intellect]." And another "premise, to the truth of which everyone assents, must also be added, namely, that everything potential and capable of being something will at some time or other necessarily pass to actuality and become the thing actually"; every

[41]Epitome of the *Metaphysics* (n. 3 above) 4, §48; German translation 127–28. Van den Bergh, n. 4 to p. 127 of the translation, assumes that Averroes is here rejecting conjunction. In the body of the Epitome of the *De anima* (n. 2 above) 89, Spanish translation 213, Averroes writes: "It is believed that having the active intellect as an object of thought is possible for us at the culmination [of our intellectual development]; . . . we would thereby necessarily receive an eternal intelligible thought. . . . This state is what is known as union or conjunction." The text does not take a definite stand on the issue.

[42]For the argument, see above, p. 22. The intent of the original *De intellectu* was almost surely that the human material intellect has what is intelligible by its very nature as an object of thought from the outset, just as light becomes an object of sight as soon as the eye sees.

potentiality is eventually actualized.[43] From the three premises—one of the moments in human thought is an actual incorporeal intellect existing independently of the human intellect and serving as the agent in the thought process, the human intellect has the potentiality of receiving that incorporeal intellect as an object of its thought, and every potentiality is eventually actualized—"the conclusion necessarily follows that at some time a potential [human] intellect will become identical with the actual intellect." Whereas the argument in Alexander's *De intellectu* established that the human material intellect has an actual intellect and, specifically, the active intellect as an object of thought as soon as man begins to think, Averroes understands the argument to establish that the human intellect has the active intellect as an object of thought at its culmination. "The active intellect consequently is cause of the [actualization of the] material intellect not solely as an agent, but also by way of being the material intellect's final perfection, as its form and end [that is, as a formal and final cause]."[44] The material intellect can develop to a point where it gains the active intellect as an object of thought, receives the active intellect as its form, and becomes one with the active intellect.

Averroes offers what he calls "Themistius' . . . true . . . demonstration" of the possibility of conjunction with the active intellect in two versions.[45] The version more faithful to Themistius runs: "If our intellect can think what is not in itself intellect, it should a fortiori be able to think what *is* in itself intellect." That is, if it can have forms that are not intrinsically intelligible and only become so when abstracted from matter as an object of thought, it should a fortiori be able to have the active intellect, which is intrinsically intelligible, as an object of thought. The other version focuses on the object, rather than the subject, of human thought and goes: "Physical beings" are rendered "intelligible [to the human intellect] by the incorporeal intellect"; an agent "gives only what is similar to that which it has in its own substance"; hence the incorporeal intellect that is the cause of the intelligibility of other things, "is more likely to be intelligible [to the human intellect] than what is rendered intelligible through it."[46]

[43]To be more precise, every potentiality in a species will come to actuality in some member, but not necessarily in all members, of the species.

[44]*Drei Abhandlungen* (n. 2 above), Hebrew text 7–8; German translation 31–36. The argument is also given in the companion opuscule, *Drei Abhandlungen*, Hebrew text 10–11; German translation 48–51. There, however, Averroes supplements the argument with additional considerations. Averroes' Commentary on the *De intellectu* (n. 2 above) 215–16, presents the argument, explains why the analogy between sensation and intelligible thought does not show that the human intellect "has the [active] intellect as an object of thought from the outset" but only at the culmination of its development, and tacitly concurs in the argument.

[45]For Themistius' argument, see above, p. 40.

[46]*Drei Abhandlungen*, Hebrew text 7–8; German translation 29, 37–38. The second version of the argument is also given in the companion opuscule, *Drei Abhandlungen*, Hebrew text 12; German translation 52, where Averroes uses it to answer a possible objection to the proof borrowed from the *De intellectu*. Averroes also records the argument, in its original version, in his Epitome of the *De anima* (n. 2 above) 89. In his Long Commentary on the *De anima* 487–

Averroes informs us that Ibn Bājja had two arguments for the possibility of the human intellect's conjoining with the active intellect.[47] The published works of Ibn Bājja preserve only one of the two arguments, and it happens to be the one that attracted most of Averroes' attention. Averroes cites it several times, sometimes, but not always, naming Ibn Bājja as the author, and he once characterizes it as, "by my life, apodictic."[48]

The composition of Averroes' giving the argument most straightforwardly, a composition that happens not to name Ibn Bājja as the source, starts with the proposition: "The proper function of intellect is to render what is accidentally many, essentially one." That is to say, from physical objects belonging to a single species, the human intellect abstracts the common form, which while accidentally many when manifested in the individual members of the species, is essentially and in itself one. Although it recovers the unity latent in plurality, ordinary "intelligible thought . . . is obviously still . . . affected by accidental plurality"; for human concepts are linked to images presented by individual imaginative faculties, "my" concept, "for example, [being linked] to different images from" those to which your concept is linked. After the initial act of abstraction, successively more unified levels of abstraction are, however, possible, and "a time must arrive when the material intellect strips away the [final] aspect of plurality," when it transcends its link to images in a particular imaginative faculty. Individuality then disappears from human thought, and all human intellects think the identical thought that other intellects at the same level think. They all unite in a single thought, which, since it has no link whatsoever to any image, Averroes assumes to be nothing other than an immediate concept of the active intellect.[49] The rationale for this last assumption could be that the active intellect comprises in itself, indeed consists in, a single concept representing the structure of the sublunar world, and the thought man attains at the highest level of abstraction must be exactly the same, all-comprehensive concept.

88, Averroes writes that Themistius' argument is demonstrative only when the material intellect is taken to be an incorporeal being.

[47]Averroes, Epitome of the *De anima* 91; Spanish translation 215–16 (imprecise); Long Commentary on the *De anima* (n. 10 above) 491.

[48]For Ibn Bājja's statement of the argument, see above, p. 145, n. 104.

[49]*Epistle on the Possibility of Conjunction* (n. 21 above) §11, p. 79, without mention of Ibn Bājja. The argument is also given in Averroes' Epitome of the *De anima* 91–94, Spanish translation 216–19, which is an appendix to the body of the Epitome. There Averroes names Ibn Bājja as the author of the argument and characterizes it as "by my life, apodictic," but the preserved texts do not bring the argument to a clear-cut conclusion. The two versions disclose identical secondary motifs, most notably, a reference to the error of the Sufis, who thought that they could attain conjunction without undergoing the requisite scientific preparation. The argument is also recorded in the Long Commentary on the *De anima* 491–92, again in Ibn Bājja's name, but the Long Commentary does not find it to be cogent.

The foregoing arguments, borrowed from Alexander's *De intellectu*, from Themistius, and from Ibn Bājja, are the primary grounds[50] that Averroes' works give for the possibility of the human intellect's having the active intellect as an object of thought and thereby conjoining with the active intellect. Averroes also responds to the challenge thrown down by Alfarabi's Commentary on the *Nicomachean Ethics*, and he does so most fully in the three compositions that he devoted specifically to the subject of conjunction. Two of the three compositions agree on what Alfarabi's objection was, although disagreeing in their responses, while the third credits Alfarabi with a completely different objection.

The two former compositions report that Alfarabi's Commentary on the *Nicomachean Ethics* ruled out conjunction with the active intellect because of the Aristotelian principle that nothing generated can become eternal.[51] Alfarabi, according to the two compositions, assumed that the human material intellect comes into existence. If the material intellect should have the active intellect as the object of its thought, it would perforce become "identical" with the active intellect, and thereby be rendered "eternal." The supposition that something generated becomes eternal is, however, excluded by the Aristotelian principle. Alfarabi, Averroes reports, therefore rejected the possibility of the human intellect's having the active intellect as an object of thought and conjoining with it.[52]

In one of the two compositions crediting Alfarabi with the foregoing reasoning, Averroes responds that the human material intellect is not in fact a generated object and is hence exempt from the rule about generated objects' not becoming eternal. And, he contends, it makes no difference which construction of the material intellect one accepts. On the thesis that the material intellect is an incorporeal substance, the material intellect obviously is not generated. But even on the contrary thesis, according to which the material intellect is a disposition in the human organism—Alexander's view and a view endorsed by Averroes in his early career—the material intellect is still not generated. On the latter thesis, the human material intellect "has no nature except that of possibility and disposition." It consequently is not an actually "existent" object and, not being actually existent, cannot properly be described as "having come into existence," despite its happening to emerge at a given point in time. Since the material intellect, however construed, is not a generated object, it does not fall under the Aristotelian rule about generated objects'

[50]The *Epistle on the Possibility of Conjunction* has six arguments. One of them is Ibn Bājja's argument, and the others are dialectical arguments unique to the *Epistle*.

[51]Aristotle, *De caelo* 1.12.

[52]*Drei Abhandlungen* (n. 2 above) 6–8, 13; German translation 27–28, 37, 53–54. Averroes also conjectures—Hebrew text 9; German translation 46—that in his old age, Alfarabi became skeptical about the possibility of conjunction, because he had failed to achieve it.

The works of Alfarabi which espoused a theory of conjunction with the active intellect did not, in fact, hold that conjunction entails the identity of the human intellect with the active intellect. See above, pp. 54, 69.

not becoming eternal; and Alfarabi's charge that conjunction would lead to the absurdity of a generated object's becoming eternal loses its cogency.[53]

In the second composition crediting Alfarabi with the same grounds for rejecting conjunction, Averroes takes another tack. He acknowledges that the material intellect is indeed "generated," but now he counters that the generated material intellect does not become eternal in its own right. It becomes eternal by "intermixing" with, and receiving, something "intrinsically ungenerated and indestructible," that is, by combining with the ungenerated active intellect. Averroes goes no further, leaving us with the mere assertion that since the material intellect gains eternity through the eternal being with which it combines, rather than through itself, it somehow avoids the impossibility of generated objects' becoming eternal.[54]

The third of Averroes' compositions dealing specifically with the subject of conjunction is known as the *Epistle on the Possibility of Conjunction*. Here Averroes mentions the Aristotelian rule about generated things' not becoming eternal and that rule's bearing on conjunction,[55] but he credits Alfarabi's Commentary on the *Nicomachean Ethics* with a different reason for rejecting conjunction of the human intellect with the active intellect. The reason he now reports is that if the human intellect could receive both "intelligible thoughts derived from material objects" as well as "[direct thoughts of] incorporeal intelligences," it would be a disposition receptive of diametrically opposite kinds of thought. Yet "a single disposition cannot, by its nature, receive two different things, nay diametrically opposite things." Consequently, the human intellect cannot have the forms of both physical and incorporeal beings as the object of its thought. The passage in the *Epistle* recording the objection calls it "the strongest that can be raised" against conjunction.[56]

Once again Averroes is not at a loss for an answer. He accepts the premise that a single disposition for thought can receive thoughts of only one kind. He submits, however, that men possess two separate human dispositions for thought, a disposition for receiving intelligible thoughts of physical objects, and a disposition for having incorporeal beings as an object of thought. The first disposition makes its debut at infancy, whereas the second appears at the culmination of human intellectual development, as an accompaniment of a man's mastery of all the philosophic sciences. Since not one but two separate dispositions are operative,

[53]*Drei Abhandlungen*, Hebrew text 6, following the reading of MS A; German translation 22–27. Averroes may have in mind Aristotle's remarks about things that, although not generated, exist after not existing; see Aristotle, *Metaphysics* 8.5. (Brought to my attention by Michael Blaustein's Harvard doctoral dissertation, *Averroes on the Imagination and the Intellect* 244.)

[54]*Drei Abhandlungen*, Hebrew text 13–14; German translation 55. The full argument is longer and rambles somewhat, but I could not see that it says anything more than what I have given in the text.

[55]*Epistle on the Possibility of Conjunction* (n. 21 above) §8, pp. 50–51.

[56]Ibid. §14, p. 108.

each receptive of its own class of intelligible thought, the new objection to the human material intellect's having the active intellect as an object of thought, and thereby conjoining with the active intellect, also misses the mark.[57]

The conclusion Averroes draws in at least seven compositions, on divers grounds and with divers rebuttals of the demurring view, is that the human intellect can attain a crowning state in which it has the active intellect as the object of its thought and conjoins with the active intellect. Sometimes, Averroes represents conjunction as a condition wherein the human intellect becomes identical with the active intellect.[58] Sometimes, he indicates that it is a condition wherein the human intellect has the active intellect as the object of its thought, but that the thought entering into the human intellect is not identical with the active intellect, and therefore the material intellect remains distinct.[59] And sometimes he does not indicate exactly what he understands by conjunction.[60] He gives two explanations of the manner whereby conjunction is achieved: an explanation borrowed from Ibn Bājja and discussed earlier in this section which implies that the state of conjunction renders the human intellect identical with the active intellect, and another offered in the Long Commentary on the *De anima* and to be discussed below which does not carry that implication. Conjunction with the active intellect occurs, in Averroes' several accounts, during the life of the body and not in the hereafter. None of the accounts envisions anything ecstatic or properly mystical in the conjunction of the human intellect with the active intellect.

The Long Commentary on the *De anima*, which belongs to the last stage of Averroes' thought, is one of the works espousing a doctrine of conjunction. There Averroes falls into a predicament from which he has trouble extricating himself.

Like other works of Averroes, the Long Commentary defines the issue as the question whether the active intellect is "related to man as [both] form and efficient cause, not as efficient cause alone."[61] Alfarabi's "Commentary on the *Nicomachean Ethics*," Averroes reports one more time, "appears to have rejected conjunction with incorporeal beings" and to have denied "that the human end is anything other than theoretical perfection [in this life]."[62] Although Alfarabi had himself once embraced the belief in conjunction, he was, when writing the Commentary on the *Nicomachean Ethics*, led to repudiate the belief by an

[57]Ibid. 108–10.

[58]*Drei Abhandlungen* (n. 2 above), Hebrew text 7; German translation 35 (p. 35, line 1, misses the point, which is that the material intellect becomes the active intellect); Epitome of the *De anima*, appendix 91 taken together with 95; Spanish translation 215, 220.

[59]*Epistle on the Possibility of Conjunction* §5, p. 35 (in the state of "conjunction," the human intellect "*in a certain respect* becomes one of the eternal incorporeal beings"); Commentary on *De intellectu* (n. 2 above) 214; Long Commentary on the *Metaphysics* (n. 21 above) 1612–13.

[60]*Drei Abhandlungen*, Hebrew text 14; German translation 55.

[61]Long Commentary on the *De anima* 502.

[62]Ibid. 433.

argument with which we are familiar. He reasoned—according to the account in Averroes' Long Commentary on the *De anima*—that the human material intellect is generated, that if it "should . . . have incorporeal forms as an object of thought and become one with them," it would be rendered eternal, whereas "a generated-destructible substance" cannot be transformed into something eternal.[63] Alfarabi therefore "finally" arrived at the "opinion . . . that the active intellect is solely the efficient cause [of human thought]" but never its formal cause, that the human intellect cannot have the active intellect as an object of thought and enter into conjunction with the active intellect.[64]

Whereas Averroes' earlier works devised stratagems to evade Alfarabi's challenge, the Long Commentary on the *De anima* concedes that Alfarabi's reasoning was watertight after all: "Anyone who assumes the material intellect to be generated-destructible can, it seems to me, discover no natural way for man to conjoin with the incorporeal intelligences."[65] Philosophers who, like Alexander and Ibn Bājja, construed the human material intellect as a disposition generated together with the human organism, were thus guilty of inconsistency when they also affirmed the possibility of conjunction.[66] Averroes neglects to mention that his own earlier works likewise construed the material intellect as a disposition generated together with the individual man, and hence they too were, from the vantage point of the Long Commentary on the *De anima*, guilty of inconsistency when they affirmed the possibility of conjunction with the active intellect.

By construing the material intellect as a substance eternal and incorporeal by its very nature, the Long Commentary obviously sidesteps the objection that conjunction of the material intellect with the active intellect would entail a generated material intellect's becoming eternal. But it remains to be shown how the conjunction of an eternal material intellect with an eternal active intellect can profit individual men who play out their lives on the temporal stage. The Long Commentary on the *De anima* struggles to furnish an explanation.

Adapting an argument of Themistius' which we have already met, Averroes contends that the eternal material intellect has the active intellect as an object of its thought; and his intent, if I understood him correctly, is that the material intellect enjoys such cognition in its own right, on the eternal and transcendent plane.[67] Averroes' present version of Themistius' argument goes: Inasmuch as the material intellect is "eternal and . . . able to be perfected by material forms, it is all the more likely to be perfected by nonmaterial forms, forms that are in themselves intelligible." The material intellect consequently "has the active intellect, which

[63]Ibid. 481.

[64]Ibid. 485.

[65]Ibid. 481. Similarly on 502.

[66]Ibid. 481–85, 488–89, refutes the arguments for the possibility of conjunction given by Alexander and by the *De intellectu* attributed to Alexander. Ibid. 494–95, refutes Ibn Bājja's arguments.

[67]See above, p. 292, n. 154.

stands to it . . . in the way light stands to the transparent [medium], as an [eternal] object of thought." And when it does so, the material intellect and active intellect are "one."[68] Averroes, if he is being consistent, can hardly mean that having the active intellect as an object of thought renders the material intellect truly identical with the active intellect. For if the material intellect were rendered identical with the active intellect, it would have been rendered so from all eternity, and there would in fact be not two eternal intellects, the material and active, but only one.

Since, as was seen in the previous chapter,[69] the single material intellect common to all mankind is linked to individual men through their imaginative faculties, individual men can, through their imaginative faculties, participate in the material intellect's immediate thought of the active intellect. "At the outset," the material intellect is "not joined to man in the respect" we are considering, that is, insofar as the material intellect has the active intellect as an object of thought. The material intellect does, however, become joined to man in the critical respect, insofar as it has the active intellect as an object of thought, "when the development of the [human] intellect *in habitu* is complete," that is to say, upon man's mastering a full corpus of theoretical thought.[70] "When the material intellect is joined [with man] in the respect wherein it is perfected through the active intellect, man is joined with the active intellect; and the condition is called . . . acquired intellect."[71] In a word, individual men tap into the material intellect's thought of the active intellect by developing their own intellects *in habitu*, by acquiring a complete corpus of intelligible thoughts. It still remains to be shown how the link between the material intellect and the human soul allows the latter to participate in the thought that the eternal material intellect has of the eternal active intellect, and why the link allows the human soul to do so only after man develops his intellect, and not from the outset. Averroes promises to provide an explanation "later,"[72] and a later section of the Long Commentary on the *De anima* does undertake to fulfill the promise. I found the explanation to be far from crystal clear, but Averroes seems to be saying the following.

In all instances "where a single act is performed by the compound of two distinct beings, one of the two must be a sort of matter or instrument [*quasi materia et instrumentum*], and the other a sort of form or agent [*quasi forma aut agens*]." Since new human thought comes about through an interaction of intellect *in*

[68]Ibid. 450–51. On pp. 487–88, Averroes writes that Themistius' a fortiori argument is demonstrative only when the material intellect is taken to be an incorporeal being, while if the material intellect is taken to be a destructible object, the argument is merely rhetorical and "persuasive."

[69]Above, pp. 289–290.

[70]Ibid. 450. A definition of intellect *in habitu* as an individual man's corpus of theoretical thoughts comes out of Long Commentary 496–99. On the term intellect *in habitu*, see above, p. 10.

[71]Ibid. 411.

[72]Ibid. 411, 450.

habitu—the corpus of human intelligible thoughts already existing at a given moment—and the active intellect, those two intellects must play the roles of matter and form. "Intellect *in habitu*" must be the "matter" or, if one prefer, the "instrument" in discursive thought of the world, while the "active intellect" is the "form" or, if one prefer, the "agent."[73]

Now, Averroes continues, if the eternal active intellect and thoughts constituting intellect *in habitu* were related as form to matter—or as agent to instrument—in the strict sense, something generated-destructible would serve as the matter, or instrument, of something eternal. And a situation of such a sort is "impossible." Intellect *in habitu* cannot therefore be a "true matter," or "true instrument." Intellect *in habitu* and active intellect must stand to each other merely in the "relation" of matter to form, not as a genuine matter to a genuine form. The one must be matter, and the other form, in no more than a loose sense. Determining "the respect" in which they are related as matter and form will make it "easy to understand the respect in which the human intellect *in habitu* conjoins with the incorporeal intelligences."[74]

Intellect *in habitu*, the corpus of already acquired theoretical thoughts, and the active intellect meet thanks to the eternal material intellect, which acts as their common "subject." The material intellect "has as an object of thought [*intellegit*] both . . . the forms of material [things] and incorporeal forms," both the "theoretical intelligible thoughts [constituting intellect *in habitu*] and the active intellect," in a manner analogous to that in which "the transparent [visual medium] . . . receives color and light at the same time." And whenever two things present in the same subject are so related that one of the two is the "perfection" of the other, "the relation of the more perfect to the less perfect is *like* [*sicut*] that of form to matter." Here then is the sense in which the active intellect is the form of the corpus of thoughts constituting intellect *in habitu*: The active intellect and theoretical thought abstracted from the physical world meet in a common subject, inasmuch as the material intellect has both as an object of thought; within the material intellect, the active intellect is the more perfect, and the corpus of abstracted theoretical thoughts, the less perfect; and when one thing is more perfect than another that is present in the same subject, it is in a sense its form.

The link, obtaining within the material intellect, between the active intellect and the material intellect's corpus of theoretical thought is then tapped into by individual imaginative faculties: "Inasmuch as theoretical intelligible thoughts join with man through forms [that is, images] in the imaginative faculty, and the active intellect is joined with theoretical intelligible thoughts—the same thing, namely, the material intellect, having both [theoretical thoughts and the active intellect] as an object of

[73]Ibid. 497, 499. The analysis appears in the passage where Averroes spoke of secondary propositions that are "produced from already known principles [of thought] and the active intellect"; above, p. 320.

[74]Ibid. 497–99.

thought [*comprehendit ea*]—the active intellect necessarily joins with man by reason of [its] conjunction with those intelligible thoughts." In what seems to be an afterthought, Averroes also writes that the factor "whereby something performs the act proper to it is its form," man "performs the act proper to him through the active intellect," and therefore in this sense too, the active intellect may be considered man's form. Averroes concludes that the active intellect becomes "a form in man in no other respect than" the sense or senses just given.[75]

Such is the account of conjunction of the human soul with the active intellect, set forth in Averroes' Long Commentary on the *De anima.*

The Long Commentary was seen in the preceding chapter to posit two subjects for human theoretical thought. It located theoretical thought both in the human imaginative faculty, characterizing that guise of theoretical thought as generated-destructible, and in the eternal material intellect, characterizing that guise as eternal.[76] To make sense of what Averroes has now said about conjunction, his intent, it would seem, must be as follows: The eternal material intellect has the eternal side of human theoretical thought as well as the eternal active intellect as objects of thought; in a certain sense, the active intellect hence conjoins with the eternal guise of human theoretical thought; the individual human imaginative faculty receives its side of theoretical thought, the generated-destructible side, through the medium of the eternal material intellect; and the imaginative faculty thereby participates in the active intellect's conjunction with the other guise of theoretical thought, with theoretical thought insofar as it is present to the material intellect.

At all events, if conjunction with the active intellect is defined as the joining of the active intellect with the human soul, or a faculty of the human soul, as its form, whereas the active intellect can become the form of the human soul only in the very attenuated sense, or senses, that have been outlined, Averroes' Long Commentary on the *De anima* has salvaged only a very attenuated conjunction of the active intellect with the human soul.[77]

Averroes nevertheless goes on: Since "theoretical intelligible thoughts join with man through forms [images] in the imaginative faculty, and the active intellect is joined with theoretical intelligible thoughts," the active intellect's conjunction with an individual human imaginative faculty and, through it, with an individual soul is proportional to the man's store of theoretical thoughts. The greater the store of thoughts, the greater the degree of conjunction. "Plainly, when theoretical intelligible thoughts are all potential in a man, the active intellect is joined to him potentially. When all theoretical thoughts exist in the man actually, the active intellect will be joined to him actually. When some theoretical thoughts are present

[75]Ibid. 499–500.

[76]Above, p. 290.

[77]Ibid. 502, Averroes writes that if he had not construed the material intellect as an eternal substance, he would not have been able to show how "the active intellect conjoins with the intellect *in habitu* in a proper [*propria*] conjunction, namely, in a conjunction *similar* to that of form with matter."

potentially and some actually, the active intellect will be partly joined and partly not; the man is said to be moving toward conjunction." At the apex, where "the process is complete, . . . the active intellect at once conjoins with the person in every respect," and the individual man "will, through the intellect then belonging to him, think all beings." He will, "as Themistius said, be like unto God, inasmuch as he too has become all things in a certain manner and knows them in a certain manner. . . . How marvelous is that state, how extraordinary that mode of existing!"[78] Despite the rhapsodic tone, the Long Commentary, as far as I could see, does not, and could not, ever expressly say that the active intellect becomes the direct object of human consciousness.

The foregoing account of conjunction is, Averroes concludes in the Long Commentary on the *De anima*, "what appears to me." He assures readers that "should anything more occur to me later, I shall write it."[79]

Immortality. While for other philosophers, lucubrations on conjunction were a preface to the equally or more important issue of human immortality, Averroes treats conjunction as by far the primary issue, and immortality as a minor corollary.

Aristotle had asserted that "it is presumably impossible for the entire [soul] . . . to survive," yet "nothing will prevent . . . the intellect . . . from surviving."[80] Philosophers taking Aristotle as their guide accordingly affirmed the immortality of the human intellect in some form, while excluding the immortality of all other aspects of the human soul.[81] Averroes follows in the same track. On occasions when he addresses a mixed readership of philosophers and nonphilosophers he does allow himself to speak of an immortality of the "soul,"[82] but in those

[78]Ibid. 500–501. Cf. Themistius, *In Aristotelis Metaphysicorum librum Λ paraphrasis*, ed. S. Landauer (medieval Hebrew translation from the Arabic; the Greek original and the medieval Arabic translation are lost) in *Commentaria in Aristotelem graeca* 5.5 (Berlin 1903), 20–21. The Themistius passage is an expansion on Aristotle, *Metaphysics* 12.7.1072b, 18–26.

[79]Ibid. 502.

[80]Aristotle, *Metaphysics* 12.3.1070a, 24–26. See above, pp. 34–35.

[81]See above, pp. 37, 40, 57, 145. Avicenna's position was that the substance of the human soul is intrinsically immortal, but even he held that the nonintellectual faculties of the soul perish. Above, p. 96.

[82]*K. al-Kashf ʿan Manāhij al-Adilla*, in *Philosophie und Theologie von Averroes*, ed. M. Müller (Munich 1859) 120, 122–23; German translation, with pagination of the Arabic indicated, in *Philosophie und Theologie von Averroes*, trans. M. Müller (Munich 1875); *Tahāfut al-Tahāfut*, ed. M. Bouyges (Beirut 1930) 557, 586; English translation, with pages of the original Arabic indicated: *Averroes' Tahafut al-Tahafut*, trans. S. Van den Bergh (London 1954). *Tahāfut al-Tahāfut* 557 quotes Koran 39:42: "God receives souls at their death as well as that [soul] which does not die in its sleep." In explanation of the verse, Averroes writes as follows concerning the link between sleep and death: "The analogy of death to sleep" provides a "proof . . . of the survival of the soul," a proof that is "common to all," since it both is "appropriate to ordinary folk" and also "points out to scientists the way through which the survival of the soul can be grasped." The proof, according to Averroes, is that "the action of the soul comes to a halt in sleep by reason of the inoperability of the soul's organ, yet the soul itself does

instances, he undoubtedly expected the enlightened reader to take *soul* as a code word for *intellect*. His strictly philosophic writings are unambiguous about the mortality of the nonintellectual soul.

His Epitome of the *De anima* states that the "senses" and "imaginative faculty" are subject to "destruction."[83] The Middle Commentary on the *De anima* paraphrases a passage from Aristotle with the statement: Since soul is defined as "the form or entelechy" of the body, "it . . . as well as its parts," or, to be more precise, "most of its parts," are "inseparable from the body."[84] The Long Commentary on the *De anima*, when commenting on the same passage in Aristotle, says virtually the same: The Aristotelian "definition" of soul—"first entelechy of an organic natural body"[85]—entails that "the soul is unable to separate itself from the body either in respect to all of its [the soul's] parts or in respect to some." "Faculties" of the soul which "are entelechies of parts of the body"—the nonintellectual faculties—"cannot separate themselves" from the parts of the body of which they are entelechies.[86]

Not only are the nonintellectual faculties mortal. "Practical intelligible thoughts" likewise do not survive; they are tied to the "imaginative faculty" and perish together with it.[87] Human theoretical thoughts that grow out of images presented by the imaginative faculty suffer an identical fate. As explained most fully in the Long Commentary on the *De anima*, the "material intellect thinks nothing [related to the physical universe] without the [cogitative] faculty and imaginative faculty," which present images for perusal. Those faculties operate through ventricles of the brains of individual men, the cogitative faculty having the "middle ventricle of the brain" as its "instrument," and the imaginative faculty being located in the "front of the brain." The two faculties are, like the brain in which they reside, "generated-destructible,"[88] and individual human consciousness of theoretical thoughts

---

not cease [to exist]. And the soul's situation in death must be like its situation in sleep." I take him to be intimating that scientists and philosophers, who are alone qualified to judge, will reason: Intellect, not being dependent on physical organs, is not affected by their absence, while the nonintellectual functions of the soul, which are dependent on physical organs, disappear when their organs disappear. Therefore the only part of the soul which can survive the death of bodily organs is the intellect.

For the survival of soul-heat, see above, p. 253.

[83]Epitome of the *De anima* (n. 2 above) 70; Spanish translation 189.

[84]Middle Commentary on the *De anima* (n. 2 above), Arabic text 119b; Hebrew translation 197a. Averroes is paraphrasing Aristotle, *De anima* 2.1.413a, 3–5.

[85]Aristotle, *De anima* 2.1.412b 5–6.

[86]Long Commentary on the *De anima* 147.

[87]Epitome of the *De anima* 69–70; Spanish translation 189.

[88]Long Commentary on the *De anima* 415, 476. Averroes writes that the location of the "imaginative faculty . . . in the front of the brain, the cogitative faculty in the middle, and the memory in the back" is the "order" given by Aristotle's *Parva naturalia*. The section of Averroes' Epitome of the *Parva naturalia* which parallels Aristotle's *De memoria* offers an argument for locating those three faculties in the three parts of the brain, but the argument does

perishes together with the faculties on which consciousness of such thoughts depends. Hence "we do not remember [theoretical thoughts] after death."[89] The Long Commentary, from which the last quotations are taken, has a unique conception of the material intellect and its relation to the human soul. But compositions belonging to other stages of Averroes' career make equally plain that "theoretical intelligible thoughts,"[90] that is to say, human scientific knowledge at the "mathematical," "physical," and even the "metaphysical" levels, all "perish" together with the human imaginative faculty. Metaphysical knowledge, no less than physical knowledge, is rooted in images furnished by the imaginative faculty, since it consists in abstractions made from propositions presented by the science of physics.[91]

The nonintellectual faculties of the soul are, then, mortal, and human thoughts of both a practical and theoretical sort, including even thoughts at the metaphysical level, are mortal as well. Put in another way, the actualized human intellect, which Averroes often calls intellect *in habitu*, perishes with the body.[92] The sole remaining candidate for human immortality is the material intellect.

We saw in the previous chapter that works belonging to Averroes' earlier period construe the material intellect as a disposition residing in, but unmixed with, the human organism or, specifically, as a disposition residing in the human imaginative faculty. When Averroes also recognizes the possibility of conjunction with the active intellect, whether or not he takes conjunction to be a complete union of the material intellect with the active intellect, he maintains that conjunction guarantees the survival of the material intellect.[93] The surviving material intellect will be void of all scientific thoughts acquired during the human lifetime, seeing that those thoughts are successive levels of abstraction, all of them ultimately rooted in images

---

not come from Aristotle. See Averroes, Epitome of the *Parva naturalia*, Arabic text, ed. H. Blumberg (Cambridge, Mass. 1972) 42; medieval Latin translation, ed. A. Shields (Cambridge, Mass. 1949) 57–58; medieval Hebrew translation, ed. H. Blumberg (Cambridge, Mass. 1954) 28; English translation, trans. H. Blumberg (Cambridge, Mass. 1961) 26, and Blumberg's note.

[89]Long Commentary on the *De anima* 476–77.

[90]*Epistle on the Possibility of Conjunction* (n. 21 above) §2, p. 13; cf. Long Commentary on the *De anima* 469.

[91]Epitome of the *De anima* (n. 2 above), appendix 91–94; Spanish translation 216–19. The section is dependent on Ibn Bājja.

[92]Epitome of the *Metaphysics* (n. 3 above) 4, §46; German translation 126; *Epistle on the Possibility of Conjunction* §8, p. 50; §10, p. 65; Long Commentary on the *De anima* 496, 497, 499. The Long Commentary on the *De anima* does recognize a collective and nonpersonal intellect *in habitu*—human scientific knowledge present to the material intellect—which exists as long as the human species exists. See Long Commentary 407, and above, p. 292.

[93]*Drei Abhandlungen* (n. 2 above), Hebrew text 7, 13–14; German translation 34–35, 54–55; Epitome of the *De anima* 95; Spanish translation 220; *Epistle on the Possibility of Conjunction* §5, p. 35; §8, pp. 50–51; §12, p. 90; §16, p. 145; appendix 152. *Epistle* §9, p. 55 (end) has to be harmonized with the other passages.

presented by the imaginative faculty.[94] The state of conjunction with the active intellect, Averroes wants us to understand, is not just one further level of abstraction, but a leap beyond. In conjunction, the material intellect transcends discursive science. It catapults itself beyond thought rooted in the impermanent images presented by the imaginative faculty, to a condition wherein the active intellect, an eternal being consisting in pure thought, is the direct object of its thought. Since at this stage of Averroes' philosophy, the material intellect is a mere disposition and not a substance, what conjoins permanently with the active intellect and survives apparently is, as Alexander of Aphrodisias had held,[95] nothing more than a disembodied thought with the active intellect as object. Obviously, no shred of anything resembling a human personality remains.

The immortality of the material intellect is also recognized by the Long Commentary on the *De anima*. But since the Long Commentary has given up the struggle to exempt the material intellect from the rule about generated objects' being destroyed, it accommodates the immortality of the material intellect only by doing away with the material intellect's generated and individual character. The material intellect is immortal only because it is an eternal incorporeal substance, existing independently of individual men. No room is left for the survival of anything whatsoever originating in, and belonging to, the individual man.[96]

Résumé. At least eight works of Averroes, belonging to various periods in his philosophic career, take up the question whether the human intellect can have the active intellect as an object of thought and thereby conjoin with it. One of the eight, Averroes' Epitome of the *Metaphysics*, exhibits doubt about the possibility of conjunction in the sense of a total unification of the human intellect with the active intellect, and that is the only sense Averroes contemplates there. The other seven affirm the possibility of conjunction. Sometimes conjunction designates for Averroes a condition in which the human intellect has the active intellect as a direct object of thought and becomes identical with the active intellect; sometimes conjunction is a condition wherein the human intellect has the active intellect as a direct object of thought while remaining distinct; sometimes Averroes leaves unclear which of the two he might mean. In defending the possibility of conjunction with the active intellect, Averroes repeatedly adduces arguments from the *De intellectu* attributed to Alexander, from Themistius, and from Ibn Bājja. He also answers the objections to conjunction which he reports in the name of Alfarabi's Commentary on the *Nicomachean Ethics*. The sole explanation that the earlier works give of the

[94]Stated explicitly in *Epistle on the Possibility of Conjunction* §8, p. 50; §10, p. 65.

[95]See above, p. 37.

[96]The statements on intellect made by Averroes' Long Commentary on the *Metaphysics* are problematic. But the Long Commentary on the *Metaphysics* 12, comm. 38; Arabic text (n. 21 above) 1612–13, does seem to reflect the position of the Long Commentary on the *De anima* when it states: "Human eudaemonia . . . consists in conjunction with the [active] intellect"; man can "conjoin with that incorporeal intellect at the apex" at least for "a short time."

manner whereby man achieves conjunction is borrowed from Ibn Bājja. It is the contention that the human intellect is capable of higher and higher levels of abstraction, that the human intellect must therefore be able ultimately to attain a single, supremely abstract thought, that the ultimate abstract thought is common to all men, and that the thought common to all men and having no link to any image can be nothing other than a direct concept of the active intellect.

The Long Commentary on the *De anima* offers Averroes' final views on the subject. Averroes explains in the Long Commentary that the eternal active intellect and the corpus of human theoretical thoughts meet on the common ground of the material intellect; they meet thanks to the material intellect's having both as an object of thought. In the sense that the active intellect is the more perfect of the material intellect's two objects of thought, it is the *form* of the other object of thought, that is, of human theoretical thoughts. Human theoretical thoughts have not only the material intellect but also the human imaginative faculty as a subject, and as an individual man's corpus of theoretical thoughts grows, the connection of the active intellect with the man's imaginative faculty likewise grows. At the culmination, the active intellect "conjoins" with the man "actually," and the man becomes "like unto God inasmuch as he too has become all things in a certain manner and knows them in a certain manner." Since, however, the active intellect becomes the human intellect's form only in a highly attenuated sense—the active intellect is the form of human theoretical thought only in the loose sense of being the more perfect of the objects thought by the material intellect, and, besides, the human imaginative faculty possesses a different guise of theoretical thought from the guise present to the material intellect—the Long Commentary apparently surrenders all but a very attenuated sense of conjunction. The Long Commentary accordingly does not, as far as I could discover, ever hint at a direct human thought of the active intellect.

Averroes' Long Commentary on the *De anima* thus ensnarls itself in one more difficulty growing out of its hypothesis of a single material intellect serving all mankind. The Long Commentary never explained when and how the eternal material intellect becomes linked to individual human imaginative faculties; how human effort can induce the material intellect to do its bidding, seeing that the material intellect is an eternal being only tenuously linked to man; nor how the eternal material intellect can reciprocate and endow individual men with an intellectual consciousness. Now the hypothesis of an eternal material intellect prevents the Long Commentary from putting any content in the doctrine long dear to Averroes, the conjunction of the active intellect with the human intellect.

Like Aristotle and philosophers standing in the Aristotelian tradition, Averroes rules out the immortality of the nonintellectual parts of the human soul. He further rejects the immortality of theoretical human thought linked in any way to perceptions of the physical world, his grounds being that such thought depends upon nonintellectual parts of the soul, which perish with the brain. The only aspect of man capable of immortality, in Averroes' view, is therefore the material intellect. In works where he construes the material intellect as a disposition for thought in the human organism, and where he defends the possibility of the material intellect's conjoining with the active intellect, he recognizes the immortality of material intellects that achieve conjunction. What he is in effect defending is disembodied thought with the active intellect as its object, and nothing that can properly be called a human personality survives. In his final position, spelled out in the Long Commentary on the *De anima*, the material intellect is immortal merely because it is an eternal substance existing independently of individual men. Here, in the Long Commentary on the *De anima*, nothing whatsoever belonging to the individual man is capable of surviving the body.

Prophecy

Alfarabi recognized two levels of prophecy, both attained when the analogue of light which every human rational faculty receives from the active intellect affects the imaginative faculty (*mutakhayyila*). The lower of the two levels, to which Alfarabi attached the specific name of *prophecy*, is enjoyed by men who have not perfected their intellect, whereas the higher, which he sometimes called *revelation* (*w-ḥ-y*), is the exclusive province of those whose intellects are perfected. At both levels, the emanation from the active intellect furnishes knowledge of future events and of present events occurring at a distance; at the lower level, and perhaps at the higher as well, the emanation from the active intellect also furnishes "clairvoyance [*kahānāt*] in divine matters," that is to say, a figurative depiction of theoretical truths.[97] Avicenna likewise recognized, and attached the name *prophecy* to, knowledge produced when an emanation from above—from the active intellect and probably from the souls of the celestial spheres—acts on the human imaginative faculty (*mutakhayyila*, which in Avicenna is, more precisely: the *compositive* imaginative faculty). A figurative depiction of theoretical truths and knowledge of the future again result. But Avicenna departed from Alfarabi by crediting, and naming as prophecy, an additional sort of knowledge, namely, genuine theoretical knowledge received effortlessly by the human rational faculty from the emanation of the active intellect.[98]

A passage in Ibn Bājja is also pertinent here. In the course of analyzing nontheoretical true beliefs, Ibn Bājja called attention to a type of true belief which comes "from the active intellect through the intermediacy of the rational faculty" and is concerned "especially with future affairs." Such true belief regarding the future is arrived at "without cogitation or syllogistic reasoning," and it takes the form "of true dream [or: vision (*ru'yā*)] and clairvoyance [*kahānāt*]." Ibn Bājja adds that

[97]Above, pp. 59–61.
[98]Above, pp. 117–22.

the "topic" was discussed by Aristotle "at the end of Part 2 of the *Parva naturalia*," that is, in Aristotle's *De divinatione*.[99]

What the word *topic* refers to in the last remark quoted from Ibn Bājja is unclear. Ibn Bājja may be saying merely that Aristotle's *De divinatione* discussed the topic of true dreams, as it in fact did. He can, however, be interpreted as saying more, as saying that Aristotle's *De divinatione* discussed the role of the active intellect in true dreams. On that interpretation, he read a good deal into Aristotle. Aristotle's *De divinatione* never mentioned the active intellect, and it labeled as "absurd" the notion that dreams "are sent by God" and are "divine"—although with the qualification that dreams have "something divine-like [δαιμόνια]" about them, inasmuch as all "nature has something divine-like about it."[100] The second interpretation, albeit unjustified by the text of Aristotle, does find support in another source, in an eclectic Arabic composition of uncertain date which treats of dreams. The composition in question evinces a mediocre level of argumentation, and although it represents itself as a work of Avicenna, its contents betray little of an Aristotelian or Islamic Aristotelian character. What is significant for us is that we find there an isolated comment to the effect that in the "*Parva naturalia*," Aristotle called the divine force responsible for true dreams "the active intellect."[101] Averroes' Epitome of the *Parva naturalia*, as will appear, ascribes a role to the active intellect in dreams, thereby implying that Aristotle's *Parva naturalia* had done so as well.

The available preserved works of Ibn Bājja do not, as far as I could discover, ever recognize an emanation from the active intellect which circumvents the ordinary processes of ratiocination to provide man scientific knowledge, as distinct from knowledge of the future. Nor does Ibn Bājja speak of the active intellect's giving man a figurative representation of theoretical truths.

As for Averroes, he refers to prophecy in a number of his writings, but the only preserved full account is found in the section of his Epitome of the *Parva naturalia* which reworks Aristotle's *De divinatione*. The position set forth there is closest to that of Ibn Bājja.[102]

[99]*Tadbīr al-Mutawaḥḥid*, ed. and Spanish trans. M. Asín Palacios, as *El régimen del solitario* (Madrid 1946), Arabic text 23–24, Spanish translation 54–55; cf. M. Ma'sumi, "Ibn Bājja on the Human Intellect," *Islamic Studies* 4 (1965) 127, 131.

The structure of Averroes' Epitome of the *Parva naturalia* suggests that the medieval Arabic version of the Aristotelian collection known as the *Parva naturalia* rearranged the parts. Averroes' Epitome regards the first six of the nine compositions in the *Parva naturalia* as three treatises, and it regards the *De divinatione* as the third chapter of the second of the three. See Averroes, Epitome of the *Parva naturalia*, English translation (n. 88 above) xi–xii; H. Gätje, *Die Epitome der Parva Naturalia des Averroes* (Wiesbaden 1961) vii.

[100]Aristotle, *De divinatione* 462b, 20–21; 463b, 13–15.

[101]Attention was called to the text, which is entitled *al-Risāla al-Manāmiyya*, "Epistle concerning Dreams," by S. Pines, "The Arabic Recension of *Parva naturalia*," *Israel Oriental Studies* 4 (1974) 120.

[102]Echoes of the eclectic composition on dreams referred to in the previous note are also discernible. Most distinctive is the appearance of an anecdote about "king Hercules" in both the

"The common people," Averroes writes, "believe" that "[true] dream" (*ru'yā*), "clairvoyance" (*kahāna*), and "revelation" (*waḥy*), are distinct and separate phenomena having different causes, true dreams being the work of "angels," clairvoyance of "the jinn," and revelation of "God, with or without an . . . intermediary."[103] People further believe that true dream and clairvoyance differ from revelation inasmuch as the first two provide knowledge "only" about "transient matters," while revelation provides knowledge "only" of "scientific matters such as . . . the essence of [human] eudaemonia" and the way "eudaemonia is achieved."[104] As he proceeds, Averroes introduces the term *prophecy* (*nubuwwa*) into the discussion, stating that "prophecy" is "ascribed to God and the divine entities, or angels."[105] He must mean either that the first and third of the supposedly distinct phenomena—true dreams, which are thought to be produced by angels, and revelation, which is thought to be produced by God—are also called prophecy; or else that all three are called prophecy.

He rejects out of hand the belief that the terms denote three separate phenomena. True dreams, clairvoyance, and revelation are, he insists, essentially the same, the difference between them being "merely . . . [one of] degree." All three are produced by an "actual intellect" that is wholly "incorporeal"; and as we shall see, this incorporeal actual intellect is none other than "the active intellect."[106] When the appropriate faculty of the human soul receives the ever-present action of the active intellect with higher than ordinary intensity, people stop calling the effect *true dream*, and rename it *clairvoyance*. When the effect is still more intense, people coin a still more flattering term and name it *revelation*.

Averroes also rejects the supposition that revelation can parallel reason as an alternate source of scientific knowledge.

He writes: Although a "theoretical thought" might come to a man "occasionally and rarely" through the phenomena we are considering,[107] man cannot receive

---

eclectic composition and in Averroes. See Pines, "The Arabic Recension of *Parva naturalia*" 130–33; Averroes, Epitome of the *Parva naturalia* (n. 88 above), Arabic text 86; medieval Latin translation 118; medieval Hebrew translation 56; English translation 50. Averroes reports the anecdote in the name of Aristotle, but without naming the work of Aristotle from which it supposedly comes. The "Epistle on Dreams" records the anecdote in the context where it makes the comment that Aristotle's *Parva naturalia* traced true dreams to a divine force called "the active intellect."

103Epitome of the *Parva naturalia*, Arabic text 66–67; Latin text 94–95; Hebrew text 43–44; English translation (inadequate in this whole section) 39–40.

104Ibid., Arabic text 67; Hebrew text 44; English translation 40.

105Ibid., Arabic text 73; Latin text 102; Hebrew text 48; English translation 43.

106Ibid., Arabic text 67, 72–74; Latin text 95, 101–3; Hebrew text 44, 47–48; English translation 40, 42–44.

107Averroes may, in part, be echoing statements Aristotle made about predictions that do "not occur invariably or on the whole" and hence are merely "coincidental." See Aristotle, *De divinatione* 463a, 2–3; 463b, 9–11. Averroes does not explain how the occasional and rare

fully developed "theoretical science" through a true dream or the like, "unless, by God, we suppose a portion of mankind who have cognition of the theoretical sciences without study. That portion—were they to exist!—would be men in an equivocal sense, and it would be more reasonable to call them angels than men." After the rhetorical preamble, Averroes offers a carefully articulated argument to show that the existence of an angelic class of men who possess scientific knowledge without study is indeed "impossible."

Assume, he submits, that "theoretical knowledge" were accessible to man both "through study," that is, through the drawing of conclusions from properly framed syllogisms, and also "without study." The assumption would lead to one of two unacceptable results. Either (1) the term *theoretical knowledge* would be predicated "equivocally" of knowledge acquired by man through study and knowledge revealed to him without it. The revealed kind would, in other words, be something completely different from the reasoned kind and consequently not theoretical knowledge at all. Or alternatively, (2) "a single thing would exist through different causes, . . . and the relation of a thing to the causes whereby it exists would not be necessary, which is an absurd outcome." That is to say, should theoretical knowledge come about in the form of conclusions flowing from syllogistic reasoning—the syllogism's premises being the cause, of which the conclusion is the effect—and also in some other fashion, then theoretical knowledge would exist through different sets of causes; but, Averroes takes for granted, every class of thing exists solely through its own unique kind of cause. Since both ways of construing the assumption that theoretical knowledge comes to man in two forms, with and without study, are untenable, man plainly attains theoretical knowledge through only a single method, through scientific and philosophic reasoning.

The phenomena we are discussing—true dream, clairvoyance, and revelation—cannot, Averroes goes on, even have the function of furnishing a "segment of mankind" with an "imaginative" and figurative representation of "theoretical matters." Such a function would be "superfluous, since man also attains theoretical knowledge through his [mental] tools." Nature does not, in other words, act redundantly, and where it provides superior and well-adapted means to an end, it does not duplicate them with other, inferior means. Should "someone" press on and propose that the figurative representation of scientific truths "perhaps" ministers to those who are "by nature or for some other reason incapable of learning the theoretical sciences," Averroes responds much as he began. The hypothetical class—"if they existed"—would not in fact be men but another species of creature which is called "*man* equivocally." By virtue of the definition of man, normal members of the human species all have the ability to learn science in the proper manner.[108]

---

theoretical thought comes to man through a dream, and hence does not explain why his argument against theoretical knowledge through a true dream does not apply to the occasional, rare instance.

[108]Epitome of the *Parva naturalia*, Arabic text 89–91; Latin text 121–23; Hebrew text 58–59; English translation 52. Averroes does not quite mean that true dream and related phenomena never

Averroes is making an extremely radical statement for a medieval philosopher, a statement from which he appears to retreat elsewhere. He is asserting that the phenomena we are considering, including revelation and prophecy, give no reliable information about matters belonging to the domain of science, not even by furnishing the uneducated with a figurative representation of theoretical truths. Revelation and prophecy do not, either expressly or allusively, instruct mankind about God, the universe, creation, the human soul. They promulgate no rules of human behavior leading to eudaemonia. Revelation as well as the written record of revealed knowledge thus contribute nothing to the soul's well-being.

Averroes has stated that true dream, clairvoyance, and revelation are essentially the same phenomenon, and he has told us what they cannot do. His explanation of what they can do builds—like the explanations of Alfarabi and Avicenna[109]—on a general description of dreams.

Aristotle had identified the imaginative faculty as the faculty of the soul which is operative in all dreams, both the usual, false dreams and true dreams.[110] Averroes, for his part, explains that in the "waking state," perceptions enter from the outside and ascend through the hierarchy of internal faculties, or internal senses, of the soul. At the top, they are processed by the imaginative faculty (*mutakhayyila*) and transmitted to the memory. In the dream state, a man seems to "perceive with his five senses, although no sense objects are present outside [the soul]." Since the percepts do not originate from without, they must originate from within and travel "in the opposite direction." Memory is not the initiator, since memory is quiescent in sleep. The inner sense that remains awake and "in constant motion" when the other faculties are asleep is "the imaginative faculty," and it must be the faculty responsible for dreams. The imaginative faculty recovers impressions from "the memory," recombines them, and projects them out through the sense faculties, so that the dreamer seems "to perceive sense objects, although none are [in actuality] present outside the soul."[111]

---

touch on scientific topics. When he takes up dream interpretation, he notes that the interpreter must be familiar with the presuppositions of the dreamer's culture as, for example, the culture's opinions on the "first cause, angels, and the character of human eudaemonia"; by implication, those topics are alluded to in dreams. See ibid., Arabic text 85; Latin text 117; Hebrew text 56; English translation 50.

[109]Above. pp. 58, 61, 118–19.

[110]Aristotle, *De insomniis* 1.459a, 8–22. In Aristotle the imaginative faculty is a guise of sensation; see *De insomniis* 1.459a, 15–17; *De anima* 3.3. 429a, 1–2. The terms *internal senses* and *internal faculties* are post-Aristotelian; see H. Wolfson, "The Internal Senses in Latin, Arabic, and Hebrew Philosophic Texts," reprinted in his *Studies in the History of Philosophy and Religion* 1 (Cambridge, Mass. 1973) 250–51.

[111]Epitome of the *Parva naturalia*, Arabic text 69–70; Latin text 96–99; Hebrew text 45–46; English translation 40–41. In ordinary dreams, the random scenes that the imaginative faculty depicts are suggested by the subject's preoccupations; ibid., Arabic 91; Latin 124; Hebrew 59–60; English 53; Aristotle, *De insomniis* 3.

The foregoing covers all dreams. In true dreams, Averroes goes on, "most" information coming to man "plainly . . . concerns future affairs, the knowledge of which [ordinarily] belongs to particular applications of the cogitative faculty [*al-quwā al-fikriyya al-juz' iyya*]"; and the particular applications of the cogitative faculty which true dreams replace are those having as their object a "knowledge of what is beneficial and harmful in future affairs." In other words, one function of the human cogitative faculty is to reason forward from present events, in order to make judgments regarding beneficial and harmful events in the future. True dreams communicate judgments of the same sort without calling upon the cogitative faculty's services.[112] The qualification that "most," and therefore not all, information communicated in true dreams concerns future events recalls Ibn Bājja's remark that the true beliefs communicated in dreams are concerned "*especially* with future affairs." In Averroes, the qualification is intended to accommodate: the rare instances where bits of theoretical knowledge happen to appear in a dream; an opinion held by some that "matters" pertaining to the "practical sciences," such as the details of the art of "medicine," can be learned in dreams; and the possibility that dreams may furnish information not only of the "future," but also of the "past and present."[113] That true dreams are a substitute for the operation of the cogitative

[112]Aristotle, *De anima* 3.7, 431a, 14–16, states: When the "dianoetic soul" judges things to be "good or bad," it "pursues" or "flees" them. In medieval Arabic psychology, the dianoetic soul (διανοητικὴ ψύχη) becomes the cogitative faculty (*mufakkira, fikr*, etc.); see H. Wolfson, "The Internal Senses" 259.

[113]Epitome of the *Parva naturalia*, Arabic text 88–89; Latin text 120–21; Hebrew text 57–58; English translation 51–52. In a note, the English translator quotes Gersonides' commentary, which in turn quotes Galen to the effect that the latter discovered medical knowledge in dreams. That true dreams provide information about about future events, was Gersonides' position; see Gersonides, *Milḥamot ha-Shem* (*Die Kämpfe Gottes*) (Leipzig 1866) 2.1–4; English translation: Levi ben Gershom, *The Wars of the Lord*, trans. S. Feldman (Philadelphia 1987).

Averroes' evidence that true dreams actually occur is, in an echo of Aristotle's *De divinatione*, empirical. True dreams, he writes, are so well attested that "to deny their occurrence is to deny the evidence of sense perception. . . ; for no one exists who has not had a dream forewarning him of what would happen to him in the future." See Epitome of the *Parva naturalia*, Arabic text 66; Latin text 94; Hebrew text 43; English translation 39; and Aristotle, *De divinatione* 462b, 15–16. Within the economy of nature, or, if one wish, within the plan of divine "providence," true dreams serve a purpose. "The intellectual cogitative faculty, the faculty whereby man has [prior] knowledge . . . of beneficial and harmful matters in the future, in order to prepare himself" for future eventualities, is not sufficient to its task. Nature and providence therefore supplement the efforts of the cogitative faculty by furnishing information about the future through true dreams. See Epitome of the *Parva naturalia*, Arabic text 84; Latin text 116; Hebrew text 55; English translation 49. Averroes has already been seen to deny that nature might supplement the intellect's activity with an alternative route to theoretical knowledge, on the grounds that all theoretical knowledge accessible to man can be learned through the scientific method, and the alternative route would be superfluous. Here, in connection with true dreams, he is maintaining that since the cogitative faculty is insufficient to its task of forewarning man regarding future events, nature does supplement the cogitative faculty's activity with an alternative route to knowledge of the future.

faculty was suggested by Ibn Bājja, when he wrote that those dreams furnish knowledge about the future "without cogitation"[114]; the implication was that cogitation is the usual means for attaining knowledge of the future. Alfarabi had similarly stated that prophecy furnishes information of a kind usually attained through *deliberation*,[115] deliberation having been classified by him as an operation of the cogitative faculty.[116]

An agent must lead the imaginative faculty from its potential possession of knowledge of the future to the actual knowledge of the future which is disclosed in the true dream. To help identify the agent, Averroes notes that predictions of the future in dreams are peculiar in a critical respect: The premises "effecting" the prediction are not known to the human subject prior to his dream. There is one other instance where premises do not precede human knowledge of a proposition, and that is knowledge of the "first principles" of theoretical thought. The agent "effecting" actual human knowledge of the first principles of thought is perforce a being that itself possesses the knowledge in actuality, hence "an actual [and incorporeal] intellect," the transcendent active intellect. Averroes accordingly infers that predictions through true dreams, where knowledge likewise comes without previously known premises, must be the work of the same wholly "incorporeal" intellect, "the active intellect."[117]

But a difficulty raises its head. "Incorporeal intelligences [or: intellects] have been shown in the metaphysical sciences to have universals as the sole object of their thought; and they are able to give only the likes of what they have in their own substance." They "cannot give anything whatsoever that is individual; for their nature does not contain knowledge of the . . . particular," seeing that the particular or individual is tied to "matter," whereas they are "free of matter." "How, then—I wish I knew—can the active intellect furnish the individual form [constituting the content of a true dream], a form particular in respect to time, place, and . . . the individual man?"[118]

Averroes' solution is that while the active intellect does not know events in their particular aspect, it does know them in their general aspect. Every "individual [natural] substance" in the sublunar world is "determinate in respect to its efficient causes," and some, though not all, accidents are so as well. "Individual accidents" of the type that "exist by chance . . . do not have determinate causes," but other individual accidents are "determinate in respect to their causes"; they "have a universal, intelligible nature, which is the primary cause of their existence." The physical laws governing the coming into existence of individual substances and

[114]Above, p. 341.

[115]Above, p. 59.

[116]Alfarabi, *Fuṣūl al-Madanī*, ed. D. Dunlop (Cambridge 1961) §6: One action of the "cogitative faculty [*fikrī*]" is "deliberating" about "how" to do things that we "wish to do."

[117]Epitome of the *Parva naturalia*, Arabic text 71–72, 74; Latin text 100–101, 103; Hebrew text 46–48; English translation 42–44.

[118]Ibid., Arabic text 74; Latin text 103; Hebrew text 48; English translation 43–44.

determinate individual accidents are so intricate that man cannot ascertain "syllogistically" anything about substances and accidents "standing at a distance from him in time." Human knowledge does not penetrate beyond the "highest and most universal" of the world's causes to the myriad secondary causes determining the existence of individual objects—with the exception of objects lying within a man's immediate ken. Most of the causes determining events are therefore, "from the human point of view, not circumscribed" and knowable. Nevertheless, since the causes of individual substances and of the determinate individual accidents are "circumscribed in themselves," the manner in which those substances and accidents are determined is in principle knowable. "Their [general] nature, which stands to them as the form [in the mind] of the artisan stands to the artifact made [by the artisan], is necessarily an object of intelligible thought for the incorporeal form [i.e., for the active intellect]."

The active intellect contains, indeed consists in, a single unified thought embracing the general nature of the determinate part of the world. True dreams come about when the active intellect "emanates" and "gives to the imaginative [faculty of the] soul, the universal nature pertinent to an individual [substance or individual determinate accident] that is about to come into existence—in other words, the intelligible thought of its causes." The "imaginative [faculty of the] soul, residing as it does in matter, receives the intelligible thought in a particularized mode." "Just as a skilled physician" makes a prognosis by combining a "universal intelligible . . . premise" and a "particular, sense-derived [premise], so too" the inspired imaginative faculty spontaneously and unconsciously applies the "universal [premise]" received from the active intellect, to its own knowledge of particular circumstances. The imaginative faculty either sees an "exact" picture of what the future holds; or, alternatively, it unconsciously recasts the information received, and it sees a "representation" merely symbolizing future events.[119]

In short, Averroes' Epitome of the *Parva naturalia* denies that true dream, clairvoyance, revelation, and prophecy are distinct phenomena, that any of them provides systematic theoretical knowledge, or that any of them even provides a figurative representation of theoretical truth. The function of true dream and its variations is to predict the future. When Averroes explored the active intellect's role in human intelligible thought, he ignored Avicenna's theory that the active intellect emanates thoughts directly.[120] In the present context, he—like Alfarabi and Ibn Bājja, both of whom also recognized no direct emanation of intelligible thoughts—traces predictions of the future to an emanation of the active intellect affecting the imaginative faculty. The active intellect's unitary thought embodies the universal

[119]Ibid., Arabic text 76–81; Latin text 105–12; Hebrew text 49–53; English translation 44–47. The "Epistle on Dreams," as cited by Pines, "The Arabic Recension of *Parva naturalia* " (n. 101 above) 111, also distinguishes between true dreams in which matters are presented explicitly and true dreams in which they are presented in a figurative guise.

[120]Above, p. 320, he did write that the active intellect imparts the first principles of thought.

laws governing the physical world, and an emanation from the active intellect can communicate those laws. The imaginative faculty receives the universal laws in a particularized mode, bringing the universal to bear on its own concerns. Future events—the future emergence of natural substances and of those accidents that are subject to natural law—appear to the inspired dreamer.

Two compositions of Averroes belonging, like the Epitome of the *Parva naturalia*, to the early period of his thought make brief passing comments that are consistent with the Epitome's position. One of the two, which is preserved only in Hebrew, states that "the imaginative faculty performs its functions best when the senses are quiescent" and do not distract it; consequently "visions and revelation [or: prophecy (*pil'e ha-nebu'a*)] generally occur in dreams."[121] The other composition states that the active intellect knows the order of nature in a "more noble mode" than man does, that it comprehends "things, the causes of which cannot be known" to man, and that it therefore can "give dreams and other forewarnings of the future."[122]

Averroes' *Tahāfut al-Tahāfut* (*Destructio destructionum*), which addresses a mixed audience of philosophers and nonphilosophers, also touches on prophecy. *Tahāfut al-Tahāfut*, as will be recalled, is a point-by-point refutation of Ghazali's *Tahāfut al-Falāsifa* (*Destructio philosophorum*). When Averroes reaches the section where Ghazali takes up miracles and prophecy, he declares his admiration for the "early philosophers," who refrained from discussing sensitive subjects publicly. He indicates that he too would have preferred "to remain silent."[123] Since the indiscretion of his adversary has, however, prevented him from doing so, Averroes permits himself a few remarks regarding prophecy. He writes: (1) "The early [philosophers] held that . . . revelation [*waḥy*] and [true] dream . . . come from God through the mediacy of a spiritual and incorporeal being, . . . the active intellect, which is called an angel in the religious texts [*sharīᶜa*]." (2) In the view of "the enlightened, . . . the attribute thanks to which a prophet is called a prophet" expresses itself in "making hidden things known, and in promulgating religious laws that harmonize with the truth and teach behavior leading to the eudaemonia of all mankind."[124] The first statement stays within the spirit of what

121 *Epistle on the Possibility of Conjunction* (n. 21 above) §2, p. 11; English translation 27. Ibid. §15, p. 139, speaks of "prophecy of what is about to come into existence."

122 Epitome of the *Metaphysics* (n. 3 above) 4.46; German translation 127.

123 *Tahāfut al-Tahāfut* (n. 82 above) 514, 516. In another composition intended for a mixed readership, Averroes discusses the allegorical interpretation of sensitive religious dogmas, asserts that that is a subject properly pursued only in works reserved for philosophers, and apologizes for having had to deal with it in a work accessible to nonphilosophers. See *Faṣl al Maqāl*, ed G. Hourani (Leiden 1959) 29; English translation: *Averroes on the Harmony of Religion and Philosophy*, trans. G. Hourani (London 1961) 62.

124 *Tahāfut al-Tahāfut* 516. The passage is cumbersome. It reads in full: "The way [used] by the enlightened in establishing the genuineness [*taṣdīq*] of prophets is a different one, one that Ghazali alludes to in several places. It [the proper criterion for evaluating a prophet] is [the

we have found in Averroes' Epitome of the *Parva naturalia*; and the words "making hidden things known" in the second statement could well refer to the predictions of the future which, according to the Epitome of the *Parva naturalia*, are the sole content of true dreams and prophecy.[125] But the comment about prophets' promulgating religious laws "that harmonize with the truth and teach behavior leading to . . . eudaemonia" appears to contradict the Epitome of the *Parva naturalia*. There, as just seen, Averroes contended that revelation cannot possibly provide theoretical knowledge or guide man to human eudaemonia, that it cannot even recast philosophic knowledge in figurative images. The *Tahāfut*'s comment affirms, in apparent contrast, that the prophet does guide mankind on questions of human eudaemonia, that the ability to offer such guidance is in fact the criterion for judging whether a man is a genuine prophet or not.

In still another passage, Averroes' *Tahāhut* asserts that "every religion comes about through revelation with which intellect is mixed" and that a "religion through intellect alone would necessarily be inferior to religions derived from intellect and revelation."[126] Here revelation is plainly understood to work hand in hand with reason, with the suggestion that revelation performs for certain members of the human species what reason performs for others. Additional statements in the same vein can be cited from Averroes' semipopular works. He writes, for example:

---

presence of] the act that flows from the attribute thanks to which a prophet is called a prophet; that act consists in making hidden things known, and in promulgating religious laws. . . ." Van den Bergh (n. 82 above) does not translate the present passage with precision; and his translation of the previous page of the *Tahāfut* contains a misleading sentence that gives an erroneous picture of Averroes. Van den Bergh's translation of the earlier passage reads: "and what is true of the prophet, that he can interrupt the ordinary course of nature, is impossible for man, but possible in itself"; see Van den Bergh 315. The translation should read: "[in the view of Avicenna] what establishes the genuineness [*taṣdīq*] of the prophet would then be that he produces something extraordinary, something impossible for the [ordinary] man, although possible in itself." Averroes is there contrasting two opinions on what "establishes the genuineness" of a prophet: an opinion attributed by Averroes to Avicenna and considered by Averroes to be philosophically incorrect, namely, the opinion that the criterion for judging whether someone is a prophet is the performing of miracles (not, in fact, a fair account of Avicenna); and the enlightened opinion, according to which the criterion for judging whether someone is a prophet is the man's message.

[125]It should be noted that the Epitome of the *Parva naturalia* recognizes the emanation of sublunar natural forms by the active intellect; and Averroes there compares the active intellect's emanation upon the imaginative faculty to its emanation of natural forms. See above, p. 234, and Epitome of the *Parva naturalia*, Arabic text 79; Latin text 109–10, 103; Hebrew text 52; English translation 46. The *Tahāfut al-Tahāfut* belongs, by contrast, to the later period of Averroes' thought, when he rejected the proposition that the active intellect emanates natural forms; see above, p. 252.

[126]*Tahāfut al-Tahāfut* 584. Ibid., 255–56, Averroes writes: "Knowledge [or: science (*ᶜilm*)] received from revelation comes to perfect the branches of knowledge [or: to perfect the sciences] of the intellect," and one area in which the supplement occurs is where intellect has "absolute inability, that is, where intellect insofar as it is intellect is naturally unable to know." Predictions of the future are presumably the area where the human intellect is naturally unable to operate.

"Demonstration" is beyond some men "either because of inborn nature, habit, or lack of the means for study"; "God" has, for the use of those men, "coined images and likenesses" of "things . . . that can [in their proper guise] only be learned by demonstration"; and the figurative images are recorded in Scripture.[127] "Revelation" establishes a regimen guiding man to his perfection; "religions" teach that regimen together with "the theoretical matters, knowledge of which is indispensable for all mankind"; the indispensable subjects taught by religion are "knowledge of God, of the angels, of the superior beings, and of [human] eudaemonia."[128] The finest of all Scriptures is the Koran, for it contains the best figurative representation of philosophic truths.[129] The Koran teaches truth—for instance, the existence of God—at different levels and for different groups; for while on the surface the Koran speaks a nontechnical language appropriate for the uneducated, by subtle hints it also directs the enlightened toward philosophic demonstration.[130]

The discrepancy is harsh. The Epitome of the *Parva naturalia* advanced carefully reasoned arguments to show that the phenomenon of revelation cannot conceivably provide knowledge about subjects belonging to the domain of science and philosophy, that revelation cannot even recast theoretical knowledge in figurative images for the use of common people. Averroes' *Tahāfut al-Tahāfut* and semipopular works affirm, on the contrary, that the prophet and the phenomenon of revelation do teach theoretical matters to the unenlightened in a figurative language comprehensible to them, and that revelation hints to potential philosophers where the purer expression of truth lies.

Two ways of handling the discrepancy suggest themselves. After writing the Epitome of the *Parva naturalia*, Averroes may have changed his mind and accepted the topos that prophecy and revelation recast scientific truths for the use of the unenlightened. Alternatively, in contexts that are not purely philosophic he may be using the terms *revelation* and *prophet* in a peculiar sense. The inner intent of *Tahāfut al-Tahāfut* and the semipopular works would then not be that a prophetic imaginative faculty fashioned the figurative representations of scientific truths embodied in Scripture. The intent would be instead that the human author of Scripture first acquired theoretical knowledge through proper scientific methods and then coolly and deliberately—not through an inspired imaginative faculty—recast his hard-won philosophic knowledge into language appropriate for his less enlightened brethren. The term *prophet* would, on this reading, mean nothing more than the human author of Scripture; and the term *revelation* would mean a

[127]*Faṣl al-Maqāl* 23; English translation 59. When Averroes speaks here of "God," he of course has no divine intervention in view, since he understood the First Cause to be impersonal and unchanging. He merely means that the eternal structure of the universe is such that some people formulate images and likenesses to help educate others.

[128]*K. al-Kashf* (n. 82 above) 119–20.

[129]Ibid. 122, and cf. 98. *Tahāfut al-Tahāfut* 585.

[130]*K. al-Kashf* 27, 46; cf. *Faṣl al-Maqāl* 23–24, 30; English translation 59, 63–64.

high level of philosophic knowledge. Support for such a reading may perhaps be found in the circumstance that Averroes generally calls the author of Scripture a "law giver" (*shāri*ᶜ) rather than a prophet.[131] There are other significant instances where Averroes' semipopular works employ expressions not in their obvious sense but as code words for something else.[132]

Averroes' Shifting Picture of the Universe and of Man's Place in It

Up to a point, Averroes' picture of the universe remains constant throughout his preserved writings. It is a deistic picture, one that Averroes shared with Alfarabi, Avicenna, and Ibn Bājja, and one that he assumed to be the correct reading of Aristotle. Although he was quite capable of changing his own mind on philosophic issues, Averroes never dreamt that Aristotle had done the same, and he treated the Aristotelian canon as the repository of a single, consistent body of doctrine.

What Averroes held fast to throughout is the location of an eternal stationary earth at the center of the physical universe, the rotation of celestial spheres—in which the sun, moon, and stars are embedded—around the earth, and the maintaining of the spheres in eternal motion by incorporeal intelligences. An impersonal, unchanging incorporeal being presides over the whole, serving, in some sense, as the First Cause of the existence of everything outside itself. At the lower end of the hierarchy of incorporeal intelligences stands an intelligence that, unlike those above it, is not associated with a celestial sphere. This is precisely the *active intellect* posited by Aristotle on the grounds that an intellect must exist which is what it is "by virtue of making all things," that is, by virtue of making all thoughts.

While Averroes remained faithful throughout his career to the skeleton just outlined, he was seen, in the two preceding chapters, to change his mind radically on certain issues; and the present chapter has uncovered additional, although less

[131]E.g., *K. al-Kashf* 28, 67; *Faṣl al-Maqāl* 34; English translation 66.

[132]Those instances are admittedly more transparent than the statements in the semipopular works regarding the scope of revelation and prophecy. Averroes writes, for example, that Scripture was judicious in describing God anthropomorphically, that the man in the street should not be disabused of his belief in an anthropomorphic deity, but that the best way of representing God is as "light"; *K. al-Kashf* 60–63. Averroes is apparently using the term *light* as a metaphor for incorporeality. See Ghazali's use of the metaphor of light, above, p. 132. *K. al-Kashf* 65–66, states that God dwells in the outer heaven. The statement, when deciphered, means that God's action manifests itself in the movement of the outermost sphere, although God himself does not dwell in any place. See Aristotle, *Metaphysics* 12. Averroes speaks of the immortality of the soul, using *soul* as a transparent code word for *intellect*; above, pp. 335–36. He carefully avoids casting any doubt on the resurrection of the body, but adds that what is resurrected is "images" of bodies, and not the identical bodies that died; see *Tahāfut al-Tahāfut* 586, and cf. *K. al-Kashf* 122. He means that when bodies die and disintegrate, they are replaced by new, different bodies, or possibly that bodies do not themselves survive, but that intellect survives.

weighty, changes of mind on other issues. His earlier and later positions fit together into distinct systems within the common framework.

His early works are imbued with an emanationism close to that of Alfarabi and Avicenna.[133] From the First Cause of the universe, the early Averroes concurs with his two predecessors, there eternally emanates an incorporeal being consisting in pure thought. That emanated being, the first intelligence, contains multiple aspects, and from the multiplicity, two further things eternally emanate: another incorporeal being consisting in pure thought, and the form, or soul—but not the body—of the first sphere. The second incorporeal intelligence eternally gives rise to similar effects. And the process replicates itself over and over again, until the intelligence governing the sphere of the moon eternally produces the form, or soul, of its sphere and the concluding link in the incorporeal hierarchy, the active intellect.

On the question whether or not the First Cause governs a sphere, Averroes continues to follow Alfarabi and Avicenna. He repeats Avicenna's rule that "from one only one can proceed" and infers that the First Cause, being wholly unitary, can have no more than a single effect. Since each of the intelligences governing a sphere has at least two effects, none of them is wholly unitary. None therefore can be the ultimate cause of the universe. The ultimate cause resides beyond the movers of the spheres and has no sphere of its own.

Averroes does not, even in his early writings, recognize a cause of the existence of sublunar matter, just as he does not recognize a cause of the bodies of the spheres. Following the example of one work of Alfarabi as well as the examples of Avicenna and Ibn Bājja, he does, however, trace the forms of animals and plants to the active intellect. In organic reproduction, plant seed or male sperm renders a portion of matter receptive of a plant or animal form; in spontaneous generation, a heat emitted by the heavenly bodies prepares matter for a given form; and in each instance, the properly prepared portion of matter automatically selects the form appropriate to it out of the ever-present emanation of the active intellect. A passage in one of Averroes' early works goes further and adds that since the human mind abstracts intelligible forms from natural substances below the animal and plant level, the forms of nonorganic substances too must, from the metaphysical—or epistemological—perspective, derive from a source consisting in pure intelligible thought. Here, the active intellect is the source of the forms of all natural substances, inanimate as well as animate.

Averroes' early works thus follow Alfarabi and Avicenna in decking Aristotle's cosmology out in Neoplatonic trappings. The translunar region and at least the animate segment of the sublunar region are, in their formal aspect, brought forth through processes of emanation.

Among the forms emanating from the active intellect upon properly prepared portions of matter is the human soul with its potential, or material, intellect. The

[133]For the divergences from Alfarabi and Avicenna, see above, pp. 223–25.

material intellect hence has its origin in the transcendent realm. As regards the essence of the material intellect within its human purlieu, Averroes had sharply divergent constructions to choose from. His early works, despite their emanationism and despite their tracing of the material intellect to a transcendent emanating source, elect the naturalistic option. Averroes dismisses the possibility that the human material intellect might be a substance similar in nature to the incorporeal intelligences, and his reasoning conducts him now to one, and now to another, version of the material intellect's being a disposition for thought present in, although not mixed with, the human organism.

Besides performing the function never contemplated by Aristotle and emanating a range of natural forms, the active intellect performs the function for which Aristotle had devised it. It is the agent that leads the material human intellect from potentiality to actuality and that enables the material intellect to think intelligible thoughts. Averroes ignores Avicenna's thesis that just as natural forms are emanated upon properly prepared portions of physical matter, so too are intelligible thoughts emanated directly on properly prepared material intellects. Instead, he follows Alfarabi as well as the Greek commentators Alexander and Themistius in representing the active intellect as a sort of light that illuminates images in the imaginative faculty as well as the material intellect itself. When the material intellect and images in the imaginative faculty are illuminated, the material intellect becomes capable of beholding the intelligible thoughts latent in the images. The active intellect does send forth an emanation that brings information to one part of the human soul. It emanates the general laws of nature upon the imaginative faculty, and human imaginative faculties capable of receiving the active intellect's emanation in a particularized mode make predictions of the future.

Works from Averroes' early period argue repeatedly that the material intellect can develop to the point where it has the active intellect as a direct object of thought and conjoins with it—becoming identical with the active intellect in the version of conjunction espoused by some of Averroes' works, remaining distinct in the version espoused by others. Conjunction is achievable during the lifetime of the body. And it is the warrant for human immortality. The human soul's nonintellectual parts and theoretical human thought tied in any way to perceptions of the physical world ineluctably perish with the death of the body, and the sole aspect of man attaining immortality is the material intellect when in a state of conjunction with the active intellect. Man's goal in life is to develop his material intellect to the level where it conjoins with the active intellect, the reward therefor being the immortality of the individual man's material intellect.

Such was Averroes' early system. It plainly misreads Aristotle when it follows the earlier Islamic philosophers and propounds an emanationist cosmogony, it captures Aristotle's spirit when it opts for the naturalistic account of the human material intellect, and it adds to Aristotle when it affirms the possibility of conjunction with the active intellect.

A pair of works belonging to an intermediate period of Averroes' career reveal him rethinking two critical points and in both instances striking a compromise. One work contends that natural sublunar forms do not after all emanate directly from the active intellect, but are produced, as Aristotle's biological writings explained, by a physical substance called soul-heat. The work in question nevertheless traces soul-heat itself to the active intellect or, perhaps, to another of the incorporeal beings subordinate to the First Cause. An excursus in a second work that almost surely belongs to Averroes' intermediate period arrives at a compromise position regarding the nature of the material intellect. After "assigning the due share of doubts" to the theory of Alexander, according to which the material intellect is a disposition in the human organism, and to the theory of Themistius, according to which the material intellect is an incorporeal substance, the excursus settles on a "combination" of the two. A material intellect is, Averroes determines, engendered for each individual man when the transcendent active intellect joins an individual inborn human disposition for thought. Here Averroes' efforts to do full justice to the text of Aristotle's *De anima*—indeed, one may venture, to inconsistent language in the text of the *De anima*—lead him to a hybrid entity that his master would have found extremely odd.

In the final stage of his thought, Averroes jettisons emanation. He still takes the First Cause to be, in a certain sense, the cause of the intelligences' existence. Each incorporeal intelligence, he now understands, possesses a stratum of existence in its own right, the underlying stratum eternally turns its mental gaze upon the unitary First Cause, and the conception of the First Cause which each receives gives it the "perfection" befitting its rank in the cosmic hierarchy. The intelligence thus receives its form and its full measure of existence through its concept of the First Cause. Inasmuch as the First Cause no longer emanates anything and, although unitary, can have more than one effect in the manner described, the principle that from one only one can proceed no longer applies. The objection to taking the intelligence coordinated with the outermost celestial sphere as the First Cause of the universe has vanished, and Averroes accordingly concludes that the First Cause is identical with the intelligence moving the outermost sphere.

He continues to identify the active intellect as the last link, or, to be more precise—because of the new status to be assigned to the material intellect—as the last link but one in the incorporeal hierarchy. Since emanation has been ruled out, the active intellect is no longer the product of a process of emanation. Like the other intelligences, it possesses a stratum of existence that eternally turns its mental gaze upon the unitary First Cause, and the conception of the First Cause which it thereby gains gives it its full measure of perfection. Nor does the active intellect emanate natural forms or even soul-heat. In Averroes' final view of things, soul-heat is engendered by the heat of the sun blended with the heat of the other stars; and physically engendered soul-heat brings potential animate forms, which are latent in matter, to actuality. The active intellect's operation in the sublunar world recedes to what it had been in Aristotle—the actualization of the potential human intellect. When a human soul is drawn forth from matter by soul-heat, the active intellect, acting as a quasi light, stands ready to help the soul acquire intelligible thought.

Averroes' motive in rethinking his early philosophic positions was the self-imposed pious task of restoring the genuine Aristotle. Not everyone will agree that he succeeded completely. It is highly doubtful whether Aristotle considered the incorporeal mover of the outermost sphere to be an indirect cause of the full measure of existence of the other incorporeal movers; and still more doubtful whether he considered the active intellect to be a final link in the hierarchy of incorporeal intelligences—even on the assumption that his active intellect is a transcendent substance. Nevertheless, by stripping away the Neoplatonic trappings with which Alfarabi, Avicenna, and Averroes' own early works had embellished Aristotle, Averroes clearly has made substantial progress in his task. Unfortunately, he did not leave well enough alone.

His early works had espoused a naturalistic construction of the human material intellect, and an intermediate work experimented with the construction of the material intellect as a hybrid entity. In order to reapproach Aristotle, Averroes should have dropped the experimental position, returned to his original naturalistic construction of the material intellect, and incorporated the original construction into his new, hard-won naturalistic account of biological processes. He should have maintained that human souls with their disposition for thought, called material intellect, are latent in the matter of the sublunar world and are drawn forth from matter by soul-heat.

But as Averroes studied Aristotle's statements concerning the material intellect, he became more and more convinced that he had originally been misled, that the naturalistic account of the material intellect fits neither the Aristotelian text nor the facts. He was very likely also swayed by his long-standing attachment to the possibility of conjunction with the active intellect; for in his late period he became persuaded that a generated-destructible material intellect could not conceivably conjoin with an eternal active intellect. Instead of returning to his original conception of the human material intellect, the late Averroes moves still further away from it than the intermediate experiment did. The crowning achievement of his restoration of genuine Aristotelianism is the discovery that a single eternal and transcendent material intellect serves all mankind. His final model of the universe yokes a transcendent material intellect to a naturalistic account of biological processes.

In Averroes' final view of things, the single eternal material intellect shared by mankind links itself to individual men through their imaginative faculties. The active intellect is still represented as a kind of light that illuminates both images in the imaginative faculty and the material intellect itself. To accommodate the active intellect's role in human thought with the conception of a single eternal material intellect, Averroes explains that the material intellect receives the light of the active intellect and gains actual concepts not as the eye receives light and colors, but as the medium in the visual process does. The material intellect, acting as a medium, permits individual imaginative faculties to acquire individual intelligible thoughts.

Averroes still struggles to uphold the possibility of conjunction of the human soul with the active intellect. A new problem raises its head, however, for nothing would seem to redound to an individual man from the material intellect's conjoining with the eternal active intellect, if the material intellect is, as Averroes has taken it to be, likewise an eternal substance and not a part of the human individual. Within the constraints of his final conception of the material intellect, Averroes salvages a conjunction of the human soul with the eternal active intellect only in the loosest of senses. He accordingly no longer speaks of man's having the active intellect as a direct object of thought. And now that the material intellect is immortal merely because it is an incorporeal substance from the start, no shred whatsoever of the individual man will be able to survive the body's demise.

In sum, Averroes' early model of the universe is shot through with an emanationism wholly foreign to Aristotle, yet at the same time it endorses a naturalistic construction of the human material intellect. It also insists on the possibility of the material intellect's having the active intellect as a direct object of thought and conjoining with the active intellect, notions never expressed in the Aristotelian canon. Averroes' final model of the universe dismisses emanationism and explains the generation of living beings in the sublunar world naturalistically, all in the name of a more genuine Aristotelianism. Yet it abandons the earlier naturalistic conception of the human material intellect and transforms the material intellect into something wholly un-Aristotelian, a single transcendent entity serving all mankind. It nominally salvages human conjunction with the active intellect, but in words that have little content.

Medieval Hebrew readers had the early, intermediate, and later works of Averroes that bear upon the subjects we have discussed, with the crucial exception of the Long Commentary on the *De anima*. Latin readers, although they did possess the Long Commentary on the *De anima*, worked with a more limited corpus. Nevertheless, they too had texts[134] in which the development of Averroes' thought can be discerned. The members of both groups were, however, unaccustomed to expect radical shifts on the part of authoritative philosophers, and they consequently did not realize that Averroes' earlier views differed extensively from his later views. Because the two groups worked with different bodies of texts, they obtained different perceptions of Averroes. The most significant difference concerned Averroes' position on the nature of the material intellect, Hebrew readers supposing his considered view to be the hybrid conception proposed by the excursus in the Middle Commentary on the *De anima*, and Latin readers supposing it to be the single eternal substance serving all mankind, as set forth in the Long Commentary on the *De anima*.

[134]Notably, the Epitome of the *Parva naturalia*, from which the Long Commentaries on the *De anima* and the *Metaphysics* diverge.

Index

Lightning Source UK Ltd.
Milton Keynes UK
UKOW04n2112181115

263010UK00001B/41/P

9 780195 074239